THE ONLY ASTROLOGY BOOK
YOU'LL EVER NEED

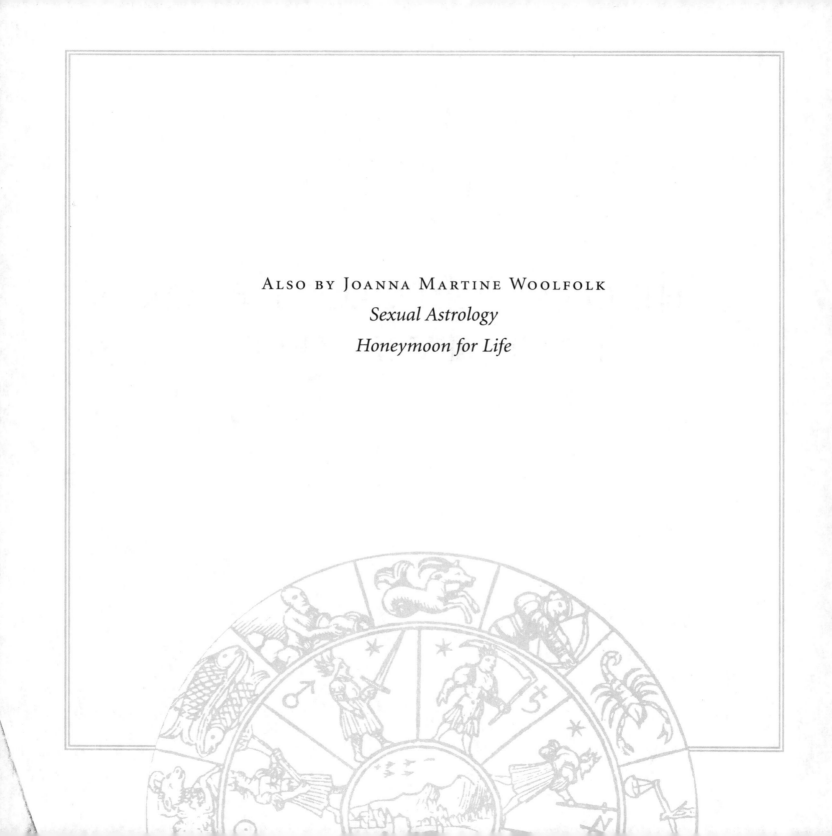

ALSO BY JOANNA MARTINE WOOLFOLK

Sexual Astrology

Honeymoon for Life

THE ONLY ASTROLOGY BOOK YOU'LL EVER NEED

New Edition

JOANNA MARTINE WOOLFOLK

Taylor Trade Publishing

Lanham | New York | Boulder | Toronto | Plymouth, UK

First Taylor Trade Publishing edition 2006

This Taylor Trade Publishing paperback edition of *The Only Astrology Book You'll Ever Need* is a revised and updated edition of the work first published in hardcover in 1982 and in paperback in 1990 and then issued by Taylor Trade Publishing in 2006. It is published by arrangement with the author.

Published by Taylor Trade Publishing
An imprint of The Rowman & Littlefield Publishing Group, Inc.
4501 Forbes Boulevard, Suite 200
Lanham, Maryland 20706

Estover Road
Plymouth PL6 7PY
United Kingdom

Distributed by National Book Network

Library of Congress Cataloging-in-Publication Data
Woolfolk, Joanna Martine.
    The only astrology book you'll ever need / Joanna Martine Woolfolk.
—new ed.
        p. cm.
    Includes bibliographical references and index.
    ISBN-13: 978-1-58979-377-4 (pbk.: alk. paper)
    ISBN-10: 1-58979-377-3 (pbk.: alk. paper)
    1. Astrology. I. Title

BF1708.1 .W68 2001
133.5—dc21   2001031798

Manufactured in the United States of America.

PHOTO CREDITS

p. 12   Colin Powell (Corbis), Peyton Manning (© Frederick M. Brown/Getty Images), Maya Angelou (Photofest)

p. 17   John Paul II (© Porter Gifford/Getty Images), Stephen Colbert (© Scott Wintrow/Getty Images), Audrey Hepburn (Photofest)

p. 22   Marilyn Monroe (Photofest), John F. Kennedy (Courtesy of the Library of Congress), Paul McCartney (Corbis)

p. 27   Princess Diana (Corbis), George W. Bush (Corbis), Ernest Hemingway (Photofest)

p. 32   Mick Jagger (Photofest), Madonna (Corbis), Bill Clinton (Corbis)

p. 37   Richard Gere (Corbis), Mother Teresa (Photofest), Lance Armstrong (© Rob Loud/Getty Images)

p. 42   Jesse Jackson (Photofest), Barbara Walters (© Brad Barket/Getty Images), Simon Cowell (© Jeffrey Mayer/Getty Images)

p. 47   Whoopie Goldberg (© Brad Barket/Getty Images), Hillary Rodham Clinton, Julia Roberts (Corbis)

p. 52   Frank Sinatra (Photofest), Jon Stewart (© Jeff Vespa/Getty Images), Miley Cyrus (© Kevin Mazur/Getty Images)

p. 57   Martin Luther King Jr. (Photofest), Elvis Presley (Photofest), Tiger Woods (© Donald Miralle/Getty Images)

p. 63   Oprah Winfrey (© Evan Agostini / Getty Images), Franklin Delano Roosevelt (Photofest), Justin Timberlake (© Steve Granitz/Getty Images)

p. 68   Kurt Cobain (Corbis), Carrie Underwood (© Alberto E. Rodriguez/Getty Images), Albert Einstein (Photofest)

I dedicate this book to William,
who, with his Sun in Cancer, taught me
the meaning of love
and, with his Moon in Virgo,
the meaning of work.

CONTENTS

ABOUT THE AUTHOR

Photo by Fran Collin

ASTROLOGER Joanna Martine Woolfolk has had a long career as an author, columnist, lecturer, and counselor. She has written the monthly horoscope for numerous magazines in the U.S., Europe and Latin America—among them *Marie Claire, Harper's Bazaar, Redbook, Self, YM, House Beautiful,* and *StarScroll International.* In addition to the best-selling *The Only Astrology Book You'll Ever Need,* Joanna is the author of *Sexual Astrology,* which has sold over a million copies worldwide, and *Astrology Source,* an interactive CD-ROM.

Joanna is a popular television and radio personality who has been interviewed by Barbara Walters, Regis Philbin, and Sally Jessy Raphael. She has appeared in a regular astrology segment on *New York Today* on NBC-TV and on *The Fairfield Exchange* on CT Cable Channel 12, and she appears frequently on television and radio shows around the country. You can visit her website at www.joannamartinewoolfolk.com.

ACKNOWLEDGMENTS

I AM GRATEFUL for having known the late Capel McCutcheon, the brilliant astrologer who devised the unique, comprehensive, and easy-to-use Planetary and Ascendant Tables in this book. None of these tables requires more than the simple laying-down of a ruler (or two) in order to read the information that applies to you. These tables are computer accurate and are based on United States time, rather than Greenwich, England, time usually found in other planetary tables.

Capel McCutcheon was a caring and inspiring teacher, counselor, and lecturer, as well as the founder of the Astrological Society of Connecticut. I miss his warmth, support, and generosity.

And I give special thanks to Matrix Software. This innovative astrological computer-software company graciously supplied for this revised edition additional Planetary Tables updated to the year 2100. Matrix Software was founded in the early 1980's by Michael Erlewine, a visionary genius in the field of computer astrology.

Matrix Software also created the CD-ROM that is packaged with this book. You who have computers can now cast astrological charts within seconds. Just enter the birth information, and your chart is ready. The CD will even give you the page numbers in this book on which key information about your chart is to be found.

We are born at a given moment, in a given place,
and like vintage years of wine, we have the
qualities of the year and of the season
in which we are born.

CARL GUSTAV JUNG

INTRODUCTION

THE LONGER I AM AN ASTROLOGER—which at this point is half my lifetime—the more I realize that what we all want to know is about ourselves. "Who am I?" you ask. You want to know what makes you tick, why you have such intense feelings, and whether others are also insecure. People write me asking questions like "What kind of man should I look for?" "Why am I discontented with my job?" or "The woman I'm dating is a Gemini; will we be happy together?" They ask me if they'll ever find true love and when they will get out of a period of sadness or fear or the heavy burden of problems. They ask about their path in life and how they can find more fulfillment.

So I continue to see that the reason astrology exists is to answer questions about you. Basically, it's all about *you*. Astrology has been described as a stairway leading into your deeper self. It holds out the promise that you do not have to pass through life reacting blindly to experience, that you can within limits direct your own destiny and in the process reach a truer self-understanding.

One surprising thing about the science of the stars is its constant newness. Down through the centuries philosophers, mystics, and spiritual teachers have studied, written about, refined, and pondered astrology's significance. It is the world's oldest science and our own generation's newest subject of inquiry. According to a Gallup poll, 35 percent of American adults believe their lives are influenced by the position of the heavenly bodies. The great majority of newspapers and magazines published in the United States carry an astrology column. Astrology as a serious subject is being offered in over a dozen university courses.

Despite this new surge of interest, however, the general public has only a smattering of knowledge about the subject. The average person will say, "I'm interested, but I don't know much about astrology."

One of the problems people encounter when trying to learn more about astrology is that most books deal with only one phase of the subject. If you want to know about your Sun sign, there are many books on this topic. If you want to know about your Moon sign, you will find books on this topic also. If you want to learn about your birth chart, you will have to look for yet another book that explains charts (these are harder to find).

Not long ago, while talking to a friend, I casually mentioned that my birth chart shows I have three planets in

Taurus. "Oh," she said, "can you tell me where *my* three planets are?" She did not know that everyone has *ten* planets* in his or her birth chart.

But how would my friend know this? Most astrology books don't deal with birth charts. Unless you are willing to hunt down esoteric volumes hidden in the occult section of bookstores or in special libraries, where would you go to get that information? Any astrology book will tell you whether your Sun sign is Aries or Pisces or one of the other signs of the zodiac. But then what?

This book tells you all you should know about the whole topic of astrology. You will learn about Sun signs—and also about Moon signs, Ascendants, Planets, and Houses. You will come to understand how these factors interact to shape your life. You will discover the meaning of Aspects in your horoscope, and how to compare your birth chart with another person's to reveal areas of compatibility. You will learn how astrology began and developed. And if you have access to a computer, the CD-ROM packaged with this book will enable you to cast a birth chart within seconds.

However, I want to say a word about what this book is not. It is not an encyclopedia—nor does it encompass all the astrological wisdom that has been discovered during the last 5,000 years. No single book could possibly do that even if it were twenty times as long as the present volume.

This book is an easy-to-understand, all-in-one guide to what astrology is about. If you want to know where all your planets are in your birth chart or how compatible your Sun sign is with your lover's Sun sign or what the influence of the Moon is in your life—it is here in *one* book.

I'd like to make one more important point. Astrology cannot transform your life—only *you* can do this. We astrologers are often guilty of overpromising or encouraging people to become overdependent. Astrology will not change the ups and downs of your life drama. What it *can* do is give you insight on how to deal with your drama. Astrology offers information and direction and, best of all, reassurance. Sometimes all one is looking for is a nugget of guidance, and I know you will find many, many nuggets in this book.

I assume you picked up this book because you are interested in astrology. And I hope this is only the beginning of your exploration. One can easily spend a lifetime exploring the uncountable facets of this ever-evolving, ever-new topic. Together we are about to enter more deeply into this fascinating, vast, and complicated arena of knowledge. I hope this will not be the only astrology book you'll ever want—merely the only one you'll ever *need*.

JOANNA MARTINE WOOLFOLK
Stamford, Connecticut
June 2008

---

*In a birth chart (which is a chart of the heavens at the time of your birth), the Sun and Moon are counted as planets. The Earth, because it is our home-planet, is not.

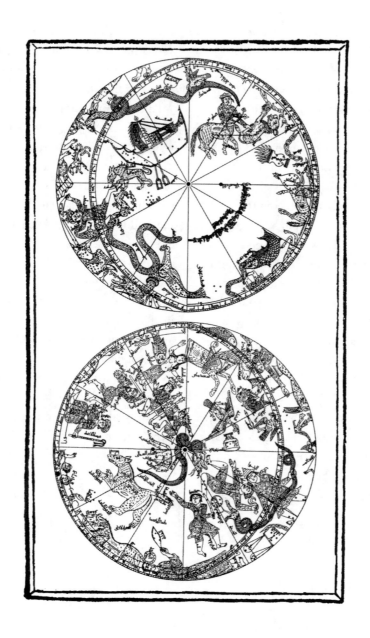

ABOUT THE BOOK

THERE HAS NEVER BEEN an astrology book like this. Here is a book that with a few hours of reading will help you to see yourself better, interpret your own chart, and use your chart year after year to understand and predict trends and opportunities.

The Only Astrology Book You'll Ever Need gives explanations of the influences that are often given scant attention in conventional astrology books: the Moon sign, the Rising sign, the placement of the planets, and the significance of the twelve Houses.

The value of this book is that an immense amount of knowledge is put into easy-to-understand language. The book is also easy to use, for it supplies simplified Tables that in most cases require only the laying down of a ruler across the birthdate.

Even simpler, for those who have access to a computer, is to utilize the CD-ROM packaged with this book. Just by typing in the birth information, this CD gives you a complete chart within seconds. The CD even provides the page numbers of this book on which to find the meaning of every influence in your chart.

The Only Astrology Book You'll Ever Need, first published in 1982, is a classic in its field. On its original publication it was a choice of Book-of-the-Month Club, the Literary Guild, and One Spirit Book Club, and has since become one of the best-selling astrology books published in the last 25 years. This new revised edition contains sections on the inner life of each sign; insights on one's relationship, emotional needs, and drives; and how others see you. This edition is also updated to include the latest information about new discoveries in astronomy, projections of world events in the 21st century, and extended Planetary Tables for every year from 1900 to 2100.

Part One

SUN SIGN ASTROLOGY

1

SUN SIGNS

WHEN A MAN SAYS to an attractive woman at a party, "I'm a Leo. What's your sign?", he is not only using an opening conversational gambit (and behaving just like Leo), he is also talking about Sun signs.

What is a Sun sign?

From our viewpoint here on Earth, the Sun travels around the Earth once each year. Within the space of that year the Sun moves through all twelve signs of the zodiac,* spending approximately one month in each sign. The sign that the Sun was traveling through at the time of your birth is your Sun sign.

The Sun is our most powerful planet. (In astrological terms, the Sun is referred to as a planet even though it, like the Moon, is actually a "luminary.") It gives us life, warmth, energy, food. It is the force that sustains us on Earth. The Sun is also the most important and pervasive influence in your horoscope, and in many ways determines how others see you. The position of the Sun in your birth chart governs your individuality, your distinctive style, and your drive to fulfill your goals in life.

I often liken your Sun sign to the role you've been given in your grand drama. One can think (as Shakespeare did) of life as a play that one enters into at the time of birth. You are the leading actor in this drama, and the role you are acting is your Sun sign.

Another analogy is that your horoscope is a painting of you. The characteristics of your Sun sign are the broad strokes that the artist first lays down on the canvas. The artist outlines your general shape, the planes and angles of your face, the way in which you hold your body. In the same way, your Sun sign delineates your general character. Are you introspective? Do you make friends easily? How do you cope with responsibility? Are you high-strung or easygoing? The answers may be found in a study of your Sun sign.

*A detailed explanation of the zodiac appears on page 383 (chapter 12, "The Zodiac").

Yet a typical remark often made to astrologers goes something like this: "I'm a Capricorn, but when I read those descriptions of Capricorn, they don't describe me very accurately."

Remember, the Sun sign is just the start of your portrait, the broad strokes. You also have a Moon in your birth chart, and it's probably in a different sign from the one the Sun is in. You have planets in your birth chart, and each may be in a different sign.

You are a complex and unique combination, unlike anyone else. Any attempt to give an accurate description from only a Sun sign falls into the kind of error H. L. Mencken was referring to when he remarked that "for every complicated problem, there is a solution that is short, simple, and wrong."

Only by studying the entire birth chart can an astrologer begin to get a complete picture of a personality. Even then, there is a certain latitude for error simply because human beings are not carved in stone. We change a little every day and with every person we meet. Love, tragedy, success—each circumstance of life alters us. However, the essential person remains. And the Sun sign is the outline of that essence.

Astrology is a fascinating tool for the study of human nature. When you first meet someone, that person is a mystery. You see the color of eyes and hair, the mode of dress, whether he or she is tall or short. You must wait for further information to know anything more. If you know the person's Sun sign, you can put a few pieces of the puzzle together. But, just as when you are beginning a complex jigsaw puzzle, too many pieces are missing. The Sun sign merely gives you an edge, an extra insight that you would not otherwise possess.

Of course, knowledge of Sun signs is not only useful in casual social meetings. It is invaluable in close relationships. If your Cancer husband nags and criticizes, you'll know it's just his way of showing how much he cares about you. If your ten-year-old Virgo daughter acts like a premature old maid, fussing about putting everything exactly where she wants it, you'll understand why she needs to have her possessions neatly arranged. Knowing how scattered and forgetful a Gemini can be, you will find it easier to forgive your Gemini lover when your birthday present shows up two days late.

Most important of all, an understanding of your own Sun sign will give you an added measure of self-knowledge, a deeper insight into the stranger that is yourself.

Some Astrological Background on the Twelve Signs of the Zodiac

In the 5,000 years that have passed since the study of astrology was first recorded, the twelve signs of the zodiac have acquired special associations, characterizations, and meanings.

Hundreds of years before the time of Christ, Greek philosophers formulated the theory of Man in Microcosm—that is, the human being is a miniature version of the cosmos. According to this concept, everything in nature has a parallel in human beings, and thus humankind and the universe are linked together in a system of correlations. Out of this idea, known as the Hermetic Theory, sprang such divinatory arts as palmistry, which holds that the solar system corresponds to various parts of the human hand.

In keeping with the Hermetic Theory, a vast body of correspondences grew up surrounding the twelve signs of the zodiac. Many of these affinities date back thousands of years. Most were known when Claudius Ptolemy recorded them in his definitive astrological treatise, the *Tetrabiblos*, during the second century A.D. Some knowledge is more recent: the three modern planets, for example, were only discovered within the last 250 years,* and with their discovery have come new associations and definitions.

One could say that each astrological sign is a miniature Book of Knowledge, and all twelve put together give a picture of human beings, our bodies, minds, and emotions, and of the surrounding world in which we live.

Like an intricate Chinese box, the zodiac is a whole entity that can be taken apart and examined in different ways.

*The three modern planets are Uranus (1781), Neptune (1846), and Pluto (1930).

To begin with, the twelve signs of the zodiac are divided into several sets of groups, or numbers. They are divided into twos, threes, fours, and sixes.

Dualities

The twelve signs are divided into two groups, masculine and feminine. Six signs are masculine, and six signs are feminine. This is known as the sign's duality. In astrological terms, a masculine sign is direct and energetic; a feminine sign is receptive and magnetic. These masculine and feminine attributes were given to the signs about 2,000 years ago. Today modern astrologers try to avoid the sexism implicit in these distinctions. A masculine sign does not mean "positive and forceful" any more than a feminine sign means "negative and weak." In modern terminology, the masculine signs are defined as outer-directed and strong through action. The feminine signs are self-contained and strong through inner reserves.

ARIES	Masculine
GEMINI	Masculine
LEO	Masculine
LIBRA	Masculine
SAGITTARIUS	Masculine
AQUARIUS	Masculine
TAURUS	Feminine
CANCER	Feminine
VIRGO	Feminine
SCORPIO	Feminine
CAPRICORN	Feminine
PISCES	Feminine

Triplicities

The twelve signs are also divided into four groups containing three signs each. Each three-sign group is called a triplicity, and each of these triplicities denotes an element. The four elements are Fire, Earth, Air, and Water. In astrology, an element symbolizes a fundamental characterization of the sign.

Three signs are *fire* signs. They are Aries, Leo, and Sagittarius. Fire signs are active and enthusiastic.

Three signs are *earth* signs. They are Taurus, Virgo, and Capricorn. Earth signs are practical and stable.

Three signs are *air* signs. They are Gemini, Libra, and Aquarius. Air signs are intellectual and communicative.

Three signs are *water* signs. They are Cancer, Scorpio, and Pisces. Water signs are emotional and intuitive.

Quadruplicities

Next, the twelve signs are divided into three groups containing four signs each. Each four-sign group is called a quadruplicity, and each of these quadruplicities denotes a quality. The three qualities are Cardinal, Fixed, and Mutable. In astrology, the quality signifies the sign's interaction with the outside world.

Four signs are *cardinal** signs. They are Aries, Cancer, Libra, and Capricorn. Cardinal signs are enterprising and outgoing. They are the initiators.

Four signs are *fixed* signs. They are Taurus, Leo, Scorpio, and Aquarius. Fixed signs are resistant to change. They are perfectors and finishers, rather than originators.

Four signs are *mutable* signs. They are Gemini, Virgo, Sagittarius, and Pisces. Mutable signs are flexible, versatile, and adaptable. They are able to adjust to differing circumstances.

You will notice that each of the twelve signs falls into a different combination. No one sign in the zodiac has exactly the same duality, element, and quality as another sign. For example, Aries is a Masculine, Fire, Cardinal sign; there is no other Masculine, Fire, Cardinal sign in the zodiac.

Because each sign is a unique combination, each sign expresses the characteristics of its quality, element, and duality differently.

Example: Aries is Masculine, meaning it is active rather than receptive; Fire, meaning it is excitable and energetic; Cardinal, meaning it is outgoing and open to new experiences. The sign of Leo is also Masculine and Fire, but unlike Aries (which is Cardinal) Leo is Fixed. Therefore Leo is extroverted and passionate like Aries, but also firm in its opinions, convinced of being on the side of truth in its passions, and not as willing as Aries to abandon an unworkable plan and go on to something new.

Polarities

Finally, the twelve signs are divided into six groups containing two signs each. Each two-sign group is called a polarity (meaning "opposite"). Each sign in the zodiac has a polarity, which is its opposite sign in the other half of the zodiac. The two signs express opposite characteristics.

Aries and Libra are a polarity. Aries is the sign of self. The opposite sign, Libra, is the sign of partnership.

*When the Sun crosses the four cardinal points in the zodiac, we mark the beginning of each of our four seasons: Aries begins spring; Cancer begins summer; Libra begins fall; Capricorn begins winter.

Taurus and Scorpio are a polarity. Taurus is the sign of personal possessions. The opposite sign, Scorpio, is the sign of legacies and shared possessions.

Gemini and Sagittarius are a polarity. Gemini is the sign of self-expression. The opposite sign, Sagittarius, is the sign of philosophy and higher thinking, of expression on a wider level.

Cancer and Capricorn are a polarity. Cancer is the sign of home life. The opposite sign, Capricorn, is the sign of public life.

Leo and Aquarius are a polarity. Leo is the sign of personal pleasure and creativity. The opposite sign, Aquarius, is the sign of hopes and ideals on a large scale.

Virgo and Pisces are a polarity. Virgo is the sign of work and self-improvement. The opposite sign, Pisces, is the sign of dreams and self-delusion.

Each of the twelve signs is attached to special associations in the outer world. There are lucky numbers, lucky days of the week, special colors, plants, metals, jewels, cities, etc. Each sign also has particular pitfalls and areas of danger attached to it.

In this modern day, however, some of these associations are quoted more for amusement than for guidance and instruction. Astrologers do not seriously suggest that if you are Aries you will like only the color red and wear diamonds, or if you are Virgo you will be happy living only in Boston and raising morning glories in your window box. The affinities to various colors, jewels, places, flowers are simply part of the long, long history of symbols and connections that has grown up around the signs of the zodiac.

Sometimes, however, it is fun to experiment with your zodiacal affinities. I have a client, for example, who gives "astrological" dinner parties and chooses flowers, table settings, and food that have certain connections to the zodiacal signs of her guests. Another client, who is a Gemini, recently took a trip to Melbourne, Australia, simply because of the affinity of his sign for that distant city. He wrote me ecstatically: "The minute I stepped off the plane I just knew that I was truly at home!"

Part of the fascination of astrology is in its complexity; the various associations and symbolism surrounding the twelve signs are part of that rich tapestry. No two astrological signs are alike. Each one is different and unique. Each holds clues to who we are and the things and places to which we are drawn.

What Is Your Sun Sign?

The dates listed for each Sun sign may vary by a day or two in certain years. To be sure of *your* exact Sun sign, look up the year and month of your birth in the Sun Tables starting on page 425 or cast your chart using the enclosed CD-ROM.

ARIES
(MARCH 21 — APRIL 19)

DUALITY Masculine

TRIPLICITY (ELEMENT) Fire

QUADRUPLICITY (QUALITY) Cardinal

   Aries is active, energetic, excitable and impulsive, optimistic, open to change and new experiences,

RULING PLANET Mars: Ancient god of war, aggression, and conflict. In astrology, Mars's influence denotes courage, passion, and competition. It can foster tension and accidents, and rules over fire and danger.

SYMBOL The Ram: Assertive, sexual, able to climb to great heights.

GLYPH (WRITTEN SYMBOL)   The pictograph represents the horns and long nose of the Ram. It also pictures the eyebrows and nose of the human face (the head is the part of anatomy that Aries rules). In symbolic terms, the glyph is two half moons joined by a straight line, which indicates idealism tied to authority and leadership.

DOMINANT KEYWORD I AM.

POLARITY Libra:

   Aries is a "me-first" sign. People with Aries tendencies strongly project their own personalities and can be very self-oriented. Libra, which is Aries's opposite sign, is the sign of partnership. Natives of Libra feel incomplete without a partner or lover, and strive for happiness as a pair.

PART OF THE BODY RULED BY ARIES The head: Aries people are prone to headaches, and subject to minor injuries around the head and face.

LUCKY DAY Tuesday   **LUCKY NUMBERS** 1 and 9

MAGICAL BIRTHSTONE Diamond: Attracts love, financial success, and brings luck in new ventures. The diamond is particularly lucky for Aries people when worn on the left side of the body.

SPECIAL COLOR Red: The color of fire and excitement.

CITIES Florence, Naples, Verona, Marseilles   **COUNTRIES** England, Germany, Poland

FLOWERS Geranium, Honeysuckle, Sweet Pea   **TREES** All thorn-bearing trees

METAL Iron

ANIMALS RULED BY ARIES Sheep and, especially, rams

DANGER Aries people are susceptible to harm from fire and sharp instruments. They are also prone to accidents involving high speed, and tend to get into violent and dangerous situations.

Your Most Likeable Trait
COURAGE

ARIES IS THE FIRST SIGN of the zodiac, the sign that symbolizes new beginnings. It connotes quick changes and sudden forks in the road. Your life is marked by arriving at a certain place and then being turned in a new direction. Certainly, one can say your life is adventurous!

There is a dynamic restlessness to the Aries character. With the Sun in this sign, you are an activist and doer. If you have a new plan or idea—if an enterprise strikes your fancy—you can't wait to plunge right in. The amusing little prayer, "Grant me patience NOW!" is typical of the Arien attitude.

When others first meet you their instant impression is of someone exciting, vibrant, talkative. Others will be lucky if they can get a word in edgewise. If someone brings up a topic, you will be delighted to tell in great detail exactly what you think about it.

As an Aries person you gravitate toward the center of action. You are audacious and intent on getting your own way. Since your nature is to express power, you treat opposition as an annoyance to be brushed out of the way. You are a natural leader who exudes self-confidence. From an early age you feel you are headed for success.

Happily, you are also generous about helping others in a crisis. You are an openhearted friend who shares ideas and advice, and likes to pick up the check. You have a quality of largesse. You are not interested in the small or petty. "Go for the best" is your motto.

There is nothing faint or half-hearted about an Arien. Whereas others may be more cautious, you actually enjoy living on the edge. A touch of recklessness makes you feel alive. The chase is always more thrilling than getting the goal. (As one Aries recently remarked rather insightfully, "Wanting is always better than getting.") You are willing to take a gamble, follow a dream, set your mind on a goal, and pursue it with irresistible enthusiasm. Your supreme quality of optimism attracts others. Underneath there may lurk insecurity, but no one will ever know about it.

This is not to say you don't get depressed or moody. But the winter of despair doesn't last a week with Aries. You have an uncrackable optimism. It is true, however, that Aries people are notorious for taking offense at fancied slights and injuries. Hot tempers and childish tantrums abound, and your threshold of boredom is extremely low. If success is not immediate, you tend to lose interest and go in search of other excitement. As a result, patient, plodding types often get to the head of the class before you do.

Ariens have a well-deserved reputation for not finishing what they have begun. You are very short of patience, and your lack of stick-to-itiveness is your weak spot. Also, you spend your energy in too many different ways, like the Ring Lardner hero who mounted a horse and rode off in all directions at once.

Independence is a keyword. You can turn sulky and peevish if you have to take orders. You would much rather be the world's largest lizard than the world's smallest dragon. You want to run the whole show. If you can't, you pull up stakes and look for a situation in which you can show off your style and brilliance. Should you come up against a superior force, you will bend but never break.

Your aggressive and combative spirit cannot be broken by anyone—except yourself.

One of the pitfalls of being an Aries is that you're essentially self-involved. Unless you make an effort to look outward at others and their feelings, you can easily become a spoiled brat.

Though generally sincere and honest, you will tell a white lie if it seems advantageous. You are not a very adept liar, however; others see right through you. Sometimes you lack tact and diplomacy, but no malice is intended. Sagittarians also lack this quality of tact because they don't know how to be oblique or roundabout. With you, tactlessness is an impulsive act—a careless expression of your innate force. Too often you speak without thinking and say whatever pops into your mouth, and usually regret your impulsiveness later.

Aries is lucky with money, but has trouble holding on to it. You tend to run up big bills, live extravagantly, soar over budget. However, you usually find a way to pay off what you owe. You have too much pride to remain in anyone's debt.

In friendship you give magnanimously if someone is in need, but you want to get credit for your good deeds. In the garden of Aries, there are few shrinking violets.

You are creative, openhearted, high-spirited, pioneering, also vain, feisty, and impatient. Those who deal with you on an intimate basis will have one chief problem: How are they going to keep up the pace?

The Inner You

You like to be in charge—you want to control your own projects and plans and not be under anyone else's thumb. You have an intense drive to succeed and put a lot of pressure on yourself. Inside, you're filled with nervous energy and worry about how you're going to handle everything. You hate to be bored; you're always looking for something different—new people and places that promise excitement and adventure. You have very little patience; you need to practice sticking things out. You're also impatient with people who can't resolve a problem. You believe in taking action. What you do have are great generosity and enthusiasm. And although you suffer from occasional self-doubt, you know that if you really want to do something, you can!

How Others See You

Your upbeat, magnetic personality pulls people toward you—you bring excitement into their lives. They envy your aggressiveness in meeting a challenge. Whatever the problem, you give the impression that you have an answer ready. You're also admired for your honesty; you don't gloss over difficulties. What people don't like is your tendency toward bossiness and your deserved reputation for being sharp-tongued. They're afraid to cross you in an argument because they know you can cut them to the quick.

Famous People with the Sun in Aries

Maya Angelou	Isak Dinesen	Peyton Manning	Omar Sharif
Johann Sebastian Bach	Celine Dion	Eugene McCarthy	Stephen Sondheim
Alec Baldwin	David Frost	Steve McQueen	Edward Steichen
Warren Beatty	Robert Frost	Ann Miller	Rod Steiger
Marlon Brando	James Garner	Dudley Moore	Gloria Steinem
Matthew Broderick	John Gielgud	Eddie Murphy	Leopold Stokowski
Charles Chaplin	Alec Guinness	Leonard Nimoy	Gloria Swanson
Cesar Chavez	Hugh Hefner	Rosie O'Donnell	Arturo Toscanini
Tom Clancy	Billie Holiday	Sarah Jessica Parker	Spencer Tracy
Billy Collins	Harry Houdini	Danica Patrick	Peter Ustinov
Joan Crawford	Henry James	Gregory Peck	Ludwig Mies Van Der Rohe
Russell Crowe	Thomas Jefferson	Anthony Perkins	Vincent van Gogh
Clarence Darrow	Elton John	Mary Pickford	Andrew Lloyd Webber
Bette Davis	Keira Knightley	Colin Powell	Thornton Wilder
Doris Day	David Letterman	Sergei Rachmaninoff	Tennessee Williams
Daniel Day-Lewis	Ali MacGraw	Diana Ross	Florenz Ziegfeld

Colin Powell

Peyton Manning

Maya Angelou

TAURUS
(APRIL 20 – MAY 20)

DUALITY Feminine

TRIPLICITY (ELEMENT) Earth

QUADRUPLICITY (QUALITY) Fixed

Taurus is quiet, affectionate, patient, stable, determined and practical, stubborn, and resistant to change.

RULING PLANET Venus: Roman goddess of beauty and the arts, pleasure, emotions. In astrology, Venus's influence inclines toward a love of luxury and exceptional creative ability.

SYMBOL The Bull: Strong, stubborn, plodding, can be both fierce and gentle.

GLYPH (WRITTEN SYMBOL) ♉ The pictograph represents the horns and head of the Bull. It also outlines the chin and Adam's apple of the human throat (the part of the anatomy that Taurus rules). In symbolic terms, the glyph is a half-moon forming a cup that rests on the circle of the Sun. The cup represents material power and wealth derived through the force of will (the circle).

DOMINANT KEYWORD I HAVE.

POLARITY Scorpio:

Taurus is the sign of property and money. Its natives put a high regard on collecting possessions and are known to cling to what is theirs. Scorpio, Taurus's opposite sign, is the sign of legacies and shared wealth. The wealth of Scorpio people tends to be spiritual rather than material, which they give to others in the form of teaching, writing, and the healing arts.

PART OF THE BODY RULED BY TAURUS Neck and throat: Many Taurus people have beautiful speaking and singing voices. But they are vulnerable to colds, laryngitis, sore throats, and thyroid problems.

LUCKY DAY Friday   **LUCKY NUMBERS** 6 and 4

MAGICAL BIRTHSTONE Emerald: Protects against infidelity and deceit, ensures loyalty, and improves memory.

SPECIAL COLORS Pale blue and mauve: The soft colors of refinement and gentleness.

CITIES Dublin, Lucerne, Leipzig, St. Louis   **COUNTRIES** Ireland, Switzerland, Cyprus, Greece

FLOWERS Violet and Poppy   **TREES** Cypress and Apple

METAL Copper

ANIMALS RULED BY TAURUS Cattle

DANGER Taurus people have a tendency to get involved in violent situations that have to do with love or money. They often antagonize others and incite the passions of lovers because of their stubbornness and possessiveness.

Your Most Likeable Trait
DEPENDABILITY

YOU ARE THE PERSON others count on in the clutch, the one who perseveres when less determined spirits fall by the wayside. Because perseverance is the quality most needed for success, you tend to be successful.

You are not the pioneer who first strikes out for new territory, but the determined settler who follows and builds houses and towns and cultivates the soil. If you were born under this second sign of the zodiac, there is a pronounced stubborn streak in you. Your greatest strength resides in your tenacity and steady, relentless drive. You are a purposeful achiever who has endless patience to see a thing through, to make it a success. You are the original immovable object *and* irresistible force.

Taurus is a fixed sign, which means its natives are not fond of change. You simply cannot be rushed into anything new. A different approach creates unease and anxiety in you. You are most comfortable and secure with the familiar, and your attitude might be summed up as "If everything is working fine the way it is, why try something new?"

Everyone knows you have a temper, although you rarely show it. As a subordinate remarked of a Taurean executive, "No one actually saw him lose his temper, but no one ever doubted that he had one." Generally, you are equable and patient, as patient as time itself, and it is only when opposed (even then, it will take a lot of pushing) that you become angry. However, there is volcanic activity going on underneath your easygoing, genial exterior. Like a bull quietly grazing in a pasture, you're not looking to challenge anyone, but it would be a fatal mistake for anyone to challenge you.

However, unless someone seriously provokes the fierce side to your personality, you are like Ferdinand the Bull, the gentle cartoon character who loves to sit and smell the flowers. You are caring, giving, and affectionate, and have a great fondness for all things beautiful. Ruled by Venus, goddess of love and beauty, you are endowed with genuine creative gifts, responsive to color and design, inspired by art and music. The Taurean taste is supremely elegant. You have a keen eye for what is valuable and are usually an avid collector. Indeed, you were born under one of the two money signs in the zodiac (Cancer is the other one), for Taurus represents material possessions. It's a rare native of this sign who does not think that possessions, *objets*, wealth, and money are definitely for *having*—and the more the better.

Others are fascinated by your rare blending of a down-to-earth person who is such a romantic, poetic sort. In Taurus, the stability of an earth sign combines with the esthetic influence of Venus to create a responsible, steadfast personality with a deep appreciation for the finer aspects of life. Again and again, you'll find that the unique pairing of your artistic vision with your determination to reach a goal is one of the great secrets to your success.

You are also driven by the search for security—your byword. You look for permanence in career, love, marriage, and home. Let others gad about, jet-set, gallivant, and sleep around. You are happiest at home, surrounded by the beautiful, expensive things you have collected, secure in the warmth of a mate's devotion, steadfast and faithful to those whom you love.

Beneath the surface you are sensuous and sentimental. You don't give lavish gifts as tokens of affection because you are not a carefree spender—value is what you expect for your hard-earned dollar. Although you are willing to follow where your heart leads, you find it difficult to display your feelings openly. Your personality is private and self-contained.

Living with you isn't always easy. You can be dogmatic, secretive, stingy, opinionated, and suspicious, and your silent manner may conceal feelings of envy and rivalry. It's hard to get you moving, for you tend to be self-indulgent, even lazy.

You have great stores of energy, however, which you put to use when *you* want to—not when others want you to.

Venus emphasizes the social side of Taurus. Although basically shy and reserved with strangers, you can be a wonderful host or hostess. You like to entertain those you are fond of. You may not indulge as freely in frivolous pleasures as, say, Leo or Libra natives, but you are renowned for enjoying good food and good wine in plush surroundings. You believe in pampering yourself with the comforts of the good life.

As a person born under this sign, you are an endearing combination of the dependable and sensible, the sensitive and emotional. Inside every practical, stolid-seeming Taurean, there is a romantic dreamer struggling to get out.

The Inner You

You need order in your life—you get anxious when things are out of control. And because the unfamiliar makes you feel insecure, you tend to cut yourself off from fresh experiences. You need to be more open to change. Having beautiful things is important to you, and your instinct for collecting even spills over into relationships. You hold fast to those you care about. You have a few close friends rather than many casual acquaintances. In love, you're happiest when involved in a caring, committed relationship. You're deeply sensitive—a rebuff or harsh word is very upsetting to you—and with strangers, you often feel self-conscious.

How Others See You

You're thought of as a serene influence, someone to depend on, and you're admired for your organized mind. Not many people realize that you're sensitive and easily wounded. You are trusted as a tastemaker, and your artistic and esthetic opinion is welcomed. Because you have sound instincts about money, your financial advice is also sought. On the other hand, people resent your tendency to be dogmatic. Even if you're right, others don't understand why you have to be so unyielding.

FAMOUS PEOPLE WITH THE SUN IN TAURUS

Akon	Kirsten Dunst	Sugar Ray Leonard	Roberta Peters
Ann-Margret	Albert Finney	Leonardo da Vinci	Michelle Pfeiffer
Fred Astaire	Ella Fitzgerald	Liberace	Ezio Pinza
Mary Astor	Henry Fonda	Anita Loos	Pope John Paul II
Burt Bacharach	Sigmund Freud	Joe Louis	Sergei Prokofiev
Stephen Baldwin	Martha Graham	Karl Marx	Anthony Quinn
Lionel Barrymore	Ulysses S. Grant	Rod McKuen	Bertrand Russell
Candice Bergen	William Randolph Hearst	Shirley MacLaine	Pete Seeger
Irving Berlin	Joseph Heller	Bernard Malamud	William Shakespeare
Yogi Berra	Audrey Hepburn	Tim McGraw	Benjamin Spock
Cate Blanchett	Katharine Hepburn	Golda Meir	James Stewart
Johannes Brahms	Glenda Jackson	Yehudi Menuhin	Barbra Streisand
Carol Burnett	Janet Jackson	Patrice Munsel	Peter Ilyich Tchaikovsky
George Carlin	Reggie Jackson	Vladimir Nabokov	Shirley Temple
Cher	Bianca Jagger	Willie Nelson	Uma Thurman
George Clooney	Jasper Johns	Jack Nicholson	Harry S. Truman
Stephen Colbert	Dwayne "The Rock" Johnson	Florence Nightingale	Rudolph Valentino
Perry Como	Grace Jones	Ryan O'Neal	Orson Welles
Gary Cooper	Harper Lee	Al Pacino	
Bing Crosby	Jay Leno	Eva Perón	

Pope John Paul II   *Stephen Colbert*   *Audrey Hepburn*

GEMINI
(MAY 21 – JUNE 20)

DUALITY Masculine

TRIPLICITY (ELEMENT) Air

QUADRUPLICITY (QUALITY) Mutable

Gemini is lively, energetic, versatile, and intellectual, lives primarily in the mind rather than the emotions, and is extremely adaptable to new situations.

RULING PLANET Mercury: Ancient messenger of the gods. In astrology, Mercury rules communication and travel. Its influence emphasizes quick cleverness and a nervous temperament.

SYMBOL The Twins: Associated with duality, humanism, versatility, communication.

GLYPH (WRITTEN SYMBOL) Ⅱ The pictograph represents the two figures of the Twins. The dual symbol also pictures the human arms or lungs (the parts of the body that Gemini rules). In symbolic terms, two upright lines bounded by top and bottom lines represent wisdom, learning, and the powers of the mind to synthesize information.

DOMINANT KEYWORD I THINK.

POLARITY Sagittarius:

Gemini is the sign of thought and communication on a personal level. Natives of Gemini strive for self-expression, and try to impose their point of view on others. Sagittarius, which is Gemini's opposite sign, is the sign governing the wider provenance of philosophy and mental exploration. Sagittarian people tend to shrink from close personal involvement and, unlike Gemini, are shaped by what others think of them.

PART OF THE BODY RULED BY GEMINI Hands, arms, shoulders, and lungs: Geminis are susceptible to strains and accidents involving arms and hands; also prone to bronchitis and respiratory ailments.

LUCKY DAY Wednesday **LUCKY NUMBERS** 5 and 9

MAGICAL BIRTHSTONE Agate: A multicolored precious stone that protects from deception and falsehood, and bestows eloquence, especially in declarations of love.

SPECIAL COLOR Yellow: Bright and luminous, the color of novelty.

CITIES London, San Francisco, Versailles, Melbourne **COUNTRIES** United States, Wales, Belgium

FLOWERS Lily of the Valley and Lavender **TREES** Nut-bearing trees

METAL Mercury

ANIMALS RULED BY GEMINI Brightly colored birds and butterflies

DANGER Gemini people are prone to accidents while traveling, especially by air. Their fickle natures also tend to arouse unexpected anger in others, the depth of which Geminis often misjudge.

Your Most Likeable Trait
RESPONSIVENESS

Pᴇᴏᴘʟᴇ ʙᴏʀɴ ᴜɴᴅᴇʀ this sign are many-sided, quick in thought and action, clever with words, skillful at handling others, brimful of new ideas.

Astrologers regard this third sign of the zodiac as the quintessentially human sign, for it seems to sum up qualities that are the distinguishing hallmarks of the human race—intelligence (Gemini is an air sign), adaptability (Gemini is a mutable sign), and communicativeness (Gemini is ruled by Mercury).

Gemini people do not sit back and watch the scenery go by. As a Gemini, you are endlessly curious about everything and must be part of the busy passing scene. If all the world's a stage, Gemini must be the actor on that stage.

Unlike Leo, who wants only to be the star, Gemini wants to play *all* the parts—and be the director, the producer, and the stagehand!

Duality is your most famous trait. You usually want more than one of everything. That includes jobs, hobbies, careers, and lovers. Basically your nature is restless, on the go, in quest of new ideas and fresh experiences. Things get very dull for you unless you have a constant change of scenery. Variety is your game. As a result, you often leave a trail of unfinished tasks. Your tendency is to fritter away energy on too many projects instead of concentrating your cleverness on one task.

Gemini is the sign of communication, and its natives

have an urgent and continual need to communicate. You enjoy writing notes, chatting with strangers, surfing the web, tossing off e-mails, IM's, and text messages—and the telephone is a major means of communication. People should learn not to give you their number if they don't like to spend a lot of time on the phone!

Your astrological symbol should really be the question mark. You're a perpetual student of life who never stops asking questions. You love to talk to people, and this is the great secret of your charm. Others open to you like flowers. As a result, you're a marvelous people-manager who can rev up enthusiasm and loyalty.

Born with the gift of persuasion, you could sell ice in Greenland. Your quick mind can explain any action, defend any position, justify any course. A mental magpie, you pick up information here, gossip there, tidbits everywhere. This makes you an ideal conversationalist, for you know a little about everything, though, some have said, not a lot about anything. You also are inclined to have firm opinions on everything (subject to revision at a moment's notice). What you value most is intellectual independence, and what you lack most is perseverance.

Another Gemini weakness is superficiality. Because you are so quick to grasp an idea or size up a situation, you tend to skim its surface, not bothering to explore it in any depth. The other side of the coin, however, is that with very little preparation you can make a marvelous initial impression.

Your facile gifts of writing, speaking, and self-expression make you a success in dealing with the public. You have a quicksilver personality that can adapt to many kinds of people. You are often drawn to the stage and the dramatic arts. Among famous writers and performers born with the Sun in Gemini are Sir Arthur Conan Doyle, Dashiell Hammett, Lillian Hellman, Laurence Olivier, Marilyn Monroe, and Judy Garland.

Amusing, versatile and witty, you are a wonderful friend who lifts people out of their doldrums. Does someone need advice? Instruction? An introduction? You're right there, ready to jump in, and others are energized by your enthusiasm. It's easy to see why you are usually surrounded by friends and admirers because you're such fun to be with. True, you can be impatient with persons who aren't as quick as you are, or who can't keep up with the rapid flow of your thought and speech. However, your natural exuberance sweeps even the most reluctant and surly along with you. In almost any situation you can be as charming as you want to be—with a little extra thrown in.

Life is a jest and all things show it;
I thought so once and now I know it,

spells out the philosophy of Gemini. You don't waste time plumbing dark emotional depths, and you certainly don't want to get sucked into anyone's problems that might sabotage your freedom. Though you do have a brooding side to your Jekyll and Hyde disposition, you determinedly put on a cheerful face so you make the best impression. You try not to let anything dampen your high spirits or throw cold water on the fun and games.

Geminis have a wide range of contacts and benefit from the advice and help of influential people. You will attract financial luck, but a tendency toward extravagance often more than offsets it. In your ledger, income always adds up to something a little short of outgo.

Routine and monotony are two things you dread, and you will go to any lengths to avoid them. Change is your keyword, and what you value most is freedom. It's useless for anyone to try to pin you down. For you, the fun is in traveling, not in arriving at a destination. You love to explore new territory, see the way people live on the other side of the world. Inquisitive and imaginative, you are open to a different way of looking at things. Your trendy, up-to-date lifestyle has you constantly living off the fad of the land.

For the sheer fascination of it, people should have at least one Gemini in their lives. (Two might be exhausting.)

The Inner You

You react instantly to new situations, but because you're so keenly attuned to your environment, you tend to have a nervous temperament. And though you give off sparks of energy, excitement, and charm, inside you feel like a wound-up spring. Others are fascinated by your enthusiasm while inwardly you're already bored with this person or that project. In your relationships, you're very giving, but you also need time for yourself. You like to perform, using your wit and intelligence to move to center stage. You love to gossip, mostly because you find out such interesting things! You're generous with your time, friendship, and possessions. One problem is that instead of looking at people's deeper qualities, you tend to judge them by their reaction to you. Are you coming off well; are you *mesmerizing* them?

How Others See You

People like to be around you because you're interesting and amusing. They admire you for your talent with words and sense of humor. Although you're considered more of a cerebral type, friends trust your judgment about emotional matters. They also know you'll jump in to help when asked. Only those closest to you know you can be moody and discouraged. When crossed you can be sarcastic, which makes some people think you're arrogant.

Famous People with the Sun in Gemini

Paula Abdul
Tim Allen
F. Lee Bailey
Josephine Baker
Annette Bening
Mel Blanc
George Bush
Rachel Carson
Rosemary Clooney
Joan Collins
Courtney Cox
Jacques Cousteau
Mario Cuomo
Tony Curtis
Johnny Depp
Arthur Conan Doyle
Albrecht Dürer
Bob Dylan
Clint Eastwood

Ralph Waldo Emerson
Douglas Fairbanks
Ian Fleming
Errol Flynn
Michael J. Fox
Judy Garland
Paul Gauguin
Lou Gehrig
Allen Ginsberg
Benny Goodman
Steffi Graf
Che Guevara
Nathan Hale
Marvin Hamlisch
Dashiell Hammett
Lillian Hellman
Bob Hope
Gerard Manley Hopkins
Hubert Humphrey

Allen Iverson
Angelina Jolie
Tom Jones
Louis Jourdan
John F. Kennedy
Nicole Kidman
Henry Kissinger
Anna Kournikova
Lenny Kravitz
Hugh Laurie
Peggy Lee
Federico García Lorca
Robert Ludlum
Paul McCartney
Malcolm McDowell
Larry McMurtry
Barry Manilow
Thomas Mann
Dean Martin

Marilyn Monroe
Bill Moyers
Joe Namath
Liam Neeson
Joyce Carol Oates
Jacques Offenbach
Laurence Olivier
Frank Oz
Cole Porter
Prince
Alexander Pushkin
Basil Rathbone
Sally Ride
Joan Rivers
Isabella Rossellini
Henri Rousseau
Salman Rushdie
Marquis de Sade
Jean-Paul Sartre

Maurice Sendak
Tupac Shakur
Brooke Shields
Harriet Beecher
    Stowe
Richard Strauss
William Styron
Kathleen Turner
Donald Trump
Richard Wagner
Kanye West
Ruth Westheimer
Walt Whitman
Gene Wilder
Hank Williams Jr.
Venus Williams
Herman Wouk
Frank Lloyd Wright
William Butler Yeats

Marilyn Monroe

John F. Kennedy

Paul McCartney

CANCER
(June 21 – July 22)

DUALITY Feminine

TRIPLICITY (ELEMENT) Water

QUADRUPLICITY (QUALITY) Cardinal

Cancer is receptive, sensitive, and imaginative, sympathetic, kind, and emotional, and possesses an active, shrewd, and intuitive mind.

RULING PLANET The Moon: Earth's one satellite, which waxes and wanes and exerts a powerful magnetic influence. In astrology, the Moon governs emotions and intuitive behavior.

SYMBOL The Crab: Possessing an impenetrable exterior covering soft flesh underneath. At the first sign of danger, it withdraws into its shell and scuttles back to the sea, where it feels safe.

GLYPH (WRITTEN SYMBOL) The pictograph represents the claws of the Crab. It is also a picture of the human breasts (a part of the anatomy that Cancer rules). In symbolic terms, the glyph is two circles of the Sun connected to two crescent moons. The moons represent Cancer's desire to store memories and possessions; the circles tied to the moons represent force and energy expressed through emotions and imagination.

DOMINANT KEYWORD I FEEL.

POLARITY Capricorn:

Cancer is the sign of home and family life. Cancerians seek close personal relationships and are happiest surrounded by the familiar and those whom they love. Capricorn, Cancer's opposite sign, is the sign of reputation and public standing. Natives of Capricorn are concerned with the image they project, and they search for power and fulfillment in the outside world.

PART OF THE BODY RULED BY CANCER The breasts and stomach: Cancerians love to eat and have to fight weight gain in later years. They are also subject to digestive ailments caused by tension and emotional stress.

LUCKY DAY Monday **LUCKY NUMBERS** 3 and 7

MAGICAL BIRTHSTONE Pearl: Changes bad fortune into good and discord into harmony. It also brings support from influential people.

SPECIAL COLORS Sea green and silver: The shimmering colors of the water and the moon.

CITIES Venice, Amsterdam, New York, Algiers **COUNTRIES** Scotland, Holland, New Zealand

FLOWERS Larkspur and Acanthus **TREES** Trees rich in sap

METAL Silver

ANIMALS RULED BY CANCER Those with shell coverings

DANGER Cancer people are susceptible to accidents in the home. They are also prone to becoming victims of theft.

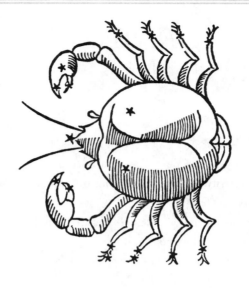

Your Most Likeable Trait
LOYALTY

No one has ever said Cancerians are easy to understand. You may appear gentle, kind, sympathetic, and a patient listener. Then someone asks for advice, and you turn cranky, snappish, and appear to be completely indifferent to anyone's problems but your own. You may wallow in self-pity and complain endlessly about how mistreated you are by the world. Turn another page of the calendar and suddenly you are back being helpful, solicitous, ready to do anything asked of you. More than any other sign, Cancer is a series of contradictions. You prize security above all else, yet love new adventure. You are the soul of caution but you're also a courageous initiator who goes out of your way to push over obstacles with your driving personality.

What's your secret? Cancer, which is ruled by the Moon and has water as its element, can be likened to the shifting tides of the oceans. Like the tides, Cancer is the sign of powerful forces moving under the surface. That surface, however, is quite difficult to penetrate, for Cancerians tend to build up an elaborate array of defenses to hide their deep feelings and extreme sensitivity.

Complex, fragile, unpredictable, temperamental, the typical Cancerian needs constant support and encouragement. You want desperately to be loved and approved of but resent needing approval so badly. Cancer's big lesson is to recognize the hidden anger you carry within you and not allow this to corrode the relationships that give you the emotional support you seek. Happily, when you get what you need, you give the best you have in return. Those who make you feel secure command your undying loyalty. When you really care for someone there is nothing anyone can say about that person that will make the least bit of difference. You have a real blind spot when it comes to seeing a failing in those you love.

If you could wave a magic wand and do the one thing that would make you happier it is to crack open that Crab shell and venture out into the world of possibility. Staying enclosed emotionally and psychically keeps you fearful. Cancer's fears are based on the fact that you have a difficult time trusting. You don't trust others or the universe or yourself. One Cancer told me recently, "We've been sold a bill of goods by the stories we were told as children. There is no joy or happiness in life. Life is just plain hard." The problem with this point of view is it leaves very little opening for any kind of abundance to flow in. It's hard to see the kindness in loved ones or the generosity of strangers or unexpected luck in an arduous situation if one has decided from the start that it's a dog-eat-dog world.

Yet most contradictory of all is the fact you're such a nurturer who gives unselfishly to anyone who needs you. Your greatest impact is in human relationships; you have an instinct for making others feel cared for and understood. Among your most endearing traits is your loyalty.

You tend to be a worrier and a silent brooder. People may pour out their hearts to you, but the flow never goes in the other direction. You are cautious about revealing too much of yourself; you guard your secrets well.

If offended, you do not strike back directly. Your method of retaliation is to sulk, and it is often very effective. The technique is somewhat like being whipped to death by a dozen strands of boiled spaghetti.

Cancer's symbol, the Crab, has a hard outer shell that protects soft, vulnerable flesh underneath. The same is true of Cancerians, who are often crusty, gruff, and grumpy, but possess a proverbial heart of gold. Beneath your tough exterior you are a sentimental softie who will make any sacrifice for someone in need. If someone asks for a favor, your first reaction will probably be no, but the final answer is always yes. You should be judged not by what you say but by what you do.

You are possessive. Anyone who becomes part of your life will never again be entirely free. You try to stay in touch with friends, ex-lovers, former spouses, business associates, persons you knew as children. Cancer is the cosmic collector—if you let anyone go out of your life, it is unwillingly and never completely. This reflects your preoccupation with the past. An aura of nostalgia dwells about you; the events and people of bygone years continue to inhabit your memory and usually grow dearer to you as time goes by. You are devoted to family and home and continue to believe in the old-fashioned idea that marriage is forever—even if the events of your own life contradict this.

It is hard to deceive you, for you can spot the tiniest nuances of behavior. In fact, you are almost psychic in your intuitions. A photographic memory added to intense powers of observation makes you extremely canny about divining other people's inner motivations.

Cancerians are crablike in their indirect approach to an intended target. Observe a crab moving on a beach and you will notice its strange sidewise movement toward a goal. People born under the sign of the Crab never take the direct approach. You step to one side, then step to the other side, and sometimes go completely around. But you get where you intend to go.

If channeled in the right direction, your enormous sensitivity can be a great source of strength. Once you overcome your shyness and touchiness and master your turbulent emotions, your intellect and imagination enable you to become a success in almost anything you undertake. You have the ability to dig into your own inner life and turn creativity into practical ideas. Contrary to the impression you often give, you can be shrewd and canny in business. Cautious, conservative in your approach, you possess an antenna that quickly gauges public taste and opinion and senses new trends in the making. You're also an on-the-mark judge of people. You are artistic and creative, and have formidable intellectual talents. This instinct for business combined with imagination is magical for acquiring financial security, and Cancer is called a "money sign" because of its ability to attract wealth.

Cancer people hold on to money as tenaciously as they do to everything that belongs to them. To you money spells security, yet no matter how much wealth you accumulate you never feel really secure. That is true of your emotional security also. A Cancerian never gets enough love and approval; you always need more. It is very easy to fall in love with this loyal, devoted, affectionate, and protective Moon-child.

The Inner You

On the surface you're the picture of calm and strength, but underneath you tend to feel insecure and inadequate. You are positive that other people know what they're doing while you're just winging it. You also imagine the worst outcome to a scenario, never the best. You are a very emotional person; you are constantly *feeling*. Hearing a song on the radio makes you feel sentimental, and a particular scent, flower, or picture can jar your memory. You

are also extraordinarily in sync with other people's feelings. In fact, you get almost as involved in your friends' problems as you do in your own. When you're close to someone, you believe you are supposed to help that person. Harmony is important to you—any kind of conflict or quarrel leaves you feeling depressed. However, you're definitely not wishy-washy; you have the courage of your convictions and the strength to stick up for what you think is right. You don't welcome change, and are hesitant about going ahead with something untried, yet this doesn't stop you from doing what has to be done.

How Others See You

Those in your circle think of you as a den mother—the one who tries to fix other people's problems and make sure everyone is happy. They like your concern for their well-being and cherish your wise counsel. But why, even if they follow your advice, do they keep it a secret from you? Because they think you're controlling and don't want to be a puppet on your string. They also think you're moody. One minute you seem to care about them, and the next you're crabby and to be avoided at all costs. In your career, you're viewed as someone who can quickly spot an opportunity for financial gain.

FAMOUS PEOPLE WITH THE SUN IN CANCER

Alexander the Great
Louis Armstrong
Polly Bergen
Ingmar Bergman
Bill Blass
David Brinkley
Mel Brooks
Yul Brynner
George W. Bush
James Cagney
Pierre Cardin
Barbara Cartland
Marc Chagall
Gower Champion
John Chancellor
Van Cliburn
Jean Cocteau
Bill Cosby
Tom Cruise
Olivia de Havilland

Oscar de la Renta
Diana, Princess
    of Wales
Phyllis Diller
Marty Feldman
M. F. K. Fisher
Harrison Ford
Bob Fosse
Stephen Foster
Erle Stanley Gardner
John Glenn
Merv Griffin
Susan Hayward
Tom Hanks
Nathaniel Hawthorne
Ernest Hemingway
Al Hirschfeld
Judy Holliday
Lena Horne
Anjelica Huston

Randy Jackson
Derek Jeter
Frida Kahlo
Franz Kafka
Helen Keller
Rose Kennedy
Ann Landers
Janet Leigh
Lindsay Lohan
Gina Lollobrigida
Sidney Lumet
Tobey Maguire
Nelson Mandela
Mary McCarthy
George McGovern
Marshall McLuhan
Bess Myerson
Clifford Odets
George Orwell
Camilla Parker-Bowles

Ross Perot
Prince William
Marcel Proust
Gilda Radner
Nancy Reagan
Erich Maria Remarque
Diana Rigg
Geraldo Rivera
Nelson Rockefeller
Ginger Rogers
Linda Ronstadt
Jean-Jacques Rousseau
Françoise Sagan
Antoine de
    Saint-Exupéry
George Sand
Carly Simon
Neil Simon
Jessica Simpson
Jimmy Smits

Sylvester Stallone
Barbara Stanwyck
Ringo Starr
Isaac Stern
Patrick Stewart
Irving Stone
Meryl Streep
Donald Sutherland
William Makepeace
    Thackeray
Twyla Tharp
Henry David Thoreau
Mike Tyson
Abigail Van Buren
James Whistler
E. B. White
Billy Wilder
Robin Williams
Andrew Wyeth

Princess Diana

George W. Bush

Ernest Hemingway

LEO
(JULY 23 – AUGUST 22)

DUALITY Masculine

TRIPLICITY (ELEMENT) Fire

QUADRUPLICITY (QUALITY) Fixed

Leo is enthusiastic, powerful, expansive and creative, generous and extravagant, dogmatic and fixed in opinion.

RULING PLANET The Sun: Center of our solar system, a star that burns with intense fire and supplies us with light, heat, and energy. In astrology, the Sun is the most powerful planetary influence, bestowing vitality and authority.

SYMBOL The Lion: Regal, brave, dominating, sometimes indolent. Possessing nobility and pride.

GLYPH (WRITTEN SYMBOL) The pictograph represents two valves of the human heart (a part of the anatomy that Leo rules). It is also the Greek symbol for the first letter of Leo. In symbolic terms, it is two incomplete circles of the Sun joined by a crescent Moon, symbolizing power derived from both the intellect and the emotions.

DOMINANT KEYWORD I WILL.

POLARITY Aquarius:

Leo is the sign that governs pleasure and creativity. Natives of Leo look for what they can get out of life for themselves, and tend to dominate others. Aquarius, Leo's opposite sign, is the sign of hopes and wishes and the higher aspirations of mankind. Aquarian people are concerned with larger ideals, humanitarian concepts, and are more impersonal and aloof in their relationships.

PART OF THE BODY RULED BY LEO Back, spine, and the heart: Emotional strain and physical overexertion cause back and spine ailments in Leo people.

LUCKY DAY Sunday **LUCKY NUMBERS** 8 and 9

MAGICAL BIRTHSTONE Ruby: Protects against physical injury and ensures faithfulness. It also brings its wearer serenity of mind.

SPECIAL COLORS Gold and orange: The magnetic colors of the Sun.

CITIES Rome, Prague, Damascus, Hollywood **COUNTRIES** France, Italy, Romania

FLOWERS Sunflower and Marigold **TREES** Orange and all citrus trees

METAL Gold

ANIMALS RULED BY LEO All felines

DANGER Leo people tend to be bombastic and challenging, and often unknowingly provoke others into impulsive violence. They are also prone to being victims of slander.

Your Most Likeable Trait
EXUBERANCE

YOUR LOYALTY is beyond question. You are devoted to yourself. All Leos possess a kingdom. The kingdom may be big or small, it may be your home or a lover or a piece of creative work or your whole career. But whatever it is, you are unquestioningly ruler of this kingdom. Self-assurance surrounds Leo people like a ghost image on a television set. While others wait in the wings, you bask in the spotlight. Whatever you do, you do with a flair for the dramatic—everything about you is theatrical. You don't have to look for a role to play in life. You've found it. You are the monarch of all you survey.

When you enter a room you secretly hope everyone will stand up and sing a few stanzas of the Hallelujah Chorus! At a party it isn't long before you assume control of the evening. Witty, vivacious, a fluent talker, you are a born entertainer who can lend spice to any occasion. Your energy is electric, and people gravitate to you as steel filings to a magnet.

Your Sun sign confers a great flair for drama and an instinct for getting attention. Because your nature is flamboyant and expansive, you despise the humdrum, the ordinary, and the dull. When real life does not supply all the excitement you need, you try to create your own. Hyperbole is second nature to you. You are born to do things in a r-r-really big way.

If you invite people to your castle (which is how you think of your home), you entertain them royally. You are a splendid host.

Others may become reconciled to accepting second best; not Leos. Born under the most royal sign of the zodiac, there is absolutely nothing Leo people can think of that's too good for them. Luxury is as vital to you as breathing. You want to enjoy the good life, and never mind what it costs. You are not a good haggler or bargainer because basically you want what you want when you want it.

Your public image is very important to you. When a Leo woman's checking account is down to two figures somehow she'll find the means to buy a glorious new dress, and when his credit cards are overdrawn a Leo man will still make reservations at the best restaurant in town. Leos are the most lavish spenders in the zodiac (Librans run a close second).

Generous, kind, and openhearted, you find it hard to believe ill of others. If injured, you strike back quickly, but you also forgive easily and never hold a grudge. Marvelously affectionate and cheerful, you have genuine joie de vivre. The Sun is your ruler, and you always bring some sunshine into the lives of others. Obviously, this is one of your most endearing traits. In many ways you are like the Sun itself—life-enhancing, radiating energy and magnetism, burning with steady fixity. Astrologers call Leos eternal children, for you take pleasure from the moment and are uninhibited in giving affection.

No one could ask for a better friend. If approached in the right way (flattery is the right way), you will do almost anything, but you expect praise and appreciation and admiration in return. Pride is your Achilles' heel. Your ego demands not respect but adoration, not compliments but flattery, and when you receive lavish praise you never stop to wonder if it is insincere. Despite your self-centeredness, you need others to give to if only to get back their appreciation. However,

because you're too proud to ask for appreciation, you often suffer silently from a wounded ego. Your hidden secret is you *need* to be needed.

In business you are the one in command. Another sign that gravitates toward authority is Capricorn, but its natives steadily climb toward a high position. Leos simply assume that they were born to high position. One of your most useful assets in career is an unerring instinct for getting along with people who are in a position to be helpful. You know the value of socializing and work best in group enterprises rather than solitary pursuits. You're an order-giver, not an order-taker, but you're usually so cheery and enthusiastic others don't mind taking orders from you. You are also a hard worker who doesn't ask more of anyone else than you do of yourself. You won't quail before a challenge or flinch from a confrontation. You will do the thing that scares you because to do otherwise spells failure to your eyes. You are ambitious, but not ruthless. All you ask is to be in the limelight.

Among your most striking characteristics is a refusal to be hampered by petty rules. Day-to-day routine quickly leads to boredom and makes you desperately unhappy. Your unhappiness doesn't last long, because you simply won't put up with it. You have an unshakable belief in your luck and quickly bounce back from despondency.

It is difficult (though not impossible) to dislike a Leo. True, you can be bombastic and overbearing at times. True, you love to give advice and tell people how to run their lives. Like your symbol, the Lion, you can be quite indolent and lazy; you like to sit back and bask in your own glory. But your great warmth and sunny disposition is very hard to resist. The world would be much less fun without Leos.

The Inner You

You have larger-than-life emotions; whether you're experiencing joy, despair, excitement, or love, it might as well be playing on a giant movie screen. You feel you have an important role to play in life and you're going to find it. You need to be involved in the world; in fact, you tend to think of any plan or project that you're part of as an extension of who you are. You believe in taking action. Your immediate reaction to any problem is to do something about it rather than sit around pondering it. But you're extremely sensitive and you try to hide this fact under a lot of bravado. It's very important to you to get others' approval. What makes you special, though, is that in spite of all your inner qualms, you jut out your chin and walk head-on into any challenge. You have a deep-seated need to prove your worth—not to others but to yourself. You'll tackle any job just so you can say, "I wasn't afraid to try!"

How Others See You

You have a regal quality, a way of standing out in a crowd. The unique combination of the excitement you project, your sense of style, your way of speaking, and your laugh is what draws people to you. They're also seduced by the fact that you think big, which feeds their own fantasies of success and power. They're attracted to your energy and enthusiasm and your take-charge attitude. They assume you'll take a leadership position. But some people dislike what they consider your king-sized ego. They think you hog the spotlight and that you're performing even when you're perfectly serious and sincere; they question your sincerity. Others regard you as a showoff who merely talks a big game. And there are those who think you have the temperament of a demanding, spoiled child.

FAMOUS PEOPLE WITH THE SUN IN LEO

Ben Affleck	Ramond Chandler	Al Gore	Madonna	Gene Roddenberry
Gracie Allen	Julia Child	Melanie Griffith	Steve Martin	Kenny Rogers
Neil Armstrong	Bill Clinton	Mata Hari	Maureen McGovern	J. K. Rowling
Lucille Ball	Paula Creamer	Alfred Hitchcock	Herman Melville	Yves Saint Laurent
Antonio Banderas	Guy de Maupassant	Dustin Hoffman	Robert Mitchum	Pete Sampras
Count Basie	Cecil B. DeMille	Whitney Houston	Benito Mussolini	Arnold Schwarzenegger
Ethel Barrymore	Robert De Niro	John Huston	Annie Oakley	George Bernard Shaw
Tony Bennett	Elizabeth Dole	Aldous Huxley	Barack Obama	Percy Bysshe Shelley
Simon Bolívar	Madame du Barry	Mick Jagger	Carroll O'Connor	Kevin Spacey
Napoleon Bonaparte	Marcel Duchamp	Peter Jennings	Jacqueline Kennedy	Danielle Steel
Barry Bonds	Leo Durocher	Magic Johnson	Onassis	Martha Stewart
Ray Bradbury	Amelia Earhart	Carl Jung	Peter O'Toole	Alfred, Lord Tennyson
Diamond Jim Brady	Zelda Fitzgerald	Garrison Keillor	Dorothy Parker	Leon Uris
Sandra Bullock	Jerry Garcia	Francis Scott Key	Maxfield Parrish	Andy Warhol
Claus von Bulow	Frank Gifford	T. E. Lawrence	Sean Penn	Mae West
Ken Burns	Kathie Lee Gifford	Monica Lewinsky	Roman Polanski	Shelley Winters
Fidel Castro	Jeff Gordon	Jennifer Lopez	Robert Redford	Orville Wright

Mick Jagger

Madonna

Bill Clinton

VIRGO
(AUGUST 23 – SEPTEMBER 22)

DUALITY Feminine

TRIPLICITY (ELEMENT) Earth

QUADRUPLICITY (QUALITY) Mutable

Virgo is reserved, modest, practical, discriminating and industrious, analytical and painstaking, seeking to know and understand.

RULING PLANET Mercury: Ancient god of communication and commerce. In astrology, Mercury rules intelligence and reason, and predisposes toward a highstrung temperament.

SYMBOL The Virgin: Representing purity of motive, modesty, industriousness, and service of oneself and one's talents toward helping others. The virgin is usually pictured holding a sheaf of wheat that symbolizes the utilization of ideas and skills to benefit (nourish) the world.

GLYPH (WRITTEN SYMBOL) ♍ The symbol represents a Virgin, for it is a pictograph of the human reproductive organs closed and untouched. In symbolic terms, the glyph is a straight line connected to two curved lines, one of which is crossed. This represents wisdom tied to feeling and emotion, and crossed by practicality.

DOMINANT KEYWORD I ANALYZE.

POLARITY Pisces:

Virgo is the sign of work and self-improvement. Its natives are perfectionists who dissect facts in order to find the truth and obtain all the information available. Pisces, Virgo's opposite sign, is the sign of illusion and self-deception. Pisceans are prone to dreaminess, imagination, vagueness, self-delusion, and escapism.

PART OF THE BODY RULED BY VIRGO The nervous system and the intestines: Virgoans are prone to illness caused by stress and nervous tension. They are particularly susceptible to ulcers.

LUCKY DAY Wednesday   **LUCKY NUMBERS** 5 and 3

MAGICAL BIRTHSTONE Sapphire: Brings tranquility of mind and protects against illness and injury while traveling.

SPECIAL COLORS Navy Blue and Gray: Classic colors of refinement and taste.

CITIES Paris, Boston, Heidelberg, Strasbourg   **COUNTRIES** Turkey, Greece, Crete, West Indies

FLOWERS Morning glory and Pansy   **TREES** Nut-bearing trees

METAL Mercury

ANIMALS RULED BY VIRGO Small domestic pets

DANGER Virgo people sometimes arouse anger and violence in others because of their tendency to interfere, their critical tongues, and their unemotional attitudes.

Your Most Likeable Trait
CONSCIENTIOUSNESS

THE REAL DRAMA of Virgo's personality is interior. To the world you may give an impression of calm authority, but you are aware of your own nervous, restless, controlled intensity, the desire to be up and doing, re-arranging, *improving*. You can exhaust yourself more by simply sitting still than others do moving around.

The planet Mercury, which rules both Virgo and Gemini, inclines its subjects toward constant activity. However, in Gemini the nervous energy is directed primarily toward stimulation and adventure, while in Virgo the ceaseless drive is to accomplish and perfect. It's impossible for Virgos to put off until tomorrow what might be done today, or to do later what might be done now. You are, in a word, organized. Your idea of taking it easy would seem like hard

work to most people. You are not a daydreamer, you're a day-*doer*.

Your emotional life is a constant striving to bring order out of chaos. Although you have a great capacity for love, love alone is not enough for you to be happy. You need more than a mate, home, children, friends. You must justify your life, conduct yourself as a good bookkeeper keeps a ledger—always ready to give a reckoning on whether there's a profit or a loss. You're ambitious, but not just for money. You want to know more, to gain in wisdom, and put this wisdom to practical use.

Your astrological symbol of the Virgin tends to be misunderstood. It does not mean you're a prude or lack sensuality. The Virgin stands for purity of purpose. You're not in the game of life to cheat or extract from others. You have higher motives. You want to be of use. In ancient times Virgo was the sign of the harvest—and the symbolic meaning of the Virgin holding a sheaf of wheat is that Virgo people take what has been sown (knowledge, information, skills) and harvest this energy to do something of practical benefit. In the same way wheat is turned into bread to feed our bodies, you want to utilize the gifts you were born with to nourish the world.

Intelligence is the hallmark of your sign. You have an excellent memory, an analytical mind, and are known for crystal-clear thinking. You also have a keen ability to probe into human motivations. People like to check their plans with you before putting them into action because you have microscopic vision when it comes to detecting a flaw. Your superb logic cuts through muddled thinking like a laser beam. You instantly zero in on a problem, take apart difficulties, and put them back together in proper order. Because you believe life should be approached rationally, you are without peer in solving knotty problems or tangled disputes. You are convinced that a reasoned presentation of the facts will carry the day. Until you have the facts before you, you are reluctant to make a decision; you want to know why and how a thing will work. Your faith is not in Chinese fortune cookies but in facts, and you distrust vague ideas that don't stand up to critical appraisal or people who make emotional judgments.

Yet it would do you a world of good to have a little more faith in general and to trust in synchronicity—that certain events occur or people connect for a fortuitous reason. Your important life lesson is to *expand your vision*, to look at things in larger terms and believe in the power of faith. Virgo is ruled by Mercury, the planet of thought and mental perceptions, and your ideas form your reality.

If you hold on to a negative attitude, then your reality will also unfold negatively.

You tend to have difficult getting in touch with your deeper feelings because your mechanism of denial is so firmly set in place. "I'm not upset," you'll say. "I feel okay about [this other person being promoted instead of me, him dating another woman, etc.]" Saying you feel "okay" covers a lot of messy feelings you'd rather not examine.

Also, you often don't see the forest for the trees. A preoccupation with neatness and precision sometimes limits your breadth of vision. That estimable faith in logic also confines your imagination and leaves you a little shy on inspiration, too dependent on established practices and methods. Your nature is to look back and analyze rather than push forward in a new direction. You must know the why and how of everything. Virgo is a mutable sign, however, so you can adjust easily to change once you find a way of fitting the new situation into your routine.

You may run into difficulty because of a tendency to complicate everything. No problem is ever simple for Virgo. For every answer you've got a question, and making mountains out of molehills is one of your specialties.

Your nature is shy and reserved; it's hard for you to relax, to make small talk or be gregarious with strangers. You prefer one-on-one encounters, in which you can offer the full benefit of your sharp insights and discerning opinions. That's also when people discover how well-read, perceptive, charming, and witty you are.

The first thing you learned about money matters is that money does matter. Although you tend to downplay your own ability in financial affairs, no one is better than you at staying within a budget. You aren't tempted into foolish ventures. Your bank balances usually jibe to the decimal point. You want the finest but rarely overpay, and you have a built-in resistance against self-indulgence.

A highly developed sense of discrimination may lead you to be hypercritical. You are unsatisfied with things as they are and continue to analyze situations and people in the hope of finding a way to make them better. At times your finely tuned sensibilities can even make you unhappy, for they give you a heightened awareness of the world's imperfections. However, you resist criticism of your faults from others. It's a rare Virgo who takes criticism well or who can admit to being in the wrong.

You are health-conscious and try to make sure you get enough vitamins and go for regular checkups at the dentist. However, in this as in other areas, you can't help being a worrier. As a result you are prone to tension and nervous ailments. Hypochondria is common among Virgos.

A warm, loving relationship brings out the best in anyone born under this sign because basically you are kind, devoted, and very loyal. When your affections are engaged you tirelessly try to serve loved ones. They will never have to worry about who's going to keep the checkbook balanced or look after them when they are ill.

The Inner You

You have plenty of willpower and dedication, and you work harder than anyone to make sure something is perfect. Why? Because if you can't do everything superbly, you begin to fear that you're failing. You are much too critical of yourself. Actually, you're an enigma that no one has quite figured out. You hold back with people you don't know well and are reserved even with those you love. Inwardly, though, you feel very deeply. Intensity and extreme sensitivity are part of your secret self. You like looking after others—giving advice to friends, feeding stray animals,

tending sick plants—but you need to be appreciated for the kind things you do. Above all, you want to be useful because you truly care about people.

How Others See You

You're regarded as a real go-getter. People trust you to handle any job. They think of you as a person who can analyze almost any problem in a logical way. Others come to you when they want their own actions explained to them, or are feeling confused about relationships. You are valued for your ability to set priorities and to create order out of confusion. Because you're both discriminating and truthful, people trust your judgment on books, theater, and clothes. However, you don't wear your heart on your sleeve, and as a result others often perceive you as haughty and cold.

Famous People with the Sun in Virgo

Marc Antony
Yasir Arafat
Lance Armstrong
Lauren Bacall
Anne Bancroft
Ingrid Bergman
Leonard Bernstein
Jacqueline Bisset
Charles Boyer
Kobe Bryant
Sid Caesar
John Cage
Taylor Caldwell
Agatha Christie
Craig Claiborne
Patsy Cline
Confucius
Sean Connery
Harry Connick Jr.

Jimmy Connors
Jackie Cooper
Macaulay Culkin
Roald Dahl
Cameron Diaz
Theodore Dreiser
Queen Elizabeth I (the
    Virgin Queen)
Peter Falk
Greta Garbo
Richard Gere
Johann Wolfgang von Goethe
Hugh Grant
Buddy Hackett
O. Henry
Faith Hill
Jeremy Irons
Christopher Isherwood
Michael Jackson

Jesse James
Samuel Johnson
Tommy Lee Jones
Michael Keaton
Gene Kelly
Stephen King
Peter Lawford
D. H. Lawrence
Alan Jay Lerner
Rocky Marciano
Judith Martin (Miss Manners)
John McCain
Freddie Mercury
Grandma Moses
Paul Muni
Bob Newhart
Arnold Palmer
Itzhak Perlman
Regis Philbin

Ryan Phillippe
River Phoenix
Keanu Reeves
LeAnn Rimes
Cal Ripken Jr.
Margaret Sanger
William Saroyan
Claudia Schiffer
Jerry Seinfeld
Peter Sellers
Charlie Sheen
Upton Sinclair
Oliver Stone
Mother Teresa
Leo Tolstoi
Lily Tomlin
Shania Twain
George Wallace
H. G. Wells

Richard Gere   *Mother Teresa*   *Lance Armstrong*

LIBRA
(SEPTEMBER 23 – OCTOBER 22)

DUALITY Masculine

TRIPLICITY (ELEMENT) Air

QUADRUPLICITY (QUALITY) Cardinal

Libra is active, artistic, easygoing, peaceable, prizes beauty and harmony, is diplomatic, polished, and very socially inclined.

RULING PLANET Venus: Goddess of love and beauty. In astrology, Venus rules pleasure, social pursuits, art, and adornment. Its influence also inclines toward self-indulgence and love of luxury.

SYMBOL The Scales: Signifying balance, equilibrium, order, and justice.

GLYPH (WRITTEN SYMBOL) ♎ The pictograph represents the Scale, which is in perfect equilibrium. This was the ancient Egyptian symbol for the setting sun, which was regarded as the doorway between two worlds. In symbolic terms, the glyph is a crescent moon connected to two straight lines resting above a third line. This represents emotion bounded on either side by reason; the line below symbolizes partnership.

DOMINANT KEYWORD I BALANCE.

POLARITY Aries:

Libra is the sign of partnership and marriage. Its natives are happiest functioning within a union, and often lose their equilibrium and positive outlook when forced to be alone. Aries, Libra's opposite sign, is the sign of ego, personality, and self. Aries people tend to put themselves first, and selfishness is one of their negative traits.

PART OF THE BODY RULED BY LIBRA The lower back and buttocks, and the kidneys: Librans suffer from lower back strain and problems in the lumbar region. They are also subject to kidney infections.

LUCKY DAY Friday **LUCKY NUMBERS** 6 and 9

MAGICAL BIRTHSTONE Opal: Brings financial success, frees its wearer from jealousy and greed, and imparts clear insight.

SPECIAL COLORS Blue and Lavender: The colors of romance, harmony, and refinement.

CITIES Vienna, Copenhagen, Charleston, Lisbon **COUNTRIES** Burma, China, Tibet, Argentina, Japan

FLOWERS Rose, Cosmos, and Hydrangea **TREES** Almond, Cypress, and Ash

METAL Copper

ANIMALS RULED BY LIBRA Snakes and lizards

DANGER Libra people tend to stir up ill feelings from others in situations having to do with love. Because they are indecisive and sometimes make a declaration of love too easily, Librans both anger and disappoint lovers. They also have a tendency to be fickle and faithless.

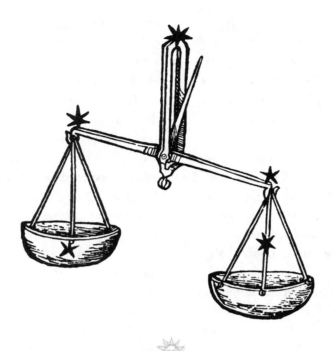

Your Most Likeable Trait
CHARM

LIBRANS ARE EASY TO LIKE, for you have a captivating charm, possess elegant taste, and are usually beautiful to look at. In addition, you have the gift of making others feel important, for you are a superb listener and instinctively know how to draw out another person. You're famous for how effortlessly you smooth ruffled feathers, bring out smiles, and make others think they're the most wonderful people in the world. You're a born charmer.

Ruled by Venus, goddess of love and beauty, you admire loveliness in all its forms, in music, art, decoration, and people. Your home will always have a touch of elegance, and you love to entertain in style. Flowers, cham-pagne, lovely jewelry and clothes, beautiful (and expensive) *objets*, luxurious surroundings—these are the ornaments of life to you. You enjoy all the things that money can buy.

A narcissist at heart, you expect admiration. You wish to be the jewel in the center of any setting, and you have a computer memory for any compliment ever paid to you. You tend to judge others by outward appearances. If someone has a charming facade, you won't look any deeper. As a result you may become easy prey for a sophisticated schemer with an affable manner.

Libra is the zodiacal sign of Partnerships—in psychological terms the sign is outer-directed. Your energies are focused on melding and combining with other people; you are at your best in personal relationships. Your real energy, however, goes into people. Whether they be partners, lovers, mates, family, friends, business associates, or even guests at your party—relationships are your metier. You're simply not a loner. Instinctively, you try to magnetize and pull others toward you. However, your main interest is on yourself within the relationship. You deal intuitively with other people's emotions, and no one is better at understanding and taking into consideration another person's point of view. Yet all too soon that outside viewpoint will be lost or subsumed within your own subtly self-centered concerns.

In the professional world you're a superb team player. You're able to meld many disparate egos into one smooth-working union. Your friendships and associations bring opportunities, and your best luck comes when you pool your creative talents and intelligence with powerful individuals who open doors for you.

Born under the sign of the Scales, you strive for balance and harmony and are happiest when your environment is ordered and serene. Peace is worth any price to you and usually you will go a long way out of your way to avoid friction and dissension. Because you see clearly every side of an argument, every possibility of a given course, you have the tact and ability to smooth over disputes. You are a born diplomat. In order to avoid an unpleasant scene, you will even stifle your own true feelings. In fact, far too often you are not sure what your true feelings are. Because you try to be all things to all people, there is a general impression that you are indecisive. You appear to be constantly poised on an edge, seemingly un-able to move one way or another, balancing pro with con, advantage with disadvantage, risk with gain. Underneath your genial, calm surface, you have to struggle in order to make decisions.

The problem is that at Libra's center is someone who does not feel complete in himself or herself. Beneath your brilliance and charm, you feel a psychic lack, something missing—whether this something is a perfect lover, a fulfilling career, a wonderful project that shows off your talents, etc. And so you spend a lot of time feeling you're not "real," that you've conned others into thinking you're smart and successful, but very soon they'll find out you're a fraud. One of Libra's best-hidden secrets is how shaky your self-confidence is—and certainly your sense of not being whole and creating a false front is at the core of your insecurity.

Although you have superb instincts, you don't trust them enough. You are likely to be an underachiever because of your easygoing attitude. For the most part, you don't want anything badly enough to fight for it. The exception is when you're denied a privilege to which you feel entitled. That ruffles your fur. Librans have a reputation for stubbornness, but that's because you are sticklers for *fairness*. You resent being treated unfairly and become upset at inequity in the world at large. In general, it seems your strength is only brought out by crisis. This is when you're at your most courageous.

You get along harmoniously with people who are even-tempered, particularly those who can laugh in the face of difficulties. You are particularly appreciative of talent in any field, whether art, literature, or music, and if you lack talent yourself you often indulge in artistic hobbies. Often people are surprised at the wide range of your interests because you hide your superior intellect under an agreeable, easygoing exterior. Libra is a cardinal sign, which means you're an initiator. You love new projects, unusual people, different ideas, and you'll travel anywhere. Gifted with imagination, flair, and *enthusiasm*, you have an open, independent mind that tries to evaluate the world dispassionately and rationally. You also have a good head for money (though your great weakness is a love of luxury).

Indeed, money has a way of slipping through your fingers because it isn't money you love, it is the *things* money can buy. Essentially frivolous, people born under this sign dislike hard work—unless someone else is doing it. A love for beauty leads many natives of this sign to careers in art, decorating, the theater, and composing, but the approach often remains that of a dilettante who enjoys the reward but avoids the effort needed to attain it.

You are an incorrigible idealist and quintessential romantic. Affectionate, warmhearted, sentimental, naturally optimistic, you do everything in your power to please. Your stock-in-trade is charm.

The Inner You

You work hard trying to please others and as a result, they find you captivating. However, beneath your friendly exterior, you desperately long for love and approval. You have trouble saying no to others' requests and you take on too many jobs or commitments—and then to prove how nice you are, you keep smiling through the strain while you hide a lot of resentment. It might be more useful to spend time building up your self-esteem rather than looking to others to give it to you. Basically, you give away your power. You hate anything unpleasant and avoid conflict,

vulgarity, or strife. If life were a play, you'd always insist on a happy ending. The problem with trying to have constant peace and harmony is that you have trouble making decisions. At times you fear that any move you make will bring something terrible crashing down around you. If you could just lighten up and not be so hard on yourself, you'd be much more satisfied with what you do achieve. You have every ingredient for happiness!

How Others See You

People feel important when they're with you because you always seem to understand their point of view. You are considered warm and outgoing because you know how to draw people out, and you're thought of as someone with an unparalleled ability to deal with the public. However, because you want others' approval, you tend to go along with what they want—and this sometimes makes you look wimpy. To some people, you also appear vain and overly concerned with your appearance.

Famous People with the Sun in Libra

Julie Andrews	Hilary Duff	Donna Karan	Arthur Miller	Paul Simon
Hannah Arendt	Eleanor Duse	Buster Keaton	Yves Montand	Ashlee Simpson
Armand Assante	Dwight D. Eisenhower	Deborah Kerr	Martina Navratilova	Will Smith
Brigitte Bardot	Britt Ekland	Evel Knievel	Admiral Horatio Nelson	Annika Sorenstam
David Ben-Gurion	T. S. Eliot	Angela Lansbury	Louise Nevelson	Bruce Springsteen
Joyce Brothers	William Faulkner	Ralph Lauren	Eugene O'Neill	Gwen Stefani
Art Buchwald	Carrie Fisher	John LeCarré	Gwyneth Paltrow	Wallace Stevens
Truman Capote	F. Scott Fitzgerald	Ursula K. LeGuin	Luciano Pavarotti	Sting
Al Capp	Annette Funicello	John Lennon	Juan Perón	Ed Sullivan
Miguel de Cervantes	John Kenneth Galbraith	Walter Lippmann	Luke Perry	Margaret Thatcher
Ray Charles	Mohandas K. Gandhi	Carole Lombard	Paul Potts	Cheryl Tiegs
Montgomery Clift	George Gershwin	Yo-Yo Ma	Mario Puzo	Desmond Tutu
Jackie Collins	Bryant Gumbel	Mickey Mantle	Christopher Reeve	Usher
Simon Cowell	Linda Hamilton	Wynton Marsalis	Anne Rice	Giuseppe Verdi
e. e. cummings	Helen Hayes	Groucho Marx	Kelly Ripa	Ben Vereen
Matt Damon	Rita Hayworth	Marcello Mastroianni	Rex Reed	Gore Vidal
Catherine Deneuve	Jim Henson	Johnny Mathis	Tim Robbins	Barbara Walters
Angie Dickinson	Vladimir Horowitz	Walter Matthau	Mickey Rooney	Sigourney Weaver
Michael Douglas	Lee Iacocca	John Mayer	Eleanor Roosevelt	Oscar Wilde
William O. Douglas	Julio Iglesias	Mark McGwire	Susan Sarandon	Serena Williams
Alfred Drake	Jesse Jackson	Melina Mercouri	George C. Scott	Thomas Wolfe

Jesse Jackson

Barbara Walters

Simon Cowell

SCORPIO
(OCTOBER 23 – NOVEMBER 21)

DUALITY Feminine

TRIPLICITY (ELEMENT) Water

QUADRUPLICITY (QUALITY) Fixed

    Scorpio is imaginative, passionate and emotional, subtle, persistent, intense, obstinate, and unyielding.

RULING PLANET Pluto: Ancient god of the netherworld and of the dead. In astrology, Pluto rules regenerative forces, and the beginnings and ends of phases in life.

SYMBOL The Scorpion: A secretive, deadly creature that can poison its enemies. Its sting is often fatal.

GLYPH (WRITTEN SYMBOL) ♏ The pictograph is the stinger of the Scorpion connected to a representation of the human reproductive organs (the part of the anatomy that Scorpio rules). This was the symbol in ancient times for the phoenix, bird of immortality and regeneration. In symbolic terms, the curved lines and arrow represent strong emotions tied to practicality and aiming toward higher consciousness.

DOMINANT KEYWORD I DESIRE.

POLARITY Taurus:

    Scorpio is the sign of inheritance and legacies. Its natives are given a sense of purpose and destiny, and find truest happiness in dispensing their life-force to others. Taurus is the sign of possessions and owning, and people born under this sign want to possess, collect, and have. They will not easily let go of what belongs to them.

PART OF THE BODY RULED BY SCORPIO The genitals: Scorpio people are susceptible to infections of the urinary system and venereal disease. In addition, their volatile emotions are often the cause of exhaustion and ill health.

LUCKY DAY Tuesday   **LUCKY NUMBERS** 2 and 4

MAGICAL BIRTHSTONE Topaz: Releases occult powers and brings serenity of mind. It also protects from enemies and illness.

SPECIAL COLORS Crimson, Burgundy, Maroon: The glowing colors of passion.

CITIES Liverpool, New Orleans, Washington, D.C., Newcastle   **COUNTRIES** Norway, Algeria, Morocco, Tahiti

FLOWERS Chrysanthemum and Rhododendron   **TREES** Blackthorn and bushy trees

METAL Plutonium

ANIMALS RULED BY SCORPIO Insects and crustaceans

DANGER Scorpio people evoke anger in others by their secretiveness and jealousy. Their sharp, stinging tempers can also enrage others to the point of violence.

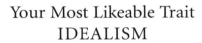

Your Most Likeable Trait
IDEALISM

THIS IS THE SIGN of extremes. Scorpio people are variously described as powerful, weak, independent, clinging, passionate, and cold. Clearly, you are a bundle of contradictions encompassing the best and worst in human nature.

The key to your personality is intensity. You do nothing by half-measures. Magnetic, emotional, capable of exerting tremendous force, your strength is hidden in the depths. In the sign of Scorpio the element of water is fixed, an image that suggests an iceberg or a bottomless well. You may appear impassive, sometimes unapproachable, but turbulent passions are always roiling underneath, invisible on the surface.

You live on many levels. While you present a calm and smiling face to the world, you're ferociously persistent and extremely strong-willed. You're also flexible when it comes to working out solutions. When thwarted, you don't just accept defeat. You're extremely agile when it comes to sidestepping obstacles and figuring out a dozen new ways to get to your goal. In a wonderful paradox, flexibility is one of your most effective methods of controlling situations.

Scorpio is the most misunderstood sign in the zodiac because of its complications and convolutions. Basically, you always have a hidden agenda. You're someone of incredible depth and brilliance, and your inner psyche is a labyrinth of wheels within wheels, boxes within boxes. Even when you seem to be at ease and relaxed, you are always evaluating, figuring out your moves, working out strategy. Much of this has to do with control, which is what you are all about. For Scorpio to be out of control is to be in psychic danger. Nothing is worse for you than to feel swept away by outside forces. When you control you are safe. Your Scorpio evolution is the journey toward controlling in positive ways—putting order into chaotic situations, being of use to others and therefore meeting an unfulfilled need, arranging your personal environment so it works smoothly for you. The unevolved Scorpio tries to control other people and manipulate situations for its own greed. Thus, as you see, the forces of light and dark continually oppose each other in your turbulent psyche.

What you need is to transmute your fervor into positive relationships and meaningful work. It is very easy to waste yourself on what is unworthy of you, and then your feelings turn inward, become imprisoned, at times even destructive. More than natives of any other sign, Scorpios live at a high pitch of emotion. Its negative aspects are brooding, jealousy, resentment, even vengefulness. The positive aspect is your unswerving dedication once your emotions are engaged. The Scorpion energy, drive, and endurance are legend. Above all, you seek to give your life a meaningful pattern, to find a deeper purpose.

You have a philosophical turn of mind and may become interested in religion and the occult. Your sixth sense enables you to intuit things before they happen. You are blessed with a native understanding of the human heart and a great awareness of life's secrets. All the water signs (Cancer, Scorpio, Pisces) tend to be psychic, but you Scorpios delve into the powers of the mind that others are

afraid of. This is the zodiacal sign of birth, sex, death, and regeneration—areas of human existence in which a person confronts the mysteries of the universe. Many Scorpio natives are brilliant doctors, surgeons, scientists, and spiritual leaders. Jonas Salk, Christiaan Barnard, Marie Curie, and Martin Luther are among them.

The complexity of your mind makes it difficult for you to skim the surface; you must uncover what lies beneath. Whether you are studying a new subject, learning a language, hunting down a fact, or just reading for amusement, there is a quality of penetration in the way your mind works.

Your finest attributes—and your worst—are revealed in relationships. With Scorpio, relationships are usually complicated. This is not surprising when you consider that you can be simultaneously generous and affectionate, violent and unpredictable; in your sunniest moods there is always a hint of an imminent change in the weather. You are deeply loyal to friends but are also intensely jealous and possessive. You cannot tolerate the thought that anyone you love might have a yearning, or even a simple yen, for anyone else. With you, it is usually all or nothing at all. Moderation, restraint, and certainly *casual* are not in your emotional vocabulary.

You never forget a kindness and will try to repay it handsomely. Conversely, you never forgive an injury and will wait years to get even. In fact, most of the time getting even isn't enough—you want vengeance. It is strictly not advisable to do harm to any Scorpion. You make a dangerous enemy, for you are as subtle and deadly as the symbol of your sign.

You are a fierce competitor, though often you manage to conceal this from others. You file away pieces of information, facts, and names, and don't hesitate to use what you know if the occasion arises. When you spot a weakness in a rival, you move in quickly for the kill.

You are adaptable, able quickly to channel your formidable energies into new paths and to embark on an entirely different career. Confronted with disaster, you will try to turn it into success. Practical and shrewd, you believe in tangible immediate goals, and your single-minded concentration on getting what you want is formidable.

Clever with money, conservative about spending it, you have an excellent chance to amass wealth. In business, you tend to accomplish things first and announce them second. By the time an opponent is aware of your progress, it is a fait accompli.

Your nature makes you subject to obsessive drives that can be resistant to reason. You will dominate and control anyone who lets you. Suspicious and wary, you are reluctant to trust your heart to anyone. But once you do, you love deeply.

Too many astrologers, in describing the sign of Scorpio, forget to emphasize how loving, generous, kind, loyal, even gentle a Scorpio can be. Many idealists who adhere to high principles and are a great positive force for helping others are born under this sign.

What all Scorpios have in common is intensity of feeling. Emotion not only rules, it characterizes you. You are passionate in love, and passionate about everything in which you become involved: work, relationships, hobbies, causes. You are an individual painted in vivid colors; there is no such thing as a pastel Scorpio.

The Inner You

You have great strength, determination, and willpower. But no matter how calm and cool you appear on the outside, you've got a well of seething emotions underneath. For the most part, though, you keep your intensity under control by channeling it into useful activities. You're a high achiever, and you seem to "get" things in a flash—with powerful psychic feelings you've learned to trust. Your instincts tell you that you're destined to do something important and you're not going to let yourself fail along the way. When you latch on to a new opportunity, you explore it in great depth before going ahead. Deep inside you is a gladiator spirit, and if you channel this fighting energy into positive goals (your continuing lesson), you will always be one of life's great winners. At times, however, you feel you are a lone warrior in a harsh world. You're a complex person who can't always express how you feel, but one thing is certain: The things you want, you want badly.

How Others See You

It's probably your secretiveness that makes people so interested in finding out what you think. You're often the guru in a group, the one with uncanny hunches about the future and piercing insights into other people's motivations. Many believe that even your humor contains the barb of truth. People are aware of your reputation for sensuality and fantasize about you as a lover. You're frequently viewed as over-controlling and too ambitious—even power-hungry—but also as someone who can be trusted, because you never make false promises.

FAMOUS PEOPLE WITH THE SUN IN SCORPIO

Spiro Agnew
Marie Antoinette
Ed Asner
Christiaan Barnard
Roseanne Barr
Sarah Bernhardt
Edwin Booth
Charles Bronson
Tina Brown
Richard Burton
Laura Bush
Albert Camus
Johnny Carson
James Carville
Dick Cavett
Benvenuto Cellini
Charles, Prince of
    Wales
Chiang Kai-shek
John Cleese
Michael Crichton
Hillary Rodham

Clinton
Barbara Cook
Peter Cook
Stephen Crane
Walter Cronkite
Marie Curie
Rodney Dangerfield
Bo Derek
Danny DeVito
Leonardo DiCaprio
Feodor Dostoevski
Richard Dreyfuss
Sally Field
Jodie Foster
Felix Frankfurter
Indira Gandhi
Bill Gates
Whoopi Goldberg
Ruth Gordon
Billy Graham
Ken Griffey Jr.
Moss Hart

Harry Hamlin
Goldie Hawn
Shere Hite
Bob Hoskins
Rock Hudson
Mahalia Jackson
Peter Jackson
James Jones
George S. Kaufman
John Keats
Grace Kelly
Robert Kennedy
Larry King
Calvin Klein
Kevin Kline
Hedy Lamarr
Burt Lancaster
k.d. lang
Fran Lebowitz
Vivien Leigh
Martin Luther
Charles Manson

Joseph McCarthy
Joni Mitchell
Margaret Mitchell
François Mitterand
Claude Monet
Demi Moore
Mike Nichols
Georgia O'Keeffe
George Patton
Joaquin Phoenix
Pablo Picasso
Sylvia Plath
Emily Post
Ezra Pound
Claude Rains
Dan Rather
Ann Reinking
Condoleeza Rice
Julia Roberts
Auguste Rodin
Roy Rogers
Will Rogers

Theodore Roosevelt
Hermann Rorschach
Meg Ryan
Winona Ryder
Carl Sagan
Jonas Salk
Martin Scorsese
Maria Shriver
Grace Slick
Robert Louis Stevenson
Lee Strasberg
Billy Sunday
Joan Sutherland
Dylan Thomas
Leon Trotsky
Ted Turner
Voltaire
Kurt Vonnegut
Sam Waterston
Stanford White
Owen Wilson

Whoopie Goldberg

Hillary Rodham Clinton

Julia Roberts

SAGITTARIUS
(NOVEMBER 22 – DECEMBER 21)

DUALITY Masculine

TRIPLICITY (ELEMENT) Fire

QUADRUPLICITY (QUALITY) Mutable

Sagittarius is energetic, ambitious, generous, freedom-loving, and a seeker of challenge, open to new ideas and exploration.

RULING PLANET Jupiter: The most important Roman god, ruler of the heavens. In astrology, Jupiter is the planet of good fortune, optimism, expansion, abundance.

SYMBOL The Archer: Representing directness, high aims, a love of outdoor activity and the chase.

GLYPH (WRITTEN SYMBOL) ♐ The pictograph represents the free-ranging, pointed arrow of the Archer. It is also a picture of the human leg from thigh to knee (the part of the anatomy that Sagittarius rules). In symbolic terms, it is the line of wisdom angled away from trouble and earthly concerns and pointing toward higher ideals.

DOMINANT KEYWORD I SEE.

POLARITY Gemini:

Sagittarius is the sign of philosophy, higher learning, and broad concepts. Its natives are happiest discovering new ideas, exploring distant places, and not getting tied down with personal commitments. Gemini, Sagittarius's opposite sign, is the sign of personal expression and communicating "one-on-one." Gemini people are extremely verbal, love to give advice, and tend to try to guide (even to control) other people's lives.

PART OF THE BODY RULED BY SAGITTARIUS The liver, the hips, and the thighs: Sagittarian natives need lots of outdoor exercise in order to keep healthy. They have a sensitive liver and are susceptible to overuse of alcohol and to hepatitis.

LUCKY DAY Thursday **LUCKY NUMBERS** 5 and 7

MAGICAL BIRTHSTONE Turquoise: Attracts love, protects from harm, and gives its wearer the ability to see into the future.

SPECIAL COLOR Purple: Uncommon color of royalty and the artistic.

CITIES Budapest, Cologne, Toledo, Acapulco **COUNTRIES** Spain, Hungary, Australia

FLOWERS Narcissus, Holly, and Dandelion **TREES** Mulberry, Oak, and Birch

METAL Tin

ANIMAL RULED BY SAGITTARIUS Horse

DANGER Sagittarian people are subject to accidents of fire and explosion, especially while traveling. Their strong desire for freedom may also incite jealousy and possessiveness on the part of a lover.

Your Most Likeable Trait
OPTIMISM

RULED BY JUPITER, planet of fortune, you appear to breeze through life. You are Lady Luck's companion who seems always to be in the right place at the right time. Astrologers say you have the gift of providence—luck protects you. In work, friendships, career, money—a door opens just when you need it. Naturally, this makes for a cheerful and ebullient disposition. You have your dark moments, but clouds roll over quickly. You are too interested in what is going to happen tomorrow to fret long about what went wrong today. You are always sure that around the next bend of the road something wonderful is about to happen.

In Sagittarius, the enthusiasm of fire, the restless mutable quality, and the jovial influence of Jupiter combine to produce an expansive personality who cannot be confined.

Independence is your guiding principle. You are progressive, restless in spirit, eager to get on with the business of living—a free, adventurous spirit who thrives on new ideas and constant change of scene. Somewhere you picked up a chronic case of wanderlust, and you have no desire to be cured. The grass is always greener someplace else, and your restless, inquiring nature requires travel, excitement, and the unconventional. Sagittarius, like its opposite sign Gemini, wants to *know*. But whereas Geminis are happy to sample a new idea, Sagittarians will follow it as far as it will go. In the zodiac, Sagittarius symbolizes the search for wisdom; this is the sign of the philosopher and the explorer.

Sagittarians are hard to pin down emotionally. You don't want to get bogged down in messy entanglements or anything that ties you down. You've got places to go and you're not about to sign up for anything that keeps you in one spot. The way to stay unfettered is to shy away from emotion. Sagittarians rarely talk about their feelings—they talk about what they *think* about their feelings. Time and again Sagittarians are bewildered when their romantic partners ask for more passion and feeling. Because you keep one eye on the exit door and don't welcome enduring, profound relationships, sooner or later, you'll unknot the tie that binds.

Friendship, however, is a different matter. You are always willing to be a pal—and you are the nicest friend in the zodiac. Kind, openhearted, jovial, completely free of malice, you are always doing favors for others. Your way of helping doesn't put the recipient under heavy obligation. "No strings" is a guiding Sagittarian motto.

Freedom is your most valuable possession. If it comes to a choice you'll take a difficult path, accept less money, dispense with security, do anything as long as you have to answer only to yourself. Your passion for liberty underlies all your other qualities. Prizing it as you do, you also willingly grant it to others. You don't meddle in other people's plans or interfere with what they think best for themselves, and you aren't possessive or jealous.

A sense of humor is among your most endearing traits. High-spirited and congenial, you are a gifted conversationalist, a wonderful storyteller, and a born entertainer. Writing, publishing, TV, communications are enterprises in which there are many Sagittarians. Famous Sagittarians in these fields include Noel Coward, James Thurber, Mark Twain, Garson Kanin, William Buckley, and Woody Allen.

You Jupiter-ruled people are unusually versatile. You have wide-ranging interests—music, nature, philosophy, computer technology, theater, animals—and enough energy to do six things at once. What you lack is staying power. Before you finish with one project, you are off to meet the next challenge. One reason is that you become bored doing the same things, and boredom is your worst enemy, but another is simply that you must move on—and up.

In business you are imaginative and clever, ready to accept the new and to use it. But you perform best when there's something really important at stake. When you're down to your last chance to win, when it's now or never, you'll put everything you own on the turn of a card and redouble the stakes. You believe in your luck.

You are straightforward and honest. Your frankness makes you easy to deal with because one doesn't have to spend time figuring out the hidden significance of unspoken clues or nuances. There is no hidden significance. What you say is what you mean. And you're willing to tell all who ask exactly what you think of them, their lifestyle, hairstyle, choices, lovers, you name it. The best part, however, is people can trust what you tell them. Your candid remarks are not meant to hurt; they spring from a desire to tell the truth. Ironically, you are rather thin-skinned and too easily hurt by a thoughtless action or careless rebuff.

The keyword in understanding Sagittarius is *possibility*. To be restricted or feel your choices are diminished is very depressing for you. You tend not to look at life as it is but as you want it to be. In many ways, you rebel against being a grownup. Certainly, you know how to take on responsibility and you've proven yourself strong in the face of setback. Crisis brings out the best in you.

It's the "dailiness" of life that defeats you. You have grand and wonderful ideas for an adventurous career or carving out a utopian life or helping the world become a better place. Then you procrastinate, let others deal with the details, lose interest in a plan—and wonder why you're stuck in the same place.

However, Sagittarians are among the most likeable people in the zodiac. True, you can be extravagant and wasteful, even on occasion reckless and irresponsible. True, your life is full of forgotten appointments, missed deadlines, unfinished projects. True, your emotions can be shallow and your commitments almost nonexistent. Overriding everything, though, is the fact that you're fun to be with. So what if you promise the moon and everyone knows you won't deliver. You know it too. There's nothing underhanded or secretive in the way you deal. You play with all your cards on the table.

Impetuous, buoyant, charming, you hitch your wagon to the merry-go-round of life and ride it with insouciant elegance.

The Inner You

Like Scarlett O'Hara, your motto is, "Tomorrow is another day." Even in your darkest moods, you believe there's a light shining around the corner. Your confidence in the future is genuine, but you hate anything interfering with your plans. You have a hunger to experience life to its fullest—to travel, meet interesting people, and see things you've never seen before. Anything new sparks your interest. In fact, you'll usually say yes to a suggestion without weighing its merits simply because it lifts your spirits. And while you're not exactly a moody person, you are high-strung and can become irritable when you start to get

bored. You may think no one cares about you or understands you when you're feeling this way, but luckily your belief that you're someone special always sees you through.

How Others See You

People like your sense of humor and your buoyant presence. No matter what goes wrong, you're ready with an upbeat explanation and forecast for the future. You're also the first to volunteer help; colleagues and friends appreciate your willingness to do favors. People like your frankness, although sometimes they think you can be too frank and that you put your foot in your mouth too often. To some you seem fickle and undependable, perhaps a bit too detached emotionally. In general, you're viewed as an unpredictable, independent spirit.

FAMOUS PEOPLE WITH THE SUN IN SAGITTARIUS

Christina Aguilera
Louisa May Alcott
Woody Allen
Christina Applegate
Jane Austen
Tyra Banks
Kim Basinger
Ludwig van Beethoven
Busby Berkeley
William Blake
Kenneth Branagh
Leonid Brezhnev
Beau Bridges
Jeff Bridges
William F. Buckley
Hoagy Carmichael
Dale Carnegie
Winston Churchill
Dick Clark
Joseph Conrad

Noel Coward
Jamie Lee Curtis
Miley Cyrus
Sammy Davis Jr.
Emily Dickinson
Joan Didion
Charles de Gaulle
Joe DiMaggio
Walt Disney
Benjamin Disraeli
Kirk Douglas
Patty Duke
George Eliot
Chris Evert
Douglas Fairbanks Jr.
Jane Fonda
Lynn Fontanne
Jamie Foxx
Redd Foxx
Ira Gershwin

Margaret Hamilton
Ed Harris
Teri Hatcher
Jimi Hendrix
Abbie Hoffman
Katie Holmes
Jay-Z
Boris Karloff
John F. Kennedy Jr.
Billie Jean King
Fiorello La Guardia
Max Lerner
John Malkovich
David Mamet
Howie Mandel
Mary Martin
Harpo Marx
Margaret Mead
Bette Midler
John Milton

Carry Nation
Mandy Patinkin
Drew Pearson
Edith Piaf
Brad Pitt
Richard Pryor
Rainer Maria Rilke
Edward G. Robinson
Lillian Russell
William Safire
George Santayana
Charles Schulz
Eric Sevareid
Garry Shandling
Frank Sinatra
Margaret Chase Smith
Alexander Solzhenitsyn
Britney Spears
Steven Spielberg
Rex Stout

John Stewart
Kiefer Sutherland
Jonathan Swift
Michael Tilson Thomas
James Thurber
Henri de Toulouse-
   Lautrec
Tina Turner
Mark Twain
Cicely Tyson
Liv Ullmann
Dick Van Dyke
Gianni Versace
William Wegman
Rebecca West
Eli Whitney
John Greenleaf
   Whittier
Andy Williams
Flip Wilson

Frank Sinatra

Jon Stewart

Miley Cyrus

CAPRICORN
(December 22 – January 19)

DUALITY Feminine

TRIPLICITY (ELEMENT) Earth

QUADRUPLICITY (QUALITY) Cardinal

> Capricorn is reserved, prudent, patient, uses strategy instead of force, seeks security, is acquisitive, disciplined, determined, and quick to seize opportunity.

RULING PLANET Saturn: Roman god who presided over the sowing and reaping of grain. In ancient times, the outermost planet of the known universe. In astrology, Saturn represents obstacles, limitation, restriction, discipline, responsibility.

SYMBOL The Goat: A surefooted animal who is able to ascend the heights by taking advantage of every foothold. The goat butts its way through obstructions.

GLYPH (WRITTEN SYMBOL)   The pictograph represents the V-shaped beard of the Goat and the curved tail of the Fish (the Sea-Goat, which was the ancient symbol for Capricorn). It also pictures the human knee and circular kneecap (the part of the anatomy that Capricorn rules). In symbolic terms, the glyph is two straight lines that meet one another, connected to a circle and a crescent. This represents the melding of authority and responsibility that is strengthened by both energy and passion.

DOMINANT KEYWORD I USE.

POLARITY Cancer:

> Capricorn is the sign governing reputation, career, standing in the community. Its natives seek honor, praise, and approval in the world at large, but tend to be emotionally reserved in personal relationships. Cancer, Capricorn's opposite sign, is the sign of domesticity and home life. Cancerians derive security from the love and closeness of mates and family members.

PART OF THE BODY RULED BY CAPRICORN The bones, joints, and knees: Capricorn natives often have beautiful bone structure, but they are subject to stiff joints, rheumatism, and orthopedic problems.

LUCKY DAY Saturday **LUCKY NUMBERS** 2 and 8

MAGICAL BIRTHSTONE Garnet: Attracts popularity, high esteem, and true love.

SPECIAL COLORS Dark Green and Brown: Classic, comforting colors of nature and the earth.

CITIES Oxford, Boston, Brussels, Chicago, Montreal **COUNTRIES** Mexico, Afghanistan, Bulgaria, India

FLOWERS Carnation and Ivy **TREES** Pine, Elm, and Poplar

METAL Lead

ANIMALS RULED BY CAPRICORN Goats and animals with cloven hoofs

DANGER Other people may harbor hidden grudges and resentments because of Capricorn's coldness and reserve. Secrets from the past are often used against Capricorns.

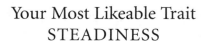

Your Most Likeable Trait
STEADINESS

Capricorns are ambitious, and the lives of those born under this sign are marked by a purposeful pursuit of their destiny. Your motivating force is desire for success, money, status, position, authority, and (though you may not realize it) for love.

Capricorn is both an earth sign and a cardinal sign, and the combination of practicality (earth) and initiative (cardinal) produces a personality geared toward leadership and power. In the zodiac Capricorn is linked to the Midheaven—the point at the top of the horoscope that represents high achievement. You're a born climber who's not content to poke along down in the valleys. As long as there is a top to get to from the bottom, you will persevere in your upward striving. Your symbol is the Goat, and every-

one knows how goats bound up impassable terrain, finding footholds where no one thought they existed. You always carry with you the knowledge that there are tasks to be fulfilled and if you can't move mountains, then at least, like the Goat, you can scale the heights.

Your ruler Saturn is the planet of limitations, which includes the limitation of time. (To the ancients, Saturn was the symbol for Father Time.) You have a heightened sense of the value of time, which helps to make you a superb organizer and planner. Unlike those who don't look beyond next month, you will carefully examine your goal, separate it into all its necessary steps, and plot out a long-term timetable that often involves years. In the sign of Capricorn the quality of patience reaches new heights. One of the hallmarks of your sign is that you learn to wait for things you want. You are willing to give up today's temptation for tomorrow's reward.

An aura of melancholy and sternness often surrounds you. Saturn has been called the Celestial Taskmaster, for it symbolizes responsibility, discipline, and restriction. As a child of Saturn, you need something to improve and to perfect. You could have been the prototype for Lewis Carroll's sly and charming jingle about industriousness: "How doth the little crocodile improve its shining tail…?" You are ambitious, practical, and, above all, determined. You are not interested in vague theory; you want to put any knowledge to use. Your active mind quickly grasps ideas, and you have an admirable ability to concentrate. You are precise and orderly, and generally don't trust others to look after details. When you give your word you stick to it, and when you undertake a task you complete it to the best of your ability. You tend to fuss over details and to make sure all contingencies are covered. It's your way of being in control.

Because of your diligence, people sometimes fail to give you credit for creativity. Yet you are highly creative—your skill is to link this to your talent for organization. You put dreams into action, and are especially drawn to the artistic arena and the performing arts.

You think of yourself as a real person in a real world that allows little time for idle pleasure-seeking. In certain ways, Saturn is an austere and strict parent that lives inside each Capricorn. Essentially, you feel you can depend only on yourself. The child in you feels unworthy—and your life-long lesson is to shed this feeling and learn to love *yourself*. You do not need to be your own parent who disciplines and keeps you toeing the line. You yourself must allow the spontaneous part of you to play and run.

Your remoteness of spirit is often misunderstood by others; it has been described as cold passion. But you are not cold as much as self-sufficient. Because you need to organize and control your surroundings, on occasion you take a strong hand in other people's lives. To you, it's not meddling but *handling* things better. Beneath your reserve there is a sensitive and sympathetic person, and anyone who needs a strong shoulder to lean on needn't look further than Capricorn.

Certainly you do not deserve your reputation for being sober and gloomy. One of your more striking characteristics is a sense of humor. Your wit may be dry, incisive, but it is extremely funny and has a way of erupting when others least expect it.

As is your nature with everything else in life, you are cautious and conservative with money. Chances are you will amass wealth during your lifetime (usually in the later years), for you know how to make sound investments. In business your success is due to painstaking preparation. The journey of ten thousand miles may begin with a single step, but you know you can't get anywhere unless you first know where you're going. You may not size up a situation as quickly as some, but this can be an advantage, for it means you won't heedlessly plunge in. Instead, you will research, examine what others have done before, and gather all relevant data. Only then, with a thorough understanding of the details, will you begin to move. And then you won't be stopped until you reach your goal.

You are not comfortable with ambiguity. You seek certainty and tend to see things in black and white. Emotional gray areas are troublesome, and you turn away from them. To the unevolved Capricorn there is only one "right" way, which is his or her way. Capricorn can be closed-minded and critical, and put value only in power and success.

Your basic concern is for security. That goal comes first and you are usually materialistic. You can be spiteful toward those who stand in the way. You have a great sense of pride and will not forgive anyone who belittles or slights you. By the same token you will repay favors done for you. Scorpios also go out of their way to repay a kindness, but in their case it is done out of a sense of gratitude and fidelity. With you the motivation is pride that does not allow you to live comfortably under an obligation.

More than any other sign of the zodiac, Capricorns marry for money and prestige. In most relationships you must dominate, because when you are in control you do not feel vulnerable to another person's power. In small ways you are continually testing the loyalty of those close to you. You are the loner of the zodiac, but have a great need to be loved and appreciated. Unfortunately, you won't let this need be known—in fact, you are a past master at concealing it.

Underneath the mask, you wear still other masks, and it can take a long time to discover the real you. To others you may appear aloof, indifferent, hard to reach because you are so self-contained. But the very elusiveness of your Capricorn personality can be hypnotically attractive. Like a riddle wrapped inside a sphinx, there seems to be a fascinating secret buried in your depths.

Anyone who cares enough to penetrate your shell of reserve will be greatly rewarded. Your affections and loyalty run deep, and you cherish and protect those you love. And you stick around when the going is toughest.

The Inner You

You don't need anyone to convince you that life is serious business; you've known it all along. That's what keeps you anxiously asking yourself: Am I fulfilling my responsibilities? Am I achieving as much as I should? Am I self-reliant enough? You *know* you have the persistence and strength of purpose to reach your goals. But you also have a deep need to connect on an emotional level in your relationships so that you won't feel separated from those you care about. You worry about keeping all that's valuable to you—which includes relationships. Despite your intelligence and the fact that you're so determined, you often feel insecure. You're a bundle of conflicting emotions. You require discipline and order—chaos drives you crazy and makes you doubt yourself and what you're capable of. But maybe the gods meant for you to have some doubt; if you believed you're as powerful as you really are, you'd be impossible to live with!

How Others See You

You're often seen as an irresistible force and an immovable object. People put you in charge because you're decisive—you're famous for having a great sense of realism. When others need a rational head in a crisis, they call on you. In personal relationships, some friends will stand in line to unload their problems on you; others avoid you because they think your outlook is too downbeat. Everyone agrees that it's difficult to divert you from your course when you've set a goal. Some people feel that in order to find the real you they have to strip away layers of secrecy, but most understand that your aloofness stems from a deep sense of personal privacy.

Famous People with the Sun in Capricorn

Muhammad Ali
Steve Allen
Matthew Arnold
Isaac Asimov
Joan Baez
Simone de Beauvoir
Robert Bly
Humphrey Bogart
Ray Bolger
Victor Borge
David Bowie
Tycho Brahe
Louis Braille
Lloyd Bridges
Nicolas Cage
Al Capone
Jim Carrey
Carlos Castaneda
Paul Cezanne
Anton Chekhov

Mary Higgins Clark
Kevin Costner
Katie Couric
Ted Danson
Ellen DeGeneres
John Denver
Marlene Dietrich
Faye Dunaway
Robert Duvall
Benjamin Franklin
Diane von Furstenberg
Ava Gardner
Kahlil Gibran
Barry Goldwater
Cary Grant
Oliver Hardy
Stephen Hawking
Conrad Hilton
J. Edgar Hoover
Anthony Hopkins

Howard Hughes
Joan of Arc
Janis Joplin
Danny Kaye
Diane Keaton
Johann Kepler
Val Kilmer
Martin Luther King Jr.
Rudyard Kipling
Gelsey Kirkland
Andre Kostelanetz
Gene Krupa
Frank Langella
Matt Lauer
Jude Law
Gypsy Rose Lee
Robert E. Lee
John Legend
Oscar Levant
Shari Lewis

Jack London
Howie Long
Mao Tse-tung
Ricky Martin
Henri Matisse
Dave Matthews
Henry Miller
A. A. Milne
Moliere
Mary Tyler Moore
Kate Moss
Sir Isaac Newton
Richard M. Nixon
Aristotle Onassis
Dolly Parton
Louis Pasteur
Edgar Allan Poe
Elvis Presley
Jean-Pierre Rampal
Paul Revere

Helena Rubinstein
Anwar Sadat
Carl Sandburg
Dianne Sawyer
Albert Schweitzer
Rod Serling
J. D. Salinger
Al Smith
Maggie Smith
Sissy Spacek
Joseph Stalin
Rod Stewart
Alfred Stieglitz
Michael Stipe
J. R. R. Tolkien
Jon Voight
Denzel Washington
Woodrow Wilson
Tiger Woods
Loretta Young

Martin Luther King Jr.

Elvis Presley

Tiger Woods

Aquarius
(January 20 – February 18)

DUALITY Masculine

TRIPLICITY (ELEMENT) Air

QUADRUPLICITY (QUALITY) Fixed

    Aquarius is assertive, independent, progressive, analytical, original, and inventive, has strong dislikes and firm opinions.

RULING PLANET Uranus: Ancient Greek sky god, first ruler of the universe. It was the first modern planet to be discovered (in 1781). In astrology, Uranus is the planet of change, disruption, the unconventional, and the unexpected. It rules invention, aerodynamics, and modern science.

SYMBOL The Water Bearer: Dispensing a gift that flows freely and equally to all; representing creation and the giving of life. The water that the Water Bearer pours out symbolizes truth, which you freely give out to the world.

GLYPH (WRITTEN SYMBOL) ♒ The pictograph represents the water that flows from the vessel of the Water Bearer. It is also a picture of the human ankle in motion (the part of the anatomy that Aquarius rules). In symbolic terms, the ridged unbroken lines represent electric energy, universal thought, and the wisdom of the future.

DOMINANT KEYWORD I KNOW.

POLARITY Leo:

    Aquarius is the sign of hopes and dreams, friends and wishes. Its natives tend to be idealistic humanitarians who are concerned with the larger issues of the world but remain personally detached in their own relationships. Leo, Aquarius's opposite sign, is the sign of pleasure, affection, and love affairs. Leo people look for fun and good times to make them happy; they need close ties with others and tend to dominate in love affairs.

PART OF THE BODY RULED BY AQUARIUS The circulatory system, shins and ankles: Aquarius natives are prone toward ankle sprains and breaks; also to varicose veins and hardening of the arteries.

LUCKY DAY Wednesday **LUCKY NUMBERS** 1 and 7

MAGICAL BIRTHSTONE Amethyst: Brings faithfulness in love and bestows the gift of prescience.

SPECIAL COLOR Electric blue: The clear color of the sky.

CITIES Stockholm, Moscow, Buenos Aires, Salzburg **COUNTRIES** Russia, Sweden, Ethiopia

FLOWER Orchid **TREES** Fruit trees

METAL Uranium

ANIMALS RULED BY AQUARIUS Large birds

DANGER Aquarians are innovative, unconventional, and sometimes eccentric, and are therefore often targets for attack by narrow-minded people. Aquarians also have a tendency to get into unusual situations and take up with oddball individuals.

Your Most Likeable Trait
FRIENDLINESS

ASTROLOGERS ARE FOND of this eleventh sign of the zodiac, for Aquarius is the sign of the future, of the visionary, some say of astrology itself. Aquarians are unorthodox, original people—sort of wacky, witty madcaps who refuse to follow the crowd and go their own way. You *like* being different. You not only march to a different drummer, you make up new music as you go along.

Intellectual independence is your most marked characteristic. In the sign of Aquarius, the combination of a fixed quality (representing persistence) and an air element (representing intellect and communication) under the influence of the planet of change, Uranus, creates a personality that is liberal, progressive, yet fixed in opinion. Your inflexibility shows up when others least expect it (in keeping with your penchant for unconventionality). It may be in defense of an idea you have, a trip you've decided on, a habit of yours that you refuse to give up—whatever the cause, someone will suddenly come in conflict with your Aquarian obstinacy. You refuse to compromise or give an inch. You're a strange mix of an avant-garde thinker whose opinions are written in stone. You cheerfully ignore what others think and strike off on new paths, unbound by precedent, because there are so many more exciting things for you to discover that way. You think boredom is a communicable disease and take every opportunity to avoid it.

Your character is a system of paradoxes. You enjoy being with people but are content to be alone. You like to travel but love relaxing at home. You are friendly and outgoing but also detached and reserved. You have both a scientific and an artistic turn of mind. In career you often are involved in two distinct areas of work.

Your astrological symbol is the Water Bearer—often Aquarius is mistaken for a water sign. Aquarius is an *air* sign. You are a communicator, an idea person. People born under this sign live most intensely in their minds. The "water" being poured out by the Water Bearer stands for truth. You are a truth-teller; you give out opinions and observations. You dispense wisdom. You are a seeker of knowledge, rational, open-minded, gifted with breadth of vision. Chock full of information, you still search for more. You always want to know what lies on the other side of the mountain. One Aquarian recently declared, "It annoys me to find out there's something out there I've never heard of. I need to know what it is!"

You can be objective in judgment, for you don't let emotion get in the way. This appears to give you the ability to stand outside yourself, to rise above ordinary human frailty. Your built-in distrust of emotion compels you to struggle against its chains, and this may become a source of inner conflict.

Problems arise when your sense of identity becomes inextricably linked to your ideas. Like Gemini, another air sign, you have a lot of ego invested in your opinions. When others disagree, you take this as an attack on your personhood. Your fixity turns into willfulness and rebelliousness for the sake of being a rebel. You deliberately refuse to recognize that your idea isn't working in the real world of your relationships or career—and you sabotage yourself by insisting on your way even if your way proves to be unfeasible.

You are very people-oriented, addicted to the study of human beings and an inveterate people-watcher. Outgoing and amiable, you attract friends wherever you go. You have a talent for making people laugh with a pithy phrase that sums up a situation—though those who tangle with you quickly discover how your sharp verbal skills can deflate pomposity and pretension. You possess a true common touch, yet never lose your own strong individuality. Whomever you meet, you remain you—that amusing, inquisitive, interested person who wants to know what makes others tick. Your gift is for dealing with all kinds of personalities from every walk of life, no matter what their station or status. You never put on airs, nor are you cowed by anyone's wealth or position. If you met the Queen of England, you would be your natural self. We're all related, you believe, because we're all human beings. You are genuinely interested in why a person thinks this way or that. The nicest part is that you do not judge. You willingly grant to others what you consider an inalienable right: the freedom to be unique. For you, the ultimate liberation is simply the freedom to be oneself.

As a student of human behavior, you have great tolerance for the weaknesses and foibles to which all mankind is heir. You are a humanitarian, concerned with the welfare of the world, but do not get deeply involved in intimate relationships. There is always a certain distant quality to you, a detachment or aloofness of spirit. You seem to disassociate yourself from emotion. However, the cool, arm's-length impression you give can be deceiving. In the zodiac Aquarius symbolizes friendship, and you can form close and enduring ties. Beneath your detached, seemingly unemotional exterior beats a stubbornly loyal heart. No one is a truer, finer friend than Aquarius. Completely free of malice, you'll do anything to be helpful. Yet you'll never let the other person become dependent on you. Your affection comes with no strings attached.

Because independence is your way of life, you will sacrifice even a close personal relationship in order to maintain it. Trying to fence you in or tie you down won't work. If you feel trapped, you try to break free at any cost. Your sign of Aquarius also represents future hopes and yearnings, and for you, what's over is done with. You want to escape the past and, like Peter Pan, head straight on to morning. You're wonderful at hatching schemes and dreams, plotting trips, setting goals. The unusual—in people, places, and projects—is what really interests you.

As an idealist you would like to see that everybody is happy, and your ambition is to do something important and meaningful. Many Aquarians go into politics or become involved in social causes. This is the astrological sign of hopes and wishes, and you are the kind who follows a dream. History is dotted with progressive Aquarian thinkers such as Charles Darwin, Abraham Lincoln, Susan B. Anthony, Thomas Edison, and Franklin Delano Roosevelt.

An Aquarian will hatch up a grandiose scheme for improving the way things are, but your main interest is in creating the idea, not translating it into action through work. Hard work doesn't interest you. You are creative, imaginative, endlessly willing to experiment, but the drudgery of detail and the minutiae of management are not your style.

You'd rather invent a new utopian scheme and let others grapple with the hard realities.

Your great weakness is a tendency to inflate your own importance, to pose as an expert on any subject.

You are so determined not to be like anyone else that you are sometimes contrary just to be different. You have the least regard for convention of any zodiacal sign, which often gives you a reputation for being eccentric. Just as you are broad-minded about the faults of others, you take for granted that your shortcomings will be overlooked.

Sometimes you will be argumentative not because you feel deeply, but simply because you enjoy the intellectual exercise. You are quickly bored and take delight in verbally provoking anyone you consider stodgy and dull.

Nevertheless, Aquarians are among the kindest people in the world. Easygoing, reasonable, slow to take offense, never mean-hearted, you believe in live-and-let-live. Honest, helpful, altruistic, and best of all never boring, you can change anyone's life for the better just by becoming part of it.

The Inner You

The most frequent question you ask is "Why?" You want to understand what makes other people tick. Their lives fascinate you because you hope they will offer you insights into your own. You have plenty of love to give, and you want nothing more than to have lots of interesting friends, a wonderful love relationship, fulfilling work, and for the world to be a better place and everyone to be happy. Not much to ask, is it? One of your best-kept secrets is how shy and insecure you are. You wonder if the people you care about feel the same way about you—this is why you work so hard to make others like you. You want to share yourself, but are afraid of losing who you are or becoming what other people think you should be. Yet somehow your feelings of insecurity manage to coexist with a belief that you are someone special.

How Others See You

You're often regarded as slightly eccentric—not necessarily *strange*, but certainly an independent character, a kind of daredevil with an unusual way of looking at things. People consider you a pathfinder, a member of the real avant-garde. They think you have a wicked sense of humor, an ability to shock and amuse at the same tine.

They know you're open to new ideas, especially when these ideas are yours. People are drawn to your friendliness and enthusiasm, but they withdraw quickly when you turn acid-tongued. Sometimes, because you need so much personal freedom, you give the impression of being uncaring or distant. Those around you may also become annoyed at your stubbornness.

FAMOUS PEOPLE WITH THE SUN IN AQUARIUS

Jennifer Aniston
Susan B. Anthony
Corazon Aquino
Tallulah Bankhead
Mikhail Baryshnikov
John Belushi
Jack Benny
Christie Brinkley
Tom Brokaw
George Burns
Robert Burns
Aaron Burr
Lord Byron
Eddie Cantor
Lewis Carroll
Carol Channing
Stockard Channing
Paddy Chayefsky
Natalie Cole
Charles Darwin
Angela Davis

Geena Davis
James Dean
Neil Diamond
Charles Dickens
Matt Dillon
Christian Dior
Placido Domingo
Dr. Dre
Thomas Alva Edison
Sergei Eisenstein
Mia Farrow
Farrah Fawcett
Federico Fellini
W. C. Fields
Clark Gable
Zsa Zsa Gabor
Philip Glass
Christopher Guest
Germaine Greer
Zane Grey
D. W. Griffith

John Grisham
Paris Hilton
Langston Hughes
Holly Hunter
Virginia Johnson-
    Masters
Michael Jordan
James Joyce
Jerome Kern
Alicia Keys
Nastassja Kinski
Eartha Kitt
Ted Koppel
Mario Lanza
Heath Ledger
Jack Lemmon
Sinclair Lewis
Joseph Lieberman
Abraham Lincoln
Charles Lindbergh
Ernst Lubitsch

Ida Lupino
David Lynch
Douglas MacArthur
John McEnroe
Norman Mailer
Edouard Manet
Christopher Marlowe
W. Somerset
    Maugham
Felix Mendelssohn
Carmen Miranda
James Michener
Jeanne Moreau
Toni Morrison
Robert Motherwell
Wolfgang Amadeus
    Mozart
Paul Newman
Jack Nicklaus
Nick Nolte
Kim Novak

Yoko Ono
Thomas Paine
Anna Pavlova
S. J. Perelman
James Pike
Jackson Pollock
Leontyne Price
Ronald Reagan
Vanessa Redgrave
Burt Reynolds
Jackie Robinson
Chris Rock
Norman Rockwell
Franklin Delano
    Roosevelt
Arthur Rubinstein
Babe Ruth
Telly Savalas
Franz Schubert
Andres Segovia
Tom Selleck

Jane Seymour
Cybill Shepherd
Susan Sontag
Gertrude Stein
Stendhal
George
    Stephanopoulos
Adlai Stevenson
Justin Timberlake
John Travolta
François Truffaut
Lana Turner
Barbara Tuchman
Jules Verne
Robert Wagner
Edith Wharton
John Williams
Oprah Winfrey
Elijah Wood
Virginia Woolf

Oprah Winfrey

Franklin Delano Roosevelt

Justin Timberlake

PISCES
(FEBRUARY 19 – MARCH 20)

DUALITY Feminine

TRIPLICITY (ELEMENT) Water

QUADRUPLICITY (QUALITY) Mutable

Pisces is receptive, intuitive and emotional, imaginative, romantic, impressionable and mystical, adaptable, and very changeable.

RULING PLANET Neptune: Ancient god of the sea; second of the modern planets to be discovered (in 1846). In astrology, Neptune is the planet of illusion, glamour, mystery, deception.

SYMBOL Two Fishes tied to one another and swimming in opposite directions: Signifying hidden depths, shifting emotional currents, conflicting desires, and extremes of temperament.

GLYPH (WRITTEN SYMBOL) ♓ The pictograph represents two Fishes tied together. It is also a picture of the human feet (the part of the anatomy that Pisces rules). In symbolic terms, the glyph is two crescent moons connected by a straight line. This represents emotion and higher consciousness tied to and limited by the material world.

DOMINANT KEYWORD I BELIEVE.

POLARITY Virgo:

Pisces is the sign of dreams and mysticism. Its natives trust their intuitions and feelings and tend to seek more spiritual values in life. Virgo, Pisces's opposite sign, is the sign of work and service. Virgo people deal in facts and reality; they are practical and strive for material success.

PART OF THE BODY RULED BY PISCES The feet: Pisceans have beautifully shaped, sensitive feet that are unfortunately prone to aches, bunions, corns. Ill-fitting shoes are a particular hazard to people of this sign.

LUCKY DAY Friday **LUCKY NUMBERS** 2 and 6

MAGICAL BIRTHSTONE Aquamarine: Magnifies occult powers and brings serenity of mind. It also protects its wearer while traveling on the sea.

SPECIAL COLORS Pale green and turquoise: The dreamy colors of the sea.

CITIES Casablanca, Alexandria, Lisbon, Seville, Dublin **COUNTRIES** Portugal, the Sahara Desert

FLOWERS Water Lily, White Poppy, Jonquil **TREES** Fig and Willow

METAL Platinum

ANIMALS RULED BY PISCES Fish

DANGER Pisceans have a high susceptibility to alcohol and drugs. They are also easily drawn into unpredictable situations and to unbalanced people.

Your Most Likeable Trait
COMPASSION

Just as the first sign of the zodiac, Aries, represents a new beginning so the twelfth and last sign, Pisces, is the end of the circle, the sign of eternity, reincarnation, and spiritual rebirth. Many astrologers say that Pisces is a link to the spirit world and that you who are born under this sign are old souls, for they believe Pisceans to have experienced other lives in the past.

Pisceans have an otherworldly quality. In mystical terms, you are described as being half-body and half-spirit, pulled between material existence and spiritual concerns, possessed of the knowledge that you will never be entirely at home in the real world.

Like natives of the other water signs (Cancer and Scorpio), you have the ability to see deeply into the human psyche. Subtle and intuitive, you are born with the gift of prophecy, and may even become involved in the occult, ESP, and spiritualism. Because you have a close relationship with astral forces, you feel things before you know them and your feelings are rarely wrong. If you get a hunch, others would be wise to pay attention. Part of your clairvoyance stems from the fact that you understand first with your heart, and only then do you rationalize what you know intuitively.

Ruled by Neptune, planet of mystery and illusion, your personality is elusive, fey, and quicksilvery. Your element is water, and the imagery of the sea is evident in how easily you adapt to the ever-shifting currents around you. More than natives of any other sign, you are enormously influenced by your surroundings and by the people who touch your life. Indeed, you have a unique ability to get under another person's skin, to take literally as your own another's problems, joys, and woes. You have tender sympathy for anyone or anything that hurts; sick plants, hungry animals, and friends in need—they all find a home with you. At times you give away the very strength and emotional security you need for yourself.

You possess superb intuitions and a seemingly bottomless understanding of other people, yet your extraordinary sensitivity can be your most vulnerable point. You are too impressionable to each passing influence, too susceptible to someone else's hard-luck story or plea for help. For you, learning to say no can be a lifetime project and you may never learn how to do it at all.

Ancient astrologers called Pisces the sign of Sorrow from Self-Undoing, and you can easily become the creator of your own downfall. You are impractical and fall prey to overindulgence. You also have a penchant for picking the wrong companions. A fatal flaw in Pisces is the tendency to flee from what you don't want to deal with, and this can lead you into a world of addictive behavior. At times, your life may become so punctuated with trouble and heartache that you try desperately to escape, and then you are like Eliza jumping from ice floe to ice floe, with no clear sense of where you are headed. Your symbol, two fishes tied together swimming in opposite directions, represents conflicting emotions and desires that pull you to and fro. You must fight hard for stability, for the strength of purpose and balance needed to combat the negativity of laziness, carelessness, and emotional confusion. You need to develop a positive self-image, play on your strengths and ability to take responsibility, not let yourself fall victim to bad choices and your predilection for self-undoing. Your life lesson is to learn self-*doing*.

Certainly, you do not lack backbone. Indeed, you are ca-

pable of great sacrifice and hard work in the service of a cause or an ideal. Intellectually you are curious and like to explore the unusual and hidden. Although you can be impractical, even lazy, you are also capable of prodigious work when you are involved in a project you truly care about. The thing is that despite the fact that you work unselfishly for others, you find it hard to be strict and disciplined with yourself. Not many natives of this sign are suited to the harsh, rough-and-tumble world of business and commerce. Pisces is the mystical sign of the poet and the dreamer, and you are more successful as a writer, musician, or artist. You're intensely imaginative and addicted to make-believe, and you strive to create a world that comes closer to your own unique vision. When you put your energy into creating fantasies, you're the most creative artist in the zodiac. Among famous Piscean creators are Pierre-Auguste Renoir, Frederic Chopin, Enrico Caruso, Vaslav Nijinsky, Rudolph Nureyev, Elizabeth Barrett Browning, and Edna St. Vincent Millay.

Because you blend compassion and understanding with great verve, you exert a unique power on people whose lives touch yours. You may feel you lack self-confidence to be a leader, but you are definitely a guide, teacher, and role model to many. You are also a fey charmer and a mischievous wit who loves to laugh. Yet because you are fundamentally unsure of yourself, you prefer to work alone rather than with people. You have an instinct for finding what appears to be the easy way out, and founder in the shallows of least resistance. This is why so many talented, charming, superior natives of this sign never attain the position in life to which their gifts entitle them.

You are a very special person whose sensitivity and awareness will always appeal to a select group. You are capable of high intellectual achievement and your magnetic, mysterious, engaging and delightful personality is heightened by an intriguing sense of drama.

You are also loyal, unselfish, and generous, always ready to help a friend who has fallen on hard times. In fact, you often create a special kind of magic—when you concentrate on the best and reject what is ugly and mean-spirited, people are likely to live up to your vision. You have a deep appreciation for the inner qualities of others; you are not concerned with the superficial and with what others see on the surface. You look at the inner soul, the essence. There is no more sensitive, perceptive friend, nor one more warmhearted, caring, devoted, and sentimental.

Your Inner Self

You absorb impressions, images, and emotions from everything around you, and then filter them through your rose-colored view of how you'd like things to be. This is not to say you cannot deal with reality—it's just that you like to think of life as an ultraromantic movie filled with happy endings and where everyone has the best possible motives. You're a big bundle of feelings. You feel intense joy and happiness when you're involved in a creative project or a loving relationship. The opposite is also true: you can suffer greater depths of sadness than most. Yet you're tougher than most people think. Push you down and you keep bouncing back like a rubber bathtub toy. You're charged with energy and get caught up in what's going on around you. Your greatest strength is in giving to others; you're always ready to help whoever needs you.

How Others See You

Everyone thinks you are his or her special friend, that they have your undivided attention. You're thought of as solicitous and concerned. You're also known as a sparkling social presence—witty, vivacious, and always interested in new activities. People consider you artistic and somewhat bohemian, and are impressed by your psychic sensibility. They value you as a confidant but, oddly, the more people lean on you, the weaker they think you *are*.

Famous People with the Sun in Pisces

Edward Albee
Mario Andretti
W. H. Auden
Tammy Faye Bakker
Drew Barrymore
Harry Belafonte
Alexander Graham
    Bell
Osama bin Laden
Erma Bombeck
Elizabeth Barrett
    Browning
Luther Burbank
Michael Caine
Karen Carpenter
Enrico Caruso
Johnny Cash
Edgar Cayce
Cyd Charisse
Frederic Chopin
Glenn Close

Kurt Cobain
Roy Cohn
Nat King Cole
Nicolaus Copernicus
Tom Courtenay
Cindy Crawford
Billy Crystal
Honore Daumier
Michael Dell
Jimmy Dorsey
Lawrence Durrell
Wyatt Earp
Albert Einstein
Bobby Fischer
Peter Fonda
Galileo Galilei
Ruth Bader Ginsburg
Jackie Gleason
Mikhail Gorbachev
Kelsey Grammer
Cedric Hardwicke

Jean Harlow
George Harrison
Rex Harrison
Patricia Hearst
Ben Hecht
Jennifer Love Hewitt
Winslow Homer
Ron Howard
Victor Hugo
William Hurt
Henrik Ibsen
John Irving
Steve Jobs
Jennifer Jones
Barbara Jordan
Jon Bon Jovi
Kiri Te Kanawa
Edward M. Kennedy
Jack Kerouac
Ring Lardner
Spike Lee

Sybil Leek
Jerry Lewis
Rob Lowe
James Madison
Anna Magnani
Gabriel García
    Marquez
Michelangelo
Edna St. Vincent
    Millay
Glenn Miller
Liza Minnelli
Piet Mondrian
Zero Mostel
Rupert Murdoch
Ralph Nader
Kate Nelligan
Vaslav Nijinsky
David Niven
Pat Nixon
Rudolph Nureyev

Merle Oberon
Shaquille O'Neal
Sidney Poitier
Aidan Quinn
Tony Randall
Sally Jessy Raphael
Lynn Redgrave
Carl Reiner
Rob Reiner
Pierre-Auguste Renoir
Miranda Richardson
Bobby Riggs
Nicolai Rimsky-
    Korsakov
Philip Roth
Kurt Russell
Willard Scott
Neil Sedaka
Dr. Seuss
Irwin Shaw
Dinah Shore

John Steinbeck
Dean Stockwell
Sharon Stone
Darryl Strawberry
Jimmy Swaggart
Elizabeth Taylor
James Taylor
Ellen Terry
Franchot Tone
Tommy Tune
Carrie Underwood
John Updike
Gloria Vanderbilt
Irving Wallace
Earl Warren
George Washington
Kurt Weill
Lawrence Welk
Vanessa Williams
Bruce Willis
Joanne Woodward

Kurt Cobain

Carrie Underwood

Albert Einstein

2

THE SUN SIGNS IN LOVE

LOVE, *L'AMOUR*, ROMANCE—it makes the world go round. In this chapter you will discover the basic amorous nature of the Sun signs. Because men and women have a somewhat different approach to love and sex, I have divided the signs into *Woman* and *Man*. Also, for those readers interested in how to attract a person born under a particular sign, I have included tips that should prove helpful.

Remember, however, that the descriptions are based on Sun signs alone, not on the other important influences in a person's chart. This chapter merely gives you clues to a person's amorous nature, but you can *never* judge a person entirely on his or her Sun sign.

Let's say a woman has just met an attractive Taurus man and he has invited her to have dinner with him. By all means, she should read the description of Taurus man's amorous nature to get an inkling of the kind of man he is. But she should not cancel her dinner date if she doesn't like everything she reads. The Taurus she dines with will have other planetary influences in his chart, and he will not exactly match his Sun sign description. On the other hand, he is a Taurean and his basic nature will have Taurean characteristics. She should go to dinner and find out more about the man. When it comes to *l'amour*, take a chance.

Later on in the book you will find a chapter on how to compare a lover's horoscope with your own. That takes you further into the various planetary influences. By the time you reach that chapter, you will know a great deal more about astrology.

Meanwhile, this preliminary survey provides a general guide and a useful insight into how each Sun sign deals with love. In addition, I include for each Sun sign a guide, called "Amorous Combinations," that tells how the sign relates to all the other signs in the zodiac.

Let me caution you, however, that the descriptions in this guide are painted in broad strokes, and should not seriously affect a decision about whom to make love with, whom to marry, or even whom to have dinner with—decisions that should be based on many other factors.

With the above caveat, I include in this chapter a summary of general compatibilities for your Sun sign in the hope that it may prove both instructive and amusing.

Vive l'amour!

ARIES
The Amorous Nature

You and Aries Woman

If you fall in love with an Aries woman, you'll never lack for excitement. But are you the kind of man who can handle a full-blooded independent, forceful female? Because that's what Aries woman is.

This passionate, intense creature can't give a tepid response. She's a fully stocked fireplace, with logs, kindling, and paper, waiting for the touch of a match to set her on fire.

What Aries woman wants, she gets. When a man meets an irresistible force like her, he tends to become a highly movable object. Indeed, when she is first attracted to a man she throws herself into the enthralling game of seeing how fast she can capture him. For her, one of the peak experiences of an affair is the *beginning* of the stalk. She's fascinated by challenge. The more aloof you are, the more she wants you; her goal is to make you her love slave.

A love affair with her is not easy. She wants freedom and total togetherness and ecstasy all at once. She has an enormous need for love and gets more than her share, but no man becomes her lord and master. She meets a man on equal terms. If he offers loyalty, she repays him in kind. If he is untrustworthy, she also repays him in kind. Basically, in her relations with men she is domineering. You can either accept it or leave. If you stay, you've made the first concession on a long road. At the end, you're likely to find you've been molded and shaped to fit her image of what her lover should be.

In love she will be faithful, but she expects total fidelity in return. Her jealousy is rooted in possessiveness. She doesn't want a lover who has too many other interests. She wants all of him—or nothing at all.

There is an important distinction to make about her jealousy that may be useful in helping to understand her fundamental character. She isn't jealous because of a feeling of insecurity (the root cause of most jealousy), but because she has to be number one. She'll become a towering inferno if her man so much as *thinks* about two-timing her.

The Aries woman finds happiness in a long-term relationship. She enjoys sharing everything with a lover, and is a giver of and partaker in pleasure. She is a highly affectionate and demonstrative lover who exudes sexuality and magnetism. Every sex encounter (even with the same lover) takes on the drama of a conquest. She will also be your staunchest ally, fight side by side with you, believe in you, encourage you. She's a marvelous companion for a man on the way up or fighting to stay at the top because she'll give him all the strength and determination she has. She's definitely ambitious.

When she does not feel she is loved she can become shrill and demanding. Above all, she won't tolerate being ignored or neglected. The straight road to perdition is a relationship with an unhappy Aries woman.

She wants to be understood and appreciated for her unique qualities. If you handle her with tact and give her the admiration she needs, this vivacious, active, mischievous, sensual, fascinating woman will do anything you ask.

You and Aries Man

It would be superfluous to say he has fiery emotions because he has practically no other kind. He's always in search of something that will satisfy his pioneering, ever-aggressive lust for adventure. He moves within a self-created aura of excitement and somehow things happen wherever he is.

He won't be easy to resist. Think it over before you say even a tentative no. Where else will you find a lover as adventurous, original, virile, and vital? A woman who is attracted to an Aries male should be willing to settle for a brilliant, exciting—and generally *short*—affair. Romantically, he dotes on challenge and novelty. To him, the world is a garden of feminine flowers and he can't afford to miss the scent of a single lovely bloom.

There are so many delights to sample before winter comes. He is always eager for a new experience. At first, that's all a woman represents to him.

However, there is a vulnerable side to this man. He believes in the Eternal Woman, a romanticized version of the beautiful goddess whom he will sweep off her feet. He doesn't understand deviousness in a relationship, and if a woman *appears* innocent and yielding he won't look further. If he discovers that he has been duped and taken advantage of, his bewilderment and hurt quickly turn to anger.

Aries acts out sexual fantasies. The minute he finds himself daydreaming about a sexual situation, he sets to work trying to make it a reality. And something about his blunt, direct approach, "the battering ram," gets results where more subtle means might fail. He leaves no doubt of his intention from the first, but comes at you directly. His manner is forceful, aggressive, and winning. He is used to winning. On your first date you'll learn that you cannot take the lead. He will tell you where you're going and when; you can simply relax and leave it all in his capable hands.

He is impulsive to the point of rashness. When he wants you, he wants you. He has no control over his passions and must go anywhere his desires impel him. He doesn't worry about consequences.

This man has energy, imagination, and sheer physical exuberance. Any woman who has had an Aries man around the house will tell you she had an exciting time—while it lasted.

How to Attract Aries

Don't be timid. Faint heart never won Aries, male or female. Let Aries people know how much you admire them right at the beginning. Aries people will never think you brash if you are paying them a compliment. They feel they deserve it. Be a bit careful, though, about laying it on too thick. They can always spot insincerity.

Aries people think of themselves as intellectuals, so don't appeal to them purely on a physical plane. They will enjoy a lively discussion of theater, music, politics, or even more esoteric subjects such as history, art, or philosophy.

A good suggestion for a date early in the relationship is a sporting event. (With Aries, it can never be more than a suggestion.) They are enthusiastic sports fans. If you don't know much about the game you're watching, let them explain it to you. They'll do so in a way that will make it interesting and exciting.

Before an important date, take a nice long nap. Aries is no clock-watcher, and the fun may go on and on into the wee hours. Aries people pick up steam while everyone else is running out of gas.

By all means, bring your problems to Aries. There is nothing they like better than to be asked for advice. They are generous with their time, counsel, money, and sympathy. And there's an additional advantage. No Aries is in doubt as to what should be done in any given situation. You'll get a forthright, black-and-white, no-quibbles-or-evasions answer.

Important: Never try to dictate to an Aries. They don't know how to take orders. If you want to put an idea into his or her head, do it so that Aries thinks the idea originated there.

Aries's Amorous Combinations

ARIES AND ARIES This can be a passionate affair, but neither is content with an inferior role. The Aries female tends to dominate (generally because domineering females have to try harder to get their way than domineering males). However, there will be fierce competition to be number one. Eventually, the flare-ups and heavy cannonading take their toll in the bedroom, and what starts out so promisingly ends in disharmony. The prognosis is a little better if each has outside interests and/or a career separate from the other. When their energies are diverted into other areas, conflict between the two becomes a bit more playful and less destructive.

ARIES AND TAURUS Both are highly sensual, but Aries may be annoyed by the deliberate pace and unimaginative lovemaking of Taurus. Taurus is a homebody, while Aries is definitely not. Aries is impulsive, and looks for new experiences and freedom. Taurus is possessive and jealous, set in its ways, and views Aries's need to be an individual as a rejection. Taurus is good at making money, but Aries is even better at spending it. The long haul can be hard going, though if they hang on long enough Aries will come to appreciate Taurus's steadiness and dependability.

ARIES AND GEMINI They won't bore each other because both love to talk. (It's a close contest, but Gemini will probably win.) And they share a special compati-

bility, for Gemini is as restless and eager to try new things as Aries is. There are no inhibitions on either side. Gemini is clever enough to counter Aries's need to dominate. Gemini may seek extra outside stimulation, but is discreet about it. Their minds mesh well; Aries is dynamic and intelligent, Gemini is versatile and ingenious. Aries is likely to be the leader sexually, and Gemini delights in thinking up variations to keep Aries's interest at a peak. The signals are definitely go.

ARIES AND CANCER These two are fascinated with each other at the beginning, but sexual attraction fades in the face of many temperamental differences. Aries leaps without looking; Cancer is cautious. Cancer loves hearth and home; Aries hates being tied down. Resentments build up and they argue over trifles. Aries has a sharp tongue that wounds vulnerable Cancer. The more aggressive Aries is, the more defensive Cancer becomes. There's too little compatibility to work with. When Cancer starts to nag, Aries looks for the way out.

ARIES AND LEO Both have got egos to burn and both like to lead. Aggressive Aries wouldn't dream of taking second place, and kingly Leo needs constant admiration. Usually they can work it out by having Leo play the emperor and Aries play the general. The trick is for neither to take the other all that seriously. It's a fine combustible sexual match, for both are fiery and romantic. Aries is optimistic and open to life; Leo is generous and good-hearted. If neither tries to deflate the other—and if they can find room to compromise about who dominates whom—this should be a happy mating.

ARIES AND VIRGO Aries's boldness should intrigue shy, reserved Virgo for a time. But they have totally different ideas about what should happen in the bedroom—and elsewhere. Aries's passions are impulsive and direct. Virgo's sexuality is more enigmatic and takes time to be revealed. In other areas Aries is full of exciting new plans and ideas, and insists on being boss. Virgo is critical and fussy, and likes things to be done the way Virgo wants. Virgo disapproves of Aries's extravagance; Aries thinks Virgo cold and carping. They end up making war, not love.

ARIES AND LIBRA There is a powerful initial attraction between these two opposites, for in certain areas each supplies what the other lacks. For one, Aries's aggressiveness arouses Libra's sensual potential. Their love life may be unconventional. However, Libra really wants peace, quiet, and harmony, while Aries wants action and adventure. Both like social life, entertaining, and pleasure, but both are restless in different ways. In time Libra will look for someone less demanding, and Aries will find someone more adoring. Marvelous affair; poor marriage.

ARIES AND SCORPIO Love can be a bonfire between these two. They're both physical, energetic, and passionate. Sexually, everything should be fine—it's the emotional side of the relationship they can't handle. Each has a forceful personality and wants to control the other. In the end, Scorpio's jealousy may prove the undoing. Aries's many outside interests make Scorpio feel insecure and that brings out Scorpio's tyrannical streak. Aries won't take orders and Scorpio will never take a backseat. This is an unstable partnership with a low ignition point.

ARIES AND SAGITTARIUS Sagittarius is a perfect temperamental match for Aries. They are both active, spontaneous people who like socializing, have extravagant tastes in common, and enjoy the good life. There may be a little conflict because both are impulsive and brutally frank. Arguments can reach the boiling point. Aries's forceful sexual approach is not always playful Sagittarius's style. However, they have wonderful senses of humor and enjoy each other's company. If they make it in the bedroom, they'll make it everywhere else.

ARIES AND CAPRICORN Aries's taste for innovation and experimentation may not please conservative Capricorn. Aries is restless, fiery, impulsive; Capricorn is ordered, settled, practical. Capricorn needs to dominate and so does Aries. Problems also crop up over money—Aries is extravagant, Capricorn is security-minded. Oddly enough, the auguries are better for the long haul than the short. Aries's responsive sexual nature meets its match in Capricorn's deep-seated passions. And Capricorn's strength and endurance will in time win Aries's respect.

ARIES AND AQUARIUS They're well suited temperamentally—both are active, ambitious, enjoy a wide range of interests, and are equally eager for sexual adventure. Depending on whim, Aquarius may or may not let Aries take the lead. Both are independent—Aquarius even more than Aries—and Aries may at times feel neglected. Aries finds the Aquarian unpredictability exciting, but also never feels entirely secure. However, with a bit of tact and understanding on both sides, this is a great affair that could turn into something even better.

ARIES AND PISCES Aries will draw Pisces out of that shell, and in turn will be hypnotized by Pisces's seductive and mysterious sexuality. The boldness and confidence of Aries plus Pisces's intuitions and fantasies add up to an eventful union. Personality differences complement each other. Aries is self-assured and vivacious; Pisces is somewhat shy and easily led. Aries likes to be dominant; Pisces likes having someone to lean on. For a happy coupling this requires only a little more tact on Aries's part.

TAURUS
The Amorous Nature

You and Taurus Woman

She is a da Vinci in the art of seduction. From her Mona Lisa smile to the sensual look in her eyes, she is a consummate mistress of love. However, she is not promiscuous, and any hopeful male who picks up her seductive signal had better turn off his antenna if all he wants is a casual affair. Taurus woman is not a lady for a day, or even for a weekend. Her need is for security and stability, and casual is not a word in her vocabulary of love.

In many ways Taurus woman is the perfect personification of the old-fashioned woman, for she is devoted and protective, a natural earth mother who loves and nurtures and gives of her strength. She is also earthy in her passions—once she falls in love. Being in love brings out the best in her. She isn't coy or provocative in a love relationship. She is open, affectionate, and demonstrative with the man she cares for, and abundantly generous with her affection, caresses, and verbal endearments. Her sexual appetite borders on the lusty—indeed, she has a great appetite for *life*. Her first sexual experience is likely to be with an older, sophisticated man who teaches her the pleasures of fine food and wines and traveling first class.

A passionate bed partner and a devoted mate, Taurus woman has a great deal to offer. But she demands a lot in return. She believes in giving her all and taking all she can get. No bargain hunters need apply.

She likes to be courted, pursued, and wooed—but is never really won. She makes up her own mind long before what you may consider the decisive moment. She plans ahead, for she doesn't believe such an important matter as sex should be left entirely to chance. The stage is set carefully. Every attention will be given to detail, for the woman born under this sign is marvelous at detail. While you preen yourself on your supposed conquest, she never lets you know that you never had a choice.

If she loves you, nothing anybody can say against you will affect her in the slightest degree. She has a secure sense of her own judgment and her own needs, and she trusts her instincts.

Taurus woman is a true romantic—serene, unaffected, sexy, artistic, good-natured, yet with elegance and taste. If you capture this woman's fancy, count yourself blessed.

You and Taurus Man

He won't sweep you off your feet and ride away with you into a crimson sunset. It's not that he's afraid to do this, it's just that the idea would never occur to him. If his maiden fair were locked up in a tower, he'd be far more likely to call at the front gate to negotiate for her release. That's the sensible thing to do.

Above all, this man is sensible, down-to-earth, and practical about love. In his approach to women he is deliberate, looking over the field before he decides. You won't find him trying to win the prize every other man is after. He wants a woman who will satisfy him for the long haul, not a glittering chromium-plated model that's all too soon ready for the junk heap. He prizes security and stability. This is not to say he will turn down an invitation to a weekend frolic with a beautiful blonde. The world is populated with millions of sexy, sensual, casual-*seeming* Taurus men who certainly enjoy making love. But scratch the surface and you'll uncover a man who doesn't want a *relationship* unless he thinks it's going to last. When it comes to his emotional life he can afford to be patient.

He is very sensitive to a rebuff, but is so good at concealing this that most women never suspect it. He may appear too stolid to be really sensitive, but his tough-looking hide is only tissue thin. It isn't always apparent at first meeting, but, in his own way, Taurus is supremely romantic. He puts the woman he cherishes on a pedestal, though he certainly doesn't treat her like a statue. Unlike some men who have an idealized vision that they try to superimpose on a woman, Taurus loves the real you.

This man isn't able to say "I love you" as readily as the more verbal types such as Gemini or Libra, but he will show his devotion by being unexpectedly generous. Of course, his gifts won't be frivolous because he never loses sight of the value he gets for money spent. He's the kind of man who will buy you a single high-priced piece of jewelry rather than a dozen gaudy trinkets.

Beneath a Taurus male's reserve is a passionate, highly physical nature. For him, romance and sensuality are practically interchangeable. Like his female counterpart, he is simple and direct about his sexual pleasures.

He sees no need for variations on the theme, but on the other hand, he has all the stamina a woman could ask for. His immense physical vitality more than makes up for any lack of variety.

Here is a sensual, strong-willed, sensible man you can depend on. He's loyal, affectionate, kind, and faithful, with a fine understated sense of humor. A lot of women who are looking for Mr. Right need look no farther than a Taurus male.

How to Attract Taurus

Taureans are not going to be rushed. They like everything, including a friendship or a love affair, to be built on a firm foundation. That may require restraint and patience, but these are qualities Taureans appreciate, for they possess those traits themselves.

Hint: The first move is up to you. Taurus is slow to make up his or her mind, and the opportunity will be gone if you don't seize the initiative.

Show them you like to be in their company, and try to amuse them. These quiet, easygoing people respond to those from whom they can borrow laughter. You'll find them charming companions, interested *and* interesting. A tendency to be somewhat ponderous or to go on at excessive length can be corrected with an apt remark at the right time.

If you tell a joke, remember that Taurus's sense of humor tends to be broad, robust, Rabelaisian. Physical jokes strike their funnybones.

If you're feeding a Taurus, feed him or her well. Take her to a restaurant where the chef knows his business and where you can get a good bottle of wine. Cook him a meal at home that shows you know your way around a kitchen, and don't skimp on the portions.

If the conversation starts to lag, try that never-failing topic of interest: money. By all means, show off your prized possessions, from stamps to ivory miniatures to jade, or even Indian-head pennies. To a Taurean, it's all endlessly fascinating.

Don't monopolize the conversation. Once Taureans get started, they like to talk. And don't be niggardly with praise—for their home, their car, clothes, jewelry, their just plain good taste, and, above all, for them.

Taurus's Amorous Combinations

TAURUS AND ARIES Taurus is not as quick on the trigger as Aries, but both have a mutual interest in making love. Aries is emotional and Taurus is sensual, and they're bound to have fun while the affair lasts. In time, though, Taurus's possessiveness will strike angry sparks from fiery Aries. They'll also argue about money—Taurus tends to be careful and conservative, Aries is reckless and a spendthrift. Aries's impulsiveness in making decisions annoys fixed Taurus, who dislikes a sudden change in routine. An affectionate affair can turn into a difficult marriage.

TAURUS AND TAURUS This isn't the most exciting union ever, for both are domestic creatures who prefer safety to adventure. However, both share a fondness for money and, are hardworking, loyal, and affectionate. She tends to be more sentimental than he, but each is as possessive as the other, which works out fine. Because they are both earthy and direct about sexual needs, there should be no problem in that department. Boredom is the threat. The perfect solution is for each to develop some outside hobbies and friends without raising the possessive hackles of the other.

TAURUS AND GEMINI These two are completely unalike in temperament. Taurus is stolid, fixed in opinions, resistant to change. Gemini is flighty, restless, vacillating. But they may find each other intriguing for that very reason—for a little while. Gemini is attracted to Taurus's passions, but in time Taurus's instinct for security and stability will be offended by volatile Gemini. Taurus is too much a creature of habit to go along with Gemini's constant need for new stimulation. Eventually, Taurus's demands are simply too much for Gemini, who seeks escape.

TAURUS AND CANCER They have a lot going for them. Both are home-lovers, sentimentalists, and highly sexed. Taurus's easy-going, placid nature is a good antidote for Cancer's moodiness, though sometimes plainspoken Taurus must be careful not to slight Cancer's feelings. Cancer needs someone strong like Taurus to depend on; in turn, Cancer gives Taurus the loyalty and feedback it needs. Taurus is ambitious for money and security, and Cancer has exactly these same goals. Similar interests and desires make for a harmonious mating.

TAURUS AND LEO Leo demands constant praise and adulation, and is forever competing with Taurus. As a result, Taurus digs in its heels and gets more sullen with each passing day. Taurus needs appreciation and Leo needs worship, but neither will get what it needs from the other. In addition, Leo is extravagant and Taurus parsimonious. There is a basic conflict between Taurus's desire for a well-ordered schedule and Leo's need for a larger-than-life existence. Sexually, these two are well matched, but Leo thinks life is a circus and tries to perform in all three rings at once. Taurus finds that hard to take, or even to watch.

TAURUS AND VIRGO It's love at first sight. Both are homebodies and they share the same intellectual pursuits. Taurus's tenacity and Virgo's sharp mind are a good combination for success as a team. And Taurus keeps a careful eye on expenditures, which pleases thrifty Virgo. Although they lack what might be called a spontaneous approach to life, neither puts a high value on that. They may have to adjust sexually, for Taurus is more physical. However, Taurus will probably waken Virgo's sleeping passions. And they have everything else in common.

TAURUS AND LIBRA Taurus finds Libra a warm, romantic, vibrant partner. Libra was born to charm and titillate. Steady Taurus balances Libra's indecisiveness. Money may be a problem, for Libra doesn't share Taurus's reverential attitude toward a dollar, but both tend to be acquisitive and like to collect beautiful things. Both signs are ruled by Venus and have sensual natures, but each expresses this quality differently. In time, Libra's fickleness and casual air toward love can drive Taurus wild; and Libra will certainly resent Taurus's possessiveness. This romantic pairing may not last long.

TAURUS AND SCORPIO These two are opposites in the zodiac, but they have more in common than other opposites. Both are determined and ambitious, and neither is much of a rover. However, there are two strong wills at work here. Taurus's passionate sexual nature meets more than its match in Scorpio—in fact, the sexual element in this affair borders on the obsessive. But Scorpio's overbearing, possessive, jealous nature makes Taurus simmer with resentment. This is a tempestuous affair, and neither has the tolerance to make the union last.

TAURUS AND SAGITTARIUS This might work if Taurus can tie a string to Sagittarius's kite and hold on tight. They are attracted to each other physically, for Taurus's passions are ignited by Sagittarius's uninhibited lovemaking. But Taurus finds it difficult to deal with Sagittarius's roving eye and search for novelty. Sagittarius has an easy, live-and-let-live attitude about sex and everything else, whereas Taurus is both serious and possessive. Sagittarius refuses to stay under someone else's thumb. No dull moments—but a good deal of quarreling. An affair can be fun.

TAURUS AND CAPRICORN Capricorn is a strong match for Taurus, for they both have passions that are straightforward and uncomplicated. There won't be much romance but plenty of healthy sex. They share the same goals and like the same kinds of friends, and both are fond of security and money. Capricorn is a bit more secretive than Taurus would like, but all the same Capricorn's loyalty makes Taurus feel secure. And Taurus is charmed by Capricorn's unexpected sense of humor. Auguries for the long term are promising.

TAURUS AND AQUARIUS Neither is likely to approve of the other. Taurus is conservative, careful, close-mouthed. Aquarius is unconventional, innovative, and vivacious. Taurus is lusty and passionate, while Aquarius operates on a mental plane. Taurus finds it hard to keep Aquarius at home or satisfied with the delights of domesticity. Aquarius looks for openness and self-expression in a relationship, while Taurus needs security and comfort. Aquarius, a fancy-free loner who resents ties that bind, sooner or later slips away from possessive Taurus.

TAURUS AND PISCES Pisces may not altogether understand Taurus's materialistic approach to life. But the dependability of Taurus supplies the anchor Pisces needs to keep from drifting away into a private sea of fantasy. Hardworking Taurus sets a good example for lazy Pisces. Also, Taurus's practical, easygoing nature helps Pisces through its frequent changes of mood. In love, Taurus is devoted and Pisces is adoring. Though Pisces can be a little fey for Taurus, they're well suited sexually. Taurus is passionate, Pisces is sensual, and what's wrong with that?

GEMINI
The Amorous Nature

You and Gemini Woman

When you meet this coquette you are likely to become enchanted, for she casts a spell better than Merlin. However her love affairs have a touch of the casual, and even when she becomes deeply involved or marries there will be as much friendly feeling as heavy-breathing passion.

Many men who agree that Gemini women are fascinating think they are too difficult to figure out. If you keep her dual nature firmly in mind you won't be so confused. There is a part of her that needs love and security: to be coddled, catered to, looked after, made to feel she is the most important woman in the world. But the stronger part of her nature needs stimulation and novelty. There is an irrepressible frivolity to the personality of this high-spirited, pleasure-loving woman.

Gemini's secret fantasy is to be a smoldering and languorous femme fatale. But in real life she just doesn't have the patience, much less the *time*. Besides, half the men she meets aren't worth the effort: They're too dull.

She has a connoisseur's appreciation for a really interesting man, but if an affair loses zest, she looks for the escape hatch. When love goes out the window she doesn't waste time wondering where it went. A bad experience is quickly put out of mind. In order to fall in love again, she knows that she must forget having been in love before.

Sometimes in the game of seduction she can appear heartless because, while trying to keep you head-over-heels

about her, she's also calculating whether you're worth her attention. She experiences sexual desire in her *mind* before it becomes a reality. As a lover, she's quick tinder—she has an endless sexual curiosity and a charming willingness to experiment. Sometimes she tends to emphasize too much the physical responses of sex and fails on the emotional follow-through. That's because, basically, she doesn't commit herself too deeply or reveal herself too openly.

Gemini woman is inclined to be restless and changeable, and is often not satisfied with just one man on her string. Her dualistic and fickle nature demands more than one man can usually provide. To fulfill all her needs, he must satisfy on several planes at once—mental, emotional, *and* sexual. Variety is the name of her game.

All this makes a problem if you are out to become number one in her life. You have to be a composite man who can interest her on both a sexual and a mental level. If you can, she will be your devoted companion, faithful lover, and all-seasons charmer. You can *almost* be sure of her.

She likes to think her love is greater than that of the one she loves, a subtle form of control that is both a reproach and an encouragement for him to prove otherwise. Don't take what Gemini woman says at face value. Even if she believes what she says, there's another motive behind the apparent one.

Underneath her bewildering variety of masks, however, there is a solid, enduring person who shows her real face when she is in love. Then she may become quite possessive and is even inclined to be jealous. It's a rare lover who can deceive her and get away with it.

But why would he want to? Tempestuous, brilliant, vibrant, and witty, she's more than enough for any man.

You and Gemini Man

He's the world's best date—quick-witted, charming, interested in his companion, generous, and imaginative about places to go and things to see. A date with him is like an entertainment that never ends.

Women are drawn like moths to the bright flame of his vivacity, his zest for living. And like moths, women flare briefly in his life and are gone. It won't do any good to try to pin him down. See that bright flash of color in the garden? It's a living butterfly, not a specimen in a case. Enjoy it while you can; its stay will be brief.

This Mercury-ruled man loves women, which is one of his secrets of success with them. The Gemini man is genuinely interested in what women have to say, how their minds work, what he can learn from them. But he also needs his minimum daily requirement of fun, and when the fun leaves a relationship so does he. Just as a woman begins to take him seriously he vanishes in a puff of smoke.

The truth is that the Gemini male is made uneasy by too much emotion, by a woman who takes love too seriously. He thinks sex is fascinating because it continually renews itself; but love is terminal. Curiously, though, many Gemini men tend to get involved with intense, emo-tional women. (Of course, they don't usually *stay* involved.) Something about women who live on a dramatic level, who really feel emotions and express them, intrigues and fascinates Gemini. It's as if through them he hopes to uncover a new facet in himself.

If you ask him why he flits from one female to another, he'll tell you it's because he's searching for his own identity, or the perfect love, or some elusive goal of perfection. He was born under the sign of the Twins, and in a way he is looking for his astral twin, the spiritual soulmate who will complete his nature and put an end to his duality.

It's all too easy for you to fall into this man's silken web. He's a past master at the art of seduction. Many a woman has begun a friendly relationship with a nice, seemingly unaggressive, intellectual Gemini, only to find herself in bed with him—and not quite sure how she got there. A variation of this approach is when he seems not to be interested, or is acting cool and indifferent, or is even pursuing someone else for a time. Then when you start making an effort to attract *him*, it's too late. He's slipped the halter around your neck.

As a lover he has imagination, assurance, and *flair*, but he may not seem fully committed. His attention is always partly occupied elsewhere.

A romance will prove intriguing and exciting but may not survive the rough spots. The initial glow rubs off, the flame starts to sputter. No regrets, though, when smoke gets in your eyes. He's been fascinating to know.

How to Attract Gemini

Meet them on the high ground. Geminis' interests are wide rather than deep—they know a little about everything, but not much about any one thing. If you know one thing well, you'll impress them.

Gemini likes to give a friend or a lover a kind of IQ test. If you pass, you're welcome. You can even choose the subject on which you're being tested. Books, music, art, politics—Gemini is interested in all.

Beware of being too smugly conservative or conformist. In Gemini's scoring this rates as dull. However, speak your mind frankly on any subject. Gemini admires candor and honesty, and a good exchange, even of contrary opinions, can be a firm foundation for better acquaintance.

Don't try to match wits, unless you're sure you have the verbal ammunition. Geminis of either sex wield words as weapons. Geminis enjoy intellectual talk but they also love gossip. If you know any interesting anecdotes about the famous, near famous, or even just mutual acquaintances, you'll have an appreciative audience. Geminis are also fond of anyone who can make them laugh.

Want to give a gift? Bracelets and rings will set off their expressive hands. Or give them something to stimulate their busy minds: books, word games, puzzles, interesting computer software, the latest dictionary.

Warning: Geminis are deeply sensitive, and need to have people around they trust. Never give them a reason to suspect you are playing fast and loose with them (even if you are). And don't you be suspicious of them; nothing distresses Geminis more than to have their motives distrusted.

Gemini's Amorous Combinations

GEMINI AND ARIES This lively, energetic pair can be good friends as well as good lovers. They thrive on activity, adventure, and variety; enjoy each other's humor; and like social life. Aries will probably make the decisions because Gemini has difficulty in that area. There will be bedroom high jinks, for both are enthusiastic about sex. Aries's domineering streak will give Gemini the firm direction it needs—and Gemini's occasional wanderings from the straight and narrow will keep Aries on its toes.

GEMINI AND TAURUS An unpromising match, though at the beginning Taurus responds to Gemini's sparkle and Gemini is intrigued by Taurus's uncomplicated directness. But Taurus wants life to be stable and ordered, while Gemini is easily bored and looks for new experiences. Taurus is devoted to home sweet home, while Gemini follows the lure of the open road. Gemini finds Taurus's lovemaking a bit on the dull side, and also resents the restrictive net Taurus tries to construct. In turn, jealous, possessive Taurus can't handle Gemini's outside dalliances. Passions cool.

GEMINI AND GEMINI You won't find a more versatile, charming, or vivacious pair. These two will never bore each other, for they are interested in everything. The pace is frenetic, but neither would dream of slowing down. They are fascinating conversationalists, have tons of friends, and together they'll throw some marvelous parties. Sex is fun and games. But this couple is also superficial, unstable, and very restless. When they move out of the bedroom, everything becomes too chaotic—even for twin Geminis.

GEMINI AND CANCER Passionate Cancer fulfills Gemini's physical needs, and Gemini's cheerfulness brightens Cancer's disposition. But all too soon Gemini's tendency to play at love wounds oversensitive Cancer. Flirtatious Gemini makes Cancer feel very insecure and an affair is likely to be volatile. These two have too little in common for a long-term relationship. Cancer needs security and domesticity; Gemini loathes being tied down. Gemini hasn't any patience with Cancer's moodiness, and Gemini's sharp tongue is too biting for Cancer's fragile ego. They are doomed to a downhill run.

GEMINI AND LEO An affectionate pair who really enjoy each other. Gemini's amorous playfulness finds a responsive partner in eager, extroverted Leo. Leo's self-confidence blinks at Gemini's flirtatiousness with others. Gemini's penchant for ridicule can annoy regal Leo, though, and Leo will probably demand more adoration than Gemini is willing to give. Socially, each tries to upstage the other, but they have a lot of fun together doing it. They both love to laugh, and in bed they set off sparks. What more can they ask?

GEMINI AND VIRGO Both are Mercury-ruled and have a mental approach to life. But similarity ends there; these two are star-crossed from the beginning. Virgo considers Gemini scatterbrained and immature. Gemini thinks of Virgo as a stick-in-the-mud and a bore. Virgo's analytical approach seems like indifference to Gemini. Virgo looks on Gemini's busy social life as superficial and a waste of time. Virgo is critical; Gemini is tactless. Passions run on a low thermostat; their sex life soon turns chilly. Gemini's eye is certain to rove.

GEMINI AND LIBRA These two air signs are well suited intellectually and every other way. They are stimulating companions who will enjoy a lighthearted, lovely affair. Neither is combative and they're likely to agree on everything. They are affectionate, fun-loving, and like social life, entertaining, and travel. Sexually both are fervent, neither is jealous or demanding, and Libra goes along with Gemini's taste for experiment. Their one problem is that they both love to spend money. Otherwise it's a perfect match.

GEMINI AND SCORPIO Gemini's imagination and Scorpio's dynamism would make a good combination if only these two were able to get along together. There is combustion in the bedroom, but they soon find out that sex isn't everything. Scorpio is sensual, passionate, demanding, jealous, inflexible. Gemini is fickle, flighty, superficial, lighthearted, changeable. Gemini is a social creature, Scorpio likes privacy. Scorpio's suspicious nature is in constant turmoil over Gemini's casual attitude about love. It won't be long before enough becomes too much.

GEMINI AND SAGITTARIUS These two are opposites in the zodiac and are attracted to each other like magnets. They'll especially enjoy each other's minds, for both have wide-ranging and varied interests. Sagittarius tends to be more intellectual, Gemini more social. Both are too restless and argumentative, and both need freedom. They may be disappointed sexually, since neither is demonstrative—and Gemini is very quick to criticize. This affair probably began impulsively and will end the same way.

GEMINI AND CAPRICORN Gemini's freewheeling, anything-goes attitude meets opposition from conventional, steady, conservative Capricorn. Capricorn worries about security, while Gemini frets about losing its liberty. Order and routine keep Capricorn content, but drive Gemini to distraction. Gemini's need for a stimulating existence does nothing to make Capricorn feel secure. And Capricorn's sober outlook puts a damper on Gemini's high spirits. This isn't an affair with high voltage—but Gemini can help develop Capricorn's sensual potential.

GEMINI AND AQUARIUS Versatile Gemini and innovative Aquarius get along famously. They share a taste for novelty, travel, meeting new people. Because both are unpredictable, things can't always go smoothly. But love keeps getting better, for Aquarius adores Gemini's wit and good cheer. If Gemini is somewhat inconstant or unstable, Aquarius understands. If the affair should end, they'll still remain friends. In marriage, these two are affectionate, devoted companions more than passionate lovers.

GEMINI AND PISCES The passion quotient is high, and so are the problems. Emotional Pisces is too easily hurt by thoughtless Gemini. Gemini is mischievous and playful, but Pisces is sensitive and takes things to heart. Each practices deception in his or her own way: Gemini dissembles, Pisces won't deal with reality.

Gemini needs freedom and new vistas; Pisces needs unending adoration. Pisces just can't feel secure with gadabout Gemini, and tries to pull the net tighter. The claustrophobic atmosphere eventually makes it hard for Gemini to breathe.

CANCER
The Amorous Nature

You and Cancer Woman

She may appear like the photograph of that dream girl most men carry around in a hidden locket of their minds. But lurking just below the surface of that shy, sweet image is a superbly sensual woman. There are secret emotional depths to her, and like the story of Sleeping Beauty and her Prince it takes love to awaken her eroticism. She is a highly sensual woman, and love unlocks the smoldering fire hidden by her diffident manner.

Don't expect her to be forward, however, because she doesn't know how to be. You must pick up the subtle clue, the unspoken invitation. She may be trying to get in touch with you while your emotional phone is off the hook. If you miss that first chance, you're probably out of luck. Her feelings are too vulnerable for her to risk another overture.

As with all the water signs (Cancer, Scorpio, Pisces), the quality of trust is very important to her in a relationship. The Cancer woman is very cautious about giving her heart away. The two things she needs more than anything else are love and security, and she offers undying loyalty to a man who makes her feel secure. She has eyes only for him, and she'll cling as tenaciously as if she had pincers instead of arms. A betrayal in love is devastating, and takes a long, long time for her to forgive. In truth, she never forgives—rationally, yes, perhaps, but emotionally, never.

On first meeting Cancer woman you will find that she can be flirtatious, although in true subtle Cancerian fashion her flirting is done in a quiet way. Hers is not a flamboyant personality, but rather one of gentleness, depth, and richness. She is not only romantic, she's convinced that love, love, love is the secret of life. She wants to discover the secret with the man of her dreams. This sounds old-fashioned, but that's part of her charm: she *is* old-fashioned. It's a special quality that makes men feel protective toward her.

A confirmed sentimentalist, she loves to collect mementos from the past and pore over them. She frames old photographs, keeps old letters, stays in touch with old friends. She is devoted to her mate and to her family.

Affectionate, romantic, feminine, sympathetic, imaginative, and sweetly seductive, this quintessential woman can make home a place that a *man* never wants to leave.

You and Cancer Man

This sensual man doesn't come at you directly. He'd rather play the attentive courtier, the one who brings candy, flowers, and champagne and takes you to nice places. At most, he'll make an oblique suggestion that could as easily be taken for a mere risqué quip. That's to leave himself an avenue of escape, for he can't stand rejection.

He falls in love easily, for he is inclined to be a romantic daydreamer. His imagination becomes quickly engaged and anything will start him off: a wisp of a remembered fragrance, an almost-familiar face, the sound of a foghorn across the water. He begins to visualize scenes out of the past or to fantasize about the future. He can work up a whole romantic scenario out of very little raw material. Unfortunately, this also applies when he becomes jealous. He *must* know that his chosen mate is faithful at all times. His own fidelity runs very deep, and he demands total fealty in return. Anything else is a threat to the stability that he prizes, the security that he needs.

Cancer male is very affectionate, and he certainly doesn't insist on having a number of women around. ("If you've got one good woman, who needs two?" a Cancer male would ask.) Lovemaking is best for him when it happens at the whim of the moment.

He is intensely imaginative and expressive, with remarkable empathy and an instinctive understanding of the human heart, especially of its pain. He can actually *feel* his way into your emotions and sense your problems. Loving and attentive, he is willing to go to any lengths to please the object of his desire. He has a gift to amuse and will spoil you outrageously if given half a chance.

Above all, he wants the woman of his dreams to share his dreams with him. He is faithful and takes his role as a strong male protector very seriously. He is a very masculine man, not necessarily in an outer show of brawn and ruggedness but in his inner strength of tenderness and sensitivity. If you're the kind of woman who likes being pampered and looked after—having a constant devoted companion—Cancer is definitely your man.

How to Attract Cancer

Cancerians are vulnerable—to praise as well as criticism. Let them know directly and forthrightly how much you admire them. Nothing will draw Cancerians out of their shells more readily than the warmth of approval. Pick out a quality that you can, in all sincerity, compliment them on. Do you like what he's wearing? Her smile? Their ability to listen attentively? (No one is better at this than Cancer.) Tell them so. Don't be insincere and single out some quality merely for the sake of having something complimentary to say. Cancerians can always spot the difference between the compliment that is sincere and the one meant only to cajole.

Show Cancerians the softer side of your nature. Are you interested in charities? Talk about that. Or children? By all means. Or discuss a genuine personal problem that's troubling you. Then Cancerians will be able to show *their* best side: their empathy and ability to give constructive advice. Finances, politics, and sports are other areas that interest them greatly.

For a date, get tickets to the theater or to some art or cultural event. Cancerians respond to romantic, strongly melodic music, and are inclined to enjoy concerts and opera. A nice touch would be to pick a restaurant where there are strolling musicians.

Cancerians don't rush headlong into anything. They are essentially cautious, not to say skittish, about making a commitment. They try to avoid giving a definite yes or no. Tip: The longer they delay, the less likely that there will be a favorable outcome.

A true Cancerian sooner or later finds some cause for feeling injured. Their amazing memory dwells on the past and constantly recalls old wounds. A Cancerian who forgives and forgets is as rare as a vegetarian snake.

Cancer's Amorous Combinations

CANCER AND ARIES These two may start out like a house on fire, but it won't take long for the fire to burn out. Aries's venturesome spirit and wandering eye enflame Cancer's jealousy. And Cancer is too easily hurt by Aries's aggressiveness and sharp tongue. Cancer likes security and domesticity; Aries needs freedom to explore new worlds. Cancer wants to cherish and protect a lover, an attitude that Aries finds too claustrophobic. Both like money, but Aries wants to spend it and Cancer wants to keep it. Too many temperamental problems here.

CANCER AND TAURUS Both need security and a sense of permanence, and both are loving, affectionate, and passionate as well. Cancer adds a dash of imagination to Taurus's otherwise staid approach to sex. Taurus is possessive and that's just fine with clinging Cancer. Both are acquisitive moneymakers, and together they enjoy the delights of hearth and home. Taurus likes being catered to, and Cancer is the one to do it. Steady-going Taurus is also good for Cancer's moodiness. What each needs the other supplies.

CANCER AND GEMINI Gemini's sparkle immediately intrigues Cancer, but Cancer won't find security with fickle, fly-by-night Gemini. Basically, Cancer's nature is emotional and Gemini's is cerebral, and that makes it difficult for them to understand each other. Although sexual energies are well matched, Cancer will have a hard time adjusting to Gemini's playful, nonchalant attitude toward love. Possessive Cancer will try to keep Gemini hemmed in, and Gemini can't abide that. It's a short countdown to the finish.

CANCER AND CANCER They have a lot in common, and that's the trouble. They understand each other perfectly and can wound each other without even trying. Both are too sensitive, too demanding, too dependent. Cancers are obsessively concerned with their emotional psyches: Each needs an enormous amount of attention, coddling, and reassurance, and resents the other for not giving enough. On the plus side, they're sensual bedmates whose erotic imaginations are sparked by each other. But that's rarely enough. This treadmill goes nowhere.

CANCER AND LEO Cancer has to get used to Leo's extroverted exuberance. Otherwise, generous, open-hearted, strong Leo is just what insecure Cancer is looking for. Cancer's marvelous intuitions tell it exactly how to handle proud and flamboyant Leo. Admiration and a lot of flattery are what are needed to keep Leo purring with contentment. Leo is domineering in the bedroom and a little too forthright sexually for Cancer. But Leo's sunny disposition is a wonderful antidote for Cancer's moodiness.

CANCER AND VIRGO Cancer's responses are emotive while Virgo's are analytical, but their personalities mesh so well that it doesn't seem to matter. Cancer may have to warm up Virgo a little, but there is fire under the ice. This can turn into a secure, comfortable, and affectionate relationship. Cancer's struggle for financial security works perfectly with goal-oriented Virgo. Cancer understands Virgo's fussy ways, and steady Virgo helps balance variable Cancer. Cancer's dependency neatly complements Virgo's need to protect, and each is anxious to please the other. Good auguries.

CANCER AND LIBRA This pair operates on entirely different levels: Cancer wants love to be emotionally transcendent, Libra seeks perfect intellectual communion. Libra has no sympathy for Cancer's moods, and Cancer is made insecure by Libra's detachment and shallow emotions. Cancer is too temperamental and possessive for airy Libra. They have a hard time establishing real sexual rapport, and that exasperates Cancer. They both love a beautiful home, but Libra also needs parties and people and outside pleasures. When Cancer turns critical, especially about Libra's extravagance, Libra starts looking elsewhere.

CANCER AND SCORPIO Cancer's sensuality is ignited by Scorpio's dynamic passions, and because Cancer is loyal, Scorpio's jealousy isn't provoked. Cancer's possessiveness will actually make Scorpio feel secure. Cancer admires Scorpio's strength, while Scorpio finds a haven in Cancer's emotional commitment. Both are extremely intuitive and sense what will please the other. Together they can build a happy cocoon where they feel safe and loved. This relationship has great intimacy, intensity, and depth. Things just get better all the time.

CANCER AND SAGITTARIUS Outgoing Sagittarius can open intellectual vistas for imaginative Cancer, but unfortunately Sagittarius won't give Cancer the security in love that it always needs. Cancer's jealousy is aroused by Sagittarius's flighty, faithless ways; Sagittarius is bored by Cancer's dependency. Sagittarius likes to wander, while Cancer is a stay-at-home. Cancer's commitment to total togetherness only makes Sagittarius desperate to get away. In addition, outspoken Sagittarius's bluntness continually wounds sensitive Cancer. Better friends than lovers.

CANCER AND CAPRICORN There's an initial sexual attraction because they are a polarity in the zodiac. If they can overcome their opposites in temperament, they can make a winning combination. But career-oriented Capricorn has too many other interests to give Cancer all the attention it needs. Cancer is shy and sensitive and needs affection, while Capricorn is brusque, aloof, and domineering. Cancer takes Capricorn's reserve as a personal rebuff and becomes moody and critical. The differences may prove too great for long-term happiness.

CANCER AND AQUARIUS Cancer's warm, responsive nature is chilled by Aquarius's cool self-possession. In turn, Cancer's clinging, cloying demonstrativeness makes Aquarius feel hemmed in. Aquarius is quick-minded, unpredictable, apt to be impatient with cautious, hesitant Cancer. And thin-skinned Cancer is easily hurt by Aquarius's caustic humor. Cancer doesn't understand Aquarius's essential detachment. Cancer needs to feel close and secure; Aquarius is a lone wolf. Sex may be all right, but there's little else going for them.

CANCER AND PISCES This is an affectionate, sensitive couple who will bolster each other's ego. Pisces is an imaginative dreamer, but Cancer is an imaginative worker—together they can make their dreams a reality. Pisces provides romance in Cancer's life, and Cancer is the all-protective lover Pisces needs. Both are emotional, intensely devoted, sensitive to each other's moods. They'll hit it off in the boudoir, for both are responsive sexually. Cancer has to take the lead, but Pisces is a very willing, erotic follower. A harmonious match.

LEO
The Amorous Nature

You and Leo Woman

What she wants most is praise. A lover has to ignore her shortcomings (she doesn't really think she has any) and dwell on her virtues. In the same way applause makes the star of a play seem larger than life, the lavish admiration of a lover makes Leo woman feel plugged into a life-enhancing incandescence. If you hope to get anywhere with her, you had better begin by accepting her inalienable right to be marvelous. You may go on from there to a sounder, more realistic relationship, but that's the foundation stone on which to build.

You would be wise not to let her know if you have an eye for other women. As far as she's concerned, she's a cosmology of one. The mere suggestion that she's in competition with other women turns her off completely. She's above that sort of rivalry, and is actually a little afraid of it. She can't be a loser—and one way to avoid being a loser is not to get into the race.

However, she has to be free to rack up male conquests. You'll hardly ever see her without a man in tow, and often several. There is something about her flamboyance, her queenlike assurance, that dazzles and attracts. She wears men as other women wear jewelry—to embellish her image—and rarely lacks for admirers.

Most descriptions of Leo woman make her sound hopelessly self-centered. It would be more accurate to say that she has an intense drive toward self-realization. Leo woman feels she was born to be someone special, and she must express this feeling. Happily, she finds enormous self-expression in love.

A Leo woman in love gives her heart without reservations. Her romantic nature is intense, vital, and uninhibited. She doesn't hold anything back, but by the same token she expects her chosen mate to be just as fervid as she is. Although Leo is a marvelously sensual creature, kinky variations are not her game. She prefers to heighten and dramatize the familiar by her passionate involvement.

Leo woman thrives in marriage, but her partner may find living with her a bit overwhelming at times. It isn't easy being attendant to a queen, and Leo woman can be tyrannical. The worst scenario is when a Leo woman marries a man she can dominate completely. In this relationship she may get total submission, but that is too little compensation for the full, deep, robust kind of love she needs. When she feels shortchanged in love, Leo woman will turn bitter and carping.

On the other hand, with a genuine prince consort, a queen can bestow her truly royal gifts—and Leo female certainly has them to bestow. If you give her the affection and admiration that her nature requires, you will waken a tender passion in this extraordinary woman. And you will have a mate who is truly fit for a king.

You and Leo Man

He falls in love readily, then finds it hard to sustain the emotion. For him, falling out of love is as simple as falling out of bed.

Don't make the mistake of thinking Leo man is casual about love. He isn't; in fact, he sees love in practically mythic terms. To him, a love affair is never minor or mild or murky. It is high drama; it is a grand passion. No one else in the zodiac can more easily make you believe that you and he are the first, original, quintessential lovers in the world. The woman who wins his favor moves instantly to center stage. The spotlight is on her, she radiates in the bright circle of his admiration. It's a heady experience to have a Leo lover. Then suddenly the lights are turned off, the curtain falls, the play is over—and she doesn't know why. And he won't explain. Most likely, it's because Leo was in love with a mythical creature of his imagination— a beautiful adoring princess completely fulfilled by him. When the real woman supersedes the myth, Leo gets on his white horse and rides off.

Leo man likes a woman to cater to his every whim. Yet he would be surprised to hear himself described as demanding. He doesn't see himself that way at all. He thinks he is openhearted, trusting, asking nothing but what he is entitled to. If told that he sometimes asks too much of those close to him, he simply wouldn't understand how. After all, why should anyone refuse him? In pleasing him, they please themselves. A true democrat, he believes everyone is equal—equally ready to serve him.

If this sounds like an overbearingly self-assured type riding for a fall, look a bit closer. Underneath Leo's surface majesty is a sensitive, vulnerable man who needs reassurance—and praise. Praise is as necessary to him as food and drink.

In sexual relationships he won't voyage beyond the farthest limits of the known to find a new continent of sensuality. He's a cautious navigator who sticks close to charted waters. On the other hand, a woman will never end up with a sunken wreck.

If you rub his mane the right way, Leo the Lion is a marvelously affectionate, cheerful companion. He is kind, strong, generous, something of a spendthrift, but usually successful in business. A woman who gets this flamboyant, magnetic overachiever with the sunny disposition has only one problem. Somehow she has to teach him that the sole object of his adulation does not have to be himself.

How to Attract Leo

You can always win over anyone born under this sign if you show by your actions, your attention, and your unceasing compliments that you are completely and hopelessly lost in admiration. If you really feel that way, you're in clover. If you don't, fake it. Leos won't suspect your sincerity because they think they're fully as wonderful as you tell them they are. Leos almost never think compliments go too far.

There is another way to make an impression on Leo: be funny. They have a fine sense of humor and love to be entertained. (Didn't every monarch have a court jester?)

You can't go wrong attending a cultural event, especially a preview of some kind. Accompany Leo to a cocktail party that marks the opening of a new art gallery, an advance movie screening, or a lecture by an author about his or her forthcoming book.

Pet peeve for Leo men: Heavy makeup on women.

Pet peeve for Leo women: A tightwad date.

Bear in mind that both male and female Leos think the best is none too good for them. Leo travels first class. If you're trying to impress a Leo woman, take the rubber band off your bankroll, never wince at a restaurant check, get the best orchestra seats, and don't overlook the flowers, champagne, and telephone calls.

If you're trying to impress a Leo male, get the best cut of steak from the butcher and don't spare the wine. If he brings a good bottle of wine (and he will), exclaim over the astute choice he made, then exclaim again over the wine's bouquet and taste. And then bring out your final surprise—that flaming dessert or special after-dinner brandy.

Keep the ambiance posh.

Leo's Amorous Combinations

LEO AND ARIES These two are the superstars of the zodiac. These well-matched partners get along marvelously in the bedroom. They're an unbeatable combination for deriving sheer joy and excitement from sex. They also share the same likes and dislikes in other areas of life. However, they need all that rapport to overcome one big problem—the head-on collision of two super egos, each of whom wants to play the leading role. They have to learn to share center stage. Otherwise, a glorious mating.

LEO AND TAURUS Leo's sovereign right to rule runs smack up against Taurus's determination to have its own way. Both are fixed signs, so neither will give an inch. Leo merely becomes angrier and Taurus more obstinate. Thrifty Taurus is also appalled at Leo's careless spending habits. Taurus is cautious and deliberate; Leo expansive and extravagant. Taurus stubbornly refuses to give Leo constant worship, and Leo is too self-centered to give Taurus the devotion it needs. Leo is much more exuberant than Taurus, both in and out of the bedroom. Too many personality conflicts here.

LEO AND GEMINI They strike it off immediately because they like so many of the same things—glamorous social life, parties, theater, lots of friends. Lively, independent Gemini brings out Leo's joie de vivre. Their affair is a merry chase after variety and amusement. Leo finds Gemini's imaginative sexual high jinks great fun, but Leo may also become jealous because of Gemini's lighthearted approach to love. Leo is more intense than airy Gemini. Life together will be stimulating and exasperating, but the outlook is good if Gemini can stay faithful. Otherwise—poof!

LEO AND CANCER Both are romantics, though in different ways: Leo wants a relationship to be glorious and exciting, Cancer wants it to be meaningful and fulfilling. Leo doesn't get as overwrought as Cancer, who takes things more seriously. Cancer needs security and tranquility and is a stay-at-home. Leo is boisterous and a gadabout who loves to be on constant display. Cancer's dependency will please Leo provided a little adoration is thrown in. Leo is flamboyant in love, and Cancer is responsive, loyal, and intense; Leo likes that. Mixed signals.

LEO AND LEO When a king and queen are together, heads turn. This couple can have a royal mating—a grand passion conducted on a grand scale. Both are romantic, colorful, exuberant about life, and highly sexed. The main question is: Who's going to be in charge? It's difficult for one Leo to make room for another ego as large as its own, but that's exactly what's needed here. Each not only wants to sit on the throne, each wants to be the power behind it as well. Grand lovers and interesting rivals.

LEO AND VIRGO Leo is drawn to Virgo's intellectualism, but Virgo doesn't understand Leo's dramatic nature. Leo can't get from cool, reserved Virgo the sexual responsiveness it demands. Virgo is practical and prudent; Leo is extravagant and a spendthrift. Leo likes to live life in a really big way, but Virgo is conservative, frugal, and a nitpicker, which puts a damper on Leo's high spirits. Virgo won't be dominated either. Leo needs lots of flattery, but Virgo's tendency is to puncture inflated egos. Both of them should look elsewhere.

LEO AND LIBRA Leo's creative side meshes well with Libra's penchant for artistic and esthetic pursuits. Leo is more interested in the strictly physical side of love than Libra, but Leo's style and brio can win Libra over. Libra is indecisive and Leo will naturally take charge. The checkbook may not always balance because they're both extravagant and love a beautiful setting in which to shine. Each will also try to outdo the other in order to get attention. But in the bedroom, Leo is the master—and that's what Leo likes.

LEO AND SCORPIO There's immediate sexual fascination with each other. But Leo finds it hard to cope with Scorpio's jealousy and possessiveness. Intense, smoldering Scorpio is on a too-short fuse, while Leo is much more buoyant. Leo thinks Scorpio difficult and temperamental; Scorpio considers Leo pretentious and a showoff. Scorpio doesn't understand Leo's need to be continually surrounded by an admiring audience. Scorpio would rather dominate than admire, and that doesn't suit Leo's kingly state. Sex isn't everything.

LEO AND SAGITTARIUS Leo is enthralled by optimistic, extroverted Sagittarius, and fun-loving Sagittarius is enchanted with Leo's sunny openness to life. Together they share a liking for freedom, adventure, and meeting new people. Both are passionate and fiery sexual types, and if anyone can keep Sagittarius faithful it's Leo. Leo's natural quality of leadership brings out what loyalty Sagittarius can give. Leo is very proud, but self-confident and expansive Sagittarius is perfectly happy to let Leo strut.

LEO AND CAPRICORN Leo's romantic, expansive nature is curbed by cautious, practical Capricorn. Merry Leo likes to kick up its heels, but Capricorn disapproves of too much self-indulgence. Both are highly sexed, but with basic differences. Leo needs glamour in lovemaking and Capricorn can't supply it. Leo will think Capricorn stingy with affection because Capricorn's reserved, undemonstrative nature cannot give Leo the adoration it needs. Neither will take a backseat or let the other dominate. This affair will be on the rocks before it even leaves the dock.

LEO AND AQUARIUS There is initial physical attraction between these two, but Aquarius's tendency to analyze and criticize will shake Leo's confidence and deflate its ego. Leo views Aquarius's aloof emotions as a personal rejection. Also, Aquarius's unconventional, experimental approach to love may prove upsetting to Leo, who doesn't like to wander too far afield. Both like socializing and meeting new people, but Leo always needs to perform on center stage, which makes Aquarius impatient and irritable. Aquarius is too independent to become Leo's devoted subject. And that's where it ends.

LEO AND PISCES Leo is flamboyant, domineering; Pisces is unworldly and mystical. They intrigue each other because they are so different, but the differences don't mesh well. Leo's active, outgoing nature doesn't harmonize with Pisces's dreamy introspection. Leo needs public acclaim, while Pisces prefers the sheltered life. Both are more inclined to take than to give. Leo can't tolerate Pisces's ultrasensitivity, nor Pisces's inclination toward exotic boudoir activity. Before long, the lion will start to roam.

VIRGO
The Amorous Nature

You and Virgo Woman

She keeps her passions on a tight rein, but underneath emotions are surging. Outwardly she may appear calm, sometimes even remote and unreachable, for the quintessential Virgo has a serene, almost classic repose. Yet hers is one of the most conflicted signs.

Basically, Virgo woman distrusts and is a little afraid of emotion. To her it represents the unknown, turbulent sea on which she may be set adrift without map or compass or rudder. Because of this a man may wonder if she isn't a bit cold. She isn't. Virgo's enormous capacity for loving will pour out, as from a rich treasury, once her emotions are unlocked. Virgo is a much misunderstood sign, and Virgo women particularly are often characterized as timid, evasive, reserved. This is also untrue. What Virgo women do have is self-possession, a sense of passion that is controlled by discipline.

Virgo is an earth sign, and like all the earth signs (Taurus, Virgo, Capricorn) she is an enigmatic combination of sensuality and conservatism. The Virgo woman likes men, but she is very careful about allowing herself to become too involved with them. Even if she's wildly attracted to you, she has an aloofness. Her eyes and body may say come close, but her manner puts up a shield. To begin with, she would never stoop to be obvious. She knows she's worth a man going to a

lot of trouble for. Also, she fears being trapped into a long-term living arrangement with the wrong man. Before she marries or enters into a meaningful affair, she is careful to note where the exit doors are. For a Virgo woman, falling in love can take a long time. She moves forward step by step, revealing the layers of her deep sensitivity, learning to trust.

She is discriminating. Rather than go out with a man who doesn't interest her, she'll stay home and read a good book. This does *not* mean (as some have tried to imply) that she thinks lovemaking is a poor substitute for a good book. It's just that she doesn't mind waiting for Mr. Right to come along. When he does he will find behind her cool facade a real woman waiting, warm and responsive. Meanwhile, her off-putting manner has served a useful purpose. It kept Mr. Wrong from intruding where he was not wanted.

The real clue to understanding Virgo woman's amorous nature is to remember that she believes in true love. When she truly loves, her inhibitions are never in control of her passions. She adores pleasing her man and can be extravagantly sensual, endlessly willing to experiment with techniques that heighten the ecstasy. However, this is not a woman you can take for granted. You must strive hard to win her, please her, fulfill her. If you can, you will have a partner who pays you back in lifelong dividends of love, loyalty, and happiness.

You and Virgo Man

He gives an impression of being in firm control of his emotions, but this is often a disguise. The Virgo man is sensitive, receptive, sensuous, and cautious all at the same time. He will never sweep you into the bedroom and take you by force. For one thing, he has too much respect for a woman.

Because he does not find it easy to express his own deep feelings, he is often drawn to women who are effusive and vivacious. Yet he has a horror of getting embroiled in tempestuous scenes and angry tantrums. Emotionality upsets him, but because he is both attracted to it and disturbed by it, his love life never runs as smoothly as he'd like. This man's love nature can be described as private. At times there is even a surface quality of untouchability about him, but this is an expression of his self-containment. He has a keen sense of the dividing line between your psyche and his.

The woman a Virgo man ultimately chooses has to measure up to very high standards. What he particularly doesn't like in a woman is any suggestion of coarseness, cheapness, or loose and careless conduct. Fastidious is a good word for what he does like.

While he doesn't find it easy to express himself directly about his emotional needs, he has a way of making his dissatisfactions known. He can be demanding. He can find fault. The woman who finds this annoying has one important consolation: His demands and his fault-finding are proof he cares about her. Otherwise, he wouldn't bother.

To some women he may seem lacking in romance, at least in the cinematic tradition of moonlight, roses, and masked men riding into a cobbled courtyard. A woman will never look down from her balcony to find him strumming his guitar and singing romantic ballads. But in the cold light of dawn, in the real world we all inhabit, Virgo men have a lot more to offer than masked riders or lovesick troubadours. For one, a Virgo lover will still be there with the dawn's early light. He won't be riding off to sing ballads to someone else.

Virgo dreams about changing his image. He would like to be a love-'em-and-leave-'em type, a Don Juan, a bon vivant. The woman who taps this secret Virgoan fantasy will reap the surprisingly rich and memorable rewards of his pent-up sensuality. It's all there under the surface, and it's the kind of sensuality that improves with time. As a lover, he is simple, direct, and for real.

If you are looking for quality, not glitter, Virgo is your man.

How to Attract Virgo

The rule to bear in mind is: Don't overpower. Underplay.

Always try to be a good sport. If that drink you're invited for turns out to be at a health food store and consists of carrot and cucumber juice, smile and gulp it. Virgos are finicky eaters and careful about their health. With them, the laws of nutrition rate just behind the Ten Commandments.

In addition to the old standby of discussing work-connected topics, another good conversational subject is pets. Virgos like the smaller variety, especially the exotic kind.

Quickly establish your cultural credentials. Virgos are drawn to people whose intelligence or learning is superior to their own.

Don't probe too closely into their personal affairs. They guard their private life. Avoid noisy places or entertainment that is vulgar or offensive. Virgos pride themselves on their good taste.

Don't let Virgo's worrying upset you. People born under this sign are natural worriers. Will they be on time for the show? Will they catch the plane? Will it rain or snow? Will the mail arrive? The list of their worries is endless. It's no use pointing out that most of the things they worry about never actually happen. They'll go right on worrying anyway; it's their way of coping with what *might* go wrong.

Both male and female Virgos appreciate gifts that are useful and practical. They are also great hobbyists and are sure to have at least one special interest.

Very few special occasions with Virgo will occur on the spur of the moment—at least not if Virgo can help it. There will be careful planning; all the moves will be figured out in advance. Virgo is marvelous at working behind the scenes to accomplish this. All you have to do is relax and enjoy it.

Virgo's Amorous Combinations

VIRGO AND ARIES Virgo can be intrigued by Aries's audaciousness, but Virgo's prudent ways soon clash with Aries's colorful personality. They have difficulty communicating, because Virgo wants to talk and Aries wants to act. Their arguments will probably be more passionate than their lovemaking. Aries will think Virgo is inhibited; Virgo will consider Aries impulsive and wild. Aries likes a flamboyant social life; Virgo is happy with quiet, intellectual friends. Aries is also the type to bring out Virgo's worst habits of nitpicking and nagging. Exit romance.

VIRGO AND TAURUS Virgo is analytical while Taurus is sensuous, but Taurus's strong passions can spark Virgo. If that happens, they make lovely love. Practical, down-to-earth, satisfied with the tried-and-true, these two have much in common. Both try to build for a secure future, both are homebodies, both share a fondness for money. Virgo's rational approach and Taurus's persistence are also a good moneymaking combination. Auguries couldn't be more promising.

VIRGO AND GEMINI They are attracted to each other because of a mutual interest in intellectual ideas. Both have active minds, but the rapport ends there. Gemini's amorous nature is too impulsive and unstable to suit Virgo. Gemini dismisses Virgo as a stick-in-the-mud. Virgo considers Gemini irresponsible and adolescent.

Gemini needs freedom to pursue its varied interests. Virgo resents this, and will nag and try to dominate. Gemini will soon stray to other lovers.

VIRGO AND CANCER A stimulating affair, for they arouse each other's beneath-the-surface sensuality. Cancer isn't too forceful, which suits Virgo fine. And the little attentions won't be neglected, which suits Virgo even better. Cancer is affectionate and sentimental and makes Virgo feel secure. This couple also likes money and domestic comfort, and Cancer's dependency fits perfectly with Virgo's protectiveness. On the downside, both tend to be overcritical. On the upside, each draws the other out of its shell.

VIRGO AND LEO Highly physical Leo takes it as a personal affront if Virgo doesn't match its leonine ardor. Virgo's passive and reserved nature frustrates Leo and leads to quarrels. Virgo isn't quick to hand out praise, and Leo lives on nothing but. Leo is a spendthrift, Virgo is careful with pennies. They're both very independent, but Leo exhibits this in a temperamental way, while Virgo is very private. Virgo simply will not be dominated by tyrannical Leo, and always has its guard up. This affair has a shorter life than a mayfly.

VIRGO AND VIRGO All is smooth sailing as long as these perfectionists curb their instincts for finding fault. Actually, they bring out the very best in each other. They are responsible, sensitive, intelligent, and take love seriously. They also share passions of the mind and will never bore each other. Both think that there are more important things in life than sex; they may end up just talking in bed. There will probably be a continual contest over who is leader, but they have too much else in common for that to matter.

VIRGO AND LIBRA Libra is too frivolous and shallow for Virgo's taste. Libra enjoys spending money, going to parties, and being the center of attention. Virgo criticizes and makes Libra feel unloved. Libra may tap Virgo's hidden sensuality, but their personalities are altogether too different for real compatibility. Virgo will try to curb and dominate Libra's fickle and outer-directed nature. Virgo is reserved and practical, and Libra views this as a personal rebuff. Libra will soon drift away in search of more fun-loving companions.

VIRGO AND SCORPIO Sensual Scorpio keeps trying to entice Virgo into ever-bolder sexual adventures. But Virgo is pleased because Scorpio is also possessive and fiercely loyal, which makes Virgo feel loved and protected. They also admire each other's minds. Virgo is logical, intellectual, analytical. Scorpio is imaginative, visionary, and perceptive. Each sometimes has trouble expressing real feelings: Scorpio is volatile but secretive; Virgo is self-restrained and reserved. There may be some conflict about who runs things, but Virgo's willingness to compromise keeps Scorpio tractable.

VIRGO AND SAGITTARIUS These two are like the grasshopper and the ant. Sagittarius's free spirit has nothing in common with hardworking Virgo. Sagittarius has a reckless gambler's spirit, while Virgo carefully builds for future security. Both are intellectual signs, but the way their minds work clashes with each other. Sagittarius is expansive and extravagant, while Virgo prefers a simple, ordered, and unpretentious life. Sagittarius considers Virgo's sexual attitudes rather prudish, and won't stay long in one bedroom anyway.

VIRGO AND CAPRICORN A harmonious pairing. Capricorn's ambition and drive for success meshes well with Virgo's perfectionism and energy. Both are diligent, disciplined, and have a sense of purpose. They admire one another and take great pride in pleasing each other. Both need respect and approval (though neither will confess this), and each intuitively gives the other exactly that. Sexual compatibility becomes a mutual achievement; in lovemaking, though, Capricorn usually takes the lead.

VIRGO AND AQUARIUS They are both rational and intellectual and tend to view love in the abstract, but the similarity ends there. Aquarius has venturesome ideas and thinks Virgo unresponsive or cold. Actually, each has a distant quality: Virgo is cautious about emotional giving; Aquarius's thoughts are in the far-off clouds. Aquarius is interested in other people, in causes, and in setting the world right. Virgo seeks personal achievement and financial security. Aquarius is outgoing, inventive, a visionary. Virgo is reserved, prudent, and very practical about its ambitions. This couple may not even make it as friends.

VIRGO AND PISCES To Virgo, love means security and mental compatibility. To Pisces, love is a sweeping, all-enveloping emotion. At first Virgo is powerfully attracted to Pisces, as opposites often are: sentimental, in-love-with-love Pisces is very intriguing to Virgo, and Pisces is fascinated by Virgo's incisive, analytical mind. However, disillusion quickly sets in. Pisces's extravagance, secretiveness, and dreaminess frustrate pragmatic, orderly Virgo. Also, Virgo isn't likely to adapt to some of Pisces's sexual preferences.

LIBRA
The Amorous Nature

You and Libra Woman

As a true child of Venus, Libra woman is in love with the idea of being loved. Expert in the art of enchanting men, she views seduction as an art form. She is, first and foremost, an actress, and her lovemaking is high drama, even though there is only an audience of one.

She is the sole person on the stage. The spotlight is on her. In many ways the signs of Libra and Leo share this star quality. But Leo likes to star on a bare stage with no accompaniment—and no distracting elements—whereas Libra is the prima ballerina who moves in a special and rarified nimbus of beauty she creates around her. To her the setting is important. Libra wants to be the brightest star in the heavens; Leo wants to be the Sun and fill the heavens with solitary splendor.

The allure of Libra woman involves all the senses. She is a creative artist, knows about food and wine, has refined taste in dressing and decoration. She has a talent for bringing out beauty in life, and she also brings these esthetic skills to sexual relationships. She uses romantic touches (such as tucking little gifts and love notes in her man's pocket) to make a love affair glow.

Sometimes, though, a Libran woman in love feels that the emotional demands of the role are too much and she needs a rest from her histrionics. This is because Libra is as lazy in love as in most other areas. Besides, once she has satisfied her primary need—to enchant and dazzle you—she begins losing interest. You must wait until she's ready to give her next performance and dazzle you again.

To some people, the Libra woman appears to project a succession of images rather than an integrated personality. She deals in moods and nuances, and expects others to sense her desires without her having to declare them. She is always looking for a perfect companion to enhance her image, but that companion exists only in her mirror.

A lover is expected to provide her with the proper setting in which she can glow and glitter. And she wants all the trappings of romance—flowers, champagne, surprise weekend getaways. That is why so many Libra women are attracted to older, richer men with experience in the art of pleasing a woman. In addition to affection, understanding, and sympathy, she wants a lover who will cater to her whims. She usually attracts such men and often marries more than once.

In her youth her quest for love may lead her down different paths. In another era, she'd have fallen for the handsome cardplayer working on a riverboat out of Natchez. But as time goes on she becomes discriminating. The glamour of transient affairs fades and she is increasingly drawn to the luster of a permanent relationship.

Most Libra women actually prefer romance to sex (the physical side of love strikes them as just a little sordid). A man who tries to appeal to this woman on a primitive level isn't going to get anywhere. She will leave him like a ship deserting a sinking rat.

When a love affair fades she tries to arrange an amicable parting. Even a discarded lover can remain an admirer, can't he? She doesn't like to lose any admirers.

You and Libra Man

Libra man is almost too popular with women because he has the rare ability to relate to them on what might be called a feminine level. He has great personal charm and elegance and a refined esthetic sense. He gets so much attention from the opposite sex that he's a little spoiled. If a woman doesn't catch his interest quickly, he moves to a more promising conquest. Practice has made him a suave lover. Roger Moore and Marcello Mastroianni are typical examples of the Libran male.

Libra man spends an enormous amount of time and energy cultivating relationships. (Remember, Libra is the zodiacal sign of Partnerships.) He may claim that what he wants is a stable, long-term love affair, but if so he wants it to be the *perfect* love affair. He is an incorrigible idealist, always looking for the perfect mate, someone to appreciate and understand (even idolize) him. He also has an inclination toward indecisiveness and tries to strike a balance between what he knows is impossible for him to have and what he has.

Libra male will go a long way out of his way to steer clear of upsetting influences. A woman will find it hard to pick a fight with him, for he never wants to give even the appearance of being unreasonable. In real life it takes only one to make a quarrel, and he'll do anything to avoid being the one. He'd rather call the whole thing off.

Rarely does this happen, however. He is the diplomat of the zodiac, the one who is able to strike a perfect balance between what he wants and what you want.

Lovemaking is his favorite recreation. He enjoys it and is good at it. But he likes to be *told* how good he is, and told as often as possible. The Libran man is very responsive to admiration and flattery, and can be a most imaginative lover. His intimate, intuitive knowledge of female anatomy and his active erotic imagination are a very attractive combination. If you want love to be a sensuous experience that transcends the merely physical, Libra man is what you are looking for. If you're looking for a caveman, however, look elsewhere.

How to Attract Libra

Librans are the jewels of the zodiac—the kind you see displayed in Tiffany's windows, not on Woolworth's shelves. They exist to be admired. Their milieu is that of the social arts, the world of good manners and pleasantries.

Don't fret about what topics to discuss. Librans have a great many interests—theater, antiques, decorating, art collecting—and are marvelous conversationalists. Of course, their favorite topic is themselves. You'll discover that even when they appear to be discussing something else, they're really talking about their own interests—in disguise. Pay the most generous compliment you can think of that has some grounding in truth and they'll be charmed by you.

If this becomes a bit wearing for you, switch to some controversial problem currently in the news. Take a strong position without being challenging or disagreeable. Librans are always interested in both sides of a question, and if you express a strong opinion they will take pleasure in pointing out what's to be said for the other side. This won't lead to an argument or unpleasantness—Librans dread that—but might make for lively conversation. And if

you tell Librans how smart *they* are and how much you've learned, you won't be making a mistake.

Librans dote on luxury and often judge people by the kind of places they go to. They believe first-class people never go to second-class places—unless they're slumming. Atmosphere means a good deal, and the wrong kind of setting is psychically disturbing. They don't care how expensive the right place is. Librans always think their pleasure is worth the price.

If you're trying to please a Libran, show that you have taste. Don't dress sloppily. Librans like to be proud of their dates. If you invite a Libran to your house, be sure the ambiance is right. No noisy stereo, no garish lighting. Dinner had better be delicious (even if you order it sent up from an expensive restaurant) and served on your very best china and crystal—preferably by candlelight. Good music is always helpful. Librans respond to harmonious sounds.

In general, don't hold back on anything. Go all out. Whatever may be said against too much, too soon, Librans believe that that's a lot better than too little, too late.

Libra's Amorous Combinations

LIBRA AND ARIES While they're immediately attracted to each other, tensions also immediately arise. Libra looks for harmony and peace, while restless Aries aggressively seeks new challenges and new worlds to conquer. Libra considers Aries rude and tactless; Aries thinks Libra hopelessly unwilling to face facts. Aries needs to feel independent but wants unquestioning fidelity from its partner, and can't forgive Libra's indecisiveness about making a commitment. Passionate Aries is also offended by Libra's shallow emotions. Physical rapport is wonderful for a while, but then what?

LIBRA AND TAURUS This couple shares a love of music and art, but hasn't much else in common. Taurus is a homebody, which bores Libra, who likes to shine socially. Libra spends lots of money on luxuries; Taurus advocates financial caution. Libra dislikes Taurus's dictatorial ways and quickly loses patience with Taurus's stodgy attitudes. To boot, Taurus is jealous of Libra's romantic and fickle nature. They are sexually in tune, but when the song is ended the malady lingers on.

LIBRA AND GEMINI Pleasure-loving Libra and high-spirited Gemini are an ideal mating. Both are curious, vivacious, and affectionate. For them, love is a carousel that never stops. True, the fun and games are more frolicsome than deeply passionate, but these two don't care as long as they're having fun. No jealousy or possessiveness will spoil their good times. Both tend to be quite indecisive, so there will be lots of discussion but not a lot of action. However, both know how to use charm to get other people to do things for them.

LIBRA AND CANCER Cancer might eventually understand Libra's romantic nature, but Cancer is too cautious to press indecisive Libra for the emotional response it needs. Disappointed at Libra's shallowness, Cancer turns sharply critical, and those crab-claws cut deep. Money-oriented Cancer is also annoyed by Libra's extravagance. Libra loves the glittering social life; Cancer is happiest in the warmth of its own home. Problems might be solved in time, but the wait usually isn't worth it.

LIBRA AND LEO Libra's amorous playfulness blends marvelously with Leo's dash and energy. Leo's generous, expansive sensuality really lights Libra's fire, and the thermometer moves up to torrid. Libra does have to approach Leo carefully on matters involving ego, but that won't be a problem for tactful Libra. In a real conflict, Libra knows how to yield gracefully. Together they share a love of luxury, going to parties, and creating a beautiful home that serves as a stage set for these two stars.

LIBRA AND VIRGO Libra is too affectionate and frivolous for emotionally inhibited Virgo, who takes love very seriously. Virgo won't express flowery admiration, which is the stuff of life to Libra. Stay-at-home Virgo resents Libra's social-butterfly instincts and pursuit of pleasure. Libra's tastes are expensive. Virgo is careful, not to say miserly. Libra finds Virgo fussy, critical, completely inflexible. Love will have a short season for these two.

LIBRA AND LIBRA Equally demonstrative, lively, warm, sociable, in love with beautiful things, they enjoy pleasing each other in sexual ways. But with these two there's a great sense of playing at love. A problem is that neither wants to face reality. Though they are charming, peace-loving, and adaptable, each needs a stronger balance than the other can provide. Also, because they are so much alike, the specter of boredom lurks around the edges. But if both of them can find enough outside stimulation to whet their appetites, this can be an interesting liaison.

LIBRA AND SCORPIO At first, Scorpio's intensity in love flatters Libra, who is always looking for any new form of attention. But Scorpio is also touchy, moody, and quick to lash out in anger, which is just the kind of person Libra cannot bear. Possessive Scorpio tries to control a lover, but Libra has a need for diversion and won't stay in Scorpio's net. Libra's flirtatiousness and casual attitude toward sex infuriates sensual Scorpio. As Scorpio seethes and becomes steadily more jealous and demanding, Libra has either to submit or to leave.

LIBRA AND SAGITTARIUS Libra is stimulated by Sagittarius's eagerness for adventure, and Sagittarius is drawn to Libra's affectionate charm. Both are highly romantic, though this quality is more dominant in Libra. Libra will want to settle down before flighty Sagittarius does, but they can work that out. Charming, clever Libra knows how to appeal to Sagittarius's intellectual side and easily keeps Sagittarius intrigued. This pairing should develop into a fun-filled, free, delightful relationship.

LIBRA AND CAPRICORN Libra is drawn to Capricorn's strong sexuality, but that's as far as it goes. Libra needs flattery and attention, but Capricorn keeps its affections buried. Sentimental, in-love-with-love Libra won't get much understanding from realistic, materialistic Capricorn. And Libra's lazy, easygoing ways will offend Capricorn, who believes in hard work and achievement at any price. Libra is fond of socializing and nightlife, while Capricorn tends to be a loner, comfortable with only a chosen few. A short-lived romance.

LIBRA AND AQUARIUS Libra's indolently sensual nature is stirred to life by Aquarius's bold and experimental lovemaking. And these two have all the makings of a beautiful friendship: harmonious vibes in socializing, artistic interests, even an involvement in public affairs. These two will enjoy the friendship side of an affair as much as the romantic part. Indecisive Libra is delighted with the fact that quick-minded Aquarius likes to make decisions. With a satisfying love life and a mutual enjoyment of living, all signals are go.

LIBRA AND PISCES They start off fine, since both are sentimental and affectionate. In a way they are alike: Both want to impose their romantic visions on reality. But Pisces needs domination, reassurance, and constant attention, and Libra soon finds that cloying and restric-tive. Libra is gregarious and fun-loving. Pisces feels neglected, and whines and scolds. Pisces senses that Libra's commitment is often insincere and that Libra's charm is mostly superficial. Sexually, Libra has to take the lead and finds that most annoying.

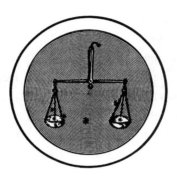

SCORPIO
The Amorous Nature

You and Scorpio Woman

Faint hearts never won a Scorpio female. It takes a man who knows exactly what he wants to hold his ground against a woman born under this sign.

Scorpio woman is very emotional, very affectionate, and very demanding. She is not interested in a light flirtation or a bed for the night. Neither does she believe in sharing. Any man who thinks it isn't necessary to sign a treaty just because he's having an affair with a woman would do well to avoid getting involved with a Scorpio female. She believes in treaties with irrevocable clauses and lots of fine print spelling out just what you can't do.

How does she get away with being so possessive and jealous? Because she is a marvelous, fascinating, irresistible woman—exciting in the bedroom, entertaining in the living room. She carries with her an enticing air of mystery. She can drive a man to the brink of despair and with a gesture summon him back to the heights of happiness.

There is no in-between with this explosive female. With any other woman of the zodiac, you can work out some sort of compromise about who has rights and who has suffered wrongs. Not with her. You have to knuckle under and make the best of your bargain, or settle for living in the middle of a permanent earthquake.

Love is very important to her, and she can turn on enough magnetism to attract any man. If a man is really special, she is willing to play the role of aggressor. Her dynamo starts to whir as soon as her remarkable intuitions tell her that this man is someone she'll be happy with. Her intuitions are rarely wrong. She is gifted with the ability to penetrate into hidden secrets of human nature. She can also see into a man's sex fantasies, and with her imaginative techniques keep him hooked.

Scorpio is a water sign, and like all the water signs (Cancer, Scorpio, Pisces) this woman is very susceptible to the feelings of others. Her most intense desire is for a close, committed union. In a relationship she cannot bear coldness or casualness or a feeling that she is being shunted aside. When she is in love she is at her most vulnerable, for then a lover can hurt her without even knowing it. Another woman might forgive and forget, but when Scorpio woman is hurt she will always strike back. If necessary, she will destroy.

However, despite what you've heard about Scorpio's willful, passionate nature, she is a faithful mate to the man she chooses for her own. Hers is a fixed sign, and she possesses an enduring capacity for loyalty. A man could not have a fiercer ally. If Scorpio woman loves you, she will defend and protect you with her dying breath. What she demands is constancy—what she offers is fidelity. She is possessive, but most men with a Scorpio woman in their lives will tell you they want nothing more than to be possessed by her.

You and Scorpio Man

Women sense in him a magnetic life force, and sexuality is only one part of this magnetism. He projects an aura of mystery and power, of a disturbing, unpredictable, thoroughly masculine presence. One reason Scorpio has such a bad press is that the flaws in his character show up more in his love life than in any other area. Nothing brings out the extremes to which his nature is subject as much as sex.

He has so much energy and passion you'll have no trouble seducing him—if that's all you want. What is harder is to form a relationship with him. This is not because he doesn't want a relationship, for it is, in fact, exactly what he does want. He is an intensely sensitive man who can be easily hurt and who often feels lonely and unfulfilled. The problem is that jealousies and unexpressed angers are very difficult to live with. He has the most indefensible defenses in the zodiac. And the one thing he will never let you see is his vulnerable side. He will never allow a woman to dominate him. If he chooses, he can keep a woman dangling on his string as long as he wants her. When he cuts her loose, no matter how ruthless the parting may be, he'll be surprised if she shows any rancor. *He's* the only one who has a right to be vindictive.

In matters of love he always knows the cost of what he wants to the last decimal point. If the cost is too high—emotionally, financially, or otherwise—he won't haggle. He'll simply walk away.

The Scorpio man is secretive and hard to fathom, although he often appears likeable, affable, and easygoing. What you see on the surface is what he wants you to see. But even when he's being most amiable, and he can be, there's a simmering danger to this man.

He is aware of how attractive he is to women and makes the most of it. In his approach to lovemaking he plans his moves carefully, not wasting time but never appearing to be in haste. He is direct and forceful, and there aren't too many women around who can avoid responding to his uncomplicated physical passion. He brings out the full sensual potential in any woman with whom he's having an intimate relationship. One of the things that makes him really unique as a lover is that he truly understands a woman's needs and, if he is not threatened, will try to meet them.

This vigorous, virile male can be a lot to handle, but Scorpio man makes a woman feel like she's the best female she can be.

How to Attract Scorpio

Scorpios are noted for their unpredictability, but here are a few general rules that may serve as a guide.

Listen to a Scorpio carefully with full attention. There's no way of faking it. Scorpios always know when you're pretending, and that will be the end before there's even a beginning.

Remember an overriding Scorpio trait: curiosity. Never tell a Scorpio that something happened without including the how or why. If you leave that out, you'll be classified as either dull or superficial. Neither type gets far with persons born under this sign.

They enjoy most forms of recreation, particularly water sports. If you're the type who likes a day at the beach or to be out on a fishing boat or to take a waterskiing lesson, you and Scorpio will have that much in common. Scorpios also enjoy parties, social affairs, charity bazaars, and places where they can associate with successful people.

If you get into an argument (and you shouldn't with anyone born under this sign), please remember to be respectful. Scorpios are proud, serious, and don't believe that any of their opinions should be trifled with, even good-humoredly.

Scorpio's Amorous Combinations

SCORPIO AND ARIES The initial attraction is strong. Sexually, Aries is more imaginative and more willing to experiment, but Scorpio's smoldering desires prove a fair match. Trouble looms in other areas, though. Both are selfish and both want to make the decisions. There is a basic clash of wills because Aries wants to dominate and Scorpio wants to control. Scorpio's secretive and brooding nature frustrates open, impulsive Aries. Aries is freedom-loving, outgoing, and flirtatious, and this enrages possessive, jealous Scorpio. Temperamental differences undermine the sexual rapport.

SCORPIO AND TAURUS Taurus has the stamina and the desire to satisfy Scorpio in the bedroom. But what will this passionate pair do with the other twenty-three and a half hours in the day? Both are very jealous and stubborn. The difference between these two is that Taurus wants to own a lover, like a valuable object, and Scorpio tries to possess in an emotional sense. Though they share an affinity for finances, Scorpio is thrifty and spurns laziness, whereas Taurus likes to spend on creature comforts. Scorpio is willful, Taurus is obstinate, and both want to be the captain of what may turn out to be a sinking ship.

SCORPIO AND GEMINI Scorpio is drawn to Gemini's vivacity, and Scorpio's complex personality fascinates curious Gemini. For a time Gemini is also intrigued by Scorpio's unceasing sexual demands. But Gemini is too changeable and inconstant for intense Scorpio, who needs and demands total commitment. Restless Gemini has a strong penchant for independence, while Scorpio wants to dominate and possess. Scorpio is basically a loner; Gemini likes to glitter in social settings. They'll have some lively frolics, but all too soon the fun palls— and Gemini starts looking for an exit.

SCORPIO AND CANCER This can be a rewarding combination. Cancer is the passive partner, but there's plenty of combustible material to catch fire from Scorpio's abundant passions. The heat in the bedroom will help cool off disputes that can arise between two jealous people. Scorpio offers strength and protectiveness, which is just what clinging, insecure Cancer is looking for. In turn, Cancer is affectionate, generous, loving, and devoted—all that Scorpio wants. These two get along together like bread and jam.

SCORPIO AND LEO Scorpio won't flatter Leo's ego or accept Leo's dominance. Scorpio seeks to plumb the erotic psyche of a lover, whereas Leo looks for a grand romance. Passions and tempers are equally strong on both sides. Fiery Leo is extravagant and likes to live on a majestic scale, but Scorpio disapproves of conspicuousness and waste. There's a great deal of physical attraction between them, but both are on a very short fuse. Scorpio's jealousy will probably provide the spark, and when the explosion comes, the sky's the limit!

SCORPIO AND VIRGO Restrained Virgo has trouble keeping up with highly demonstrative Scorpio and doesn't understand what all the fuss and bother is about. But there's a marvelous meeting of minds and a fine mixing of personalities. Both are devoted to family and to financial security. Neither is flighty or superficial; the deep feelings that each harbors lead to a strong commitment and loyalty. They have so much in common that maybe Scorpio won't mind that Virgo's passions are more intellectual than physical.

SCORPIO AND LIBRA Scorpio's unpredictable nature immediately intrigues Libra, who enjoys collecting interesting people. Scorpio satisfies Libra's need for affection—and then some—and Scorpio's jealousy will flatter Libra. But Libra is an inconstant flirt, and Scorpio is supersensitive and touchy. Intense Scorpio takes love and commitment seriously; Libra wants a partner to enhance its own image. Libra's on-again-off-again attitude toward love will frustrate and upset Scorpio. This mating isn't likely to lead to anything permanent.

SCORPIO AND SCORPIO Plenty of sexual attraction here, but the emotional temperature can't keep rising forever. These two people who are so much alike understand each other very little. They are highly jealous and demanding. They are so intense that every little storm quickly becomes a hurricane. Both are sulky, brooding, possessive. Both are in a continual struggle to force the other to relinquish control. Something has got to give, and when it does it's likely to spell The End.

SCORPIO AND SAGITTARIUS Scorpio is tantalized by Sagittarius's freewheeling, uninhibited style. Scorpio will dominate but can't keep restless, flighty Sagittarius submissive for long. Sagittarius thinks the accent should be on fun and new adventure; Scorpio wants security and constant loving. Sagittarius is open, talkative, and casual about relationships; Scorpio is reticent, secretive, and very jealous in love. Scorpio wants Sagittarius at home, Sagittarius wants to roam. An affair without a future.

SCORPIO AND CAPRICORN All of Scorpio's powerful passions find a welcome here. Scorpio's volatile emotions tend to open up brooding, inner-directed Capricorn, and the zesty goings-on add savor to a warm emotional relationship. Capricorn even likes Scorpio's jealousy—for this makes Capricorn feel secure. These two share a sense of purpose: they are ambitious, determined, and serious about responsibility, and as a team have good auguries for financial success. They should have clear sailing.

SCORPIO AND AQUARIUS Scorpio makes heavy emotional demands, but to Aquarius even a love affair is simply another way to broaden its horizons. Scorpio can't tolerate Aquarius's independence within a relationship or understand Aquarius's casual air toward love. Aquarius is altogether too impersonal and has too many outside interests to suit possessive, jealous Scorpio. Scorpio will try to dominate and will be upset by Aquarius's unpredictable moods and love for freedom. Scorpio wants to stay at home; Aquarius wants to be free to go. And so on—to the finish.

SCORPIO AND PISCES Scorpio's strength is a perfect bulwark for Pisces's indecisiveness. In turn, Pisces's imagination sparks Scorpio's creativity. Pisces is able to give Scorpio the devotion and admiration it craves, and their mutual fascination with lovemaking provides a fine romantic aura. Pisces's flair for the bizarre adds spice to Scorpio's desires, and the intense emotional needs of both signs neatly complement each other. Pisces's intuitive awareness and Scorpio's depth of feeling unite in a special closeness. This kind of mating lasts.

SAGITTARIUS
The Amorous Nature

You and Sagittarius Woman

Like all fire sign women (Aries, Leo, Sagittarius) she is at her most vibrant when she is in love. She is drawn to the excitement, passion, and sheer adventure of romance. Her attitude toward life is enthusiastic and positive, and being in love intensifies these glowing feelings. Where another woman might walk around in a dreamlike haze, a Sagittarius woman in love positively radiates happiness and energy.

Sagittarius is also the sign of mental exploration. To her, love is not just passion but a challenge. This free spirit finds domesticity boring. She is the perfect playmate but only as long as she finds the game worth playing. She is not one to make the best of a bad bargain. If she is unhappy, she won't resign herself or compromise or try to work things out. She'll just walk out.

She can't take love as seriously as other women do. It's part of life to her, not the end or the beginning. If she finds a man who's a real companion, who shares her pleasure in sports and the outdoor life, who likes to travel and hates to be tied down to any one place, then love is a wonderful extra added attraction.

Her exploratory nature may lead her to have a number of early sex experiences, especially the kind that begin quickly in an exotic setting and have a passion-in-the-moment edge (for example, a tryst on a train speeding through Europe, wild sex with a new lover on a beach in Barbados).

She doesn't always perceive the consequences of romantic entanglements. To her, life means moving forward into the future, and each new love is a learning experience. She doesn't take into account that when a romance is over it may leave behind a trail of wounded feelings. If an old lover harbors resentment, she is genuinely surprised.

She likes men and enjoys the flirtations and maneuvers of a developing affair. In turn, men like her charming, easygoing manner and her acceptance of what the world is like. Other women may prefer the straight and narrow path, but Sagittarius can't help wandering over to the primrose path to pluck whatever blooms strike her fancy. When she does find her big romance, however, this is a woman who believes in loyalty to her man. She is a romantic who will marry for love's sake rather than for money or social position. She wants a true soul-companion.

A sense of humor is one of her nicest traits, and she isn't interested in a man who lacks a sense of fun. She doesn't welcome tempestuous, heavy-breathing relationships that put her through an emotional wringer. What she looks for is a lover who can share her sense of adventure. She prefers men who are intellectually stimulating, well read, and well traveled. Sexually, she doesn't play control games. She wants sex to be truthful, genuine, very romantic, very impulsive.

Basically, Sagittarius woman enjoys life and tries to make sure everyone around her enjoys it too. When this clever, amusing, optimistic, high-spirited woman finally settles down with some lucky man, she'll be the most delightful companion he can hope to find.

You and Sagittarius Man

This charming lover can be a poor choice as a husband. The symbol of his sign is the Archer, and he is always on the hunt. He likes nothing better than the chase. As the song has it, "When he's not near the girl he loves, he loves the girl he's near."

He's perfectly sincere when he tells you he loves you. And he will be perfectly sincere when he tells someone else the same thing the next night. Whatever he believes at the moment is true.

The Sagittarian male has a deserved reputation as the Don Juan of the zodiac. This is not because he has an insatiable sexual desire, but because love to him is an elusive adventure, an unexplored path. He is the archetypal footloose and fancy-free lover searching for his feminine ideal. Along the way he manages to garner more than his share of female admirers who can't help responding to his open, honest, cheerful, intelligent lovemaking. Sagittarius has a captivating sense of humor, and the woman he squires can count on good times.

He's much more likely to ask you to an informal lunch at an outdoor cafe than to a grand dress-up dinner. This isn't because he is reluctant to spend money but simply because he prefers the easygoing approach in all things. He hates whatever is artificial, pompous, or pretentious.

If practice made perfect, he'd be the world's best lover. However, he doesn't consider love to be an experience anything like the novelists tell it. He is passionate but not intense: His great quality is enthusiasm, a sense of sheer enjoyment. What bothers him is that everyone else seems to take love so seriously. Why can't everyone be like him—relaxed, buoyant, undemanding?

Very often he isn't interested in marriage or a long-term relationship. He wants to tarry for the fun and laughter, and move on. Happiness for this man is not a fixed goal, it's a way of traveling. If you put enough happy days together, you end up with a happy life!

If he's decided that you're his kind of woman, don't be coy. He doesn't regard a romantic fling as all that important, and he won't understand if you do. If casual *amour* isn't your style, then maybe Sagittarius isn't for you.

How to Attract Sagittarius

You won't have trouble striking up a conversation. Sagittarians are interested in almost anything. When they've talked themselves out on their favorite subjects, they'll decide *you're* a fascinating conversationalist!

Ask about their work, their friends, books they have read, and their reactions to a current news event. If you happen to like animals or outdoor sports, you are already halfway home with a Sagittarian.

There is a fine line between taking an interest in their interests and prying. Don't overstep that boundary. Sagittarians are very wary of anyone who might be trying to corner them. If talking about generalities gives you the feeling that you're sliding rapidly over ice, don't worry. Matters will improve on better acquaintance. You may discover, in fact, that your problem is trying to ignore the direct, sometimes overly frank inquiries that Sagittarians will make. When they get to know you, they like you to share confidences with them or ask for their advice.

Sagittarians like outdoor dates: dancing under the stars, open-air concerts, picnics at the beach, skiing or sailing outings. They usually avoid large parties or too-close quarters because they cannot bear to be hedged in or confined. Never infringe on their freedom. Never let your emotional needs intrude on their private lives. And you'd be wise not to put too much stock in their promises. Their words are writ on water.

Enjoy being with Sagittarius but don't think you've signed a lifelong contract, because Sagittarius doesn't think so. And don't look back with regret when it's over. Sagittarius won't.

Sagittarius's Amorous Combinations

SAGITTARIUS AND ARIES Both share a similar approach to sex (they make the most of *every* opportunity). Add to this a mutual love of the outdoors and a fondness for socializing, and you can see why they get along. They're also intellectually well suited: Both have a wide range of interests and love to talk about them. Sagittarius is more philosophical about problems than Aries, who becomes more personally involved. The one question mark is their combustible temper. Arguments are heated but short-lived, and the making up will be fun. A perfect match.

SAGITTARIUS AND TAURUS Taurus wants to run things, but Sagittarius won't be controlled. Sagittarius needs change, variety, and adventure. That proves irritating to steady, disciplined, home-loving Taurus. Taurus approves of tried-and-true ways of doing things, but Sagittarius will try anything. Blunt Sagittarius will say what it thinks at the drop of a hat, and that brings Taurus's temper to a slow simmer. There are also money problems, since Sagittarius gambles today while Taurus hoards for tomorrow. A short future for this pair.

SAGITTARIUS AND GEMINI They're both restless, adventuresome, imaginative, and fun-loving. No other opposite signs in the zodiac enjoy each other more than these two. There'll be shooting stars in the bedroom for a while, but when the fireworks fizzle the bickering begins. Both have bright minds, but Sagittarius is outspoken and bossy, while Gemini likes to poke verbal fun. Too rootless and discontent to settle down, they eventually both succumb to the siren call of other interests, other loves. But parting should be amicable.

SAGITTARIUS AND CANCER Cancer's sensuality and romantic imagination intrigues inquiring Sagittarius. But Sagittarius is both venturesome and cerebral while Cancer is cautious and emotional, and this pair will never understand each other. Sagittarius can't supply the security and stability Cancer needs or endure Cancer's moodiness and jealousy. Without even being aware of it, blunt Sagittarius wounds sensitive Cancer at every turn. When Sagittarius seeks outside stimulation away from home, Cancer nags and whines and tries to hold on tighter. They'd be better as friends.

SAGITTARIUS AND LEO There are exciting times ahead for this ardent pair. Self-confident Leo holds the key to unlocking Sagittarius's deeper passions, and their love life is an adventure. They also enjoy travel, meeting new people, and each other's company. Leo loves freedom as much as Sagittarius, so there won't be problems with jealousy or possessiveness. Sagittarius has the lightness of touch necessary to cope with Leo's monumental ego. A grand mating.

SAGITTARIUS AND VIRGO Shy, reticent Virgo can't take the initiative, which makes Sagittarius think Virgo is prudish. Both have intellectual leanings, so they may end up having some interesting conversations in bed. Elsewhere, Virgo looks for order and simplicity whereas Sagittarius looks for excitement and new experiences. Virgo wants a long-term commitment; Sagittarius has to be free to roam. Sagittarius's slapdash ways irritate meticulous Virgo. When Virgo carps and criticizes this is sometimes a way of showing it cares, but Sagittarius will never understand that. Little bodes well in this affair.

SAGITTARIUS AND LIBRA Sagittarius is charmed by Libra's artistic, elegant, easygoing nature, and Libra is fascinated by Sagittarius's lust for adventure. Libra is more romantic than Sagittarius; otherwise the sexual harmony is delightful. Libra casts a tolerant eye on Sagittarius's frolicking, and may even slow down Sagittarius's pace, for Libra knows how to turn on sensual charm. Libra loves home and luxury, and Sagittarius prefers the outdoor life. But Librans are artists at working out such problems.

SAGITTARIUS AND SCORPIO Scorpio tries to clip Sagittarius's wings and keep it in a cage. Brooding, pent-up Scorpio just can't deal with open, ebullient, outspoken Sagittarius. Sagittarius's far-roaming interests constantly make Scorpio jealous. Romantically, this is a volatile combination. Sagittarius is playful about sex and finds Scorpio's intense, dominating passions too much to cope with. Soon Sagittarius's inclination is to fly. Sagittarius is also quick-tempered and cools

quickly, while Scorpio's anger seethes until it erupts in fury. A temperamental, difficult union.

SAGITTARIUS AND SAGITTARIUS Some astrologers believe the only fit mate for a Sagittarian is another Sagittarian. They do seem perfectly suited: two independent, freedom-loving roamers. But this exciting, chaotic, eventful relationship is too unpredictable to suit either of them. They have a tendency to bring out the worst in each other. Each remains uncommitted and has so many outside interests that this pair inevitably drifts apart. But they'll be good sports when the fun is over.

SAGITTARIUS AND CAPRICORN Capricorn's demands can't be satisfied by Sagittarius's flighty, light-hearted approach to love. Both have high aspirations in life, but their approaches are totally different. Capricorn wants to climb to the top of the mountain; Sagittarius wants to fly over the top. Sagittarius's frank outspoken nature is sure to rile Capricorn's sensibilities. Capricorn is restrictive, a loner, known for its dour outlook. Sagittarius is venturesome, sociable, and expansive. Capricorn is cautious with money and concerned with appearances—and Sagittarius is neither. Both should look elsewhere.

SAGITTARIUS AND AQUARIUS These two share a great zest for living and a forward-looking viewpoint. Neither will try to tie down the other. Both seek to explore possibilities to the fullest, and they share an idealism about love and life. Aquarius is innovative. Sagittarius loves to experiment. There'll be imaginative fun in the bedroom, and they'll probably find out things that would surprise even Masters and Johnson. They'll like each other too. True emotional intimacy may be slower to develop—but prospects are wonderful for the long haul.

SAGITTARIUS AND PISCES Pisces is drawn to Sagittarius's life force, and Sagittarius is attracted to Pisces's spirituality. But Sagittarius needs a pal and Pisces needs a dream lover—and neither can help the other. Sagittarius's naturally buoyant spirits are anchored by Pisces's dependency and timidity. Highly emotional Pisces is looking for more than an occasional sex partner, and restless, freedom-loving Sagittarius is looking for nothing but. Bedroom high jinks keep things going for a while, but this affair slowly sinks into a quagmire.

CAPRICORN
The Amorous Nature

You and Capricorn Woman

Though she may not show it, this woman cares a great deal about love. Deep in her inner core, she is an extravagant romantic, but she is very private, restrained, and aloof. Some women are content to leave love to fate, but Capricorn woman takes a hand in determining her own fate. She is discriminating in her choice of men, the least likely of all the zodiacal signs to fall in love at first sight. She has no time to waste in silly flirtation; love is a serious matter to her. If a man doesn't measure up, she wants him out of her way. If a man does interest her, she will observe him from an emotional distance before moving closer. She takes the time to get to know him and considers carefully the consequences of her involvement. Like all earth signs (Taurus, Virgo, Capricorn), she has a deep-rooted sensuality that flowers only when she feels safe and secure.

To Capricorn woman, happiness in love is crucial. She wants someone who will cherish and understand her, who will not rob her of her self-sufficiency or ask her to relinquish control of her life and goals. But she is a realist and knows how hard he is to find.

She will not put her neck into any man's yoke. A Capricorn woman may appear shy or submissive, but she is like a rubber ball: You can push a dent into it, but the ball always springs back to its original shape. She is self-disciplined; she has a clear mind, a commonsense approach. She is a most womanly woman, a lady with "class." Typical examples of Capricorn females are Marlene Dietrich, Maggie Smith, Ava Gardner, Faye Dunaway, Mary Tyler Moore—all intensely feminine, yet with a reserve of inner strength.

If you have your mind set on winning a Capricorn beauty, you'd better prepare for a long siege. She is not easy to win. She expects to be pursued, wooed, and put into the mood. No Don Juan can leap into her bed and leap out again. If a man lets the issue of sex become a contest of wills, he is a good bet to lose. In a head-to-head contest this woman could wear down a glacier.

She sometimes becomes involved with men who are younger than she is. One reason is that she wants to dominate in the male-female relationship. On a date, she will often try to dictate the terms. She'll pick the restaurant and the kind of entertainment and arrange for tickets. If you begin living together, she will handle the division of household chores.

Capricorn women are not particularly lucky in love. Perhaps they demand too much, perhaps they're too involved with a career to inspire the kind of love and devotion they want, or perhaps the men they choose tend to be too inexperienced or naive. Whatever the reason, it's too bad because Capricorn women, in addition to their sexuality, have many practical virtues. They are loyal, dependable, excellent at handling money, canny about people. They are very helpful to a mate and will stand by him when the going is toughest. All a Capricorn woman asks in return is to share in the spoils when the battle is won.

Her passions run deep, and so does her impact. Long after transitory affairs have run their courses, this smoldering siren will hold her place in a man's affections. Cherish her, honor her, love her, and respect her. She'll pay you back in the richest coin of the realm—the kind of loving relationship that lasts.

You and Capricorn Man

Women are intrigued by his frank, earthy approach. To him, physical desire is a necessary part of love. He doesn't see how one can exist without the other.

However, love relationships are not easy for him emotionally. There is always a certain loner quality about him. He has difficulty placing his trust in another human being. To some extent he cuts himself off from spontaneous feeling. In his career Capricorn man has complete responsibility for decisions, and in relationships he finds it hard to share responsibility.

Like his female counterpart, he has a very cool exterior. He appears totally self-assured, but he needs a woman to show how much she likes and admires him. Because he is private, even secretive, he doesn't always let this need be known—but it *is* there. Give his ego the encouragement it needs and he will tie himself to your strings for as long as you want him. He is a faithful lover who doesn't feel or even understand the need to stray.

Contrary to popular opinion, there is a romantic streak to the Capricorn man. But his sense of discipline—or, more specifically, his need to make the very best choice for the future, not just for the present—is stronger. He will sacrifice romance and look for a woman who will be useful to his ambitions. Generally, Capricorn men marry either very early in life or in their later years. The ones who marry later are usually happier. By the time a Capricorn man is successful he has become more relaxed, less wary of love; it is no longer a burden to his climb up the ladder.

Few women have reason to complain about a Capricorn lover. His charged passions are never far from the ignition point. He may not be the most imaginative or poetic partner, but he is lusty and skillful. His interest in the physical side of love never wanes. The older Capricorn male gets, the more attractive he becomes, and the more potent. When other men are resigned to their rocking chairs, Capricorn will still be inviting you into his bedroom.

He prefers a comfortable setting. Others may like to make love on a bare floor or standing in a closet. Capricorn likes a nice, spacious bed, dim lights, soft music, and, if possible, a chilled bottle of champagne close at hand.

There is a sensual, poetic side to Capricorn, although it may take a while to reveal itself. This man will probably not send you flowers or love letters, but on your twenty-fifth wedding anniversary he may charter a plane to whisk the two of you to Paris so you can spend the evening dancing on the floodlit banks of the Seine.

How to Attract Capricorn

If Capricorns appear aloof at first, it's because they are calculating the risks of a new friendship.

They are quite willing to be your audience, so don't be afraid to take the initiative in conversation. A sure way to capture Capricorns' interest is to be amusing, for they are basically melancholy types who need an emotional lift.

They often try to mask their feelings because they are afraid of exposing too much of themselves. Never mind that their fears are unfounded; this is how they feel. Even at their most open, Capricorns will be pretty hard to fathom.

Capricorns are interested in art, music, and theater and are drawn to people who are intellectually stimulating. They prefer to talk of serious subjects. When they decide to state an opinion, listen as if you were hearing the Gettysburg Address for the first time. And don't come up with radical or far-out opinions. They shun unconventionality.

You can't go wrong getting a Capricorn something practical as a gift. Be sure it is of the best quality, not something gaudy or showy. Persons born under this sign appreciate luxury, but are far too aware of the value of a dollar to respect anyone who splurges merely to make an impression. Books are always a good item, especially biographies, self-help books, and books dealing with investments.

Tip: Always be on time. Time is money—and you know how Capricorns feel about that.

Capricorn's Amorous Combinations

CAPRICORN AND ARIES They'll get along as lovers, but even in bed there'll be arguments about money, friends, socializing, and who's boss. A major difference is that Capricorn won't make a move unless sure of winning, whereas Aries is completely headstrong and impulsive. Arguments never fade away, for both are strong-willed and aggressive and need to dominate. Jealousy also raises its head as Aries's lively passions stray toward more fun-loving company. Temperamentally and emotionally, this mating is better suited to an arena than to hearth and home.

CAPRICORN AND TAURUS Taurus admires Capricorn's strength of purpose, and Capricorn is delighted with Taurus's affectionate stability. Taurus can get through to aloof, cautious Capricorn and give the encouragement and responsiveness needed. Both have earthy, passionate natures, and sensual Taurus can tap the deep well of romanticism that lies under Capricorn's reserve. Capricorn is loyal and Taurus is devoted, so jealousy is not a problem between these two. In addition, both value money and security and are homelovers. One union, strong and indivisible.

CAPRICORN AND GEMINI Capricorn will have a hard time holding the reins on excitable, flirtatious, wayward Gemini. All of Capricorn's patience is needed to deal with a partner it considers to be capricious, ex-travagant, and scatterbrained. Capricorn prizes order and control, and approaches life in a practical, determined manner. Gemini is disorganized, high-strung, and erratic. Also, Gemini's verbal quickness has a way of making Capricorn secretly feel inadequate. Neither is particularly sentimental, so whatever flamelets ignite at the beginning will quickly cool.

CAPRICORN AND CANCER These two are sexually attracted to each other, but need all the harmony they find in the bedroom to offset the discordance they create everywhere else. Sensitive Cancer will resent Capricorn's domineering manner. Capricorn isn't willing to put up with Cancer's endless emotional demands. Cancer's need for warmth will be frustrated by Capricorn's aloof coolness. Both fear rejection, but Cancer's tendency is to withdraw and Capricorn's is to become tyrannical. These two are zodiac opposites with all that implies.

CAPRICORN AND LEO Ordered, organized Capricorn neither understands nor approves of Leo's exuberant impulsiveness. Capricorn cannot stand Leo's habit of leaping first and looking afterward. Extroverted Leo will be impatient with Capricorn's secretive tendencies. Capricorn is too reserved to give Leo the adoration it needs, and proud Leo will not give in to Capricorn's domineering ways. Spendthrift Leo adores luxury, while Capricorn puts financial security above all. Also, they both want to rule in the bedroom. This unpromising couple will find their way to a quick ending.

CAPRICORN AND VIRGO Virgo's neat orderly mind meshes well with Capricorn's self-discipline and capacity for hard work. Both take pride in their home, enjoy having a few close friends rather than many acquaintances, and admire each other's intellectual abilities. There's no reason this duo shouldn't click—except in the bedroom, where Virgo's reticence needs a stronger push than reserved Capricorn likes to give. Neither finds it easy to be spontaneously affectionate. However, this is the only minus entry on a balance sheet full of pluses.

CAPRICORN AND LIBRA Capricorn is intrigued by magnetic Libra, and Libra is charmed by Capricorn's slowly revealed passions. But over the long term Libra needs more excitement, romance, and beauty than Capricorn can provide. Capricorn is not oriented toward social and artistic pursuits, which are Libra's favorite activities. Capricorn prizes discipline and responsibility, and finds Libra altogether too frivolous, vain, and self-centered. Libra turns restive and starts to look elsewhere. Throw in some Capricorn jealousy to keep the cauldron bubbling. A recipe for disaster.

CAPRICORN AND SCORPIO Scorpio's powerful sensuality kindles Capricorn's slumbering passions. Scorpio is the more imaginative lover, but Capricorn's stamina is a delightful match. Scorpio's possessiveness spells security to Capricorn. These two work well as a team—Capricorn is highly organized and Scorpio has native shrewdness. Both prize discipline and accomplishment. Each is strong-willed, and sometimes Scorpio's renowned temper comes up against Capricorn's stubbornness. Their battles will be royal, but so will their makings-up.

CAPRICORN AND SAGITTARIUS Capricorn is cheered by optimistic Sagittarius, and Sagittarius is intrigued by Capricorn's depth and self-containment. All too soon, though, Capricorn becomes annoyed by Sagittarius's fickle attitude and total need for freedom without strings. Capricorn senses that it cannot count on Sagittarius's loyalty through thick and thin, and is frustrated by Sagittarius's nonchalance in love. Also, Sagittarius is impetuous and has free-and-easy spending habits, while Capricorn is serious-minded and a stay-at-home. The ties that bind are soon cut.

CAPRICORN AND CAPRICORN Capricorns approve of people like themselves, so with these two there's no lack of mutual respect and regard. Both are cautious, reserved personalities who work hard and love to save money. But even compatibility can sometimes be dull. They're well matched sexually, but in other areas they encourage each other's tendencies to be gloomy and pessimistic. Neither one can relax or let down its hair. As partners they're okay, but not too much fun. Love travels an almost imperceptibly downhill road.

CAPRICORN AND AQUARIUS Capricorn finds Aquarius too unpredictable, and Aquarius's impersonal attitude makes Capricorn uneasy. Capricorn's conventional approach quickly irritates adventurous Aquarius.

Aquarius believes in self-expression; Capricorn believes in self-discipline. Aquarius is somewhat a rover, while Capricorn prefers home and hearth. Freedom-loving Aquarius won't stay bound for long to earnest, staid Capricorn. However, they should like each other, and love can turn into friendship.

CAPRICORN AND PISCES Capricorn provides ballast for Pisces's drifting dreaminess and supplies the stability that Pisces needs and admires. And there's nothing Capricorn likes better than being admired. Capricorn is the boudoir captain, but Pisces is a willing crew. Pisces's taste for the bizarre may even influence Capricorn's conventional passions. Pisces's generous affections and Capricorn's strong sense of loyalty combine to make each feel safe and protected. These very different people meet each other's needs.

AQUARIUS
The Amorous Nature

You and Aquarius Woman

This charming, funny, brainy, tantalizing woman doesn't have to play games to fascinate a man. She plays herself. There is a special magnetism to Aquarius that some astrol-ogers have called distant glamour. Like all the air signs (Gemini, Libra, Aquarius), she lives in a world of ideas and possesses a certain detached quality. Curiously, this attracts men who want to stir her emotions.

She is not aloof, cold, or removed from feeling, but warm, vibrant, friendly, and outgoing, concerned with others. She's a woman with a strong romantic streak. Romance for Aquarius is an idea, an ideal, not a sweeping passion. In truth, she is wary of emotion, for it can be troublesome and tiresome. She is above that; she is able to deal rationally with life.

Aquarius female is subject to no man's whim and follows no dictates but her own. She was a liberated woman before anyone ever heard of the women's movement. This supremely independent woman cares little what the rest of the world thinks. She is definitely unpredictable. Part of her attitude is reflected in her imaginative approach to sex. Her boudoir behavior is usually innovative and creative; she seeks novelty and diversion more than heavy-breathing passion.

However unconventional her attitudes may be, and however flirtatious she may seem, a man will have to convince her that she's not simply his target for tonight. He cannot make the mistake of treating her as a sex object.

She expects to be courted, and a man should not press matters to a conclusion until he knows more about her than her telephone number. Passion is not important to her; communication is. Aquarius sees a man as an individual first and a bed partner second.

In marriage or a serious relationship she often finds it hard to give of herself. She is an unconventional person who lives most intensely in her mind. She's too concerned with her projects, hobbies, interests, and friends, so her love tends to be diffuse. She has been accused of loving mankind rather than one particular man.

Once her passions are aroused and directed toward a specific man, however, she is loyal and devoted. When Aquarius makes a promise she stands by her word. After all, that is what honor and idealism are about, and those are hallmarks of this sign.

Some say Aquarian woman is the perfect mate because she is easy to deal with—tolerant, slow to take offense, never jealous or unreasonable, never overemotional or clinging. All she asks is for a man to respect her privacy and not stand in the way of her far-reaching interests.

The quickest way to lose her is to try to hold her fast. What intrigues her is the hill beyond the unexplored horizon. She is never content to stay where she is. There's too much out there waiting to be discovered. A man has to share her love of a challenge or he will soon be left behind. She will move on without a backward glance, a grand ship sailing on without an inkling of the tragedy in her wake.

You and Aquarius Man

His first contact with a woman has to be made through the mind. Before he can become physically stimulated, he must be intellectually stimulated. For Aquarius the meeting of minds always precedes the meeting of bodies. He wants to make love to *somebody*, not just *any* body.

Give him half a chance and he'll fall in love. He thinks that that is a natural—and delightful—condition. But falling in love and loving mean two different things to this man, and the latter is likely to bring out his inner conflicts. One reason is that Aquarius tends to repress emotion. His is a cerebral sign, and he's somewhat unnerved and embarrassed by emotion. Also, love represents a demand on him, and he has a fierce need for independence. In addition, loving means making room for another person, and in common with the other fixed signs (Taurus, Leo, and Scorpio), Aquarius does not adapt easily to others. Others have to adapt to *him*.

He is very attractive to women, but he may not linger long in a liaison. To him, love passes like a train in the night and there is always another train coming along the track. Yet Aquarius isn't a Don Juan. He is remarkably true to his women—in his fashion. He doesn't try to keep many women on his string at one time. Rather, he believes in consecutive monogamy. Even if he marries, he doesn't consider the bond to be forged in steel. Aquarius men are the most often married in the zodiac.

The Aquarius man does not expect any woman to be easily won. His patience is proverbial and a woman may finally make the proposition herself. Then, surprisingly, she'll discover how intensely and passionately her Aquarius lover has wanted her. When a love affair is under way he makes up for lost time. A woman will find that making love with him is like living in the midst of a carnival—there's always a new exciting ride.

Aquarius is the sign of truth, and this man doesn't lie or misrepresent himself. This is, of course, a winning quality—though in Aquarius's case it sometimes has unexpected consequences. One young woman I know spotted this quality in her Aquarius lover. She compelled him at various times throughout the day to tell her how he felt about her at that exact moment: "To tell you the truth, right now I'm not as much in love with you as I was this morning."

In a love affair Aquarius is generous and tolerant, the kind who tries never to encroach on your rights or to give orders. A love relationship with him has many of the elements of friendship—intellectual interests and social compatibility. He won't be selfish or domineering either. He may be less than fiery, but he is a surprising, stimulating, broad-minded, and inventive lover.

Don't fence him in. Once this man is in love with you he will stay pretty much in his pasture. But he must feel the escape routes are open.

How to Attract Aquarius

These highly social creatures make friends easily. They are amusing, interesting conversationalists who nonetheless prefer to discuss what is significant or important. Don't be surprised if they don't reach any conclusions, though. When you're dealing with eternal verities, it's hard to come to the point.

Aquarians are usually courteous but elusive. There is no way to breach this demeanor, especially not with a direct attack. When faced with a head-on approach, Aquarians tend to retreat.

It is easy to draw out their compassionate qualities. They are humanitarians whose interests stretch far beyond the horizon. They see the big picture, not its little flaws.

They are interested in books, art, or scientific matters. Most Aquarians have an interest in science. They are also fascinated by hobbies and gadgets. If you can't share all their interests, at least try not to be jealous of the fact that Aquarians have so many. They can't help it; it's in their stars.

Aquarians are not steak-and-potatoes people; they prefer to try the little place that features *Chinois* cuisine—a combination of Chinese and continental cooking. Aquarians are always delighted with the different.

Give them time to know you, trust you, and depend on you. Aquarians may take advice but are too smart to be fooled. They won't keep taking bad advice; they'll just avoid the adviser.

Important: Never nag Aquarians about a mistake. They will acknowledge one readily enough, but then forget it. A mistake seems genuinely unimportant to them, and if you keep harping on it they'll just think you are strange.

Aquarius's Amorous Combinations

AQUARIUS AND ARIES They'll enjoy plenty of fun and frolicking. Aquarius's imaginativeness meshes well with Aries's forcefulness. Sexually, Aries's passion inspires Aquarius's originality. They won't try to tie each other down, for each understands the other's need for freedom, adventure, and outside interests. Neither likes to be dominated, however, and Aries *must* take the lead. If this problem can be worked out satisfactorily, the track is clear ahead as far as anyone can see.

AQUARIUS AND TAURUS Aquarius's careless attitude toward love will baffle and finally enrage highly passionate Taurus, who doesn't want someone just to play with. Taurus's possessiveness and jealousy make Aquarius anxious to pack a suitcase and go. Aquarius loves to wander anyway, while Taurus loves home. These two are stubborn in very different ways: Aquarius refuses to be conventional, while Taurus rigidly adheres to the values of family and security. Aquarius is interested in humane concerns; Taurus is single-minded about itself and its possessions. And so on and on and on.

AQUARIUS AND GEMINI Gemini is willing to go along with Aquarius's taste for experiment. In addition, Aquarius calms down Gemini's flightiness and is a stabilizing influence. They enjoy each other's quick, intelligent minds and will have fascinating conversations about people, ideas, and places. Both desire harmony and companionship with not a lot of emotional Sturm und Drang. They love to socialize, they have a wide range of outside activities, and neither is particularly jealous or proprietary. They'll be fine bedmates and fascinating friends.

AQUARIUS AND CANCER Aquarius bristles at Cancer's possessiveness and can't understand why Cancer won't hang loose. Aquarius is careless and free with affection, making sensitive Cancer feel neglected and rejected. Aquarius hates Cancer's clinging restrictiveness and complaining, which stem from Cancer's constant need for proofs of love. Cancer wants a safe, secure home, but Aquarius needs a very flexible living arrangement. Cancer wants Aquarius to stay, but soon Aquarius is inclined to wander away.

AQUARIUS AND LEO Leo is delighted by Aquarius's sexual inventiveness, and Aquarius is drawn to Leo's fire and robust zest for living. These two opposites in the zodiac start off on a high note, but then the notes go sour. Basically, Leo is physical and Aquarius is mental. Leo can't get the cooperation or the admiration it requires, and Aquarius resents Leo's attempt to rule. They have different views of independence: to Aquarius it means freedom to explore new horizons; to Leo it means pursuing a glamorous, extravagant lifestyle. Aquarius is interested in the world; Leo is strictly interested in Leo.

AQUARIUS AND VIRGO Both are mental signs rather than emotional, but Virgo looks on the darker side of life while Aquarius is imaginative and optimistic. Aquarius needs activity, social events, a wide circle of acquaintances. Virgo enjoys a quiet existence with a few close friends. Their goals are very different: Aquarius wants to be as brilliant as possible; Virgo wants to be as efficient as possible. They're compatible intellectually but won't celebrate many anniversaries.

AQUARIUS AND LIBRA Warm, sensual Libra joins with enthusiasm in Aquarius's erotic fun and games. Also, diplomatic Libra knows just how to get around Aquarius's quirky stubborn streak. They like the way each other's minds work and share interests in music, theater, and the arts. Both love parties and other people and have numerous projects in common. There won't be arguments about who leads and who follows because they are both great egalitarians. This should be a lovely affair, but for the long term *someone* will have to settle down.

AQUARIUS AND SCORPIO Fueled by Scorpio's volatility and Aquarius's imaginativeness, sex is quite out of the ordinary. But Aquarius is turned off by Scorpio's powerful and jealous passions, and Scorpio is upset by Aquarius's unpredictable moods. Aquarius is looking for a companion in adventure, whereas Scorpio wants a committed consort. Aquarius is aloof, unemotional, and restless; Scorpio is demanding, critical, and intensely possessive. Aquarius starts looking for happiness outside the home and might as well keep right on traveling.

AQUARIUS AND SAGITTARIUS These two are so innovative about lovemaking that they ought to charge admission. In addition, they inspire each other intellectually, for Aquarius has far-out, inventive ideas and Sagittarius is optimistic and visionary. Aquarius can be dogmatic in its libertarian views, but that doesn't bother live-and-let-live Sagittarius. Both are highly social, fun-loving creatures who like people, seeing new places, and whatever is unpredictable. The best part is that neither one is jealous when the other isn't home.

AQUARIUS AND CAPRICORN Both signs have a strong sense of self, but Aquarius wants to be free and Capricorn wants to dominate. Aquarius has a great many opinions about everything and welcomes neither advice nor orders from rigid Capricorn. Aquarius is continually on the go and likes to spend money. Capricorn considers that frivolous and tries to impose strict controls. Capricorn is cautious, solid, and straightforward, and doesn't understand Aquarius's adventurous ideas. A brief rapport at best before boredom sets in and damps the fire.

AQUARIUS AND AQUARIUS They admire and like each other, and especially enjoy each other's sense of humor. Inventive, progressive, attracted to the new and unusual, they are sexually suited and share wide-ranging interests. Each is involved in all kinds of projects and friendships. With so many outside activities going, they are likely to be apart as much as they are together and that's fine with them. They haven't a thing to quarrel about since they agree on everything: Both of them are much more rational than emotional. Their love won't be as deep as a well, but it will draw water.

AQUARIUS AND PISCES Aquarius is intrigued by Pisces's romantic charm, and Pisces is drawn to Aquarius's visionary ideals. Sensual, imaginative Pisces will go along with anything Aquarius wants, and they achieve an unusual intimacy. However, things begin to go downhill as Pisces insists on more and more testaments of love. Dependent, indecisive Pisces needs someone strong to take control. Aquarius shuns *any* kind of emotional demands. When Aquarius feels hemmed in by that all-enveloping Piscean web, it will struggle free and go its own way.

PISCES
The Amorous Nature

You and Pisces Woman

Pisces woman is a fascinating mixture of earthly passion and unworldly fantasies. It's no wonder that men are captivated by her at first glance and haunted by her forever after. They may try to recall what it is about her that's so enchanting, but they can't plumb the depths of her enticing allure.

Her knack for getting around men is uncanny. She has an instinctive ability to make men feel masculine. Her gentleness and softness and innocence bring out their need to be strong and protective.

Pisces lady doesn't pick her mate on the whim of the moment. Like all water signs (Cancer, Scorpio, Pisces), she has a mysterious way of uncovering the secrets that lie beneath a person's social mask, and her psychic vision sees through to real motives. Sensitive to the slightest nuance in what someone says or how someone behaves, she'll quickly beat her way to the exit if what she sees and hears isn't quite right.

The lovers that Piscean woman chooses tend to fall into two extremes. Because she needs to be needed, she finds herself attracted to emotionally handicapped men whom she can mother and envelop with compassionate care. She also falls in love with the opposite kind of man—one who is strong, decisive, with a great sense of self, a man who will protect and cherish her, and give her the support and firm direction that she needs.

To her love is the ballast, the center from which all else radiates. When she is happy in love, everything else in life seems marvelous. When she is miserable over a love affair, nothing else matters. Her greatest need is to lose herself in someone else, to unite in an almost mystical communion. She wants to enter into the psyche of her lover.

More than any other woman in the zodiac, Pisces will change herself to fit the image that her partner wants. Hers is a mutable sign and she is completely adaptable. Yet this woman of a thousand faces remains uniquely herself: elusive, untouchable, mysterious. She has a fascination that no one quite understands.

The Piscean woman's charms can be a little too otherworldly. Daydreams are her truest reality. One of the many things men find bewitching about her is that she can give full expression to her sexual fantasies. Pisces woman is accomplished at all varieties of erotic play and can employ the skills of a courtesan to heighten the delight of her lover.

Sometimes her abundantly affectionate nature goes over the brink into dependency. But her psychic intuition lets her know when she's reached the limits of a man's patience. She can, if she wishes, take steps to win back a man's favor. Sometimes though, she becomes touchy and oversensitive at another's lack of understanding. What she needs most is patience and sympathy. She can't stand the least hint of rejection. When she's treated with care and affection, however, the sensual, ultrafeminine side of her nature comes shining through. She has the ability to blend a grand romance, an intense sexual bonding, and profound spiritual communion all within the same relationship.

The secret of pleasing this ethereal, unworldly, quick-silvery, sensitive woman is never to come up short on romance. Romance is the breath of life to her.

You and Pisces Man

Pisces man has rare charisma. The secret of his extraordinary appeal to women is a deep and sensitive appreciation for their inner qualities. He always sees a woman at her best. Pisces male is a real charmer, the eternal romantic.

All the water signs have the quality of emotional imagination. Cancer uses it to create a protective environment; Scorpio seeks to delve into the secrets of the human psyche. Pisces tries to live in a world of dreams and romance. He lives for the whim of the moment, and while the moment lasts he can make it seem enchanted, everything a woman ever dreamed of, champagne and caviar, moonlight and poetry and passion. Unfortunately, when the sun comes up the words don't quite rhyme and the champagne is flat. In the cold light of day you may reflect on what a fool you were to have thought it could be otherwise.

Basically, he would like to find happiness with one woman, but the vagaries of his character and the constant appeal to him of change make that unlikely. He is unable to steer a steady course between his conflicting desires. He prefers clandestine meetings and secret affairs with high risk quotients. Married women are his natural prey. Pisces man falls in love easily, but his is the sign of self-undoing, and he has an instinct for choosing the wrong woman. His love life often tends to be chaotic and turbulent, and over his lifetime he may lose his heart many times to the wrong partner. Indeed, it's been said that in every woman's past there is a Pisces man.

He is intensely emotional about making love because he considers it not a merely physical act but the culmination of a romantic yearning. His bedroom behavior, like that of female Pisces, tends toward the offbeat. But he is tender and loving and considerate, and won't insist on having his way. He is a marvelously sensuous, understanding, innovative lover.

As a husband, he probably won't be a good provider. His career problem is that he looks for the easy way—not realizing there is no easy way. But he won't neglect you and is generously willing to share what he has. This man is a giver in an emotional sense. He will do almost anything for someone he cares for. Once he commits himself to a woman, he will give unselfishly of his time, energy, sympathy, and concern.

If you're looking for an attentive, romantic lover, a kind and compassionate man to fulfill your spiritual needs as well as your physical ones, Pisces male is for you. He may be a dreamer, but he can make the right woman's dreams come true.

How to Attract Pisces

You can always interest them in conversation about the world of entertainment, art, books, poetry, and dramatics. Another sure way to get their attention is to discuss any topic touching on the occult, mysticism, spiritualism, and the supernatural, particularly anything involving reincarnation. Pisceans who don't actually believe in it (there aren't many) are fascinated by discussions about it.

Tell them your problems. They're great listeners and their sympathy is mostly genuine. But avoid giving the appearance of being overwhelmed by your problems. While Pisceans have an unusual compassion for losers, they prefer people who are strong and supportive, with definite goals and a positive approach to life.

A good compromise tactic is to discuss your difficulties humorously. Pisceans like to laugh and will be impressed by your ability to smile your troubles away.

Ask them about a subject they know well. (Tip: Pisceans are artistic, or at least have a real appreciation for the arts, so you can hardly go wrong moving in that direction.) Pisces will soon open up. In fact, your problem may be getting back in control of the conversation. Pisceans love to expound and explain and expatiate.

Always greet them with a compliment about their appearance or social presence, or remember to repeat a flattering comment someone else made about them. Pisces soaks up flattery like the Sahara soaks up water.

Above all, be sentimental. Remember each birthday and anniversary. Pisceans are grateful and they don't forget kindness or thoughtfulness. You'll be richly rewarded.

Pisces's Amorous Combinations

PISCES AND ARIES Sensual Pisces is drawn to Aries's dynamic passions, and Pisces's desire to shower affection on a lover will flatter Aries. Pisces's imagination and mysterious allure bring out a new sensitivity and romanticism in this aggressive lover. Aries will handle decisions and fight battles for Pisces, which is just what Pisces is looking for. Headstrong Aries will dominate, but that doesn't necessarily displease Pisces, who likes to have someone to lean on. What may trouble Pisces more is Aries's tendency to criticize. Tact is needed to cement this otherwise sexy partnership.

PISCES AND TAURUS Taurus is a strong, authoritative figure who can provide security and stability for vacillating Pisces. Also, Taurus's artistic bent enhances Pisces's creative imagination. Pisces will accentuate Taurus's taste for comfort, and together they'll furnish a luxurious setting for love. Both are highly passionate and sensual, although Pisces is volatile and more emotional than Taurus. While Taurus's possessiveness makes Pisces feel secure, Taurus is a bit too practical and down-to-earth to satisfy Pisces's romantic nature. If they work out this problem, all goes well.

PISCES AND GEMINI Pisces is drawn by Gemini's wit and communicativeness, and Gemini is fascinated by Pisces's mystery. But this combination is as unstable as nitroglycerin—and likely to blow up. Pisces can't stand Gemini's fickleness and thoughtlessness. Gemini can't stand Pisces's emotionalism and dreaminess. Insecure Pisces is possessive and clinging, while Gemini wants to have fun and move on. In different ways, each is as shifting and changeable as the other. Pisces lacks direction, while Gemini goes off in too many directions. Both need more dominant partners.

PISCES AND CANCER Pisces enjoys Cancer's sexual demands, for Cancer is equally sensual. This romantic duo finds passion, sensitivity, and tenderness in each other. Pisces doesn't mind if Cancer makes most of the decisions; Cancer's concern for security and excellent money sense provide a very practical stability. These two are sentimental types who like to stick close to home. Loyal Cancer devotes itself exclusively to insecure Pisces, and, in turn, Pisces idolizes Cancer. A very compatible pair.

PISCES AND LEO Pisces's tendency to think rather than act annoys Leo, who considers Pisces wishy-washy. These two are very unalike: Pisces is shy, introverted, and vulnerable, while Leo is arrogant, brash, and domineering. Both behave emotionally, but Leo is given to temperamental outbursts while Pisces withdraws into private fantasy. Leo won't tolerate Pisces's sensitivity and dreaminess. Highly social Leo needs lots of feedback, while Pisces demands exclusivity. Leo likes to roam; Pisces doesn't. This combination is like fire and water—they won't mix.

PISCES AND VIRGO Pisces's affectionate nature intrigues Virgo at first, but these two personalities are just too opposite for any rapport. Virgo, being a mental sign, distrusts emotions, whereas Pisces runs its life emotionally rather than intellectually. Reserved, fault-finding Virgo won't satisfy sexually, and when Virgo's sexual rebuffs start, this awakens all the Piscean insecurities. Virgo also can't give Pisces the romance or ego-bolstering Pisces needs, and Pisces proves to be too unstable for exacting Virgo. Virgo will resent Pisces's dependency. This soon becomes a toboggan to nowhere.

PISCES AND LIBRA These affectionate, creative, artistic people take to each other immediately. But Pisces is looking for emotional support and won't find that with Libra. Libra wants romance and harmony, but flees from the responsibility of any kind of demands or entanglements. They both like luxury and a lovely home, but Pisces is too lazy about making money and Libra is too extravagant about spending it. Libra has numerous outside interests and feels stifled by Pisces. Physical rapport isn't enough for the long term. But as long as it lasts, this is likely to be fun.

PISCES AND SCORPIO Pisces finds its match here—and then some. Scorpio will provide a deep, exciting sexual union for Pisces, and gives Pisces valuable emotional support, strength and leadership. Scorpio's jealousy and possessiveness won't bother Pisces—in fact, it makes Pisces feel loved. Pisces's dependency is just what Scorpio is looking for. These two share a special communion, much of it on a sensual, unspoken level. Both have intense feelings and are loyal, intuitive, and interested in the mystical and the unusual. An ideal mating.

PISCES AND SAGITTARIUS These two ignite in the bedroom, but the compatibility ends there. Pisces is an imaginative dreamer, not a doer, whereas Sagittarius thrives on constant activity. Independent Sagittarius is too much of a rover to satisfy Pisces's need for attention and devotion. Sagittarius's sharp tongue will hurt Pisces's romantic sensibilities. Pisces wants to get close but is constantly confused and rebuffed by Sagittarius's struggle to free itself of the heavy emotional demands. Pisces is dependent and home-loving, but restless, adventurous Sagittarius won't stay home long.

PISCES AND CAPRICORN These two very different people please each other. Capricorn's strong, dominant personality is just what Pisces needs. Pisces feels secure with practical, determined Capricorn, who can take charge and make decisions. In turn, Pisces brings a breath of romance and idealism to Capricorn's staid approach to life, and Pisces's lavishness with praise and affection delights Capricorn. Capricorn does not easily verbalize its deep feelings, but Pisces intuitively recognizes Capricorn's loyalty and passion. Sex is fine, and their contrasting temperaments neatly complement each other.

PISCES AND AQUARIUS Pisces's romantic eroticism inspires Aquarius to experiment in new areas. Sexually, this might be fun since they are both venturesome in entirely different ways. But Aquarius is detached, interested in ideas and the world at large, while Pisces is interested in sensual fulfillment. Eventually, outgoing, social-minded Aquarius will start looking around, and Pisces can't endure that. Independent Aquarius needs freedom and after a while resents Pisces's struggle to keep Aquarius caged at home.

PISCES AND PISCES If all life's problems could be resolved in the bedroom they'd be happy, but both need what the other does not have. Each is weak-willed and dependent and drains the other emotionally. Both have a tendency to sink into a mire of self-pity and negativity, and they accentuate each other's confusion, self-indulgence, and muddled thinking. They find it hard to cope with practical realities, and there's no strong partner around to push either one in the right direction. This sexy affair has no place to go.

3

THE DECANATES AND CUSPS OF SUN SIGNS

ROM TIME TO TIME when looking through astrology books or magazines you may have run across the terms *decanate* and *cusp*, but you probably don't have a clear idea of what these words mean. These are astrological terms that subdivide your Sun sign. The subdivisions further define and emphasize certain qualities and character traits pertaining to your Sun sign.

Everyone is born within a particular decanate of a sign, and some people are also born on the cusp. In this chapter I hope to make clear the meaning of decanates and cusps in your life.

What Is a Decanate?

Each astrological sign is divided into three parts, and each part is called a *decanate* or a *decan* (the terms are used interchangeably).

The word comes from the Greek word *dekanoi*, meaning "ten days apart." The Greeks took their word from the Egyptians, who divided their year into 360* days. The Egyptian year had twelve months of thirty days each, and each month was further divided into three sections of ten days each. It was these ten-day sections the Greeks called *dekanoi*.

Astrology still divides the zodiac into decanates. There are twelve signs in the zodiac, and each sign is divided into three decanates. You might picture each decanate as a room. You were born in a certain sign, for example, Gemini, that consists of three rooms (decanates). Which room of Gemini were you born in?

The zodiac is a 360-degree circle. Each decanate is ten degrees of that circle, or about ten days long, since the

*The Egyptians soon found out that a 360-day year was inaccurate, and so added on five extra days. These were feast days and holidays and not counted as real days.

Sun moves through the zodiac at approximately the rate of one degree per day. (This is not exact because not all of our months contain thirty days.)

The decanate of a sign does not change the basic characteristics of that sign, but it does refine and individualize the sign's general characteristics. For example, if you were born in the second decanate of Gemini, that does not change the fact that you are Geminian. It does indicate that you have somewhat different and special characteristics from those Geminians born in the first decanate or the third decanate.

Each decanate has a constellation in the heavens that represents it. These constellations have special mystical meanings that also add to the unique quality of your decanate.

Finally, each decanate has a specific planetary ruler, sometimes called a subruler because it does not usurp the overall rulership of the sign. The subruler can only enhance, or add to, the distinct characteristics of that decanate. For example, the entire sign of Gemini is ruled by Mercury, but the second decanate of Gemini is subruled by Venus. The influence of Venus, the subruler, combines with the overall authority of Mercury to make the second decanate of Gemini unlike any other in the zodiac. In the following guide, I have outlined the subtle differences and special characteristics of your own unique decanate.

THE DECANATES OF ARIES

FIRST DECANATE: MARCH 21 THROUGH MARCH 31

Keyword: Inspiration
Constellation: Andromeda, the Chained Woman. She was freed of her chains by Perseus, the Rescuer. The constellation symbolizes the power of love.
Planetary subruler: Mars

Mars is both your ruler and subruler, giving your personality extra force and impact. You are a dominant person and can sometimes be too aggressive. In an argument or clash of wills, you ride right over the opposition. You are impetuous and energetic and tend to throw yourself into activities with all your heart. A person of conviction, you will never take an action that you think is wrong. You are a clear, incisive thinker and can carry a plan to conclusion. Your best quality is your ability to inspire confidence in others. At times you tire yourself out because you don't know when to stop. You also tend to monopolize conversations.

SECOND DECANATE: APRIL 1 THROUGH APRIL 10

Keyword: Innovation
Constellation: Cetus, the Whale or Sea Monster, tied to two fishes and led by a lamb. Cetus symbolizes energy harnessed to imagination and love.
Planetary subruler: Sun

The Sun in this decanate adds to the power of Aries's Mars, which gives your character dignity, pride, and vitality. You have an ardent and excitable love nature, and your sexual energy is high. The Sun here indicates a great fondness for change. You are never content to take things as they come. Because you are ambitious, you go out and try to put your mark on the world. Others tend to cluster around you, for you have joie de vivre and a magnetic personality. More than the other two decanates of Aries, you seek pleasure out of life. You have a taste for the expensive and can be quite imperious if you don't get what you want. A liking for too much good food is one of your downfalls.

DC

THIRD DECANATE: APRIL 11 THROUGH APRIL 19

Keyword: Foresight
Constellation: Cassiopeia, a beautiful queen seated on her throne who symbolizes good judgment. Down through the ages she has been a celestial guide to travelers.
Planetary subruler: Jupiter

The expansive qualities of Jupiter combine with Aries's Mars to give you a wide or lofty outlook, a love of ambitious ideas and of travel. You resent restriction of any kind and prize your personal freedom. For you, the perfect life is to be successful doing something creative, where you are in charge and call all the shots. Your sense of adventure often takes you far from home. You like to find out new information, to explore different fields of knowledge. The occult interests you. You are shrewd and clever in business matters and may possess an insight or sixth sense about other people. There is a warm-hearted geniality about you that allows you to make friends easily. At times you can be too extravagant with money.

THE DECANATES OF TAURUS

FIRST DECANATE: APRIL 20 THROUGH APRIL 30

Keyword: Acquisition
Constellation: Triangulum, the Triangle, mystic symbol of truth and harmony.
Planetary subruler: Venus

Venus is both your ruler and subruler, and its gracious influence is prominent in your character. Though you have strong likes and dislikes, you are not abrasive about them. You have a charming social touch, and many friends are devoted to you. Your kind and sympathetic nature is easily imposed on. You have an artistic eye for beauty and design and may possess musical ability. Venus in this decanate indicates a love of beautiful possessions. Generally, your instinct for value is useful; in time many of your possessions should be worth more than you paid for them. Sometimes you are too acquisitive and materialistic. Your worst faults are your stubbornness and a refusal to venture out into new areas.

SECOND DECANATE: MAY 1 THROUGH MAY 10

Keyword: Evaluation
Constellation: Eridanus, the River Po, a winding current that symbolizes justice.
Planetary subruler: Mercury

Mercury combines with Venus (Taurus's ruler) to give you an inquisitive mind and a great talent for organization. You are conservative in approach, but also possess intuitive powers that you should use more often. Because you are a determined worker, you inspire trust on the part of others. You have an instinct for cooperation, but you also need the independence to set your own pace, free from distractions. Your mental powers are very strong, and you can take complex ideas and make them understandable to others. Mercury here bestows an ability to speak and write effectively, perhaps even eloquently. Sometimes you meddle too much into other people's affairs, and you have a tendency to forget small details.

THIRD DECANATE: MAY 11 THROUGH MAY 20

Keyword: Determination
Constellation: Perseus, the Rescuer, the hero with winged feet and a sword who slew the Gorgon Medusa. Perseus is symbolic of victory.
Planetary subruler: Saturn

The meditative qualities of Saturn combine with harmonious Venus to give you quiet determination and strength of character. People think of you as stable and reliable, for you are not easily deterred once you are set on a goal. You possess an active mind and are keenly observant. Usually you deal with problems by thoroughly analyzing them before you act. You are not wishy-washy about letting others know where you stand; you'd rather confront a difficulty than evade and worry about it. You have strong, deep feelings, and in romantic relationships are loyal and protective. A fault is that you tend to be too serious. Sometimes you are hurt by what others say because you take things too much to heart.

♊
THE DECANATES OF GEMINI

FIRST DECANATE: MAY 21 *Jim*
THROUGH MAY 31

Keyword: Ingenuity
Constellation: Lepus, the Hare, who triumphs over enemies by
 outwitting them.
Planetary subruler: Mercury

Mercury is both your ruler and subruler, and your mental acumen is sharp. You enjoy new ideas and look for chances to express yourself. Your ability to speak or write influences the direction of your life. You have a forceful personality because you are
able to decide quickly and then act. Logic and rationality are two
rules you live by; you try not to cloud issues by sentimentalizing
them. This is not to say you don't have warm feelings. You have a
unique capacity for forming close relationships, and if you love
someone you tend to involve yourself completely in that person's
affairs. Underneath you are a tense worrier who suffers and frets
too much. You try to handle all details brilliantly, but often they
overwhelm you.

SECOND DECANATE: JUNE 1
THROUGH JUNE 10

Keyword: Union
Constellation: Orion, the Giant Hunter of magnificent strength
 and beauty. Orion was placed in the heavens to commemorate
 his great bravery.
Planetary subruler: Venus

Harmonious Venus combines with Gemini's Mercury to give you
a deft social touch. People respond to your warm and effusive nature. The approval and esteem of others are important to you,
and you tend to function best with people rather than as a loner.
There is a sense of adventure in your outlook, and you enjoy
travel because it exposes you to new experiences. Once you have
made up your mind about a pursuit, you eagerly give it your best
effort. Sharing is part of your life; you are generous with your
time and friendship, and also with possessions. You have a great
deal of sex appeal and are ardent in your expression of love. At
times you can be argumentative because you are so fond of your
own ideas.

THIRD DECANATE: JUNE 11
THROUGH JUNE 20

Keyword: Reason
Constellation: Auriga, the Charioteer. He was the serpent-footed
 king who invented the four-wheeled chariot, which symbolizes communication.
Planetary subruler: Uranus

Uranus, planet of knowledge, combines with Gemini's Mercury to
give you clear and perceptive reasoning powers. You are known
for your original point of view, and other people often seek your
advice. You tend to be intellectual and approach life on a mental
rather than an emotional basis. Though you have many friendships and love affairs, it is your mind that must be first engaged
before your heart can follow. In your work you take the practical
approach and disregard anything you cannot put to use. You are
both witty and loquacious and are never reluctant to say what you
think. At times you are too demanding and domineering, for you
expect others to live up to your high standards.

THE DECANATES OF CANCER

FIRST DECANATE: JUNE 21 THROUGH JUNE 30

Keyword: Receptiveness
Constellation: Canis Minor, the Small Dog, who symbolizes reason.
Planetary subruler: Moon

The Moon is both your ruler and subruler, and so you tend to be very receptive and sensitive to other people. You see deeply into human nature, and your insights and guidance are often sought after. You would make an excellent teacher or instructor. Rationality is important to you. Even though you are an emotional person, you are able to sift through facts and arrive at a fair decision. You have an excellent memory for feelings and impressions (both yours and those of others), but ordinary day-to-day details escape you. In relationships, you look for harmony and security. You dislike quarrels and dissension, and any kind of emotional disturbance leaves you depressed. At times you are too moody and pessimistic.

SECOND DECANATE: JULY 1 THROUGH JULY 11

Keyword: Intensity
Constellation: Canis Major, the Great Dog, companion to the mighty hunter Orion. He symbolizes triumph.
Planetary subruler: Pluto

Pluto is the planet of depth and intensity, and combines with your Cancer Moon to give you a forceful yet thoughtful personality. Of the three Cancer decanates, yours is the most mystical and interested in things unseen. People are drawn to your sensitivity and often tell you their secrets. Your intellectual talents are formidable even though your strong feelings predominate when making decisions. Both curious and intuitive, you are able to gather facts and information from all sources and use them for your benefit. In work you are disciplined and practical; in relationships you are the opposite—sentimental, emotional, and often possessive. You have a tendency to become too fixed and rigid once you've set your mind.

THIRD DECANATE: JULY 12 THROUGH JULY 22

Keyword: Empathy
Constellation: Argo Navis, the magical ship of adventure that symbolizes strength of mind. Placed in the heavens by Poseidon to be a guide to travelers on the southern seas.
Planetary subruler: Neptune

The spiritual planet Neptune is your subruler, which joins forces with the Cancerian Moon to accentuate an impressionable and romantic nature. You may be very artistic, and you try to create beauty and harmony around you. Your adaptability to different kinds of people is one of your secrets of success. Many of you are destined for some kind of public life. You have an ability to touch people's feelings and to form close ties. In love you have deep emotions. You are loyal and protective toward your family and mate, and you believe only the best about them. Cautious and conservative are the words that best describe your approach to problems. Even in the midst of crisis, you look for balance. Often you are prone toward discontent and dissatisfaction.

♌ THE DECANATES OF LEO

FIRST DECANATE: JULY 23 THROUGH AUGUST 1

Keyword: Self-expression
Constellation: Ursa Minor, the Small Bear. This is the constellation of the Little Dipper. The Small Bear symbolizes goals and true direction.
Planetary subruler: Sun

The Sun is both your ruler and subruler, and you are doubly under its beneficent influence. You enjoy being in the spotlight and may be known as a colorful personality. You have an artistic flair. You also have a knack for drawing attention because of the way you speak and present yourself. The role of a leader comes easily, for you are able to excite and stimulate others. In general, you don't keep your feelings to yourself. When you are happy the world knows about it. When you are melancholy you are usually vocal in expressing your moods. You are impulsive in love and tend to follow the dictates of your heart without thinking. At times, you can be very stubborn about wanting your own way.

SECOND DECANATE: AUGUST 2 THROUGH AUGUST 12

Keyword: Expansion
Constellation: Ursa Major, the Great Bear. This is the constellation of the Big Dipper. The Great Bear symbolizes wisdom.
Planetary subruler: Jupiter

The expansive planet Jupiter co-rules your decanate with Leo's Sun, accenting intellectual and visionary qualities. You have a very proud nature and a quick temper. Your ability to dissect problems and see immediately what needs to be done gives you an authority that others respond to. Though you are jovial and good-humored, it's hard for you to laugh at yourself. You are ambitious, but not just for money; what you want is to know more, to gain in intelligence. While you can do manual labor, you much prefer mental pursuits. Sometimes you are thought of as being brash and overconfident, but this is simply a genuine expression of your enthusiasm and willingness to try.

THIRD DECANATE: AUGUST 13 THROUGH AUGUST 22

Keyword: Creativity
Constellation: Hydra, the water-serpent, who symbolizes activism and mental energy.
Planetary subruler: Mars

The aggressive planet Mars combines with Leo's Sun to underline your impetuousness and willpower. You plunge into new projects with verve, but you want tangible results for your efforts. Day-to-day routine quickly bores you; you need fresh ideas, new stimulation, and challenge to keep you at your best. Your life is often marked by furious bursts of energy, followed by periods of complete lethargy. In personal relationships, people are never in doubt about where they stand with you. Love may be troublesome because you want it to be perfect and you can be too demanding of a lover. You find waiting very difficult. Since you are outspoken, you dislike secretive people. Sometimes you have a reputation for being temperamental.

THE DECANATES OF VIRGO

FIRST DECANATE: AUGUST 23 THROUGH SEPTEMBER 1

Keyword: Analysis
Constellation: Crater, the Cup, the goblet of Apollo. The Cup symbolizes emotional giving.
Planetary subruler: Mercury

Mercury, planet of the mind, is both your ruler and subruler, giving you a formidable intellect. You approach problems rationally; you want to find out the reason things happen, and then apply your knowledge to working out a better system. Often your insights are thought of as prophetic, but they are the result of keen observation. You have a warm and witty personality that draws friends and admirers. However, your standards are high and you expect intelligence and decorum in the people you associate with. In love you are romantic and devoted and have great sensitivity toward a lover. There is much nervous energy churning beneath your surface. You tend to worry secretly and to fuss over small problems.

SECOND DECANATE: SEPTEMBER 2 THROUGH SEPTEMBER 12

Keyword: Efficiency
Constellation: Hercules, the strong and virtuous hero who triumphs over evil.
Planetary subruler: Saturn

Saturn, planet of determination, combines with Virgo's Mercury to give special force to your personality. You are concerned with details and want to plot your moves in advance so there won't be any mistakes. Though you are versatile and adaptable, most people think of you as persistent and tenacious. Your fixity of purpose is simply that you demand perfection of yourself and try to give your best performance. In truth you are too exacting and suffer needlessly when you don't live up to your expectations. When you are in love you have a gentle and sympathetic nature, and you do all in your power to please. You are easy to live with as long as no one arouses your strong stubborn streak.

THIRD DECANATE: SEPTEMBER 13 THROUGH SEPTEMBER 22

Keyword: Discrimination
Constellation: Bootes, the Bear Driver, the ancient herdsman who every day chased the Great Bear around the North Pole. Bootes symbolizes the utilization of knowledge.
Planetary subruler: Venus

The gregarious and social qualities of Venus combine with Virgo's Mercury to signify a winning way with people. What motivates you is a desire for approval. You have a special talent for using words and can write and speak charmingly. An artistic flair and use of color is usually present in your surroundings or dress. You possess a sense of style and project a strong personal image. Poise and confidence are assets in your work or career, and you are known for your tact and diplomacy. Since you are unhappy living under restrictions, you are drawn to creative pursuits where you are free to be your own master. In love you are warmhearted and generous, though you demand a lot of attention in return.

THE DECANATES OF LIBRA

FIRST DECANATE: SEPTEMBER 23 THROUGH OCTOBER 2

Keyword: Magnetism
Constellation: Corvus, the Crow, symbolizing idealism and a sense of duty.
Planetary subruler: Venus

Venus is both your ruler and subruler, which intensifies your Libran love for beauty, pleasure, and luxury. You tend to have extravagant tastes and often have trouble holding on to money. Blessed with great social charm, you strive to make an impact. To a large extent, the way you feel about yourself is determined by how much love you receive from others, and in general you try to achieve your goals through other people. Sometimes you cover up a lack of self-confidence by being the aggressor or the one who initiates projects. You have a creative nature that welcomes new ideas, and you are fond of travel. In love you are romantic and impulsive, but you have a tendency to choose lovers who take more than they give.

SECOND DECANATE: OCTOBER 3 THROUGH OCTOBER 13

Keyword: Endurance
Constellation: Centaurus, the Centaur, the magical half man, half horse that symbolizes duality in human beings.
Planetary subruler: Uranus

Uranus, planet of the intellect, rules your decanate, giving power to the romantic qualities of Libra's Venus. Often people are surprised at the sharpness of your mind, since your personality tends to be serene and charming. The Scales (Libra's symbol) also represent a duality that often makes you feel like two different people. There is a radiance to you, an artistic and original style, matched with a determination to accomplish what you set out to do. You are an independent person, yet you need companionship and love. Endurance and conservatism are hidden in your depths. You are at your best in social situations; this is where you come to life and shine.

THIRD DECANATE: OCTOBER 14 THROUGH OCTOBER 22

Keyword: Order
Constellation: Corona Borealis, the Northern Crown, the bridal crown of Ariadne. Christian astronomers called it the Crown of Thorns. Corona Borealis symbolizes achievement.
Planetary subruler: Mercury

The energy and quickness of Mercury join with Libra's Venus to give you an attention-getting personality. You have both vitality and likeableness, a combination that indicates success working with the public. Your mind is forceful, curious, open to new ideas. In general, you tend to follow your head rather than your heart. You enjoy sifting through information and making a reasonable and balanced judgment. Your pronounced intellectual capabilities are part of your allure; you have much sex appeal and enjoy attention from a wide range of people. Sometimes the depth of your true feeling for a lover is not apparent on the surface. Though you have a talent for the written word, you find it difficult to speak of your emotions.

♏ THE DECANATES OF SCORPIO

FIRST DECANATE: OCTOBER 23 THROUGH NOVEMBER 1

Keyword: Integrity
Constellation: Serpens, the Serpent, symbolizing power and occult knowledge.
Planetary subruler: Pluto

Pluto is both your ruler and subruler, which gives a hypnotic intensity to your personality. You are loyal and steadfast, and others quickly sense they can depend on you. You will stand by a lover long after others in the same situation would let go. Once you let go, however, there is usually no turning back. You have fixed opinions, but also a scientific turn of mind that will examine ideas and arrive at a new opinion should the facts warrant it. You are drawn to the mysterious and the occult, but may keep this a secret. Should you choose to use it, you have great power of self-discipline. Sometimes you let things slide by because you don't care enough to exert yourself.

SECOND DECANATE: NOVEMBER 2 THROUGH NOVEMBER 11

Keyword: Regeneration
Constellation: Lupus, the Wolf, held aloft by Centaurus. The Wolf symbolizes offering.
Planetary subruler: Neptune

Neptune, planet of sensitivity, combines with Scorpio's Pluto to accentuate an idealistic personality. In both work and love, you tend to reach out toward others and give of yourself. You would make a superb teacher, healer, or physician; you have a talent for inspiring and helping others. It is important to you to find deeper meaning in your relationships. You are romantic and intense; love fulfills and completes you. Once you can find contentment in love, you reach your true potential in other areas of life. Generally, your luck comes through other people when you least expect it. You are not a patient person and find it difficult to wait for the slow unfolding of events in your life.

THIRD DECANATE: NOVEMBER 12 THROUGH NOVEMBER 21

Keyword: Clarification
Constellation: Aquila, the Eagle, whom the Greeks considered the only creature able to outstare the Sun. The Eagle is symbolic of rising above earthly limitations.
Planetary subruler: Moon

The sensuous Moon combines with Scorpio's Pluto to give an allure to your personality. You are at your best dealing with groups of people, and tend to choose work that projects you into the public eye. Your magnetic social touch wins popularity. Fate seems to thrust you into situations or relationships that you do not pick, but are often the most successful for you. You have a strong sense of ethics, and injustice brings out your fighting spirit. At times you can be moody, especially when the actions of other people discourage you. You have deep emotions that you have difficulty sharing. Once you reveal yourself, you are direct and honest and don't evade the truth.

Rush — Jupiter — Wisdom

THE DECANATES OF SAGITTARIUS

FIRST DECANATE: NOVEMBER 22 THROUGH DECEMBER 1

Keyword: Honesty
Constellation: Ophiuchus, the Serpent-Holder, who as a child vanquished his serpent enemies. Ophiuchus symbolizes victory over adversity.
Planetary subruler: Jupiter

Jupiter, planet of wisdom, is both your ruler and subruler, which accentuates lofty ideals and a love of knowledge. You look for experience and adventure. You want to deepen your understanding of life and are usually a student of human nature. People know they can trust what you tell them, for you are open and aboveboard. In addition, you have a special talent for pleasing others by what you say. You believe strongly in freedom, in the right of each person to choose an individual pathway. Because you have such wide-ranging interests, you may find it hard to commit yourself completely to a marriage or love affair. Emotional discord is extremely distressing to you; you strive to surround yourself with harmonious relationships.

SECOND DECANATE: DECEMBER 2 THROUGH DECEMBER 11

Keyword: Drive
Constellation: Sagitta, the Arrow that killed the eagle who fed upon Prometheus. The Arrow symbolizes the destruction of evil in its path.
Planetary subruler: Mars

Mars, planet of initiative, combines with Jupiter's expansiveness to give you a courageous and generous nature. You have the rare gift of being able to influence and inspire others. Often the kindnesses you show have a much greater impact than you know. Your life is usually geared toward a goal; your real respect is for achievement. You are dependable, efficient, and thorough when you undertake to do a job. At times you may be discouraged, but the face you show to the world is one of humor and strength of character. You are a person of fierce independence; you want to do things your way, though you will try not to step on any toes. In love you may seem detached, but you are devoted and loyal.

THIRD DECANATE: DECEMBER 12 THROUGH DECEMBER 21

Keyword: Intuition
Constellation: Ara, the Altar of Dionysus (Bacchus). Christian astronomers called it the Altar of Noah. Ara symbolizes unity and triumph.
Planetary subruler: Sun

The Sun, which stands for pride and vitality, joins forces with beneficent Jupiter; together they give great magnetism to your personality and a charming talent for making people laugh. Often your profound intellect is hidden under a social and gregarious exterior. Gifted with intuition and insight, you have a deep capacity for learning and discovering deeper meaning. You enjoy travel and meeting new people, for you want to widen your experience. The world of teaching or writing beckons to you. You have a refined and elegant nature that responds to art and beauty. In love, you are passionate and impulsive. You tend to fall head over heels quickly, but these crushes fade away just as quickly.

THE DECANATES OF CAPRICORN

FIRST DECANATE: DECEMBER 22 THROUGH DECEMBER 31

Keyword: Responsibility

Constellation: Corona Australis, the Southern Crown, garland of the gods. The constellation symbolizes commitment to knowledge.

Planetary subruler: Saturn

Saturn, planet of discipline, is both your ruler and subruler, which gives you a serious mien and a talent for handling responsibility. You are precise and orderly and generally don't trust others to look after details. When you undertake a task you complete it to the best of your ability. Once you've set your mind on a goal, you are relentless and determined. There is a quiet force to your personality; other people are always aware of your presence. You are both subtle and aggressive; you have an instinct for knowing how far you can push. Ambition usually motivates you, for you are never content to be an underling. Love brings out your affectionate and demonstrative nature. When aroused you are a passionate person.

SECOND DECANATE: JANUARY 1 THROUGH JANUARY 10

Keyword: Fairness

Constellation: Lyra, the Harp, formed by the god Mercury from a tortoiseshell. Lyra symbolizes harmony.

Planetary subruler: Venus

Venus, planet of love, softens Saturn's stern influence and gives a gentleness and serenity to your personality. People respond to your warmth and charm. Venus here also indicates an interest in beauty and design, and perhaps some creative ability. In your work, you are practical and persistent. You are a doer who does not waste precious time. You enjoy periods of solitude to read, think, explore new subjects. Possibly you carry on a large correspondence, for you write well. Travel holds fascination for you. Your lover, family, and friends take first place in your heart; you are devoted to their wants and needs. You are reticent about your feelings. Love is a deep emotion, and you don't readily speak of it.

THIRD DECANATE: JANUARY 11 THROUGH JANUARY 19

Keyword: Honor

Constellation: Draco, the Dragon, the "seeing one" who guarded the Golden Apples. The Dragon symbolizes observation and intuition.

Planetary subruler: Mercury

Mercury, planet of mental energy, adds impetus to the discipline of Saturn. You have a quick intellect and flexibility of character that allows you to adapt to different people and situations. When you give your word you stick to it; you treat others fairly and with respect. Friends and admirers are drawn to your spiritual nature. You are an idealist and a dreamer, but when motivated you are also an indefatigable worker. Money and material comforts are important to you, and you usually quickly spot where your best financial interests lie. You are a person of deep desires, though this may not be apparent on the surface. Life is often marked by a struggle to fulfill your inner needs.

THE DECANATES OF AQUARIUS

FIRST DECANATE: JANUARY 20 THROUGH JANUARY 29

Keyword: Knowledge
Constellation: Delphinus, the Dolphin, ancient savior of the shipwrecked. The Dolphin symbolizes spirituality.
Planetary subruler: Uranus

Uranus, planet of originality, is both your ruler and subruler, which accentuates your perception and quick mentality. You are capable and intelligent and deal easily with people. Your wit and sense of humor are advantages both socially and in your work. What others may consider obstacles, you think of as challenges. Finding solutions and a better, quicker way of handling things is what you emphasize. You are intrigued by new problems and need change in your activities to keep you from going stale. You have an affectionate and kindhearted nature, although a lover may complain of your detachment. This is probably because you try to apply logic to emotional situations. You are fond of analyzing why a person behaves in this way or that.

SECOND DECANATE: JANUARY 30 THROUGH FEBRUARY 8

Keyword: Frankness
Constellation: Piscis Austrinus, the Southern Fish that symbolizes knowledge and fertility of mind. The Fish drinks from the Fountain of Wisdom.
Planetary subruler: Mercury

Mercury, planet of versatility, adds its energy to Aquarius's Uranus, which gives a liveliness and sparkle to your personality.

You have a spontaneity and genuine warmth that draws others to you. One of your most outstanding traits is your honesty and frankness in speech. People know they can depend on what you say, for you speak your true mind. Mercury bestows a gift for language, and you may have literary interests. You probably have the ability to sum up a person or situation in a clever and witty phrase. You enjoy knowledge for its own sake and are always interested in learning more. You want love to be a consuming and passionate experience, but you are too self-sufficient to be swept away.

THIRD DECANATE: FEBRUARY 9 THROUGH FEBRUARY 18

Keyword: Association
Constellation: Equuleus, the Little Horse, brother of Pegasus. The Little Horse symbolizes loyalty and the harnessing of strength.
Planetary subruler: Venus

Venus, planet of sociability, combines with Aquarius's Uranus to make you the most people-oriented of the three decanates. You have the ability to form close and enduring ties. Often your success in work comes through other people. You probably have an artistic nature and take pride in making your surroundings as beautiful as you can. You like people who do what they say they will and who show up on time. In your own life you are careful about details and tend to be critical about the lax ways of others. Travel and new adventure always excite you, for you are a forward-looking person. In love, you are romantic and affectionate and you tend to have a flirtatious eye.

THE DECANATES OF PISCES

FIRST DECANATE: FEBRUARY 19 THROUGH FEBRUARY 29

Keyword: Imagination
Constellation: Pegasus, the Winged Horse who bears the rider of good fortune.
Planetary subruler: Neptune

Neptune, planet of illusion, is both your ruler and subruler, which emphasizes creativity and imagination. There may be involvement in artistic or literary work; you have a talent for expressing your inner thoughts. You are particularly sensitive to the people with whom you share your life. Discord is unbearable to you, and you will do your best to shield yourself from unpleasantness. Your keen mind is open to ideas, and personal achievement is important to you. Often you must struggle to accentuate positiveness instead of letting negative feelings overwhelm you. You may suffer from physical ailments, but your character is very strong. Love is probably tempestuous, for you have deep passions.

SECOND DECANATE: MARCH 1 THROUGH MARCH 10

Keyword: Compassion
Constellation: Cygnus, the Swan. Also called the Northern Cross. The Swan is the celestial symbol of grace and beauty.
Planetary subruler: Moon

The receptive Moon combines with the spiritual influence of Neptune and heightens your awareness of others. You have an uncanny way of knowing what those around you think or feel, and can use this power on a much wider scale. You are, or have the potential to become, well known not only in your circle but in the larger world. Your observations are keen; you are able to gather ideas or art forms and transform them with your own unique vision. Social occasions enable you to display your special charm with people and a knack for witty conversation that is one of your strong points. You are a romantic at heart, and love is a transforming experience for you. Unfortunately, you don't find love easy to hold on to.

THIRD DECANATE: MARCH 11 THROUGH MARCH 20

Keyword: Action
Constellation: Cepheus, the Monarch who rests one foot on the Pole Star. He symbolizes constancy.
Planetary subruler: Pluto

Pluto, planet of power, gives force to Pisces's Neptune and underlines your need for activity and outlets. You possess imagination and vision; if you harness your energy you can soar to great heights of achievement. Intellectually you are curious and like to explore the unusual or hidden. You are especially drawn to religious, spiritual, or occult matters. Solitude and periods of withdrawal from others are necessary for you to think, review, and meditate. You have a talent for writing or speaking that can move and influence other people. Your emotions are deep and strong; you understand first with your heart and only then with your head. Love motivates many of your decisions.

What Is a Cusp?

A CUSP IS THE POINT at which a new astrological sign begins.* Thus, the "cusp of Aries" means the point at which Aries begins. (The word comes from the Latin word *cuspis*, meaning "point.")

When someone speaks of being "born on the cusp," he or she is referring to a birth time at or near the beginning or the end of an astrological sign. For example, if you were born on July 23, you were born on the cusp of Leo, the sign that begins on July 23. Indeed, depending on what year you were born, your birth time might even be in the last degree of Cancer. The Sun does not move into a new sign at *exactly* the same moment each year, and the dates for the different Sun signs may vary by a day or so. Even if the Sun were moving into Leo on that day, what time of day did this happen? Were you born while the Sun was still in Cancer or after the Sun entered into Leo? If your birthday is near the beginning or end of a sign, check the Sun Tables starting on page 425 or cast your chart using the enclosed CD-ROM to be absolutely certain which sign you were born in.

Astrologers differ about when a person is born on the cusp. Some astrologers claim it means only within the first two days or last two days of a sign. Others say it can be as much as within the first ten days or last ten days of a sign. The consensus, however, is that you were born on the cusp if your birthday is within the first *five* days or last *five* days of a sign.

With cusp-born people there is always the question, "What sign am I really?" They feel that they straddle the border of two different countries.

To some extent, this is true. If you were cusp-born, you are under the influence of both signs. However, much like being a traveler leaving one country and crossing into another, you must actually *be* in one country—you can't be in two countries at the same time. One sign is always a stronger influence, and that sign is almost invariably the sign that the Sun was *actually* in (in other words, your Sun sign). The reason I say "almost" is that in rare cases a chart may be so heavily weighted with planets in a certain sign that the person more keenly feels the influence of that specific sign.

For example, I have a friend whose birthday is December 22. On the day of his birth the Sun was leaving Sagittarius and entering Capricorn. At the moment of his birth the Sun was still in Sagittarius, so technically

---

*There are two kinds of cusps in astrology—sign cusps and House cusps, i.e., the point at which a sign begins and the point at which a House begins. Houses are the twelve divisions of a birth chart that represent various departments of life (for example, career, marriage, wealth and possessions). Astrologers carefully study House cusps when interpreting a birth chart because planets on or near the cusps of the Houses have a stronger influence than other planets in the chart. For more about Houses, see chapter 8, "The Houses of Astrology."

speaking he is a Sagittarian. However, the Sun was only two hours away from being in Capricorn, and this person has the Moon, Mercury, and Saturn all in Capricorn. He has always felt like a Capricorn and has always behaved as a Capricorn.

This, obviously, is an unusual case. Generally, the Sun is the most powerful planetary influence in a chart. Even if you were born with the Sun on the very tip of the first or last degree of a sign, that sign is your Sun sign, and that is the sign you will most feel like.

However, the influence of the approaching sign or of the sign just ending is present, and you will probably sense that mixture in yourself. If you are cusp-born, you should recognize yourself in one of the following descriptions.

THE CUSPS OF ARIES

BORN MARCH 21 THROUGH MARCH 25

You are Aries with Pisces tendencies. You are headstrong and impulsive, but there is a part of you that longs for peace and solitude. You resent it when others intrude on or interfere with your plans. Your intellectual powers are keen, and you enjoy probing into new areas and coming up with different ideas. You are clearly an individual. Warmth and sympathy come easily to you. Generally you are fond of entertaining and get along well with people. Your lovemaking tends to be passionate.

BORN APRIL 15 THROUGH APRIL 19

You are Aries with Taurus tendencies. You are impatient, high-strung, and volatile, but also determined and at times very stubborn. Ariens have the reputation for not finishing what they begin, but you are able to see a project through to the end. You like to be the one in charge, and your reaction to disorder and sloppiness is irritation. Emotions are a dominant factor in your life. People always know they can get an honest reaction from you. You are fiery and romantic. You have strong feelings, whether it be anger or joy or love.

THE CUSPS OF TAURUS

BORN APRIL 20 THROUGH APRIL 24

You are Taurus with Aries tendencies. You are self-sufficient and determined, but also spirited and independent. You cannot bear being restricted by other people's rules, and whatever the situation you always assert your own personality. People often come to you for advice; you may be known as having great style and confidence. In truth, you sometimes feel insecure, but you hide it very well. You take the intellectual approach to solving problems. In love, however, you are impulsive and extravagant.

BORN MAY 16 THROUGH MAY 20

You are Taurus with Gemini tendencies. You are ambitious, have strong willpower, and are also imaginative and intellectually inclined. You have an attractive personality and possess a special persuasive touch that works well with people. Generally, you deal in a straightforward manner because you prefer to cut through deception or secretiveness and lay things out in the open. You dislike taking orders. Words come easily to you unless you are emotionally involved; then you are often unable to express your deepest feelings. This is especially true when you are in love.

Jim

Ⅱ
THE CUSPS OF GEMINI

BORN MAY 21 THROUGH MAY 25

You are Gemini with Taurus tendencies. You are inquisitive and changeable, but you also have a stubborn streak and are not easily moved off your course. At times you become irritable when others don't measure up to your expectations. Generally, though, you deal tactfully with others and you have many friends. Artistic talent may be evident, but you are practical and realistic about making money. Your attitude in new situations is, "Where do *I* fit in?" Usually you make a marvelous first impression.

BORN JUNE 16 THROUGH JUNE 20

You are Gemini with Cancer tendencies. You are quick-witted and communicative, and also analytical, cautious, and conservative in your approach. When you give your word, others know they can trust you to do exactly as you say. You like to be surrounded with familiar objects and people, and you put a lot of weight on charming manners and appearance. Yours is a sensitive nature that is easily hurt by carelessness or selfishness. You are not satisfied with being ordinary; you want to create beauty or be known for your brilliance.

THE CUSPS OF CANCER

Tc

BORN JUNE 21 THROUGH JUNE 25

You are Cancer with Gemini tendencies. You have a sympathetic and generous nature, and an incisive, intellectual mind. You may be famous for your brain, but those close to you know you are a softie inside. Sometimes your heart and mind are at odds with each other; emotions affect you more than you like to admit. You have a special touch for getting along with people from all walks of life. You need stimulation and change, and will become discontent if stuck in one place for too long.

BORN JULY 18 THROUGH JULY 22

You are Cancer with Leo tendencies. You are idealistic and sensitive, and also clever and forceful, and you probably you have a temper that quickly comes and goes. In work, you like doing things your own way. You possess a pleasing social grace that mixes easily with people, but you take a long time to form truly close relationships. Love is not impulsive. You may be instantly attracted to someone, but you are careful because you fear rejection and won't let yourself become too vulnerable

THE CUSPS OF LEO

BORN JULY 23 THROUGH JULY 27

You are Leo with Cancer tendencies. You have high aspirations and tend to be creative, and at the same time are methodical and studious. You want to make the "right" decisions and hate to be caught unprepared or off-guard. Mental work stimulates you; you have good powers of concentration and an ability to express yourself. Because of your ebullience and warmth, you attract many friends. You are often extravagant with money because you love to buy beautiful things. You also are headstrong and possessive in love.

BORN AUGUST 18 THROUGH AUGUST 22

You are Leo with Virgo tendencies. You gain attention because of your strong personality and sense of style. Determination is one of your dominant qualities; you climb over obstacles to reach a goal or get something your heart is set on. You have a taste for elegance and like to travel first class. Though you are very levelheaded when analyzing other people's problems, you are basically an emotional person. You make decisions first with your heart and then rationalize with your head.

THE CUSPS OF VIRGO

BORN AUGUST 23 THROUGH AUGUST 27

You are Virgo with Leo tendencies. You are kind, gracious, and reliable, and you also possess great flair and personal style. Your optimism, wit, and sense of fun magnetically draw people toward you. Projects you undertake are likely to be successful because of your eye for detail and quick intelligence. Often you end up handling the whole show because of your organizational abilities. Sometimes you are impatient with the irresponsibility of others. You shine in social settings. In love, you tend to be effusive, warm, and loyal.

BORN SEPTEMBER 18 THROUGH SEPTEMBER 22

You are Virgo with Libra tendencies. You are an idea person, intellectual and perceptive. You have a gregarious nature and are most successful dealing with and through other people. Your mind is alert and lively, and you probably have a facile flair for conversation. Your particular gift is for using your social talents in your work. Your finely honed esthetic sense sets high standards. You may be a collector of beautiful objects or be drawn to creative pursuits. In love you are sincere and expressive but need a lot of attention and devotion from a lover.

THE CUSPS OF LIBRA

BORN SEPTEMBER 23 THROUGH SEPTEMBER 27

You are Libra with Virgo tendencies. You are people-oriented and possess a talent for making others like you. You are also industrious and have a keen eye for detail but sometimes take on more than you can handle. It is important to you to be admired. You are aware of your public image and always strive to make the best impression. You would like to keep your emotions on an even keel, but you tend to be either enthusiastically happy or else dejected over some little thing going wrong. Love makes you feel fulfilled, and you are probably flirtatious.

BORN OCTOBER 18 THROUGH OCTOBER 22

You are Libra with Scorpio tendencies. You have magnetic personal charm and usually try to maneuver situations so you are the one who controls or directs. You know how to work hard, and you apply yourself wholeheartedly to achieve a goal. You are skillful in dealing with people. Your sensuality attracts others, even when you are not aware of it. At times you can be impatient and quick-tempered, but basically you don't like arguments and you are willing to keep peace. You have a captivating social nature. Punctuality is not one of your strong points.

THE CUSPS OF SCORPIO

BORN OCTOBER 23 THROUGH OCTOBER 27

You are Scorpio with Libra tendencies. There is an elegance to your personality, a charm and good-naturedness that people respond to. You have a talent for expressing your opinions in an apt and amusing way. You have a strong will, but unless you are crossed or thwarted you don't often show it. In general, you are cooperative and friendly, even though you prefer to work alone at your own pace. This is especially true in any creative enterprise. In love your feelings run deep and you tend to be cautious. You don't commit yourself easily because you fear being hurt or rejected.

BORN NOVEMBER 17 THROUGH NOVEMBER 21

You are Scorpio with Sagittarius tendencies. You are sensitive, intuitive, and likely have a lot of nervous energy. You enjoy a variety of interests and hobbies and attract different types of friends. Mental activity stimulates you. You are fond of discussion and are never reluctant to share an opinion. Those you love are aware of your loyalty and warm feelings; others usually see you as someone who makes dispassionate judgments. The truth is that you are sentimental, but able to stand back and be objective if this is in your best interests.

THE CUSPS OF SAGITTARIUS

BORN NOVEMBER 22 THROUGH NOVEMBER 26

You are Sagittarius with Scorpio tendencies. You are high-strung and excitable and may be known as a colorful personality. You are also intelligent, versatile, and forward-thinking. Life is full of activity for you. Because you dislike being alone, you surround yourself with people and projects and sometimes spread yourself too thin. You know how to spot an advantage and how to make yourself the center of attention. You have good psychic powers and an ability to probe into other people's minds. In love you are passionate but changeable.

BORN DECEMBER 17 THROUGH DECEMBER 21

You are Sagittarius with Capricorn tendencies. You are genial and good-natured and have charming social manners. You are also ambitious, know how to take responsibility, and are thorough when doing a job. Since you have both imagination and a strong sense of self, you like to work without interference from others. People sometimes look to you for advice, since your quick mind can zero in on important matters. You have a sensitive nature and a capacity for loving deeply. You do not always make wise decisions in love, however.

THE CUSPS OF CAPRICORN

BORN DECEMBER 22 THROUGH DECEMBER 26

You are Capricorn with Sagittarius tendencies. Underneath your practical and sometimes unemotional approach, you have a kind and loving heart. People instinctively rely on your integrity. You do not betray their confidences and are a sympathetic listener. There is an adventurous quality to you; you like to travel and to explore new places and ideas. Even though you are conservative and cautious in your judgments, you are always willing to examine another point of view. You often pick up unspoken signals from others because of your keen sensitivity.

BORN JANUARY 15 THROUGH JANUARY 19

You are Capricorn with Aquarius tendencies. You are a deep person who possesses insight and vision, but you are also generous and fun-loving and like to be in the company of people. You enjoy entertaining and the "good life," and may be known as an excellent host or hostess. Success is likely working with the public. In general, you look on the positive side, but when things go wrong you are able to see only the negative. Your loyalty is unshakable, and you are always ready to help someone you love. In romance you tend to settle for less than you deserve.

THE CUSPS OF AQUARIUS

BORN JANUARY 20 THROUGH JANUARY 24

You are Aquarius with Capricorn tendencies. You have a quick mind and are versatile enough to handle many varied projects. In addition you have a good memory and a methodical approach. Generally you are most successful in enterprises where you can run things your own way. Your sociable nature attracts people, and you may be known for a witty sense of humor. At times you need complete privacy and periods of reflection. You have a strong streak of independence. You try to deal with love analytically because you dislike falling prey to feelings.

BORN FEBRUARY 14 THROUGH FEBRUARY 18

You are Aquarius with Pisces tendencies. You have an easygoing charm that fits in well with almost any group. Whereas you may have many acquaintances, those who know you really well are few. You have a lighthearted exterior that often hides deeper feelings. In work you are forward-thinking and progressive, but also cautious. You view life with a somewhat jaded eye and won't rush into anything new without investigation. Nothing offends you more than being unfairly dealt with. You tend to have extravagant tastes and enjoy spending money.

THE CUSPS OF PISCES

BORN FEBRUARY 19 THROUGH FEBRUARY 23

You are Pisces with Aquarius tendencies. You have an elegant and refined nature, and also an infectious sense of fun. You possess both determination and good organizational ability, and generally are successful at making money. In your work, you can be incisive and objective about solving problems. People are often surprised at the variety and extent of your interests. You have strong likes and dislikes, but also an open mind that enjoys toying with new ideas. You need change in scenery to keep from becoming bored. Love may be elusive because you need a special kind of person to fulfill you.

BORN MARCH 16 THROUGH MARCH 20

You are Pisces with Aries tendencies. You have keen powers of observation and are drawn to the unusual in people and in ideas. You have a strong personality that makes an impact, and you possess the ability to execute personal plans in spite of obstacles. In short, you are a most original person. You have learned that luck comes when you least expect it. You have a magnetic social touch and are usually surrounded by friends and acquaintances. You are flirtatious and changeable, but in love you are capable of intense devotion.

4

ASTROLOGY AND HEALTH

AMONG THE MOST IMPORTANT QUESTIONS a client asks an astrologer is, "What does my chart say about my health?" Health and well-being are of paramount concern to human beings. Love, money, or career take second place, for without good health we cannot enjoy anything else in life.

Astrology and medicine have had a long marriage. Hippocrates (born around 460 B.C.), the Greek philosopher and physician who is considered the father of medicine, said, "A physician without a knowledge of astrology has no right to call himself a physician." Indeed, up until the eighteenth century, the study of astrology and its relationship to the body was very much a part of a doctor's training. When a patient became ill a chart was immediately drawn up. This guided the doctor in both diagnosis and treatment, for the chart would tell when the crisis would come and what medicine would help. Of course, Western doctors in the twentieth century no longer use astrology to treat illness. However, astrology can still be a useful tool in helping to maintain our physical well-being.

The Signs and Anatomy

To begin with, each sign of the zodiac rules or governs a specific part of the body. These associations date back to the beginning of astrology. Curiously, the part of the body that a sign rules is in some ways the strongest and in other ways the weakest area for a person born under that sign. Look under your individual sign to see how this paradox of nature applies to you.

The Planets and Your Body

In addition to the sign's rulership over parts of the body, the planets are associated with various glands in the body. These glands release hormones that keep our bodies functioning.

Astrology and Diet

Each sign of the zodiac has particular diet needs for minerals that are found in certain foods. Your diet may be failing to supply these specific needs. Included under your sign is a list of foods that would be beneficial for you in a healthful eating program.

Astrology and Your Erogenous Zones

Our bodies are very sensitive to the touch of another human being. The special language of touching is understood on a level more basic than speech. For each sign in the zodiac, there are certain zones and areas of the body that are especially receptive and can receive sexual messages through touch. Many books and manuals have been written about lovemaking, but few pay attention to the unique knowledge of erogenous zones supplied by astrology. You *can* use astrology to become a better, more sensitive lover.

The association between the signs of the zodiac and the different parts of the body and the illnesses connected with them is part of the Hermetic Theory, an ancient Egyptian-Greek philosophical science that held that the entire cosmos is reflected in the human being. The signs of the zodiac, beginning with Aries and ending with Pisces, correlate to the human body, beginning with the head (ruled by Aries) and ending with the feet (ruled by Pisces). Thus, the entire zodiac is contained within the human body.

I want to say a word to you before you read this health chapter. It can be read on both a simplistic and a more advanced level. If, for example, you were born with the Sun in Aries, you will no doubt read the pages about Aries and probably discover that many of the health tips and medical issues discussed in the Aries section apply to you. But the story does not end there.

For one thing, modern medical astrology believes strongly in the "principle of polarity," that the opposite sign in the zodiac also influences the health of the native. Thus, if you are Aries, you should also read the pages on Libra (Aries's opposite sign), for there will be guidance in those pages that also relates to Aries.

In addition (as I have emphasized and will continue to emphasize), no person is a pure sign. You may discover when you cast your birth chart that your chart is heavily weighted with planets in a particular sign other than your Sun sign. Therefore, the health aspects of that particular sign will also apply to you.

Still another factor to be considered is your Ascendant (or Rising sign), which in many ways contributes to your outward appearance and health. Your Ascending sign also is a significant part of your health picture.

I have a woman client whose Sun sign is Libra, whose Ascendant is Taurus, and who has three planets in Taurus, one of them Saturn, a planet that often indicates areas of delicate health. She has had a long history of lower back problems (her Sun sign, Libra, rules the lumbar region), headaches (her Sun sign's polarity is Aries, which rules the head), and throat and thyroid problems (her Ascendant, Taurus, heavily weighted with planets, rules the throat). If this woman reads all three sections—Libra, Aries, and Taurus—she will gain a greater understanding of her health issues and needs, and get many more tips on care and exercise than if she reads only Libra (her Sun sign).

I urge you to do the same. Later on, when you discover more about your chart, come back to this health chapter and read further about the various signs that make up your whole birth chart.

ARIES

Part of the Body Ruled by Aries

Aries rules the head and face. You can often spot an Aries person by his or her fine facial bone structure and a shining, healthy head of hair. Sometimes there is a birthmark or mole on the face. The head is associated with thinking and perception, and natives of Aries tend to be sharp, shrewd thinkers who use common sense.

Aries people are subject to headaches, including migraines, head congestion, and sinus conditions. They are also prone toward minor injuries around the head and face, and should use protective headgear if taking part in strenuous sports. They have a tendency to overwork themselves and overtax their energy. They are prey to eyestrain and to having problems with their teeth.

When excited or frustrated, an Aries person will often get red in the face. If he or she has fever, it tends to reach a high degree in a short period of time. However, Ariens have strong recuperative powers and can fight off illness very rapidly.

The glands that Aries rules are the adrenals. These are the glands that pump adrenaline into the bloodstream during times of stress and emergency. The Aries personality is known for its excitability and impetuosity, and one reason may be that Mars, the planet associated with Aries, rules the muscular system and the sex glands. Aries people are active, have excellent muscle coordination, and are noted for their energetic sexuality.

Diet and Health Tips for Aries

Because the Aries person is usually busy, active, and on the go, he or she needs a well-balanced diet to maintain good health and energy. The cell salt for the sign of Aries is potassium phosphate. This mineral builds brain cells and replenishes the liver. Aries people usually expend so much energy that their supply of this element is depleted and must be replenished. Lack of potassium phosphate can cause depression.

Foods rich in this mineral and therefore beneficial for Ariens to include in their diet are: tomatoes, beans (red kidney, navy, lima), brown rice, lentils, walnuts, olives, onions, lettuce, cauliflower, cucumber, spinach, broccoli, brussels sprouts, veal, swordfish, flounder, figs, bananas, dried uncooked apricots, pumpkin. A healthy diet should also include milk, which is good for teeth and bones.

Salt and liquor are two enemies that Aries people in particular should avoid. Too much salt affects bones and arteries; liquor overstimulates and reacts negatively on the kidneys. Ariens should enjoy their meals in a quiet, serene atmosphere, and never eat too quickly or under stressful conditions. They should drink plenty of water and get adequate rest and relaxation.

Aries's Erogenous Zone

The nerve endings in the face and head are especially sensitive for Aries people, and gentle stroking of the hair and scalp is something they respond to favorably.

Aries woman loves to have her hair combed and played with. If you nibble Aries man's ear, you will send him a definite sexual message. Other stimulations that people of this sign respond to are featherlight strokes of the lips with your fingertips, and gentle kisses on their closed eyelids.

One technique that will relax Aries and put her or him in the mood for love is to travel a path with your fingertips from the base of the hairline at the back of the neck all the way to the top of the skull. Your fingers should move in small circles that vibrate the scalp. Use a light but firm pressure. Repeat this pathway from neck to top of the crown until the entire head has been massaged. This technique is also extremely useful for relieving the headaches due to nervous tension that Aries is subject to.

TAURUS

Part of the Body Ruled by Taurus

The sign of Taurus rules the throat and neck, which includes the vocal cords, palate, and tonsils. Generally, Taureans have long, expressive necks, and women of this sign have lovely skin around the throat and collarbone area. Both sexes are known for their melodious speaking voices, and many are fine singers. Taurus's taste buds are keen, and Taureans thoroughly enjoy good food. A tendency to put on weight grows more pronounced as they get older.

Taureans are particularly vulnerable to colds, coughs, sore throats, laryngitis, swollen glands, stiff necks, and minor injuries around the neck. When exposed to wintry wind and cold weather, they should take care to bundle up with scarves and mufflers. Taurus people are subject to tonsillitis and earaches. Colds seem to settle into their throats and are not easily shaken off. When they get physically tired or overtense, Taureans tend to get coughs and stiff necks. Many go through life with a semipermanent "crick" in their necks.

Taurus also rules the thyroid gland, which can cause serious weight problems if it is malfunctioning. In addition, Taurus's ruling planet Venus has an effect on the parathyroids, which control the calcium level in the body. Traditionally, Venus also rules the throat, kidneys, and lumbar region. Being Venus-ruled, Taurus people sometimes suffer from back strain, especially because they tend to be sedentary.

Diet and Health Tips for Taurus

A diet low in starch, fat, and sugar is particularly important to Taureans because so many have to fight the battle of the bulge. They are likely to eat fattening foods, to be sluggish and indolent, and to dislike exercise. They may suffer from puffy eyes and jowls, and their faces are apt to get heavier as time goes by. Moderate exercise and good diet should be a strict discipline in every Taurean's life.

Taurus's cell salt is sulphate of sodium, a mineral that controls the amount of water in the system. It is present in the liver, the pancreas, and the hormones of the kidneys. An imbalance of this mineral in the body can cause bloating, symptoms of congestion around the thyroid gland, and a feeling of being waterlogged. Foods that contain this mineral that Taureans need are asparagus, beets, spinach, horseradish, Swiss chard, cauliflower, cucumber, onions, pumpkin, cranberries, and raw nuts. Celery can help them to clear their systems after overindulgence. Carbohydrates have a way of turning into fat in a Taurean's body and should be avoided, along with heavy, rich foods. To keep the thyroid functioning at its best, Taureans should eat food with natural iodine, such as fish and seafood. Other foods that keep Taureans healthy are eggs, liver, kidney beans, wheat germ, fresh fruit, and green salads. They should drink plenty of water to keep their systems flushed out.

In general, Taurus people should coddle their throats, try not to catch colds, wear warm head-and-neck covering in winter, and keep foreign objects out of their ears. Walking is wonderful exercise for them, and stretching exercises for the neck are very beneficial.

Taurus's Erogenous Zone

The throat and neck is Taurus's sensitive area, and light touching, kissing, and fondling of this zone will quickly raise a Taurean's sexual temperature. When fixing Taurus man's tie, lightly glide your fingernails over his throat. Brush the back of Taurus woman's neck in an affectionate gesture. Both men and women enjoy kisses and gentle bites on the back of the neck and the throat.

Here is a massage technique that will surely please: 1) While Taurus lies on his or her back, gently vibrate the area under the earlobes with your fingertips, using little circular motions. Trace a path down to the collarbone. Repeat until entire front of neck has been massaged. (Be very gentle around the windpipe.) 2) Taurus likes to lie on his or her stomach while you trace vertical paths from the hairline to the top of the spine, using your fingertips to vibrate the flesh and muscles.

This technique will thoroughly relax Taurus and make him or her very receptive to lovemaking.

♊

GEMINI

Part of the Body Ruled by Gemini

The sign of Gemini rules the shoulders, arms, hands, and lungs. Natives of this sign are noted for their graceful arms and beautifully shaped hands. They are dexterous and well coordinated and often excel at sports and dancing. Geminis are often called jacks-of-all-trades, and are happiest when involved with many projects and a wide range of people. Gemini persons seem to look young longer.

Unfortunately, Geminis are vulnerable to upper respiratory infections, bronchitis, and asthma. In times of stress they may have difficulty breathing and suffer from either hyperventilation or an inability to draw in enough oxygen. They are apt to get sprains and fractures, particularly in the bones in their shoulders, arms, and hands. They are also afflicted by bumps, cuts, scratches, and bruises.

Gemini rules the nerves, so natives of this sign are often excitable and high-strung. They vacillate between despondency and euphoria, and seem to run on their nerves. The planet Mercury, which rules Gemini, has always been associated with respiration, the brain, and the entire nervous system. It also governs the delicate links between the mind and the different parts of the body, so with Gemini people the state of mind has a great deal to do with the state of their health. Anxiety and nervousness literally can make them sick.

Diet and Health Tips for Gemini

For Geminis, relaxation is not just something that's nice if they can get it. It is essential to their well-being. Because they expend so much nervous energy, they should take time to unwind, relax, and soothe their jangled nerves. Coffee and stimulants make matters worse and should be avoided. Herbal teas have a calming effect.

Gemini people are inclined to eat on the run and are notorious junk-food addicts. To keep up their energy and high spirits, they must have a proper diet. Many Geminis can't tolerate large amounts of food at one time; eating four mini-meals a day can be beneficial.

The cell salt for Gemini is potassium chloride, which builds fibrin in the blood, organs, and tissues of the body. A deficiency of this mineral leads to clots in the blood and circulatory problems. Potassium chloride also keeps the lungs and bronchial tubes unclogged. Foods high in this mineral are asparagus, green beans, tomatoes, celery, carrots, spinach, oranges, peaches, plums, apricots, and wild rice. Healthy nerve foods for Gemini include grapefruit, almonds, broiled fish and shellfish, grape juice, apples, and raisins. Lettuce and cauliflower help to combat bronchitis. Geminis need calcium to keep their bones healthy; milk, buttermilk, and cottage cheese are excellent sources.

Gemini people should protect their chests in cold, inclement weather, and never smoke tobacco. Not only is tobacco smoking detrimental to the lungs, it causes circulatory problems in the arms and hands. Geminis should practice deep-breathing or yoga exercises to help them relax and breathe easier, and should play tennis and Ping-Pong to strengthen their arms.

Gemini's Erogenous Zone

Gemini's sensitive arms and hands are very receptive to erotic stimuli. Light kisses, touches, and fingertip brushes of this area will send shivers of delight down a Gemini's spine. Gemini women are fond of handkissers. Gemini men respond to light stroking of their hands, especially the palms and inside of the fingers. As a prelude to love-making, try lightly kissing the inside of your Gemini's

arms, starting with his or her fingertips and moving up to the armpits.

A massage technique that natives of this sign find especially stimulating is to grip Gemini's wrist gently with both hands. Using light but firm pressure, turn one hand in one direction and the other in the opposite direction in a gentle wringing motion. Do this all the way up Gemini's arm and back again. Another way to relax Gemini is to travel the path of his or her inner arm, from the palm to the armpit, vibrating the flesh and muscles by using a circular motion on the skin with your fingertips.

CANCER

Part of the Body Ruled by Cancer

Cancer rules the breasts and the stomach. This part of the anatomy has always symbolized nourishment and motherhood, and Cancer natives are characterized as protective and clinging. Cancer women often have beautiful bosoms, with soft creamy skin and a curving decolletage. Men of this sign have well-shaped chests and flat stomachs. All of this changes as Cancerians grow older, for they are susceptible to gaining weight in later years. They find it very difficult to lose excess weight.

Tension, anxiety, and emotional stress are the leading causes of illness among Cancerians. They have delicate stomachs and digestive problems and are prone to ulcers,

gallbladder upsets, gas pains, nausea, and gastritis. Their health is not robust, particularly in childhood, and many suffer from upper respiratory infections such as bronchitis. Born under a water sign, Cancerians will overindulge in wine and alcohol, which they do not tolerate well. Drinking alcohol aggravates their stomach problems, increases weight, and causes fluid retention in body tissues.

The Moon, Cancer's ruler, has dominion over the breasts and the alimentary canal, heightening the susceptibility of Cancerians in these areas.

Diet and Health Tips for Cancer

Food means security to Cancer people, and they turn to pies, cakes, ice cream, and candy to make themselves feel better when they are low in spirit. This is a self-accelerating spiral, for excess sweets make their stomachs worse. Cancerians need to watch their diets very carefully in order to keep their digestive systems healthy and their weight under control.

Cancer's cell salt is calcium fluoride, which unites with albumen and oil in the body's system to keep elastic and connective tissues healthy. It is also an important ingredient in tooth enamel, fingernails, bones, and the lens of the eye. Deficiency of this mineral can cause varicose veins, receding gums, curvature of the spine, eye problems, and cataracts. Food sources for calcium fluoride are egg yolks, whole-grain rye, yogurt, beets, watercress, fish, and oysters. Cancerians are prone to skin disorders when there is a lack of calcium in their diet. They should consume milk, cheese, kale, lettuce, and tomatoes, which are high in calcium. Okra, which also contains calcium, is an aid in reducing stomach inflammations. Fresh vegetables, fresh fruit, and lean protein are a daily must for the Cancerian. Starches, sugar, and salt should be avoided. The first two cause constipation, and salt produces bloat. Cancer people should stay away from spicy, highly seasoned food and should forgo hot pepper sauce and horseradish.

Cancerians should always have meals in pleasant surroundings—no bickering or heated discussions at the dinner table. Taking a walk after a meal aids digestion and serenity of mind. Walking in warm rain (under an umbrella) or by the seashore is excellent, for the moist air soothes the lungs.

If Cancerians get sick, they recuperate faster in their own beds at home.

Cancer's Erogenous Zone

Breasts are an erogenous zone for most people, but this is especially true for Cancerians. Both men and women born under this sign respond quickly to oral and manual manipulation of the nipples. Soft caresses, gentle bites, and kisses on this area heighten Cancer's sensuality. Run your hands over the hairs on Cancer man's chest, just barely touching them, and you will ignite his passions. A Cancer woman derives pleasure from having her breasts touched and kissed by a lover.

To massage the breast and chest area erotically, begin by placing two fingers on Cancer's clavicle (the bone that juts out at the bottom of the neck). Using featherlight pressure, gently vibrate the flesh of each breast. Then stroke each nipple with the tip of one finger. Using your finger pad, gently stroke the pink area around the nipple (the areola). Finally, stroke each breast with your fingernails, just barely making contact with the flesh.

This massage technique will create urgent sensations of sexual desire in any Cancer woman or man.

♌
LEO

Part of the Body Ruled by Leo

The sign of Leo rules the spine, the back, and the heart. The heart is associated with warm emotions, the back with courage. Leo people display these qualities. They are open personalities who give wholeheartedly of themselves to others and live life to the fullest. Leos have robust constitutions, supple spines, and good coordination. They are usually excellent dancers and athletes.

Leos have a great need to excel in what they do, and often push themselves so hard that they suffer strain from overexertion and nerves. Their upper back tires more easily than other parts of their bodies. They are also subject to pains and pressure around the heart. When startled a Leo's heart will seem to jump into his or her throat. They can usually feel their pulses beat inside their heads. Heart problems may crop up later in life; however, Leos are noted for their longevity.

Leo's ruler, the Sun, has always been associated with the heart, back, and spinal column. It also influences the spleen and the entire body's vitality. In more recent times, astrologers have come to believe that it rules the thymus, an endocrine gland that secretes hormones necessary for growth during the early years of childhood. Scientific studies connect the thymus with the immunization of the body against bacteria.

Thus, the sign of Leo is characterized by growth, vitality, and good health. Leo people are not inclined to be sickly, and when they are ill they bounce back very quickly.

As a rule, Leos live healthy lives. However, they must learn to slow down in later years to avoid the risk of heart attack.

Diet and Health Tips for Leo

Leo people enjoy the good life, and eating well is part of this. They like rich food and fine wine. Fortunately young Leos have strong stomachs and good circulation, and keep in shape because they are active. However, time does catch up with them, and Leos must learn to eat correctly and cut down on fatty foods.

Leo's cell salt is magnesium phosphate, which keeps the motor nerves in top functioning order and is also necessary to the formation of the skeletal structure. It forms blood albumen, maintains the fluidity of the blood, and activates the digestive enzymes. Foods that contain this element so important to Leos are whole wheat and rye products, almonds, walnuts, sunflower seeds, figs, lemons, apples, peaches, coconut, rice, seafood, beets, asparagus, romaine, and egg yolk. Foods that aid the circulation and have blood-making properties include beef, lamb, poultry, liver, fresh fruit, salad greens, cheese, whole milk, and yogurt. Foods rich in iron, such as spinach, raisins, and dates, are recommended for Leo. Plums, pears, and oranges reduce heart strain.

Leo people should take care of their backs by doing simple strengthening exercises. They must learn how to bend and lift, and never lift anything too heavy. They benefit from developing good posture, getting enough rest and relaxation, and enjoying short periods of sunbathing.

Leos usually have thick shining hair, somewhat like manes. If they keep it clean, healthy, and conditioned, it should last them a lifetime.

Leo's Erogenous Zone

Sweeping caresses over the back and spine sexually stimulate and excite Leo. An easy and enjoyable preliminary is to sponge Leo's back in the bath with a loofah sponge. Work gently down along the spine, pausing in the small of the back, then circle out to the sides and the ribs. Sponge until Leo's skin is rosy. In the bedroom, while Leo lies on his or her stomach, shake talcum powder over the back (still tingling from the bath). Using your hands or a soft bristle brush, smooth the powder into the skin, paying particular attention to the spine and small of the back. Your Leo will be more than ready for love.

There are as many different kinds of back massages as there are masseurs, for this is an area in which tensions seem to gather. This technique will relax and soothe a Leo: Place the heels of your hands on Leo's upper back with your thumbs resting directly over the spine. Using a circular vibrating motion, describe six-inch circles with the heels of your hands. Trace a path from the shoulder blades down to the small of the back. Return. Repeat until the entire back has been massaged.

If you find this relaxes Leo so much that he or she falls asleep, erotically stimulate the back. Lightly draw long lines from shoulder to buttocks with your fingertip or fingernail just barely touching flesh. Stroke down into the cleft between the buttocks. Leo will wake up fast.

Virgo

Part of the Body Ruled by Virgo

The sign of Virgo rules the nervous system and the intestines. The intestines assimilate food into the body. By the same token, Virgoans assimilate knowledge and turn it into practical use. They have delicate and finely tuned nervous systems, which makes them intuitive and discriminating.

As with Cancer, nervous tension, anxiety, and emotional stress are Virgo's worst enemies. People of this sign can literally worry themselves sick. When things go wrong they have a tendency to turn the trouble in onto themselves, and the problem is instantly reflected in a physical ailment, usually intestinal.

Virgoans have fussy digestive systems, and suffer from indigestion, gas pains, ulcers, liver upsets, colitis, and bowel problems. In addition, they are often troubled by skin eruptions, again due to nerves. Virgoans worry about their health; they tend to be hypochondriacs.

Virgo's ruling planet Mercury has dominion over the brain and the nervous system. It also controls the links between the mind and the functions of the body. This intensifies Virgo's proclivity for turning mental tension and upsets into illness of the body.

Diet and Health Tips for Virgo

Virgoans have to coddle their sensitive digestive systems. A proper diet is essential to good health and to keeping up energy. In addition, food should not be highly seasoned, spicy, laden with sauces or gravies, or fried.

Virgo's cell salt is potassium sulphate, which regulates oil in the body, carries oxygen to cells, and is essential to muscle contraction. This mineral keeps the skin pores unclogged and ventilated. Lack of potassium sulphate in the diet causes dandruff, hair loss, eczema, acne, and dry, flaky skin and hair. A deficiency also leads to extreme fatigue and constipation. Foods high in this mineral that Virgoans need are green leafy vegetables (endive, chicory, romaine), whole wheat and whole-grain breads, wheat germ oil, oats, almonds, cheese, oranges, bananas, lemons, lean beef, and lamb. Healthy foods that are easy to digest are corn bread, yogurt, brown rice, eggs, and cottage cheese. Melons, apples, pears, and papaya are particularly good for Virgoans, and lemon juice in the diet will ease skin eruptions and dandruff. Honey should be used as a sweetener instead of sugar. Herb teas soothe upset stomachs. Virgoans love chocolate, which unfortunately does not love them; it causes upsets of the skin and digestive system. They do not tolerate drugs well, and medicine should be taken only under a doctor's supervision.

Sunshine (in moderate amounts), mild exercise, and periods of relaxation are important for Virgo. It's hard not to worry when one **is** a worrier, but it helps to get away from it all and think about something else.

Virgo's Erogenous Zone

As a prelude to love, a playful tête-à-tête in the bath is just the thing to please Virgo. One reason: Virgo is very attracted to cleanliness. While in the bath, gently lave Virgo's stomach area with a sponge, soap, and warm water. For Virgoans, the entire stomach area is responsive to erotic touching, kissing, and stroking. They also enjoy the feeling of a spray of warm water over this area. A handheld shower nozzle will do the trick nicely.

In bed it is very easy to arouse Virgo sexually with this massage: 1) Begin by slowly and gently stroking the abdomen, starting just under the chest and going down to the top of the legs. Use your fingertips and cover the entire area. 2) Using a featherlight touch, stroke long lines from the navel to the genitals with your fingertip. Do the same thing using just fingernails and scarcely touching flesh. 3) Moving in a large circle, stroke the stomach area with your fingertips, describing smaller and smaller circles until you are at the rim of the navel.

By this time Virgo is your slave.

LIBRA

Part of the Body Ruled by Libra

The sign of Libra rules the kidneys, lumbar region (which includes the lower spine and back), and the buttocks. Libra women tend to have graceful lower spines and curvaceous buttocks, and Libra men have well-shaped, muscular backs. As a rule, natives of this sign enjoy good health, although sometimes in adolescence it is delicate and then balances out in adulthood.

Venus, the planet that rules Libra, holds sway over skin, hair, and veins, as well as the throat, kidneys, and lumbar region. Librans are known for their fine (though sensitive) skin, pleasing features, and good bone structure. When called upon, their energy level can keep up with the best, although they are usually slow starters in the morning.

Librans are prone toward weakness in the lower back, and this is the first place in the body to suffer when Librans overexert themselves. They also are predisposed toward kidney ailments and skin breakouts. In winter they may be afflicted with cold hands and feet because of poor circulation.

In many ways, their health is influenced by their surroundings and relationships. Any disturbance, dissension, or disagreement makes Librans wretchedly unhappy and undermines their ability to work or function.

Diet and Health Tips for Libra

Balance is the key to Libra's health and well-being—balanced diet, balance of work and recreation, and balanced relationships with other people.

Libra's cell salt is sodium phosphate, which equalizes the balance of acids and alkalis in the body and rids the body of waste material. It's important for Librans to keep a proper balance between acids and alkali in the body, for too much acidity will interfere with proper kidney function. The skin is a good indicator of whether more sodium phosphate is needed in the diet: Skin tends to get yellowish and sallow when there is a deficiency. Good food sources for this mineral are strawberries, apples, raisins, almonds, asparagus, peas, corn, carrots, spinach, beets, radishes, tomatoes, wheat, brown rice, and oatmeal. Librans function best with a high-protein diet that is low in fat, sugar, and acid-producing foods. They should eat lots of broiled fish, seafood, and poultry (not too much beef or pork), low-fat cheeses, yogurt, plenty of fresh fruits and vegetables, salad greens, and whole-grain breads.

Librans's sensitive skins immediately show the effect of lack of sleep, rich food, and too much champagne. They should drink plenty of water to keep their systems flushed out and free of toxins, and should avoid alcohol and carbonated drinks, which are bad for the kidneys. They should also use caution when trying new skin preparations, many of which cause the skin to break out. Mild exercise, especially back exercises, will strengthen a weak lower back and keep the body supple. Good posture will free Librans from vague aches and pains in the back.

In general, Librans should try to surround themselves with beautiful things, pleasant music, and harmonious people. This is good advice for everyone, but emphatically important for Librans.

Libra's Erogenous Zone

If you want to get on more intimate terms with Libra, try unobtrusively caressing his or her lower back when dancing or strolling together. The small of the back and the buttocks are very sensitive. When the relationship has progressed to the point where you are both in the bath or shower together, pay particular attention with a sponge or washcloth to Libra's lower back and buttocks. Gently sponge this area and lave with warm water until the skin is rosy.

Both male and female of this sign are very partial to having their buttocks rubbed, fondled, patted, and gently pinched. An erotic massage technique that is sure to put Libra into the mood for love is: 1) With Libra lying face-down, begin the massage by gently clutching one buttock in each hand and moving them in a circular motion. 2) With fingertips barely touching flesh, stroke buttocks up and down with featherlight touches. 3) Do the same, using just fingernails. 4) Using four fingers of each hand, place fingertips lightly on the buttocks, one finger at a time. Move quickly and lightly so that all the fingertips touch the skin in rapid succession. Position hands so that the fingertips will land in the cleft between the buttocks.

By now Libra will be sexually aroused.

♏ SCORPIO

Part of the Body Ruled by Scorpio

The sign of Scorpio rules the sexual organs. Symbolically, this part of the anatomy represents life-giving force, and Scorpio people are renowned for their fund of energy and imagination. They have a reputation for being highly sexed, passionate, and possessive, the kind who do nothing halfway. A healthy sex life is essential to their well-being. Scorpio people even take out their anger in sexual ways; they use or withhold sex as a weapon. Sexual frustration or suppression of their intense feelings results in erratic and cruel behavior on their part.

Natives of this sign are prone to problems and infections of the sex organs. Skin eruptions on the genitals, cystitis and diseases of the urinary tract, and venereal infections are ailments to which Scorpios are most susceptible.

In addition, Scorpio people are subject to ill health brought on by emotional difficulties. Their intense natures brood and seethe over insults and injuries (often imagined). They seem unable to rest and relax, and as a result may suffer from exhaustion.

The sign of Scorpio is ruled by the planet Pluto, which governs the formation of cells and the reproductive function of the body. Thus, Scorpio's link with sex and regenerative forces is strengthened. As a rule, Scorpios have strong, voluptuous bodies and excellent recuperative powers—though some astrologers have remarked on the fact that more people born under Scorpio come to a violent and unexpected end than do natives of other signs. It's been said that Scorpios look old when they are young, and young when they are old.

Diet and Health Tips for Scorpio

A healthful diet is important for Scorpio people in order to keep up their energy and a positive outlook on life. When problems strike they have a tendency to overindulge in alcohol and forget about food, which in turn makes them more unhappy, listless, and ill.

Scorpios have a problem handling liquor. Of all the signs in the zodiac, alcohol has the worst and most immediate effects on Scorpio's looks and skin. It is toxic for their system, it intensifies their already volatile emotions, and most Scorpios don't know how to say no to a second drink.

Scorpio's cell salt is calcium sulphate, which is the prime factor in the repair of tissues and resistance to infectious diseases. The nose, mouth, throat, esophagus, reproductive organs, and intestinal pathways need this mineral for healthy functioning. A deficiency opens the way to colds and sinus infections that hang on forever, skin eruptions that do not heal, and infertility. Foods rich in calcium sulphate that Scorpios should include in their diet are asparagus, kale, cauliflower, radishes, onions, parsnips, watercress, tomatoes, figs, prunes, black cherries, and coconuts. Scorpios need calcium foods such as milk, cheese, yogurt, and cottage cheese. They should concentrate on a diet high in protein, fresh fruits and vegetables, and whole-grain breads. The following are particularly good for Scorpio: fish and seafood, green salads, beets, escarole, romaine, brussels sprouts, artichokes, lentils, wheat germ, almonds, walnuts, citrus fruit, berries, apples, bananas, and pineapples. Scorpios should not eat large meals, and the evening meal should be light. Bottled spring water is often better for them to drink than regular tap water.

In general, Scorpio people need rest and recreation, exercise, and peaceful surroundings. Born under a water sign, they benefit from sea travel, vacations at the seashore, and long soaks in warm baths.

Scorpio's Erogenous Zone

The genitals are everyone's erogenous zone, but for Scorpio the genitals are where sexual energy is exclusively focused and concentrated. Scorpio starts off with intense sexual feelings, and genital contact adds fuel to the fire. Even a light fingering of Scorpio's genital area will turn him or her into a volcano of passion.

There is almost no wrong way to touch and fondle Scorpio's genitals, unless you are inflicting pain. The following technique of erotic touching is one good way to begin sexual arousal: Using fingertips or fingernails, stroke very lightly starting at one knee, up one thigh across the genitals, and down the other thigh to just short of the other knee. Repeat in the opposite direction, but this time shorten the stroke by a few inches. Continue making each stroke shorter and shorter until you are just inches away from the genitals.

Since much of the excitement in erotic touching comes from anticipation, any manual or oral stimulation of the genitals should be done very slowly, and you should not always follow through as expected. "Teasing" with your fingertips can spur Scorpio on to the sexual heights.

SAGITTARIUS

Part of the Body Ruled by Sagittarius

The sign of Sagittarius rules the hips, the thighs, and the liver. In human anatomy the hips and thighs represent locomotion and volition, and it should not be surprising that most Sagittarians are active people who love freedom, fresh air, sunshine, and the great outdoors. Physical activity is a must; they will stagnate and become ill if they don't get enough exercise.

Both men and women tend to have long, well-shaped legs. Sagittarians are graceful, coordinated, and well-developed and are often described as having a buoyant walk. Indeed, walking is their favorite form of relaxation and exercise.

Though usually lean and slender in their early years, they have a tendency to put on weight as they get older. In Sagittarian women the weight unfortunately seems to settle on the hips and thighs.

Sagittarians are likely to incur injuries and ailments of the hips and thighs. The upper legs are the first part of the body to tire and weaken when Sagittarians are under strain. They often have chronic aches in the hips and thighs, and are very susceptible to fractures, sprains, and bruising in this area. They are vulnerable to sciatica, gout, hip disease, and sometimes lameness.

Sagittarius's ruling planet Jupiter governs the liver. In addition, recent astrologers have traced Jupiter's influence on the pituitary gland. The pituitary, known as the "master gland," regulates hormone production and physical growth. Sagittarians tend to have an active, sensitive liver that instantly suffers from overuse of alcohol. They are also susceptible to hepatitis.

With a minimum amount of care, however, they enjoy long, healthy lives. There are more octogenarians who were born under Sagittarius than under any other sign.

Diet and Health Tips for Sagittarius

Proper diet is important for on-the-go Sagittarians. A poor diet heavy in fats, starches, and alcohol places an extra burden on Sagittarius's sensitive liver and makes it harder for them to sustain a high energy level.

Sagittarius's cell salt is silica, which strengthens the nervous system, keeps the connective brain tissue healthy, and prevents numbness in fingers, legs, and feet. Deficiency of this mineral results in lank hair, dull skin, and sores and receding of the gums. Best sources for the silica that Sagittarians need are the skins of fruits and vegetables, raw salads, green peppers, figs, prunes, strawberries, pears, apples, potatoes, oats, the husks of grains, whole-grain cereals, and egg yolk. Foods that particularly do not agree with Sagittarius are fats, gravies, cream, butter, candy, and chocolate. They should go very easy on alcoholic beverages, to avoid damage not only to the liver but also to the skin, which coarsens and ages under the effects of liquor. To keep their weight at optimum level Sagittarians should eat a high-protein diet, with lots of broiled poultry and fish, fresh vegetables and fruit (such as brussels sprouts, beets, tomatoes, asparagus, plums, cherries, oranges, and lemons), eggs, skim milk, yogurt, brown rice, and whole wheat.

Sagittarius people need constant mental stimulation, which can lead them to overwork and overplay. More than most people, Sagittarians have to have recreation and exercise, but moderation is the keyword. They should avoid the blistering effects of sun and wind, for their skin is apt to be quite thin and tender.

Other good tips: they should drink lots of pure water, avoid smoking tobacco (which constricts blood vessels), eat four mini-meals a day rather than three large ones, and be careful when walking, riding, or participating in sports. Injuries to the hips and thighs are common among people born under this sign.

In general, Sagittarians are healthy and optimistic, recuperate quickly from illness, and keep their good looks and sparkling smiles well into old age.

Sagittarius's Errogenous Zone

The hips and thighs are special erotic areas for Sagittarians. They like to be touched and caressed in these places. Both male and female enjoy kisses, nibbles and delicate fingering along the inside of the thighs and around the hips.

Try giving Sagittarius a rubdown of the upper legs with warm body oil. He or she is sure to find it sexually arousing. Use circular motions on the hips and vertical strokes on the thighs.

Another erotic massage technique is to begin stroking the outside of Sagittarius's thighs with four fingers while exploring the inside of the thighs with your thumbs. Stroke upward toward the genitals. Then stroke the inside of the thighs with the palm of your hand. Switch to using fingertips or fingernails and just barely touch the skin. Stroke upward along the inner thigh so that your fingertips touch the thighs and your knuckles brush against the genitals.

By this time erotic sensations are shooting up the spine of your Sagittarius.

♑
CAPRICORN

Part of the Body Ruled by Capricorn

The sign of Capricorn rules the bones, joints, knees, and teeth. Capricorns are known for their beautiful bone structure and stately carriage. Capricorn women often have a striking angular beauty, especially in their facial bones, which makes them very photogenic. Both men and women have strong constitutions, vigorous and enduring, capable of withstanding stress and illness. Their health seems to get better as they get older. Along with Leo and Sagittarius, Capricorn is noted for its longevity.

Capricorn's bones, joints, and knees, however, are vulnerable to accidents, fractures, bumps, bruises, and cuts. The knees tire more easily than other parts of the body. Many Capricorns complain of a bothersome trick knee and of bone aches throughout the body. Chief dangers to Capricorn are rheumatism, arthritis, neuralgia, stiff joints, and orthopedic problems.

Capricorn's ruling planet Saturn holds sway over the gallbladder, spleen, bones, skin, and teeth. Capricorns usually have good-looking teeth, but they require a great deal of care and dentistry. The skin tends to be dry and sensitive.

Capricorn people are inclined to be introspective, moody, and depressed. Ill health and indefinable aches and pains can be brought on by their negative emotions. Worry drains their energy and spirits. Capricorns tend to have trouble with the demon drink.

Diet and Health Tips for Capricorn

A diet high in protein and calcium is a must for Capricorn in order to keep the bones, skin, and teeth in prime condition. Capricorns tend to do things in excess. They overwork, skip meals, then eat too much at one time. They should go easy on the highly seasoned and spicy food they are fond of, for it causes intestinal upsets. Gloomy Capricorns often seek solace in alcohol, which they do not handle well.

Capricorn's cell salt is calcium phosphate, which is the most important element in bone formation and composition of the skeleton. Lack of calcium phosphate causes rickets, misshapen bones, spinal curvature, tooth disorders, and pains in the joints. Foods rich in this mineral that Capricorns need are oranges, lemons, figs, celery, cabbage, kale, dandelion greens, spinach, broccoli, corn, peas, potatoes, walnuts, almonds, whole wheat, oats, and brown rice. Capricorns should include in their diet every day a fresh raw salad, fresh fruits and vegetables, lean protein, fish, eggs, and whole-grain breads. They need lots of calcium foods, such as cheese, buttermilk, and yogurt. Capricorns tend to get into a rut about food likes and dislikes, and often eat the same things every day. They should try to vary their diet with different vegetables, fruit, meat, and fish.

They are bothered by dry, itchy skin, especially in wintertime. Oils from apricots, sesame, and almond are soothing and moisturizing, and drinking plenty of water will keep the skin clear and plump. Eating chocolate and refined sugar is bad for Capricorn's skin. They should never overdo when sunbathing, for their skin will quickly take on the patina of old cracked leather.

Other tips for Capricorn: They should keep warm and wrapped up in cold, damp weather. If they surround themselves with color, flowers, soothing music, and pleasant people, their mood should lighten. They should strive for good posture, sit up straight, and loosen their gait. Warm baths, moderate exercise, and long walks in the country are very relaxing for Capricorn.

Capricorn's Erogenous Zone

The special erotic area for Capricorn is the knees. Capricorn's slumbering passions are instantly awakened if you gently brush, stroke, fondle, or kiss the area around the knees.

Either male or female Capricorn will be sexually stimulated by a sensual massage that starts in the small of the lower back. Use your fingertips or fingernails, and stroke lightly, just touching the skin. Make long strokes from the lower back, down along the buttocks, the backs of the thighs, and on to the backs of the knees. Return the same way, but this time shorten the stroke. Keep shortening your featherlight strokes until they are concentrated around the back of the knees. A variation would be to use your tongue and lips in slow short circles on the skin around the knees.

The effect on Capricorn is volcanic!

AQUARIUS

Part of the Body Ruled by Aquarious

The sign of Aquarius rules the circulatory system and the shins, calves, and ankles. The lower leg represents active locomotion, and Aquarius people are characterized as progressive and forward-thinking. They are generally strong and healthy, with good coordination, well-shaped legs, and slender ankles. They tend to be very active mentally, more than they are physically, and there is a slight tendency to put on weight if they are not careful. Often their health will take an unexpected sudden turn for the worse, and just as quickly reverse again. Their illnesses come on without apparent reason.

The lower part of the legs and ankles is an area that is very susceptible for Aquarians. At times, their ankles swell and cause problems. They are prone to varicose veins and cramps in the lower legs. Accidents, cuts, bruises, sprains, and fractures are suffered more frequently on the shins, calves, and ankles than on other parts of the body. They suffer circulatory problems, hardening of the arteries, anemia, and low blood pressure. Cold weather is particularly hard on Aquarians, and they are prone to frostbite.

Uranus, Aquarius's ruling planet, governs the circulatory system and the pineal gland. The exact purpose and function of the pineal gland, which is found at the base of the skull, remains unknown. The ancients called it the "seat of the soul," and thought it was what remained of man's "third eye." The sign of Aquarius is associated with the concept of unusual and mystical knowledge.

Diet and Health Tips for Aquarius

Aquarians need a healthy diet to maintain vitality and to keep their weight at the perfect level. Aquarius people like to immerse themselves in projects and activities, and that leaves little time for balanced meals. They are inveterate snackers, and often eat the wrong things while on the run.

Aquarius's cell salt is sodium chloride, which is common table salt. This does not mean, however, that Aquarians should heavily salt the food they eat. That will only lead to bloating, kidney disorders, hardening of the arteries, and problems with sluggish circulation. On the other hand, lack of sodium chloride in the blood results in dehydration. Aquarians need to absorb sodium chloride naturally, by eating the right foods. These include ocean fish, lobster, tuna, clams, oysters, spinach, radishes, celery, cabbage, lettuce, corn, romaine, squash, lentils, almonds, pecans, walnuts, apples, peaches, pears, lemons, and oranges. Aquarians should follow a diet that limits fattening foods and is high in protein, fresh fruits and vegetables, and whole-grain breads. Fruits high in vitamin C will keep the veins in their legs healthy. Other foods that are very good for Aquarians are chicken, veal, beets, broccoli, carrots, peppers, tomatoes, strawberries, pineapple, pomegranates, figs, dates, brown rice, buckwheat, whole wheat, yogurt, and natural cheeses.

Fresh air and exercise are very important for Aquarians in order to relieve tension and rev up energy. They should take great care, however, when doing anything that might injure the calves and ankles. Brisk walks are excellent, for that gets circulation going in the legs. Aquarians should not run even when they are in a hurry; they are likely to trip and fall. Puffiness in the legs and ankles can be counteracted by elevating the legs, and an afternoon nap keeps up vitality. They should cut down on coffee, which makes them nervous.

Aquarians are apt to get gray hair fairly early in life; they shouldn't worry that this means the onset of premature old age!

Aquarius's Erogenous Zone

The sensitive area is the calves and ankles. Touching, rubbing, fondling, or kissing this part of the anatomy will significantly arouse Aquarius's sexual desire.

Absentmindedly caress the ankle, moving up to the calf, and see how quickly Aquarius responds. Aquarians love having their lower legs and ankles laved with a sponge while reclining in a bath.

As a preliminary move to lovemaking, give Aquarius an erotic massage. Use your fingertips or fingernails, and stroke ever so gently. Begin at the ankles, and slowly describe circles around the ankle bone. Make long strokes up the calves until you reach the knees. The area in back of the calves is particularly sensitive.

While making love, any position that allows contact with the calf and the ankle will increase Aquarius's sexual satisfaction.

PISCES

Part of the Body Ruled by Pisces

The sign of Pisces rules the feet and toes and the mucous membranes. Pisceans are noted for their graceful, well-shaped feet, and many become excellent dancers. Their senses of taste and smell are exceptionally acute. In general, health is not robust in Pisces. Natives of this sign tend to have delicate constitutions that do not easily fight off disease. They are vulnerable to colds, sinus trouble, and water retention in the body. Pisceans have sensitive, emotional personalities, and illness is frequently emotionally based.

The feet tend to be a source of trouble for Pisces people. They find it difficult to do work that requires long hours of standing. Many suffer from corns and bunions. Ill-fitting shoes are particularly troublesome, for many Pisceans cannot seem to find shoes that will properly fit their sensitive feet. They usually kick off their shoes at the first opportunity and walk in slippers or barefooted. Pisceans are prone to athlete's foot and other fungus infections. Gout often afflicts the toes. Bruised, stubbed, or broken toes are also common injuries to Pisceans.

Neptune, the planet that rules Pisces, acts on the general nervous system and specifically on the thalamus. The thalamus is the part of the brain that transmits stimuli to and from the sensory organs.

Pisces people are especially sensitive to stimuli around them. They are very impressionable, and often involved in creative work, music, art, and drama. Unfortunately, they easily fall prey to the influence of alcohol and drugs.

Diet and Health Tips for Pisces

Pisceans are attracted to glamorous living, which often includes overindulging in eating and drinking and keeping late hours. The key to their good health is to establish moderate habits. With a minimum of care—a well-balanced diet, moderate exercise, rest—Pisceans can feel younger than they are and keep their good looks well into old age.

Pisces's cell salt is ferrum phosphate, which is iron. Iron is needed for the manufacture of hemoglobin in the bloodstream. Hemoglobin is the essential element in the red blood cell and is responsible for the transport of oxygen from the lungs to other body cells. Lack of iron in the system leads to anemia, low blood pressure, inflammations, glandular problems, and heart irregularities.

Foods rich in iron that Pisceans should include in their diet are liver, lean beef, lamb, egg yolks, oysters, kidneys, whole-grain cereals, barley, dried beans, beet tops, spinach, onions, lettuce, raisins, dates, prunes, apricots, peaches, grapes, apples, lemons, and oranges. Pisceans function best with a high-protein diet that is low in fat and sugar. Lean broiled meat, chicken and fish, natural cheeses, yogurt, and nuts are excellent sources of protein. They should cut down on table salt, for this makes bloat (something Pisceans are quite prone to). Coffee overstimulates Pisces and should be cut down to a bare minimum.

Pisceans are particularly susceptible to the effects of alcohol, which will age a native of this sign quicker than one of any other in the zodiac. Caution: Drugs and medicine should be taken by Pisceans only under the supervision of a doctor.

Pisces people need lots of rest to keep up vitality, which tends to be low. Wonderful exercises are swimming and dancing; both will keep them fit and glowing. They should take extra care of their feet and wear comfortable, well-fitting shoes. A warm footbath before going to bed will aid relaxation and a good night's sleep. They should never walk around with wet feet or sit on the beach in a wet bathing suit.

Pisces's Erogenous Zone

The feet are the special area for Pisces that is sensitive to erotic touch. The practice of reflexology is based on a school of thought that maintains that the foot represents the body in microcosm—that different parts of the foot correspond to various parts of the body. Thus, massaging, touching, and treating different parts of the foot can stimulate and treat the whole body. If this theory is valid, it should be particularly true for Pisces.

You can use massage on Pisces's feet both to induce re-laxation and to increase sexual desire. Here is a relaxing technique: 1) Grasp all five toes and bend them toward and then away from the ankle. Repeat ten times. 2) Using thumbs and fingers, knead and rub the soles of the feet. Knead the top of the foot, using lighter pressure. 3) Gently pinch and knead the Achilles tendon. 4) Grasp the foot with both hands and gently wring, starting near the toes and working up to the ankle.

The best beginning to an erotic massage is a foot soak in warm, scented water. Follow up with an application of skin lotion all over the feet and toes, paying special attention to the soles of the feet and to the skin between the toes. Then, using just fingertips or fingernails, gently caress the heel and arch. At the ankle bone, use a featherlight circular motion with your fingertips. Move around to the top of the foot and then down to the toes. If you rub Pisces's toes between the pads of your fingers, you will send a very definite sexual message.

Pisceans often use their feet to enhance the act of love. Pisces woman will gently masturbate her lover using the balls of her feet. Male Pisces gets added stimulation by rubbing his feet over the vaginal area.

Cochin Filius inv. et Sculpsit.

Part Two

LESS WELL-KNOWN
INFLUENCES

5

MOON SIGNS

Everyone is a moon and has a dark side
That he never shows to anyone.
SYBIL LEEK

THE POSITION OF THE MOON in your horoscope is second only in importance to the position of the Sun. The Sun sign is the part of you that is most apparent on the surface; it is what others see. The Moon sign is the part of you that *you* see.

In astrology the Moon stands for emotions, instincts, the unconscious. Whereas the Sun represents your will, the Moon represents your instinctive reactions. Evangeline Adams, the most famous astrologer of the early twentieth century, wrote that the Sun signifies your individuality and the Moon signifies your personality. Other astrologers define the Sun's influence as a vital force and the Moon as an unconscious force. In essence, the Moon represents the side of you that reacts before you have time to think.

The distinction in astrology between the influence of the Sun and the Moon is a forerunner of Sigmund Freud's theory of the ego and the id in human personality. According to Freud, the ego is a person's *consciousness* (symbolized in astrology by the Sun), and the id represents a person's *instinct* (the Moon).

In many ways your Moon personality is the one you keep hidden. Human beings tend to disapprove of instinctive behavior. We call it uncivilized, primitive, animalistic. Thus, in certain respects, your Moon personality is a part of yourself that you find disturbing. It is your inner core, which feels hate and jealousy, broods and is fearful, and has fantasies that you often deny even to yourself.

Of course, this is not the complete picture of the Moon's influence on your personality. It is also your Moon side that can spontaneously feel and express joy and pleasure, the side that reacts to emotional stimuli. It is the part of you that enjoys the little sensualities of life—the perfumed aroma of flowers, the smell of the grass after it rains, the delight of a long, hot shower. The Moon is inextricably linked to what might be called your reaction to your environment, for the Moon has rulership over the five senses—sight, hearing, taste, smell, and touch.

In astrology, the meaning of the Moon can become very esoteric. The Moon also stands for infancy, childhood, your dreams, memory, and your past. All these words might be summed up as your inner psyche. As the astrologer Landis Knight Green says, "The Moon is the threshold of the subconscious." Often your Moon personality is expressed in dreams—both the daydreams you brush aside as you go on with your daily responsibilities and the sleeping dreams that haunt your waking hours.

Because the Moon holds dominion over the emotional sphere, it influences your receptivity to others and also how others feel about you. Obviously, therefore, the Moon is an extremely important factor in love relationships. A strong and lasting bond is indicated in a relationship when the woman has her Moon in the same sign in which a man has his Sun. For example, if he is a Scorpio Sun sign and she has her Moon in Scorpio, they have an excellent chance of a long relationship because each will have a deep understanding of the other.

Many people ask me, "How can two people who have the *same* Sun sign be so different from each other?" I usually answer this question by asking another question: "What are the Moon signs of these two people?"

Let's take a brief look at two well-known Sagittarian entertainers: Woody Allen and Bette Midler. They were born on the same day, December 1—Woody Allen in 1935 and Bette Midler in 1944. In both people we see the strong Sagittarius qualities of humor, independence, frankness, and a candid openness of expression. Woody Allen has a brilliant, funny, barbed wit that appeals to intellectuals. He is an auteur who produces, writes, directs, and stars in his own films made totally outside the studio system. Bette Midler began her career doing over-the-edge comedy routines in the bathhouses of lower Manhattan, playing to mostly homosexual audiences. She has gone on to major stardom in films, stage, and television, as a comedian, singer, and dramatic actress—always playing someone a bit outrageous, wacky, and rule-bending. Both entertainers have had long careers in which they broke free of boundaries and expressed their forward-thinking ideas through a sense of humor.

Let's look further: Woody Allen has his Moon in Aquarius. He displays the rebellious attitude of the free-thinking Aquarius-Moon person who lives life his own way. In his politics, creative work, and private life he is controversial, radical, and progressive. He also exhibits the emotional detachment of an Aquarius Moon. His film roles are not deeply passionate; his characters speak trenchantly about the human condition, but don't grab the audience's emotions. Instead, they offer Aquarian intellectual stimulation and tickle the funnybone. Aquarius-Moon people can coldly break off relationships, and the public has witnessed this in Woody Allen's ongoing private soap operas with the women in his life.

Bette Midler has her Moon in Cancer, and in her we see an emotional quality. She communicates great feeling in her work, and her characters exhibit a certain Cancerian vulnerability. She plays lovable, spunky, and endearing women who reach out and care for others (a Cancer-Moon specialty). As a singer, Bette Midler has recorded hit songs that have a deeply emotional appeal, including "The Wind Beneath My Wings," a song about being supported by love (a Cancer-Moon theme). In her private life (which in Cancer-Moon fashion she keeps private), she has been in a stable and enduring marriage and raised a family.

Throughout history the Moon has been studied, revered, and worshipped. In ancient civilizations the Moon deity (usually a goddess) reigned side by side with the Sun. In some religions the Moon was even more powerful than the Sun because it dispensed wisdom and spiritual knowledge. The Romans set aside a sacred feast day for the Moon. The name for it persists to modern times, though we now call it Monday rather than Moon Day.

Scientists are still studying the Moon's power over plant life, tides, emotions, fertility, menstruation, biorhythms, and crime. Astrologers continue to find new and subtle ways in which the Moon influences our daily lives.

The Moon in your horoscope modifies your Sun sign; it brings new forces, different motivations, and special elements to the character of your Sun sign. Your Sun sign personality and Moon sign personality are a blend, a marriage. As in a marriage, disparate elements sometimes work together to form a compatible partnership, each lending the other its strengths. But sometimes there is conflict in which opposing traits collide with each other.

If you feel that you are in constant conflict with yourself—if you feel you are two different people torn and pulled by each other—astrology can help you. Study both your Sun sign and Moon sign. Learn the positive and negative sides to these signs and try to recognize these elements within yourself. You may find that with a deeper understanding of the forces that motivate you, you will learn to be less hard on yourself and to reconcile what seems to be a confusing whirl of contradictions. On the other hand, if your Sun and Moon are in the same sign, you will probably find the characteristics of that sign doubly reinforced in your personality.

Know thyself. This is what the ancient Greeks carved on the temple at Delphi. It is an ideal that human beings have struggled toward for thousands of years. It is what astrology can teach us.

What Is Your Moon Sign?

To find out your Moon sign, look up your year and month of birth in the Moon Tables starting on page 429.

MOON IN ARIES

A Moon in Aries modifies your Sun sign in this way:

THE BRIGHT SIDE OF ARIES MOON You are more energetic, enterprising, optimistic, open to change, idealistic.

THE DARK SIDE OF ARIES MOON You are more impulsive, opinionated, domineering, impatient, vain.

ARIES IS AN ACTIVE, FIERY SIGN, but the Moon is cool and passive. This disparity gives great brilliance and sharpness to the senses, but also results in a nervous temperament. If you have the Moon in Aries, you have a high-strung disposition. Your sense-impressions of the world around you are swift and instantaneous, and you never doubt them for a moment. As a result, you tend to be very sure of your opinions and don't like it when people question or contradict you.

Patience is not your long suit. You won't spend time laboriously wading through details; you prefer to plunge right in and see what happens.

In the vibrant sign of Aries, the Moon endows you with charm, vivacity, and a special knack for getting others to do what you want. You are extremely fond of talking (about almost anything) and sound knowledgeable on a wide range of subjects. But you have a short attention span. Although enthusiasm and energy abound, the long, hard necessity of really performing often causes you to fall short of your goal. But you are quick to pick yourself up and move on to something new and exciting, leaving the old project to wither away. However, if you are pursuing a goal you really have your heart set on, you will drive yourself to the limit of your endurance.

Where you really excel is on the social scene. You are able both to stimulate and to delight, and no party should be without the wit and sparkle of an Aries Moon. In addition, you are generous when you feel kindly disposed toward someone. You give unselfishly of your time, attention, concern, and even your money. However, a Moon-Arien who feels slighted or unappreciated will sulk and pout and complain about the world's harsh treatment.

On the plus side, you have a great passion for life. A basic optimism underlies your personality, and unless your Sun is in a water sign (Cancer, Scorpio, Pisces), you don't hold a grudge for long. Your most striking characteristic is a hatred of restriction. You will do what you want without any interference, thank you. Because you resent advice, you rarely are willing to listen to other people's opinions. This obviously has its drawbacks. But in a situation in which a decision must be made instantly, no one is more decisive and forceful than you. You perform best under pressure and handle emergencies as quickly as a firefighter answering an alarm bell.

In emotional relationships you struggle against being tied down or dominated. You have to be the one in control. You demand freedom in a relationship, but this is exactly what you won't give in return. You insist on being the center of your lover's attention. You want to be loved passionately, and you want love to be always exciting and romantic. If an affair dwindles into ordinariness, you quickly grow dissatisfied and restless.

The sign of Aries symbolically represents a fork in the road, and the lives of Moon-in-Aries people are marked by sudden change. They often reach positions of authority and are successful in the world of business and government. As a Moon-Arien the essence of your emotional life is the love of the chase. You view life as a grand quest, and impulsively pursue love, success and attention from others. The chase, in fact, is far more satisfying than the prize itself. Achieving the prize is never as thrilling as *wanting* the prize and galvanizing your energy into going after it.

No matter what your Sun sign may be, an Aries Moon confers a quality of self-confidence and an adventurous spirit that runs through your personality. If your Sun is in a fire sign (Aries, Leo, Sagittarius), an Aries Moon underlines your impulsiveness and enhances your magnetic ability to sway others; you have great dash and energy. If your Sun is in an air sign (Gemini, Libra, Aquarius), an Aries Moon bestows a shrewd intellect and persuasive powers of expression. If your Sun is in an earth sign (Taurus, Virgo, Capricorn), an Aries Moon accentuates your leadership ability and lends your personality a certain positiveness and advanced outlook. If your Sun is in a water sign (Cancer, Scorpio, Pisces), an Aries Moon emphasizes imagination and intensity; you have an increased ability to create striking original work.

Whatever your Sun sign, an Aries Moon confers quickness of mind, an outspoken nature, and an inability to live under other people's strictures.

FAMOUS PEOPLE WITH THE MOON IN ARIES

Dante Alighieri	Charles de Gaulle	Friedrich Nietzsche
Leonard Bernstein	Isadora Duncan	Jacqueline Kennedy Onassis
Marlon Brando	Bobby Fischer	Albert Schweitzer
Robert Browning	Bill Gates	Robespierre
Al Capone	Henry VIII	Mark Twain
Salvador Dalí	Whitney Houston	Stevie Wonder

♉ MOON IN TAURUS

A Moon in Taurus modifies your Sun sign in this way:

THE BRIGHT SIDE OF TAURUS MOON You are more trustworthy, determined, warm, affectionate, artistic.

THE DARK SIDE OF TAURUS MOON You are more obstinate, possessive, rigid, overcautious, a slave to routine.

THE MOON IS AT ITS BEST in Taurus (in astrological terminology, the Moon is exalted in this sign). The stable sign of Taurus steadies and strengthens the Moon's otherwise changeable, erratic influence. The Moon in this position gives you great powers of concentration. You live your life the way you tackle a job: systematically and getting it done right. Whereas others complicate their lives, when you're confronted with a problem you look for the most effective way to deal with it, and even if it's personally painful for you, you get it handled.

The sign of Taurus also brings out the quiet, reflective qualities of the Moon: you carefully ponder the sense-impressions you receive from the world around you before you reach a conclusion. With a Moon in Taurus you do not form opinions quickly and are quite the opposite of impressionable. It takes a while for you to come to a decision—you must be sure of all the facts—but when you do there is no way to make you change your mind. One can't change a Moon-Arien's mind either, but the difference here is that Aries Moon quickly reaches its decision. With a Taurus Moon you take your time assimilating information. Once you have done that, you will purposefully, relentlessly, and unchangeably follow your course.

Taurus is the astrological sign of earthly possessions, and a Moon in Taurus indicates a person who is resourceful, someone who gathers material things. As a Moon-in-Taurus person, you are also blessed in that you seem to have the least emotional problems of any Moon sign. This may be because Taurus is practical and positive in its outlook, as well as methodical, patient, and responsible. Small wonder that history is dotted with the achievements of lunar Taureans. A few among many are William Shakespeare, Karl Marx, and John Milton.

The sign of Taurus is ruled by Venus, planet of romance and the arts, and a Moon in this beauty-loving sign endows you with a keen artistic sense. You are romantic, have elegant manners, and usually display a distinctive style of dressing. The Moon is a sensual influence and in Taurus indicates a great love of creature comforts. You enjoy serene surroundings, the pleasures of a luxurious home, the joys of good dining. Although socially adept, you dislike big parties and large, noisy groups. Your idea of a wonderful evening is a small, candlelit dinner party at home with four close friends.

In love, lunar Taureans are the one-man/one-woman type, and are happiest in a close, committed union. Sometimes it may seem otherwise (especially if the Sun is in a flirtatious or highly sexed sign), but at heart Taurus-Moon wants the comfort of a committed relationship. Your security is heightened by sharing your home and pleasures with the person you love and who, in turn, is devoted to you. You look for a true soulmate, and when you find him or her you happily and faithfully settle down.

The other side of the coin is that a Moon-Taurean has a tendency to stay too long in an unhappy love affair or marriage. Because of your need for security and resistance to change, you shut yourself off from new experiences and settle for what you have.

No matter what your Sun sign may be, the Taurus-Moon qualities of patience and determination run through your character. If your Sun is in an earth sign (Taurus, Virgo, Capricorn), your remarkable endurance is underlined by the stability and persistence of a Taurus Moon; this is an excellent combination to achieve success and material wealth. If your Sun is in a water sign (Cancer, Scorpio, Pisces), a Taurus Moon heightens your personal magnetism and gives strength and perseverance to your creative imagination. If your Sun is in an air sign (Gemini, Libra, Aquarius), a Taurus Moon gives you firm resolve and inclines your intellectual powers toward practical, moneymaking pursuits. If your Sun is in a fire sign (Aries, Leo, Sagittarius), a Taurus Moon adds to your physical strength and your fiery exuberance, and gives your personality great force and the ability to win popularity with the public.

Whatever your Sun sign, a Taurus Moon gives you endurance, a conservative outlook, and a sensitive, sensual personality that needs love and security.

FAMOUS PEOPLE WITH THE MOON IN TAURUS

Bjorn Borg	Katharine Hepburn	John Milton
Bill Clinton	Hubert Humphrey	Joe Namath
Prince Charles	Mick Jagger	Gregory Peck
F. Scott Fitzgerald	Carl Jung	Ronald Reagan
Greta Garbo	Frida Kahlo	George Bernard Shaw
Billy Graham	Peter Sellers	William Shakespeare
Che Guevara	Karl Marx	C. P. Snow

Ⅱ
MOON IN GEMINI

A Moon in Gemini modifies your Sun sign in this way:

THE BRIGHT SIDE OF GEMINI MOON You are more versatile, witty, charming, lively, amusing.

THE DARK SIDE OF GEMINI MOON You are more disorganized, inconsistent, superficial, cunning, manipulative.

IN THE LIVELY, RESTLESS SIGN of Gemini the Moon's sway becomes more mutable and erratic. This does not make all Moon-in-Gemini children flighty, frivolous, and frenetic, but almost always indicates an active mind, an imaginative and creative personality, and someone who is inclined toward intellectual pursuits. If you have a Moon in this position you are extraordinarily quick to receive sensory impressions from the outside world. You rapidly sift through information and make your judgments. Because Gemini is a mental sign, your snap decisions tend to be more intellectual than emotional. It is not that you are unfeeling, simply that your immediate reaction to stimuli is on a mental plane.

You are a fast learner, probably have a high IQ, and are an excellent critic, for you have an ability both to analyze and to verbalize. A Moon in the communicative sign of Gemini inclines you toward loquaciousness and endows you with great personal charm. You have enchanting vivacity that draws others to you. Conversations with you tend to run off on unexpected tangents and take sudden turns and reverses. At heart, a lunar Gemini is essentially restless and needs constant stimulation. If forced to be indoors or solitary or inactive, you are unhappy and should try to set aside a part of the day to get out and be among people.

A Moon in Gemini makes you extremely impressionable to the changing scene around you. Skill in speaking and writing predisposes many lunar Geminis to become writers, teachers, and journalists. John Keats, Rudyard Kipling, Jack London, and George Bernard Shaw are only a few famous Moon-Geminis of the past.

As a Moon-in-Gemini person you are always mentally assessing what you are feeling. You tend to dissect your feelings and emotions to analyze why you think this way or behave that way. The most famous lunar Gemini who possessed this quality is Sigmund Freud. Freud also had his Sun in Taurus and Scorpio Rising, giving him extraordinary tenacity and depth of insight.

You are quick-witted and vibrant, and when you come across a new fact or a different way of looking at something, you are likely to undergo a change of mind. One can't count on your firm convictions, but your openness to life makes you a fascinating companion.

In emotional relationships lunar Geminis display a certain free spirit. Here is where you are most intensely restless. You resent being subject to the whims and vagaries of other people's emotions, and struggle to retain independence. At the same time, you search for the "perfect" love, which of course does not exist. If your would-be lover is elusive or hard to figure out, this especially piques your interest. The Moon-in-Gemini personality is high-strung. You have a streak of discontent that sometimes shows up as irritability and snappishness. On the other hand, you are amusing, witty, and have a wonderful sense of humor. When you are in the right mood you are a delight to be with.

At times your talent can be stymied by the fact that you lose interest in things so quickly and drop what you so eagerly began. You thrive on travel, change, and meeting different kinds of personalities. In business, your best qualities are versatility and a winning way with people. You perform very well when linked in partnership with someone practical and hardheaded. Having to make a final decision is torture for you; you need a strong, decisive partner.

No matter what your Sun sign may be, the Gemini-Moon qualities of versatility and intellectualism can be discerned in your personality. If your Sun is in an air sign (Gemini, Libra, Aquarius), your keen intelligence is accentuated by a Gemini Moon and you have a superb gift of self-expression. If your Sun is in a water sign (Cancer, Scorpio, Pisces), your emotional nature is sharpened by the Gemini-Moon mental acumen; you have strong creative instincts and a talent for research. If your Sun is in an earth sign (Taurus, Virgo, Capricorn), a Gemini Moon gives you quickness of mind that you can use in a practical way in combination with your Sun sign persistency. If your Sun is in a fire sign (Aries, Leo, Sagittarius), a Gemini Moon bestows high mentality that combined with your passion and adventurism indicates superior leadership ability.

Whatever your Sun sign, a Moon in Gemini imparts a witty intellect, an independent spirit, and an imaginative sparkle to your personality.

FAMOUS PEOPLE WITH THE MOON IN GEMINI

Fred Astaire	Steffi Graf	Mary Pickford
Joan Baez	Buddy Holly	George Bernard Shaw
Brigitte Bardot	John Keats	Spencer Tracy
Jack Benny	Rudyard Kipling	Queen Victoria
Pablo Casals	Gypsy Rose Lee	Barbara Walters
Bette Davis	Jack London	Andy Warhol
Sigmund Freud	Louis Pasteur	Christopher Wren

69

Moon in Cancer

A Moon in Cancer modifies your Sun sign in this way:

THE BRIGHT SIDE OF CANCER MOON You are more imaginative, sympathetic, protective, tenacious, loyal.

THE DARK SIDE OF CANCER MOON You are more possessive, moody, critical, self-pitying, a nag.

The Moon is in its natural home in Cancer, for this is the sign that the Moon rules. Here the best qualities of the Moon—devotion, patience, sensitivity—are brought out. The romantic, intuitive sign of Cancer and the sensuous, receptive Moon are in harmony with each other. If you have the Moon in Cancer you have strong emotions and perceive the world around you through your feelings rather than your intellect. However, because you do not openly show your feelings, it is sometimes difficult for others to figure out where they stand with you.

In general, you are more receptive than active. You store away impressions, reactions, and information until the time comes when you can use them. Lunar Cancerians often excel in an artistic or literary way. Jean-Paul Sartre, Lord Byron, and Ethel Barrymore are famous and typical Moon-Cancerians. Imaginative and creative, you work best when you set your own pace and are not subject to the tyranny of time clocks.

Any impression that sinks into your mind makes an indelible mark. You have an extremely retentive memory. Lunar Cancerians are often found in professions where memory plays an important role: historians, teachers, actors, writers. Famous Moon-Cancerians in these walks of life

are Franklin Delano Roosevelt, Benjamin Spock, Humphrey Bogart, and Harrison Ford.

At heart, you are refined, delicate, and gentle. You may appear to be aggressive and forceful, especially if your Sun or Mars is in a fire sign (Aries, Leo, Sagittarius), but underneath you are vulnerable and easily hurt. You tend to let your feelings fester, and indeed, touchiness, moodiness, and a kind of quiet self-pity always lie near the surface. Though you are subject to greater mood swings than other Moon signs, your ups and downs don't last long. If you are left alone for a while, the dark clouds will soon blow away. One of the most striking characteristics of Cancer is the continual ebb and flow of emotions, which combined with the waxing and waning influence of the Moon produces quick shifts in temperament and at times makes you emotionally exhausted.

You are at your best in a deep and committed love relationship. Unfortunately, you often have to go through an unhappy love affair before you find the contentment and security you seek. Even though you are motivated strongly by your feelings, in a curious way you are also afraid of them. It is your nature to mistrust love, to feel you are somehow unworthy of someone else's devotion. You will hold on too long to a relationship that's destructive because deep in your psyche you don't believe you'll ever find another love. You also believe that to be alone is a fate worse than death. Very often early in life a Moon-in-Cancer person must go through an emotional trial. But when at last you find love that feeds your soul and you feel secure, your personality blossoms.

You have a tendency to hold on possessively to a loved one, and a knack for subtly instilling guilt in someone you love, usually to test the person's depth of feeling. However, among your most endearing traits are intense loyalty and dedication.

No matter what your Sun sign may be, the Cancer-Moon qualities of creativity and emotionalism will be evident in your personality. If your Sun is in a water sign (Cancer, Scorpio, Pisces), your intensity and depth of feeling are accentuated by a Cancer Moon; you have superb intuition and almost hypnotic power in creative work. If your Sun is in an earth sign (Taurus, Virgo, Capricorn), you have unshakable loyalty and strong passions under the influence of a Cancer Moon; this combination gives you an ability to capture the imagination of the public. If your Sun is in an air sign (Gemini, Libra, Aquarius), a Cancer Moon gives your intellectualism a magnetic, daring quality; you have the ability to touch other people's feelings. If your Sun is in a fire sign (Aries, Leo, Sagittarius), a Cancer Moon directs your enthusiasm and energy into creative channels; you have a flair for drama and the theater.

Whatever your Sun sign, a Moon in Cancer gives you sensitivity and imagination, enormous personal charisma, and a warmhearted, romantic nature.

FAMOUS PEOPLE WITH THE MOON IN CANCER

Humphrey Bogart	Clark Gable	Isaac Newton
Lord Byron	Farrah Fawcett	Eleanor Roosevelt
Tom Cruise	Aretha Franklin	Franklin Delano Roosevelt
Phyllis Diller	Janis Joplin	Jean-Paul Sartre
Ralph Waldo Emerson	Princess Margaret of England	Paul Simon
Harrison Ford	Bette Midler	Benjamin Spock

♌

MOON IN LEO

A Moon in Leo modifies your Sun sign in this way:

THE BRIGHT SIDE OF LEO MOON You are more exuberant, creative, broad-minded, colorful, fun-loving.

THE DARK SIDE OF LEO MOON You are more self-indulgent, self-centered, conceited, overbearing, bullying.

IN THE MAGNETIC, flamboyant sign of Leo the Moon's power is positive and robust, and even its dark side is less dark than in other signs. Leo is a wonderful placement for the Moon because it gives great warmth and stability to the Moon's influence; it also imparts an idealistic quality.

If you have the Moon in Leo you have strong emotions and can be reached through your heart rather than your head. You are a quick and accurate learner when your feelings are involved. But if a subject does not arouse your affections, you have no interest in exploring it further. The sensory impressions you receive from the world around you come to you on an emotional level. In order to make you change your mind, someone first has to change how you *feel*.

One of your most striking characteristics is a refusal to be hampered by other people's rules. You tend to be extremely intelligent and are hospitable to new ideas, but you have little sympathy for petty or narrow thinking. You like to be the center of attention and enjoy taking on public roles. You are highly expressive, and are especially drawn to the world of theater, music, painting, and the arts. In a way, it might be said that you, like all lunar Leos, have a "show biz" personality.

You possess a wonderful sense of humor and great personal charm, which makes you fun to be with. There is a sense of excitement about you. If nothing is happening that is interesting or amusing, you'll try to create it. Sincere, open, very sociable, you have a way of lifting the spirits of people around you.

Moon-in-Leo people work very well in group enterprises because they have a talent for inspiring people to do their best. Your immediate reaction to a problem is to confront it rather than sit around moping about it. A natural leader, you often feel you have a mission in life. Sometimes you may become bossy and overbearing—you are an order-giver rather than an order-taker—but at heart you are so cheerful and enthusiastic that people find it easy to forgive you. You have a fund of optimism and energy that others draw upon.

Vanity is a chief weakness; you are a sucker for anyone who can deliver an artful compliment. You always need an audience and are inordinately fond of attention. It must also be said that you will probably get more than your share of attention because the Moon in Leo imparts a lovable quality to your personality.

You are drawn to the luxuries of life—good food, fine

wines, striking clothes. You are an excellent host or hostess who delights in giving glittering parties. Unless Taurus or Capricorn is prominent in the horoscope, a Moon-Leo will always pick up the check. Fortunately, you usually are able to pay for your extravagant tastes.

In love, you are a great romantic, yet your flamboyant romanticism would never be sparked by someone who won't make you look good. You need a partner who sets you off to best advantage and keeps up your image to the world. Your tendency is to put the object of your affection on a pedestal, to credit a lover with superlative virtues that may have no basis in reality. When a lover does not live up to your expectations you are disappointed—not only because you take love seriously but because your lover always becomes an extension of yourself, and his or her failure to be wonderful is very wounding to your pride and ego. Also, though you are jealous and possessive toward your loved ones, you yourself are flirtatious and a bit of a rover

because you need everyone to admire you. You are an attention addict.

No matter what your Sun sign may be, the Leo-Moon qualities of warmth, vitality, and charisma will appear in your personality. If your Sun is in a fire sign (Aries, Leo, Sagittarius), a Leo Moon accentuates your creativity and leadership abilities. If your Sun is in an air sign (Gemini, Libra, Aquarius), a Leo Moon lends a dynamic, compelling quality to your people-oriented personality. If your Sun is in an earth sign (Taurus, Virgo, Capricorn), a Leo Moon gives you an even stronger passionate nature and good moneymaking skills. If your Sun is in a water sign (Cancer, Scorpio, Pisces), a Leo Moon heightens your already powerful emotional impact on others.

Whatever your Sun sign, a Moon in Leo gives you dignity, an affectionate, outgoing nature, and an instinct for leadership.

FAMOUS PEOPLE WITH THE MOON IN LEO

P. T. Barnum	Tom Hanks	Prince Philip
Pearl Buck	James Joyce	Margaret Chase Smith
Clint Eastwood	Mao Tse-tung	Diane Sawyer
Queen Elizabeth II	Paul McCartney	Gloria Steinem
Ralph Waldo Emerson	Ralph Nader	Oscar Wilde

♍ MOON IN VIRGO

A Moon in Virgo modifies your Sun sign in this way:

THE BRIGHT SIDE OF VIRGO MOON You are more intellectual, meticulous, industrious, steadfast, responsible.

THE DARK SIDE OF VIRGO MOON You are more critical, high-strung, standoffish, argumentative, hypochrondriac.

THE SIGN OF VIRGO stabilizes the shifting effect of the Moon. Virgo is the sign of intelligence and practicality, which gives a sharp analytical bent to the Moon's influence. If you have the Moon in Virgo you have a fine, discriminating mind. You do not pursue knowledge merely for the sake of learning; you figure out how to use what you learn. Your immediate reaction to the sense-impressions you receive from the world around you is to analyze what you have just seen and heard. You are meticulous in sifting through information and you tend to question whatever is told to you. Moon-Virgos are sometimes so skeptical they don't even believe in what they see with their own eyes. You love to discuss ideas and probe into opinions held by others, though you yourself hold fast to preconceived notions. You are not so stubborn, though, that you will hold on to a theory once the facts prove you wrong. You are a seeker of truth, and you believe truth is what is left after falsehoods have been exposed.

No one would call you a Pollyanna or the kind who looks at the world through rose-colored glasses. It's not that you are dour or pessimistic, it's just that you deal with life as it is. This practical realism makes you good at business and at handling money. Your eye is on the long-term profit rather than immediate gain, and you are concerned with security and providing for your old age.

As a Moon-in-Virgo person you bring an extra touch of perfectionism and professionalism to everything you do. Methodical in your approach to problems, you figure out exactly what needs to be done and then tackle the issue a step at a time. But you have a tendency to worry, to fret over the things that might go wrong and try to cover all contingencies. You think that too much good work is ruined by the lack of just a little more effort, so you don't spare yourself and are often fussy and critical with others.

Logic is the discipline you live by, and you find it frustrating to deal with minds that are illogical or scatterbrained. You think such people belong in Disneyland, not in the real world. Discriminating in the people you choose for friends, you are also selective about the cultural activities you take part in. There is a certain judgmental quality that you bring to almost any situation. No experience washes over you aimlessly; you always learn a lesson from it.

Moon-in-Virgo women are sometimes thought of as

unfeminine because they are usually so efficient, thorough, and well organized—qualities that most people don't associate with the word "feminine." Both male and female of this Moon sign are reserved and shrink from sentimentality or gushiness, and therefore are often perceived as cold. In truth, the less developed types who pick other people apart and exhibit a stingy pettiness *are* cold. Generally, however, Virgo-Moon people are caring and giving in practical ways; one can count on them. Virgo is the sign of service, and lunar Virgos want to be useful to others.

In matters of love Virgo-Moon people don't have a lot of self-confidence. One might think that the ideal mate for you would be someone intelligent, logical, nice looking, and neat, but how many can marry a clone? Actually, you are attracted to people who are quite unlike you—more emotional and effusive, less calculating, more readily able to express their feelings. In love relationships, Virgo-Moon people take on the role of a critical but caring parent. Unconsciously, lunar Virgos are afraid of anger and feeling

vulnerable, and tend to live in the illusion that their love lives are calm, stable, and under control.

No matter what your Sun sign may be, the Virgo-Moon qualities of caution and seriousness show up in your personality. If your Sun is in an earth sign (Taurus, Virgo, Capricorn), practicality and industriousness are even more pronounced; you are also very money-conscious. If your Sun is in a fire sign (Aries, Leo, Sagittarius), Virgo Moon brings strength and endurance to support your expansive creativity; this is an excellent combination for politicians and people in the theater. If your Sun is in an air sign (Gemini, Libra, Aquarius), Virgo Moon contributes an even sharper intelligence and a flair for original work. If your Sun is in a water sign (Cancer, Scorpio, Pisces), Virgo Moon lends greater dimension to your emotional nature, for you are blessed with a rare combination of psychic truth and hardheaded realism.

Whatever your Sun sign, a Moon in Virgo gives you keen mental powers, a strong vein of common sense, and an intelligent, thoughtful approach to life.

FAMOUS PEOPLE WITH THE MOON IN VIRGO

Ingrid Bergman	William Faulkner	Edward M. Kennedy
Andrew Carnegie	Gabriel Garcia Marquez	John F. Kennedy
Winston Churchill	Mel Gibson	Shirley MacLaine
Bill Cosby	William Randolph Hearst	J. Pierpont Morgan
Marlene Dietrich	Lyndon B. Johnson	Leo Tolstoy

MOON IN LIBRA

A Moon in Libra modifies your sun sign in this way:

THE BRIGHT SIDE OF LIBRA MOON You are more adaptable, creative, charming, good-natured, diplomatic.

THE DARK SIDE OF LIBRA MOON You are more indecisive, self-indulgent, dependent, frivolous, changeable.

LIBRA IS THE SIGN of esthetic perceptions, and here the Moon's romantic, glamorous influence is accentuated. If you have the Moon in Libra you have a keen appreciation for beauty and art, and an artistic eye unmatched by any other Moon sign. You also have a heightened awareness of your environment and of other people. However, what you truly value are those experiences that make life more beautiful and pleasing. You abhor coarseness, vulgarity, or strife. Your immediate reaction to anything unpleasant is to deny it, or, if that is impossible, at least to put it in its best possible light. You try to surround yourself with comfort and lovely *objets* in a tranquil and luxurious environment. If it were possible, you would live forever in a flower-filled room with soft music playing in the background.

Because you enjoy beautiful things, you are happy to spend your (and sometimes other people's) money on possessions that catch your fancy. You are the kind who will walk into a shop and instantly spot the perfect thing to go with what you have in a closet at home. The presentation and ritual surrounding a thing is as important to you as the thing itself. A meal served on fine china and crystal with embroidered linens, flowers, and candles on the table is as important as the taste of the food itself.

The Moon in the balanced sign of Libra endows you with an open, independent mind that tries to evaluate the world dispassionately and rationally. A Moon in Libra also confers great personal charm and enhances the ability to get along with people. You are marvelous at understanding the other person's point of view (though you never lose sight of your own self-interest). For the most part you are pleasing and easy to live with and have a genial disposition. Libra is the astrological sign of partnership, and as a Moon native you function well in that relationship. Very often your destiny is tied up with a strong and influential person with whom you form a connection early in life. To a large extent, what you accomplish depends on other people.

Essentially you love with your head rather than your heart. There is something a bit calculated about your carefully balanced emotional nature. To become your lover, a person has to possess certain qualities, such as good looks and elegant social manners. It is not that you are unemotional, but love is more an esthetic pleasure than steamy passion. You try to create something beautiful—fanciful if need be—from every intimacy. You may go through a number of affairs and marriages before you finally settle down with someone with whom you are mentally compatible (more necessary to you than sexual compatibility). When you are in a contented marriage, it is a source of great satisfaction to you because it answers your need for security and reassurance, and you truly enjoy sharing.

No matter what your Sun sign may be, the Libra-Moon qualities of refinement and grace can be traced in your character. If your Sun is in an air sign (Gemini, Libra, Aquarius), Libra Moon accentuates your keen mentality and gives you an unsurpassed ability to win favor with other people. If your Sun is in an earth sign (Taurus, Virgo, Capricorn), Libra Moon endows your strength of purpose with a creative bent; this is a winning combination for entrepreneurs and those dealing with the public. If your Sun is in a water sign (Cancer, Scorpio, Pisces), Libra Moon underlines the intuitive, imaginative side of your personality and gives a strong, balanced intellectual approach. If your Sun is in a fire sign (Aries, Leo, Sagittarius), Libra Moon heightens your magnetism and flair, and aids your ability to put original ideas into successful action.

Whatever your Sun sign, a Moon in Libra gives you a polished, charming manner with people, an instinct for fairness, and artistic vision.

FAMOUS PEOPLE WITH THE MOON IN LIBRA

Marie Antoinette
Louis Armstrong
Arthur Ashe
Elizabeth Barrett Browning
Maria Callas
Frederic Chopin
Agatha Christie
Walt Disney

Amelia Earhart
Henry Fonda
Rose Kennedy
Rudolph Nureyev
Sylvia Plath
Sydney Poitier
Wallis Simpson, Duchess of
   Windsor

Bruce Springsteen
Sylvester Stallone
Twyla Tharp
Henri de Toulouse-Lautrec
Lana Turner
Rudolph Valentino

♏

MOON IN SCORPIO

A Moon in Scorpio modifies your Sun sign in this way:

THE BRIGHT SIDE OF SCORPIO MOON You are more imaginative, determined, ambitious, emotional, idealistic.

THE DARK SIDE OF SCORPIO MOON You are more obstinate, secretive, jealous, resentful, domineering.

SCORPIO IS THE ASTROLOGICAL sign of death and regeneration, also of extremes of emotion. The effect of Scorpio is to underline the Moon's sensuous power and at the same time bring out its forcefulness. If you have the Moon in Scorpio you have a spiritual nature and intense feelings that motivate your actions.

You are very clever at hiding your true feelings. A Moon in Scorpio is one of the more difficult lunar positions. Though you are driven by strong passions you tend to deny that they are your motivation. You often disapprove of your emotions (for example, your anger or jealousy), and therefore keep your reactions hidden under a calm, agreeable surface. You can exercise great self-control. If an experience becomes painful, you cut yourself off from your feelings (in effect, kill your pain) rather than continue to suffer. You particularly dread any form of rejection.

Your ability to deaden feelings allows you to feel in control, but it is also the path to slow destruction of the spirit. In Scorpio, the lesson of finding your Moon's true potential for wisdom and self-mastery is often difficult. Basically, you must learn to let go emotionally and *feel*

your pain, and through the experience expand your phenomenal ability to love.

A Moon-in-Scorpio person possesses enormous willpower and acute powers of observation. Your judgments are shrewd and accurate. You are blessed (and/or cursed) with a phenomenal memory. This is usually a great aid to you in your work, but it causes you to brood over an emotional wound or injury. Some Scorpio-Moon types will never forget and will wait years to get revenge. This does not necessarily mean that you are cruel and vengeful, but at any time in life you can instantly recall a slight to your pride—remember exactly what the other person said and how bitter you felt at the time.

Your persistence and determination enable you to rise above obstacles, and this Moon position unfortunately has more obstacles than others. There is usually a secret sorrow or trouble in the lives of Moon-Scorpios that very often concerns family problems or health. This lunar position creates a need for escape into fantasy, although higher Scorpio-Moon types use the spiritualism that is so much a part of this sign to do work that benefits humanity.

Though passion is always a factor with you, your sexuality can be sublimated in other areas, such as creative work or a career that demands self-sacrifice. Work is important to you, for it is through work and effort that you are best able to express yourself. You have high standards, and pride of craftsmanship is visible in all your endeavors. You tend to be ambitious and are endowed with executive ability. This is especially true if your Sun or Ascendant is in an earth sign (Taurus, Virgo, Capricorn).

Without even being aware of it you possess a sensuality that attracts the opposite sex. This is often a source of difficulty in your love life, and many lunar Scorpios marry more than once. A fear of being controlled is at the core of your relationship issues. For you to be in a position of emotional vulnerability puts you in a classic Scorpio deathlike situation, for to be unsafe means you are at the mercy of another person. It is almost impossible for you to put complete trust in someone else, and it takes a long time for you to commit yourself fully. The secret is your great need for emotional security and, in a sense, there is

no security that is secure enough. However, once you feel unthreatened, you are capable of deep love.

No matter what your Sun sign may be, the Scorpio-Moon qualities of persistence and intensity run through your personality. If your Sun is in a water sign (Cancer, Scorpio, Pisces), a Scorpio Moon confers energy and creativity, a true gift for turning a dream into reality once you set your mind to it. If your Sun is in an earth sign (Taurus, Virgo, Capricorn), a Scorpio Moon accentuates your managerial talents and capacity for authority and leadership. If your Sun is in an air sign (Gemini, Libra, Aquarius), a Scorpio Moon bestows deep mental powers and an ability to captivate the public. If your Sun is in a fire sign (Aries, Leo, Sagittarius), a Scorpio Moon emphasizes your compelling personality, your vitality and drive for success.

Whatever your Sun sign, a Moon in Scorpio gives you a strong inner core of self-reliance, an arresting sensuality, and a magnetic flair for influencing others.

FAMOUS PEOPLE WITH THE MOON IN SCORPIO

Julie Andrews	Charles Chaplin	Alfred Hitchcock
Warren Beatty	Miles Davis	Henry Miller
Truman Capote	J. Paul Getty	Nelson Rockefeller
Jimmy Carter	George Harrison	Elizabeth Taylor

Moon in Sagittarius

A Moon in Sagittarius modifies your Sun sign in this way:

THE BRIGHT SIDE OF SAGITTARIUS MOON You are more adventurous, optimistic, exuberant, open-minded, sincere.

THE DARK SIDE OF SAGITTARIUS MOON You are more restless, extravagant, irresponsible, careless, uncommitted.

IN SAGITTARIUS, the Moon takes on a sparkle and brightness that it does not have in other signs. Sagittarius is the astrological sign of higher learning and breadth of vision. Here the Moon's influence loses its passivity. If you have the Moon in Sagittarius you are noted for your quick, sharp mind, extraordinary insights, and an ability to get things done in a flash. Your clear-thinking intelligence sifts through sensory impressions swiftly and with startling lucidity.

You are the kind of person who envisions great goals and then, undaunted by possible failure, sets about achieving them. You rarely listen to advice about pitfalls and drawbacks, nor do you wait to find out if a plan is impractical or unworkable. With energy and enthusiasm you rush in and usually accomplish what you set out to do. One reason for your success is your keen judgment. With a Moon in this sign of lofty vision, you have a way of seeing farther than people with the Moon in other signs.

As a Moon-Sagittarian you are fond of open spaces, travel, new people, different surroundings. Among your most winning traits is *adaptability*—to different kinds of personalities and to foreign and strange places. Your immediate reaction to a new experience is to explore and learn more. To you a chance to expand your horizons is always welcome, and you are not exclusively interested in making a profit. Money, in fact, does not stay long in your pocket or checking account. You feel that the whole purpose of money is to buy pleasure. You want to enjoy life.

At times you can be quite careless and reckless. Since you believe in your luck, you tend to abandon yourself to whatever fate has in store. You operate on the theory of optimistic fatalism. The danger is that you may push your luck too far. However, a setback does not keep you down for long. With renewed high spirits and a fresh outlook, you hitch up your wagon once more to the stars.

Because of your charm and geniality, you have a knack for making friends. You also have a witty way with words and a buoyant sense of humor. Your social gaiety sweeps others along on a tidal wave of goodwill. One of your most endearing qualities is your ability to perceive the best in people. When you criticize, you do so with such openness and candor that it is comparatively easy to take.

Unlike the other fire Moons (Moon-Aries and Moon-Leo), Moon-Sagittarians are not highly sexed and passionate. You look on love more as an adventure. You enjoy the thrill of discovery, the stimulating high of being in love, but you are unwilling to immerse yourself in deep emotional intensity. After a while your lovers may complain of your detachment or unreachableness. A perfect soulmate for you is someone who looks more outward than inward, and in time your love affairs become more like friendships. You are also noted for a roving eye and a refusal to be tied down to one person or one place. You need a lot of personal space and independence. This does not necessarily make you a bad marriage partner—you are a marvelous companion—it is just that you do have a certain lightheartedness about love and fidelity. Life to you means change and variety, and this attitude has a way of also applying to love.

No matter what your Sun sign may be, the Sagittarius-Moon qualities of optimism and expansion express themselves in your personality. If your Sun is in a fire sign (Aries, Leo, Sagittarius), a Sagittarius Moon accentuates your self-confidence, adventurous nature, and appetite for experience. If your Sun is in an air sign (Gemini, Libra, Aquarius), a Sagittarius Moon lends you vitality, enthusiasm, a keen intellect, and a talent for salesmanship. If your Sun is in an earth sign (Taurus, Virgo, Capricorn), you combine commonsense practicality with a lofty, creative outlook; this is an excellent position for people in politics and law. If your Sun is in a water sign (Cancer, Scorpio, Pisces), your emotional, imaginative personality is galvanized by the energy and philosophical vision of a Sagittarius Moon; this is a successful combination for writers and artists.

Whatever your Sun sign, a Sagittarius Moon gives you a love for learning, humanitarian instincts, and a gift for being an independent thinker.

FAMOUS PEOPLE WITH THE MOON IN SAGITTARIUS

Neil Armstrong	Albert Einstein	T. E. Lawrence
Anne Bancroft	Vincent van Gogh	Henri Matisse
Lewis Carroll	Bob Hope	Wolfgang Amadeus Mozart
Bing Crosby	Anthony Hopkins	Pablo Picasso
Charles Dickens	Howard Hughes	Oprah Winfrey

♑

Moon in Capricorn

A Moon in Capricorn modifies your Sun sign in this way:

THE BRIGHT SIDE OF CAPRICORN MOON You are more determined, responsible, disciplined, patient, committed.

THE DARK SIDE OF CAPRICORN MOON You are more rigid, pessimistic, opinionated, materialistic, overexacting.

CAPRICORN HAS BOTH a stabilizing and restrictive effect on the shifting influence of the Moon. The Moon represents the emotional, sympathetic side of a personality whereas Capricorn is an unemotional and undemonstrative sign. People with the Moon in this position have to overcome obstacles and complexities within their own natures to find the happiness they constantly seek.

If you have the Moon in Capricorn you have an alert mind and are very eager to learn. However, you are not interested in vague theory; you want to put your knowledge to use. An example of this talent for practical application is Thomas Edison, a Moon-Capricorn whose Sun was in Aquarius. In Edison we see the inventive, far-reaching vision of the Aquarian truth-seeker, but the focus of his work was to make his experiments useful, to put them into everyday utilization. His inventions of the telegraph, phonograph, electric light, and moving picture changed the way we live. Another example of a Capricorn-Moon is Gene Kelly, whose Sun was on the Leo-Virgo cusp. In his life we saw the creativity and exuberance of Leo, the hard work ethic of Virgo; his Capricorn Moon was evident in how he took his knowledge of dancing and applied it in a practical way to film choreography. In the process he in-troduced an entirely new genre of musical comedy and changed the very way such movies were filmed.

If you have a Moon in Capricorn you are organized, ambitious, and usually a prodigious worker. Self-sufficient and a bit solitary, you are haunted by a feeling of responsibility, of a task you must fulfill.

You are a determined person but your singlemindedness can sometimes turn into obsession. You pin your hopes on one idea, turn all your energies in one direction; if you fail you may suffer serious depression. Of course, because of their unshakable commitment, most lunar Capricorns succeed and often make an imprint on the world. Napoleon Bonaparte, George Washington, and Abraham Lincoln all had their Moon in Capricorn. Lunar Capricorns who have their Sun or Ascendant in one of the cardinal signs (Aries, Cancer, Libra, or Capricorn) have particularly auspicious auguries for leadership.

Money is important to you, not so much for what it can buy as for the status it bestows in the world of business, politics, finance, and high society where you wish to shine. You have charming social manners and an instinct for getting to know the right people.

Unknown to all but your closest intimates, you suffer

from feelings of insecurity and loneliness. Often you conceal this with a dry sense of humor. Your secret terror is of being abandoned or having someone you love cease to love you. You find it hard to reveal your deepest feelings and therefore may be perceived as being cold or calculating. For many lunar Capricorns, authority and power are a compensation for the difficulties they encounter in emotional areas.

Lunar Capricorns tend not to find true love in youth. Cautious and reserved, you tend to turn your feelings inward, and you need a lot of emotional reassurance before you allow them to be drawn out. You also have difficulty putting your complete trust in someone else. But at some point, usually when you are past thirty, you find the person you can become totally involved with, and then your love is durable. When you feel secure within an emotional relationship your commitment may last your entire lifetime. You are loyal and steadfast, generous and giving. In fact, you often give more than you get back. This is especially true about the relationships of female lunar Capricorns to their lovers and friends.

No matter what your Sun sign may be, the Capricorn Moon qualities of steadfastness and dedication manifest themselves in your personality. If your Sun is in an earth sign (Taurus, Virgo, Capricorn), a Capricorn Moon underlines your executive talent and ability to achieve great rewards; you have hidden depths to your character. If your Sun is in a water sign (Cancer, Scorpio, Pisces), a Capricorn Moon lends force and dynamism to your creativity; this is an excellent position for attracting wealth and fame. If your Sun is in an air sign (Gemini, Libra, Aquarius), a Capricorn Moon brings strength and intensity to your resourcefulness and encourages far-ranging interests; this is a good combination for people in communications, television, and publishing. If your Sun is in a fire sign (Aries, Leo, Sagittarius), a Capricorn Moon confers a special gift for authority and self-reliance; you have a mesmerizing personality.

Whatever your Sun sign, a Capricorn Moon gives you persistence, an ambitious and powerful personality, and an instinct for excellence.

FAMOUS PEOPLE WITH THE MOON IN CAPRICORN

Lucille Ball	Thomas Alva Edison	Robert Kennedy
Yogi Berra	Margot Fonteyn	Abraham Lincoln
Napoleon Bonaparte	John Glenn	Anaïs Nin
Johnny Carson	Ernest Hemingway	Stephen Sondheim
Dick Cavett	Gene Kelly	George Washington

MOON IN AQUARIUS

A Moon in Aquarius modifies your Sun sign in this way:

THE BRIGHT SIDE OF AQUARIUS MOON You are more idealistic, creative, tolerant, a humanitarian with a progressive outlook.

THE DARK SIDE OF AQUARIUS MOON You are more unpredictable, contrary, aloof, fixed in opinion, tactless.

AQUARIUS IS A MOST favorable sign for the Moon to be in, for here the Moon's influence confers admirable qualities of sensitivity and perception. Aquarius is the astrological sign of rational thinking and humanitarianism; in this sign the Moon's effect is to bestow clear logic with altruistic concerns. If you have the Moon in Aquarius you are rational, intuitive, and imaginative. Your senses are well balanced and accurate. Your immediate reaction to impressions you receive from the outside world is to deal with them in a scientific, open-minded way and at the same time try to understand them from the human point of view. There are no extremes of temperament in this lunar position. You are neither too emotional nor too cerebral; you are visionary but not eccentric.

A Moon-Aquarian has a wonderful gift for expression. You crackle with vitality, are a witty conversationalist, and make a delightful companion. Your friendliness charms all types of people—indeed, you're people-oriented, sociable, and outgoing, interested in other people's problems. However, unlike Moon water signs (Moon-Cancer, Moon-Scorpio, Moon-Pisces), you never become so emotionally involved that it changes your own life. There is a balance that runs through your relationships.

The passions of Aquarius-Moon people are passions of the mind. You are interested in ideas, philosophy, higher learning. You enjoy science and mathematics, as well as art, music, literature. Again, I repeat, you are not a person of extremes. You are well-rounded intellectually, for you have a wide range of interests in many different fields and associate with a large number of varied people.

Aquarius is the sign of future knowledge, and as a Moon-native you are interested in the unknown and what lies ahead. Many lunar Aquarians seem to be clairvoyant, to see things before they happen. On the other hand, you are not especially practical or down to earth. It can be said that you have a wide outlook but short sight. You tend to see things in terms of large concepts, but when it comes to the hard work and sweaty toil of turning a concept into a reality, you are likely to drift off in search of a new idea. Moon-Aquarians are often known as giants in promise and pygmies in performance. The unusual—in people, in places, and in projects—is what interests you most.

In love, lunar Aquarians have a butterfly quality—alighting for a while to sample an experience, flitting off to find something new. You are inclined to be somewhat ambivalent about love affairs. While you have a strong romantic streak, you also have a horror of being suffocated by another person's demands. You cannot bear possessive, jealous lovers, and you're often drawn to emotionally unavailable types. Unconsciously, you choose people who shun you; the less interested someone is in you, the more interested you become. In your early years you spend a lot of time trying to figure out what you want as opposed to what you *think* you want, swinging back and forth between romantic longing and feeling totally detached.

You seek a fine balance between commitment and independence, and many Aquarius-Moon people go through a number of unsatisfactory amours. When you do marry (often in later years), the relationship quickly becomes as much friend-and-companion as husband-and-wife. To you, the most important glue in a relationship is communication. In general, male lunar-Aquarians have a somewhat easier time emotionally than female Moon-Aquarians, apparently because it is still more socially acceptable for males to be intellectual and emotionally detached.

No matter what your Sun sign may be, the Aquarius-Moon qualities of intelligence and individualism run through your personality. If your Sun is in an air sign (Gemini, Libra, Aquarius), an Aquarius Moon emphasizes your superior mental gifts and ability to deal successfully with different kinds of personalities; this is a successful combination for people in the field of communication. If your Sun is in a fire sign (Aries, Leo, Sagittarius), an Aquarius Moon lends imagination and the common touch to your dynamic, exuberant forcefulness; this is a wonderful combination for people in public life. If your Sun is in an earth sign (Taurus, Virgo, Capricorn), an Aquarius Moon adds to your practicality a gift for innovation and original work; this placement is excellent for performing artists. If your Sun is in a water sign (Cancer, Scorpio, Pisces), an Aquarius Moon accentuates your imaginative, clairvoyant qualities; you have a unique talent for self-expression.

Whatever your Sun sign, an Aquarius Moon gives you an independent, stimulating mind, a persuasive charm with people, and a side to your personality that is always titillated by the unconventional.

FAMOUS PEOPLE WITH THE MOON IN AQUARIUS

Muhammad Ali	Arthur Conan Doyle	Eugene McCarthy
Woody Allen	George Gershwin	Marilyn Monroe
Fidel Castro	Cary Grant	Richard M. Nixon
Marc Chagall	Timothy Leary	Adlai Stevenson
Angela Davis	John Lennon	H. G. Wells
Diana, Princess of Wales	Sophia Loren	William Butler Yeats

♓

MOON IN PISCES

A Moon in Pisces modifies your Sun sign in this way:

THE BRIGHT SIDE OF PISCES MOON You are more compassionate, sensitive, loving, creative, loyal.

THE DARK SIDE OF PISCES MOON You are more indecisive, discontented, vague, secretive, easily confused.

PISCES AND THE MOON have a natural affinity; Pisces is the sign of depths of emotion, and the Moon represents your instinctive emotional reactions and sometimes your hidden dreams. Pisces is also the astrological sign of sorrow and self-undoing. If you have the Moon in Pisces you have deep feelings and an innate understanding of the human condition.

A peculiar danger for anyone with this Moon position is that the impressions received from the outside world will not accurately reflect the world as it is. Instead, they are filtered through an intense romanticism. Your instant reaction to stimuli is to interpret things as you would like them to be rather than as they are. You wear the reality-distorting glasses of the incurable optimist, the dreamer, the poet.

Your romantic emotionalism is not always apparent on the surface, for you try to keep this part of your nature well hidden. However, even the most pragmatic person with a Moon in Pisces feels the need to escape into a world of private imagination.

As a Moon-in-Pisces person you are artistic and have a keen love for beauty and the arts. Many Moon-Pisceans have a flair for acting, writing, composing, or painting.

Gifted with vision and imagination, you express yourself well in creative areas. It is through the senses and emotions rather than the intellect that you perceive things. You are extraordinarily intuitive and sometimes are gifted with psychic vision; you seem able to strip away the veil that separates the real world from the spiritual world, and to know things that others cannot comprehend.

In the real world, unfortunately, you do not always have an easy time. You tend to let your emotions get the better of you. Though you seem confident and completely in charge (especially if your Sun is in a fire sign [Aries, Leo, Sagittarius]), you have a weakness for letting those with strong wills and definite opinions lead you onto unsuitable paths.

Although you can work tirelessly and unselfishly for others, you find it hard to be strict and disciplined with yourself. Having to make final decisions causes you conflict and anxiety. There is a strong tendency to escape harsh realities and obligations. Sometimes you are perceived as gullible, but it is only your emotional nature that makes you appear that way. You are easy prey for unprincipled types who play on your tender feelings. It is an axiom in astrology that Moon-Pisceans are born under a special vibration that impels them to befriend humanity. Indeed, it is through helping others that you liberate yourself.

In love, as in the rest of your life, you prefer the illusion to the reality. It is the wild passion, the feeling of being swept away, that you desire. Your most favorite life-moments are when you feel the euphoria of love enveloping your entire being. You are a romance addict, and many Moon-Pisceans who drift from affair to affair keep wanting to experience the fabled glow of love as a form of psychological escapism.

You are a romantic who will do everything you can to make a mate happy. It is your nature to do this, even if you do not get an equivalent return from the other person. At the same time, you feel vulnerable and dependent and build up an elaborate array of defenses to avoid being hurt. However, once you get past playing the role of the victim, you are able to sustain a truly joyful relationship of honesty and depth.

No matter what your Sun sign may be, the Pisces-Moon qualities of creative imagination and sensitivity affect your personality. If your Sun is in a water sign (Cancer, Scorpio, Pisces), a Pisces Moon accentuates your intuitive nature and spirituality, and confers unique artistic talent. If your Sun is in an earth sign (Taurus, Virgo, Capricorn), you combine strength of purpose with the Piscean-Moon perceptiveness and idealism—an excellent placement for those in politics and humanitarian work. If your Sun is in an air sign (Gemini, Libra, Aquarius), a Pisces Moon combines with your keen powers of communication to endow you with clairvoyant ability and a gift for touching the emotions of others. If your Sun is in a fire sign (Aries, Leo, Sagittarius), a Pisces Moon gives your dynamic energy more depth and profundity; people with this placement have a hypnotic effect on the public.

Whatever your Sun sign, a Pisces Moon gives you a sympathetic heart, an artistic temperament, and a great capacity for doing work that will make a lasting impression.

FAMOUS PEOPLE WITH THE MOON IN PISCES

Paul Cezanne	Martin Luther King Jr.	Percy Bysshe Shelley
Hillary Rodham Clinton	Michelangelo	Frank Sinatra
Marie Curie	Paul Newman	Susan Sontag
Audrey Hepburn	Edgar Allan Poe	Robert Louis Stevenson
P. D. James	Elvis Presley	Leonardo da Vinci
Helen Keller	Martin Scorsese	Stanford White

6

YOUR ASCENDANT AND
ITS POWER

Your Ascendant or Rising sign (the terms are interchangeable) is a very important part of your horoscope. Your Ascendant is the sign that reflects your outward demeanor and to a great extent determines how the outside world looks at you.

The word *outer* is significant in defining your Rising sign, for this is the sign that represents your outer personality. In modern terminology, it is your image. Very often your Ascendant is what the world first sees in you, the impression that you first make on other people. Many astrologers believe that your Rising sign is more *immediately* revealing than your Sun sign. Your Rising sign has been likened to the door of a house, the entranceway that visitors first see and must pass through in order to look into the house itself.

In my own work as an astrologer, I have found that the personality you outwardly project is almost always a perfect blend of your Sun sign and Rising sign. It is this combination that makes your unique impact on the world. Your Moon sign is a more hidden aspect of your personality. It is a pervasive influence, but it is likely that other people *sense* the influence of your Moon sign in your character rather than see it on the surface.

Your Ascendant is the sign that was rising over the eastern horizon at the time of your birth (hence, your Rising sign). When you were born you left the condition of being a fetus and became a separate, fully formed human being. Therefore, the sign that was rising at this precise moment denotes your first experience as a separate human being; it expresses the moment in which you began independent existence in this world. As such, it characterizes the way you deal with others and your distinctive style of interacting with people. It speaks of your coping mechanisms and how you react to anything new that life throws at you. In many respects, your Ascendant is the sign that makes you feel most comfortable psychically. Its behaviors reassure you that you are coping well and will be safe as you enter unfamiliar emotional territory.

Your Ascendant is called the sign of your *self*—your self-awareness, your self-sufficiency, your self-interest. In many ways your Rising sign signifies your goals, aims, and objectives, and indicates the main thrust of your creative powers. To some degree, this sign also influences your physical characteristics and mannerisms. It is your mask of outward appearance. Like any mask, it may hide your real face, but more likely it is simply a part of your real face. It is the face that you most easily and naturally show to others.

What exactly is an Ascendant? In its simplest definition, your Ascendant is the astrological sign that was rising on the eastern horizon at the moment of your birth. To get a picture of what this means, imagine the Earth as a small circle in the center of a larger circle. That larger circle represents the heavens, the sky bubble that is all around us. You, as a newborn baby, are lying on that small inner circle (Earth) and looking all around you at the sky at the very moment of your birth. If you draw a line from the eastern horizon of the Earth outward to the edge of the sky bubble, that line marks the exact degree of your Ascendant. (Some clairvoyants claim they can actually see this astral line in a person.) The Ascendant in your birth chart is always pictured this way:

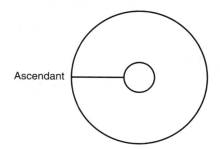

When a layperson talks about being "born under a sign," he or she means the Sun sign (the sign that the Sun was transiting at the time of birth). However, when some astrologers refer to the sign that an individual was born under, they are talking about the Ascendant. In an earlier era the Ascendant was thought more important than the Sun sign, but since the twentieth century this view is no longer held. However, most astrologers feel that the line of the Ascendant is the single most important point in a birth chart, for many other calculations in a horoscope can be made once that point is established. One thing is certain: Unless the Ascendant can be determined in a horoscope, interpretation of that horoscope remains limited; it can never become a truly personalized *natal* chart.

If you know the approximate time of your birth, the Ascendant Tables on pages 481–84 should make it easy for you to find your Ascendant.* Or utilize the enclosed CD-ROM, which will provide you with this information within seconds.

In reading the description of your Rising sign, keep in mind that this is not a delineation of you. You are a blend, and your Ascendant is only part of your personality. Only by self-examination can you discern which parts of you are your Sun sign, which are your Moon sign, and which are your Rising sign.

*If you do not know the time and place of your birth, it is still possible to discover your Ascendant. This is done by a process called "rectification" of your chart, in which a competent astrologer determines the time of your birth using as guideposts the time at which major events in your life have taken place.

What Sign Is Your Ascendant?

Consult the Ascendant Tables starting on page 481 in order to calculate your Rising sign.

Note: The Ascendant Tables in this book were designed for ease and simplicity. Using them, you can quickly ascertain your Rising sign.

However, for the purposes of analyzing your horoscope, you really need to know the *exact degree* of your Ascendant. Calculating this without the aid of a computer requires making some mathematical computations. First you must know the precise moment of your birth and also the exact latitude and longitude of the spot on earth where you were born. You must then convert the local time of your birth to Greenwich Mean Time (named for the town of Greenwich, England, the official point from which time is reckoned). Then you must convert Greenwich Mean Time into sidereal time at Greenwich. (Sidereal time, meaning *star* time, is measured in relation to

the fixed stars; a sidereal day is four minutes shorter than twenty-four hours.)

All of this can be quite complicated and involve a number of mathematical processes. For those of you who are interested, there are some excellent books that will help you to make these calculations in detail. You will find some of these books listed on page 520 in my Recommended Reading List.

Of course, these days we let the computer make these computations. The enclosed CD-ROM will calculate your birth chart instantly—providing you with the exact degree of your Ascendant as well as of every Planet and House cusp in your horoscope. And should you want to purchase a different program, on page 522 I list companies that specialize in an array of interesting astrological computer programs.

♈

ARIES ASCENDANT

ARIES IS A VERY STRONG ascendant. If you were born with Aries rising, you are adventurous and pioneering. You like to take on the role of a leader, even if the leadership is in a small area. For example, in your friendships you are the one who tries to dictate where you will meet, what restaurant or movie you will go to. An Aries-Rising child will be the most domineering and ego-centered among his or her brothers and sisters.

As an Aries-Ascendant person you have strong likes and dislikes and are never shy about expressing them. Your dealings are straightforward and honest. You are uncomfortable with lies, fraud, and elaborate deceptions. You will always try to get right to the point, say whatever is on your mind, and see what happens.

There is a contagious enthusiasm about you. You are an activist and doer rather than a thinker. Warm, generous, lively, you have a very friendly people-oriented quality. You like to be noticed.

Sometimes Rising-Aries people have a reputation as troublemakers. This is not because you are malicious (quite the opposite is true). But you like to throw off old, conservative ways of doing things and try a new, brasher, more direct approach. You plunge right into whatever the problem is and give it your best. As far as you're concerned, obstacles are just there to be butted down. However, if the obstacle won't move you won't butt your head off. You will quickly lose interest and bound off to find a new challenge, further excitement. You may be a groundbreaker, but if you should get stuck in the middle of a furrow, you'll drop the plow and move on to new ground.

Aries is the sign of beginnings. What you're really best at is the beginning of a job. You have the exuberance, verve, and energy. Once you master an idea, you won't stick around until all the how-to-do-its are in place.

Aries-Ascendant people are accident-prone. Because you are impulsive and quick to rush in headlong, you usually don't look where you are going. You tend to trip and fall, bump into things, cut yourself. Often your face and head are more prone to injury than other parts of your body.

As a person with Aries rising, you are likely to have a flashing smile, piercing eyes that move quickly from object to object, gold or reddish coloring in the skin or hair, a muscular body, and an agile quick movement to your step.

The planet Mars, which rules Aries, is very prominent in your chart. The influence of Mars bestows great willpower, stamina, an aggressive sex drive, and a need for achievement and recognition. It also brings on strain, tension, conflict, selfishness, a quick temper, and accidents with fire and sharp instruments.

TAURUS ASCENDANT

THERE IS A STEADFASTNESS, a basic calm about a Taurus Ascendant. If you have Taurus rising you tend to be placid and easygoing. You also have charming social manners and a strong artistic bent, for the sign of Taurus is ruled by Venus, planet of love and esthetics. You want to create beauty and harmony in your life, and many Taurus Ascendants have a flair for writing, decorating, or composing music.

Taurus-Rising people don't push their opinions on others. On the other hand, once you make up your mind (after due deliberation), you rarely change it. You hold on to your opinions and can be very stubborn and obstinate. You are also quite set in your ways, though this is not always apparent at first. It's the little clues that give you away: you may eat the same breakfast day in and day out; if you are fond of a particular color (possibly in the blue or rose family, which are Taurean colors), you may use it repeatedly in your clothes and throughout your house. Doing things the same way you've always done them gives you a sense of stability, and this is a fundamental need.

Taurus-Rising people have a reputation for laziness that is not entirely deserved. It is true that you love creature comforts, elegance, luxury, physical ease, and lots of leisure. However, you can and do work very hard, especially if motivated by the promise of money or by the approval of someone you love. Determined, persistent, and strong-willed, you possess endless patience to see a thing through, to make it a success.

Taurus is the sign of wealth and material possessions, both of which are extremely important to you. You have a tendency to brood about your future security: Will there be enough to keep from starving? Are you going to be able to pay the rent next year? The fears and worries do not require a basis in reality. In fact, though you may have to struggle for money when you are young, Taurus-Rising people tend to accumulate wealth as the years roll by. Owning things can sometimes become a mania; you covet possessions and once you own something you guard it jealously and are heartbroken should you lose it. You never resign yourself to the fact that things break, tear, wear out, get lost, and are stolen.

In relationships, as well, you tend to be jealous and possessive, although you are adept at hiding this. One of your weak points is your vanity, and you rarely forgive anyone who ridicules you. Having to cope with rivalry is hard for you. You may try to pretend the prize is not worthy of your talents.

As a person with Taurus rising, you tend to have an unusually good-looking face, large round eyes, and clear skin. Often your neck is short and thick, and your body gives the impression of weight and sturdiness. Becoming overweight is a problem, especially in later years.

The planet Venus, which rules Taurus, is very prominent in your horoscope. The influence of Venus bestows grace; charm; a love of pleasure, art, and adornment; and social awareness. It also encourages overindulgence, superficiality, jealousy, and conceit.

♊
Gemini Ascendant

THE FIRST IMPRESSION others receive of you is of someone in constant motion: your hands gesticulate, your eyes dart here and there, your body does not sit still in a chair. Restlessness underlies your personality; it is the symptom of your yearning for something that is just beyond your reach. You need change and variety and are often discontent with your present lot. Gemini is the sign of duality and this is evident in the lives of Gemini Ascendants. You can be happy and unhappy at the same time, satisfied yet dissatisfied. Of course, this can be said of many people, but in your case you are discontent for a specific reason: You feel you have not lived up to your potential. You sense that there is an experience just over the horizon that will make you feel truly fulfilled, and you resent the strictures that you may think keep you from venturing out to find it.

A striking characteristic of Gemini-Rising people is their ability to use words to say exactly what is meant. To you, clarity is a tribute that words pay to ideas. You are well informed, witty, mentally quick. Gemini-Rising people tend to move into positions of prominence not by force of will but by their facile way of handling people. You adore having an audience. Many of you become actors and writers and are successful in the entertainment industry, TV, journalism, and the literary world.

As a Gemini-Rising person you have an excitable nature that is quick to react to any stimulus, to come up with an answer to any question—and also to get upset easily. You throw yourself into a project with verve and enthusiasm, then worry and fret (usually quite audibly) about this thing going wrong

or that person not liking you, about how *long* everything is taking. However, you have a marvelous mercurial quality, and your high spirits and interest are quickly revived. You go out of your way to keep busy, if not at your vocation then at your avocation. You love puzzles, games, books, and the computer—anything that will amuse and occupy the mind.

There is a basic coolness to the Gemini-Rising personality. Even though you love to be with people and appear to have charming warmth, yours is a mental rather than emotional outlook. You deal with feelings and relationships exactly as you do with facts and figures—as things that can be analyzed. There is also a tendency to be egotistical, for fundamentally you know that you know better than others.

You like to encounter many different situations and people. You travel, change residences and occupations, and often marry more than once. Blessed with a natural sense of drama, you know how to heighten and brighten any experience.

As a Gemini Ascendant, you tend to have small sharp features, twinkling eyes that are filled with humor, a friendly smile, and graceful arms and hands that you use to great effect. You move with quickness and agility and hold on to your youthful looks well into old age.

The planet Mercury, which rules Gemini, is very prominent in your horoscope. The influence of Mercury bestows a high intellect, acute perceptions, cleverness, adroitness in speaking and writing, and a flair for foreign languages. It also encourages arrogance, sarcasm, snobbishness, cynicism, and disorganization.

♋

CANCER ASCENDANT

IF YOU HAVE CANCER RISING, you are very sensitive to emotional signals from other people. You have extraordinary insight into human motivation. There is a reserve about you that is sometimes difficult to penetrate, but underneath is a warm, affectionate, loving, and giving nature. You are adaptable to different kinds of people even though you are not liable to make instant friendships. It takes a while for you to let someone get really close.

Cancer-Rising people tend to moodiness, and others may not always find you in a receptive frame of mind. Sometimes you can be crabby and impatient and exhibit a snappish temper. You are touchy, and others have to be careful of what they say lest they hurt your feelings. Your sensitivities are so heightened that you sometimes take offense where none was intended.

However, this same sensitivity is what sets you apart from the crowd. You possess great imagination and awareness. Many Cancer Ascendants are extraordinarily gifted as writers, poets, and painters. Because you are so tuned in to the nuances of other people's motivations, you are able to absorb what others are feeling and thinking. You pick up opinions, thoughts, facts from all around you and, being very clever and practical (as well as visionary), you are able to put all this information to work for you. Cancer Ascendants are also clever with money, prudent and cautious, and have a native shrewd-ness in business. You know how to make wise investments and where to get the best value. Though you usually have to climb the ladder through your own efforts (rather than the efforts of others), you are likely to accumulate material success as the years go by.

You won't hog the spotlight, but on the other hand you want public recognition for your talents. With Cancer rising, acclaim and applause can be hard to come by, so you tend to have a way of feeling sorry for yourself. You complain that the world does not appreciate you, but your complaint is usually an effort to win reassurance that quite the opposite is true.

As a Cancer Ascendant you have obstacles in your path, especially when young. However, as you surmount each difficulty and succeed (Cancer Rising has great tenacity of purpose), you become stronger and more self-assured.

If you have Cancer rising, you are likely to have a round expressive face, pale luminous eyes, slender arms and legs, and a rolling gait to your walk. Your body may be thickset through the middle, and you are prone toward putting on weight as you get older.

The Moon, which rules Cancer, is very prominent in your horoscope. The influence of the Moon bestows kindness, imagination, sympathy, deep emotion, an ability to cherish and protect, a retentive memory. It also encourages laziness, inconstancy, restlessness, passivity, and untidiness.

♌

LEO ASCENDANT

LEO ASCENDING SIGNIFIES nobility of character, high ideals, and great personal magnetism. If you have Leo rising, you are big-hearted, expansive, benevolent, and kind. You consider it beneath you to stoop to pettiness, carping, stinginess, or narrow-mindedness. Because you are so magnanimous in spirit, you find it hard to believe ill of others. You are the opposite of the Irish as Dr. Samuel Johnson described them: "A fair people; they never speak well of each other."

Of course the world does not always live up to anyone's expectations, and Leo Ascendants are puzzled and hurt by meanness and ungenerosity. At such times you simply put on your regal air and make sure the underling knows in what contempt and low esteem he or she is held.

Rising-Leos have a great sense of showmanship. You love to put on lavish displays—whether it is decorating your house with expensive and elegant things or dressing in attention-getting clothes or throwing a splendid dinner party. To less flamboyant types you may appear ostentatious, show-offy, and extravagant. But your showy displays are not only to get attention; you see life in larger-than-life terms and aspire to the highest and the best. This quality draws others to you and, in itself, attracts power and influence.

Leo-Rising people seem surrounded by luck in money, career, and friendship. You are not an especially hard worker but tend to achieve success through the influence and pull of others. Fame and fortune come to you when you aren't looking for it.

You are efficient at organizing groups of people and inspiring them to give their best. You are happiest in the role of leader. In fact, you feel wounded if your public doesn't put you in that position. When not given what you feel is your due, you can turn haughty, temperamental, and arrogant. Leo is the sign of pride, and Ascendant natives have this in abundance. You are self-confident and have a resolute faith in yourself.

There is a basic likeableness about you, partly because you give the distinct impression that life is fun. You have a wonderful sense of humor. (Note: Rising-Leos have a particularly soft spot for children and spoil them outrageously.)

As a Leo-Rising person, you tend to have a large, beautifully shaped head, thick shining hair, a dazzling smile with bright, even teeth, and a stately bearing. Many of you are benefited by an inheritance later in your lives. Whatever path you choose to follow, you usually emerge on the sunny side of the hill.

The Sun, which rules Leo, is very prominent in your horoscope. The influence of the Sun bestows enthusiasm, generosity, power, warmth, creative self-expression, passion, and courage. It also encourages egotism, arrogance, snobbism, conceit, pomposity, and condescension.

♍
VIRGO ASCENDANT

VIRGO ASCENDING INDICATES an analytical outlook. Though the degree of emotionalism depends on other influences in your horoscope, it is generally through the mind that you perceive the world. This is not to say you are cold and insensitive. Indeed, the opposite is true, for Virgo Ascendants have deep and tender emotions and care a great deal about others.

However, it is the process of thinking logically that gives you the deepest satisfaction. You appreciate the finely tuned mechanics of sifting through facts and information, finding the truth of the matter, introducing order and reason into almost any situation. Rising-Virgos are rather fixed in opinion, but not so inflexible that they will not change their minds upon careful review of opposing facts. To you, the cardinal sin is to be ignorant of one's ignorance.

A fault sometimes is your inability to put things in perspective, a proclivity for getting bogged down in minutiae and losing sight of the big picture. You magnify the importance of a petty detail and then become resentful if others fail to see its significance.

Work is important to you, and you usually accomplish a great deal during your lifetime. Often you are at war within yourself, both wanting things to come easily and needing to achieve solely through your own efforts. Control—both of self and of events—is what makes you feel secure. As it turns out, most Rising-Virgos do gain through their own hard work rather than through the influence of others.

You have a charm and elegance that is difficult to pin down. You are not always easy to know intimately. Your shyness and aloofness (sometimes well disguised by a social veneer) must be penetrated by anyone who wishes to become truly close. Emotionally, it's hard for you to show your feelings, though a great deal is always going on under the surface.

As children, Rising-Virgos sometimes suffer from poor health. Happily, health improves the older you get. For many of you, a marriage partner brings property or wealth. Later in life Rising-Virgos frequently become property owners, often in a foreign country. Success for you is often linked to dealings in and travel to places far from home.

As a Rising-Virgo person, you tend to have a gentle, oval face, eyes that sweep around a room and take in everything, and a body that gives the impression of frailty but is actually very strong.

The planet Mercury, which rules Virgo, is very prominent in your horoscope. The influence of Mercury bestows a logical mind, acute powers of observation, an intellectual outlook, perception, and a flair for science and writing. It also encourages fussiness, a nervous temperament, sarcasm, fault-finding, and worry.

LIBRA ASCENDANT

L IBRA IS A MOST PLEASING and harmonious Ascendant. If you have Libra rising, you have natural charm, grace, and poise. You are extremely social-minded and take pleasure in being with other people in a convivial atmosphere. Parties, holidays, laughter, fun, and good times are what Libra Ascendants revel in. You have a gay and genial personality and are full of hope for the future. No matter what disappointments today may bring, Rising-Librans fantasize happy tomorrows and look forward to living them.

Of course, you are not this way all the time. One of your problems is that you are easily thrown into despair and depression, especially by downhearted and discouraging people. Libra is the sign of balance, but it doesn't take much to push Libra Ascendants off balance. Basically, however, your spirits are optimistic and blithe.

You are born with a great sense of fairness, and nothing angers you more than to see injustice go uncorrected. You are deeply upset by cruelty, violence, bloodshed, strife. To you life should be serene and content, but it must, above all, be fair.

Libra Ascendants are refined, neat, and discriminating. You breathe rarefied air. Your aloof quality is sometimes hard for others to figure out, but it will never leave you even though you function so well with other people.

You gravitate toward artistic and creative endeavors, but sometimes your artistic flair lies dormant and unused, for you dislike hard work and prefer to take the easy way out. You don't have to seek the spotlight, however; it shines on you. You don't struggle to find success; luck often comes to Libra Ascendants through a partner, mate, or close association.

You like travel, new people, new projects. You happily throw yourself into enterprises that promise excitement or diversion. The trouble is you don't have much perseverance, so a great many things go unfinished. Another difficulty you have is making up your mind. You weigh a decision carefully, vacillating between one course of action and another; when you've finally decided you still hesitate. There is a timidity behind all this pondering, a fear of taking risks.

You are unhappy when single and fond of being married. (This does not necessarily mean that you will stay married to the same person.) Somewhere along the way Libra Ascendants are likely to gain wealth and material possessions through a marriage partner. As a rule you don't have a lot of children, but you take great delight in those you do have.

As a Libra-Rising person, you tend to have a strikingly good-looking face, graceful and symmetrical bone structure, and a radiant smile. Your body is usually curving or round, though not necessarily fat.

The planet Venus, which rules Libra, is very prominent in your horoscope. The influence of Venus bestows beauty, charm, social graces, a romantic nature, an appreciation for art, music, and decoration. It also encourages superficiality, jealousy, laziness, dependence on others, and a weak will.

♏ SCORPIO ASCENDANT

I F YOU WERE BORN WITH Scorpio ascending, you put the whole force of your personality behind everything you do. You are not a halfway person. Rising-Scorpios have an intensity, a dynamism that seethes and roils under the surface. Your willpower and determination are formidable.

Though you are sometimes viewed as a lone wolf, you do have an ability to work with people—actually, to lead people. You are strongly persuasive and zealously pursue your goals, and in addition have the power to make others pursue the same goals.

Clever, creative, and resourceful, your fertile mind seems to be an inexhaustible source of ideas and suggestions. Your brain behind your cool facade is always ticking away. One of the things you must do is find out how something works, to dissect it, study it, and put it back together so that it works better. This is also true in artistic terms; you can do great visionary work if you have Scorpio rising in your chart.

As a Scorpio Ascendant you are happiest when you can control from behind the scenes. You tend to be secretive and reserved, and shun the spotlight because you can't work there unnoticed. If you are domineering, it is a subtle dominance, a kind of mind control. Some people claim that they are hypnotized by Scorpio Ascendants; it's true that you have a way of knowing what others are thinking. Much of this comes from your acute powers of observation. You are a charming, witty conversationalist, but the acute observer will soon notice that it is the *other* person who is doing most of the talking. You are usually quietly watching, waiting, observing—filing away information that will be useful later on.

Rising-Scorpios have a reputation for a sharp temper; the reputation is deserved. When crossed, you can be cruel and biting. You tend to use any weapon at your disposal—from ridicule to playing on a person's fears. In the heat of that moment, Rising-Scorpio must be the victor. Later, you are remorseful for having dealt wounds, though it is extremely hard for you to say so.

Scorpio is the astrological sign of hidden passion; Scorpio Ascendants tend to have a secret love affair at least one time in their lives, and usually marry more than once. Astrologers have observed a strange pattern in which Rising-Scorpios often lose their first spouse to death. They seem to suffer more financial setbacks and disappointments than other rising signs; but no other sign is more victorious in the end.

As a Scorpio Ascendant you tend to have sharp features, a prominent nose, and large, hypnotic eyes. Sometimes your brows are thick and dark. Your body is agile and moves decisively.

The planet Pluto, which rules Scorpio, is very prominent in your horoscope. The influence of Pluto bestows powerful feelings and emotions, a sense of purpose, persistence, determination, plus the imagination and ability to make a successful start in a new direction. This planet's influence also favors secrecy, suspicion, jealousy, and cruelty.

SAGITTARIUS ASCENDANT

A SAGITTARIUS ASCENDANT favors independence and freedom. You cannot bear to be stifled by outmoded ideas or difficult lovers or tedious work. You are progressive, full of optimism about the future. You are also restless in spirit, anxious to get on with the business of living, ready to accept a new challenge.

Sometimes your impatience is misunderstood. Your sensitivity toward other people and your need for freedom are part of the same personality. You grant freedom to others and never try to limit or restrict another human being.

Sagittarius Ascendants are basically humanitarians, idealists who care deeply about injustice. On a personal level, you are honest and generous to others and easily wounded when confronted with selfishness or thoughtless cruelty. It's true that you can expect too much of your fellow man.

You have a knack for making friends, for you are very open to new people and new ideas. You enjoy a spirited discussion, an exchange of opinion. (Rising-Sagittarians have a reputation for frankness: other people always know where they stand with you.) You are interested in research, blessed with imagination, foresight, and clear thinking. You like to travel, see new places, learn how the rest of the world lives. Usually you tend to read a great deal, watch the news, subscribe to periodicals, plug into the latest information on the computer, talk about current events with friends. You prefer the simple life, with not too many trappings or obligations. You like money, but your real appreciation is for the independence it affords. You fear that if you take success too seriously, life will become boring.

One of your problems is that you don't measure the consequences of what you do. You are impulsive, sometimes reckless. To take action is the main thing, to do *something* about a problem. You don't always stop to consider where all the activity may lead.

Marriage is not the most important thing in your life. Sagittarian Ascendants have a tendency to marry the wrong person (at least once) and get into unhappy romantic situations from which they must extricate themselves. Travel is a major theme in your life, and luck surrounds you in foreign countries. Many Rising-Sagittarians live out their later years in another country.

As a person with Sagittarius rising, you tend to have a pleasant, cheerful face, a broad forehead, bright, humorous eyes, and a friendly smile. You often make sweeping gestures with your arms and hands, and have a strong, active body.

The planet Jupiter, which rules Sagittarius, is very prominent in your horoscope. The influence of Jupiter bestows good fortune, happiness, generosity, breadth of vision, sincerity, and a genial social manner. It also encourages restlessness, self-indulgence, conceit, impatience, wastefulness, and gambling.

♑ CAPRICORN ASCENDANT

IF YOU HAVE CAPRICORN ascending, you tend to have a serious turn of mind. One would not call you melancholy, but you certainly aren't frivolous. Cautious in your dealings, you are reluctant to commit yourself until you know the score. With strangers you are often quiet, reserved, perhaps a bit shy. But once you open up you can be lively, friendly, warm, and expressive.

Capricorn Ascendants have strong personalities, possess great willpower and determination, and diligently pursue their goals. These goals are usually for a better life—money, status, a higher standing in the community for your family. It's important to you to feel that your life is meaningful. You have self-esteem and are reliable, dependable, and stable. Sometimes, though, you will strive toward a goal and when you achieve it will still not be happy. You have a sense that something is missing, and you continue your search.

You have an active mind with quick intelligence and an ability to concentrate. You can ferret out information, see flaws in a plan, map things out ahead in detail. Sometimes you may be accused of being too calculating, because you add up all the pros and cons before embarking on a project. If an opponent has a weakness, you are also quick to spot it—and not entirely above using it to your advantage.

You tend to fuss over details to make sure all contingencies have been covered. It's your way of being in control—you don't want bad luck to catch you unprepared. Rising-Capricorns are worriers; in youth you worry about life, in old age about death. In middle age you worry about success.

It isn't always easy for Rising-Capricorns to show their feelings, though powerful feelings do exist. You love deeply, are loyal and protective, and go out of your way to do kind deeds for others. However, you are often torn by jealousy and resentment (which you hide), and down deep you never really forgive someone who does you an injury.

What you achieve is mainly through your own efforts rather than through the influence of others. Though it happens that Rising-Capricorns seem to benefit financially through marriage, your own hard work within the union is largely responsible for your gain. With Capricorn Ascendants there is often a rivalry with brothers and sisters, or some kind of disagreement with their fathers.

As a person with Capricorn rising, you tend to have a small, well-shaped head, deep and penetrating eyes, and a beautiful smile with good-looking teeth. You have strong feet and usually enjoy walking or jogging.

The planet Saturn, which rules Capricorn, is very prominent in your horoscope. The influence of Saturn bestows discipline, ambition, patience, determination, good endurance, and thrift. It also encourages stubbornness, hardship, melancholy, aloofness, pessimism, and selfishness.

AQUARIUS ASCENDANT

IF YOU HAVE AQUARIUS ascending, you usually make friends easily. You are quick-witted and lively, open in your dealings, honest and truthful. You are an inventive conversationalist who paints word pictures that amuse and fascinate. Intelligent and charming, you are particularly suited to a position of leadership.

You are idealistic in your outlook and want nothing more than for all the world to be happy and harmonious. Even the idea of conflict upsets you. You want to see the best in humanity and are hopeful about the future.

Though you have a reputation for fairness and tolerance, there is a strong streak of inflexibility to your nature. Much of this is the impatience you feel toward those who do not have your visionary or lofty ideas. Rising-Aquarians are modern, forward-thinking, and progressive, yet you are as set in your ways as Capricorn or Taurus. One could say that you hold firmly far-out opinions. The choice for most people is to accept society as they find it or try to improve it. You want to construct a new society that will correspond to your vision of the ideal.

You are often intolerant of other people's shortcomings and can be wickedly sarcastic and very funny at the same time. Your razor-sharp powers of observation help you to uncover flaws that you can poke fun at.

You are a system of paradoxes. You enjoy being with people but are perfectly content to be alone. You like to travel but love relaxing at home. You are friendly and outgoing but, at other times, moody and reserved. You have both a scientific and an artistic turn of mind. In your career, you often are involved in two distinct areas of work.

Fame comes rather easily to Aquarius-Rising people, and many times it is just as easily taken away from them. Your life tends to be marked by unexpected triumphs and reversals. When good fortune smiles there is often a dark underside to it. For example, many Rising-Aquarians inherit money, but it often turns out that the legal entanglements are more trouble than the inheritance is worth.

Aquarius Ascendants approach new places and situations with a spirit of adventure, even though the spirit does tend to wear thin. You become quickly bored. Rising-Aquarians usually marry early in life and find contentment with their mates. Though most of you are comfortably off by the time you reach middle age, you never quite make all the money you'd like. Friends are helpful to you in both career and personal matters.

As a person with Aquarius rising, you tend to have a wide forehead, fine bone structure in your face, and dreamy, wandering eyes. Many of you are quite tall and rangy-looking.

The planet Uranus, which rules Aquarius, is very prominent in your horoscope. The influence of Uranus bestows independence, originality, friendliness, a reforming spirit, versatility, and a hatred of restriction. It also encourages rebellion, unpredictability, tactlessness, eccentricity, and contrariness.

PISCES ASCENDANT

IF YOU WERE BORN with Pisces rising, you carry within yourself a strong artistic gift that must sooner or later find expression. You have an active fantasy life and a pronounced romantic outlook. You want life to be perfect and since it isn't, you choose not to see what you don't want to see. Down deep, many Rising-Pisceans believe that they alone are destined to suffer disillusionment in life; sometimes others sense this secret sorrow in you. Often you feel you were born at the wrong time in the wrong place, and you are strongly drawn to the past.

Basically, you have a dauntless goodwill toward others. You tend to be very sociable, fond of entertaining, and enjoy the warmth of companionship. You love the good life—fine food and drink especially, beautiful clothes, and travel. At parties Rising-Pisceans are vivacious and verbal (sometimes you talk *too* much); you enjoy performing in front of a group. A talent for mimicry makes many Pisces Ascendants turn to the theater.

The word *sentimental* comes to mind when describing you. Your tender feelings are easily moved by sad stories, lost animals, unhappy human beings. Your personality is also changeable, at times moody and distressed. Worry and imagined fears overtake and sometimes overcome you.

In your private life you tend to be disorganized, a bit careless, the kind who is forever losing or misplacing belongings. In work, however, you are knowledgeable and creative and can be quite disciplined when working within a group, especially in artistic projects. You are also successful in occupations that involve writing and travel. Many Rising-Pisceans frequently change their residence.

It often happens with Pisces Ascendants that a person who was an adversary in early years becomes a valuable friend later on. You may sometimes have trouble with a first marriage because of in-laws and relatives. As a Rising-Piscean you are probably fond of children; your own children usually bring you pride and happiness.

If you have Pisces rising, you tend to have large, luminous eyes and a sensuous mouth. You are likely to have wavy hair and well-shaped feet.

The planet Neptune, which rules Pisces, is very prominent in your horoscope. The influence of Neptune bestows compassion, sensitivity, keen intuition, imagination, creativity, and an interest in spiritual things and the occult. It also encourages confusion, indecisiveness, worry, vagueness, carelessness, and self-deception.

7

YOU AND THE PLANETS

Their Role in Your Destiny

Our solar system as we know it today consists of the Earth, the Sun, the Moon, and eight other planets that revolve around the Sun in a precise and ordered pattern. The dependability of this pattern allows us to go to bed each night knowing that morning will arrive on schedule tomorrow. This pattern marks not only our days, but our seasons, our years, and our lives. This "conformity to certain known laws" (as the *Columbia Encyclopedia* expresses it) enables us here on Earth to calculate exactly where a given planet has been, is, or will be at any given point in time.

Because each entity in our solar system moves at a different speed and rate, and in a separate path or orbit, the combinations of the placement of the planets are almost endless. At the moment of your birth, the Sun, Moon, and planets were in a particular arrangement in the heavens. This exact arrangement will not be repeated for 4,320,000 years. This means another person with your *exact* horoscope will not walk on this earth for another 4,320,000 years! Even then, of course, that person will never be exactly the same because of the entirely different genetic and environmental factors.

What about twins, one might ask. Wouldn't they have the exact same horoscope? The answer is no. Every four minutes the Ascendant changes by one degree. This means that twins born as little as four minutes apart might have Ascendants in two different signs if one of the twins was born in the last degree of an Ascendant and the second twin born in the first degree of a new Ascendant. Even a difference of one degree in the same Ascendant makes a change. When the Ascendant shifts, the entire birth chart shifts. True, the changes are slight and the horoscopes are very similar—but then, twins *are* very similar.

And what of people born at the same second, perhaps in the very same hospital? People born at the same time are known as astral-twins or time-twins. A great deal of research is currently being done by astrologers and scientists into the life-patterns of time-twins. The results are astounding. In case after case, it has been documented that the life-patterns of time-twins are eerily similar. In many cases, they marry at the same time, have the same number and same sexes of children; they divorce, travel, and change jobs and residences at the same time; in many cases they die at the same time and from the same causes.

Obviously time-twins are very, very rare. The unique pattern of Sun, Moon, and planets in your horoscope is most likely unduplicated by *anyone* else. Your Sun sign might be Taurus or Scorpio, but you may be as different as night and day from another Taurus or Scorpio. Just as your fingerprints are like no one else's, your birth chart is like no one else's. And if you wish to gain further insight into the knowledge astrology can provide you, you must know where the various planets are placed in your (or anyone else's) birth chart.

Each planet has a specific influence in astrology and governs a certain area of your personality or your approach to life. For example, Mercury relates to your mental outlook; Venus governs your love nature. It is the placement of these planets in the various zodiacal signs that determines how you *express* the different facets of your personality. If your Mercury is in Gemini, you tend to be extremely verbal and quick-witted. If your Mercury is in Capricorn, you handle detail work very well and carefully plot out your plans in advance. If your Venus is in Leo, you are not happy unless you receive a great deal of attention from a lover. If your Venus is in Aquarius, you consider freedom of expression for each person to be the most important thing in a love relationship.

In the following pages you will find a rundown of each planet, its power and influence, and what that influence means when it is in each sign of the zodiac. There are

Planetary Tables on pages 485–513 that will give you the exact position of each planet in your chart for your particular day of birth.

⚬

Note: The astrological community has taken a great interest in a tiny planet or asteroid (it has not yet been determined which, and is often referred to as a planetoid) discovered by Charles Kowal on November 1, 1977. This tiny planetary body is named Chiron, who in Greek mythology was the wise centaur, a teacher, and a healer. Chiron has a diameter of between 100 and 400 miles and an orbit that lies between Saturn and Uranus. The astrological significance of Chiron is still under observation. In general it is thought of as an influence for spiritual regeneration and the search for meaningful work. Some astrologers connect it to Scorpio and Sagittarius, and others to Virgo. A group has been formed called the Association for Studying Chiron; this society feels that Chiron has no sign rulership and that its nature is, in their word, "maverick." Many astrologers (and computer astrology programs) now routinely note the position of Chiron in horoscopes and, when doing chart readings, include an interpretation of Chiron's placement in a birth chart.

In August 1989, an interesting discovery about Neptune's moon Triton was made. Data sent back to Earth from our space probe, *Voyager 2*, has led many astronomers to believe that Triton may once have been a planet that revolved around our Sun, and eons ago was drawn into Neptune's gravitational embrace.

In accordance with ancient prediction, many astrologers down through the years have believed that more planets will be discovered within our solar system. A prevailing theory (one among many) is that two more planets remain to be discovered—the planet Apollo and the planet Vulcan. Apollo is said to be the true ruler of Taurus (which now shares the planet Venus with the sign of Libra), and Vulcan to be the true ruler of Virgo (which now shares the planet Mercury with the sign of Gemini).

Indeed, astronomers continue to search for two other planets in our solar system. One, named Vulcan, is thought to be close to the Sun, between Mercury and the Sun. The other, called Planet X, is being looked for beyond Pluto. Something out there is exerting a gravitational pull on Uranus, but Pluto (the planet beyond Uranus) is far too tiny in size to influence the orbit of a planet as big as Uranus, and so astronomers continue to search for Planet X. In fact, in April 1998, the scientific world was thrilled when it seemed that a tenth planet had been discovered,

and disappointed when it turned out to be a comet briefly orbiting the Sun.

When a new planet is discovered and assigned to a zodiacal sign, that sign undergoes a slow change in appearance. For example, before the end of the eighteenth century (and therefore before the planet Uranus was discovered), the rulership of Aquarius belonged to Saturn. Back then Aquarius was a much more sober, practical, melancholy, and restrictive sign than the bright, modern, forward-thinking, and electric Aquarius we know today. In the grand plan of the universe according to astrology, the true ruler of a sign brings out that sign's true characteristics.

Of course, it is perfectly possible that the ancient predictions will not take place and the number of planets in our solar system will remain exactly the same as today. Only time will tell.

MERCURY

⟨⟩

IT HAS BEEN SAID that Mercury makes life understandable, for it is the planet of intelligence.

How does the power of Mercury express itself in your personality?

Do you easily strike up conversations with strangers or do you only open up with friends? Are you the kind who on a moment's notice will have a bag packed and rush off on a trip, or do you prefer quiet evenings at home listening to music, delving among your favorite books? Do you enjoy speaking in front of a group, or would you rather tell stories in your own living room? Do you take hold of one idea and see it through to fruition, or do you prefer working on many projects at once?

You can start to answer these questions by looking at your horoscope to find the position of Mercury, planet of the mind.

From the very beginning of man's observation of this elusive planet, Mercury has been associated with speed and agility. In ancient mythology, Mercury was the messenger of the gods. He was young, beautiful, and swift as the wind, for his feet had wings. His province was communication, commerce, everything requiring skill and dexterity. Not only was he clever in speech, he also invented music, mathematics, and astronomy. In Roman times, Mercury also became the god of thieves, for he was a cunning trickster, full of guile.

In astrology, Mercury is the planet of mental activities, communication, and intellectual energy. It rules over your

An Astronomical Look at Mercury

Mercury is the second-smallest planet in our solar system (only Pluto is smaller), and the planet nearest the Sun (about 36 million miles away). Its diameter is 3,000 miles compared to Earth's diameter of almost 8,000. Mercury moves very quickly, completing a revolution around the Sun every 88 days, as opposed to Earth's orbit around the Sun of 365¼ days.

Because Mercury is so near to the Sun it is not easily seen through telescopes; when nearest to Earth, Mercury is between us and the Sun, and therefore invisible. The planet is never visible long after sunset nor long before sunrise, and so our observations have always been made in daylight when it is difficult to see. Mercury's orbit is very near our horizon, and the haze of the Earth's atmosphere further clouds our vision of the planet.

Recent space probes, however, have given us a much clearer picture of the planet. Until well into the second half of the twentieth century, astronomers believed that Mercury did not turn on an axis the way Earth does. However, we now know that Mercury does rotate on its axis, once every 59 days. Thus the planet makes three rotations during two revolutions around the Sun, resulting in the rather unusual phenomenon of there being exactly three Mercury-days in every two Mercury-years! According to photographs made in 1975 by the *Mariner* 10 probe, the surface of Mercury is similar to our Moon's—riddled and pitted with craters—and a magnetic field around the planet protects it from the Sun's harsh particle wind.

Mercury appears as an evening star in March and April, and as a morning star in September and October. The ancient Greeks thought it was two stars—a morning star they named Apollo and an evening star called Mercury. In Egypt it was also regarded as two stars, Set and Horus, which were known as the stars of thought.

intelligence, perception and reason, memory, speaking and writing. It reflects the way you see, hear, understand, and assimilate information. Day-to-day travel, short trips, and the various means of transportation are under its dominion. It also controls the functions of the nerves, arms, hands, and fingers.

When Mercury is prominent in a person's horoscope, that person is likely to be facile in speech; a lively and amusing storyteller; a clever, shrewd bargainer. He or she will probably have a good memory, a talent for debate, and quick, highstrung movements.

Mercury also rules the voice, and people with strong Mercury influences are successful at public speaking, singing, and acting. Mercury protects travelers and benefits education and research. Its rulership ranges from such major areas as the nervous system and the ability to communicate to such minor things as handwriting, pens and pencils, communication via the computer, and deliveries.

The negative side of Mercury's influence produces a tendency to be critical, sarcastic, argumentative, and sly. Lies, deceit, and certain types of crime, such as fraud, swindling, and forgery, are examples of Mercury's negative power.

Because Mercury travels so close to the Sun, it is never very far from the Sun in your birth chart. It is always either in your Sun sign or in the sign immediately preceding or following your Sun sign.

Where Is Your Mercury?

To find out what sign Mercury was in on the day of your birth, consult the Mercury Tables on page 485.

MERCURY IN ARIES This is a strong position for Mercury because Aries imparts aggressiveness and brilliance to the intelligence. If you have Mercury in Aries, you tend to be witty, outspoken, and original. There is a sharp edge to your conversation, an ironic or sarcastic tone that can sometimes be biting and sometimes very funny. You use highly expressive language and throw a lot of slang into your speech. You exaggerate. An Aries-Mercury makes you impatient, eager to get things done and wanting your way in the proceedings. You can be argumentative and tactless. Fond of both speaking and writing, you may become active in the literary world. Even if not a professional writer yourself, you like to talk to writers and attend literary cocktail parties. A problem is that you are too impulsive; not enough planning goes into your actions. However, you are blessed with luck in this respect: Your first decisions tend to be the right ones. Mercury-in-Aries people suffer from headaches, especially in a raucous and noisy atmosphere.

MERCURY IN TAURUS As a Mercury-in-Taurus person, you never embark on a project without being completely prepared. You have a practical, stable, and constructive mind. There is a rigidity to your intellect: You are quite sure your opinions are the wisest and you have little use for what others think. You have an excellent memory and are a good observer, but you are apt to listen inattentively; since you're not about to change your mind, why listen to what someone else has to say? You also have a tendency to repeat yourself, to state what you've just said over again in different terms, usually to make sure everyone has gotten the point. Although you are sociable and attractive, and have a certain refinement about your manners, you're a bit shy with strangers. You're more at ease reading a book while lounging in a comfortable overstuffed chair than holding court in the middle of a crowded gathering. You read a great deal, but it is experience that teaches you the lessons you value in life. A Mercury in Taurus promotes a knack for handling money. Possessing an eye for both beauty and value, Mercury-Taureans are often successful art and antique dealers.

MERCURY IN GEMINI If you have Mercury in Gemini, it's hard to pin you down. You have a quicksilver duality to your mind. You tend to change opinions quickly based on the latest news you're listening to. You often hold down more than one job or work on a number of projects at once. Extremely quick, versatile, interested in the world at large, you live mostly on a mental plane. You must have facts and information; what you want is to *know*. You are good at languages and math and love to read, study, travel, and talk to new people about what you think. However, because you have such a variety of interests, your grasp of knowledge tends to be superficial. You always know a bit about everything, but sometimes not a lot about anything. You are clever enough to conceal this and to give a marvelous impression of being well informed. Another problem is your lack of stick-to-itiveness. At times there is a distinct lack of order in your life. You would make a wonderful debater, public speaker, or actor, and you have lots of friends because of your infectious good humor. Many popular TV interviewers and talk-show hosts have their Mercury in Gemini.

MERCURY IN CANCER As a native of this Mercury position, you are sensitive to what others think about you. You have an almost sixth-sense intuition and pick up signals from all around you. You believe that if we had to depend only on our eyes we would see very little. You are chameleonlike in the way you are able to adapt yourself to different kinds of people. This does not mean you don't cling possessively to your own ideas. Indeed, you are a bit narrow-minded, but others would need to be as psychic as you are to discern this. On the surface it is not evident; you maintain a charming social face. Your outlook is always intensely personal—you're fond of discussing large events in terms of your own feelings. Gifted with powerful imagination, a sense of poetry, and a fine memory, Mercury-in-Cancer people are successful as scholars, historians, teachers, and writers. You are likely to make a profit in real estate and may inherit money from the maternal side of your family. Sometimes you are plagued with irrational phobias, such as a fear of flying.

MERCURY IN LEO Mercury in Leo bestows a gift for eloquence and a skill for leading others. If you are a native of this position, you have a magnetic flair for dealing with people. You are a superb organizer who knows how to direct, manage, and control. It's true that you can be boastful, arrogant, and bombastic; and if things don't go your way your fiery temper may ignite. But basically you have such a kind heart and sunny disposition that people usually forgive you. There is a showy expansiveness to your outlook. Though you would rather play than work, you are determined to be successful. You have great enthusiasm and sometimes get so caught up in a project you ignore everything else. People with Mercury in Leo are in love with the theater and the performing arts, and are happiest when they are on display. Creative fields attract you; you resent tedious work.

MERCURY IN VIRGO This position of Mercury gives a fine analytical quality to the mind. You like to deal in facts; before you make up your mind you must know all sides to the question and get all the information available in order to analyze it. Once you form a theory, you're quite convinced it is the truth. Thenceforward, you expect reality to conform to your ideas, rather than vice versa. You have an intellectual intolerance for people who are sloppy in their thinking; you don't really understand human failings. Your emotional detachment makes you an excellent scientist, researcher, teacher, or reporter. You are very quick to learn and can usually memorize long pages of material. A fault is your eagerness to take on too much work or too many projects. You wear yourself down, and at times become nervous and hypercritical. As a Mercury-Virgo you have a superb talent for creative crafts.

MERCURY IN LIBRA Mercury is the planet of rationality and Libra the sign of balance. If you have this Mercury position, you love to make comparisons by listing all the pros and cons, looking at both sides, weighing all the factors. What you want is to make the *perfect* choice. Even after you've made up your mind, however, it isn't definite. A favorite ploy is to adopt a wait-and-see attitude. In truth, you have fine intuitions and often know things in a flash. But then you tend to intellectualize and go off in the wrong direction. Toward other people, your attitude is gentle, sympathetic, friendly. You are fond of socializing. Not wishing to stir up controversy (oh, never!) in company, you will go along with someone else's opinion even if you privately disagree. Mercury-in-Libra people do their best creative and intellectual work within a partnership. You are especially successful if you team up with a strong person who can direct you. Left alone, you may become lazy and not apply yourself with diligence.

MERCURY IN SCORPIO As a Mercury-in-Scorpio person, you are questioning and probing. You must dig beneath the surface to discover the real facts. You are especially drawn to things hidden: many of you go into the fields of medicine, science, religion, and the occult. Mercury-Scorpios are particularly suited for investigative work because you are unflagging in your pursuit and nothing eludes your keen observation. You take great pride in your ability not to be fooled. You also have a stubborn, obstinate mind and are enamored of your own ideas. One cannot budge you from a point of view unless you want to be budged. You consider other people's "proofs" to be variations of their opinions, and listen to neither one nor the other. Solitary work and research are better suited to your temperament than cooperative ventures. You probably have a volatile temper, and Mercury-Scorpios are known for their biting sarcasm when crossed or upset. You have an emotional intelligence. You will fight for a cause even if it is hopeless, or sacrifice your time and energies for someone you love.

MERCURY IN SAGITTARIUS If you have this position of Mercury you are quick and bright, breezy, to the point. You prize freedom of expression and cannot bear the thought of any power of censorship over what you have to say. Your mind is restless, inquiring, always looking for stimulation. You may jump from project to project or change jobs frequently. Travel is often involved in your work. Mercury-Sagittarians never stop learning; yours is an ongoing, lifetime education. You love to read, explore new ideas, learn about other people. You are fast on your feet and can grasp ideas instantly, but a frequent failing is your lack of concentration. Some people find you too blunt and outspoken, but that quality springs from Sagittarius's basic honesty. You never deliberately set out to deceive or dissemble; if you are tactless it's because you don't think before you speak. Sometimes you find it difficult to complete a long, sustained piece of work.

MERCURY IN CAPRICORN If you have Mercury in Capricorn you tend to be ambitious and methodical, careful, calculating, and patient. You are not only superb at handling detail, but you also never lose sight of the whole picture. When it comes to making decisions you are extremely rational. Logic, the steady progression from point to point, is what you put your faith in. You always have an objective; you always have a secret goal you are pursuing. Mercury-Capricorns often attain positions of leadership because they are so dependable and have an air of authority. (This is evident even in very small children who have Mercury in this position.) A problem you have in relating to people can be your dictatorial manner. You also tend to have a disapproving air about the foibles and frivolities of others. Life is serious to Mercury-Capricorns and you see its dark side—though a redeeming trait is your dry sense of humor.

MERCURY IN AQUARIUS Mercury in Aquarius indicates a fine and clever mind, inquisitive, accurate, and inventive. As a native of this position you take a great interest in other people and have excellent judgment of human nature. You love to analyze character and motivation, and with your finely tuned powers of observation are able to predict accurately how someone will react in a certain situation. You are a notorious people-watcher—in trains, buses, airports, and restaurants. Yours is a broad and emotionally detached outlook. Aquarius is the sign of the truth-seeker, which charac-terizes the way your mind works. You enjoy intellectual discussions about philosophy, metaphysics, and the future of mankind. Chances are you have read the classic writings of our great thinkers. You are especially suited for work in progressive professions—science, inventions, the world of television and electronics. Sometimes you may seem eccentric, for your ideas are advanced and you also enjoy saying things that shock other people.

MERCURY IN PISCES Pisces is the sign of psychic revelation, and Mercury in this sign gives you a subtle and intuitive mind. There is an intriguing air of mystery about the way you think. You don't logically arrive at conclusions; you seem to get flashes of knowledge or sudden feelings that are not based on previous facts or circumstances. Sometimes you will make a pronouncement, and afterward what you say will turn out to be true. You have accurate intuition. As a Mercury-Piscean you are imaginative and creative, but you tend to lack self-confidence. At times you appear timid or confused. You have deep sympathy and understanding for the foibles, failings, and follies of other people. In your opinion everyone, including a liar, has his own truth. You have such sensitivity to your environment that you cannot work or think straight when there is anything or anyone upsetting or jarring around you. An apt image for Mercury-in-Pisces is the absentminded professor.

VENUS

〜

V ENUS IS THE PLANET of love and pleasure. It rules over your capacity to express affection and to enjoy beauty. In addition, Venus lends your personality allure and desirability, and tells what kind of sex appeal you possess.

By looking at the position of Venus in your birth chart, you can answer such questions as: What kind of lovers do you attract? Are you flirtatious? Do you find happiness in your love affairs, or are you often disappointed? Where do your creative talents lie?

From early times, Venus in mythology has been a goddess whose dominion is love and the emotions. It was Venus who taught the arts of seduction to mortal men and women. Her power over the heart is legend; she "stole the wits even of the wise." She was extremely beautiful, and flowers grew wherever she walked. The goddess was also temperamental and self-indulgent, and at times could be treacherous and spiteful.

In astrology Venus rules over love affairs, art and beauty, adornment and decoration, the social graces, affection, harmony and friendship. The planet governs the higher emotions; its greatest gift is the gift of happiness. It can be said that Venus makes life beautiful.

The influence of Venus in your chart indicates how you relate to the opposite sex, whether you are popular and make friends easily, and also what artistic leanings you have. It rules your ability to love and to share with another person, and also governs your choice of gifts, cosmetics, flowers, and art objects. Being the planet of pleasure, it points to the kinds of amusements you are drawn to and in what ways you spend your money.

An Astronomical Look at Venus

Venus, the second planet from the Sun (a little over 67 million miles away), has long been known as Earth's sister-planet because it is very similar to Earth in size, mass, and density. Also, no other planet comes as near to us in its orbit. The orbit of Venus lies between us and the Sun and is an almost perfect circle.

Venus takes 225 days to complete its journey around the Sun. Like Mercury, the planet at times appears to us as a morning star and an evening star. In ancient days astronomers thought it was two separate stars—one that heralded the morning and the other that closed the doors of twilight.

Though Venus is so near to us, until the early 1960s its surface was a mystery due to the impenetrable veil of clouds that envelops it. Since that time space probes have shown that Venus has a hard crust like the Earth and a rocky surface covered with volcanoes, mountains, and craters. The most recent space probe to study Venus was the *Magellan* from 1990 to 1994. Venus's thick and heavy cloud covering has been analyzed as composed of carbon dioxide and sulphuric acid. The light of the Sun is reflected on these clouds, which is what makes Venus shine so brightly in the heavens. The planet's soft and beautifully luminous appearance has always fascinated earthlings.

When Venus is prominent in your horoscope you are usually a delightful companion, very easy to get along with. Venus also endows its natives with an unerring eye for design and beauty, and knowledge of how to dress and present themselves appealingly.

The other side of Venus's influence is that it can encourage a person to put more importance on pleasure, ease, and luxury than on self-discipline. A strong streak of narcissism and a lack of willpower indicate an afflicted* Venus in a chart.

The planet Venus never travels far from the Sun. In your horoscope, it is always either in your Sun sign or in one of the two signs immediately preceding or following your Sun sign.

*A planet is "afflicted" when the negative side of its power is stressed.

Where Is Your Venus?

To find out what sign Venus was in on the day of your birth, consult the Venus Tables on page 491.

VENUS IN ARIES This position of Venus gives a responsive and impulsive love nature. You are the kind of person who falls in love at first sight and never thinks once before following the dictates of your heart. You are strongly sensual and feel at your most complete when you are emotionally involved with someone. Physical appearance is what first attracts you, but to sustain a love affair you must also find mental compatibility. You are turned off by a sloppy appearance or loud, vulgar behavior. As a Venus-Arien you attract friends because of your demonstrative and enthusiastic attitude. You like to bring unexpected gifts to those you love. People with Venus in Aries are a curious mixture of sentimentality and aggressiveness. Your emotions are easily touched but you are also demanding and somewhat selfish. Others should not expect you to settle down into calm domestic peace; you are too restless and flirtatious, too enamored of *amour*.

VENUS IN TAURUS As a Venus-in-Taurus person you are affectionate and romantic, but you don't give your love away too quickly. A bad love affair is hard on you emotionally, so you take your time deciding on the right person to love. This process, however, is done by feeling rather than thinking logically. Yours is a very physical and earthy love nature. To you, love does not exist without sex. You are very demonstrative and generous toward a lover, sometimes too much so. Your passion can be smothering; you have an all-consuming need to make a lover belong to you. With friends, you are willing and ready to help, but you are as cautious about forming instant friendships as about love. This position of Venus brings money luck, sometimes through inheritance or marriage. Venus-in-Taurus people have a keen artistic eye and are interested in music. You also love to eat and have to fight overweight.

VENUS IN GEMINI If you have Venus in Gemini you must have an intellectual rapport with someone before your affections begin to blossom. Basically, you have a lighthearted attitude toward love. Intense, heavy emotional commitments are like an anchor around your neck. You have such a wide range of interests—travel, literature, music, seeing new places (and meeting new people)—that a lover just can't be the single focus of your life. This lends a certain coolness to your emotions. Your inconstancy sometimes causes you difficulties in love or marriage, but you bounce back quickly. Not even a frustrated lover can be angry at you very long—you are too charming, witty, and funny. You enjoy being with people and have lots of friends, and often more than one lover. (Venus exerts its most flirtatious influence in Gemini.) This position of Venus also stimulates a careless and free hand for spending money.

VENUS IN CANCER As a Venus-in-Cancer person you are romantic and sensitive. Being loved is more important to you than almost anything else, though you often conceal this need under a shell of reserve. You are not, however, so blindly romantic that you don't carefully consider future security. For example, if you are a man you may not propose marriage until you have some reliable means of earning a living; if you are a woman you make sure you won't end up sharing your lover's poverty or struggling to support him. In a love affair you would much rather be pursued than do the pursuing; you need the reassurance that someone wants you enough to go after you. Once you feel secure you are demonstrative and sensual. You have a wonderful gift for eloquence and you are also intensely sentimental. You will make a big fuss over your lover's birthday and remember the anniversary of the day you first met. This position of Venus indicates strong family loyalty. Venus-Cancerians are delightfully content to be at home and often love to cook.

VENUS IN LEO Without doing anything, Venus-Leos are able to attract warm feelings on the part of others. There is something so magnetic, so irresistibly *likeable*, about you that you enjoy great popularity. You are extravagantly affectionate and generous, buying expensive gifts for those you love and praising them to the skies in front of other people. Of course, what you must have back is intense devotion, loyalty, and lots of attention. You must always be dominant in a love affair. "All the world's a stage" was written about your emotional nature. No one can make a scene or confrontation as dramatic as a Venus-Leo. Needless to say you are drawn to the world of theater, and many of you are blessed with superb creative gifts. You also love fine possessions—money, clothes, jewels, furs. Though self-indulgent and pleasure-seeking, you are capable of making a great self-sacrifice for the happiness of someone else.

VENUS IN VIRGO If you have Venus in Virgo, you tend to be cautious about falling in love. You sometimes avoid involvement by taking small defects in a person and blowing them up out of proportion as major character flaws. You hold yourself on a tight rein, because you fear that your feelings will be exploited by someone unworthy. What you want in a love relationship is someone who will regard you as special. Curiously, however, when you do give your heart away it's often to the wrong person, who will not appreciate your fine qualities. (For some reason, this position of Venus tends to promote scandal.) Venus-Virgos have many virtues. You are refined and intelligent, loyal and sympathetic. Often you are an imaginative writer and

teacher; you have an excellent business sense and a quiet but witty sense of humor. Many of our brilliant government leaders and humanitarians are Venus-Virgos who have given their love to the world at large rather than to one person.

VENUS IN LIBRA You are in love with love. However, you are much more romantic than sensual. You skate gracefully over the profundities of love. Anything coarse, crude, vulgar, or earthy repels you. To you, true love is of the spirit. This is not to say you are sexually chaste. Indeed, you fall in love too easily and often have more than one *amour* going at a time. However, a love affair for a Venus-Libran must have all the right trappings and ritual. The ambiance created by champagne, intimate candlelit suppers, poetry written expressly for you, and beautiful gifts quite undoes your resistance. You put great store by charming social manners. People who don't measure up are summarily dismissed no matter what their deeper qualities may be. Venus-in-Libra can be cold and aloof toward anyone who presumes. This position of Venus is superb for an artistic talent or a flair for design and decoration. You are successful working in creative projects within a partnership or marriage (sometimes you combine both). Venus-Librans adore creature comforts and luxury and tend to be extravagant with money.

VENUS IN SCORPIO With your Venus in Scorpio, being in love is an all-consuming experience for you. There is a profound intensity to your emotions. Your sex life is passionate and demonstrative, and in a love affair it is the sexual side of the relationship that is emphasized. However, you also put love on a spiritual plane. Your deep need is to possess a lover wholly, to make your partner surrender to you body and soul. This, predictably, leads to stormy scenes; it is not easy for anyone to deal with such possessiveness. You are very sensitive to any rebuff; you can bristle like a porcupine. If someone does not respond to your love, you may even become vindictive. (If you have the Sun in Libra or Sagittarius, however, the jealous drive is lightened.) Venus-Scorpios tend to become involved in lucrative marriages or business partnerships. You have a sweeping compelling imagination, and many of you do highly original artistic work.

VENUS IN SAGITTARIUS Venus-Sagittarians begin love affairs with a spirit of adventure. You like to experience the excitement of love in the same way you search for diversion in the rest of your life. First attractions are always wildly romantic; as a Venus-Sagittarian you never seem to have commonplace or banal love affairs. However, you cannot sustain the emotion, and therefore never completely sacrifice your freedom to another person. What you want is the unobtainable—perfect love—and even if you could find it you would shrink from being possessed by it. With such contradictory attitudes, it's no wonder you leave your lovers terminally puzzled. Basically, Venus-Sagittarians are high-spirited, outgoing, and highly imaginative. You tend to attract powerful and influential friends and find it much easier to deal with friends than with lovers. For one thing, friendship is less demanding. Luck in creative affairs surrounds projects undertaken in foreign countries or far from home.

VENUS IN CAPRICORN Venus-Capricorns are as careful and cautious about love as about anything else. You may sometimes be thought of as cold and calculating because you believe in the dictate "it's just as easy to fall in love with someone rich as with someone poor." In fact, this was probably said originally by a Venus-Capricorn. However, it is far from telling the whole story. When in love, you are loyal, faithful, and dependable. If you don't marry rich, you work to give a mate security, and that includes material comforts. You may not be demonstrative and flowery, but what you say you mean. There is a dichotomy between your emotional life and your sexuality: You have earthy passions but keep them separate from your mental attitude. You can be sexually involved and detached at the same time. Venus in this position indicates a personality that is jealous, possessive, and fearful of rejection. Once snubbed, Venus-Capricorn's reaction is complete coldness.

VENUS IN AQUARIUS Venus in Aquarius promotes a kind and loving nature. You are helpful, charitable, and giving, but you are not an *emotional* person. You have an intellectually detached attitude toward love. To you, personal freedom is most important, and any relationship must leave you free to explore varied interests and hobbies, meet new people, and enjoy a wide range of friends. You cannot tolerate jealousy and will walk away from emotional scenes. You believe in fairness and openness. As a Venus-Aquarian, you are most likely to have platonic friendships because sexual involvements are more emotionally binding than you like. You are immensely popular, and can attract a great many lovers; often, however, you choose to direct your personal magnetism toward larger concerns and more enduring verities than mere romance. Aquarius is the sign of hopes and wishes, and Venus in this sign usually grants you what you dream of (though not until midlife or later).

VENUS IN PISCES As a Venus-Piscean you are inclined to have tender emotions and a deep capacity for devotion. In love, you are gentle, kindhearted, extremely sensitive—and fickle. It is not that you mean to be inconstant. It's simply that being in love is such a wonderful feeling, and *being loved* makes you feel complete.

You have an unfortunate penchant for choosing the wrong kind of lover, the kind who will take emotionally but not give back. Venus-Pisceans often have a secret love affair that causes them grief. You are completely intuitive about love, never logical. No other position of Venus can be as self-sacrificing or places more importance on the happiness of loved ones. You have true empathy for the problems of another person. Venus also indicates an imaginative and creative artistic flair, which helps you to put your feelings into writing, acting, or music. Venus-Pisceans are so generous that money slips through their fingers.

MARS

⟨⟨⟨⟨⟨⟩⟩⟩⟩⟩

MARS IS THE PLANET of physical energy. It governs your sex drive, your forcefulness, and your aggression. Mars is the planet that spurs you into action.

Are your sexual relationships ardent, tempestuous, and quarrelsome? Do you lose your temper quickly, or do you simmer for a while and then explode? In a conflict do you display cold contempt or heated anger? Is your willpower strong or weak? Does competition bring out your fighting spirit?

To learn more about your assertive power, you must study the position of Mars in your birth chart.

From early times Mars has excited and stirred the imagination. Because of its red color, Mars has always been known as a "fiery" planet. It is named after the Ro-

man god of war. Mars, whose name means "bright and burning one," was a warrior who exulted in battle and strife. Aggressive and quarrelsome, he never hesitated before leaping into the fray.

In astrology Mars governs energy, boldness, the will to win, the ability to turn ideas into action. It is the planet of passion and sexuality and force. It signifies ambition and desire, courage and strength. A large part of the planet's domain are your sex impulses, for Mars governs the sex organs. Mars's position in your chart indicates what stirs your passions and whether you can get your own way. It tells what kind of physical endurance you possess and how accident-prone you are.

An Astronomical Look at Mars

As we travel away from the Sun, Mars is the first planet whose orbit falls outside that of the Earth. It is the fourth planet from the Sun (about 141¼ million miles away). Mars is about half the size of the Earth, with a diameter of 4,200 miles compared to Earth's 8,000 miles. Like the Earth, it rotates on an axis, and its day is very near in length to ours, approximately 24 hours and 37½ minutes. However, a year on Mars (the length of time it takes to travel once around the Sun) is 687 days, nearly twice Earth's 365¼ days.

We have seen Mars very clearly through telescopes and noted its craters and rock formations, and when *Viking* 1 landed there in 1976 it confirmed that the planet has a barren, desertlike landscape scattered with rocks. We also found giant volcanoes, one of them over 15 miles high and 350 miles wide, and a 2,000-mile-long canyon. The planet has two white caps in the polar regions (very like Earth's North and South Poles), which we believe to be a mixture of ice water and carbonic acid ice. In 1996 scientists analyzing rocks taken from Mars announced the discovery of markings that might be microscopic fossils of a bacterialike organism that may have lived on Mars more than 3.6 billion years ago. Scientists continue to debate whether these are traces of a primitive Martian life form.

From Earth, to the ordinary observer, the most striking and beautiful characteristic of Mars is its color. It glows with red and ochre hues and is very bright in the heavens. Our space probes indicate that Mars's surface material is iron oxide, which accounts for its reddish color. The sky surrounding the planet is also a reddish-pink, most likely because of fine dust particles stirred up by the wind. Once every fifteen years, Mars comes nearer to the Earth than any other planet except for Venus. At that time Mars shines with a red splendor that rivals anything in the sky.

Mars's influence also brings strife and conflict, tension and anger, accidents and destruction. It rules heat, fire, earthquakes, violence, and war. The negative side of Mars's power can cause sudden injury or illness.

When Mars is prominent in your chart you have a go-getting personality with enormous energy and a rugged constitution. You tend to be enterprising, quick, and active, and you hate to be ordered around. Depending on how you use Mars's force, you may be argumentative, quarrelsome, and reckless and encounter a great deal of discord in your sex relationships. You may be a strong leader, adventurous and pioneering, but may also be quick-tempered, brash, impulsive, and impatient.

In its highest form Mars represents your unleashed energy and your human will. It is up to you to use this force constructively.

Where Is Your Mars?

To find out what sign Mars was in on the day of your birth, consult the Mars Tables on page 497.

MARS IN ARIES Mars is in its natural home in Aries (the sign that it rules), and emphasizes qualities of brilliance, force, and energy. As a Mars-Arien you are given self-confidence and force of character. Others always know how you feel about a subject because you tell them in no uncertain terms. You are courageous and honest, but the opposite side of the coin is that you can be tactless, blunt, and combative. Your passions are fiery and are quickly ignited. Active and assertive in your sex life, you aggressively go after what you want (whether it's a long-term lover or just a bedmate for the night). The professions of big business and politics are populated with Mars-Ariens, for natives of this position have a domineering will to win. You are able to make others respond to your ideas. Your youthful springy appearance lasts a lifetime.

MARS IN TAURUS If you have Mars in Taurus, you tend to triumph through your own determined and persistent efforts. Your vitality is a slow and steady force that drives you on to success. Success to you means money, material possessions, and true love. A great deal of your energy is spent in sexual pursuits; your passions are earthy and voluptuous. In love affairs you try to dominate and to possess, and the firmness to your nature can become downright obstinate. Difficulties tend to arise because you are unwilling to see anyone else's point of view. Because of your tenacity, you have the power to create almost anything you can envision. Sometimes a bent toward depression or temper tantrums mars your happiness. During your lifetime you often accumulate money and are known as a big spender.

MARS IN GEMINI Mars in Gemini favors energetic activity of the mind. You are brilliantly intellectual, with a steel-trap brain that quickly grasps concepts and spins new ideas. You are incisive and practical and arrive at conclusions in a flash. The problem is that you lack force of will. You hesitate, vacillate, and think of yet another delay. In matters of sex, you experience desire in the *mind* before it becomes a reality. You enjoy the adventure leading up to lovemaking and have passions that are easily aroused. However, as soon as an affair loses zest and becomes ordinary you look for the escape hatch. You tend to have a number of affairs and marriages. Mars-Geminis are able to inspire and to lead others through the power of the spoken and written word. Often you have a magnetic voice and a compelling talent to convince others of what you say.

MARS IN CANCER Mars's power turns subtle in Cancer. You have great strength of will, but it is never thrust into the open. Like the tides, you wear down opposition by repeated assault. Each wave may accomplish little, but the accumulated effect is overpowering. In sex, Mars-in-Cancer's approach is emotional. You are sensuous but refined, and your lovemaking is a highly intuitive art. Your passion, however, is dependent on what is forthcoming from a lover. If a lover is insensitive or unresponsive, he or she may find that your get-up-and-go just got up and went. Yet, as a native of this Mars placement, you will cling to a relationship that does not make you happy. You react only in outbursts of temper and nervous irritability. What you often require is an outlet for your pent-up energies. You are noted for your breadth of vision and highly emotional work.

MARS IN LEO In Leo, Mars's fire is accentuated. With this Mars position in your chart you are never ordinary. You make grand plans and possess the force and drive to put them into action. No one else can grab the attention and affection of others the way you can. You also have a dramatic sex drive. Hot-blooded and impulsive, you are successful in sex relationships because of your dynamism. You must dominate in affairs and demand a great deal of attention, but you are also warm, expressive, ardent, and affectionate. You prefer to make love in luxurious, rich surroundings. You are creative at work, but at times can be overbearing, authoritative, and a bit condescending. Mars-Leos see events in terms of themselves; it would never occur to you to be an anonymous observer. You are lucky in speculation and gambling, and often attract powerful friends.

MARS IN VIRGO As a Mars-in-Virgo person, you are a prodigious worker who finds your best success in a systematized approach. You are ambitious and proud, though this is not always apparent on the surface. Extremely strong-willed, you can separate yourself from your emotions when it comes to making decisions. In your work you are shrewd, calculating, and quietly determined. You suspect people who only want to deal with big problems because somehow such people never seem to reach any useful conclusions. Mars-in-Virgo may appear sexually cool, but in truth you glamorize sex. You want it to be both physically rapturous and mentally exciting. Your passions are strong but kept under tight rein. Mars-Virgos tend to be successful in professions where control of emotions is advantageous

(such as politicians, psychologists, and investigators). When putting a plan into action you must beware of getting bogged down in detail.

MARS IN LIBRA When Mars is in Libra the power of this planet seems to fluctuate. You are impulsive and sensuous in your sex drive. A great deal of your energy is spent forming emotional relationships. Yet you have a languid attitude toward sex and often must be sought after rather than be the aggressor. You are idealistic and esthetic; crudeness of any kind turns you off. You prefer liaisons with cultivated, sophisticated lovers, but tend to become involved in unhappy sex relationships. This position of Mars is excellent for a unique artistic or literary talent. There is a great beauty and balance in your work. You have an enviable ability to make a pleasing impression on the public. Mars-Librans believe passionately in fair play. Your actions are always preceded by a careful weighing of the pros and cons.

MARS IN SCORPIO Mars in Scorpio underscores persistence and intensity. As a Mars-Scorpio you are a hard-driving and resourceful person whose strength is not so much shown in the heat of action as in determination and relentlessness. Your efforts are well disciplined, always directed toward a purpose. There are no wasted movements or needless expenditures of energy. You have a strong and deeply felt sexuality. However, it is sometimes an *emotional* sexuality, displayed in jealousy, anger, hurt feelings, and resentment. Though it is possible for you to be ruthless in your relationships, you are far more often simply quarrelsome and touchy.

This position of Mars enhances imagination and a powerful creative drive. You are always able to move an audience. Often you are attracted to professions or situations that contain an element of danger or death.

MARS IN SAGITTARIUS In Sagittarius, the power of Mars exhibits itself in brilliant flashes. It promotes courage, independence, and daring. Dashing and exciting as your actions may be, you are easily distracted. Your attention becomes riveted to a new plan, and your meteoric enthusiasm turns in that direction. This does not mean you do not accomplish anything, for you can produce remarkable results in a short time. Passionate and sensual, you may have numerous affairs because of your open, exploratory nature. You look on emotional commitments as a form of personal restriction. A sex relationship quickly begins, and just as quickly ends. You tend to be impulsive and act rashly. Quick-witted in speech and writing, you have the power to amuse and delight. You make a marvelous first impression.

MARS IN CAPRICORN Mars in Capricorn signifies force and energy kept under control, to be used when necessary. As a person with this Mars position, you are fierce, magnetic, and commanding. Your strength lies in your obstinacy and ability to endure. When obstacles block your path you run over them roughshod. You have vigor and dynamic force, and also quiet self-reliance. Your sexual nature is earthy and passionate, but the element of self-control marks your relationships. At times hot-blooded, sexy, even romantic, at other times you are chilly and disinterested. What you

usually do is channel your formidable power into the direction that serves you best. In their youth Mars-Capricorns often have a secret love affair with an older person. At some point in their lives, strong personal ambition tends to project Mars-Capricorns into the public eye.

MARS IN AQUARIUS In Aquarius, the energy of Mars is expressed on a mental plane. You are quick in your actions, but before you act you must be committed intellectually. You tend to be very people-oriented and involved in a variety of projects. There is an element of reform or fighting for freedom in your outlook. High-strung and unpredictable, you struggle between wanting to do things alone and getting involved in group activities. There is also ambivalence in your sexual nature. You have strong desires that are not always reachable. You try to deal with sex relationships rationally, and swing back and forth between passionate involvement and detachment. You acknowledge sexual desire but don't want to be fettered by it. This sometimes leads to your having a number of affairs (often simultaneously); that way, each affair can't be a total commitment. As a Mars-Aquarian you have acute insights into human nature.

MARS IN PISCES Pisces is an emotional sign, and your strength with Mars in Pisces is your power to stir the feelings and grab the emotions. If you have this Mars position you may be noted for your compelling imagination. Many artists, writers, and actors have Mars in Pisces. Enormously receptive to your environment, you store impressions in your subconscious and then produce them at the opportune time. You shoulder the responsibilities of others without complaint. Intensity of feeling is evident in your sexuality. You are sensuous, have deep passions, and display a high level of fervor. You seek to involve yourself totally in a sex relationship, for this is a way in which you can draw closer to another human being. You may suffer disappointment in love. During your lifetime you attract influential friends and gain monetarily from these associations.

Jupiter

JUPITER IS THE PLANET of good luck, optimism, success, and generosity. Jupiter brings joy to life.

Are you a generous person? Do you seem to attract success through your close associations? Are you able to turn your ideas into profit? Does your luck work for you when you need it most?

If you answer yes to these questions, Jupiter is well aspected in your horoscope. The position of Jupiter in your birth chart can indicate where your fortunate opportunities are to be found. This benevolent planet shows where you have the most room to expand and the areas in which you will get the best out of life.

Jupiter has always been identified with the idea of expansiveness and abundance. In mythology, Jupiter was the ruler of the heavens, supreme god of gods. He was an all-powerful and benign guardian who symbolized honor, good faith, and wisdom.

In astrology, the planet Jupiter is known as the Greater Fortune (Venus is the Lesser Fortune). Jupiter's kingdom is luck, health and happiness, wealth and worldly goods, power and high position. It rules over knowledge, higher learning, breadth of vision, and honesty. Its influence bestows a willingness to partake of life, to gather new experiences. The knowledge that Jupiter imparts is on a philosophical level, as opposed to the day-to-day cleverness that Mercury confers.

Jupiter's position in your chart indicates how outgoing and genial you are, whether you attract money and posses-

♃

AN ASTRONOMICAL LOOK AT JUPITER

The fifth planet in our solar system is Jupiter, approximately 483½ million miles away from the Sun. It is our largest planet, more than 300 times as massive as Earth, and has a diameter of 89,000 miles compared to the Earth's 8,000. Jupiter is a colossal world so big that it could contain the Earth and every other planet in our solar system, and still have lots of room to spare. At certain times (every 13 months or so) Jupiter is the most brilliant object in the sky, shining with a flashing white luster that rivals any star.

Jupiter completes its orbit around the Sun in a little under 12 years. Like the Earth, it rotates on its own axis, and for a planet its size spins very quickly indeed. A day on Jupiter takes only nine hours and 50½ minutes. Because it rotates so rapidly, Jupiter has a noticeable bulge at the equator.

Astronomers have long noticed that the distances between the planets in our solar system follow a definite sequence or formula (known as Bode's Law). Mercury, Venus, Earth, and Mars all follow this sequence. However, between Mars and Jupiter there is an enormous gap, and for years astronomers searched for a lost planet in this vacant space. On January 1, 1801, a very small body, an asteroid 485 miles in diameter, was discovered traveling in the orbit that was supposed to have a planet. Since that time thousands more asteroids have been discovered in this area, which is now known as the asteroid belt. One theory is that these particles are the result of the breaking up of an ancient planet in our solar system. Another theory is that the asteroids are part of a planet that has not yet formed.

In 1973 *Pioneer 10* discovered that Jupiter emits about twice the amount of heat that it receives from the Sun. Jupiter, therefore, has an internal heat source and is, in effect, a miniature sun. The famous astronomer Carl Sagan called Jupiter a "failed star," meaning that Jupiter is made up of the same elements as our Sun (hydrogen and helium), but it does not have planets the way our Sun does. However, it is theorized that Jupiter may once have been the center of its own planetary system, and possibly the parent of Mars, Venus, Earth—and the lost planet that is now the asteroid belt.

In 1979 a new discovery about Jupiter was made when *Voyager 1* and *Voyager 2* sent back pictures of dusty rings around the planet. (In the following ten years *Voyager 2* found rings around Uranus and Neptune as well.)

In December 1995, after a six-year journey, a probe from our spacecraft *Galileo* landed on Jupiter. The probe sent back thousands of detailed photographs of Jupiter's hot surface, rings, and sixteen moons, until the probe was vaporized by Jupiter's extremely hot temperature: 3,400 degrees F.

sions, and in what career you will have the most luck. Jupiter signifies the good things that come to you easily and with little effort—this is the planet of "free lunch." It is said that when Jupiter is working for you, you will never go under. You will often find that Jupiter's power comes to your rescue at the last minute. However, it is also true that unless you put Jupiter's gifts to good use and not waste them, they can be taken away as quickly as they were given.

When Jupiter is prominent in your horoscope you tend to be well liked and popular, friendly, broadminded, and cheerful, successful in career and business. (An interesting sidelight: You will probably discover that a large number of the people with whom you have an immediate rapport have Jupiter in the same sign as your Sun sign.)

Jupiter can also be too much of a good thing, for its influence can make you extravagant, lazy and luxury-loving, profligate with money, and blindly optimistic. If things fall into your lap too easily, you never develop strength of character or spiritual wisdom.

Jupiter is the planet of blessings—blessings we must learn to use wisely.

Where Is Your Jupiter?

To find out what sign Jupiter was in on the day of your birth, consult the Jupiter Tables on page 501.

JUPITER IN ARIES Luck follows you in professions where you can be your own boss. You are discontent when you have to follow other people's orders and, being independent and brash, you immediately try to change that situation. Confident and enthusiastic, you are a natural leader capable of running organizations, groups, social clubs, and businesses. You have original ideas and make swifter progress by relying on your own opinions and abilities. You can be a bit bullying and are sometimes quite extravagant in your spending. This position of Jupiter fosters an ability to win over influential people and obtain their help in your career. Jupiter-Ariens often achieve high rank in politics, literature, science, and the military. Your luckiest times of the year are when the Sun is in the signs of Aries, Leo,

and Sagittarius. Also, people who have those Sun signs are likely to bring you financial benefit.

JUPITER IN TAURUS Jupiter and Taurus are very harmonious; Taurus is the money sign of the zodiac and Jupiter brings abundance. You are successful in fields where finances are prominent, such as banking and stocks and bonds, and investments are likely to bring reward. You are conservative about the way you handle money; security is extremely important to you. (If Jupiter is afflicted, however, you will overspend on luxuries for yourself; this is also true if Venus is prominent in your chart.) As a Jupiter-Taurean you have an eye for beauty and art. You tend to collect paintings and sculpture, jewelry, and antiques that often increase in value. In this sign, Jupiter bestows a lovely voice and artistic talent. Natives are also successful in careers they conduct at home, such as writing, interior decorating, and art collecting. Jupiter-Taureans tend to marry well; career opportunity often comes to you through the opposite sex. Your luckiest times of the year are when the Sun is in the signs of Taurus, Virgo, and Capricorn.

JUPITER IN GEMINI If you are a Jupiter-Gemini, you are blessed with an adventurous attitude and a knack for getting into advantageous situations. Though you don't necessarily look for moneymaking opportunities, these usually come to you through the many friends and contacts that you acquire. You achieve best success in intellectual areas, such as teaching, lecturing, diplomatic careers, and law. You would also do well in the airline industry. Gemini is the sign of communication, and if your Jupiter is in Gemini you profit financially in ventures where communicating is prominent—publishing, magazine writing, TV reporting or commentating, and acting. As a Jupiter-in-Gemini person you are versatile and clever, and often you make a name for yourself in more than one profession. A change in vocation at one point in your life is almost certain. Your luckiest times of the year are when the Sun is in the signs of Gemini, Libra, and Aquarius.

JUPITER IN CANCER This is one of the luckiest positions Jupiter can be in. As a Jupiter-Cancerian you have a wonderful disposition, are good-humored, funny, and optimistic. You are popular wherever you go, and this opens many doors for you. Retentive Cancer is a sign that holds on to money; people with Jupiter in this sign are lucky with investments, real estate, inheritances, and the stock market. You are imaginative and sympathetic, and do well in creative pursuits. Old things have a special appeal to you; you would be successful in the antique business and museum work. Anything involving food and drink also brings luck; many of you make successful chefs, restaurateurs, and cookbook writers. You will probably acquire enough material possessions by the time you reach middle age to ensure that your later years are peaceful and secure. You make excellent parents and your children tend to bring you benefits. Your luckiest times of the year are when the Sun is in the signs of Cancer, Scorpio, and Pisces.

JUPITER IN LEO Jupiter in Leo bestows an extraordinary public appeal. If you are a native of this position you are well suited for the theater, television and movies, politics, advertising, and public relations. Your full potential is achieved through leadership; you are wretchedly unhappy if forced to stay on the lowest rung. You think big, are ambitious, and have a penchant for grandeur and extravagant display. In professions where this is useful, such as the entertainment industry, the world of fashion, and high-powered selling jobs, you are predestined to succeed. The problem is that success may come too easily. In that event, Jupiter-Leos can become boastful and power-hungry. Fortunately, this does not happen often, for Jupiter gives you personal charm and warmhearted vitality. Other people want to do things for you, and you often benefit from influential friends. Your luckiest times of the year are when the Sun is in the signs of Leo, Sagittarius, and Aries.

JUPITER IN VIRGO Jupiter in the practical sign of Virgo gives you a capacity for making a success of a hobby or a pastime. Many famous Jupiter-Virgos start out with a shoestring and build empires. If you have this Jupiter position you are smart, analytical, and persevering. You figure out the surest route to the largest dividends. The power of Jupiter surrounds you in intellectual pursuits, but the difference between Jupiter-Virgos and other intellectual signs is that Virgos have an uncommon amount of *common sense*. You are also superb at handling detail and do your best work a step at a time. You would make a successful teacher, accountant, literary critic, journalist, or news commentator. Your ability to grasp facts and then apply them systematically makes careers in the fields of space technology, science, and medicine accessible to you. Your luckiest times of the year are when the Sun is in the signs of Taurus, Virgo, and Capricorn.

JUPITER IN LIBRA Jupiter in this sign bestows a magnetic and charming personality. Luck comes to you through your artistic talents and your eye for beauty and harmony. Many of you are talented musicians, painters, interior decorators, fashion designers, and art collectors. You have a knack for getting your talent on display and winning friends in high places. You like to entertain, and many of your allies are won in the relaxed and genial atmosphere you are able to create. More than natives of any other Jupiter position, you benefit from marriage. Marriage often brings social position and wealth, and sometimes an entrée into the business world. Jupiter-Librans are most successful in partnerships; you should never start a business completely on your own. Your finely balanced reason and impartiality would make you an excellent judge, lawyer, or diplomat. Your luckiest times of the year are when the Sun is in the signs of Gemini, Libra, and Aquarius.

JUPITER IN SCORPIO Jupiter in Scorpio is a very powerful influence on willpower and personal magnetism. If you have this Jupiter position you tend to be successful in artistic work. Many Jupiter-Scorpios excel at ferreting out hidden information. This would make you an excellent psychiatrist, researcher, politician, or security agent in government. Luck comes to you through your strong attraction for the opposite sex. Often the door is opened to career and financial op-

portunity because of sexual liaisons. Scorpio is the sign of death and regeneration, and Jupiter in this sign promotes skill in medicine, surgery, and therapy. You possess shrewdness in money matters, and many of you have a Midas touch for picking lucrative investments. Sometimes you benefit from inheritances during your lifetime. Your luckiest times of the year are when the Sun is in the signs of Cancer, Scorpio, and Pisces.

JUPITER IN SAGITTARIUS Sagittarius is the sign that Jupiter rules, and the planet's expansive, generous qualities are emphasized. With this Jupiter position, you are a person who likes to live well; you have a free hand when it comes to spending. Fortunately, you usually attract financial luck. No other Jupiter position augurs as much success in this area. As a native, you have an instinct for turning ideas into cash; you think big and profit accordingly. You also tend to marry well, and many of you inherit money. Jupiter in Sagittarius, though, does not make the personality crass or materialistic. You are high-minded and idealistic. You will often give up a well-paying position if it doesn't suit your inner calling. Gifted with great intellectual capacity, you are drawn to professions in law, government, diplomacy, and the world of literature and philosophy. Your luckiest times of the year are when the Sun is in the signs of Aries, Leo, and Sagittarius.

JUPITER IN CAPRICORN In the strong, materialistic sign of Capricorn, Jupiter's power is expressed through ambition. As a native of this placement, you gain high position in life through hard work and fierce willpower. Capricorn is an earth sign, and Jupiter's influence is propitious for enterprises that involve earth in some way: mining, construction, land development, real estate, and the oil industry. Success isn't a flash in the pan with you. It is achieved gradually, but over the long term you tend to reach the top because you are disciplined. Jupiter in Capricorn confers an instinct for business; you are a canny trader and tend to handle finances conservatively. Others may notice a curious mixture of economy and extravagance in your spending habits. You may pinch nickels but will be lavish with large sums. This can be useful in business: You are able to keep to a budget but are not afraid to spend when you have to. The luckiest times of the year for you are when the Sun is in the signs of Taurus, Virgo, and Capricorn.

JUPITER IN AQUARIUS Jupiter in Aquarius contributes to a magnetic ability to win friends. You usually find good fortune through your friends and unexpected opportunities. Aquarius is also the sign of the future, and as a native of this Jupiter position you tend to be successful in professions of the modern era—television, computers, electronics, aviation, and the space industry. You easily become bored when the sole purpose of an activity is to make money. You usually find your best opportunity in professions where a broader view is necessary. You are also endowed with a special aptitude for music, and many Jupiter-Aquarians

become well known in that world. One of the nicest benefits of Jupiter in this sign is that you bring luck to others. You have a sharp intuition about human nature coupled with idealism. The most auspicious times of the year for you are when the Sun is in the signs of Gemini, Libra, and Aquarius.

JUPITER IN PISCES Jupiter is strong here because it endows you with the power to appeal to the emotions. Work in which you deal directly with others, especially where there is a high level of feeling, will bring success. This is especially true for those of you who enter the healing arts. Jupiter also accentuates imagination, wisdom, and high ideals. In general, you do your best work in fields in which you help humanity. Jupiter-Pisceans are singled out for success in social or religious work, politics, and philanthropic organizations. Work that involves travel over water brings other opportunities into your life. You also have a deft touch with animals, would make a fine veterinarian, and many of you have lucrative businesses breeding horses, owning cattle ranches, and raising cats and dogs for show. Jupiter in Pisces usually grants you your secret ambition. You attract fortune because of your likeableness and popularity. The luckiest times of the year for you are when the Sun is in the signs of Cancer, Scorpio, and Pisces.

SATURN

S ATURN IS THE PLANET of responsibility and symbolizes the ethic of hard work. Under its influence a person's character is strengthened through trial and difficulty. It has been said that Saturn disciplines us until we can learn to discipline ourselves.

Are you able to stick with a task until you have it completed? Do you at times feel beset by problems or see obstacles at every turn? Would other people call you stubborn? Have you sometimes felt lonely and depressed?

If you answer yes, then you have felt the presence of Saturn in your life.

The planet is named after the Roman titan-god who was the father of Jupiter, Neptune, and Pluto. Saturn was also a symbol for Father Time, for he brought to an end all things that had a beginning.

In astrology Saturn is the planet of diligence, selfcontrol, and limitation. Its domain is patience, stability, maturity, and realism. Its influence is stern and restrictive, cold and severe.

Saturn is called the Celestial Taskmaster, for it teaches us the lessons we must learn in life. In the grand plan of the universe, Saturn does not give us more than we can handle. Under Saturn's influence we achieve by overcoming obstacles and hardship. Sometimes the effort itself is

AN ASTRONOMICAL LOOK AT SATURN

Until the end of the eighteenth century Saturn was the most remote planet in our solar system. It is the sixth planet from the Sun, over 887 million miles away—almost twice as far from the Sun as Jupiter is. Saturn is a large planet (second only to Jupiter), measuring over 75,000 miles at its equator compared to Earth's 8,000 miles. Saturn moves very slowly around the Sun, taking 29½ years to complete one orbit. For such a large planet it spins with great velocity on its own axis: A day on Saturn is only 10 hours and 14 minutes.

To the ordinary observer here on Earth, Saturn shines with a steady, yellowish light, rather dim compared to brilliant Jupiter. In ancient days Saturn was considered the least interesting planet of all, since it does not have Venus's soft luminosity, Mars's red color, or Jupiter's radiance.

The ancients were wrong about Saturn's lack of interest as a celestial body. We only recently discovered that Saturn is a multihued planet, with bands of yellow, golden-brown, and reddish-brown on its surface. Saturn is now considered our most interesting planet because of its dramatic rings.*

First seen in 1610 by Galileo through his telescope, these bright and dark rings circle Saturn at its equator in a magnificent spectacle. Until 1969 astronomers believed there were only three rings; in that year a fourth ring was discovered, shortly followed by the observation of a fifth and sixth ring.

Then, in November 1980, America's space probe *Voyager 1* swept by Saturn and sent back to Earth pictures of this astronomical wonder that went far beyond our imagination. There were not six, but thousands of separate ringlets—like the grooves in a phonograph record 170,000 miles wide. *Voyager 1*'s photographs showed there are rings within rings, like concentric ripples in a cosmic pond. The rings are made up of swarms of icy particles, ranging in size from snowballs to a few giant chunks the size of mountains. One of the largest rings, what we call the F-ring, is composed of twisted strands of ice, each 500 miles long, entwined into a gigantic braid.

When *Voyager 2* flew by Saturn in August 1981 the spacecraft reported that a cloud of gases circling the planet is 300 times hotter than the Sun's corona! This is the hottest spot ever detected in the solar system. In June 2004 the *Cassini* spacecraft is expected to arrive at Saturn and begin orbiting the planet over a four-year period. Astronomers continue to study the complex and "mind-boggling" (as one expressed it) data that our space probes are giving us about this spectacular planet.

---

*Saturn's rings were once thought to be unique in our solar system, but we now know that Saturn is not the only planet that has rings. In 1979, *Voyager 1* and *Voyager 2* flew by Jupiter, sending back evidence of dusty rings around that planet. In 1986, *Voyager 2* found nine dark rings around Uranus. In 1989, *Voyager 2* discovered that Neptune has five rings.

the reward, for effort is what builds character. In the end, what we learn under Saturn's influence we keep for the rest of our lives.

Saturn's position in your chart indicates how well you accept responsibility, whether you are self-disciplined, and what delays and opposition you can expect to encounter. When its influence is prominent you tend to be reliable, trustworthy, and patient. Saturn gives the power to endure and provides the tenacity and perseverance to realize your potential.

Saturn's effect is to delay rewards until they are earned. It perfects human nature while it bestows an ability to wait. It is the planet of courage, steadfastness, and integrity.

Many people shrink from accepting its burdens, but Saturn is not to be feared. If you look into your past, you will probably see that you have achieved lasting strength and satisfaction from triumphing over obstacles.

As a negative influence, Saturn can make a person overly ambitious, calculating and selfish, solitary, inhibited, and unhappy. Its negative influence is associated with inflexibility, cruelty, humorlessness, and pessimism. Saturn also represents illness, handicaps, and misfortune.

Keep in mind, however, that Saturn is only one of many influences in a chart. Obviously, it is an important influence, but Saturn's power is not necessarily felt in an overwhelming way.

In its symbolic form, Saturn is our destiny. It rules fate, the things we cannot escape, and the payment we must make for what we receive.

Where Is Your Saturn?

To find out what sign Saturn was in on the day of your birth, consult the Saturn Tables on page 506.

SATURN IN ARIES Saturn brings delay to Aries, the sign of initiative, and the result is confusion. If you are a Saturn-Arien, you can be strong and powerful one minute and irresolute and wavering the next. This position is not an easy one, for you must continually fight against obstacles placed in your way. Many of you achieve success, but not without disappointment and setback. Saturn in Aries makes you ambitious and determined, and promotes your power to control other people. On the negative side, Saturn-Ariens can be stubborn, dictatorial, and sometimes solitary and grumpy. In general, your hardest times come early in life. It is then that you develop the strength of character that serves you well in later years. As you grow older, each year brings less struggle and more success. Natives of this Saturn position tend to suffer from headaches and dental problems.

SATURN IN TAURUS In Taurus, the obstinate and tenacious qualities of Saturn are emphasized. With this Saturn position you are determined and capable, and take responsibility seriously. Your strong willpower borders on stubbornness and rigidity. You usually try to amass possessions and wealth because of your underlying fear that you will be left alone and bereft, without material resources or love. Unfortunately, Saturn in Taurus does not predict an easy time financially. Money tends to come in slowly and to be dissipated along the way. You tend to spend a lot of effort trying to put away the savings, stocks, bonds, and real estate you feel you must have. As a result, you are sometimes considered materialistic and selfish. However, once you achieve material comfort (usually later in life), you are generous to others in need, for you understand what it means not to have enough. Saturn in this position makes you susceptible to colds, sore throats, and thyroid problems.

SATURN IN GEMINI Gemini is a good home for Saturn. This versatile sign's intellectual qualities are emphasized by Saturn. With Saturn in Gemini, you have a sharp mind that is deepened with understanding under this planet's steadying influence. You can, however, be cynical and sarcastic, skeptical and coldhearted. Much more likely, you have a happy combination of native wisdom and a youthful wish to learn. Saturn-Geminis sometimes have a difficult childhood during which you suffer loneliness or sorrow. You may have a hard time obtaining an education. Later in life, you are likely to encounter obstacles while traveling. However, Saturn endows you with a good head for finances, and also a musical ability. You prosper when engaged in work that requires both patience and intelligence. Saturn-Geminis are susceptible to ailments of the chest and lungs.

SATURN IN CANCER Saturn encourages too much dependence on others in this emotional and clinging sign. As a Saturn-Cancerian, you love to overindulge in eating, drinking, and other sensual pleasures. In this position, though, Saturn also gives a shrewdness and tenacity to your personality. You are superb at seeing a task through to completion. You are also ambitious and strive to find material wealth to make your life secure. The obstacles that Saturn places in your path are insecurity and lack of confidence. Sometimes your early life is marked by problems with parents, especially a mother. Many of you Saturn-Cancerians had to take on family responsibility at a very young age. Natives of this position tend to marry someone older in an effort to find an anchor and stability. Saturn endows you with good business sense, although you must be cautious in dealings with relatives. The negative side of Saturn in Cancer is a tendency to melancholy and self-pity. You are prone to digestive and stomach problems; if you are not careful, you can become quite overweight.

SATURN IN LEO Restrictive Saturn and the expansive sign of Leo are not in harmony. Saturn in Leo is likely to bring a chill to the emotions and disappointment in love. There are, however, many good points to this Saturn position: You are proud and strong-willed, self-assured and authoritative. You are good at organizing people and assuming responsibility. As a Saturn-Leo, you have an instinct for knowing how to draw a public to you. You are inclined to be cold and analytical in choosing your associations, though you are subtle enough to keep this from being obvious to the casual observer. You fear appearing mediocre and ordinary, and you hide feelings of envy and jealousy because this is a weakness you will never admit to. You strive to make a dramatic impression, but tend to be suspicious of compliments and dislike excessive displays of affection. In your career you often rise to great heights, but Saturn in Leo has a way of causing a downfall when you are at the peak. Natives of this position are susceptible to high blood pressure and heart ailments.

SATURN IN VIRGO The responsible planet Saturn and the conscientious sign of Virgo work well together. This Saturn position heightens Virgo's intellectual ability and practical turn of mind. You are methodical and organized, willing to work hard to achieve goals. To you, theory and practice are one and the same; you immediately put what you learn into use. Saturn does place hardship in your path, usually early in life when you must sometimes cope with sorrow, disappointment, or frail health. You can become bogged down in trivialities because you are a stickler for details. You are also capable of becoming a petty tyrant when others don't see things your way. Saturn gives you wisdom but not necessarily vision. Too often you see the dark side of life and fear the unknown—that is, what you cannot categorize and control. On the plus side, Saturn endows you with an ability to make money, especially in real estate. Natives of this Saturn position are vulnerable to intestinal upsets and ulcers.

SATURN IN LIBRA Libra is a favorable sign for Saturn. As a Saturn-Libran you are gifted with good judgment and an instinct for making the right impression on others. You know when to be aggressive and when to be diplomatic. Though it is part of Saturn's lessons to bring some sorrow and disappointment in relationships, you usually benefit from the stability of marriage. However, there may be a divorce before you find happiness with a mate. Sometimes an early love affair turns out to be the love of your life but ends in loss. Saturn in Libra may suppress the desire to share and be close to another person, which often results in loneliness. In general, this is an excellent position for success in public life, and also for a strong showing in artistic pursuits. It has been said that if your Saturn is in Libra, you will only get into trouble when you are doing what you ought not to be doing. Saturn-Librans are susceptible to back injuries and kidney problems.

SATURN IN SCORPIO Saturn is powerful in this secretive and passionate sign, lending subtlety and force to the personality. As a native of this position you understand human motivation, which enables you to control others. Your dominating strength is often hidden under a pleasant and genial exterior. Saturn, however, places obstacles in your path in the form of emotional difficulties and sometimes scandal. You tend to be drawn to secret love affairs that bring sorrow or trouble into your life. When you achieve power you sometimes undergo a downfall because of rumor and gossip. When young you often have health problems, but you get through this and tend to live to a ripe old age. This is an excellent planetary position for executive ability and an unswerving commitment to a goal. Your strong will can become inflexible. Once you set on a course, you see it through to the end. You are prone to secret brooding, but there is usually a touch of dry Saturnian humor to relieve it. Saturn-Scorpios are liable to suffer the loss of loved ones early in life.

SATURN IN SAGITTARIUS In Sagittarius, Saturn has the effect of delaying success until the lessons of patience and perseverance are learned. You may encounter adversity and setbacks early in life, and often must work hard and long to receive what is due you. However, as you get older you acquire wisdom, vision, and a depth of understanding that fashions you into a leader. Saturn gives your mind a philosophical bent; you can usually face up to what life offers because you put your faith in the long-term outcome. This is an excellent position for success in law, politics, writing, and foreign affairs. Saturn, however, emphasizes Sagittarius's tactlessness and cynical point of view. It is possible you may suffer a blow to your reputation because of something heedless you have said. As a Saturn-Sagittarian you experience inner conflict between your need for order and security and your desire to seek adventure and challenge. Natives of this Saturn position are susceptible to accidents involving the hips and thighs.

SATURN IN CAPRICORN Saturn rules the sign of Capricorn, and thus its power is strong here. Both the positive and negative qualities of Saturn are powerfully emphasized in you. You are ambitious and independent, dedicated and unswerving, but your methods can be dictatorial and overbearing and you may sometimes be thought of as selfish and mean. Saturn puts many obstacles in your path, and you learn early in life to be self-sufficient. You want to do everything yourself. It would be easier to take a cub away from a mother bear than a task away from a Saturn-Capricorn. You also have an instinct for doing things the hard way; you

don't listen to advice. However, you do learn from experience. As a child you may have been insecure and timid, but as you grow older you gain in authority. Loneliness and an inability to share is a running thread throughout your life. Many of you are prone to melancholy, but you usually have a witty, dry sense of humor. Generally, you attract faithful friends, but Saturn in Capricorn tends to bring disappointment in love. Natives of this Saturn position are prone to aches in the joints and knees.

SATURN IN AQUARIUS In the humanitarian sign of Aquarius, Saturn's qualities of trustworthiness and self-discipline are well placed. As a Saturn-Aquarian, you have a talent for dealing with people and appealing to the masses. Many of you achieve fame in both the entertainment world and politics because of this ability. Saturn in Aquarius enhances a rational and original mind, capable of learning and study. Like those with Saturn in the other fixed signs of Taurus, Leo, and Scorpio, you are likely to encounter obstacles and difficulties early in life, but you tend to gain the wisdom and maturity that serve you well as you get older. You like to run the show and get your own way, and you are clever about manipulating people so you can. You can be obstinate and cunning at the same time. Saturn gives you the aggressiveness to take leadership, but you know how to avoid rubbing others the wrong way. You have humor and wit, though your need for independence sometimes leads to a lonely life. Natives of this Saturn position are prone to injuries to the lower legs and ankles.

SATURN IN PISCES Saturn in the mystical sign of Pisces does not favor material success. What you gain in life are sagacity and discernment. Your vivid imagination can be translated into creative work; your sympathy and intuition enable you to draw others to yourself. However, more than people of any other Saturn position, you are sensitive to the woes and harshness of the world. Saturn often brings disappointment and loss; the way it does so for you is to force you to make personal sacrifices for others or dictate that you take an inferior position even though your talents are superior. In time you can change this, but you must first develop the courage and determination to do so. Pisces is the sign of self-undoing, and your greatest power comes when you learn not to be the cause of your own unhappiness. You are drawn to philosophy, writing, and teaching of a spiritual or occult nature. Natives of this Saturn placement are vulnerable to ailments and problems involving the feet.

URANUS

⟨⟩ᴍᴍᴍ⟩

URANUS IS THE PLANET of change and originality, symbolizing the element of surprise in your life. Uranus brings about sudden events and opportunities. It awakens, shocks, and revolutionizes. It is responsible for the flash of human genius that creates something new—whether it be in art or science.

Do you often take an action that has no rhyme or reason? Are you attracted to an unusual line of work or to odd, colorful people? Do you feel that you are a more inventive thinker than those around you? Do you take an interest in modern science and the latest discoveries in the world? Are you known for your startling pronouncements or being an unusual character?

A person who has a strong Uranus in his or her birth chart will answer yes to these questions. It is important for you to know the sign that Uranus occupies in your horoscope in order to see where your *own* originality and special self-expression can best be utilized.

Uranus was not known to the ancients, for the planet was discovered only in 1781. Uranus is the first of the three modern planets, and the first ever to be found through a telescope. On March 13, 1781, at Bath, England, the British court astronomer Sir William Herschel discovered what he thought was a comet. After a year of careful observation, he verified that this heavenly body was a new planet in our solar system.

Herschel named the planet Georgium Sidus (Star of George) in honor of King George III of England, but the name never caught on. For a while it was called Herschel, and finally was changed to Uranus. (The letter H, for Herschel, is still embodied in the symbol for Uranus: ♅.)

Uranus was the Roman sky god, the first ruler of the universe. In astrology Uranus is the planet of the future, associated with modern science, invention, electricity, humanitarian movements, and revolution. It is the planet of sudden upheaval and swift, unexpected happenings. Its domain is all that is new, original, different, and unorthodox.

Uranus relates to your inner will and your secret power. In certain respects its power is similar to that of Mars. The difference is that Uranus is a deep-seated energy within the personality, an unconscious purpose that is revealed over a lifetime. As the great astrologer Evangeline Adams explains, a person can be powerful even if he or she is physically crippled, and another person may have enormous energy that he or she scatters about to no purpose. The first person has a strong Uranus and an afflicted Mars. The second has a powerful Mars and a weak Uranus.

Uranus's position in your chart indicates whether you have an inventive or unconventional mind and if you are attracted to odd and peculiar ideas. It designates what kind of genius you possess, whether you encounter unusual circumstances in work, travel, and relationships, and your propensity for sudden and dramatic events that mark your life.

If Uranus is prominent in your horoscope, you are inclined to be independent and resourceful. You may dress in an unusual manner, create your own style, and invent new gadgets. People may be attracted to you because of your "far-out" point of view. You may even be psychic. Uranus is the guiding force behind the visionary.

Uranus's influence also tends to make a person eccentric in behavior, undisciplined, reckless, and perverse. He or she may be difficult to get along with because of an abrupt manner, rebelliousness, or unpredictable moods.

In addition to having a personal meaning in your horoscope, Uranus is one of three planets in astrology that have a generational influence. The three modern planets, Uranus, Neptune, and Pluto, are so far away from the Sun that they travel very slowly through the zodiac. They spend a long time in each of the signs: Uranus takes seven years to transit one sign, Neptune spends fourteen years in one sign, and Pluto takes from thirteen to thirty-two years to go through one sign. Astrologers believe that these planets influence a whole generation as well as individuals. Uranus was first discovered at the time of the industrial revolution, the beginning of the modern age. The planet's journey through the zodiac corresponds with the new discoveries of science. For example, between 1996 and 2003, Uranus traveled through the sign of Aquarius, the sign that it rules. Aquarius represents the airwaves, space, freedom of opinion and far-flung communication. During Uranus's transit, the computer and micro-technology literally took charge of every aspect of our lives—how we communicate, do business, file information. Indeed, the world is run by the microchip, and scientists say the computer has changed the very way human beings think. Uranus is the ruler of the new Age we are in, the Age of Aquarius (see chapter 13).

Uranus brings change into our lives, new situations, and new people. Its gifts are always sudden and ephemeral; you have to take immediate advantage of them before they flash by. The message of Uranus is to move with change and not be afraid of the future.

An Astronomical Look at Uranus

Uranus is the seventh planet from the Sun, and is 1,784,800,000 miles distant from the Sun. Uranus is four times larger than the Earth, with a diameter of almost 32,000 miles compared to Earth's 8,000. Its orbit around the Sun is an almost perfect circle, and it takes 84 years and 7 days to complete one journey. It spins very quickly on its own axis, however; a day on Uranus lasts only 10 hours and 49 minutes. This means that there are 68,000 Uranian days in one Uranian year!

Uranus tilts rather oddly on its axis, inclined at an angle only eight degrees from being horizontal. In other words, it practically lies on its side. The Sun, therefore, shines first on one pole and then on the other pole (depending on where Uranus is in its orbit), while the opposite pole is in complete darkness. When the South Pole has sunlight, the North Pole is plunged into darkness, and vice versa; each of these periods of night and day on Uranus lasts for 21 Earth years. Uranus also rotates on its axis in a direction contrary to the other planets in our solar system. On Uranus, the Sun rises in the west and sets in the east.

These unusual characteristics of Uranus correspond to the planet's astrological reputation for eccentricity. Uranus has been called the black sheep of the solar system.

When *Voyager 2* flew by Uranus in January, 1986, it photographed ten previously undiscovered moons (bringing the total to fifteen), and two new rings around the planet (bringing this total to eleven). *Voyager 2* also discovered a corkscrew-shaped magnetic field around Uranus that stretches for millions of miles.

Where Is Your Uranus?

To find out what sign Uranus was in on the day of your birth, consult the Uranus Tables on page 510.

URANUS IN ARIES Uranus in the active sign of Aries favors an original and inventive mind. You need to be in charge and, given the chance, you will run other people's lives. You can be brusque and blunt because you feel that you know better than others. What you want is to see things clearly and not be a victim of con-

fused or disorganized thinking. You immediately try to put your own ideas into action and have little patience with tried-and-true methods. You believe that people who play it safe are usually sorry. Often you have an inimitable style of dressing, a look all your own. You tend to change jobs or residences often and are fond of traveling.

URANUS IN TAURUS Uranus is very strong in Taurus and its influence promotes willpower and determination. Uranus in Taurus helps you to produce results through patient and concerted effort. You have a need to build, to be constructive, and to achieve. You tend to be blessed with financial luck, particularly with possessions that gain in value. Often you have a mania for owning new and different objects, and Uranus sometimes brings a sudden find into your life. A taste for bright colors and vivid patterns is evident in the way you dress and decorate. Uranus in Taurus usually indicates a happy and prosperous marriage.

URANUS IN GEMINI In Gemini, Uranus shows its power through ideas. You are intellectual and imaginative. You possess a magnetic mind that draws people to you, and you have the ability to sway others to your point of view. Your energy is forceful in mental pursuits. You are attracted to offbeat ideas and fascinated by psychic phenomena and unexplained events. Uranus in Gemini produces a strong urge to express yourself in writing and speaking and to create something striking and startling. Even in ordinary communication, such as phone calls and letters, you are original and captivating and your amusing way with words is evident. You enjoy traveling, easily pick up foreign languages, and have an aptitude for music.

URANUS IN CANCER In Cancer, the power of Uranus is expressed through heightened sensitivity to other people. You have a highly developed imagination and a subconscious that borders on psychic awareness. Your intuitions can be trusted. Valuable insights come to you through sudden and unexpected feelings that arrive in a flash. You receive opportunities through the intervention of other people, often in chance encoun-

ters. Uranus in Cancer also promotes success through home-oriented activities, such as gourmet cooking, collecting antiques, and interior decorating. Many of you have a reputation for being eccentric and unpredictable and for having an artistic temperament.

URANUS IN LEO Uranus exerts a formidable influence in the expansive sign of Leo. As a native of this position, you have a forceful personality and express yourself through leadership. You have a desire to be a hero or heroine. Your creative mind constantly spins new ideas, but you are not content merely to see your concepts carried out. You must be on display as well; you want the credit and the attention. Uranus in this position often brings sudden opportunity through romantic relationships. Uranus also takes you far afield in your search for new and different pleasures. You tend to have luck in gambling, especially on sporting events. At times you give an impression of being too defiant and independent.

URANUS IN VIRGO In Virgo, Uranus shows its power in the ability to analyze and use facts. Uranus in Virgo bestows a marvelous combination of intuition and common sense. You have a great need to improve the world. You seek complete autonomy when carrying out your ideas, and rebel against routine and the restrictions of others. Your independence is sometimes so marked as to be considered eccentric by others. Uranus brings you luck through sudden changes in work situations, often a reshuffling of staff or a complete relocation to a new place. Uranus-Virgos are known for unusual ideas about health and food. You are the first one to know all about the latest reducing or rejuvenating diet.

URANUS IN LIBRA In the harmonious sign of Libra, Uranus expresses its power through partnerships. As a native of this position, you are drawn to unusual relationships and are often thought of as unconventional in your choice of friends or lovers. Uranus brings you luck through your relationships and also many opportunities through persons of foreign birth. In this Uranus position, love affairs and marriages tend to begin quickly and to have abrupt endings. Libra is an artistic sign, and Uranus bestows style and imagination. You are known for your unusual or exotic taste in art and decoration. You possess an appealing charm in the way you present yourself or dress. Uranus confers an ability to make a memorable first impression.

URANUS IN SCORPIO Uranus is strong in the intense sign of Scorpio. You have a dominating quality that wells up from deep within you. You possess a magnetic sexuality that is sometimes known as star quality. You are blessed with a penetrating mind. You are able to bring concentration and willpower to bear, and thus can move mountains through sheer effort. Uranus brings you luck through intuitive flashes of knowledge about people or situations in which you are involved. Unusual financial turns and reverses can be expected during your lifetime. Often you benefit through a partner's money or by an inheritance. At times you may be thought of as stubborn, secretive, and shrewd.

URANUS IN SAGITTARIUS In the freedom-loving sign of Sagittarius, Uranus exhibits itself as pioneering and adventurous. You are very independent and rebel against anything overly organized and structured. At times you are restless and quite reckless. You are proud and courageous and often have an unconventional point of view. Though you don't necessarily seek it, Uranus promotes financial luck through investments and speculation. Often while traveling, unexpected events or new people bring opportunity into your life. Uranus in this position also endows you with prophetic vision and insight, and you can often tell when something important is about to happen.

URANUS IN CAPRICORN Uranus's energy is channeled into constructive effort in the disciplined sign of Capricorn. You have a strong inner will to succeed. You need to be in authority and have difficulty accepting the rule of other people. Uranus in this position signals unexpected shifts in career or working conditions. You have an ability to spot future trends and to move in a more lucrative direction. Uranus gives you confidence to break through old established ideas. You are thoughtful, forceful, and able to organize people. You can also be tyrannical and domineering; there is always a fighting spirit to your personality. However, Uranus lightens Capricorn's seriousness and gives you a lively satirical wit.

URANUS IN AQUARIUS Aquarius is the sign Uranus rules, and the Aquarian qualities of inventiveness and originality are strongly emphasized. You have a touch of genius plus the ability to make your impact on a wide group of people. Others are drawn to your unique mind, for you are an advanced thinker. You are a curious blend: You believe in freedom of thought and expression but are convinced that you alone are right. Uranus causes unexpected turnabouts in your life. You may work for years toward a goal, then success will come through something you did not give a second thought to. Friends and associates bring you luck in career. As a Uranus-Aquarian you are noted for your wry sense of humor.

URANUS IN PISCES Uranus's power becomes subtle and emotional in the sensitive sign of Pisces. You have a unique talent for understanding and expressing human feelings, which often shows up in creative work. Uranus brings you luck through your sharp psychological insights and your ability to uncover what is secret and unknown. You are blessed with psychic awareness; many of you are serious students of philosophy, religion, astrology, and the occult. In career and business affairs, your intuitions tell you when to act and alert you to when others are most receptive to your ideas. Uranus in this position, however, does not indicate a strong will. At times you must withdraw from the world and recharge your psychic batteries.

NEPTUNE

NEPTUNE IS THE PLANET of mystery and illusion. Its power is that of the imagination. Neptune represents your dream life and your mystic qualities. It is the planet of bewitchment.

Do you have an active fantasy life? Have you been told there is a hypnotic quality to your personality? Do you have compassion for the suffering of others? Are you interested in occult and psychic phenomena?

If you answer yes to these questions, Neptune exerts a strong influence on your life. Anyone who has had an artistic vision, or is drawn to spiritual matters, or has experienced an unusual and unexplainable event has felt the power of Neptune. Knowing the position of this planet in your horoscope will help you to understand better its action in your affairs.

Neptune is named after the Roman god of the sea, who ruled over oceans, rivers, streams, fountains, and all things hidden by watery depths. In astrology Neptune is the planet of idealism and spirituality. Its realm is the subconscious world, hidden memory, intuition, and clairvoyance.

The positive side of Neptune's influence represents glamour and mystery, artistic imagination, dreams, and visions. Its negative side is characterized by deception, confusion, fraud, treachery, and sham. Neptune rules over a wide domain of human activity, from motion pictures, drama, dance, and poetry to hypnosis and anesthesia, hospitals, institutions and prisons, poison, and drug addiction.

This planet's position in your chart indicates what kind of ideals and goals you have, how psychic and visionary you are, and whether you possess a magnetic allure that people respond to. Neptune's influence brings great depth of understanding, ESP ability, and creative genius. Unlike the power of Uranus, which is sudden and forceful, Neptune's power is subtle, ethereal, inspirational, and otherworldly. Many astrologers claim that Neptune brings a person into contact with a higher plane of consciousness. When this planet is prominent in an individual horoscope, that person is likely to become involved in mysticism, psychic phenomena, or dream interpretation.

When Neptune is afflicted, a person cannot separate fantasy from reality. He or she may seek release from life's problems in drugs and alcohol or even exhibit criminal tendencies.

Like the other two modern planets, Neptune has a strong generational influence. Because it moves so slowly through the zodiac, Neptune spends approximately fourteen years in each sign. The year 1846, when Neptune was discovered, was a time of renewed interest in spiritualism. Hypnosis became a new medical treatment, and anesthetics were first introduced into general use. Ten years later Sigmund Freud was born. During his lifetime, Freud's theory of the unconscious and his new science of psychoanalysis revolutionized the treatment of mental disorders and changed the very way that human beings looked at themselves.

All through the decade of the 1960s, Neptune was in Scorpio. During this time we saw the rise of the drug culture. From the 1970s until 1984, Neptune transited the sign of Sagittarius, and there was an upsurge of interest in so-called New Age topics—reincarnation, channeling, and a quest for deeper meaning. While Neptune was in Capricorn between 1985 and 1998, drugs became an international trade and governments rose and fell over issues of

religion and ideology. Between 1998 and 2012 Neptune journeys through Aquarius; a negative aspect of this transit may be a rise in anarchy, but a more optimistic view looks for greater brotherhood among nations and a more spiritual altruism throughout the world. Interestingly, the final year of Neptune's presence in Aquarius, the year 2012, is predicted by the Mayan calendar to be the "end of the world." Many astrologers and spiritual guides predict this means that on a global level there will be a change in "consciousness" among human beings, and our values will shift toward creating a utopian society.

Because Neptune has a generational influence, you share Neptune's characteristics with the people of your era. The sign that Neptune is in determines how you and your generation will make history. The influence of Neptune will be perceived much more clearly by historians once it has passed into a new era.

Keep in mind that we have never observed even one complete journey by Neptune through the zodiac. This is because the planet takes almost 165 years to make one orbit around the Sun and we only discovered Neptune in 1846. Of course, mankind has always felt Neptune's influence even though we did not know of the planet's existence. By the year 2011 we will have finally noted Neptune's transit through all twelve signs of the zodiac.

In its highest form Neptune symbolizes perfection. It represents your unselfish ideals, your spiritual quest, and your search for the Impossible Dream.

Where Is Your Neptune?

To find out what sign Neptune was in on the day of your birth, consult the Neptune Table on page 512. I also give Neptune's dates of transit in the following descriptions of the planet in the different signs of the zodiac. Be-

An Astronomical Look at Neptune

Neptune is the second of the three modern planets to be discovered, and the achievement is considered a mathematical triumph. In the years following the first sighting of Uranus in 1791, astronomers noted that planet's tendency to wander from its prescribed orbit. The erratic motion led some to believe there was yet another lost planet exerting a gravitational pull on Uranus.

The position of this unknown planet was finally computed by two astronomy students, working separately and independently. In October 1845, John Couch Adams of Cambridge, England, sent his data about the discovery of an unknown planet to the royal astronomer. The royal astronomer ignored it because he himself was working on this own theory to explain Uranus's orbit. In June 1846, Urbain Jean Joseph LeVerrier of Paris, France, announced his discovery of the unknown planet's position. LeVerrier was also ignored. Finally in September of that year, LeVerrier sent his data to Johann Gottfried Galle, director of the observatory in Berlin, Germany. Galle turned his telescope to the designated spot and found a planet only one degree away from where LeVerrier claimed it would be. Both Adams and LeVerrier were subsequently given credit for discovering Neptune, and happily became fast friends.

Neptune is the eighth planet in our solar system, and is 2,795,700,000 miles distant from the Sun—thirty times farther from the Sun than Earth. The planet cannot be seen by the naked eye, and it is difficult to pick out even with a telescope, for there are over 200,000 stars in the heavens brighter than Neptune.

When *Voyager 2* flew by Neptune in August 1989, the spacecraft had been traveling for twelve years but it did not disappoint scientists with its discoveries. One discovery is that Neptune (like Saturn, Jupiter, and Uranus) has rings, five of them. *Voyager 2* also discovered six more moons (bringing the total to eight). One of Neptune's eight moons is Triton, a moon that orbits the wrong way—in a direction opposite to Neptune's orbit. This leads astronomers to believe Triton was once a small planet that orbited around our Sun but long ago came too close to Neptune and was captured by its gravitational field.

cause of Neptune's generational influence, it is interesting to look back at the planet's effect on an entire era. Note: In the dates for Neptune's and Pluto's transits through the signs, you will note in some cases more than two dates are given for a particular sign. This is because Neptune and/or Pluto were in retrograde motion for a while, entering a new sign, then returning to the previous sign before finally settling down into the new sign. For a detailed explanation of retrograde movement, see page 417.

NEPTUNE IN ARIES (1861/62–1874/75) To Aries, the sign of active energy, Neptune brings a reforming spirit and high ideals. Neptune-Ariens favor new methods in politics, medicine, and science that will better the lot of mankind. They are idealists and revolutionaries. When Neptune was last in Aries, it was a time of upheaval. Darwin's theory of evolution shook long-established concepts about man's history. The American Civil War was fought for the ideal of equality among human beings. During this era the Red Cross was established, with its emphasis on caring for the sick and needy; the Theosophical Society was founded, which renewed popular interest in philosophy and spiritualism. Neptune-in-Aries bestows a vivid imagination, and natives get true hunches about the future.

NEPTUNE IN TAURUS (1874/75–1887/89) Neptune in the materialistic sign of Taurus brings a deeper awareness of what is truly valuable in life. Neptune-Taureans are attracted to artistic and spiritual quests; many possess psychic ability. These people are able to make practical use of (and sometimes profit from) their interest in mysticism. When Neptune was last in Taurus we had the great expansion of American industrialism, and along with it a revival of interest in mysticism and the occult. During this era the writings of Karl Marx gave rise to a new idealism about the distribution of wealth. On a personal level, Neptune in this position favors an unusual source of income. Love and marriage bring happiness and inner wisdom. However, there is danger of financial loss through deception or fraud.

NEPTUNE IN GEMINI (1887/89–1901/02) In Gemini, Neptune bestows mental genius, imagination, and creativity. Neptune-Geminis have a magnetic ability to express themselves, a hypnotic way of communicating. Many create a lasting impression on the public. Neptune in this position gives inspiration for new inventions in science and mechanics. When Neptune was last in Gemini, Henry Ford perfected the automobile and the Wright brothers built a prototype of the first airplane (Gemini rules both transportation and the air). In science the first experiments in relativity laid the groundwork for Albert Einstein's epochal theory. On a personal level, Neptune-Geminis are resourceful, versatile, and perceptive. They have a tendency to attract unusual friends and to have impractical ideas.

NEPTUNE IN CANCER (1901/02–1914/16) In the emotional sign of Cancer, Neptune's influence gives a psychic, spiritual, and idealistic quality. Neptune-Cancerians are sensitive and compassionate. They tend to hold home and family in high regard and believe in old-fashioned values. However, Neptune also brings a striving for change and innovation to make the world a better place. When Neptune was last in Cancer, the American movement of social protest was part of a change affecting Western civilization. Also, while Neptune transited this sign of imaginative depths, Sigmund Freud explored the unconscious and Carl Jung formulated his theory of a collective unconscious. On a personal level, Neptune in this position promotes a love of luxury. At some point in their lives, Neptune-Cancerians are likely to experience an unusual or strange occurrence in their home or with relatives.

NEPTUNE IN LEO (1914/15–1928/29) In the noble sign of Leo, Neptune confers great courage and ability for leadership. Neptune-Leos are generous, dignified, and ambitious. They have high aspirations and the force to make their dreams a reality. Many of the world's heads of states and political leaders dedicated to a cause were born with Neptune in Leo (e.g., John and Robert Kennedy). Leo is also the sign of drama, and during Neptune's transit of Leo we saw the rise of the motion picture industry to dominance in the field of entertainment. The decade of the Twenties saw the radio become an everyday source of entertainment. This was also the flamboyant era of the Roaring Twenties (Leo is the sign of showy ostentation). On a personal level, with Neptune in this position there is a tendency for its natives to be egotistical and quite sensual.

NEPTUNE IN VIRGO (1928/29–1942/43) The spiritual planet Neptune in the practical sign of Virgo gives a strong instinct for service to mankind. Neptune-Virgos are discontent with the status quo, critical of accepted conventions. Many of those born when Neptune was in Virgo—the tumultuous years of the Great Depression and the onset of World War Two—have in our day become active in civil rights, the women's movement, and environmental concerns. When Neptune transited Virgo, the sign of health, treatment of disease with penicillin became widespread and chemotherapy was introduced. On a personal level, Neptune-Virgos possess clairvoyance and psychic ability in which they should put more faith. Neptune in this position sometimes shows a tendency to be hypercritical and confused in thinking.

27

NEPTUNE IN LIBRA (1942/43–1955/57) Neptune in the romantic sign of Libra emphasizes idealism and love. Those born while Neptune transited Libra have been called the love generation. Neptune-Librans seek harmony and balance, and are deeply bothered by injustice in the world. Many of the people who were born during the early years of Neptune's journey through Libra became active in the antiwar movement of the 1960s. Neptune-Librans strongly believe in the concepts of brotherly love and resistance to inequity. While Neptune transited this sign of peace the United Nations was founded. Libra is also the sign of partnership and marriage; this era brought a new questioning of the values of marriage, with a resultant rise in divorce and search for happiness in love. On a personal level, Neptune in this position produces a magnetic attraction to the opposite sex, and at times a lack of willpower and determination.

NEPTUNE IN SCORPIO (1955/57–1970) In the powerful sign of Scorpio, Neptune's influence is shown in depth and intensity of feeling. Neptune-Scorpios are drawn to what is hidden from public view and want to uncover the truth. In years to come, this generation will continue to fight for more open government and to rectify the probable secret damage done to our environment by ruthless profitseekers. Neptune-Scorpios have a true capacity for innovation and invention and are attracted to science, medicine, and genetics. While Neptune traveled through this sign of sex and mysticism, there was a breakdown of sexual taboos in society and a revival of interest in the supernatural. On a personal level, in this sign of spiritual regeneration

Neptune brings an extraordinary psychic awareness and interest in the occult.

NEPTUNE IN SAGITTARIUS (1970–1984) In the altruistic sign of Sagittarius, Neptune has an uplifting influence. Astrologers put great store in the generation born when Neptune was in this sign, for Sagittarius is the sign of higher learning, philosophy, and freedom. Neptune-Sagittarians have fine intellects, high purpose, and humane natures, and as these young people reach their adult years we look forward to new philosophers, sages, and humanistic leaders. Neptune in this position brings a desire for liberty and truth, and a visionary outlook. Neptune-Sagittarians will play an important role in improving living conditions in the Third World countries and in discovering new advances in medicine and science. While Neptune transited this sign of travel and expansion, more people had access to foreign cultures through travel, research, and the World Wide Web.

NEPTUNE IN CAPRICORN (1984/85–1998) In the disciplined sign of Capricorn, Neptune's power is practical and concrete. Neptune-Capricorns are destined to be thorough and painstaking and to possess great courage once they are committed to a purpose. The generation born during Neptune's transit through Capricorn will make use of the inspirational ideas of the previous generation, particularly in science, chemistry, and medicine. Neptune in this position gives creative insight into the things of the earth—water, timber, natural resources, oil, and minerals—and these

people will find a way not only to use them efficiently but also to conserve and replenish the gifts of the earth.

NEPTUNE IN AQUARIUS (1998–2012) In the humanitarian sign of Aquarius, Neptune's power brings high ideals and social justice. Neptune-Aquarians are concerned about the welfare of others less fortunate. This generation will have visionary concepts that they put into practice. As revolutionaries, they will not tear down and destroy; rather, they will build for a grand future. Neptune in this position has been called by astrologers "the flame of conscience." The generation born during Neptune's transit of Aquarius will be the authors of unusual and undreamed-of discoveries to aid mankind.

NEPTUNE IN PISCES (2012–2026) In Pisces, Neptune will be the sign it rules, and therefore its qualities of spirituality and creative genius will be enhanced for those born in this era. Neptune-Pisceans will be deep thinkers with profound understanding about the meaning of life. Their compassion will be complemented by intense psychic powers. Astrologers believe that this generation, born when Neptune next transits Pisces, may usher in the ultimate period of self-realization. Their ascendancy will help to bring peace and tranquility to the world. Neptune in this position does not value materialism, so Neptune-Pisceans no doubt will explore the inner man and woman, and develop a new philosophy based on what they find.

PLUTO

P<small>LUTO IS A PLANET</small> of awesome power, but it is a power that we still find largely inexplicable and difficult to understand.

Pluto was discovered as recently as 1930, and astrologers continue to study this planet's influence in astrology. What is certain is that wherever Pluto appears in your horoscope, that area of life will show a marked change, perhaps a transformation. If you have ever experienced one of those blinding moments in which you suddenly see your life in an entirely new light and decide to change everything, you have felt the energy of Pluto. Pluto's action brings to light things hidden in the depths of your subconscious, releases your dormant forces, and causes your suppressed energies to erupt suddenly.

Pluto is named after the Roman god of the underworld and the nether regions of Hades, and of the spirits of the dead. Originally called Planet X, Pluto was given its name by a young British girl whose letter suggesting a new name for the planet was the first to arrive at the Lowell Observatory, where Pluto was first discovered.

The planet is well named, for in astrology Pluto signifies death and rebirth. It is the planet of regenerative forces, of destruction and annihilation, and then complete transformation. Its keyword is *elimination*; Pluto wipes the slate clean.

Pluto's immense power is felt in world events and in the great tides of history. It influences masses of humanity, enormous groups of people, and large organizations. Mass media and giant conglomerates are in its domain. Pluto rules over such disruptive elements in nature as earthquakes and volcanoes. Its negative influence is shown in mob violence, demonstrations, murder, wide-scale terrorism, and bombing.

Pluto's power has been likened to that of nuclear fission, which both destroys and creates. There are two sides to Pluto's influence, and like the two sides of a coin they are opposite but part of the same.

Pluto has a powerful generational influence and also a personal meaning in your chart. The planet governs the beginnings and ends of the phases in life. If your life has taken a dramatic shift—if, for example, you have worked hard for a goal, only to see it destroyed or ended and an entirely new direction opened up—Pluto is likely to be prominent in your horoscope. People who have had to leave their homes behind to begin anew in a foreign country, or those whose lives were irrevocably altered because of the death of a key figure, are under Pluto's influence. The Plutonian character has a deep need to dominate and control, and often will rise to great heights. People who have brilliant careers in politics and government, in medical research and archeology are under Pluto's influence; the planet governs the uncovering of secrets of the past in order to clear ground for the future.

Even in the most civilized personality, Pluto's force is felt as an undercurrent of turbulence and uncontrolled energy. Its strong negative power may cause some people to be cruel, sadistic, or treacherous, or even lead a life of crime. Pluto's power is seen in both idealistic leaders and brutal dictators.

Pluto represents the highest and lowest of which humankind is capable. Some astrologers believe Pluto's power is too arcane and mysterious for human beings to

analyze properly now, but that the planet will continue to govern impulses in our secret psyches that we do not yet fully understand.

Where Is Your Pluto?

To find out what sign Pluto was in on the day of your birth, consult the Pluto Table on page 513.

⟨⟩

Each of the three modern planets has foreshadowed coming events of the era during which it was discovered. In the case of Pluto, the planet was discovered exactly three months after the great stock market crash set off a worldwide economic depression. The decade that followed saw the rise of gangsterism and criminal mobs that were a law unto themselves. During this decade Adolf Hitler began his demonic rise, which ended by plunging the entire world into war. During the latter years of the twentieth century, while Pluto transited Scorpio (the sign of sexuality, death, and rebirth), we witnessed the rise of the AIDS virus and genetic engineering.

Because Pluto is so new, astrology has not had much time to study and refine its knowledge of the planet. It is not always easy to see what influence a particular planet has on an era until time provides perspective.

Since its discovery in 1930, we have noted Pluto's journey through only six signs of the zodiac. Pluto is now transiting a seventh sign, Capricorn, in which it will stay until 2024. Reckoning backward into the 1800s as well as projecting forward a few years into the twenty-first century, here is a glance at what we are able to discern of Pluto's influence.

AN ASTRONOMICAL LOOK AT PLUTO

In 1914, two years before his death, the American astronomer Percival Lowell began his computations on the position of an unknown planet beyond Neptune. He was looking for a planet (then called Planet X) to explain disturbances in the orbit of Uranus. Not until February 18, 1930, however, was Pluto actually discovered, by Clyde W. Tombaugh, who based his work on Lowell's reckonings. After years of search, Pluto was at last identified on a photograph taken with the giant telescope at Lowell Observatory (established by Percival Lowell in 1894). The discovery of Pluto was a mathematical feat, for the planet is an enormous distance from the Sun and is quite small in size, a mere pinpoint among the over 15 million stars in the heavens that are brighter than it is.

Pluto is the ninth planet in our solar system, and is 3,680,000,000 miles distant from the Sun. Pluto's distance from Earth is approximately 50 times Earth's distance from the Sun. Pluto is a tiny planet with a diameter of 1,440 miles, less than one-fifth the width of Earth and less than half the size of Mercury. Because Pluto is so far away from the Sun, it receives relatively little sunlight. So great is the Sun's brilliance, though, that noon on Pluto is still 600 times brighter than a night here on Earth when the full moon is shining.

Pluto has an eccentric orbit. All the other planets in our solar system travel in paths around the Sun that are virtually circular and are more or less on the same plane as Earth's orbit. Pluto's orbit, however, tilts rather wildly, so much so that at certain times Pluto is nearer to the Earth than Neptune is. In 1989, Pluto was at perihelion (closest to the Sun in its orbit) and until 1999, contrary to popular belief, it was not our outermost planet. During the years 1979 to 1999 Neptune was the planet farthest from the Sun. After that, and for the next 228 years, Neptune reverted to being the eighth planet from the Sun and Pluto the ninth.

When speaking of Pluto's orbit, one must deal in terms of many years, for Pluto takes nearly 250 Earth years to make one journey around the Sun. This means Pluto dwells for many years in each sign of the zodiac. The number of years varies because of the planet's odd orbit, and may range from as low as 13 years to as many as 32 years.

In January 2006 NASA (National Aeronautics and Space Administration) sent a space probe, *New Horizons*, out toward Pluto, which is expected to reach Pluto in July 2015.

Meanwhile, in 2001, controversy erupted over the status of Pluto. It was declared an asteroid, but quickly reinstated as a planet. Then in August 2006 the International Astronomical Union formerly downgraded Pluto to a "dwarf planet." According to new standards, one of the criteria for a planet is it must have cleared away all other objects out of its orbit. Yet Pluto orbits through the icy wreckage of asteroids in the Kuiper Belt—and thus has now been relegated to the status of dwarf planet.

Though to astronomers Pluto may be a dwarf, in astrology it looms as large as ever. Pluto continues to represent profound psychological transformation and the beginnings and endings to the stages of our lives (as well as historical events).

PLUTO IN ARIES (1822/23–1851/53) Pluto's influence in this adventurous sign set off the great pioneering trek westward in America. The first railroad was introduced in America. It was during this era that the world became larger as mankind ventured to explore the far reaches of this planet. There were struggles for supremacy as strong nations acquired colonies. It is particularly notable that England (which is specifically an Aries country) achieved world ascendancy during Pluto's transit of Aries, becoming the empire on which the sun never set. When Pluto is in Aries, the planet's personal influence gives courage, self-reliance, and a strong sense of individuality; recklessness and egotism are its negative effects for individuals.

PLUTO IN TAURUS (1851/53–1882/84) In Taurus, the sign of wealth and possessions, Pluto brought upheaval. In America, a bloody civil war was fought over the question of slavery—whether one human being could properly be the possession of another. All over the world the very wealthy exploited the very poor; child labor flourished and the have-nots endured lives of misery and hardship. During this era Karl Marx formulated his revolutionary theories, based on the elimination of the class system and a more equal distribution of wealth. Pluto-in-Taurus saw capitalism finally triumph over the last vestiges of feudalism and virtually take over the world. When Pluto is in Taurus, the planet's personal influence gives its natives determination and endurance. People with this Pluto position seek stability and are often obsessed with material advancement.

PLUTO IN GEMINI (1882/84–1912/14) When Pluto was last in Gemini, the sign of communication, it revolutionized the way information reached the masses. This was the era when newspapers came into prominence. The phonograph and photography reproduced sounds and visual information for wide use by the public. The first motion pictures were invented and gave rise to a new industry (which flowered when Neptune transited the theatrical sign of Leo). Gemini rules the airwaves, so it is not surprising that during Pluto's transit the telegraph, the radio, and the telephone came into being. This era also introduced two new forms of travel that would revolutionize the world: the airplane and automobile. When Pluto is in Gemini the planet's personal influence gives its natives an inventive and restless mind that seeks change and freedom from old restrictions.

PLUTO IN CANCER (1912/14–1937/39) Pluto's stormy transit through Cancer, the sign of home, brought upheaval to family life in America. By the millions people left the country to settle in towns and cities. The negative side of Pluto-in-Cancer was shown in the hideous loss of life in World War One, and the preparations for World War Two under the leadership of militaristic Nazi Germany, a nation that espoused glorification of the homeland. Our country and our way of life (Cancerian values) were imperiled. Cancer is the sign of agriculture; during Pluto's transit in the 1930s, we saw the great drought and the misery of the migrant farmworkers forced from their land. We also saw the rise of industrial unions formed in violent struggles against the power of the great corporations. When Pluto is in

Cancer, the planet's personal influence gives intense emotions and creative imagination. Negatively, it produces a deep resentment of other people's good fortune.

26°

PLUTO IN LEO (1937/39–1956/58) During Pluto's journey through the masterful sign of Leo, the United States entered World War Two and helped the Allied powers win a victory over Germany and Japan. Leo is also a magnanimous sign (after the war the United States gave money and assistance to the defeated countries in order to help rebuild them). On October 24, 1945, the United Nations was formed, where each country would express its point of view and attempt to work out its differences with other nations. The Korean War was fought to save a nation from aggression. Pluto in the power sign of Leo also points to abuse of power, and during this era people's lives and careers were crippled and destroyed by the rise of McCarthyism. When Pluto is in Leo, the personal influence is to emphasize love of power, a domineering ego, and self-aggrandizement, but it also confers on its natives strong pride and a will to prevail despite obstacles. There is a tendency toward arrogance, selfishness, and sensual pleasures. The generation that was born when Pluto transited Leo introduced the era of the pleasure principle; there is also strong emphasis on mass hero-worship of personalities in the media.

But I hate abuse of power

PLUTO IN VIRGO (1956/58–1971/72) During Pluto's transit of Virgo, the sign of service to others, the Kennedy and Johnson administrations were committed to social programs. This was the era of the Great Society, of achievement in the fight for civil rights and, in the mid 1960s, a growing feminist movement. In this sign of health, some of Pluto's influences on its generation are a new awareness of toxic food additives, an emphasis on holistic medicine, and concern over pollution of the environment. Virgo is also the sign of practicality, of putting facts to useful work. During Pluto's transit of this sign, the two world superpowers were actively involved in space exploration. In 1969 a human being first walked on the Moon. The dark side of Pluto's power was shown as the United States was plunged into turmoil by the assassinations of John Kennedy, Robert Kennedy, and Martin Luther King Jr. Southeast Asia was torn by an unending war in Vietnam, which not only took its toll in lives and misery but also divided the nation emotionally. When Pluto is in Virgo, the planet's personal influence bestows a profound analytical quality to the personality. People under this influence seek perfection but are also suspicious and ready to find fault with the world around them.

PLUTO IN LIBRA (1971/72–1983/84) Libra is the sign of peace and harmony, and early in Pluto's journey through Libra the agonizing war in Vietnam finally came to an end. On a larger scale, two enormous hostile world powers, the United States and the People's Republic of China, moved toward peace and a new rapprochement in their relationship. Pluto-in-Libra also indicates deep concern for law and balancing injustice. The era of Watergate, with its shocking revelations of corruption, ended by bringing new order to government and restoring the balance of powers be-

tween the executive branch and Congress. A conse-
quence was the adoption of the Freedom of Information Act. Libra emphasizes egalitarianism and equality,
and Pluto's transit saw the passage of equal opportunity laws, support for the Equal Rights Amendment,
and greater equality for homosexuals. Libra also signifies a love for luxury, and the early 1980s ushered in a
period of opulence and ostentation. When Pluto is in
Libra, the planet's personal influence promotes a deep
need to seek harmony and cooperation. Its negative
side brings unforeseen problems and disruption in
close relationships.

PLUTO IN SCORPIO (1983/84–1995) The entry of
Pluto into the sign of Scorpio coincided with George
Orwell's predictions of a totalitarian government and
loss of individual rights in his famous book *1984*.
Pluto is extremely powerful in Scorpio, the sign that it
rules, and this period was one of turmoil and revolution. During this era the Berlin Wall fell, the Soviet
Union disbanded and became a commonwealth, Iran
turned militantly conservative, Yugoslavia was torn
apart by warring Serbs and Croats. Scorpio is the sign
of destruction, and Pluto's transit was rife with worldwide terrorism. Pluto's link to the underworld was
seen in the rise of an international drug trade. The
sign of Scorpio rules sexuality, birth, death, and rebirth, and Pluto's journey gave rise to test-tube babies,
surrogate parenting, cloned animals, and all manner of
genetic engineering. The AIDS virus became rampant,
underlining the themes of sex and death. Pluto's personal influence in Scorpio produces individuals with
penetrating minds and strong wills. These people are

imaginative and passionate, possess psychic ability, and
can be ruthless about getting their own way.

PLUTO IN SAGITTARIUS (1995–2007/08) Pluto zips
through Sagittarius in a relatively short time, thirteen
years, and its influence promises to be less heavy. Sagittarius is the sign of truth and open knowledge, and the
years just prior to the turn of the millennium are characterized as the Information Age. Television reported
events in full detail almost before they took place; the
Web links us to information within seconds; endless
streams of memoirs have left no one's secrets untold.
In keeping with full disclosure, we witnessed a U.S.
president's impeachment (and acquittal) that began
with the exposure of his extramarital sexual affair.
Sagittarius also represents foreign lands and far-flung
places and, through the computer and the Internet,
Pluto has transformed the concept of distance. International trade and business takes place in seconds, re-
tailers sell to the public directly through the computer,
and e-mail instantly connects people on opposite sides
of the Earth. We are hopeful that the first decade of the
twenty-first century is an era of new values in philosophy, religion, education, and foreign affairs, areas all
under Sagittarius's influence. Sagittarius is the sign of
freedom, adventure, and exploration. There should be
a new spirit of friendliness and spiritual sharing
among nations. Europe has already joined in a Common Market. Pluto-in-Sagittarius brings deep hope
and profound understanding. Its negative influence is
toward impractical extremes, but the optimism and
enthusiasm that characterizes this transit should make
this an uplifting time for human beings everywhere.

PLUTO IN CAPRICORN (2008/09–2024) Because Capricorn is the sign of discipline and ambition, Pluto's influence here should stress responsibility and the ethic of work. Capricorn is the sign of government and long-term security, and Pluto may have the effect of bringing a new world order into being. Individual nations may join in a system of world government that leads to greater stability. Star-watchers are focused on the year 2012, which the Mayan calendar marks as the "end of the world." Many spiritual movements believe this is a metaphor for a change in "consciousness" when the human race will adopt a more spiritual value system. Astrologically, Pluto in Capricorn holds out the hope there will be an end to war.

By the time Pluto enters the following sign of Aquarius, the world will be in the Age of Aquarius (see chapter 13). Pluto will bring even greater emphasis to the humanitarian and freedom-loving qualities of Aquarius. This should be a time of unimaginable scientific discovery, for Aquarius is the sign of science and future knowledge.

When Pluto is in Pisces, human beings may at last comprehend the fullness of Pluto's power and add to their knowledge of the meaning of life. Pisces represents the completion of the circle, the last step before moving on to the first rung of a higher ladder. By this time the human race may have evolved to a higher and more noble plane.

Part Three

UNDERSTANDING ASTROLOGY

8

THE HOUSES OF
ASTROLOGY

A S FAR BACK AS BABYLONIAN TIMES, ancient astrologers divided life into different categories. They understood that a life's journey consists of a myriad of activities and emotions, of work, ambition, hopes and dreams, and relationships.

Babylonian astrologers named twelve separate categories of life, which have come down to us from that time almost unchanged. These twelve divisions are called Houses. I recently saw a modern definition for Houses—"existential arenas"—but this is just a fancy way of saying that each House represents a separate area and specific function of your life. There is a House of domestic life, a House of personal wealth, a House of marriage, a House of career, etc.

Your horoscope—which is a map of your individual personality—consists of all twelve Houses. Here, beginning with the first, are the twelve Houses of a horoscope. After you have set up your horoscope (see chapter 9), you will have a clearer understanding of what the Houses of astrology mean in your life.

Self Image

Self Worth

FIRST HOUSE This is the House of Self. It is the most personal and most powerful House in your chart, for it symbolizes *you*—your mannerisms, your style, your disposition and temperament. This is the House of your outward behavior, your likes and dislikes. The First House reveals both the way you present yourself to others and the way the outside world sees you. It often indicates your physical characteristics, especially your head and facial features. Sometimes called the House of self-interest, it denotes what you want in life and how you go about achieving it. The place in your chart at which this House begins is the most important point in a horoscope, for it determines where all the other Houses will follow. In astrology the First House is thought of as a giant lens through which the rest of your chart is seen and interpreted.

ARies / MARS = natural

SECOND HOUSE This is the House of Money and Possessions. It relates to what you own in life and what you will acquire, your income, and your financial prospects. This is the House of movable possessions, the things you physically take with you as you move through life. The Second House also tells how you feel about money and possessions, and gives a clue to the kinds of objects with which you like to surround yourself. To a certain extent it gives a picture of your earning power and ability to handle money. The Second House often shows what activities and projects may be a lucrative source of income for you.

Taurus / venus = natural

THIRD HOUSE This is the House of Communication. The Third House relates to your immediate environment in three major areas: self-expression, your family ties, and day-to-day travel. This House governs the way you think, speak, and write. Logic, memory, and manual skill are in its domain. The Third House often indicates what kind of early education you received, and your ability to study and learn. Your relationships with brothers and sisters, aunts and uncles, cousins and neighbors are part of this House's influence. Short trips and the vehicles for this type of travel are governed by the Third House—especially the travel you do for work or education.

Natural Ruler: Gemini — Mercury

Jup — □ Sat — indiff. to success, mistrustful, ventured
sex Jup = helps people generous — imag. Art
☿ — Pluto — directs + intelligent

MINE

Cancer ⊕

empty Ⓔ

Cancer / Leo

Uranus in Leo XI 38°

Uranus unique found here

Leo ♌

Jup in Leo 27°

Pluto 26° Leo

UR

Jup

Mine

VIRGO ♍
Ⓔ

④

Angular house:
Cusp is the NADIR
natural ruler is CANCER & planet is MOON

mine EMPTY —

Empty

FOURTH HOUSE This is the House of Home. The Fourth House governs your home life in the past, the present, and the future. It indicates the kind of home you had in childhood and your relationship with parents. What you have brought into this life from your ancestors is in its domain. In the present, the Fourth House relates to the kind of home you make for yourself. Your current domestic affairs are under its influence, as are real estate holdings and the ownership of land. This House also rules over the closing years of your life, the kind of security you seek for old age. The Fourth House is one of the more mystical houses in your chart, for it represents what you keep protected and secluded from the rest of the world—the place you call home in both a physical and an emotional sense.

LIBRA ♎
Intercepted 5th
SCORPIO

Neptune ♆
Saturn ♏

Play —
attitude:
Romance
Relationships
fun drama
costume

27 Saturn in
in Scorpio
trine th

27 Neptune
in Libra

FIFTH HOUSE This is the House of Creativity and Sex. The Fifth House rules over everything you do for pleasure and to express yourself creatively. Your sexual nature (the most basic creative urge in your psyche) is a large part of its domain. Children and the joy you receive from them are governed by this House. The Fifth House also relates to entertainment, holidays, amusements, and the arts. It rules love affairs, new undertakings in life, speculation and gambles, and games of chance. It is the House that expresses your artistic talents as well as your ability to enjoy yourself in life. In childhood, pets and playmates are part of this House, for it holds sway over all the things to which you instinctively give affection. This is the House of your heart. Natural - LEO - SUN

SAG ♐
☾ Moon
☊ NN

48 MOON
tr Pl

08 North Node
Asc Node

SIXTH HOUSE This is the House of Service and of Health. Often called the House of service to others, it indicates your need to help others and to be useful in the world. In the old days it governed a person's attitude toward servants and those of inferior standing. In the modern day, this House rules your relationship with the people you work with, with those who are subordinates, and with your employers. The Sixth House also relates to your state of health and especially applies to illness brought on by worry or emotional upsets. This House often signifies whether you have a robust or delicate constitution, and what kinds of diseases you may be subject to. natural VIRGO - mercury

Capricorn ← Rulers Saturn who is
in Scorpio
my 5th house
(Empty)

SEVENTH HOUSE This is the House of Partnership and Marriage. On a personal level, it relates to your husband or wife, the mate you choose in life. It often indicates what kind of marriage you will have and whether you might divorce or remarry. This is your House of partnerships, not only in marriage but also in work, business, legal affairs, and sometimes in politics. It covers legal unions or contracts you enter into, and both sides of a question or dispute. The Seventh House concerns your ability to work harmoniously with others. Paradoxically, it also governs what astrologers call your open enemies, those who are usually your adversaries in the business or professional world. The Seventh House is the opposite of the First House of Self; here you blend your personality with others in order to pursue shared goals. Natural: Libra/venus

8

Emotional + soul security

for CAPRICORN / AQUARIUS ♒
(Empty)

CRISES
change
growth.
addiction
others' money
taxes divorce
inheritance

Transformation/Sexuality

EIGHTH HOUSE This is the House of Death and Regeneration. The Eighth House is one of the three mystical houses in your chart (the others are the Fourth and the Twelfth), and one of the most difficult to understand. Sometimes called the House of spiritual transformation, it rules the life forces that surround sex, birth, death, and the afterlife. It concerns legacies and what you inherit from the dead—both materially and spiritually. Money that belongs to your partner, and taxes and debt are also in this House's domain. The Eighth House may give some indication of the conditions surrounding your death, although the precise time always remains a mystery. Surgery is governed by this House, since it relates to regeneration. This is the House of psychic powers and occult studies and knowledge. Natural: Scorpio/Pluto

♒ AQUARIUS / (PISCES) ♓ learning → identity
professional
MARS in Pisces ♂ 9,5°

Belief
higher learning
exploration
travel
pers. truth
Publishing

MARS

NINTH HOUSE This is the House of Mental Exploration and Long-Distance Travel. The Ninth House can be thought of as a widening of the Third House; study, travel, and mental pursuits are expanded in the Ninth House onto a much wider plane. This is the House of the higher mind. Under its domain are higher education, philosophy, and the study in depth of profound subjects. Long journeys of both the mind and the physical body are controlled by this House. It concerns actual travel to foreign lands and business interests in other countries. It governs the meeting of foreigners who expand your way of thinking, and also the study of languages. The Ninth House rules your public expression of ideas and is therefore the House of publishing and literary effort.

SAG/Jupiter - natural

Mars in IX— deeply rooted opinions + can defend it convinced of virtue

Mars □ MARS impulsive - throws herself into thg

Pisces in X-profession success

Material Action
MIDHEAVEN ⑩

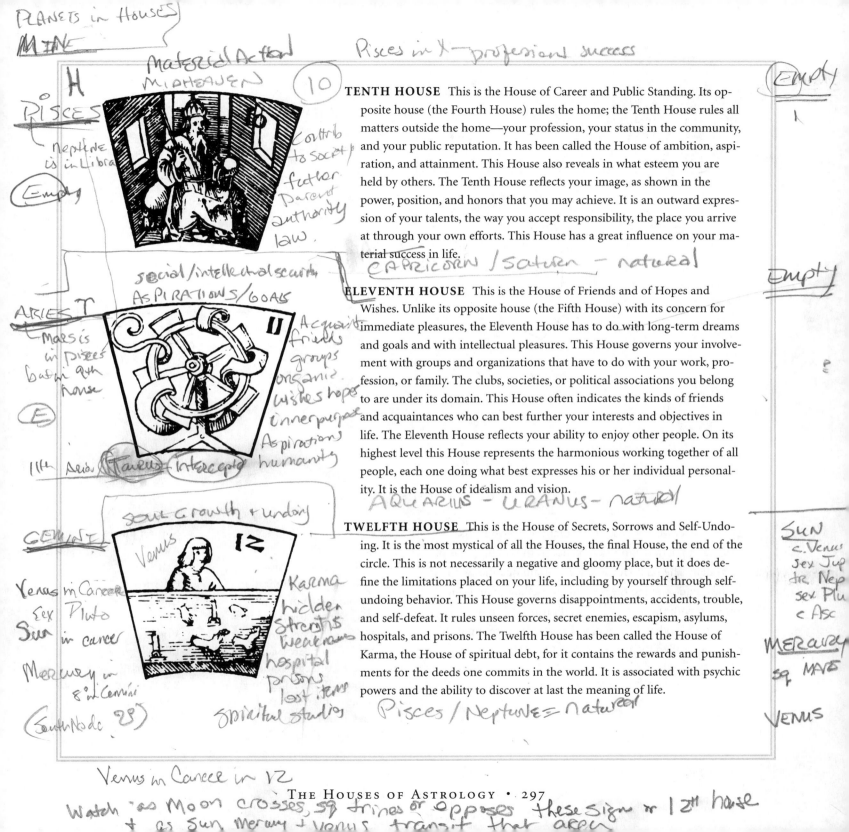

♄
PISCES
Neptune is in Libra
(Empty)

Contrib to society
Father
Parent
authority
law.

TENTH HOUSE This is the House of Career and Public Standing. Its opposite house (the Fourth House) rules the home; the Tenth House rules all matters outside the home—your profession, your status in the community, and your public reputation. It has been called the House of ambition, aspiration, and attainment. This House also reveals in what esteem you are held by others. The Tenth House reflects your image, as shown in the power, position, and honors that you may achieve. It is an outward expression of your talents, the way you accept responsibility, the place you arrive at through your own efforts. This House has a great influence on your material success in life.

CAPRICORN / Saturn - natural

(Empty)

Empty

social/intellectual security
ASPIRATIONS/GOALS

ARIES ♈
Mars is in Pisces but in 4th house

(E)

Acquaint friends
groups
organize
wishes hope
inner purpose
Aspiration
humanity

ELEVENTH HOUSE This is the House of Friends and of Hopes and Wishes. Unlike its opposite house (the Fifth House) with its concern for immediate pleasures, the Eleventh House has to do with long-term dreams and goals and with intellectual pleasures. This House governs your involvement with groups and organizations that have to do with your work, profession, or family. The clubs, societies, or political associations you belong to are under its domain. This House often indicates the kinds of friends and acquaintances who can best further your interests and objectives in life. The Eleventh House reflects your ability to enjoy other people. On its highest level this House represents the harmonious working together of all people, each one doing what best expresses his or her individual personality. It is the House of idealism and vision.

AQUARIUS - URANUS - natural

11th Aries (Taurus) (Intercept)

GEMINI

Soul Growth + undoing

Venus

12

TWELFTH HOUSE This is the House of Secrets, Sorrows and Self-Undoing. It is the most mystical of all the Houses, the final House, the end of the circle. This is not necessarily a negative and gloomy place, but it does define the limitations placed on your life, including by yourself through self-undoing behavior. This House governs disappointments, accidents, trouble, and self-defeat. It rules unseen forces, secret enemies, escapism, asylums, hospitals, and prisons. The Twelfth House has been called the House of Karma, the House of spiritual debt, for it contains the rewards and punishments for the deeds one commits in the world. It is associated with psychic powers and the ability to discover at last the meaning of life.

Pisces/Neptune= natural

Venus in Cancer
Sex Pluto
Sun in cancer
Mercury in 8th Gemini
(South Node 28)

Karma
hidden
strengths
weaknesses
hospital
prisons
lost items
spiritual studies

SUN
c. Venus
Sex Jup
tr. Nep
Sex Plu
c Asc

MERCURY
sq Mars

VENUS

Venus in Cancer in 12

Watch as Moon crosses, sq trines or opposes these sign or 12th house
+ as Sun Mercury + Venus transit that area

In a horoscope, the Houses are always pictured as follows:

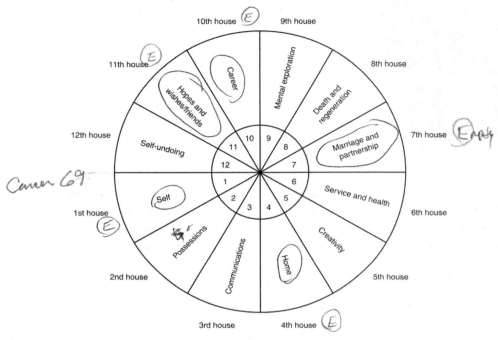

Rulers of the Houses

You may have noticed that the twelve Houses bear a relationship/resemblance to the twelve Signs of the zodiac. The First House shares certain qualities with the first sign of Aries; the Second House has qualities in common with the second sign of Taurus, and so on through the zodiac. The zodiacal sign that corresponds to a House is called the *natural ruler* of that House.

House	Natural Ruler
First House of Self	ARIES
Second House of Possessions	TAURUS
Third House of Communication	GEMINI
Fourth House of Home	CANCER
Fifth House of Creativity	LEO
Sixth House of Service	VIRGO
Seventh House of Partnership	LIBRA
Eighth House of Regeneration	SCORPIO
Ninth House of Mental Exploration	SAGITTARIUS
Tenth House of Career	CAPRICORN
Eleventh House of Hopes	AQUARIUS
Twelfth House of Self-Undoing	PISCES

Kinds of Houses

In astrology, the Houses are categorized in groups of three and in groups of four. These groups have special meanings that help us to see the overall picture of how Houses relate to life.

Houses Divided into Three Groups

1. ANGULAR HOUSES (called Angular because they mark the four "Angles" of a chart. See pages 343 ff.) These are the First, Fourth, Seventh, and Tenth Houses. Planets in these Houses indicate that you will achieve some kind of prominence in the world.

First House of self and personality.
Fourth House of home and the latter part of life.
Seventh House of fortune in partnership or marriage.
Tenth House of honor and position in career.

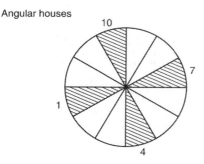

Angular houses

2. SUCCEDENT HOUSES (called Succedent because they "succeed" or follow the Angular Houses.) These are the Second, Fifth, Eighth, and Eleventh Houses. Planets in these Houses indicate that you have stability, willpower, and fixity of purpose.

Second House of finances.
Fifth House of creativity.
Eighth House of regeneration.
Eleventh House of hopes.

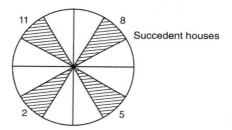

Succedent houses

3. CADENT HOUSES (called Cadent because they "fall away" from the Angular and Succedent Houses. The word *cadent* comes from the Latin *cadere*, meaning "to fall.") These are the Third, Sixth, Ninth, and Twelfth Houses. Planets in these Houses indicate that you are mentally active and communicate your ideas.

Third House of day-to-day communication.
Sixth House of employment.
Ninth House of mental exploration.
Twelfth House of the subconscious.

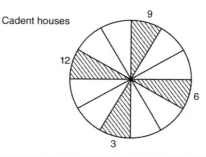

Cadent houses

Houses Divided into Four Groups

1. HOUSES OF LIFE These are the First House of energy and vitality, the Fifth House of creativity and offspring, and the Ninth House of learning and conviction.

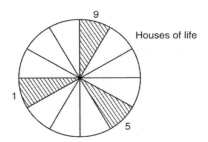

Houses of life

2. HOUSES OF WEALTH These are the Second House of personal property, the Sixth House of employment and work, and the Tenth House of career and public status.

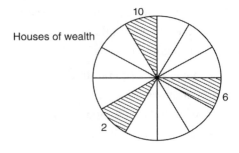

Houses of wealth

3. HOUSES OF RELATIONSHIPS These are the Third House of relatives and neighbors, the Seventh House of partnership and marriage, and the Eleventh House of friends and organizations.

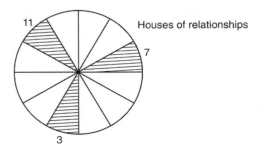

Houses of relationships

4. HOUSES OF ENDINGS These are the Fourth House of the latter years of life, the Eighth House of death and regeneration, and the Twelfth House of spiritual reward and debt.

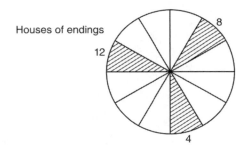

Houses of endings

Planets in the Houses

ONE OF THE GUIDEPOSTS an astrologer looks at when interpreting your birth chart is which Houses in your horoscope are occupied by planets. Any House in your chart that has one or more planets in it is emphasized and strengthened by their presence in specific ways. For example, Jupiter (planet of luck) in your Second House of Possessions indicates ease in making money, whereas Jupiter in your Seventh House of Partnership means you tend to make gains through your partnerships or marriage. Mars (planet of assertiveness) in your Third House of Communication designates intellectual sharpness and a powerful talent to communicate effectively, whereas Mars in your Eighth House of Regeneration indicates strong willpower, volcanic passions, and an interest

in the occult. Venus (planet of love and beauty) in your First House of Self accentuates social ease, a refined esthetic nature, and a goodlooking physical appearance, whereas Venus in your Fourth House of Home indicates that you are likely to have a comfortable, beautiful domicile and to have enjoyed a happy childhood.

Each planet in each House has a special meaning, and the following rundown will serve as a useful guide. In order to apply these descriptions to yourself, however, you must first set up your birth chart. Instructions for doing that are outlined in the next chapter, "How to Cast Your Own Horoscope." Once you set down your Houses and discover which planets occupy which Houses, the following descriptions will help you to interpret your horoscope.

FIRST HOUSE (House of Self)

SUN in (Planet of vitality and individuality): You have a strong will and sense of self, and you like lots of attention. You are an independent person with leadership ability. Good points: healthy constitution, generous, confident, dignified. Bad points: authoritative, egotistical, dictatorial.

MOON in (Planet of emotions and instincts): You are imaginative in the way you express yourself and intuitive about other people. Home and family mean a great deal to you, and you remember your childhood with nostalgia. You

want to be appreciated and admired, and would like to be famous. Good points: receptive, romantic, curious. Bad points: oversensitive, moody, a tendency to dissipate energies.

MERCURY in (Planet of the mind): You are mentally alert, inquisitive, and humorous, and you need intellectual challenge. You like to travel and enjoy talking to people. You may be known as an idea person and are probably a good mimic. Good points: adaptable, active, good at writing and speaking. Bad points: restless, indecisive, think too much about yourself.

VENUS in (Planet of love and pleasure): You are affectionate, flirtatious, and usually quite good-looking. You have charming social manners and like to have companionship. Your appearance is important to you and you tend to spend too much money on yourself. Good points: sympathetic, artistic, a cheerful personality. Bad points: lazy, narcissistic, too fond of pleasure and luxury.

MARS in (Planet of energy and assertiveness): You are impulsive and independent, and dislike taking advice from others. You approach new projects with energy and confidence, and are capable of hard work. You have strong sex desires and are passionate in lovemaking. Good points: strong body, self-assertive, courageous. Bad points: inconsiderate, pushy, domineering, accident-prone.

JUPITER in (Planet of luck and expansion): You have a buoyant, cheerful disposition, and are a success socially. You inspire confidence, are optimistic, and tend to be generous with your time and energy. You are blessed with luck, and things usually turn out for the best in life. Good points: jovial, broad-minded, expansive, kind. Bad points: self-indulgent, gullible, with a marked tendency to gain weight. You are sometimes faithless in love.

SATURN in (Planet of discipline and limitation): You are persistent, have organizing ability, and are capable of self-discipline. You are patient and a bit shy, feel nervous underneath (which you keep under tight self-control), and

you want your talents and work to be recognized. Good points: industrious, good powers of endurance, a keen sense of responsibility. Bad points: stubborn and set in ways, afraid of new beginnings, secretive.

URANUS in (Planet of change and originality): You have an inventive mind and may take up unusual interests or hobbies. Your life is often marked by sudden and unexpected beginnings. You have a high-strung personality and an independent way of looking at things. You can be strong-willed about getting your own way. Good points: original, creative, intuitive. Bad points: inconsiderate, stubborn, eccentric.

NEPTUNE in (Planet of spirituality and illusion): You are imaginative and impressionable and can use this in artistic work. You tend to be absentminded because you like to daydream. You are fond of luxury and are sometimes lazy. A lot of your time is spent on or near the sea. Good points: visionary, idealistic, sensitive to other people. Bad points: procrastinating, changeable, weak-willed, never satisfied.

PLUTO in (Planet of transformation): You have an intense and magnetic personality, and you seek adventure. You learned to be self-sufficient when you were young and are inclined to be a loner. Good points: great strength, relentless in pursuing a goal, potential for self-transformation. Bad points: inscrutable, vindictive, ruthless.

SECOND HOUSE (House of Possessions)

SUN in (Planet of vitality and individuality): You need security and tend to attract money, but it comes into and goes out of your life rather quickly. You like to spend on luxuries, and many of your possessions increase in value over time. You often gain through influential people. Good points: generous, great reserves of strength, persistent, creative in financial affairs. Bad points: possessive, greedy, ostentatious, money and possessions become status symbols.

MOON in (Planet of emotions and instincts): You are able to earn money creatively, by using your imagination, and through the public—selling to the public, appearing in public, etc. Your financial affairs fluctuate and tend to be unsettled. You are sometimes thrifty and careful, at other times wasteful and careless. Good points: tenacious with a keen sense for what is lucrative, security-minded with an ability to plan for the future. Bad points: greedy, extravagant, you spend money emotionally and often unwisely.

MERCURY in (Planet of the mind): You are able to earn money in intellectual enterprises—writing, teaching, lecturing—or in any field of communications. You like to spend money on travel and education, and for gadgets that make your life easier. Sometimes you have more than one source of income. Good points: quick mind for financial opportunity, good bargaining powers, talent for salesmanship. Bad points: careless with money, impractical, vulnerable to trickery and theft.

VENUS in (Planet of love and pleasure): You tend to prosper through social connections, marriage, or artistic pursuits.

Business ventures with a partner are lucrative. You like to spend on clothes, jewels, personal adornment, and pleasures. If you are a man you tend to spend money on women. Good points: generous, fair and honest in financial dealings, an ability to use beautiful things profitably (fashion, decorating, art gallery, etc.). Bad points: extravagance, love of luxury and expensive possessions, inadequate willpower.

MARS in (Planet of energy and assertiveness): You have good earning power and make gains through your own effort and competitiveness. Money is important to you, and you aggressively go after it. You tend to have frequent financial crises, but you recover quickly. Good points: efficient, enterprising about new profit-making ideas, often have your own business. Bad points: impulsive spender, lavish, careless, vulnerable to losses because of fire, haste, or rashness.

JUPITER in (Planet of luck and expansion): You tend to make money easily and have a talent for financial dealings. Other people are attracted to your expansive ways and you often benefit through social contacts. Depending on the other factors in your chart, you will gain affluence or spend all you get in wild extravagance. Traveling or the travel industry is another source of wealth for you. Good points: honest in dealings, generous, visionary about new moneymaking ideas. Bad points: materialistic, careless, apt to suffer loss through legal entanglements.

SATURN in (Planet of discipline and limitation): You are ambitious about acquiring material comfort and tend to make long-range financial plans. You are thrifty and shrewd, cautious about your investments; blue-chip stocks are more your style than get-rich-quick schemes. Money doesn't come in quickly; gain is slow and steady, and you must put in considerable effort. Good points: practical, persevering, hardworking. Bad points: stingy, may encounter delays and obstacles in acquiring money.

URANUS in (Planet of change and originality): You tend to have an unusual source of income or your money opportunities pop up suddenly and unexpectedly. Your long-term financial picture will probably have spectacular fluctuations. If there are no opposing influences in your chart, you can expect to gain overall. Antiques, curios, and collectibles are lucrative for you. Good points: inventive, resourceful, unusual eye for value. Bad points: sudden losses, erratic money dealings, financial problems with friends.

NEPTUNE in (Planet of spirituality and illusion): You are intuitive and imaginative about making money. A more logical person would say your financial affairs are not run in a businesslike way. In acquiring objects, you tend to be more interested in their esthetic value (their meaning to you), rather than their material value. Good points: generous to others in need, gain through creative work, unmaterialistic. Bad points: a careless or indifferent attitude toward money, too easily imposed on or swindled, lazy.

PLUTO in (Planet of transformation): You are adventurous about money and not afraid of taking risks. You like to diversify, and during your lifetime there may be several changes in your source of income. You tend to become obsessed with possessions and finances. Good points: unique fiscal talent, resourcefulness, ability to win high return on your effort. Bad points: squanderer, selfish, tendency to be unscrupulous.

THIRD HOUSE (House of Communication)

SUN in (Planet of vitality and individuality): You have an active, creative mind and need to communicate your ideas. Chances are you will be successful in writing, teaching, or lecturing. Your ability to express yourself often makes you a leader in your field. Good points: ability to study, fluent, cheerful personality. Bad points: disorganized, arrogant, tendency for misunderstandings with relatives.

MOON in (Planet of emotions and instincts): You tend to think emotionally and have a strong imagination. You dislike routine and your life is marked by many short trips. You have a good memory, often change your opinion, and make a good impression when working with or appearing among the public. Good points: inquisitive mind, good common sense, successful writing about self or family. Bad points: moody, unstable, tendency to interfere in the lives of others.

MERCURY in (Planet of the mind): You have an alert manner and are versatile in handling both people and projects. You are practical and efficient at coping with details. People are drawn to your wit and humor and your eloquence in expressing yourself. Good points: curious, logical, intelligent, sociable. Bad points: nervous worrier, indecisive, apt to quarrel with relatives.

VENUS in (Planet of love and pleasure): You are artistic, have an innate sense of taste and design, and win attention for your ideas in a way that people find charming. Your social life may involve taking a number of trips. Love may come about because of travel or through correspondence. Good points: cheerful, creative, eloquent in both speech and writing. Bad points: mentally lazy, superficial, too swayed by emotion.

MARS in (Planet of energy and assertiveness): You are determined and active and usually speak your mind. You like to be a leader and often get your way in things because you are so persuasive. You tend to drive too fast or encounter difficulties while traveling. Good points: alert, full of new ideas, can express yourself creatively. Bad points: argumentative, especially with relatives, vulnerable to loss in legal disputes.

JUPITER in (Planet of luck and expansion): You have an optimistic outlook and like to keep busy with a variety of intellectual interests. Your mind is not content with a little knowledge; you want to know more. Travel is a beneficial influence for both pleasure and profit. Good points: curious and open to new experience, able to share ideas, good relationships with relatives. Bad points: restless, impractical, reckless.

SATURN in (Planet of discipline and limitation): You have a practical and rather serious mind; you want to learn things so you can put them to use. You have good powers of observation, and prefer to deal in facts rather than theories. You sometimes procrastinate because you wait to make the right decision. You may encounter difficulties or obstacles in getting an education. Good points: contemplative, persevering, conscientious. Bad points: prone to pessimism, estrangement from relatives.

URANUS in (Planet of change and originality): You have an independent and inventive mind and like to follow your own road rather than someone else's. Travel in your life often comes up suddenly. At times you can be strikingly original in the way you speak and write. Good points: creative, ingenious, versatile. Bad points: restless, friction with relatives because of unconventional ideas, prone to accidents while traveling.

NEPTUNE in (Planet of spirituality and illusion): Your mind is impressionable and imaginative, and you may have psychic feelings about other people. You have a deep need to learn about life and are attracted to occult studies. You like to daydream and fantasize. Good points: idealistic, intuitive, artistic. Bad points: discontented, may undervalue your capabilities, confused dealings with relatives.

PLUTO in (Planet of transformation): You have a penetrating mind and seek to learn as much as possible. There is an intensity to the way you speak and write, which you can often use creatively. Travel opens new experiences for you and sometimes marks a significant turning point in your life. Good points: curious, good concentration, original in your thinking. Bad points: suspicious, manipulative, you want to dominate others.

FOURTH HOUSE (House of Home; also of the Early and Latter Parts of Life)

SUN in (Planet of vitality and individuality): You take pride in your home and family; from the time you were young you had a deep need to establish roots. One or both of your parents was a dominant influence in your life; in some cases you had to struggle for independence. Conditions surrounding the end of your life promise to be fortunate. Good point: you may benefit through inheritance. Bad point: you have a tendency to feel insecure.

MOON in (Planet of emotions and instincts): You are protective toward your family and are (may become) a devoted parent. During your lifetime you can expect to change residences often, and you like to live near water. During the latter part of life you may achieve public recognition. Good point: financial acumen in real estate or family possessions. Bad point: you resist facing up to reality.

MERCURY in (Planet of the mind): Your home is often a place of study or work, and the work you do may lead to changes in your residence. Your parents and early home life stimulated your curiosity to learn. In your latter years you can expect to be mentally active and to have many contacts throughout the world. Good point: you deal rationally with family and as a parent. Bad point: restlessness and difficulty in settling down.

VENUS in (Planet of love and pleasure): Your home is usually your showplace and you like to surround yourself with beautiful things. You tend to have happy memories of childhood and are probably attached to your mother. Circumstances at the end of your life promise to be peaceful. Good point: you promote harmony in domestic relationships. Bad point: you are extravagant in buying possessions for your home.

MARS in (Planet of energy and assertiveness): You have a great desire to own your own home so that you can live independently. In your childhood you may have been in conflict with parents, especially your father. Your latter years promise to be active, and you are unlikely to be dependent on others for a place to live. Good point: enterprising about making money at home. Bad point: quarrelsome in domestic relations.

JUPITER in (Planet of luck and expansion): You tend to be happy and comfortable at home, and take pride in your family. In childhood you probably felt secure and loved by your parents, and you inherit from them in either a spiritual or material way. The latter part of your life should find you in comfortable circumstances. Good point: you should find material success in the city or country of your birth. Bad point: extravagant and overgenerous in domestic affairs or as a parent.

SATURN in (Planet of discipline and limitation): You are concerned about and devoted to your family. In childhood you may have assumed responsibility at an early age. Saturn in the Fourth House sometimes indicates an early loss of a father. You will look after those who cared for you as a child when they are old. You plan carefully for security in your old age, and are likely to spend your last years alone and independent. Good point: gain through real estate. Bad point: difficulty expressing feelings to family members.

URANUS in (Planet of change and originality): You are not a domesticated creature and need a certain amount of independence. You have had a different childhood from your friends, or your parents may have had unusual careers. Your life may take a sudden turn and your latter years will be spent in an environment you cannot yet envision. Good point: successful at entertaining groups in your home. Bad point: you can be a disruptive influence in family relations.

NEPTUNE in (Planet of spirituality and illusion): You probably have an idealized picture of what home life should be like and are vaguely dissatisfied with what it really is. There may be family skeletons hidden somewhere. Your latter years will likely be spent in a faraway place. Good point: you are (may become) an imaginative and stimulating parent. Bad point: tendency for confusion and misunderstandings in family affairs.

PLUTO in (Planet of transformation): You care intensely about family matters and want to dominate in your own home. Your parents were probably a profound influence on you but you may never resolve your mixed feelings about your early home life. Your latter years may be spent secluded and isolated, perhaps working on an important project. Good point: you feel responsibility toward the family. Bad point: may suffer early loss of parent or guardian.

FIFTH HOUSE (House of Creativity and Sex)

SUN in (Planet of vitality and individuality): You are energetic and creative, fond of pleasure and good living. You are interested in art, theater, sports, and like to be with people. You may have many love affairs, and you spend money with a free hand. Good point: joy in children. Bad point: pride interferes with love relationships.

MOON in (Planet of emotions and instincts): You are impulsive about love and tend to follow your heart rather than your head. You seek out pleasure in life; one of your love affairs is likely to become public knowledge. You may have a child who becomes famous. Good point: romantic and creative imagination. Bad point: overprotective and possessive of lovers and/or children.

MERCURY in (Planet of the mind): You like change and new people, and probably have a number of love affairs. A lover must keep you intellectually interested or you become bored. You have a dramatic way of expressing yourself, and may possess artistic talent. Good point: flair for communicating with the public. Bad point: overcritical with loved ones.

VENUS in (Planet of love and pleasure): You like social life and being in the spotlight. You attract romance, and usually have many lovers. You take pleasure in creative work and are affectionate with children. Good point: you have the talent to succeed in the artistic and entertainment world. Bad point: self-indulgent and overly fond of applause.

MARS in (Planet of energy and assertiveness): You are rash and impulsive in love affairs, and sometimes too impatient in lovemaking. You are competitive (in love, sports, socially) and need to be a winner. You have a personal magnetism that draws people to you. Good point: leadership ability. Bad point: conflicts with loved ones because of ego.

JUPITER in (Planet of luck and expansion): You enjoy most forms of recreation—sporting events, parties, and theater are special favorites. If there are no opposing influences in your chart, you will be lucky in speculation. You are sometimes indiscreet about love affairs. Good point: children bring happiness. Bad point: extravagant; sometimes gambling losses.

SATURN in (Planet of discipline and limitation): Because you are disciplined and take life seriously, you often don't allow yourself to relax and have fun. You have strong feelings about those you love, but you also need their respect. You may be stern with children. Your periods of unhappiness have taught you a lesson in life. Good point: conscious of duty and responsibility to loved ones. Bad point: fear of giving too much of yourself in love.

URANUS in (Planet of change and originality): You are prone to sudden infatuations that also end abruptly. You may be engaged to marry and then break the engagement. You like novelty and experimentation in sex. Good point: innovative and inventive in creative expression. Bad point: may be estranged from children.

NEPTUNE in (Planet of spirituality and illusion): You love pleasure and luxury (sometimes too much); you are very drawn to the theater or cinema. You bring a fantasy quality to lovemaking. You may be involved in one or more illicit love affairs, which may cause sorrow. Good point: artistic talent, especially as actress or actor. Bad point: vulnerable to loss through gambling or fraud.

PLUTO in (Planet of transformation): You are impetuous and passionate and will follow your desires where they lead you. You exaggerate the importance of your love affairs until you become intensely involved. You have a strong artistic bent. Good point: you feel responsibility to loved ones. Bad point: you harbor resentment against a past love.

SIXTH HOUSE (House of Service and of Health)

SUN in (Planet of vitality and individuality): You take pride in your work and have a talent for organization. You need to feel appreciated. Health tends to be good, with strong recuperative powers, though you are subject to occasional nagging health problems. Good point: you're an efficient problem solver. Bad point: you can be fussy and difficult to work for.

MOON in (Planet of emotions and instincts): You may change jobs frequently until you find something that truly suits you. Unhappiness at work may affect your health adversely. You may be especially prone to stomach trouble. Good point: intuitive and imaginative in work. Bad point: unstable and indecisive about responsibility.

MERCURY in (Planet of the mind): You are something of a perfectionist, which can make day-to-day problems seem overwhelming. You take an interest in health, diet, and hygiene, and are usually well informed about the latest on these subjects. You have a tendency to be nervous and may have respiratory or stomach problems. Good point: practical and efficient, especially in work involving writing or communications. Bad point: a worrier about health and work.

VENUS in (Planet of love and pleasure): You strive for harmony and good relationships with associates on the job. You don't like hard or gritty physical labor. Health is good, though you tend to overindulge in eating and drinking. Good point: work situation may bring romance.

Bad point: tendency to laziness and letting others do the chores.

MARS in (Planet of energy and assertiveness): In your work you set out to accomplish things. Keeping impulsiveness under control will make you more efficient. You drive yourself hard and expect others to perform at your level. You have vitality and energy, but are prone to careless accidents. Good point: can initiate new work methods. Bad point: at times intolerant and argumentative with coworkers.

JUPITER in (Planet of luck and expansion): You tend to be successful in work and get along well with associates. You are loyal and dependable, and Jupiter usually brings monetary reward. You love good food and tend to gain weight. Good point: work brings opportunity for travel and expansion. Bad point: health problems because of overindulgence.

SATURN in (Planet of discipline and limitation): You are a conscientious and reliable worker and handle responsibility well. You are exacting in your demands on yourself. Health may be under strain due to overwork or because you tend to neglect looking after yourself. Good point: you are admired by colleagues and associates. Bad point: you can't accept that there are limitations and obstacles beyond your control.

URANUS in (Planet of change and originality): You think of new methods or original ideas in plying your trade. You are also erratic and impatient, and sometimes don't achieve as much as a more thorough and disciplined worker. Your health is subject to unusual complaints that are difficult to diagnose or treat. Good point: ability to modernize, streamline, or improve old ideas. Bad point: inconsistency in output and devotion to a task.

NEPTUNE in (Planet of spirituality and illusion): You are idealistic about your work, sensitive to your surroundings and associates. You may have difficulty finding the right circumstances in which you can be happy and comfortable. Health is subject to strange ailments; drugs are a

particular hazard and their use should be supervised by a doctor. Good point: a desire to help the unfortunate. Bad point: inclined to laziness and merely drifting along.

PLUTO in (Planet of transformation): You have great power of concentration and are intent on seeing results. You tend to overwork yourself. You take an interest in medicine and health and are sometimes gifted in the healing arts. Good point: the work you do can inspire others. Bad point: physical energy is often sapped by job pressures.

SEVENTH HOUSE (House of Marriage and Partnership)

SUN in (Planet of vitality and individuality): You are promised success in marriage and in partnerships. Both should bring material, monetary, and social benefits. You may not marry young; your spouse will probably be prominent or of good and honorable character. Sex is important to you in marriage. Good point: you are popular and know how to attract people. Bad point: clashes at times because of your need to be dominant in relationships.

MOON in (Planet of emotions and instincts): Security is very important to you in marriage and relationships. Chances are you will marry a parental figure of some kind. Your spouse will probably be protective of you. You are likely to become popular with the public at some time in your life. Good point: responsive in partnerships; sensual in marriage. Bad point: changeable in your love relationships; possible divorce.

MERCURY in (Planet of the mind): You seek intellectual compatibility in marriage and partnerships. You will probably marry someone lively and talkative; verbal give-and-take characterizes your intimate relationships. Business partnerships in law, literary, or communications world are beneficial. Good point: you are sociable, adaptable to all kinds of people. Bad point: stress in relationships because of quarrels and arguments.

VENUS in (Planet of love and pleasure): You look for harmony and fulfillment in both marriage and partnerships. You are affectionate, romantic, and popular with the opposite sex. At some point in your life you are likely to gain prestige or financial benefit through a mate or partner. You tend to marry early and possibly more than once. Good point: you are a natural peacemaker. Bad point: resentful if others do not make the first move toward you.

MARS in (Planet of energy and assertiveness): You are a highly independent individual and won't give that up in a marriage or partnership. Your relationships begin impulsively, and you are usually the aggressive one. Mars in the Seventh House indicates that you may marry more than once, or that a marriage or business partnership may end because of the death of partner. Good point: ardent and sexually passionate in marriage. Bad point: arguments and quarrels in relationships; possible early divorce.

JUPITER in (Planet of luck and expansion): You are successful in marriage and partnerships, and are likely to gain power and prestige through both. Jupiter in the Seventh House often means you will marry twice and that one of your mates is likely to be powerful or wealthy. During your lifetime your adversaries often become friends, and conflicts have a beneficial ending. Good point: legal partnerships tend to be fruitful. Bad point: overgenerosity and placing your trust in the wrong person.

SATURN in (Planet of discipline and limitation): You are cautious about marriage and partnerships, and may delay getting involved until you are sure. You often marry a widow or widower or someone older than yourself. If there are no opposing influences in your chart, you benefit monetarily or socially through marriage. Good point: you take commitment to another person seriously. Bad point: possible legal problems and a setback because of them.

URANUS in (Planet of change and originality): Partnerships or marriage may come about suddenly for you. You are drawn to unusual people and are likely to marry someone intellectually stimulating. As a team you will draw attention. However, Uranus in the Seventh House indicates the possibility of sudden divorce and remarriage. Good point: you are able to achieve goals through a marriage partner. Bad point: your need for independence may cause disruption or jealousy in marriage.

NEPTUNE in (Planet of spirituality and illusion): In marriage and partnerships you look for compatibility of spirit, common goals in life, or an artistic or religious vision that you share. However, an unrealistic or confused attitude about what you want in a partner may lead to the possibility of an illicit love affair while married. Good point: sensitive and responsive to needs of partner. Bad point: too easily swayed; open to disappointment.

PLUTO in (Planet of transformation): You are intense and dominating in relationships. You seek fulfillment in marriage and are emotionally demanding. Pluto in the Seventh House indicates that you may marry in secret or elope. Business partnerships are likely to be successful. Good point: you are intuitive about partner's needs. Bad point: strife, jealousy, and emotionalism in relationships.

(E) except chiron

EIGHTH HOUSE (House of Death and Regeneration; also of Legacies)

SUN in (Planet of vitality and individuality): You are philosophical and have deep insights; you strive for self-improvement. You may benefit from inheritance or from money through a marriage partner. There is the possibility of achieving fame near the end of your life or after death. Good point: you take pride in responsibilities. Bad point: may suffer the early loss of father or husband.

MOON in (Planet of emotions and instincts): You are a deeply sensitive person with a talent for healing. You have strong powers of suggestion. You are interested in questions about death and an afterlife, and quite possibly have psychic ability that you can use in a practical way. You are highly responsive sexually. Finances may be unsettled because of marriage or inheritance. Good point: you can guide others in a spiritual way. Bad point: may suffer the early loss of mother or wife.

MERCURY in (Planet of the mind): You have a penetrating mind and look for some way to communicate your insights. You have a talent for research and analysis. Money comes to you through other people or a marriage partner, but there may be insurance or legal problems. Good point: ability to see into human motivation. Bad point: may suffer the early death of a relative.

VENUS in (Planet of love and pleasure): You are intense about sexual involvements and look for fulfillment in them. You are likely to inherit money from a loved one or a marriage partner, or to gain from the career advance-ment of someone who loves you. Circumstances surrounding your death promise to be peaceful. Good point: sexual relationships tend to be harmonious. Bad point: laxness and reluctance to handle responsibilities.

MARS in (Planet of energy and assertiveness): You are passionate about life and have a strong sex drive. You are attracted to the occult, also to medicine and the healing arts. There may be conflicts in your family over wills or legacies. Good point: powerful and brilliant researcher. Bad point: need to protect yourself against financial loss because of an extravagant partner.

JUPITER in (Planet of luck and expansion): You tend to have an optimistic and healthy attitude toward life and death, and an abundant sex drive. You will probably enjoy financial gain through inheritance or marriage. Jupiter in this House promises easy and peaceful conditions at your death. Good point: your philosophy of life can inspire others. Bad point: possibility of wasting other people's money.

SATURN in (Planet of discipline and limitation): You take responsibility for others and may become involved in their financial affairs. You are inclined to be somewhat inhibited sexually or to have difficulty expressing yourself emotionally in sex. Saturn in the Eighth House usually indicates that you will live until ripe old age. Good point: you are careful about putting aside money to protect loved ones. Bad point: difficulties over property matters or inheritance.

URANUS in (Planet of change and originality): You have an unusual outlook on life and death, and possibly an interest in the mystical. Sexual tastes or involvements are likely to be unconventional. You may receive sudden financial benefits from unexpected sources. Good point: you feel a responsibility to others. Bad point: risk of loss through business deals.

NEPTUNE in (Planet of spirituality and illusion): You are something of a visionary and seek to give your life more meaning. You may be gifted as a medium or possess strong ESP powers. Finances that you share with a mar-riage partner are a source of trouble or confusion. Good point: an idealistic desire to help others in need. Bad point: may suffer disappointment or be deluded in a sexual relationship.

PLUTO in (Planet of transformation): You have a strong drive toward achievement combined with a need to analyze what you do. You are dominant and passionate in your sexual nature. Pluto in this House indicates that your death will be of public concern. Good point: self-reliant and resourceful. Bad point: prone toward developing unhealthy obsessions.

NINTH HOUSE (House of Mental Exploration)

SUN in (Planet of vitality and individuality): You enjoy seeing new places and exploring new ideas. You are a person who stands by your word and tends to be idealistic. You may spend a good deal of time traveling abroad. Good point: you believe in and pursue an education. Bad point: may become fanatical about your ideas.

MOON in (Planet of emotions and instincts): You have a receptive, imaginative mind capable of delving into philosophical ideas. You are attracted by the unknown; in your work you may delve into history or the past. At some time in your career you are likely to benefit from in-laws or relatives of the person you marry. Good point: you will have happy experiences on voyages or travel. Bad point: tendency to be vague, dreamy, and impractical.

MERCURY in (Planet of the mind): You are alert and adaptable, quick to establish rapport with new people. Yours is an exploratory nature, interested in gaining further knowledge. During your middle years you may travel a great deal, both for health and your work. Good point: mentally advanced. Bad point: inclined to be meddlesome and to make promises too readily.

VENUS in (Planet of love and pleasure): You have warmth and understanding for people from different backgrounds. You are open to new ideas and experiences. Chances are good that you will receive some kind of honor in life. You may possibly be married abroad or marry a foreigner. Good point: high ideals. Bad point: you long for the unattainable.

MARS in (Planet of energy and assertiveness): You are independent in thought and open to change, and you enjoy travel and adventure. You will fight for your convictions. You seek out experience because you want to live life to the fullest. Good point: will gain in honor or financially through higher education. Bad point: can be headstrong and fanatical about ideas.

JUPITER in (Planet of luck and expansion): You have strong principles, are adventurous and optimistic. Travel and education open new doors for you and may lead to monetary gain. You have a flair for languages or an ability to express yourself well. Good point: foreign places and/or people contribute to your success. Bad point: can be arrogant and self-righteous.

SATURN in (Planet of discipline and limitation): You are thoughtful and contemplative and have a desire to learn. You delve seriously into questions of philosophy, faith, or religion. Contacts with foreigners are beneficial in your life, especially with older people. Good point: idealistic principles. Bad point: obstacles or limitations to receiving an education.

URANUS in (Planet of change and originality): You have an independent mind, and seek to widen your intellectual horizons. You may be known for your unorthodox views or interest in unusual branches of study. Opportunities for travel may come up suddenly, or you may experience exciting events in foreign countries. Good point: adventurous and open to new experience. Bad point: inclined to be rebellious.

NEPTUNE in (Planet of spirituality and illusion): You are drawn to deeper concerns in life, perhaps mystical or philosophical questions. You have imagination and insight, and probably make a fine teacher or counselor. There may be complications or difficulties in traveling abroad. Good point: visionary and idealistic. Bad point: a tendency to be discontented with your lot.

PLUTO in (Planet of transformation): You have an urge to discover the truth and perhaps change things for the better. You take an intense interest in other cultures and in different religions and philosophies. Travel and foreign people may affect you deeply. Good point: a desire for deeper understanding. Bad point: you try to impose your views on others.

TENTH HOUSE (House of Career)

SUN in (Planet of vitality and individuality): You have a strong sense of self and a drive to succeed. Chances are you will achieve success, but most likely in the middle of your life. Problems may arise if ambition and career take precedence over other concerns, such as marriage and relationships. Good point: leadership ability and power to influence others. Bad point: sometimes arrogant and dictatorial.

MOON in (Planet of emotions and instincts): You are involved with the public in career, professional, or social activities, and perhaps will not have much private life. There is the possibility that you will change your occupation in midlife. The Moon in this House brings career benefits through women or female members of your family. Good point: you are intuitive about what the public wants. Bad point: a risk of public scandal.

MERCURY in (Planet of the mind): You are able to use facts profitably and can adapt to different kinds of people. Your career should be intellectually stimulating, for you have talent in writing or communications. Travel is frequently involved in your work. Good point: success dealing with persons in authority. Bad point: unforeseen disruptions or uncertainty in career.

VENUS in (Planet of love and pleasure): You have an ability to use charm and diplomacy to further your interests. You may be involved in artistic or cultural work or in creating beauty. You are likely to be popular with the public. Good point: partnership (possibly marriage) should enhance career. Bad point: risk of scandal or disappointment through or because of women.

MARS in (Planet of energy and assertiveness): You have energy and initiative in career matters and will likely dominate other people. You are ambitious and competitive, and you strive for independence or to get rid of interference. Your self-reliance and executive ability should bring status within your occupation. Good point: you deal with practical problems rather than vague theories. Bad point: possibility of frustration due to unrealized goals.

JUPITER in (Planet of luck and expansion): Your desire to achieve in life will likely have good results in your career. You are confident, sociable, able to deal successfully with people. Jupiter in this House often confers public honor or esteem. Good point: ability to win favor of influentials. Bad point: tendency toward an arrogant, devil-may-care attitude.

SATURN in (Planet of discipline and limitation): You are self-reliant, ambitious, and likely to achieve success. You have the stamina and perseverance to attain your ambition step-by-step. There is the possibility that you will reach high position toward the end of your life, but that it will be a lonely place. Good point: self-disciplined and responsible. Bad point: selfish; susceptible to discredit or disgrace.

URANUS in (Planet of change and originality): You are an independent type who looks for freedom from interference. You achieve success in your work because of your unique or unconventional way of doing things. Your career tends to be marked by sudden or unusual turns and changes. Good point: original and inventive mind. Bad point: difficulty dealing with persons in authority.

NEPTUNE in (Planet of spirituality and illusion): You have high aspirations and are likely to be talented in a creative way. Your imagination and intuition are helpful tools in your career. Neptune in this House indicates an unusual profession or possibly success using a different name. Good point: idealistic and spiritual outlook. Bad point: liable to become confused by going in too many directions at once.

PLUTO in (Planet of transformation): Your intense personality makes its mark in career matters. You usually have a flair for business and knowledge of how to elicit support from others. During your lifetime you are likely to achieve a position of power and independence. Good point: forceful and dynamic energy. Bad point: subject to unforeseen twists of fate with loss of prestige.

ELEVENTH HOUSE (House of Hopes and Wishes; also of Friends)

SUN in (Planet of vitality and individuality): You are socially popular, able to attract and keep friends. You usually benefit through their faith and support. You have high goals in life, and an optimism that wins others to your cause. Good point: idealistic and creative. Bad point: a tendency to be domineering with others.

MOON in (Planet of emotions and instincts): Your easy social charm attracts admirers. At some time in your life your goals shift and friendships are likely to change. You have a flair for entertaining in your home. Good point: emotionally intuitive in dealing with people. Bad point: accessible to unreliable friends and scandal not of your making.

MERCURY in (Planet of the mind): You should have a large number of acquaintances, for you adapt yourself to a variety of different people. Your friendships tend to be based on an intellectual rapport. You are socially minded and usually become involved with groups, clubs, and societies. Good point: clever at thinking of ways to achieve your goals. Bad point: inclined to be impractical and/or cynical.

VENUS in (Planet of love and pleasure): You are sociable and fond of people and usually have lots of friends. You will likely benefit from your associations in both a social and a monetary way. You are drawn to marry a friend or someone you meet through a group or association. Good point: a tactful, diplomatic touch with people. Bad point: you are likely to confuse friendship with love.

MARS in (Planet of energy and assertiveness): You actively involve yourself with friends and tend to be a leader in your circle. Your associations with others are likely to be based on mutual assistance or favors. You have definite goals and objectives in life that you energetically pursue. Good point: willingness to help or be responsible toward others. Bad point: you can be quarrelsome and argumentative.

JUPITER in (Planet of luck and expansion): You are popular with others, and your associations bring you luck and happiness. You have high ideals and will likely gain your objectives. You know how to deal successfully with prominent and important people and will benefit from their influence. Good point: cooperative and generous with friends. Bad point: you rely on undependable or parasitical friends.

SATURN in (Planet of discipline and limitation): You form a few true and lasting friendships rather than cultivate many superficial acquaintances. You have high aspirations, but must often cope with mundane delays and obstacles. The discipline you learn early in life brings freedom later on. Good point: determination to reach objectives. Bad point: victimized by unscrupulous or selfish motives on the part of others.

URANUS in (Planet of change and originality): Your attachments and friendships often form suddenly. You are attracted to people with unusual interests and from different walks in life; you may be involved with the occult. Your ideals and ambitions are not run-of-the-mill, and you are often thought of as a unique personality. Good point: lively and inventive attitude toward achieving goals. Bad point: suffer estrangements from friends, and consequent emotional upsets.

NEPTUNE in (Planet of spirituality and illusion): You are drawn to artistic, sensitive people and are likely to form friendships because of goals you share in common. You are inclined to be an idealistic, compassionate person, concerned with giving help to others. You may join a humanitarian organization or a group with visionary aims. Good point: intuitive to the needs of others. Bad point: you suffer because of unreliable or treacherous friends.

PLUTO in (Planet of transformation): You are a strong, vital force in the lives of your friends, and involve yourself deeply with them. You are something of a reformer, and seek to bring about a change for the better in any situation. You feel intensely about your goals and may even have an obsessive personality. Good point: strong loyalty to friends. Bad point: vulnerable to separation or sorrow through death of friends.

TWELFTH HOUSE (House of Secrets, Sorrows, and Self-Undoing)

SUN in (Planet of vitality and individuality): You like privacy and quiet and the joys of meditation and reflection. You may be reticent or have difficulty expressing yourself and are close to only a few people. Success comes later in life rather than earlier. Good point: a deep spiritual understanding. Bad point: you tend to lead a secluded or lonely life.

MOON in (Planet of emotions and instincts): You are sensitive, receptive, and intuitive toward other people. Too easily hurt, you hide your real feelings. Often you need to get away to restore yourself, think, and meditate. Good point: a creative imagination. Bad point: often insecure; possible disappointment comes through mother or family.

MERCURY in (Planet of the mind): You tend to be a contemplative, self-absorbed, insightful thinker who works things out for yourself, alone or in secret. You worry over trifles and inconsequentials, and may be very shy. Good point: an instinctive researcher or investigator. Bad point: vulnerable to slander.

VENUS in (Planet of love and pleasure): Emotional and sensitive, you are capable of giving true and selfless love. You are most content when leading a private and secluded life. There is the possibility of a secret love affair. Good point: artistic and creative urges. Bad point: danger of an unhappy marriage or sexual alliance.

MARS in (Planet of energy and assertiveness): You keep your deep and vehement feelings secret from the world. You have strong intuitive powers that can be used to advantage in personal relationships. Your sexual nature is intense but repressed. Good point: active imagination. Bad point: danger from secret enemies.

JUPITER in (Planet of luck and expansion): You lean toward the spiritual or have an uplifting religious or philosophical faith. Your success in work helps or benefits others, and you are most attracted to medicine or social work. You also have a gift for producing inspired thoughts in seclusion. Good point: a compassionate and charitable nature. Bad point: impractical; you rely on others too much.

SATURN in (Planet of discipline and limitation): You are reserved, somewhat solitary or reclusive. You place limitations on yourself because of cautiousness or fear. You find it hard to share your feelings with others and may carry a secret sorrow with you. Good point: successful when working alone and in seclusion. Bad point: possibility of loneliness or isolation later in life.

URANUS in (Planet of change and originality): You are very intuitive, perhaps psychic, and are attracted to unusual beliefs in religion or metaphysics. Your need to be independent in thought fights against limitations placed on you by others. During one period in your life you may spend time alone in foreign countries or strange places. Good point: you are humanitarian and compassionate. Bad point: you are subject to sudden and unexpected adversities.

NEPTUNE in (Planet of spirituality and illusion): You are deep and sensitive and likely to possess a strong artistic bent. You prefer to work and live in a quiet atmosphere where you can create or meditate. There may be a mysterious or otherworldly quality to your personality. Good point: kind and helpful toward others. Bad point: afraid of life or harsh experiences.

PLUTO in (Planet of transformation): You have a compelling desire to understand, to see deeply into philosophical questions. There may be a secret sex involvement in your life. You are a private person and do not share your emotions easily. Good point: profound imagination. Bad point: may hide feelings of anger or resentment.

9

HOW TO INTERPRET
YOUR HOROSCOPE

IN THIS CHAPTER YOU WILL LEARN, step by step, how to interpret your birth chart or horoscope. The terms *birth chart* and *horoscope* here are used interchangeably, although they are not precisely the same. A horoscope is simply a map of the heavens—specifically the part of the heavens we call the zodiac.* A horoscope can be cast for any given point in time; for example, at the beginning of a new business enterprise. A birth chart is a horoscope for the *moment of birth*. When a person speaks about "my horoscope," he or she means a map of the zodiac for his or her birth time.

There was a time, not too long ago, when setting up a horoscope was a laborious process. Many complicated mathematical steps were involved and, by and large, people were dependent on professional astrologers to do the job. Happily, though, we are now living in the age of information—the computer has given everyone access to his or her complete, detailed, *accurate* natal chart. This book, for example, comes packaged with a CD-ROM that you can easily slip into your computer. Just key in the birth data and within seconds you can obtain a chart for anyone.

Casting a chart is easy—the *interpretation* is more complex. Charts are filled with astrological detail, and every one of these scores of details has a meaning. Putting together all the intricate denotations is a fine art. It is similar to the process a physician or therapist goes through looking for a diagnosis. In addition to extensive knowledge of astrology, this synthesis requires keen observation, an understanding heart, insight, and something more—an "extra-sensory" sense, a flash of seeing. And like finding a good therapist, finding someone who can offer an interpretation that is incisive, penetrating, compassionate and revelatory can be tricky.

But this does not mean you cannot read a horoscope. You can—and you can do this using some easy exercises that offer much information. This chapter provides you with simple tools that start delineating an overall

*A detailed explanation of the zodiac is given on page 383.

begin with your own horoscope (yours is the most fascinating). Shortly you'll amass a good ... ormation about your strengths and talents, your likes, weaknesses, needs, and hidden agendas. ... this chapter, I illustrate each exercise with a Sample Chart. For this Sample Chart, I chose the ... Oprah Winfrey, the charismatic talk show host and media super-celebrity who has touched an ex- ... ord with the public.

What Is a Birth Chart?

JUST AS YOUR FINGERPRINTS, blood type, and genetic code were all set at the moment of your birth and all comprise a picture of you, so your birth chart was imprinted at the time of your birth and is a composite portrait of you.

What is a birth chart? It is a diagram of the zodiac at the moment you were born. As explained earlier, you can think of it as a pictograph of you as a newborn baby, lying on the circle of Earth, looking all around you at the sky bubble that surrounds you.

⟨⟨⟨⟨⟨⟩

Nowadays a horoscope is drawn as a circle, though in old astrology books you will find horoscopes in the shape of a square. The circle is far easier to use and clearer to see at a glance.

Every horoscope is divided into twelve parts, like a pie cut into twelve pieces:

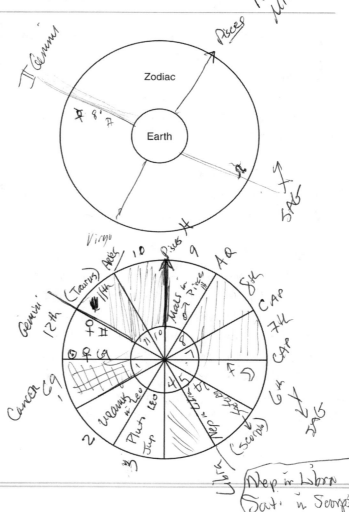

Each of the twelve segments in a horoscope represents one of the houses of astrology, which were described in the previous chapter. The lines (which look like the spokes of the wheel) are known as the cusps of the houses. A cusp is the point at which a house begins.

The houses of a horoscope always follow the same pattern. The First House begins at the "nine o'clock" position. The houses then go *counterclockwise* around the wheel of the horoscope. The Second House begins at the eight o'clock position. The Third House begins at the seven o'clock position, and so on through the twelve houses. Here is what the houses look like pictured in a horoscope:

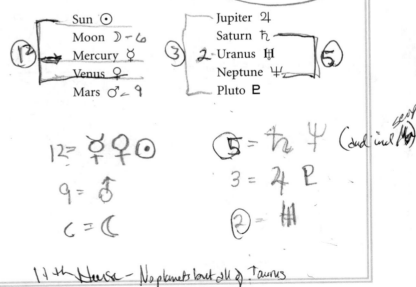

Generally, charts use symbols rather than words. If you are looking at a chart produced by a computer, you will see that the signs, planets and aspects are indicated in symbols. The symbols (called glyphs) for each zodiac *sign* are:

Aries ♈
Taurus ♉
Gemini ♊
Cancer ♋
Leo ♌
Virgo ♍

Libra ♎
Scorpio ♏
Sagittarius ♐
Capricorn ♑
Aquarius ♒
Pisces ♓

The symbols for each *planet* are:

Sun ☉
Moon ☽
Mercury ☿
Venus ♀
Mars ♂

Jupiter ♃
Saturn ♄
Uranus ♅
Neptune ♆
Pluto ♇

Oprah Winfrey's Birth Chart

Oprah Winfrey
Born January 29, 1954, at 4:30 a.m. Central Standard Time,
in Kosciusko, Mississippi
Latitude 33'03" North, Longitude 89'35" West
Ascendant is 29 Sagittarius

The Sun is in 9° Aquarius in the Second House
The Moon is in 4° Sagittarius in the Eleventh House
Mercury is in 19° Aquarius in the Second House
Venus is in 8° Aquarius in the Second House
Mars is in 23° Scorpio in the Eleventh House
Jupiter is in 16° Gemini Retrograde in the Sixth House
Saturn is in 9° Scorpio in the Tenth House
Uranus is in 20° Cancer Retrograde in the Seventh House
Neptune is in 26° Libra Retrograde in the Tenth House
Pluto is in 24° Leo Retrograde in the Eighth House

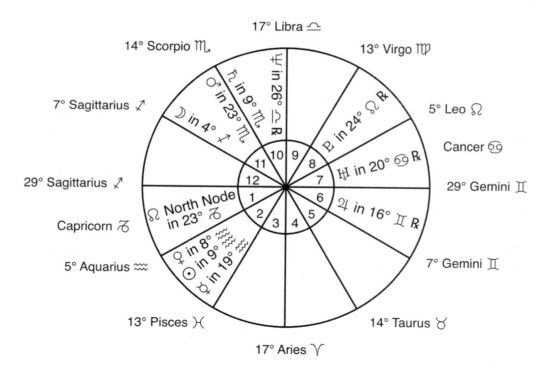

Interpretation

Now you have your computer birth chart. What next?

You will notice that a chart is made up of three components: Planets, Signs, and Houses. These are the three tools of a chart. Planets are the forces that act. Signs represent *how* the planets act. Houses represent *where* the planets act.

To begin your interpretation, make a list of your planets, signs, and houses. List your Sun, Moon, and planets in one column called *Planets*,* the signs in which they are found in a second column called *In What Sign*, and the houses in which they are found in a third column called *In What House*.

At this point, you will find it useful to go back into chapter 8, "The Houses of Astrology," and read the description for each of your planets now that you know in which houses they belong.

For example, Oprah Winfrey has the Sun in her Second House. On page 303, we will read she needs security and attracts money that can go in and out of her life quickly. She gains through influential people, and her possessions tend to increase in value. She is generous, has great strength and persistence, but can be possessive and ostentatious. As you read through the descriptions for the planets in your particular houses, you should jot down some keywords next to the houses in the third column. For example, in Oprah's birth chart I would write down the following:

PLANET	IN WHAT SIGN	IN WHAT HOUSE
Sun	Aquarius	**Second House** Needs security. Attracts money that comes and goes quickly. Gains through influential people. Possessions increase in value. Strong, persistent, possessive.

*For the sake of convenience, the Sun and Moon, which are luminaries, are referred to as Planets.

When you have finished going through all ten planets in their houses and made your notes, turn to chapter 7, "You and the Planets," and read the descriptions for the planets in the various *signs* that apply to you. This time, you should jot down notes in the second column. For example, in the above entry I would write the following:

PLANET	IN WHAT SIGN	IN WHAT HOUSE
Sun	**Aquarius** Intellectually independent. Enjoys ideas and learning. Friendly. A communicator, visionary and humanitarian. An idealist who searches for answers. Gift for dealing with all kinds of personalities. Likes to be contrary and different, can be argumentative.	**Second House**

Go through this process for each of the ten planets in your chart, making notes in both the *Signs* column and the *Houses* column. When you are finished, look down your list. You will see that you have various pieces of information. You can put together these pieces of information to form an accurate description of the person.

This is the beginning of the fine art of synthesis—of learning how to interpret a chart. It is not only fun but also will sharpen your observation of other people as well as your insights into yourself. The more you do it, the better you will become at it.

Sample Chart

In Oprah Winfrey's birth chart, the list of Planets, Signs, and Houses would look something like this:

Ascendant in Sagittarius

Needs independence and freedom. Cannot bear to be stifled. Is progressive, restless in spirit, ready to accept new challenges. A humanitarian and idealist who cares deeply about injustice. A knack for making friends. Open to new ideas and enjoys exchange of opinions. Honest, frank, impulsive, self-indulgent (food, money), and can make wrong choices in love.

PLANET	IN WHAT SIGN	IN WHAT HOUSE
Sun	**In Aquarius** Intellectually independent. Enjoys ideas and learning. Friendly. A communicator, visionary and humanitarian. An idealist who searches for answers. Gift for dealing with all kinds of personalities. Likes to be contrary and different; can be argumentative.	**In Second House** Needs security. Attracts money that comes and goes quickly. Gains through influential people. Possessions increase in value. Strong, persistent, possessive.
Moon	**In Sagittarius** Adventurous, exuberant, open-minded and sincere. Has expansive outlook and breadth of vision. Loves higher learning. Envisions high goals and rushes forward to achieve them. Sense of humor; witty way with words. Has talent for salesmanship, great adaptability. Perceives the best in people. Needs personal space and independence.	**In Eleventh House** Social charm attracts admirers. Goals and friendships may change throughout lifetime. A flair for entertaining. Emotionally intuitive in dealing with people. May encounter unreliable friends or scandal.

PLANET	IN WHAT SIGN	IN WHAT HOUSE
Mercury	**In Aquarius** Inquisitive, inventive, interested in people and their motivations. Is drawn to philosophy, metaphysics, the future of mankind. Advanced ideas. Especially suited for progressive professions, such as work in science and television. Can shock people.	**In Second House** Able to earn money in writing, lecturing, any field of communications. Spends money on travel, education; has more than one source of income. Quick mind for financial opportunity; can be impractical and vulnerable to trickery.
Venus	**In Aquarius** Helpful, charitable and giving. Kind and loving nature. Needs love relationship that allows freedom to explore her interests, hobbies, new people, and many friendships. Is immensely popular, but tends to direct personal magnetism toward larger concerns than mere romance. Will realize her dreams, often later in life.	**In Second House** Prospers through social connections. Businesses with partners are lucrative. Generous, fair, attracts money though beautiful things (fashion, decorating). Often extravagant and has lack of willpower in spending habits.
Mars	**In Scorpio** Hard-driving and resourceful. Has great persistence, relentlessness, intensity and determination. Disciplined efforts are directed toward a purpose. A powerful creative drive, as well as sexual drive. Attracted to danger or issues around death. Able to move audiences.	**In Eleventh House** A leader in her circle; actively involved with friends, groups and causes. Involvements with people based on helping each other. Responsible toward others. Has definite goals she energetically pursues. Can be quarrelsome or argumentative.
Jupiter	**In Gemini** Adventurous attitude; knack for finding advantageous situations. Moneymaking opportunities come through friends and contacts. Best success in intellectual areas, such as teaching, lecturing, and profits financially in communications (publishing, TV reporting, commentating, acting). Versatile, clever, makes name in more than one profession.	**In Sixth House** Loyal, dependable, has success working with associates. Personal fulfillment and financial gain being of service. Finds work with opportunity for travel and expansion. Has weakness for good food; tends to gain weight and possible health problems because of overindulgence.

PLANET	IN WHAT SIGN	IN WHAT HOUSE
Saturn	**In Scorpio** Strong will. Has subtlety, force, and dominating strength under a genial exterior. Understands human motivation. Executive ability; unswerving commitment to goals. Obstacles in her path in the form of emotional difficulties and scandal. Secret love affair may bring sorrow or trouble. Liable to suffer loss of loved ones early in life.	**In Tenth House** Self-reliant, ambitious, disciplined and responsible. Has stamina and perseverance to attain ambitions. Achieves success. Will reach high position, though it may be a lonely place. Is susceptible to discredit.
Uranus	**In Cancer** Heightened sensitivity to others. Insight comes through sudden and unexpected feelings. Intuitions can be trusted. Highly developed imagination. Opportunity comes through chance encounters and intervention of other people. Has artistic temperament; can be eccentric and unpredictable.	**In Seventh House** Drawn to unusual people; partnerships or marriage may come about suddenly. Element of the unusual in a marriage-like relationship; may be broken quickly, or be in relationship without marriage. Achieves goals through partnerships. Need for independence may cause disruption to marriage or marriage plans.
Neptune	**In Libra** Emphasizes idealism and love; a belief in brotherly love and resistance to inequity. Deeply bothered by injustice in the world. Possesses a magnetic attraction; can have unrealistic or unconventional view of marriage.	**In Tenth House** High aspirations. Idealistic and spiritual outlook. Creative talent. An unusual profession; imagination and intuition are helpful tools in career. May run into confusion going in too many directions at once.
Pluto	**In Leo** A love of power, domineering personality, strong pride and will to prevail despite obstacles. Can be arrogant and pleasure-seeking. Tends to hero-worship personalities in the media.	**In Eighth House** Dominant and passionate in feelings. Strong drive toward achievement. A need to analyze. Will move through some kind of ending or death (or death-like experience) and create new beginning.

The most prominent theme in Oprah's birth chart is the power to achieve. Again and again, her planets and their placements speak of persistence, drive, determination, and making the most of opportunity. Certainly, she has needed this in a life that reads like a soap opera. She is black, a female, an illegitimate child born in extreme poverty in an area of the United States known for its racism and segregation. In earliest childhood Oprah was raised by her maternal grandmother (who took in laundry) on a farm that had no indoor plumbing. As a child she had no shoes or toys, no TV, telephone or store-bought clothes, and only the food that was grown on the farm. Yet she has become one of the most wealthy, influential, instantly recognizable women in the world.

Oprah's Sun sign is Aquarius, and she has Mercury and Venus also in Aquarius with Venus in almost exact conjunction to her Sun. Thus the Aquarian qualities of reaching out to a larger life, a belief in learning and ideas, and having humanitarian ideals are triply emphasized. Her Sun-Venus conjunction shows enormous likeability—Oprah has warmth and genuineness, and seems to speak from the heart. Aquarius is noted for intellectualism, evident in everything Oprah has done in her career in TV, film, magazines and the media. Yet Venus being joined to her Sun says that love is a strong theme—her love of learning, finding out about people, her humanitarian efforts, her love of performing, and especially the way her audiences love her.

She does have Mercury (planet of communication and thinking-processes) in Aquarius, which denotes an independent, inquiring mind, someone interested in a wide range of subjects and who is a brilliant communicator. Her love of ideas and gift for communicating are also un-derlined by Jupiter (planet of luck and blessings) in Gemini, the sign of communication. As a very young child Oprah was taught to read by her grandmother, and Oprah has said books became the most profound influence in her life. "When I didn't have friends I had books, and books opened a window to a world full of possibilities"—a statement that embodies her Moon in Sagittarius (the sign of possibilities) and her expansive Jupiter in Gemini (the sign of writing and ideas). By the time she was three, Oprah was memorizing and performing dramatic readings in front of the congregation in her church; the church ladies called her the "talkingest child" and a "champion speaker."

Oprah has been successful in numerous career venues—TV, movies, book and magazine publishing, theater—but all of them revolve around communication. From her start as a talk-show host in 1984 in Chicago, Oprah's shows have won a phenomenal following; currently *The Oprah Winfrey Show* is seen in 122 countries. *Oprah's Book Club* has become one of the most powerful tools in the world to promulgate reading, not to mention create overnight bestsellers. In 2000 Oprah launched a magazine, called *O*, which (like her other projects in the field of communication) became an immediate and huge success. The magazine concentrates on inspirational and self-help articles designed, in Oprah's words, "to help readers live their best life" (Sun in Aquarius, Moon in Sagittarius). Some critics have called Oprah—and her TV show and magazine—preachy, self-indulgent, New Agey, and egotistic. Interestingly, these are some of the negative qualities of Aquarius (where Oprah has her Sun, Mercury, and Venus).

From the beginning, Oprah's upward climb and the "finding of herself" can be traced to her love of communicating. It also helps that she has benefited from others' opening a door, a chance to try, and especially a willingness to leap into the lion's den of situations she knew nothing about. When she was in high school she joined the debating team, made the honor list, was elected president of the student body, appeared in school plays, was a prominent speaker in her church. In her senior year, she was voted Most Popular and won a scholarship to college. She also snagged a part-time job reading news stories on a small local radio. This, in turn, lead to her doing a five-minute spot on TV when she was a sophomore in college.

Her career is marked by a pattern in which she was recognized as a natural on air and offered opportunities (first as a newscaster, then as interviewer) that she snatched up and made good at. Step by extraordinary step, Oprah would find her niche and turn a small success into a bigger one. The Saturn-in-Scorpio themes of persistence, jumping into a scary place, not giving up, are repeated. In those early years she was described as a "warm, bubbly personality who could get people to open up" and a "universal woman" (apt descriptions for the Sun, Mercury and Venus in Aquarius, Jupiter in Gemini, an Ascendant and Moon in Sagittarius, and Neptune in Libra in the 10th House).

One of the most interesting parts of a chart is the "dark side"—and another theme in Oprah's horoscope is struggle, pain, separation, and death (in both a literal and figurative manner). Pluto (planet of darkness and transition, as well as power and profound experiences) is in her Eighth House of Sex, Death (or death-like experiences), Endings and Rebirthing. Oprah has spoken of the sexual abuse she suffered starting when she was nine. The abuse, by an older male cousin and later an uncle, went on for years, and Oprah hid this terrible secret. When she was 14

Oprah became pregnant, a fact she hid from her father and his wife, and gave birth to a premature baby who died two weeks later (Saturn in Scorpio, Pluto in the 8th House). In her teens, Oprah took a self-destructive path of sexual promiscuity, experimentation with drugs, lying, running away from home. Her mother was about to place her in a home for wayward girls, but the home had no immediate room for her. Oprah remembers thinking at the time, "I am a smart girl. How did I get here?" She was sent back to live with her father, and at that point Oprah's essential belief in herself (Sun in Aquarius), and her determination (Mars and Saturn in Scorpio), took hold and she turned her young life around.

Oprah's childhood, home and family life are marked by disruption and conflict (Aries, sign of independence as well as conflict is on the cusp of Oprah's 4th House of Home and Childhood). She was first raised by her grandmother because her 18-year-old mother could not care for her. At the age of six, Oprah was sent to live with her mother, who over the next several years had two more out-of-wedlock children (half-siblings to Oprah). At eight, Oprah was sent to her father, Vernon, and his wife. Throughout her teens Oprah was shunted back and forth between her mother and father, which resulted not only in a lack of emotional security but in conflict in parental expectations. Her mother, gone much of the time and working long hours, did not care for Oprah's "book learning," whereas her father was adamant about education and discipline. In her horoscope, Oprah's Moon (an indicator of one's relationship to mother) is in the sign of Sagittarius, which points to distance and space to her mother. Oprah's Saturn (an indicator of relationship to father) is in Scorpio, which shows a far more intense connection to a strong, controlling figure. In Oprah's life, her father's control was a key element in her "rescue" as a young teenager.

In her open Aquarius-Sagittarius fashion, Oprah has shared, on-air and in her magazine, about her personal demons—her shame and guilt about her hidden sexual abuse, her early history with men who treated her badly, her weight problems, and struggle to love herself. She has said much of the pain she has experienced was the result of worrying about what people would think of her.

Another theme in Oprah's chart is money. The public's perception of Oprah centers on her superstardom, media presence, power, influence, the humanitarian work. Yet her chart definitely outlines major money. Three planets (Sun, Mercury, and Venus) in her House of Money, plus Pluto, Neptune and Saturn in Houses that relate to money, show an overwhelming theme of financial gain. Indeed, Oprah is a billionaire (she became a millionaire at 30 when she made a syndication deal for her Chicago TV talk show). Interestingly she does not spend her wealth only on her-self, her real estate holdings, etc. She has created two huge charities, the Oprah Winfrey Foundation and the Angel Network, to which she has given more than $60 million of her own money and raised millions more. Her humanitarian work (Sun, Mercury, and Venus in Aquarius, Moon in Sagittarius, Neptune in 10th House, Moon and Mars in 11th House) has aided lives around the world, contributed to schools, libraries, hospitals, established educational and health centers in South Africa for poor children, and helped to change laws in this country (the Oprah Bill signed into law in 1993 tracks convicted child abusers).

Oprah says, "You become what you believe—not what you wish or want but what you truly believe." So it would seem that with her Sun in Aquarius, and Moon and Ascendant in Sagittarius, she truly did believe she was special (she told this to her teacher in kindergarten) and she was going to "fly all over this world" (said to her mother when she was eight).

Other Things to Look for in a Chart

The Elements Formula

There are ten planets in a chart (remember that the Sun and Moon are referred to as planets), and each planet is in a sign. The astrological signs fall into four basic groups called elements. The elements are fire, earth, air, and water.

FIRE SIGNS   Aries, Leo, Sagittarius
EARTH SIGNS   Taurus, Virgo, Capricorn
AIR SIGNS   Gemini, Libra, Aquarius
WATER SIGNS   Cancer, Scorpio, Pisces

What do the four elements mean in a chart?

ELEMENT	KEYWORD
FIRE	Energetic. Active. Enthusiastic. Passionate. A need to express oneself. Impulsive. Takes the initiative. Outgoing. Tends to be extroverted.
EARTH	Practical. Stable. Places importance on security. Patient. Industrious. Strong-willed. Able to apply oneself toward long-range goal.
AIR	Communicative. Intelligent. Likes to deal on a mental plane. Quickly grasps ideas. Can speak or write effectively. Takes a rational viewpoint.
WATER	Emotional. Intuitive. Sensitive to surroundings and to other people. Creative. Good powers of imagination. Empathetic. A person of hidden depths.

One of the things to look for in a chart is which elements are dominant and which are weak or lacking. Is there more earth than fire? Does this chart accent water more than air? Does one element dominate or is one element missing? Is this chart evenly balanced among all four elements?

To come up with the answer, you must calculate the Elements Formula in your chart. This is extremely simple to do. You just count the number of planets that are in fire signs, in earth signs, in water signs, and in air signs.

Calculate the Elements Formula for your chart. Now note which elements are most stressed, which elements are least stressed, and which are not present at all.

- If a chart is deficient in *fire*—The subject is likely to have difficulty putting ideas into action. He or she does not tend to promote himself or herself aggressively, and may wait to be motivated by outward circumstances and other people.
- If a chart is deficient in *earth*—The subject is likely to be impractical and may have trouble holding on to money. He or she often lacks the ability to work hard and tends to grow impatient if the results of effort are too long in coming.

- If a chart is deficient in *air*—The subject is likely to have difficulty expressing exactly what he or she means to say. There may be misunderstandings or crossed wires in communicating. He or she is probably not too interested in abstract ideas or intellectual pursuits.
- If a chart is deficient in *water*—The subject likely does not have a lot of sensitivity to other people's feelings. He or she may be self-oriented or selfish. Also he or she may have difficulty expressing emotion and may keep feelings bottled up.

The Elements Formula is a simple but useful device for seeing the overall picture of a personality at a glance.

SAMPLE CHART

Let us add up the elements in Oprah Winfrey's birth chart. There are:

2	planets in fire signs	0	planets in earth signs
5	planets in air signs	3	planets in water signs

Her chart therefore has the following Elements Formula:

Fire 2　Earth 0　Air 5　Water 3

(Since every chart contains ten planets, the Formula must always add up to 10. Some leading astrologers, like Charles Jayne, suggest that the Sun and Moon be given *double* weight because they are such important influences in your horoscope. If you do that, the Sun would count for 2, the Moon would count for 2, and the rest of the planets would be 1 each. The total would therefore be 12.)

Oprah's chart is heavily weighted toward Air (communication, intelligence, an idea-person, speaks effectively), with a secondary emphasis on Water (emotion, intuition, sensitivity and empathy to others). She also has two planets, one of them the powerful Moon, in Fire, which points to her energy, emotional courage, enthusiasm and need to express herself. She has no planets in Earth, showing that she is far less directed toward finding security than in exploring new ideas. Her chart says her work in the world is her true "stable home."

If the Sun and Moon are given double weight, the Elements Formula looks like this:

Fire 3　Earth 0　Air 6　Water 3

With this formula, Oprah's chart is still overwhelmingly weighted toward Air, with a secondary emphasis on Water and Fire.

The Qualities Formula

Just as you look at a chart to determine what elements are dominant, you should study a chart to see which "qualities" are prominent.

The astrological signs fall into three groups of Qualities. They are Cardinal, Fixed, and Mutable.

CARDINAL SIGNS   Aries, Cancer, Libra, Capricorn

FIXED SIGNS   Taurus, Leo, Scorpio, Aquarius

MUTABLE SIGNS   Gemini, Virgo, Sagittarius, Pisces

[handwritten notes in margins: 4, 4, 3; Give Double to Sun + Moon; Cardinal - 5; Fixed - 4; Mutable - 4]

What do these four qualities mean in a chart?

In the same way that you arrived at an Elements Formula for your chart, count up the planets in the chart that are in Cardinal, Fixed, and Mutable signs and write down the Qualities Formula.

QUALITY	KEYWORDS
CARDINAL	Open to change. Emphasis on action. Tries to change environment. Projects self onto surroundings.
FIXED	Resistant to change. Single-minded in pursuits. Not easily swayed. Tries to mold environment to the will.
MUTABLE	Changeable and flexible. Mentally explorative. Emphasis on intellectual activity. Adaptable to environment.

If a chart is weighted with the Cardinal quality—The subject is likely to be restless, impatient, or domineering. If a chart has too little of the Cardinal quality, the subject may lack initiative.

If a chart is weighted with the Fixed quality—The subject is likely to be stubborn, rigid, tyrannical, or afraid of change in life. If a chart has too little of the Fixed quality, the subject may have little endurance or stability.

If a chart is weighted with the Mutable quality—The subject is likely to be vacillating, unreliable, or unable to accept responsibility. If a chart has too little of the Mutable quality, the subject may lack adaptability.

SAMPLE CHART

For example, in Oprah Winfrey's birth chart there are:

- 2 planets in Cardinal signs
- 6 planets in Fixed signs
- 2 planets in Mutable signs

Therefore, the Qualities Formula is:

Cardinal	2
Fixed	6
Mutable	2

Here we find a heavy emphasis on Fixed (single-minded in pursuits; tries to mold environment to her will). She is strongly directed toward what she wants to make happen and turns her force into those quests. She has an equal secondary emphasis (two planets apiece) on the Cardinal and Mutable qualities, meaning she is also open to change, an initiator, likes to explore mentally, and can go with the flow.

If the Sun and Moon are given double weight, the Qualities Formula looks like this:

Cardinal	2
Fixed	7
Mutable	3

The emphasis is still overwhelmingly on the Fixed quality, underlining Oprah's persistence and stubbornness. Her Mutable quality (of mental exploration) is now ahead of the Cardinal quality.

What Chart Type Are You?

THIS INTERESTING personality guide was devised by the well-known American astrologer Marc Edmund Jones in his book *The Guide to Horoscope Interpretation.* Jones formulated seven distinct personality types based entirely on the *pattern* that the planets form in a chart.

In this chart analysis, you look only at the picture of the chart. To begin, draw a blank horoscope circle and divide it into twelve sections. Now, referring to your birth chart, place a large dot (one for each planet) in the section of the horoscope in which each planet appears. There should be ten dots in all.

For example, Oprah Winfrey's birth chart, which looks like this:

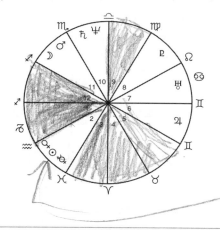

has a pattern that looks like this:

No

Study your pattern, and match it up to one of the following seven types:

The Splash

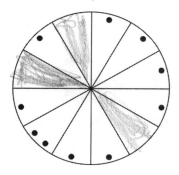

In this chart the planets occupy as many signs as possible, scattered all over the twelve sections. This type of person has a great many interests in life, studies or reads about a wide variety of topics, and may be proficient in a number of areas. The problem is that sometimes the Splash type scatters his or her energies.

SPLAY

The Splay

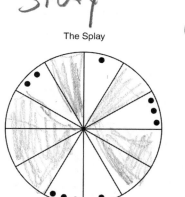

This chart is similar to the Splash, but the key difference is that there is at least one stellium in the chart. (A stellium is a grouping of three or more planets in one sign.) A Splay person is very individual and refuses to be regimented by other people's rules or conventions. He or she tends to have unusual tastes and interests and will follow those dictates and no one else's.

The Bundle

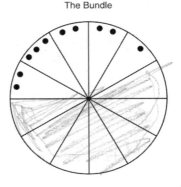

In this chart the planets are closely grouped together in very few signs. In addition, the signs must all be *consecutive*. This is the rarest pattern of all seven types. Here, the individual is a specialist—someone whose work or interests revolve around one concern or point of view. Bundle types do best applying themselves to one subject and becoming expert at it.

The Locomotive

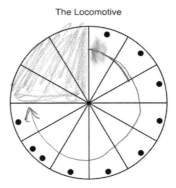

This pattern is easy to spot because it looks something like a train. The planets range over a large number of signs, and all the signs are consecutive. The locomotive (which is the planet that *leads* the others in a clockwise

position) is usually dominant in the chart, and this segment of the chart is one of the strongest houses. Locomotive people attack problems with drive and energy, and have a great many resources. The dominant planet and house usually give an indication of what area the person is strong in.

The Bowl

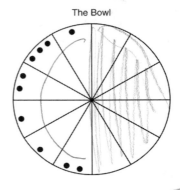

In this chart all ten planets fall within six consecutive signs, which gives the pattern the half-circle look of a bowl. The Bowl type tends to be thoughtful and self-contained; these people learn and profit from their experiences in life. They have particularly forceful personalities if the bowl is entirely in the top half or the bottom half of the horoscope circle, or is entirely on the left-hand side (as pictured) or the right-hand side of the horoscope circle.

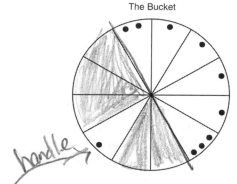

The Bucket

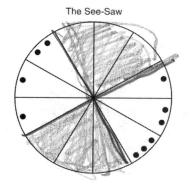

The See-Saw

handle

In this chart eight or nine planets fill one-half of the horoscope circle, and the remaining planet (or two planets together) is in the opposite half of the circle. This tenth planet forms the handle of the Bucket, and is called the Singleton. Bucket people tend to have a single-minded drive toward achieving a goal. They marshal their energies in one direction. Often the Singleton planet indicates the goal or direction that the Bucket type pursues.

This chart has a number of planets on one side of the horoscope circle in consecutive signs, and a number of planets on the opposite side of the circle in consecutive signs. In between the two populated sides of the circle are empty spaces. There must be at least two empty signs on either side of the seesaw. Seesaw personalities are always able to see two sides of a question. They take into consideration opposing viewpoints and opinions, and weigh these when making their decisions. As one astrologer put it, they "see life through a contrasting set of windows."

SAMPLE CHART SPLAY

The birth chart of Oprah Winfrey (page 335) most closely resembles the Splay pattern. She is a highly individual person who even as a child stood out from others; she has definitely directed herself toward her unusual interests, tastes and projects. Her chart also bears a secondary resemblance to the Bucket pattern—but in her case the Singleton (the "handle") is not one but three planets in Aquarius. Thus her goal-oriented, single-minded drive is triply emphasized, and her direction is toward Aquarian pursuits of knowledge, new ideas and humanitarian concerns.

Studying the patterns of different charts is both fun and informative. With a bit of practice you'll soon be able to tell at a glance what type is pictured is in a birth chart.

In What Part of the Horoscope Are You Strong?

WHEN LOOKING at the pattern that the planets form in a birth chart, another thing to consider is where the planets appear in the horoscope circle. The various parts of the horoscope circle all have specific meanings.

To make this chart analysis, all you will need is your horoscope circle that has the large dots (representing the planets in the chart). Study the layout of the dots in your horoscope, and note which parts of the circle contain the most dots.

To begin with, the horoscope circle is divided into halves. There are *four* halves in the circle—the left half, the right half, the top half, and the bottom half.

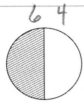

The left half of the circle, called the *eastern hemisphere*,* represents a person's impact on the world. The keyword for people who have many planets on this side of the horoscope is that they *mold circumstances*. These people are able to stamp their environment with the imprint of their own personalities.

The right half of the circle, called the *western hemisphere*, represents the impact of the world on a person. The keyword for people who have many planets in this

half of the horoscope is that they are *molded by circumstances*. These people are influenced by their surroundings and by the people in their lives; each experience becomes a part of their personality.

The top half of the circle, called the *southern hemisphere*, emphasizes social and public life. The keyword for this half of the horoscope is *outer aim*. People with many planets in this top half of the horoscope tend to be oriented toward career or professional life. They are usually involved with the community or the world at large; the approval of the public gives them satisfaction.

*You will notice that in a horoscope east, west, north, and south are exactly opposite to a geographical map. The reason is that as a horoscoper you are looking upward at the heavens whereas a mapmaker is looking downward to the earth

The bottom half of the circle, called the *northern hemisphere*, emphasizes self and family. The keyword for this half of the horoscope is *inner aim.* People with a majority of planets in this hemisphere are primarily interested in personal pursuits and pleasures, inner goals and satisfactions. This does not mean they don't achieve in life; it means their primary motivation for achievement is to satisfy themselves.

SAMPLE CHART

In Oprah Winfrey's birth chart, the left hemisphere has a marked preponderance of planets, seven, while the right hemisphere has only three—a clear indication that she molds circumstances to her liking. When confronted by obstacles, she takes immediate action to change the situation rather than allow her environment to shape her. She also has the force to seize opportunity and mold it into what she wants to make happen.

Oprah's chart has six planets in the top hemisphere (outer aim), and four planets in the bottom hemisphere (inner aim). She is oriented toward public life, professional success, and making her mark in a larger world and gaining public approval. However, she does have four planets in the bottom hemisphere, not an insignificant number, which shows introspection and great satisfaction in achieving her inner goals.

THERE IS ANOTHER way in which the horoscope is divided. It is divided into quarters.

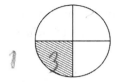

The first quarter of the horoscope consists of Houses One, Two, and Three. People having many planets in this quarter are highly individual and have strong personalities. They are primarily self-assertive and self-motivated. In their early lives they usually develop the character that will make a mark on the world later in their lives.

The second quarter of the horoscope consists of Houses Four, Five, and Six. Those who have many planets in this quarter are relationship-oriented. They need companionship in their lives to feel satisfaction and harmony. In their early lives they usually develop an instinct for dealing successfully with other people; their associations are likely to bring them contentment later in their lives.

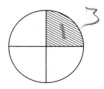

The third quarter of the horoscope consists of Houses Seven, Eight, and Nine. People who have many planets in this quarter are outer-directed and ambitious, but need the cooperation of others to achieve their goals. They are adaptable to a wide variety of situations and people. In their early lives, they usually develop an instinct for cooperation and diplomacy; their relationships are likely to bring them success in their careers.

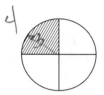

3 planets close conjunction in 12 (10 + 11 are Empty)

The fourth quarter of the horoscope consists of Houses Ten, Eleven, and Twelve. People with many planets in this quarter are the most independent and ambitious of all. They make their own way in life, and gain through their own efforts rather than those of other people. In early life they usually learn to depend on themselves; their self-sufficiency is likely to bring them success later in life.

SAMPLE CHART

Oprah Winfrey has four planets in the fourth quarter of her horoscope, and three planets in first quarter. A strong fourth quarter shows independence and great ambition; she is self-directed and from an early age depended on her own hard work and determination. Oprah's first quarter contains three planets (in close conjunction), underlining again the theme of a strong and highly individual person who is motivated and self-assertive.

Handwritten annotations at top: Moon rules Cancer — my Moon is in SAG → See next page Box insert

What Is the Ruling Planet of Your Chart?

Every chart has a ruling planet, which is easy to discover. Simply look at the sign that represents your First House. The planet that naturally rules this sign in the zodiac is the ruling planet of your chart. For example, if Virgo is your First House, the ruling planet of your chart is Mercury. If Sagittarius is your First House, the ruling planet of your chart is Jupiter.

Now carefully note in what sign and in what house your ruling planet appears in your chart. Its position has great influence in your life and to a large extent colors your personality.

Be sure to find your ruling planet and check its position in your chart. This is an important clue when interpreting a horoscope.

Handwritten annotations: TAURUS — 11th | SCORPIO is my INTERCEPTER — 5th house

SAMPLE CHART

Oprah Winfrey's First House is Sagittarius, and therefore the ruling planet of her chart is Jupiter. This planet of expansion and freedom is evident in her independent persona and need to express herself. She loves to explore and wants to "fly" (her wish when she was eight). Jupiter is the planet of luck; Oprah has always benefited from being in the right place at the right time and others giving her a chance to perform—the happy "accident" of others recognizing her talent and offering her opportunity to use it. Oprah's Jupiter is in Gemini, sign of communicating and dealing with people, and in the Sixth House of utilizing one's skills, focusing on getting the job done, and serving the world—exactly the trajectory of her career. The Sixth House also speaks of digestion and utilization of food, and Jupiter here points to issues around weight gain.

Special Note: Now and again, a birth chart will have Houses that contain "intercepted" signs. This means an entire sign is totally contained within the doorways of one House (a phenomenon based on the longitude and latitude of the birthplace). Oprah's First House contains an intercepted sign. The First House begins with 29 degrees Sagittarius, then Capricorn is completely contained within the House, and the House ends with Aquarius. Because houses that lie opposite each other mirror each other, Oprah's Seventh House also contains an intercepted sign, Cancer (the opposite sign to Capricorn). Houses with an intercepted sign speak of complexity; these signs are said to have "difficulty getting out." The native of the chart must work extra hard to express these signs. Capricorn in Oprah's First House shows a drive to control, to ascend to authority, and certainly executive ability. Capricorn's ruler is Saturn, planet of discipline and hard work—and in certain respects, Saturn is the subruler of Oprah's chart. Certainly her capacity for hard work, her driving passion, and the obstacles she has had to overcome (personally and professionally) demonstrate the force of Saturn in her First House. In her Seventh House, Oprah's intercepted Cancer shows that her nurturing instinct has revealed itself more in her work than in marriage or motherhood. Having Uranus (planet of uniqueness) here in Cancer also points to Oprah's "unusualness" in this respect.

What Is the Ruler of Your Sun?

In a chart, the planet that rules the Sun sign has great significance. This planet (called the *dispositor* of the Sun) strengthens the power of the Sun in your chart.

If, for example, your Sun sign were Libra, you would study the position of Venus (the ruler of Libra) to see how it influences you.

It is useful to study the planet that rules your Sun and to see its influence in your chart.

SAMPLE CHART

In Oprah Winfrey's chart, the Sun sign is Aquarius and therefore the dispositor (ruler) of the Sun is Uranus. Oprah's Uranus is in her Seventh House (of Partnerships & Marriage or marriage-like relationships). Uranus is the fascinating planet of being different, not bound to rules, of having a free spirit and special genius. It speaks of out-of-the-blue events and a disruptive, sudden breaking apart. Oprah's teenage pregnancy that ended in the death of her baby was a breaking apart of motherhood (a Cancerian instinct). Oprah's love relationships have not ended in marriage; an early affair with a married man caused her enough grief to contemplate suicide. Oprah's 20-year "marriage-like" relationship to Stedman Graham has still not resulted in a legal marriage. Oprah's Uranus points instead to her love of education, her special talent for connecting to people from all walks of life, and her caring humanitarian efforts poured into the world. Her latest TV show, *Oprah's Big Give,* has contestants giving out bundles of money to strangers in need.

What Is the Ruler of Your Moon?

Just as you looked at the ruler of your Sun sign in your chart, you should study the planet that is the ruler of your Moon sign. If, for example, your Moon were in Aries, the planet Mars (which rules Aries) would be important in your chart.

The Moon, as you remember, gives an indication of your emotional life, of the hidden currents in your personality. The position of the ruler of the Moon in your chart underlines the kind of emotional impact you have on others.

Be sure to look at the ruler of your Moon sign. You will find it interesting to figure out how this planet motivates you.

SAMPLE CHART

In Oprah Winfrey's birth chart, the Moon sign is Sagittarius, and therefore the ruler of the Moon is Jupiter. Jupiter is also the ruler of Oprah's chart (see page 341), which doubly underlines Jupiter's expansive power. The Moon denotes the emotional impact one has on others, and Oprah's TV talk shows and acting work are filled with emotion. She connects to people and sheds tears on-air with them as they tell their life stories. Her magazine accents believing in one's gut instincts, trusting one's own feelings of what is right. Larger-than-life Jupiter is reflected in the incredible numbers of people around the world who hear her inspirational messages, watch her shows, and are recipients of her charitable work.

The Four Power Points in Your Chart

The first things an astrologer examines in a chart are the four Angles of a horoscope. These four Angles are the most important points in a chart; they indicate power, strength, and activity. In astrology, they are sometimes called wide-open doors, because planets here can act freely and unimpeded.

The four Angles (Power Points) of a horoscope are:

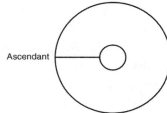

1. the Ascendant.

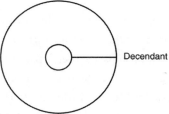

2. the Descendant.

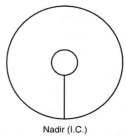

3. the Nadir (also called the Imum Coeli, the Latin word for "lowest part of the heavens"; often written on charts as I.C.).

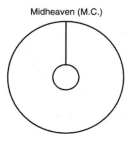

4. the Midheaven (also called the Medium Coeli, the Latin word for "middle of the heavens"; often written on charts as M.C.).

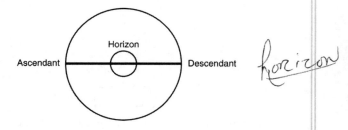

The line in a horoscope connecting the Ascendant and Descendant is called the Horizon.

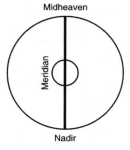

The line in a horoscope connecting the Nadir and the Midheaven is called the Meridian.

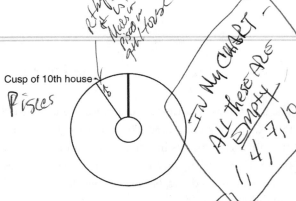

69 Cancer

Cusp of 1st house

(1)

In a chart, the line of the *Ascendant* marks the cusp of the First House.

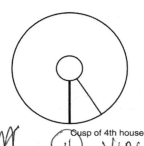

Cusp of 4th house

MP *(4)* VIRGO

The line of the Nadir marks the cusp of the Fourth House.

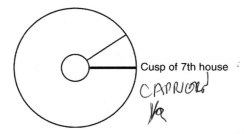

Cusp of 7th house

CAPRICORN
♑

The line of the *Descendant* marks the cusp of the Seventh House.

(handwritten margin notes): What constitutes "at" here? Can it be before? or in 12th house?

(handwritten notes top): before it is, Mars in Pisces in 12th house

(handwritten note): Cusp of 10th house → ♓

Pisces

(handwritten note): IN MY CHART — ALL THESE ARE EMPTY — 1, 4, 7, 10

The line of the *Midheaven* marks the cusp of the Tenth House.

PLANETS are extremely forceful in your chart if they are on or near the cusps of the First, Fourth, Seventh, or Tenth Houses (called Angular Houses). Indeed, any planets in these four houses are prominent and powerful.

Planets at the Ascendant or in the First House represent strength of character and personality—the power of a person's self.

On the opposite side of the horoscope, planets at the Descendant or in the Seventh House represent strength through relationships, partnerships, and marriage—the channeling of power in tandem with another person.

Planets at the Nadir or in the Fourth House represent strength through a person's beginnings—what he or she inherits from previous generations. The Fourth House is a mystical House, and therefore planets here indicate the subconscious motivation behind a person's actions. Planets in this House also give an indication of what the latter part of life will be like.

The opposite side of the Nadir is the Midheaven. Planets at the Midheaven or in the Tenth House represent strength in the public or outer world—the world of ambition and status. Planets in the Tenth House indicate the conscious motivation behind a person's actions.

Check the four power points in your chart to find out what are the most active and prominent planets in your horoscope.

(handwritten margin): 7 ... 4 ... motives — 1 ... CAREER ... CANCER

SAMPLE CHART

In Oprah Winfrey's chart, her Midheaven (the Fourth Angle Tenth House) is occupied by two planets, Neptune and Saturn. Also, her Descendant (the Third Angle Seventh House) contains a planet.

At her Midheaven Oprah's first planet is Neptune, which represents imagination, deep creativity, going for the dream, a desire to put ideals into action, and exerting a fascination on others. The Tenth House is the House of Career, and the force of her Neptune in Libra (sign of affectionate relationships and equality) points to her ability to fascinate the public and build a strong career based on her utopian principles.

The second planet at her Midheaven is Saturn, representing drive, discipline, concerted effort and ability to push through obstacles. Saturn is in Scorpio, sign of resilience, relentlessness, and profound power to control. These qualities of Saturn and of Scorpio also define aspects of Oprah's career life.

The other Power Point occupied by a planet is the Descendant—with Uranus in Oprah's Seventh House of relationships and partnerships. Uranus, planet of genius and unusualness, shows a marked propensity for long-standing relationships of loyalty that serve her well, personally and in her work. Uranus in the Seventh also underlines being drawn to powerful and unusual people who open opportunity and to forming a dynamic relationship with the public.

in my 2d house

Have You Any Planets in Their Dominion?

Each planet in astrology has a sign that it naturally rules—for example, Mars rules the sign of Aries. If, in your chart, a planet is in its home sign (in its dominion), its power is strong and it is able to express its qualities most purely. For example, Mars is very active, assertive, and energetic when it is in its home sign of Aries.

If you have a planet (or more) in its dominion in your chart, study that planet's power and also take into account the House that it occupies. Ask yourself, What kind of power does this planet possess and what house is it in?

The reason for these two questions is that a planet in its own sign has the strength to advance the affairs of the specific house it is in.

For example, suppose that in your chart Jupiter (planet of luck) were in Sagittarius (the sign that Jupiter rules and the sign of higher learning) and in your Second House (the House of Wealth). You would be likely to earn a very comfortable living and have an easy time financially doing work that involved your higher intellectual faculties, such as in the professions of law, publishing, teaching, or writing.

Have You Any Planets in Mutual Reception?

Two planets are in mutual reception when each one occupies the sign that the other one rules. You might think of it as two planets visiting each other's home. For example, if in your chart Venus is in Sagittarius (ruled by Jupiter) and Jupiter is in Libra (ruled by Venus), Venus and Jupiter are in mutual reception.

This is a very positive position for two planets to be in, for each one strengthens the power of the other. They will work in cooperation with each other, each one emphasizing the effect of the other planet.

Analyze your chart to see if there are any planets in mutual reception. They augur strength and luck in a chart.

[handwritten: MERCURY is in GEMINI]

[handwritten: 08° ♊ 50' ... ℞ ... Mer]
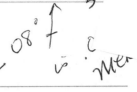

Where are the Head and Tail of Your Dragon?

YOUR BIRTH CHART contains two Lunar Nodes (the North Node ☊ and South Node ☋). These are not planets but a pair of points that speak of positive qualities you need to develop and negative qualities to release. In classical astrology, the North Node was called the Dragon's Head and the South Node the Dragon's Tail, symbolizing a celestial Dragon. A person entered life "head first" carrying positive qualities to work with, and trailing a "tail" of negative qualities to dispense with. In your computer chart, <u>only the North Node appears (shown as ☊)</u>; it denotes qualities to expand, gifts to use, your life purpose, and tasks to be mastered. Your South Node, located in the House opposite to your North Node, shows negative behavior to release and destructive patterns to let go of.

The following list delineates what the placement of your Nodes mean:

North Node in First House
Courageous, plucky, having true grit and initiative, popular, spontaneous, full of energy, vivacious, charismatic.

North Node in Second House
Decisive, persevering, practical, stable, responsible, offers security to others, a talent for financial gain.

North Node in Third House
Curious, imaginative, communicative, intelligent, quickwitted, cheerful, skilled in handling people, good verbal expression.

North Node in Fourth House
Emotionally strong, loyal, nurturing, family oriented and home-loving, deep understanding of others' feelings.

North Node in Fifth House
Creative, good-natured, confident, passionate, self-expressive, socially skillful, leadership ability.

North Node in Sixth House — *[handwritten: SAG]*
Diligent, able to work with others, high standards, seeks to be service, good with detail, sensible about health.

North Node in Seventh House
Cooperative, sociable, creative, charming, fosters harmonious relationships, willing to commit, good at partnership.

South Node in Seventh House
Indecisive, calculating, lacks backbone, tries too hard to please, superficial in relationships, sees partner as rival.

South Node in Eighth House
Manipulative, over-controlling, scheming, subject to extremes of emotion, chasing after the forbidden, sexual misbehavior.

South Node in Ninth House
Conceited thinker, moral superiority, arrogance, insincerity, cannot admit weakness.

South Node in Tenth House
Stingy, withdrawn, gruff, a grumbler, egotistical, pushy, power-hungry, greedy for success, ruthless.

South Node in Eleventh House
Feelings of inferiority, over-dependent on being liked, eccentric, too high expectations of friendship, feels misunderstood, isolates self from group.

South Node in Twelfth House *[handwritten: GEMINI]*
Rebellious, takes flight from reality, addictive personality, clandestine relationships, self-destructive behavior.

South Node in First House
Selfish, impatient, narcissistic, can hurt others through thoughtlessness, exaggerated need for freedom.

North Node in Eighth House
Profound in thinking, analytical, wise advisor, can keep secrets, strong powers of healing, fearless, dedicated.

North Node in Ninth House
Courageous, idealistic, can achieve long-range goals, strives toward higher education, faithful to commitments, love of travel.

North Node in Tenth House
Diligent, dependable, honorable, an achiever, sense of responsibility, assumes authority, strives for the top.

North Node in Eleventh House
Accepting, open, altruistic, able to form deep friendships, trustworthy, a reforming spirit, group leader.

North Node in Twelfth House
Devoted, nurturing, spiritual, sensitive to others, able to love deeply, champion of the underprivileged, love of humanity.

South Node in Second House
Stubborn, greedy, a glutton, concentration on materialism, a show-off, shady tricks in moneymaking.

South Node in Third House
Contradictory, intellectual snob, sarcastic know-it-all, superficial, fickle.

South Node in Fourth House
Moody, childish behavior, over-dependent, narrow-minded, fears change, a petty tyrant.

South Node in Fifth House
Needs constant attention, overbearing, exaggerator, a boaster and self-aggrandizer, indolent pleasure-seeker.

South Node in Sixth House
Fussy, finds fault, nerve-racking perfectionist, fear of rejection, argumentative.

SAMPLE CHART

In Oprah Winfrey's chart, the North Node (Dragon's Head) is in her First House, which indicates she came into this life with a strong personality—endowed with the gifts of courage, pluck and charisma. Her task was to express her power of *self* and not be afraid of her ambitious nature. With her South Node (Dragon's Tail) in the Seventh House, she needed to stop trying so hard to please, to be trustworthy in her relationships, keep from being competitive in her partnerships, and learn to make definite decisions.

If you have gone through these exercises, you have now amassed a great deal of information about your chart. At this point, some of you may want to delve more deeply into chart analysis. For those who are interested, there are a number of excellent books on chart-casting and analysis, and I list some of these on page 520 in my Recommended Reading List.

1 0

ASPECTS AND SYNASTRY

Probing Deeper into Your Birth Chart

The Aspects in a Chart

CHART ANALYSIS IS THE CORNERSTONE of modern astrology. Twentieth-first-century practitioners of this oldest science are putting less emphasis on divination and prediction than on exploring the human psyche. Through the study of astrology they hope to reveal the many facets of the human personality.

As you begin to learn more about chart interpretation you will become familiar with another very important branch of astrology. This is called *aspects*.

Astrologers consider the study of aspects an integral part of horoscope delineation. Modern astrologers are doing more research on aspects than ever before, and some call this the astrology of the future. Aspects are not a new study, but they lend themselves to deeper and more complex refinements the more they are studied.

In order for you to calculate the aspects, you will need to know not only in what signs your planets are, but in what degree of those signs your planets are. For example, in my own birth chart, Jupiter is in Taurus in the First House. But Jupiter is precisely in 14° of Taurus in the First House.

If you want to do the research, you can find the exact degree of all your planets by consulting an ephemeris (an almanac listing the planetary positions for each day of the year) or consulting a detailed Table of Planets for your year of birth. These publications are available in bookstores specializing in astrological publications, and I list some good sources in the appendix.

However, it is far easier to utilize the computer. These days, astrologers, teachers, students, and the general public rely on computers to construct horoscopes. Any astrological computer program will give you the exact degree of all your planets in your birth chart—and will calculate every aspect between those planets. In addition to making every calculation for you, computers avoid the human error that tends to creep into mathematical computations.

Computer service is relatively inexpensive and most services take only a day or two to construct your chart. If you yourself have access to the Internet, you can easily find astrological sites that will cast a chart for you free. You can also purchase an astrological computer program for your computer that allows you to cast far more complex charts than a simple birth-chart and provide you with in-depth horoscope analyses. Some reliable astrological sources that provide computer charts and sell computer programs are listed in the appendix on page 522.

Simplest of all is to utilize the CD-ROM packaged with this book. With this CD you can instantly cast a detailed birth chart, and the program also gives you the page numbers of this book on which to find descriptive information about every planet placement and aspect in your chart.

What Is an Aspect?

AN ASPECT IS SIMPLY the *relationship* between two planets and is based entirely on how many degrees apart they are in a chart. Remember that the horoscope circle contains 360 degrees. The planets within that circle form different relationships depending on how many degrees apart they are from each other.

Aspects are categorized as major (most powerful) and minor (less powerful). The major aspects were classified by Claudius Ptolemy in the second century A.D. In modern astrology they are still considered the most powerful aspects in a birth chart.

The major aspects and their influences are:

NAME OF ASPECT	DEGREES APART	SYMBOL	MEANING
CONJUNCTION	0° Two planets in the same degree in the same sign (or within 10° of each other).	☌	Powerful. A conjunction is the strongest aspect in astrology. It is usually a beneficial influence, though not necessarily so. If the planets have other difficult aspects in the chart, a conjunction may intensify them. A conjunction means the two planets involved have a powerful influence and are a focal point in the chart.
TRINE	120° Two planets 120° apart (or within 9° either way of 120°).	△	Most harmonious. A trine is the most favorable aspect, bringing advantage and ease. The only problem is that too many trines in a chart may make a person weak and lazy.
OPPOSITION	180° Two planets 180° apart (or within 9° either way of 180°).	☍	Unharmonious. An opposition brings strain, discordance, or separation. Modern astrologers look at oppositions less negatively than they were regarded in ancient times. Oppositions in a chart are thought of as challenges to growth and achievement.
SEXTILE	60° Two planets 60° apart (or within 6° either way of 60°).	⚹	Harmonious and favorable. A sextile brings opportunity. Unlike trines, sextiles require effort on the part of the native to work their beneficial influence.
SQUARE	90° Two planets 90° apart (or within 9° either way of 90°).	□	Challenging and stressful. A square places obstacles and teaches lessons. This aspect usually indicates an area where the person can develop drive and strength of character by overcoming difficulties.

Minor (less powerful) aspects were first introduced early in the seventeenth century by Johannes Kepler, the renowned astronomer who is called the father of modern astrology, and by Jean-Baptiste Morin, a French mathematician and astrologer. The minor aspects and their influences are:

NAME OF ASPECT	DEGREES APART	SYMBOL	MEANING
QUINCUNX	150° Two planets 150° apart (or within 2° either way of 150°).	⚻	Originally classified as mildly adverse, the modern tendency is to consider its influence unpredictable and also more powerful than first thought. Some astrologers connect a quincunx with health problems; others say it brings "offbeat wisdom."
SEMISQUARE	45° Two planets 45° apart (or within 2° either way of 45°).	∠	Mildly adverse. Brings tension that precipitates events but is much less powerful than a square.
SESQUISQUARE (sometimes called a SESQUIQUADRATE)	135° Two planets 135° apart (or within 2° either way of 135°)	⛫	Mildly adverse. Similar influence to a semisquare.
SEMISEXTILE	30° Two planets 30° apart (or within 2° either way of 30°).	⎴	Mildly favorable. Brings opportunity but is much less powerful than a sextile.

The Meaning of the Aspects

WHEN INTERPRETING A BIRTH CHART an astrologer will calculate which planets form an aspect to other planets. In Ptolemy's time an aspect was thought of as one planet "looking at" another planet; an archaic meaning of the word *aspect* is *to look* at or *glance*. This is still a useful way of regarding aspects. For example, if there is a Sun-Jupiter aspect in your chart, you might ask yourself, "Does the Sun look at Jupiter in a friendly way (a good aspect) or an unfriendly way (an adverse aspect)?"

To look further at this example: If the Sun in your chart were at 15° Gemini and Jupiter were at 15° Aquarius, you would have a *trine* in your chart. The Sun trine Jupiter is a very good aspect, so harmonious in fact that it helps to outweigh other adverse aspects in your chart. Its influence tends to make you well liked, popular, broad-minded, and generous. You would make money easily and influential people would be likely to help you. If instead the Sun in your chart were at 10° Taurus and Jupiter were at 10° Scorpio, you would have an *opposition* in your chart. The Sun in opposition to Jupiter indicates carelessness and extravagance. You would be likely to have financial problems and need to borrow money. You might make frequent errors of judgment or be susceptible to bad advice. You might be a gambler but luck would not be on your side.

Again, you must keep in mind that the aspects in a chart are a *contributing* influence in your horoscope. The combination of all influences—Sun sign, Moon sign, Rising sign, Planets, Houses, Aspects, as well as many others—make up the unique, distinct, unduplicatable, one-and-only you.

Here is a brief rundown of the *meanings* of the various aspects each planet might form with other planets:

Sun Aspects

SUN and MOON
GOOD ASPECTS Well-integrated personality; adaptable to others. Tends to have harmonious home life; gets promotions in job.
ADVERSE ASPECTS Inner conflicts about self, insecurity. Actions are contradictory. Emotionally oversensitive.
CONJUNCTION Stubborn and self-willed. Sometimes an unbalanced or one-sided personality; deep-rooted habits.

SUN and MERCURY
The Sun and Mercury are always within 28° of each other and thus if they form an aspect in your chart, it would only be a conjunction.
CONJUNCTION If 5° or less separate the Sun and Mercury, native is apt to be rigid and dogmatic in opinion.

SUN and VENUS
Because the Sun and Venus are never more than 48° apart, the only aspect considered important between these two planets is a conjunction.
CONJUNCTION A very harmonious aspect bringing warmheartedness, sociability, and charm.

SUN and MARS
GOOD ASPECTS Creative. Assertive. Enterprising. Indicates a high energy level.
ADVERSE ASPECTS Tendency to be quarrelsome, combative, headstrong. Lacks staying power; is hasty and takes risks.
CONJUNCTION Hard worker. Adventurous. Restless. Enthusiastic.

SUN and JUPITER
GOOD ASPECTS Optimism, generosity. Enjoys popularity. Attracts luck.
ADVERSE ASPECTS Extravagant and spendthrift tendencies. Person may be conceited, overbearing, indolent.
CONJUNCTION A cultured mind. A sense of humor.

SUN and SATURN
GOOD ASPECTS Ability to persevere. Good concentration; well organized. Succeeds through own efforts.
ADVERSE ASPECTS Indicates disappointment and obstacles. Subject must overcome hindrances and feelings of inadequacy.
CONJUNCTION Gives seriousness and sense of purpose. This aspect is often found in the charts of self-made men and women.

SUN and URANUS
GOOD ASPECTS Leadership ability; strong initiative. A touch of inspiration and genius in thinking.
ADVERSE ASPECTS Rash; erratic. Nervous strain. Possible separation in marriage.
CONJUNCTION Originality and independence. Inclined to be obstinate. Possible superiority complex.

SUN and NEPTUNE
GOOD ASPECTS Good imagination; artistic potential. Creative self-expression.
ADVERSE ASPECTS Vagueness of mind; unbalanced emotions. Susceptible to treachery and deceit.
CONJUNCTION Powerful artistic expression. Fine esthetic taste. Psychic ability.

SUN and PLUTO
GOOD ASPECTS Strong character. Ability to start afresh with new ideas. Self-confident.
ADVERSE ASPECTS Inclined toward selfishness, aloofness, and antisocial behavior.
CONJUNCTION Egotistical. Person may have a power complex. A dictatorial way with others.

Moon Aspects

MOON and MERCURY

GOOD ASPECTS Indicates common sense and shrewdness. A witty talker; an entertaining personality.

ADVERSE ASPECTS High-strung, frenetic nature. Native inclined to be anxious and nervous.

CONJUNCTION High intelligence, sensitivity, and imagination.

MOON and VENUS

GOOD ASPECTS Affectionate, lighthearted personality. Love of beauty; artistic talent.

ADVERSE ASPECTS Careless, self-indulgent. Moody. Disappointment in love affairs.

CONJUNCTION Friendliness; a tranquil nature. Love of luxury. An artistic eye.

MOON and MARS

GOOD ASPECTS Energetic; resourceful. Quick-acting; gets projects under way without delay. Good health.

ADVERSE ASPECTS Changeable moods; touchy; argumentative. Self-indulgent. Problems with health.

CONJUNCTION Courage. Liveliness. Strong powers of concentration.

MOON and JUPITER ♃

GOOD ASPECTS Optimistic, friendly personality. Good business ability. Native enjoys travel and literary pursuits.

ADVERSE ASPECTS Weak financial judgment. Laziness. Difficulty accomplishing goals.

CONJUNCTION Generous and protective nature. Native needs change and new challenge. May be vain.

MOON and SATURN

GOOD ASPECTS Diplomatic. Ambitious. Conservative nature; patient. Thoroughness in dealing with problems.

ADVERSE ASPECTS Shyness; lack of self-confidence. Money problems. Possible trouble in first marriage.

CONJUNCTION Thrifty. A perfectionist, though may be too critical. This aspect brings stability to emotions.

MOON and URANUS

GOOD ASPECTS Strong intuition. Open to change and the future. Native attracts luck through change.

ADVERSE ASPECTS Too changeable; temperamental. Nervous tension. Perversity.

CONJUNCTION An original, highly individual personality. Native may be considered eccentric, unusual—will not conform or be restricted.

MOON and NEPTUNE

GOOD ASPECTS Powerful imagination. Interested in the occult. Native has strong need to create in an artistic way.

ADVERSE ASPECTS A dreamer. Danger of self-delusion. Susceptible to schemers. Problems in love affairs.

CONJUNCTION Sympathetic. Warmhearted. A preference for seclusion.

MOON and PLUTO

GOOD ASPECTS Changes in native's life are common. Strong emotions. Shrewd business ability.

ADVERSE ASPECTS Moods and emotions swing to extremes. Jealousy prominent. Aspect may bring unpleasant changes.

CONJUNCTION Impulsiveness. Tendency for changes to erupt suddenly, and for native to make thoughtless moves.

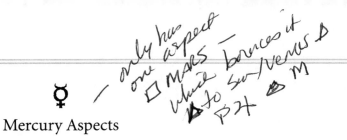

MERCURY and VENUS
GOOD ASPECTS Cheerful, lighthearted. Artistic. Native leans toward literary and creative pursuits.

ADVERSE ASPECTS These two planets never form major adverse aspects. At most, they indicate that artistic faculties are not expressed.

CONJUNCTION Charm of speech. Balance between mental activities and love of art and beauty.

MERCURY and MARS
GOOD ASPECTS Active, practical mind. Courageous personality. Literary ability. Forceful debater.

ADVERSE ASPECTS Fault-finding and irritability accentuated. Native may be belligerent and disputatious.

CONJUNCTION Potential for high intellectualism. A flair for writing, speaking. Witty and expressive.

MERCURY and JUPITER
GOOD ASPECTS An active mind with broad outlook. Good judgment. Sense of humor. Native does not like detail.

ADVERSE ASPECTS Skeptical mind. Susceptible to errors in judgment. Native may be indiscreet, open to scandal.

CONJUNCTION Above-average intelligence. Optimistic. Philanthropic bent.

MERCURY and SATURN
GOOD ASPECTS Disciplined, well-organized mind. Good concentration. Serious and practical.

ADVERSE ASPECTS Native may be rigid, a strict disciplinarian, fearful of change. Abrupt. Blunt.

CONJUNCTION Native is methodical and patient; may also be obstinate. Good powers of endurance. Prone to depression.

MERCURY and URANUS
GOOD ASPECTS Cleverness, originality. Independent mind. Self-reliant nature.

ADVERSE ASPECTS Opinionated, brusque, and tactless. Tendency to waste energy. Native may be discontent, confused.

CONJUNCTION A talent for scientific thinking. Can be stubborn and eccentric, but also a genius.

MERCURY and NEPTUNE
GOOD ASPECTS High creativity. Artistic imagination. Indicates talent for acting. May be clairvoyant.

ADVERSE ASPECTS Scheming tendencies; native disposed toward deceiving others. Hazy thinking; difficulty in concentrating.

CONJUNCTION Impulsive personality but also powerfully creative. Native interested in mysticism and spiritual subjects.

MERCURY and PLUTO
GOOD ASPECTS Native is versatile, flexible, restless. Prone to sudden changes of opinion.

ADVERSE ASPECTS Illogical reasoning. Nervous tension. Native tends to rush into commitments before considering actions.

CONJUNCTION A penetrating mind but susceptible to nervous tension. Native often has a marked talent to bring about change through the use of the written word.

♀

Venus Aspects

VENUS and MARS
GOOD ASPECTS Feelings of warmth and affection easily expressed. Enthusiastic. Passionate. Romantic.
ADVERSE ASPECTS Impulsive, quarrelsome. Difficulty and strain in sexual relationships. Hypersensitivity. Discontentment.
CONJUNCTION A sensuous personality. Optimistic outlook. Good balance between charm and aggressiveness.

VENUS and JUPITER
GOOD ASPECTS Indicates harmonious relationships. Love is easily expressed. This aspect also brings good money luck.
ADVERSE ASPECTS Too much affectation and insincerity. Numerous love affairs and unhappiness brought on by extremes of feeling. Possible weight problem.
CONJUNCTION Magnetic sex appeal. Native enjoys much popularity and a reputation for charm.

VENUS and SATURN
GOOD ASPECTS Constructive influence in business partnerships. Serious and faithful in love.
ADVERSE ASPECTS Disappointment or incompatibility in marriage and love relationships. Tendency toward a solitary, lonely existence. Marriage may be delayed early in life.
CONJUNCTION Strong sense of duty. Conservative in picking love partners. Feelings of affection sometimes sublimated or sacrificed for personal ambition.

VENUS and URANUS
GOOD ASPECTS Romantic, artistic personality. Intrigues others because of unusual ideas about sex and love. Can be very sentimental.
ADVERSE ASPECTS Too much unconventionality in relationships; imbalanced sensuality. Choice of lovers and partners may bring unhappiness.
CONJUNCTION Apt to be emotional, excitable. Native may do original, artistic work. A sensual personality.

VENUS and NEPTUNE
GOOD ASPECTS Heightened creativity. Interest in mysticism. Powerful artistic potential but native needs firm direction.
ADVERSE ASPECTS Disappointment in love. Sometimes victimized in relationships. Difficulty making decisions.
CONJUNCTION Sensitive and kind to others. Artistic talent present. Also prone to nervous tension, disillusion in love affairs.

VENUS and PLUTO
GOOD ASPECTS Passionate nature. Love life marked by sudden changes that tend to bring benefits. Good financial ability.
ADVERSE ASPECTS Reversals in love; attachments broken. Strong sexual feelings, but sex relationships cause difficulties.
CONJUNCTION Deep-rooted, intense passions. Native tends to fall in love secretly. Indicates shrewdness in handling finances.

MARS and JUPITER

GOOD ASPECTS Strong willpower, optimism, positive outlook. Inspires confidence. Good leadership potential.

ADVERSE ASPECTS Over-enthusiasm, hastiness, impulsiveness. Extremist temperament. Restless. Extravagant.

CONJUNCTION Frank. Energetic. Able to make decisions. An aggressive streak.

MARS and SATURN

GOOD ASPECTS Powers of endurance. Ability to succeed in spite of harsh circumstances. Disciplined. Indomitable.

ADVERSE ASPECTS Vacillating energy. Inner feeling of being pulled to and fro. Ill-tempered. Susceptible to injury.

CONJUNCTION Rebellious, turbulent personality. May indicate accident-proneness. Native resents any opposition.

MARS and URANUS

GOOD ASPECTS Practical. Intellectual. Energetic. Resourceful. Ability to make quick decisions.

ADVERSE ASPECTS Impatient, perverse, touchy nature. Native may be intolerant, combative. Subject to irritability and tension.

CONJUNCTION Excitable, willful personality. High energy level. Also indicates nervous strain.

MARS and NEPTUNE

GOOD ASPECTS Creative impulses. Idealistic and crusading. Powerful emotions. Imaginative.

ADVERSE ASPECTS Prone toward negative escapism in alcohol. Native may be oversensitive; wastes energies in hopeless causes.

CONJUNCTION High artistic gifts may be present. Strong sense of design and color. Romantic. Passionate.

MARS and PLUTO

GOOD ASPECTS Great physical energy. Self-confidence. Ambitious. Courageous.

ADVERSE ASPECTS Obsessive personality. Combative nature. Native unhappy when forced to accept new conditions.

CONJUNCTION High emotional level. Quick, violent temper.

♃
Jupiter Aspects

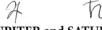

JUPITER and SATURN
GOOD ASPECTS Patience and persistence. Breadth of vision. Sound financial judgment.

ADVERSE ASPECTS Pessimistic; lack of inner satisfaction. Obstacles in the way of success. Financial miscalculation.

CONJUNCTION Ambitious and single-minded. Ability to achieve through hard work. Streak of discontentment.

JUPITER and URANUS
GOOD ASPECTS Originality combined with leadership ability. Magnetic personality. Humanitarian outlook.

ADVERSE ASPECTS Outspokenness. Willful. Tendency toward radicalism or militancy.

CONJUNCTION Freedom-loving, restless, eccentric. Sometimes an unusual physical appearance, for example, extremely tall or short.

JUPITER and NEPTUNE
GOOD ASPECTS Kind, humanitarian instincts. Drawn to spiritual concerns. Creative talent that promises financial success.

ADVERSE ASPECTS Too emotional and extravagant. Marked tendency toward self-deception. Weak and easily manipulated.

CONJUNCTION Sensitive, artistic personality. Active fantasy life. May possess ESP. Love and concern for animals.

JUPITER and PLUTO
GOOD ASPECTS Intellectual and organizational skill. Strong tendency for native to create new beginnings. Idealistic.

ADVERSE ASPECTS Scheming personality; desire to exploit others. Often destructive tendencies.

CONJUNCTION Ability to break with the past and start anew. Tendency to be domineering.

♄

Saturn Aspects

SATURN and URANUS
GOOD ASPECTS Willpower and initiative; indicates administrative talents. Inventive, efficient, resourceful.
ADVERSE ASPECTS Autocratic, arrogant personality. Prone to anxiety and depression.
CONJUNCTION Great self-reliance and determination. Indicates a masterful manner with others, an original personality.

SATURN and NEPTUNE
GOOD ASPECTS Careful, conscientious nature. Orderly common sense. Creative imagination put to practical use.
ADVERSE ASPECTS Reclusive inclinations. Suspicious, possibly paranoid nature. Life is marked by disappointment.
CONJUNCTION Hardworking and authoritative. An excellent aspect that combines idealism with practicality.

SATURN and PLUTO
GOOD ASPECTS Self-disciplined. Capable of deep concentration. A self-confident, high-principled personality.
ADVERSE ASPECTS Unpredictability. An obsessive personality. Sometimes susceptible to unusual diseases.
CONJUNCTION Inclined to be unpredictable. Native is able to deal well with disappointment. This conjunction occurs once every 92 years and is considered a generational influence.

♅

Uranus Aspects

URANUS and NEPTUNE
GOOD ASPECTS Kindness, sensitivity, intuition. Musical ability. Spiritual and mystical interests.
ADVERSE ASPECTS High emotional level. A personality that becomes easily upset. Easily led onto unproductive paths.
CONJUNCTION Potential for highly original work. Bias toward eccentricity. A visionary and prophetic nature. This conjunction occurs every 171 years and is considered a generational influence.

URANUS and PLUTO
GOOD ASPECTS Lofty aims; strong loyalty. Ability to direct energy into productive channels.
ADVERSE ASPECTS Disruptive influence. Indicates inner tension. Tendency toward sudden emotional outbursts.
CONJUNCTION Strong sense of independence. This conjunction occurs every 115 years and is considered a generational influence. Power can be positive or negative, depending on how it is channeled.

♆ ♇

Neptune and Pluto Aspects

NEPTUNE and PLUTO

Neptune spends 14 years in each sign and Pluto from 13 to 32 years in each sign. Any aspects formed last for extremely long periods of time; they are considered important in an individual's horoscope only if Neptune or Pluto are on the Ascendant or Midheaven, or Pisces or Scorpio are prominent.

GOOD ASPECTS Occult traits are positively used.

ADVERSE ASPECTS Obsessive tendencies. Easy prey to temptation.

CONJUNCTION Intellectual abilities. An interest in the occult. Promotes gift of clairvoyance.

The Art of Prediction

AMONG THE MOST IMPORTANT uses of astrology is the art of prediction. When a client consults an astrologer it is usually to ask questions about the future. Astrologers use many tools to anticipate future conditions.

One is the drawing up of a *horary chart*—a chart that represents the present moment in which a person is asking a question. The theory behind horary astrology is that there is sympathy between the cosmos and the human mind; therefore, when a question is asked, the positions of the planets at that moment can help to answer the question. This theory underlies such predictive techniques as the I Ching, Tarot, and card reading.

Another method of prediction is to study the *transits* of the planets. You (or an astrologer) would consult an ephemeris to arrive at the exact positions of the planets in the future—say, next week or next month—and then compare these positions to the planetary positions in your natal chart. Let's take a hypothetical example in which Jupiter next week was going to be in 27° of Libra, and in your natal chart your Sun is in 27° of Libra. This transit (called transiting Jupiter conjunct natal Sun) augurs a fortunate financial trend, activation of energies, and the courage to make the most of opportunity.

Another chart drawn for predictive purposes is the *solar return chart*—a horoscope cast for the exact moment that the Sun is passing through the degree of the sign it was in at the moment of your birth. The solar return chart is analyzed in respect to your birth chart, and a study is made of the new aspects formed between the two charts. This is a useful tool for seeing trends ahead for the coming year. It is also possible to cast a *lunar return chart* for the moment that the Moon is passing through the degree that it occupies in your natal horoscope. A lunar return chart foretells trends in the coming month.

One of the most popular techniques for arriving at predictions is the casting of a *progressed* birth chart. There are a number of different ways to progress a horoscope, but the one in most frequent use is the day-for-a-year method. This method of progression is based on the theory that there is a relationship in the human psyche between the earth's daily rotation on its axis and its annual revolution around the Sun. The theory postulates that the days following birth represent a person's inner development during the corresponding *years*. Astrologers also point to biblical references to this method of progression. Numbers 14:34 and Ezekiel 4:6 both speak of "each day for a year," and Genesis 29:27 tells of a week symbolically representing seven years.

To progress your chart, you would begin by drawing up an exact natal birth chart, which includes the precise degree of each House cusp and the precise degree and minute of the sign that every planet occupies in your chart.

The next step would be to decide what year in the future you wish to see. If, for example, you were born on May 1, 1975, and you wish to know about the year 2010, you would progress your birth chart ahead to 35 years after your birth. Using the one-day-for-one-year rule, you arrive at the number of 35 days. Thirty-five days from May 1, 1975 (your birthday) brings you to June 5, 1975. At this point, you draw up a brand-new horoscope for the day June 5, 1975. This horoscope is your *progressed chart*.

Now you would compare your birth chart with your progressed chart. You would calculate the new planetary aspects formed within the progressed chart, and also calculate the planetary aspects formed between the birth chart and the progressed chart.

If, for example, your progressed Mars were in opposition to your natal Sun, 2010 might be a period of strain and ill health. If your progressed Venus formed a trine with your natal Sun, there might be the possibility of marriage in 2010.

Whatever the method of prediction, it is wise to keep in mind that astrology is not soothsaying or magic. Astrologers do not predict. What they do is assess future trends and point out possible areas of success or pitfalls. The true value of prediction is to draw attention to a person's strengths so that he or she may take best advantage of them.

Synastry: For Lovers

WHEN READING HOROSCOPES in newspapers and magazines, a great many people look for advice about love. When they read astrology books, the second thing most people turn to (after reading about themselves) is a description of their lover or mate—or prospective lover or mate.

The problem, however, with most astrological analyses is that they are limited, for they are based on Sun signs alone. As I have emphasized before, you are not a "pure" Sun sign. You are a unique combination of signs and planets. If you have set up your birth chart (as outlined in chapter 9), you see in front of you a picture of how many different factors go into your horoscope. The same is true for every other person.

The most accurate and complete answers about love are to be found in a birth chart. Now that you can cast a simple birth chart for yourself, it is an easy matter to take two birth charts (yours and someone else's) and compare them in order to answer questions about compatibility and love. This comparison of two people's charts to see how they might or might not get along with each other is called *synastry*.

Before you read further about the specifics of synastry, you should be aware that chart comparison is based on the *relationship between planets in the two charts*—in other words, on the *aspects* (the harmonious and inharmonious influences determined entirely on how many degrees apart the planets are).

Here is an easy way to calculate the aspects between the two charts. All you have to do is count signs:

HOW FAR APART	INFLUENCE	NAME OF THE ASPECT
Planets in the same sign	Powerful influence. Can be beneficial.	Conjunction
Planets one sign away from each other.	Strain. Common ground is lacking.*	Semisextile
Planets two signs away from each other	Beneficial influence. Indicates harmony.	Sextile
Planets three signs away from each other	Tension, but not necessarily irreconcilable differences. There is usually a lot of energy between these two signs.	Square
Planets four signs away from each other	Very harmonious. Pleasant and easygoing. Sometimes so peaceful things may be dull!	Trine
Planets six signs away from each other	Opposite in the zodiac. There may be lots of arguments and strain, but there is also a strong and stimulating attraction between opposites.	Opposition

*The exceptions to this rule are Capricorn and Aquarius, who are one sign apart. Though they are quite different from each other (Capricorn is conservative, Aquarius is ultramodern), both are strong and can make a good pairing.

To begin your comparison of horoscopes, draw two simplified birth charts: yours and your lover's.*

The Sun and the Moon

One of the first things to look at is the position of the Sun and Moon in both charts. The Sun is often referred to as the masculine principle in astrology, since it represents a person's outward expression. The Moon is called the feminine principle, since it represents the emotional side. If a man has the Moon in his First House, he is usually the kind of man who is in touch with his emotions—someone who accepts feelings comfortably rather than someone who tries to repress them. If a woman has the Sun in her First House, she tends to have a strong sense of self or an authority and dignity about her that is a natural part of her personality.

Very often you can tell the kind of woman whose personality will appeal to a man by looking at where the Moon is in his chart. Is the Moon in Aries or Leo? He probably likes strong, assertive women who refuse to be pushed around. Is the Moon in Virgo? He's likely to be attracted to practical and stable women. Is it in Libra or Pisces? He tends to fall in love with romantic, feminine women.

Conversely, you can often find out what kind of man intrigues a woman by looking at the sign her Sun is in. Is it in Taurus? She probably likes strong, earthy types who have a knack for making money. Is it in Gemini? She tends to be attracted to brainy men, writers, and intellectual types.

Keep in mind, though, that people don't always end up with (or sometimes even go out with) the men and women who attract them. People also choose lovers on an unconscious level. For more about why we pick the people we do, consult the influence of Mars and Venus in your love horoscope (page 366).

In comparing your two charts, begin with your Sun. What is your Sun sign? Now consult the aspects table on page 288. Is your Sun in a compatible sign to your lover's Sun? For example, if you have an Aries Sun sign, is your lover's Sun sign Leo or Sagittarius (four signs away) or Gemini or Aquarius (two signs away)?

Now look at the two Moon signs. Are they compatible with each other?

Don't worry if your two Sun signs or Moon signs are not in the most harmonious aspect to each other. Remember that a square or opposition (three signs away and six signs away) may add fireworks to the relationship, and also bring interest and excitement. In any case, this is only the beginning of your comparison. The positions of your respective Suns and Moons are a factor to consider, but only *one* among many.

Here is a very positive factor: If your Moon is in the same sign as your lover's Sun, or vice versa, this is a wonderful augury. It is a green light to a happy and lasting affair and indicates that each of you should have a deep understanding of the other.

Major Points of Incompatibility

1. If your Sun sign is the same as your lover's Ascendant (Rising sign), or your Ascendant is the same as your lover's Sun sign: This is a powerful indication of happiness and contentment between you. Your personalities mesh well because you tend to think alike.

*I use the word *lover* here to mean anyone you are romantically connected to, whether it is someone you only fantasize about or someone you've lived with most of your life.

2. If your Sun sign is in opposition (six signs away) to your lover's Ascendant, or your Ascendant is in opposition to your lover's Sun sign: This is also a positive influence and bodes well for rapport. In this case, each person would be likely to supply what the other needs or even lacks. For example, if she is a Libra Sun sign and he is an Aries Ascendant, he will probably be able to give a push to her lazy nature, while she can bring a touch of elegance and romance to his aggressiveness.

3. If your Sun sign is the same as the sign of your lover's Tenth House, or your Tenth House sign is the same as your lover's Sun sign: You both mix career and love well. In this case, your aims and goals should be compatible, and each can be a source of power or inspiration to push the other.

The Sun and Ascendant

As you have just read, two powerful influences for compatibility are when the Suns and Ascendants in the two charts are in conjunction or in opposition.

If you don't fall into either category, there are other aspects to consider. Do your Sun and your lover's Ascendant (or vice versa) form a square (three signs away from each other)? There may be quarrels along the way and probably more than a little competition between the two of you. But the sparks of feeling between you should at least make the affair interesting.

Are your Sun and your lover's Ascendant (or vice versa) in sextile or trine aspect (two signs away or four signs away)? There will be a great deal of tolerance for each other's foibles. You both tend to blend with each other and work harmoniously together.

Venus and Mars

Venus, planet of love, has always been a feminine planet in astrology. It represents your capacity for affection and sharing, your geniality, friendliness, and charm. The position of Venus in your chart tells what kind of effect you have on others. In a woman's chart, it is usually the placement of Venus that gives an indication of her love nature.

Mars, which represents energy and aggression, is a masculine planet. It deals specifically with a person's sexual nature, with the fire and passion of sexual response. In a man's chart, it is the placement of Mars that gives an indication of the way he deals with women.

Just as the Sun and Moon in your chart indicate to some extent what kind of man or woman you are attracted to, so Venus and Mars point to the kind of person who sexually stirs you. In a woman's chart, the position of Mars will often tell what kind of man arouses her. Very often the arousal is on a subconscious level. This may be the film star who ignites her imagination, the man at a party she is immediately intrigued by without even thinking about it.

In a man's chart, the position of Venus usually indicates the kind of women he is drawn to. For example, if his Venus is in Gemini, he is likely to be stimulated by a woman who is amusing, lively, and witty. Venus points to the woman who, consciously or not, seizes his emotions. Astrologers always look at the positions of Venus and the Moon in a chart to see where a person's *emotions* are most strongly attracted.

There is a *powerful sexual attraction* when:

- Your Venus and your lover's Mars (or vice versa) are in the same sign: Both of you are passionate and sexually responsive. Your love life will be stimulating even if there are temperamental differences.
- Your Venus is in the same sign as your lover's Ascendant (or vice versa): You tend to be imaginative lovers and know what pleases each other.
- Your Venus is in your lover's Sun sign (or vice versa): This indicates not only a joyous sex life but also mutual interests in other areas.
- Your Mars is in your lover's Moon sign (or vice versa): Can be a volatile combination because of the emotional element; a high-keyed sex life is indicated.

I hope I have piqued your interest in learning about charts. The more you work with charts, the more proficient you will become. You will intrigue friends and family with your insights and observations.

In addition, as I have stressed throughout this book, you will gain in self-knowledge, which is what astrology is all about.

Part Four

ASTROLOGY IN HISTORY AND LEGEND

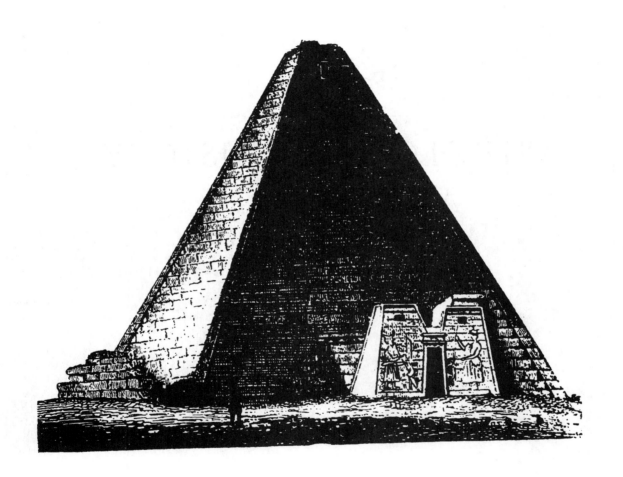

11
THE STORY OF ASTROLOGY

S A CHILD, LOOKING UP ON A CLEAR EVENING at a vast, endless sky twinkling with points of
light, did you make a wish on the "first star I see tonight"? You were doing what men and women have
done since they first turned their eyes skyward. People have always scrutinized the heavens, looking for
guidance, omens, and meanings.

The study of the Sun, the Moon, stars, eclipses, day and night, began well before recorded history. There are
reindeer bones and tusks of mammoths from the Ice Age that have notches carved on them picturing the phases
of the Moon. These bones and tusks are dated between 25,000 and 10,000 B.C., and some scientists place them as
long ago as 32,000 B.C.!

The path of the stars was recorded 6,000 years before Christ was born. As early as 2767 B.C., a horoscope was
cast in Egypt by Imhotep, the architect of the great Step pyramid in Saqqarah. That horoscope still exists!

Ancient astrologers charted the movement of planets and stars, and made predictions about eclipses, up-
heavals, famine, and fortune. They developed calendars for marking and measuring the passage of time. You can
still read star charts that were made by Egyptian astrologers in 4200 B.C.

In ancient societies, astrology and religion were inextricably linked. The astrologers were mainly priests. In
fact, the Sumerian symbol for divinity was a star. Even the patterns that the stars form in the heavens were given
names and worshipped as gods.

Not too surprisingly, the Sun was the most powerful god. The Sun gave warmth and light, nourished plant
life, and made crops grow. Druids, Egyptians, Incas, and Hindus were all sun worshippers. In the ancient Hindu
religion, Vishnu is the embodiment of the Sun, the symbol for life itself.

We can still visit some of the early observatories that primitive people built to study the skies. The fabled
Pyramids at Giza in Egypt, one of the Seven Wonders of the World, are elaborate tombs for dead royalty. They
are also giant compasses, whose triangular sides directly face the points of a compass and can still be used to
take sightings. In the old Mayan city of Chichen Itza there stands a pre-Columbian stone structure that some-

what resembles our Capitol building. It is called the Cara-col observatory. Inside, a spiral staircase leads to various windows from which the positions of the planets can be observed as they shift throughout the year.

If you should find yourself in Brittany, the seaside re-sort in northwest France, visit the Menhirs (great stones) of Carnac. These are huge upright granite blocks ranging from sixteen to twenty feet high. They were built by sun worship-pers (many historians believe they were Druids), and used for astrological calculation.

In the south of England there stands the magnifi-cent structure known as Stonehenge. Stonehenge con-sists of a series of stones, some as high as twelve feet, placed in a circular pattern. Outside the stones is a circle of holes or pits. In 1961 Professor Gerald S. Hawkins, an astronomer from Boston University, submitted the pat-tern of Stonehenge to analysis by an IBM computer. He discovered that these strange stones and holes can be used to record the positions of the Sun and Moon, and that virtually every eclipse of the Sun and Moon can be predicted from them. Obviously, the people who built Stonehenge in 2500 B.C. were not just barbarians who painted themselves blue with woad. They built what is, in effect, a sophisticated astronomical observatory!

In the United States a structure called Casa Grande, built by Hohokam Indians in Arizona around A.D. 1300, has eight openings that are aligned with the risings and settings of the Sun at both solstices and both equinoxes— the four cardinal points of the zodiac.

Clearly, there are no new ideas; there are new people discovering old ideas. Here is a brief look at the earliest as-trological lore in more or less chronological order.

HINDU (5000 B.C.–3000 B.C.)

Hindus trace their religious wisdom back to seven ancient sages known as the Rishis. The word rishi means "to shine," and the original Rishis were the seven stars of the constellation Ursa Major (Big Dipper). Hindu religion lit-erally began with the stars.

Vishnu, the reigning god of Hinduism, is the Sun in-carnate, their most divine being. Sometimes, when the world is in discord, Vishnu takes various forms and visits the Earth. Some of the shapes he takes on are the Ram, the Bull, and the Lion, and carvings of these shapes are found on temple walls dating back 7,000 years. In mod-ern astrology we still use those three symbols: Aries the Ram, Taurus the Bull, Leo the Lion.

The Hindus divided the sky into twenty-eight equal parts, called Lunar Mansions, each part representing a passage of the Moon through its twenty-eight-day cycle. The lunar cycle, in fact, is a basis of Eastern astrology. Western philosophy is founded much more on the solar cycle. As a result, astrologers often refer to the Western world as children of the Sun and to the Eastern world as children of the Moon.

The Indian zodiac has twelve signs, the same number our zodiac has. However, in India there is a concept not found in Western astrology. This is the doctrine of karma and reincarnation. Karma is the journey of the soul through various lives (incarnations). A person's karma is based on three things: 1) the influence in this life of acts committed in previous lives; 2) the influence of one's present acts on the next life; 3) unrealized acts. The practice of astrology in India is often linked to the discovery of what stage a person's soul has reached.

EGYPTIAN (3000 B.C.–300 B.C.)

Egyptian astrology was also bound up in their religion. The priests held the secrets of the heavens. Within a complicated hierarchy of gods and deities, each god had a specific power and ruled over a particular kingdom of influence. For example, Osiris was god of the dead. Isis was Osiris's wife and sister, protectress of the dead. Thoth was the god of learning, inventor of hieroglyphs, and scribe of the gods. Many Egyptian symbols and deities reappear in the present-day occult study of Tarot cards.

The Egyptians were the first people to foretell a person's character by the date of birth. They also gave to each month, and indeed to each day, a special deity who ruled that day and that month.

The River Nile was the focus of Egyptian life. The river made their barren region fertile, and so it is not surprising to find the imagery of water used again and again in their mythology. The sky was a goddess named Nut, who was also an enormous river. Lesser gods crossed the sky-river in their individual boats. When an Egyptian pharaoh died, he was provided with everything he needed for the journey across a great river into the afterlife.

At first, Egyptians divided the sky into thirty-six sections. (The Greeks later called these sections *dekanoi*, meaning ten days apart, from which we get our words *decan* and *decanate*.) These thirty-six decanates remain unchanged to the present day (see chapter 3). Later, the sky was divided into twelve parts, and each part was given a form and a name. Each part of the sky was assigned three stars to call its own,

and each was given a boat in which to cross the sky. See how similar the twelve Egyptian sky gods are to our modern astrological signs:

EGYPTIAN	MODERN
The Sheep	Aries the Ram
The Bull	Taurus the Bull
Two Men Clasping Hands	Gemini the Twins
The Scarab	Cancer the Crab
The Lion	Leo the Lion
The Maiden	Virgo the Virgin
The Horizon	Libra the Scales
The Scorpion	Scorpio the Scorpion
He Who Draws a Bow	Sagittarius the Archer
The Goat	Capricorn the Goat
The Water Man	Aquarius the Water Bearer
The Fishes	Pisces the Fishes

The Egyptians believed the Sun, another powerful deity, controlled the waters of the Nile. The Sun brought the Nile to flood stage, providing needed irrigation to the surrounding countryside and making the deserts fertile.

The Moon was also a special deity. The Egyptians designated several gods to represent it. The famous Eye of Horus, sometimes worn as an amulet to protect against danger, was a picture of the Moon. When the eye of the hawk-god Horus was completely open, the Moon was full.

Venus had her honored place among the gods. The planet Venus is a brilliant, silvery star that at times is seen in the morning and at other times in the evening. She was pictured by the Egyptians as a two-headed goddess, each head wearing a different crown.

One of the most famous astrologer-kings in ancient

Egypt was Ramses II (nineteenth dynasty). At his death in 1223 B.C., Ramses's body was placed in a sarcophagus covered with astrological symbols, and put inside a pyramid at Abou-Simbel. There the great pharaoh lay, like Merlin, in his room of wonders. Some of the wonders are still being discovered. For example, we have learned that Ramses's tomb was constructed so that on a certain date the rays of the Sun would find their way into the very pit of the grave. To this day, and on that very date, they do. When Ramses VI (a successor to the great Pharaoh) died, a star map drawn in the shape of a seated man was placed on his tomb. Modern scientists discovered that by using this map, they can chart the journey of the stars for each hour of the night throughout the year.

Not until human beings are replaced by a civilization of machines run by a great computer are we likely to get any greater precision than that!

CHINESE (2800 B.C.–PRESENT)

With Marco Polo's adventurous travels in A.D. 1275, Europeans learned for the first time of the great beauty, wealth, history, and romance of China. Untouched as they were by outside influences, the Chinese had developed their astrology along somewhat different lines from the Egyptians, Chaldeans, Babylonians, and Greeks.

Life in ancient China revolved around the Emperor. His title was Son of the Heavens, and he was an absolute ruler. Confucius wrote of the Emperor: "The sovereign who rules by virtue is like the polar star. He stays motionless in his place while everything turns around him." It was the Emperor who maintained good relations between the forces of heaven and human beings here on Earth.

Some historians mark the beginning of Chinese astrology during the reign of the Divine Emperor Fu Hsi around 2800 B.C. The Bamboo Annals (a manuscript found in a Chinese prince's grave in A.D. 281) tell about Emperor Yao, who named the twelve signs of the Chinese zodiac and divided the sky into twenty-eight Mansions of the Moon.

The Chinese zodiac differs from the zodiac of the West. There are twelve years, and each year is represented by a different animal. This twelve-year cycle is sometimes called the Yellow Road of the Sun. The twelve animals are the rat, ox, tiger, hare, dragon, snake, horse, ram, monkey, cock, dog, and boar. Legend tells us that when Buddha lay on his deathbed, he asked the animals of the forest to come and bid him farewell. These twelve were the first to arrive. The cat, as the story goes, is not among the animals because it was napping and couldn't be bothered to make the journey.*

Chinese astrology is not content to rest with a division into twelve animals. There are also five elements (wood, fire, earth, metal, and water). A Chinese horoscope is divided into interlocking sets of the numbers ten and twelve (e.g., ten Celestial Stem signs and twelve Terrestrial Branch signs). In addition, the ancient principle of Yin and Yang (negative and positive forces) is very much involved in charting a horoscope.

Astrology has been an integral part of everyday life in China. The new Communist regime, which prides itself on rationalism and materialism and derides astrology as mere superstition, has made few inroads on the people's faith in

*This is only one version of the legend. In certain Far Eastern countries (e.g., Vietnam), the cat is the astrological symbol instead of the hare.

the divinations of the horoscope. Not even the authority of the state has prevailed against astrology.

A Chinese person always knows his or her animal sign and will often give his or her age by naming the animal year in which birth occurred. Major decisions in life are still made according to astrology. This is especially true when the Chinese seek guidance about whom to marry and when. Astrology is also a guide as to when to conclude financial agreements, begin journeys, start building a new house, and even where to bury the dead.

Some modern astrologers have tried to combine Western astrology with Chinese astrology. They give each person both an astrological sign and an animal sign. One becomes, for example, a Gemini Tiger or a Libra Dragon. For those interested in learning more about this fascinating attempt to merge two cultures, there are some books on the subject.

In truth, however, the astrology that we practice owes less to these Eastern influences. We are, after all, children of the Sun and rely more on solar astrology than the Eastern world and its children of the Moon. Our astrological lore can be traced back to the Sumerians and to the fascinating fragments of documents that contain the astrological predictions of Sargon the Ancient, who ruled around 2800 B.C. in a city known as Babylon.

BABYLONIAN (4000 B.C.–125 B.C.)

In a fertile plain in the Middle East, bordered by the Tigris and Euphrates Rivers, lies a region that was once known as Mesopotamia. The southern part was called Babylonia; the north was called Assyria.

The Sumerians were the first people to settle in the area, sometime around 4000–3500 B.C. They were mostly shepherds and farmers, who apparently spent a great deal of time looking up at the sky. They soon noticed a connection between the heavenly cycles and the cycles of growth in plants and food. Based on such observations, the Sumerians began to worship three all-important gods: Sin the Moon god, who traveled in a crescent boat and was the most powerful; Shamash the Sun goddess; and Ishtar the goddess of fertility, whose home was the bright star of Venus.

As in most early cultures, the astrologers were the priests, and the priests were not only religious leaders but leaders of government as well. Each priest ruled his separate province (called city-states) and dispensed divine wisdom to his followers. Large observatories or watchtowers (called ziggurats) were built for the priests to study the movement of the stars and planets. The ziggurats in the cities of Ur, Uruk, and Babylon were almost 300 feet high. We can still visit a ziggurat built by King U-Nammu, who founded the Third Sumerian Dynasty (2079–1960 B.C.). It is widely believed that the biblical story of the Tower of Babel describes the building of a ziggurat, and tells in mythic terms of the folly of trying to master the secret of the heavens.

By the time the Babylonian culture was in full flower (between 2800 and 500 B.C.), astrology had become more sophisticated. Besides the Sun, Moon, and Venus, four other planets had been discovered (Mercury, Mars, Jupiter, and Saturn). The planets were given individual characteristics and properties, and a god was assigned to each. For example, Mars, reddish in color, became identified with the fiery god of war. Venus, seen early in the morning, was in a sense giving birth to the day; she was therefore a feminine planet, associated with love and fertility. To this day, Mars and Venus have these same characteristics in modern astrology.

The four seasons were also given symbols: Spring was a Bull, summer a Lamb, autumn a Scorpion, and winter a Turtle. These divisions of the calendar date back to the twelfth century B.C., and two symbols, the Bull and the Scorpion, are still used in modern astrology. Note also that in today's astrology, the Bull (Taurus) is the sign for late April and early May (spring), and the Scorpion (Scorpio) is in late October and early November (autumn).

The invention of the modern zodiac is credited to the Babylonians. Cicero, the famous Roman orator who lived during the last century B.C., had an explanation for why the Babylonians were such acute astrologers: "They reside in vast plains where no mountains obstruct their view of the entire hemisphere, and so they have applied themselves mainly to that kind of divination called astrology."

It was the early Babylonian priest-astrologers who set down the basic principles of astrology that have remained almost unchanged until today. They divided the sky into twelve equal parts, through which the Sun and Moon traveled. One theory is that they patterned the twelve divisions after the twelve months in the Babylonian year, one month for each lunar cycle. The sky was thought of as a circle of 360 degrees with each division being 30 degrees. This is the way astrologers measure the sky today. The twelve sky divisions, or signs as we call them, were given names: Aries, Pleiades, Gemini, Praesepe, Leo, Spica, Libra, Scorpio, Sagittarius, Capricornus, Aquarius, and Pisces. The Greeks later changed Pleiades to Taurus, Praesepe to Cancer, and Spica to Virgo. These are the names we still use for the twelve signs of the zodiac.

Each of the signs had a precise influence over events on Earth. Each ruled a plant, an animal, a precious stone, and a color. The Babylonians also named twelve Houses. These are divisions of the zodiac that govern various areas of life.

The Babylonian Houses were 1) Life; 2) Riches and Poverty; 3) Brothers; 4) Parents; 5) Children; 6) Health and Illness; 7) Wife and Husband; 8) Death; 9) Religion 10) Dignities; 11) Friendship; 12) Enmity. With some exceptions, these are more or less what the Houses in modern astrology govern.

By the time of the reign of King Assurbanipal in the middle of the seventh century B.C., the basic tenets of astrology had been set down. One of the reasons we know so much about King Assurbanipal is that he left behind a great library, much of which survives. We even have some memoranda written to the king by his astrologers. One of them (which reflects a narrowly monarchist point of view) reads in part as follows:

To my Lord the King of all Countries—If an eclipse occurs but is not observed in the capital, such an eclipse is considered not to have happened. The capital means the city in which the King is staying.

Astrology was mainly used for wide-scale predictions: weather forecasts, floods, good and bad harvests, eclipses, war, and the fortunes of the king. Around the fifth century B.C. astrology became more personal. There is a Babylonian horoscope dated 409 B.C. that is still in existence. We also have a translation of a horoscope cast in 234 B.C. for a man named Aristokrates:

The position of Jupiter means that his life will be regular. He will become rich and will grow old. The position of Venus means that wherever he may go it will be favorable for him. Mercury in Gemini means that he will have sons and daughters.

In Babylonian astrology the constellation of Cassiopeia rules over Syria and Palestine. This constellation was called the Woman with Child because every 300 years it produced an unusually bright star. Astrologers calculate that this star appeared after the birth of Christ, and may be the very Star that the Three Wise Men followed to the Manger.

The Jews of that era are also known to have practiced astrology. Among modern-day Jews the expression mazel tov is used on occasions of joy, such as birthdays, weddings, anniversaries. Few people know that mazel tov has its roots in astrology. The word *mazelot* in biblical Hebrew meant "sign of the zodiac" or "constellation," and thus to wish anyone mazel tov literally means to wish them a "good constellation."

GREEK (900 B.C.–A.D. 150)

The Greeks, who came later to the study of astrology, were not as patient observers of the skies as the Babylonians. Not until the ninth century B.C. did the Grecian astrologers learn to differentiate between the stars and the planets. When they did discover there were five planets, they gave them names based on their appearance: Venus was the Herald of the Dawn because it appeared in the morning. (The Greeks did not yet realize that at times Venus also appeared in the evening. They thought that was a different planet, which they named Vespertine.) Mercury was the Twinkling Star. Mars was the Fiery Star. Jupiter was the Luminous Star, and Saturn the Brilliant Star.

In the sixth century B.C. the philosopher Pythagoras wrote his famous *Harmony of the Spheres*. He said that the universe was a giant sphere that contained the earth and the air around it. His thoughts on the subject are poetic:

The Sun, Moon, and planets revolve in concentric circles, each fastened to a sphere or wheel. The swift revolution of each of these bodies causes a swish, or musical hum, in the air. Evidently each planet will hum on a different pitch, depending on the ratios of their respective orbits just as the tone of a string depends on its length. Thus the orbits in which the planets move form a kind of huge lyre whose strings are curved into circles.

Two hundred years after Pythagoras, in the fourth century B.C., a Greek astronomer and mathematician named Eudoxos introduced a calendar, based on the Babylonian one. Eudoxos also divided the sky into twelve equal signs. He was the first Greek astronomer to explain the movements of the planets in scientific terms. (Our word *planet*, incidentally, comes from the Greek *plenetes*, meaning "wanderer." While the stars remain fixed in their positions in the firmament, the planets move in their orbits, so they were thought of as travelers who crossed the sky and collected souls.) Eudoxos's theory was that the planets were held in place by spherical shells that kept them in their paths.

A turning point in Greek astrology came when Alexander the Great conquered Babylonia in 331 B.C. We know that Alexander consulted astrologers. There is a legend that when he was about to be born, an astrologer named Nektanebos stood by the bedside. Nektanebos asked Alexander's mother to hold back the birth until all the stars and omens were propitious. At last Nektanebos said, "Queen, you will now give birth to a ruler of the world," and Alexander was born.

There is another story about Alexander's entry into Babylon. It seems that Babylonian astrologers had predicted Alexander would die in their city. To avoid this fate, he entered the city by the west gate, which was apparently not the expected route for a conqueror. The prediction did not come true, and Alexander went on to annex all of Babylonia, Persia, and India. However, when he did die, in June 323 B.C. at the age of thirty-three, it was in Babylon.

The Greeks took over Babylonian astrology and made it theirs. They gave the five planets new names, taken from the gods of their mythology. Later, the Romans renamed the planets again, according to their gods of mythology. The Roman names are the ones we use today. Or, to be precise, they are an English translation of a Latin translation of a Greek translation of the original Babylonian nomenclature.

The father of modern astrology is Claudius Ptolemy. In A.D. 140 this Greek astronomer from Alexandria wrote a four-volume treatise called the *Tetrabiblos* (meaning The Four Books), in which he set down his observations and theories about the universe. The *Tetrabiblos* is considered the first modern textbook on astrology. Ptolemy described the function of the planets, houses, and signs of the zodiac. He formulated the theory of aspects, in which the distances between the planets in one's astrological chart have a good or bad influence. The study of aspects is still an important part of modern astrology.

Ptolemy's teachings remained unchanged for the next 1,400 years. It was not until 1543, when Nicolaus Copernicus published his treatise, that Ptolemy's vision of the earth as the center of the universe was seriously challenged.

ROMAN (300 B.C.–A.D. 476)

Astrology was brought to Rome by Greek slaves whom the Romans took captive. These early astrologers were sometimes known as "astrologers of the circus"; the Romans liked to bet heavily at chariot races and brought along their Greek astrologer-slaves to predict winners for them.

Astrology soon became a topic of great interest to Romans. By the time of Julius Caesar (102–44 B.C.) just about every important Roman statesman and military man had his horoscope cast. Julius Caesar had a detailed horoscope prepared for him, and Mark Antony's astrologer was a "gift" to him from Cleopatra. Caesar, in fact, wrote a book about different kinds of divinations. He was warned of his death by someone versed in astrology, "Beware the Ides of March."

The Roman emperors who followed Caesar took astrology very seriously. Augustus (27 B.C.–A.D. 14) ordered coins to be minted that bore his astrological sign of Capricorn. Two stories have grown up about his early experiences with astrologers. One is that on the day Augustus was born, his father, who was a senator, arrived late at the Senate because of the happy event. He explained to the assembly that a son had just been born. At that point, Nigidius, a famous Roman scholar and astrologer, stood up and predicted that the new child would grow up to be a ruler. The second story is about a time, before he was emperor, when Augustus visited an astrologer. The astrologer did not know who Augustus was. Suddenly, upon learning the birth date, the astrologer threw himself at Augustus's feet and worshipped him as the future master of the empire.

Tiberius (A.D. 14–37), who became emperor after Augustus, studied the horoscopes of political rivals. If he saw any that were likely to gain power in the future, he had those persons put to death. Life under Tiberius was equally hazardous for astrologers. If the emperor was presented with a horoscope he didn't like, he had the astrologer thrown into the sea. Clearly, Tiberius believed that astrology should be a science in which never is heard a discouraging word.

The infamous Emperor Nero (A.D. 54–68) believed in the auguries of the stars so firmly that he waited until his astrologer told him it was the propitious time before proclaiming himself emperor.

Emperor Hadrian (A.D. 117–138) announced on the first day of each year the events that his charts told him would happen during the coming year. Hadrian correctly predicted the hour of his own death. If that happened today, it would cause the kind of shock among skeptics that would register high on the Richter scale.

MODERN ERA (A.D. 1200–2000)

After the fall of Rome, astrology went into a decline—actually more of a total eclipse—from which it did not recover until after A.D. 1200.

One of the reasons for its decline is that astrology became very linked with superstition during the Roman era. When Christianity became widespread, astrology was opposed as the work of the devil and its study vigorously discouraged. St. Augustine (354–430) was one of those in the early Church who vehemently preached against the practice of astrology.

Though there was little astrology practiced in Europe during this time, it did not disappear completely. It merely changed its principal residence for a time. In the Arab world astrology remained a serious science. One of the great and most renowned Arab astrologers is Albumassar (805–886), and translations of his writings found their way into Europe and were influential in turning the tide back toward astrology.

Another influence in turning the tide was the renowned Church figure St. Thomas Aquinas (1225–1274). He lent legitimacy to the study of the stars when he declared, "The celestial bodies are the cause of all that takes place in the sublunar world."

By the time of the Renaissance, astrology was in full bloom again. The Catholic popes now used astrology as a matter of course, and Leo X (1475–1521) had many astrologers on staff at the papal court. The di Medici family, the ruling princes of Italy from around 1400 to 1600, were great patrons of astrology along with arts and literature. Catherine di Medici was influenced by Nostradamus, the famous French astrologer and physician. He correctly predicted the death of her husband Henry II—and its exact circumstances—four years before it happened.

In the sixteenth century, a lonely and frightened young princess in prison, facing possible death, had her horoscope read by a Dr. John Dee. Dee told her that she would live to ascend to the throne. Throughout the long reign of Queen Elizabeth I, Dr. Dee continued to advise her on affairs of state as well as on her more personal affairs.

One of the famous names in astrology at that time is William Lilly (1602–1681), an English astrologer who accurately predicted the Great Fire of London. As a result, he was summoned before Parliament and charged with having conspired to set the fire. He was later acquitted.

Toward the end of the seventeenth century, astrology again fell into disfavor. The succeeding century was known as the Age of Enlightenment, and astrology was linked with superstition and occultism.

During these skeptical times, in 1781, Sir William Herschel discovered a new planet, first called Herschel and then renamed Uranus. This contributed to a growing feeling by the public that astrologers simply had their facts wrong when giving their chart of the heavens. Astrologers also had to accommodate to the discovery of the planet Neptune in 1846 and the discovery of Pluto in 1930. This did not prove hard to do. Just as astronomers were doing, astrologers simply enlarged their vision of the universe. The three new planets are now very much a part of modern astrology.

The founding of the Theosophical Society in 1875 by Madame Helena Blavatsky started astrology on the comeback trail. The aims of the society were to encourage the study of comparative religions and to investigate unexplained laws of nature. The Theosophical Society played a large part in the revival of intellectual interest in astrology, and many prominent astrologers of the day were active in the society.

Around the turn of the century, two very popular astrologers helped to bring astrology to millions. In effect, they discovered the power of the media to promote ideas. Alan Leo, a British astrologer, published an influential magazine called *The Astrologer's Magazine*. In 1914 he was taken to court for being a fortune-teller. The case was dismissed. In 1917 he was prosecuted again, and this time fined twenty-five pounds. Alan Leo's magazine, renamed *Modern Astrology*, flourished and gained many new converts to astrology. Leo lectured widely and wrote a number of astrology textbooks, still in use today. His were the first books that explained astrology to the layperson.

The famed astrologer Evangeline Adams has been called the First American Astrologer. Miss Adams's reputation was established during her first visit to New York when she said that the hotel in which she was staying "was under the worst possible combination of planets, bringing conditions terrifying in their unfriendliness." That night the hotel burned to the ground.

In 1914 (the same year as Alan Leo's trial in England), Miss Adams was also brought to trial in America. She, too, was charged as a fortune-teller. In court she was given an anonymous horoscope to interpret. The horoscope was that of the judge's son. Miss Adams's reading was so accurate that the judge congratulated her, remarking that "the defendant raises astrology to the dignity of an exact science." He dismissed the charge against her. By 1930 Evangeline Adams had a very popular radio program on astrology, which won hundreds of thousands of converts.

During World War Two, Nazi leaders used astrology for propaganda purposes. Joseph Goebbels, Hitler's propaganda minister, had a number of astrologers on his staff, among them one Karl Ernst Krafft, who translated and reinterpreted the predictions of Nostradamus in ways that seemed to favor the Nazi cause. Krafft fell from grace after Rudolph Hess's defection to England. (The Nazis blamed astrology for Hess's defection, saying he was "crazed by astrologers.") Krafft later died in a concentration camp.

Beginning in the 1960s, we have seen a new resurgence of interest in astrology. It is not just popular with the younger generation or with those who read newspaper horoscopes every day. It is also the subject of serious research. More people are learning more about this oldest science all the time.

In 1988, astrology became headline news when a White

House adviser revealed that First Lady Nancy Reagan, wife of President Ronald Reagan, regularly consulted a personal astrologer. Mrs. Reagan apparently used her astrologer's advice to schedule key events and appointments, both for herself and her husband. Understandably, this created a great stir in the media and the general public, who felt that astrology should not be a controlling factor in national politics. Mrs. Reagan defended herself, saying she sought the support and counsel of an astrologer, who became her confidante, only after her husband's near-fatal brush with an assassin's bullet on March 30, 1981. The astrological community has long understood that the Reagans consulted astrologers as far back as the 1960s, when Ronald Reagan was governor of California.

Nancy Reagan's description of her relationship with her astrologer is interesting. Joan Quigley, the astrologer, became a psychological support for Mrs. Reagan, an intimate friend who listened sympathetically to her problems and anxieties. The value of this role of counselor and supporter is often overlooked when arguing the pros and cons of astrology and, indeed, is in itself a great benefit to those who seek the advice of an astrologer.

More and more, astrology has entered the mainstream of our culture. It is no longer considered out of the ordinary for people in business, commerce, banking, the law, the arts, politics—in fact, almost every major profession—to consult a personal astrologer.

1 2

THE ZODIAC

The Legend behind Each Sign

IN ANCIENT TIMES, the sky above us was seen as a giant hollow dome rising over a flat earth, much like an inverted teacup resting on a saucer. Later, this vision of the Earth and the surrounding sky changed to that of a hollow sphere—like an enormous soap bubble with the globe of the Earth in its center. The Sun made a journey every year around the edge of the sky-bubble; within the space of one year it made a complete circle.

The path of the Sun's circle around the Earth is known as the *ecliptic*. This narrow band of the Sun's path is the zodiac. The zodiac is a belt circling the earth, 16° wide (8° above the ecliptic and 8° below the ecliptic) and 360° around. Within this belt are contained the orbits of all the planets in our solar system except Pluto, which has an extraordinarily wide path. Also within this belt are stars, which the ancients arranged in patterns called constellations. To the early stargazers most of these constellations looked like animals, so this belt of constellations became known as the zodiac—from the Greek word *zodiakos*, meaning "circle of animals."

The zodiac is divided into twelve constellations, each with a name and each given the shape of an animal or figure. Using these constellations, the ancient astrologers named the twelve astrological signs.

The zodiac belt may be imagined (in the sense that it is a man-made division of the heavens), but the stars within that belt are real. If you could simultaneously stand at various spots circling our globe, you would be able to see all twelve constellations in the sky at one time. These constellations were known long before Ptolemy categorized them in his textbooks, and each constellation has a story handed down through ancient myths. This folklore has become very much a part of our knowledge of each astrological sign.

ARIES, the Ram

THE FIRST SIGN of the zodiac is represented by the Ram. In mythology, the Ram has always been courageous and enterprising, a lively, energetic animal able to bound over obstacles and rocky terrain.

The story of the Ram begins in ancient Greece with a king named Athamus who ruled the province of Boetia. Athamus married a woman called Nephele, and they had two beautiful children, a son and daughter they named Phrixus and Helle.

After a time, Athamus grew tired of Nephele and deserted her. He took a second wife, Ino, and they had two sons. Ino was a jealous and conniving woman who hated her stepchildren Phrixus and Helle, and set about plotting their deaths.

The first thing she did was convince the women of her country to roast the corn before planting it. This effectively cancelled out the crops that year. Famine swept the land. The king sent a messenger to the Oracle at Delphi to find out what caused the crop failure. Apparently, it never occurred to him to ask the women who planted the crops, but this is the sort of oversight of which some modern political leaders are also guilty.

Ino managed to bribe the king's messenger to return from Delphi and tell the king that the crops would not grow again until the lives of his children Phrixus and Helle were sacrificed to the god Jupiter. The gullible king planned to have his son and daughter killed in order to save his people.

A quick shift now to Phrixus and Helle, who were tending their sheep. In their flock was a Ram with golden fleece. This Golden Ram had been given to their mother Nephele as a present from the god Hermes (Mercury). Nephele, getting wind of what evil was afoot, begged the Ram to save her children. The Ram spoke with the voice of a man to warn Phrixus and Helle of their danger, then told them to climb onto his back. Then he flew with them across the sea.

Unfortunately, as they were crossing the strait that divides Europe and Asia, Helle grew dizzy and faint and slipped off the Ram's back. She fell into the sea and drowned. To this day, the strait into which she fell is named after her, the Hellespont.

Her brother Phrixus, however, was carried safely to the land of Colchis. This put an end to the plot of the villainous Ino, though it does not seem to have done much to relieve the famine or to have brought King Athamus to his senses.

Rather ungratefully it would seem, Phrixus killed the Golden Ram as a sacrifice to Jupiter, who in turn placed the Ram's likeness among the stars in heaven to honor him for his heroism.

TAURUS, the Bull

THE SECOND SIGN of the zodiac is represented by the Bull, an animal that is both fierce and gentle and has always symbolized strength and sexuality.

The myth of the Bull begins with Jupiter, supreme god of ancient Greece, ruler of heaven, of lesser gods, and men. Jupiter had a strong romantic streak, and had numerous love affairs, wives, and mistresses. One such love affair concerns the beautiful Princess Europa, daughter of the King of Phoenicia.

Europa led a very sheltered existence in her father's palace and knew nothing of the world outside. One night she had a prophetic dream in which a strange woman held out her arms to Europa and said, "I shall bring you to Jupiter, for destiny has appointed you his beloved."

Sure enough, that day when Europa and a group of young maidens went out to pick roses and hyacinths in a meadow by the sea, Jupiter saw her and was thunderstruck by her beauty. There and then he determined to have her.

Jupiter knew that an innocent young girl like Europa would run from him if he showed himself in his own godlike image, so he transformed himself into a Bull. He became not an ordinary bull, but a magnificent white Bull with jewel-like horns and a silver crescent moon in the middle of his forehead.

Europa was fascinated by the beautiful, gentle Bull, and began to caress him. Finally she climbed onto his back. That was just what Jupiter wanted. He sprang into the air and carried her away to the island of Crete. There, he changed himself back to his true likeness and declared his love for Europa. Under the boughs of a large tree, he and Europa became lovers.

Not long afterward Venus, the goddess of love, appeared to Europa to confess that she was the strange woman in the dream. From now on, Venus told her, the continent to which Jupiter had taken her would be known as Europe.

This adulterous love story (Jupiter was married to the goddess Juno) has a happy ending. Europa bore Jupiter three children, and Jupiter took the likeness of the Bull and placed it in the heavens.

GEMINI, the Twins

GEMINI IS THE SIGN of the Twins. It is the third sign of the zodiac and the first to have a human rather than an animal symbol.

The myth of the Twins, like that of the previous sign Taurus, also involves Jupiter and his eye for a pretty face. In this story, the object of his affections is a beautiful woman, Leda, married to Tyndareus, king of Sparta. The lustful god Jupiter, apparently unwilling to try the bull ploy twice (see Taurus), changed himself into the form of a magnificent swan. Details of the encounter are a bit sketchy, but he did manage to seduce Leda while disguised as a swan.

From this remarkable union, Leda bore two eggs. The story goes that one of the eggs was the offspring of Jupiter, and that the other was the offspring of Leda's mortal husband. The two eggs produced four children: two brothers, Castor and Pollux, and two sisters, Helen of Troy and Clytemnestra. It is unclear exactly whom Jupiter sired. Some versions of the tale say that Castor and Pollux were his immortal offspring. Others have Castor and Helen as Jupiter's children.

In either case, the twin brothers Castor and Pollux grew up strong and stalwart and inseparable. Castor became famous for his skill as a horse-tamer; Pollux was renowned as a superb boxer. When they were young men they joined Jason and his Argonauts on their expedition to find the Golden Fleece. During a storm at sea, two stars appeared over the heads of the twins and the storm miraculously ended. Because of that incident, Castor and Pollux are considered the patron saints of travelers at sea. (During storms at sea, these lights are still seen twinkling at the top of ships' masts and other tall spires. They are caused by the discharge of electricity. The legend is that if two lights are seen, the storm will cease; if only one appears, the storm will grow worse.)

The twin brothers are described as high-spirited young men. Unfortunately, during a battle Castor met his death. Pollux was inconsolable. At last he went to his father Jupiter to beg him to bring Castor back to life. In turn, Pollux volunteered to give up his own life as ransom.

Jupiter rewarded the brothers' great love and attachment to each other by placing them in the sky as stars. There they shine in the constellation of Gemini, side by side throughout the ages.

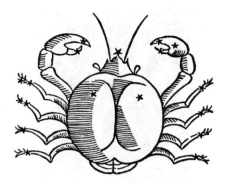

CANCER, the Crab

THE FOURTH SIGN of the zodiac is symbolized by the Crab, a water creature that is also capable of walking on land. We know that the crab symbol was placed in the zodiac some five hundred years before Christ. The Chaldeans gave it the name of Cancer, or Crab, because the crab's backward or oblique movement appeared to represent the Sun's movement upon reaching this sign. When the Sun reaches the sign of Cancer (around June 21) it seems to remain stationary for a few days. The Sun's entry into Cancer begins the summer solstice; the very word *solstice* signifies "the Sun standing still."

In Egypt, the constellation was called Stars of the Water and was represented by two turtles. (This may have been because the constellation was seen at dawn when the Nile was at its lowest; Nile turtles were rather plentiful at that time of year.) Many astrologers think that Cancer the Crab is a melding of the Egyptian turtles and a Babylonian water creature called Allul, which was apparently a kind of tortoise. All three water creatures—turtles, tortoise, and crab—are similar in important ways. They resemble each other in form, and all are hard-shelled and move slowly (like the Sun's movement on entering Cancer).

According to Greek legend, Cancer is the giant crab that attacked the foot of Hercules while he was engaged in battle with the monstrous nine-headed serpent Hydra. Hercules, son of the god Jupiter and a mortal woman Alcmena, had been sent on twelve difficult and heroic undertakings, known as the Twelve Labors of Hercules. One of Hercules's Labors was to slay the evil serpent Hydra. Hercules was having his hands full as the crab attacked, for every time Hercules cut off one of Hydra's heads, two more grew in its place.

The crab's attack on Hercules was instigated by Juno, Jupiter's jealous wife, who was set on Hercules's destruction. Unfortunately, the giant crab's attack sealed its own doom, for Hercules crushed it before proceeding to dispatch the Hydra.

However, legend has it that Juno was grateful for the crab's attempt to carry out her orders. As a reward for its obedience and sacrifice, she placed the crab's figure in the heavens along with other heroic symbols.

LEO, the Lion

LEO, FIFTH SIGN OF THE ZODIAC, is represented by the Lion, king of beasts. Traditionally, the mythology of the Lion is based on the story of Hercules and the Nemean Lion.

Hercules was the son of the great god Jupiter and the mortal woman Alcmena. Jupiter's wife Juno, understandably jealous of Jupiter's numerous love affairs, set herself against Hercules from the time he was a baby. When he was a young man Hercules was compelled to embark on twelve heroic and desperate undertakings, known as the Twelve Labors of Hercules.

The first Labor was to go to the valley of Nemea and there kill the savage and fearless Nemean lion. The skin of this lion could not be hurt by the weapons of man. Stone, iron, and bronze simply bounced off his pelt. Hercules tried to kill the lion with arrows, but they just fell away from the lion's side. Finally Hercules wrestled with the lion barehanded. Because he possessed such great strength, he managed to get a grip around the lion's neck and strangle him to death. In the process, the lion bit off Hercules's finger, which by any measure would seem to indicate he got off lightly.

After he killed the beast, Hercules skinned the magical pelt. From the skin, Hercules made himself a breastplate, and from the lion's jaw he formed a helmet. This new armor was to prove very valuable during his subsequent Labors.

The constellation of Leo is said to commemorate the bravery of combat between Hercules and the magnificent Nemean Lion.

VIRGO, the Virgin

Virgo is the sixth sign of the zodiac and the second sign to have a human representation rather than an animal one. Virgo is often depicted as a young woman holding a sheaf of wheat, for the constellation of Virgo has always been associated with the harvest. Babylonians called the constellation The Furrow, and it was represented by a corn goddess. The most prominent star in Virgo is named Spica, meaning Ear of Corn.

The legend of Virgo is found in the Greek myth of Creation. The story goes that before men or animals lived on Earth, a race of giants, called titans, ruled the world. Two titan brothers, Prometheus and Epimetheus, were given the task of creating human beings and animals. When this was done, Epimetheus set about giving various gifts to the animals—wings to one kind, claws to another, etc. He was so generous that when it came time to dispense something to mankind, he had nothing left to give, so he asked Prometheus for help. Prometheus went into heaven and came back with the gift of fire. This made man superior to other species, for with fire he could keep warm, make tools, and eventually develop commerce and science.

Jupiter, chief of gods, became so angry at the gods' secret of fire being given to man that he bound Prometheus to a rock on Mount Caucasus where an eagle constantly tore at his liver, though never entirely consuming it. He also sent a curse to Earth, brought by the first woman. Her name was Pandora, meaning "a gift of all the gods."

Pandora brought with her a box, which she was told never to open. One day, seized with curiosity, she lifted the lid of the box. Out sprang terrible plagues to haunt mankind forever after: sickness and death for the body; anger, envy, and revenge for the mind. At the bottom of the box lay the one thing that had not escaped—hope.

During the terrible times that followed, the gods deserted Earth one by one and went to live in heaven. The very last to leave was Astraea, goddess of innocence and purity. After leaving the Earth, Astraea was placed among the stars and became the constellation of Virgo. The legend is that one day the Golden Age will come again, and that Astraea (Virgo) will return to Earth.

LIBRA, the Scales

LIBRA IS THE SEVENTH astrological sign and the only one to have a symbol that is neither animal nor human. The Scales represent balance and justice, harmony and equilibrium.

Like the previous sign, Virgo, Libra is associated with the harvest, for in ancient times grains and crops were weighed on scales after they were harvested. The Scales also have a more profound symbolism. They are the scales of judgment for the dead, where souls are weighed.

In Egyptian religion the scales of judgment were the sole province of the god Anubis, Conductor of Souls. Anubis, who had the head of a jackal, guided the dead through the underworld and made sure they were weighed fairly. He was the master of the balance (the scale). There is in existence a painting, called the Papyrus of Ani, dated around 1500 B.C., that shows a judgment scene. Anubis is crouching by a large scale weighing the heart of a dead person. In one bowl of the

scale rests the heart; in the other bowl Truth sits, symbolized by a feather. In this depiction, the scale is equally balanced. In Egyptian religion, the dead heart (or soul) had to be in harmony with Truth before it could pass into the afterlife.

The Scales have also long been associated with the concept of justice and the law. We have all seen statues of the embodiment of Justice. She is a woman who is blindfolded and who holds the scale in her hands. The Scales are the symbol of impartiality, of rendering to each person his or her rightful due.

In Greek mythology Justice was represented by the goddess Themis, mother of Astraea (see Virgo). Themis and her daughter Astraea are the constellations of Libra and Virgo, who shine side by side in the firmament. The legend is that when the human race finally reaches its Golden Age, Themis (symbolizing justice) and her daughter (symbolizing innocence) will return to Earth.

SCORPIO, the Scorpion

THE EIGHTH SIGN of the zodiac is represented by the Scorpion, a poisonous creature that can paralyze its victims with the sting of its tail.

The sign of Scorpio suffers from its association with the scorpion, since its symbol is often hated and feared. The scorpion, however, was not always reviled. In ancient Egypt it was deified in the form of Selket, the scorpion-goddess. Selket was the protectress of the dead, and she is often seen on walls of tombs with her wings spread out in a protective gesture.

The classical myth of the Scorpion begins with the death of Orion, a beautiful young giant and a great hunter who was the son of Neptune (god of the sea). Tales of Orion's prowess, strength, and manliness are legend. The story of his death is related in many versions. One is that Eos, goddess of the dawn, fell in love with him and carried him away with her. Diana, the moon-goddess, became jealous that Eos should take a mortal lover and commanded a scorpion to kill Orion.

Another version is that Orion tried to rape Diana, and she brought a giant scorpion out of the earth that stung Orion to death.

After Orion's death, Jupiter placed both Orion and the Scorpion among the stars. They each became a constellation. Orion, with his golden armor and sword in hand, is one of the brightest and most spectacular constellations in the heavens on a winter night. But when the Scorpion, who was placed in the zodiac, rises in summer, the brilliance of Orion fades.

SAGITTARIUS, the Archer

SAGITTARIUS, THE NINTH SIGN of the zodiac, is depicted as an Archer, but the Archer is not an ordinary man drawing a bow. He is a centaur, that mythological creature who is half man and half horse. Sagittarius is the only astrological sign to have both a human and animal representation.

The constellation of Sagittarius, however, is not just any centaur. It is the great and wise Chiron, a son of the titan-god Saturn. Chiron was a friend and confidant of both gods and men. The gods taught Chiron the arts of medicine, hunting and riding, music, and prophecy. In turn, Chiron himself became a renowned teacher. Among his famous pupils were Achilles, Jason, Castor and Pollux, and Hercules.

One day, while the great Hercules was hunting a dangerous boar, he accidentally struck Chiron in the knee with a poisonous shaft. Chiron suffered the agony of dying, but because he was immortal he could not die. Hercules promised to find Death to release him. On his journey Hercules came across poor Prometheus, chained throughout eternity to a rock where an eagle tore at his liver. The supreme god Jupiter had put a curse on Prometheus: his torture would last until someone of his own free will consented to suffer in his place. The dying Chiron took Prometheus's place. Thus, the curse was fulfilled. Chiron was allowed to die, and Prometheus was set free by Hercules.

After Chiron's death Jupiter rewarded his noble character by placing the heroic centaur among the stars, and he became the constellation Sagittarius.

CAPRICORN, the Goat

THE TENTH SIGN of the zodiac is represented by the Goat, a sure-footed animal who scales the heights by taking advantage of every foothold.

In ancient times, the Goat was depicted as part goat and part fish, with its front half the goat and its back half the fish. In many old drawings and engravings you will see the Goat pictured with a fish tail, and in some astrology books Capricorn is known as the Sea-Goat.

The Sea-Goat in the Babylonian religion was a great and revered god named Ea, who brought learning and culture to the people of Mesopotamia. In the valley of Mesopotamia, irrigation of land and crops came primarily from the flooding of the Tigris and Euphrates Rivers. Because of this, people believed there was an ocean of fresh water underneath the earth. The god Ea lived in that ocean. Every day he came out of the underground sea to dispense his wisdom, and every night he returned there.

By the time of Greek and Roman culture, Capricorn had become associated with the god Pan, a sporting and lusty creature who ruled over woodlands and fields, flocks and shepherds. Pan was a man from the waist up and a goat from the waist down. He had goat ears and goat horns.

Pan was fond of music and was famous for playing the pipes. His shepherd's pipe, called a syrinx, was actually a nymph who had rejected his sexual advances. Pan turned her into a musical instrument, saying that if he could not have her one way she would be his in a new guise.

In time, Pan became known as the god of Nature. Certain qualities of Pan's—sexuality, impudence, a love of nature—have become part of the character of Capricorn.

AQUARIUS, the Water Bearer

THE ELEVENTH SIGN of the zodiac has as its symbol the Water Bearer, a human figure carrying a jar or receptacle from which water pours out in a stream.

The symbol of the Water Bearer goes back to both Egyptian and Babylonian religion. In Egypt the Water Bearer was the god Hap, the personification of the river Nile. Hap carried two vases of water, which represented both the South and North Nile, and was considered the sustainer of life. All living things would die without the waters of Hap.

In Greek literature the constellation of Aquarius was called the Water Pourer, and is sometimes thought to represent the god Jupiter, who at a command caused the waters to pour from heaven. It also commemorates Deucalion, the only man to come through the Great Flood unharmed.

At the beginning of creation, gods and humanity lived in harmony during an era called the Golden Age. The earth produced food without people having to till the soil; the waters flowed with wine and honey. Then Pandora opened her box of evils, and plagues and sickness of the mind and body were released on Earth.

The great god Jupiter looked down and decided to rid the world of people and create a new race worthier of life. With the help of his brother Neptune, Jupiter covered the earth with water. Only two people were saved, Deucalion and his wife Pyrrha, who were both just and pious and who worshipped the gods faithfully. They took refuge on Mount Parnassus, and when Jupiter saw them he remembered their exemplary lives. He caused the waters to recede and the earth to dry up. Then Deucalion and Pyrrha were commanded to cast the bones of their mother behind them. Deucalion interpreted "the bones of his mother" to mean the stones of the earth, and he and Pyrrha began to pick up stones and cast them behind themselves as they walked. These stones slowly turned into human beings; the ones Deucalion threw became men, and the stones Pyrrha threw became women. Thus, Deucalion became the father of a new race of mankind.

PISCES, the Fishes

THE TWELFTH AND LAST SIGN of the zodiac is represented by two fishes, tied to one another although swimming in opposite directions. The two fishes in water symbolize conflicting currents of emotion and hidden depths.

The constellation of Pisces has been known as Two Fishes as long ago as 2000 B.C. The Babylonian name for this constellation, Kun, has been translated as The Tails (of the fishes). Kun is also known as The Band or The Leash (the string that connects the two fishes). Tied to this leash were two fish goddesses, Anunitum and Simmah, who represented the Tigris and Euphrates Rivers.

In Greek mythology the Two Fishes are associated with a story of Venus and Cupid. A great and terrible monster named Typhon had a hundred dragon heads, eyes that shot fire, and a voice that was a combination of hissing snakes, bellowing bulls, and roaring lions.

One day Venus (goddess of love and beauty) and her son Cupid were walking along the Euphrates River when Typhon suddenly appeared. His hundred heads flicked dark tongues and the eyes flashed fire. Typhon was intent on the goddess's and her son's destruction. Terrified and unable to flee, Venus called on her father Jupiter for help. Jupiter quickly changed Venus and Cupid into two fishes, and they jumped into the river and escaped. Another version of this story is that two brave fishes leapt out of the water to rescue Venus and Cupid and carry them off on their backs through the river to safety. As a reward, Minerva (the virgin goddess) placed the two fishes among the stars, where they became the constellation of Pisces.

Part Five

ASTROLOGY IN OUR TIME

13

THE AGE OF AQUARIUS

EVERYONE SEEMS TO HAVE HEARD about the Age of Aquarius. Depending on which astrologer you consult, we have either begun or will soon begin the Aquarian Age.

But what exactly *is* the Age of Aquarius?

To answer that question, we must backtrack a little. As you know, looking at the Sun from our vantage point here on Earth, it travels around the Earth once every year. On its journey, the Sun travels a narrow path (called the ecliptic), and passes through the twelve signs of the zodiac.

When the foundation stones of the science of astrology were first formally put in place in Babylonian times, the signs of the zodiac were named after actual *constellations of stars* in the sky. Those early astronomers had noticed that the Sun journeyed through the same constellations every year. During the spring, the path of the Sun crossed over the constellation of Aries. In the fall, the path of the Sun crossed over the constellation of Libra.

The beginning of the astrological year is a point called the vernal equinox. This is where the Sun's path crosses the celestial equator (the line that divides the heavens into a northern half and a southern half). At that point, day and night are equal in length. The word *equinox* comes from the Latin, meaning "equal night" (i.e., night is equal to the day). There are two equinoxes during the year, vernal and autumnal. The vernal equinox begins spring; the autumnal equinox begins autumn. The vernal equinox also begins the first astrological sign (Aries) and the first half of the zodiac; the autumnal equinox begins the seventh sign (Libra) and the second half of the zodiac.

When astrology was first formalized, the vernal equinox signaled the beginning of the Sun's entrance not only into the *sign* of Aries but also into the *constellation* of Aries. At that time, the two were considered to be identical. Since then, however, astrology and astronomy have diverged. The signs of the zodiac no longer correspond to the same constellations in the sky. Thus, nowadays, when an astronomer talks about Taurus, he or she means the actual group of stars in the heavens that make up the constellation of Taurus. When an astrologer talks about Taurus, he or she refers to the second astrological *sign*, that 30° segment of the zodiac that controls a whole set of characteristics, symbols, and associations.

It was in the second century B.C. that a Greek astronomer named Hipparchus discovered a phenomenon called the *precession of the equinoxes*. He found that, ever so slowly, the Earth shifts in its position as it spins through the solar system. Scientists sometimes refer to this slight shift as the Earth's "wobble," because it somewhat resembles a top wobbling as it spins. Instead of remaining upright, the poles of the Earth, like the top and bottom of a spinning toy, lean from side to side as the Earth rotates on its axis. Over the span of a great many years, this leaning of the Earth changes the placement of the celestial equator, because the celestial equator is on the same line as the Earth's equator except that it is projected out into the heavens. Therefore, as the position of the Earth shifts, the line of the celestial equator shifts.

All of this adds up to the fact that as time passes, the vernal equinox (the point where the path of the Sun crosses the celestial equator) takes place in an entirely different *constellation*. This slow motion of the Earth's tilt is called the precession of the equinoxes because, during the span of many, many years, the equinoxes slowly travel through all the constellations of the zodiac, in backward order. (If they traveled in forward order, no doubt it would have been called the *procession of the equinoxes*.)

When the Babylonians calculated the zodiac, the vernal equinox took place in the *constellation of Aries*. Around the time of the birth of Christ (the beginning of A.D.), the Earth had shifted enough so that the vernal equinox took place in the *constellation of Pisces*. Around the year A.D.

2000, the vernal equinox began to take place in the *constellation of Aquarius*. Hence, "this is the dawning of the Age of Aquarius."

Little by little, at the infinitesimal rate of approximately 1 degree every 7½ years, the equinoxes move through the zodiac. In the space of about 2,150 years, the equinoxes move through one sign of the zodiac. In the time span of approximately 25,820 years, the equinoxes move through the entire twelve signs of the zodiac. This 26,000-year time span is called a Great Year. Each 2,100-year transit through a sign is called a Great Month; a Great Month is also referred to as an Age.

For the past 2,000 years or so, mankind was living in the Age of Pisces; we have now entered the Age of Aquarius. Because such vast amounts of time are involved, it is difficult to give an exact year to the beginning of a new Age. For example, some astrologers mark the beginning of the Aquarian Age at the end of World War Two. The venerable astrological association, the Church of Light, puts the date as early as 1881. Astrologer Capel McCutcheon believed we entered the new Age in the 1970s with the advent of the computer. The psychologist Carl Jung and the astrologer Charles Jayne both predicted that the new Age would begin during the decade of the 1990s. Others, like the Irish astrologer Cyril Fagan, set the date as far ahead as 2300–2400. The consensus, however, is that as of the year 2000 we were definitely in the Age of Aquarius.

Each Age is characterized by the astrological sign of that era. During its existence, our earth has gone through thousands of Great Years. Scientists estimate our Earth to be as old as 4.6 billion years, which means that it has passed through almost 177,000 Great Years. But humankind's ancestors, creatures who first walked upright on two legs, have been on Earth for only 115 Great Years

(3 million years). And Neanderthal Man walked this earth only nine Great Years ago.

Astrologers trace mankind's written history only as far back as the Age of Leo.

AGE OF LEO

(CIRCA 10,000 B.C. TO 8000 B.C.)

This Age is characterized by the energy and creativity of human beings learning how to use their environment. Men and women lived in caves and learned to refine highly finished and polished stone implements. The Sun, ruler of Leo, was of paramount importance to Neolithic (New Stone Age) people, for during this era human beings acquired a limited ability to raise food (agriculture) rather than merely hunt and gather it. According to astrologers, cave paintings from this age (the first written history) show a marked Leo influence.

AGE OF CANCER

(CIRCA 8000 B.C. TO 6000 B.C.)

It was during this Age that human beings abandoned their caves and formed fixed dwellings aboveground (the Cancerian influence to make a home). People learned to spin and weave and make pottery. They began to grow varied crops and to domesticate animals. Moon worship and fertility rites abounded during this era. (Cancer is ruled by the Moon and is the sign of domesticity, fertility, and motherhood.)

AGE OF GEMINI

(CIRCA 6000 B.C. TO 4000 B.C.)

This Age is marked by the development of writing (Gemini is the sign of communication). Mankind expanded its intellectual capacities by beginning to record and to store information. The invention of the wheel made rudimentary commerce and travel possible (both ruled by Gemini).

AGE OF TAURUS

(CIRCA 4000 B.C. TO 2000 B.C.)

The great Egyptian civilization, with its emphasis on cultivation of land and new technology of building (the pyramids), echoes the influence of earthy Taurus. Both the esthetic nature of Taurus and its solidity are reflected in the beautiful art and architecture of this Age.

AGE OF ARIES

(CIRCA 2000 B.C. TO 1 B.C.)

This era is known as the Iron Age, when mankind learned to fashion weapons from iron (Aries rules the metal iron). The Age is also characterized by its militancy and aggressive spirit. During this era Assyria and the Greek city-states rose to power, and Alexander the Great conquered the world. In the latter part of the Age, militaristic Rome became the most powerful empire ever known.

AGE OF PISCES

(CIRCA A.D. 1 TO A.D. 2000)

The enormous influence of Christianity changed the world during this era (Pisces is the sign of spiritual knowledge). The fish (symbol of Pisces) is also the symbol of Christianity. Drawings of fish were used as secret signs between early Christians. Christ called His apostles "fishers of men." This Age is marked by sacrifice and struggle (qualities associated with Pisces).

What will the Age of Aquarius be like?

FOR CLUES WE NEED TO EXAMINE the sign of Aquarius. Aquarius is the sign of brotherhood and humanitarianism, aglow with utopian ideals. In the coming era astrologers expect that the concept of individual nations will fade and humankind will join together as one people rather than be separated into nationalities. Within the next 2,000 years, we hope to at last reach the long-held ideal of world peace.

Right now, however, this seems an impossible dream. The Age of Aquarius has gotten off to a poor start. Warring factions are everywhere. The United States has been embroiled in a prolonged war in Iraq. Fundamental Islamism has become strongly militant, dividing the world into "them" and "us." Suspicions, greed, fear, violence, abuses of human rights and genocide throughout the world have not lessened. Indeed they have become more focused and divisive. Wealth is not distributed more evenly, and programs are not implemented to better the lives of those suffering poverty, neglect and lack of education and health care. The haves and the have nots are more separated, angry, and conflict-ridden.

Consider the negatives of Aquarius. This is a Fixed Air sign, meaning inflexibility and stubbornness of ideas.

Aquarius focuses on the betterment of society but often leaves out the betterment of the individual. It gets stuck in adamant thinking patterns that this is right and that is wrong. Extremism, radicalism, and the militant revolutionary are archetypes of this sign. Aquarius loves its own principles and, because it is such a mental sign, is easily cut off from the heart. Negative qualities are coldness and spitefulness; the shadow side of Aquarius is anger. Astrologically, the journey of Aquarius is to move away from its perversity, find the deeper truth of its humanity and tap into its idealism to create a truly better world.

Keep in mind I am not speaking of an Aquarian person but of the *sign*'s characteristics—and how these might apply to the state of the world during these beginning years of the 21st century.

Still, we are roughly only 2% of the way into the new Age of Aquarius, so perhaps we should concentrate on the positives.

Aquarius is the sign of scientific knowledge and invention, and rules the airwaves. It is impossible to imagine what mind-boggling inventions will take place in the next 2,000 years, but astrologers predict incredible journeys through space will definitely be one of them. Not just travel in our own solar system, or even our own galaxy, but to the universe beyond. There will be space arks that can transport multitudes of people, space colonies, and interstellar travel. The achievement of travel to the stars will indeed be remarkable when one considers that Pluto, our outermost planet, is only 5.0 light-minutes distant from us, while the nearest star (not counting our own Sun) is 4.3 light-*years* away!

Aquarius is a mental sign, and the future should be marked by as yet unthinkable intellectual achievement. There will be concern for the environment, and the discovery of new technology to solve the problems of dwindling supplies of energy and resources on Earth. The power of atomic energy, electronics, and aviation (all Aquarian inventions) will be harnessed for the greatest possible use. Already the computer has reshaped the world, the way we communicate, conduct all business, and keep records. Scientists and psychologists say the computer has already started to reconfigure how the human brain thinks. Aquarius is a practical sign; the purpose of knowledge is to make use of it, not simply for the sake of knowing.

Astrologers have a special place in their hearts for Aquarius because it is the sign associated with astrology. We have already seen an upsurge of interest in astrology at the dawning of the Aquarian Age. As someone once remarked, "Astrology is the religion of the new generation." In the coming Age astrology will no longer be thought of as a superstitious, arcane, or secret knowledge possessed by a few. It will be a respected scientific inquiry, available to everyone.

Perhaps it is wishful thinking to say that in the Age of Aquarius humanity will achieve universal harmony, but after all Aquarius is the sign of hopes and wishes. Predictions are there will be a great emphasis on the common man, and that special privilege for people of high birth or wealth will become an antique notion. The aristocrat of the future will be the person of learning and achievement. Astrologers hope that in the Aquarian Age we will build on past knowledge to discover new truths (Aquarius is the truth-seeker).

These predictions, of course, are based on the positive qualities of Aquarius. In our real world, we have grave problems to surmount. There is a terrible danger of so over-populating our planet that only global war, disease, and famine will reduce our numbers. We are using up our natural resources at an alarming rate, stripping our planet bare of plant and animal species and its ability to sustain life. Already, we are feeling early effects of a dire global warming. Most terrifying of all, we have the atomic power to completely destroy ourselves and, quite likely, the Earth along with us.

Still, the Age of Aquarius offers hope. Uranus, ruler of Aquarius, is called the planet of the future, for within its dominion lie modern science, invention, electricity, and humanitarian movements. Uranus is the planet of the power of will and of unconscious purpose. A promise is held out to us; we can build a wonderful new world. Or we can lose all that we have. It is up to the new universal Aquarians—in other words, ourselves.

About the System of Astrology Used in the Book

Two systems of astrology are in use today. One is traditional astrology, sometimes referred to as tropical astrology. This is the system in most common use in the Western world, and the one described in this book.

A second school of thought adheres to sidereal astrology. *Sidereal*, which comes from the Latin word for star, *sidus*, means "determined by the stars." Siderealists believe astrology should be measured according to the actual star groupings. As explained on pages 399–401, as our Earth slowly shifts position, the stars slowly shift their positions in relation to us. Sidereal astrology is based on the theory that the dates of the Sun's entrance into each sign should change along with the Earth's shift in position. They claim that this is the most scientific approach, since it is based on the position of the actual constellations in the zodiac. According to sidereal astrology, the zodiac that Claudius Ptolemy calculated back in the second century A.D. has now changed by about twenty-five days. Siderealists differ from traditionalists about the dates for the Sun's entrance into the twelve *signs* of the zodiac. They believe that as the Earth continues to shift position, the dates for the Sun's entry into each sign will also change.

Traditional astrologers point out that even in ancient times the zodiac never precisely corresponded to the actual constellations. Ancient astrologers knew that the various constellations in the zodiac were of unequal size and brilliance (for example, the constellation of Gemini is very large and bright, whereas the constellations of Libra and Pisces are quite dim). Nevertheless, they grouped the signs of the zo-diac into twelve equal segments of 30° each, and this grouping has remained valid for thousands of years. Indeed, the symbols and associations of these signs have become part of humankind's collective consciousness.

Traditionalists say that the Earth's slow shift through the signs of the zodiac relates to the zodiacal Ages of the Earth. This has nothing to do with the yearly zodiac, which is concerned with individual human experience and is marked by the seasons.

In traditional (tropical) astrology, the vernal equinox marks the entrance of the Sun into the first sign of the zodiac, Aries. That is the turning point, the beginning of the yearly zodiac cycle. (The word *tropical* comes from the Greek, meaning "turning point.") Whichever constellation the vernal equinox may take place in, what remains constant is that the vernal equinox begins the Sun's entrance into the first degree of the ecliptic—and the first degree of the ecliptic is always the first degree of Aries.

In sidereal astrology, the vernal equinox currently takes place about the fifth day of Pisces, and as the Earth moves so will that date. According to sidereal calculation, therefore, someone born on March 22 in the year 5000 A.D. would be classified as Capricorn rather than Aries.

All this may seem like making waves in a teacup. After all, ancient as astrology may seem, the science is at most only three Great Months old. Much more unfolding of our understanding of astrology lies ahead during the new Age of Aquarius—and a dispute that may loom large to us now is sure to resolve itself as we learn more.

Part Six

AN ASTROLOGER'S LEXICON

AN EXPLANATION
OF TERMS

AFFINITY A mutual attraction between signs.

AFFLICTION An unfavorable or adverse aspect between planets in a birth chart, indicating stress, difficulty, or disharmony. Modern astrology associates afflictions in a birth chart with psychological problems that the native must make an effort to overcome in order to achieve his or her full potential.

AGE, ASTROLOGICAL (Also known as a Great Month) A time span of approximately 2,150 years, during which the vernal equinox passes through all 30° of one sign of the zodiac. The phenomenon, known as the Precession of the Equinoxes, is caused by the slow but constant shift of the Earth as it spins on its axis. Astrologers believe that in the latter part of the twentieth century the world left the Age of Pisces and entered a new Great Month—the Age of Aquarius. A *Great Year* is the time span that it takes the vernal equinox to make a complete revolution through all twelve signs of the zodiac, a period that lasts about 25,800 years. (*See also* Precession of the Equinoxes.)

AIR One of the four elements under which the signs of the zodiac are classified. The four elements are fire, earth, air, and water. Gemini, Libra, and Aquarius are the air signs and comprise the air triplicity. In astrology, air signifies intellect, reason, and communication.

ANGLES The four cardinal points in a horoscope that mark the horizon and meridian. The four angles are the Ascendant, Nadir (Imum Coeli), Descendant, and Midheaven (Medium Coeli). These are the most important and sensitive points in a birth chart. Planets on or near any of the four angles have a marked influence on the subject's personality or public image.

ANGULAR HOUSES The four houses in a horoscope that immediately follow the four angles. Angular Houses are the First, Fourth, Seventh, and Tenth. In a birth chart, planets in any of these houses indicate that the native is likely to achieve prominence in the world.

AQUARIUS The eleventh sign of the zodiac, which the Sun transits each year from approximately January 20 to February 18. Aquarius has as its element air and is fixed in quality. The sign is symbolized by the Water Bearer and ruled by the planet Uranus. Aquarius natives are characterized as innovative, idealistic, humanitarian, and intellectual.

ARIES The first sign of the zodiac, which the Sun transits each year from approximately March 21 to April 19. Aries has as its element fire and is cardinal in quality. The sign is symbolized by the Ram and ruled by the planet Mars. Aries natives are characterized as impulsive, energetic, quick-tempered, and having leadership ability.

ASCENDANT (Also known as Rising sign) The sign of the zodiac that was rising on the eastern horizon at the time of birth. Also, the exact degree of the sign rising on the eastern horizon at the moment of birth, the point in a birth chart that marks the cusp of the First House. The Ascendant (or Rising sign) characterizes a person's outward approach to life. In a birth chart, planets at or near the line of the Ascendant represent strength and power of a person's self.

ASPECT The geometrical relationship between planets in a birth chart, which indicates areas of harmony, challenge, strain, ease, and/or power. Aspects are classified as major (Conjunction, Trine, Sextile, Opposition, Square) and minor (Quincunx, Semisquare, Sesquisquare, Semisextile). The study of aspects in a birth chart is an important part of horoscope interpretation.

ASTROLOGY (From the Greek, meaning "science of the stars") The art and science of studying the celestial bodies and their cyclical motion, and determining their influence on human character, behavior, experience, and events.

BIRTH CHART (Also known as natal chart) A diagram of the heavens, called a horoscope, that charts the position of the celestial bodies as they appeared at the time of an individual's birth. The terms *horoscope* and *birth chart* are often used interchangeably, although precisely speaking a horoscope is a chart for any given moment and a birth chart is specifically for the moment of birth. In a birth chart, the Ascendant (Rising sign) is the astrological sign that was rising on the eastern horizon at the moment of birth (as opposed to a solar chart in which the Sun sign is used as the Rising sign). The Rising sign is also the First House in a birth chart, and thus the houses placed around the chart are known as natal houses. A birth chart is a very personal chart, and many astrologers feel it contains the only true delineation of the native.

CADENT HOUSES (From the Latin word *cadere*, meaning "to fall") The four houses in a horoscope that immediately follow Succedent Houses, so named because they "fall away" from both Angular and Succedent Houses. Cadent Houses are the Third, Sixth, Ninth, and Twelfth Houses. In a birth chart, planets in any of these Houses indicate that the native is mentally active and able to communicate ideas.

CANCER The fourth sign of the zodiac, which the Sun transits each year from approximately June 21 to July 22. Cancer has as its element water and is cardinal in quality. The sign is symbolized by the Crab and ruled by the Moon. Cancer natives are characterized as imaginative, emotional, sensitive, loyal, and with a tendency to be moody.

CAPRICORN The tenth sign of the zodiac, which the Sun transits each year from approximately December 22 to January 19. Capricorn has as its element earth and is cardinal in quality. The sign is symbolized by the Goat (or Sea-Goat) and is ruled by the planet Saturn. Capricorn natives are characterized as disciplined, responsible and hardworking, ambitious and determined.

CARDINAL One of the three qualities under which the signs of the zodiac are classified. The three qualities are cardinal, fixed, and mutable. Aries, Cancer, Libra, and Capricorn are the cardinal signs and comprise the cardinal quadruplicity. The Sun's entrance into these four signs marks the beginning of the four seasons: spring, summer, autumn, and winter. In astrology, the cardinal quality signifies action, initiative, leadership, and outgoing activity.

CELESTIAL EQUATOR The Earth's equator projected outward onto the heavenly sphere.

CONJUNCTION A major aspect, the most powerful in astrology, in which two or more planets occupy the same degree (or are within 10° of each other) in a horoscope. Conjunctions in a chart exert a marked influence, the precise nature of which depends on the specific planets involved.

CONSTELLATIONS Groups of stars assigned names suggested by the patterns they form in the heavens. To the ancients, charting the constellations was an invaluable method of studying and organizing the universe.

CUSP 1. The point at which a sign of the zodiac begins. Persons are said to be "born on the cusp" when their birth times fall at or near the beginning or end of an astrological sign. Cusp-born people often exhibit characteristics of both their Sun sign and the previous or following sign.

2. The point or line in a horoscope that marks the beginning of a house.

DECANATE (Also known as Decan) A 10° subdivision of the zodiac that divides each astrological sign into three parts of approximately ten days each. There are three decanates in each sign, making a total of thirty-six decanates in the zodiac. Each decanate has a planetary ruler, called a subruler, and is also symbolized by a constellation. Decanates serve to refine and emphasize certain qualities and character traits pertaining to the overall sign.

DESCENDANT One of the four angles in a horoscope (the four most important points in a chart). The Descendant, which marks the cusp of the Seventh House, is the point in a birth chart directly opposite the Ascendant. The Descendant represents the channeling of power through partnerships and relationships; planets at or near the Descendant indicate that the native may come to prominence through his or her associations.

DIRECT The forward-moving motion of a planet in its orbit through the signs of the zodiac. Direct motion is the normal course of a planet. At various times, however, a planet may appear to turn backward in its orbit, a movement known as retrograde motion. The retrograde motion of a planet is an optical illusion caused by the angle of observation from earth. (*See also* Retrograde.)

DISPOSITOR A term used in horoscopes to describe the ruler of a sign in which another planet appears. For example, if in a birth chart Mercury is in Sagittarius, Jupiter (which rules Sagittarius) is called the dispositor of Mercury.

DRAGON'S HEAD *See* Nodes.

DRAGON'S TAIL *See* Nodes.

DUALITY One of the classifications under which signs of the zodiac are grouped. A sign's duality is either masculine or feminine. Six signs are masculine: Aries, Gemini, Leo, Libra, Sagittarius, Aquarius. Six signs are feminine: Taurus, Cancer, Virgo, Scorpio, Capricorn, Pisces. In astrology, masculine signs are outer-directed, energetic, strong through action; feminine signs are receptive, magnetic, strong through inner resources.

EARTH 1. One of the four elements (fire, earth, air, and water) under which signs of the zodiac are classified. Taurus, Virgo, and Capricorn are the earth signs and comprise the earth triplicity. In astrology, earth signifies practicality, conservatism, stability, and materialism.

2. The planet Earth, which we inhabit.

ECLIPTIC The great circle in the heavens that marks the apparent path of the Sun on its yearly journey around the Earth. The ecliptic is the path of the Sun when viewed from the Earth (although in reality it is the Earth that revolves around the Sun, and the ecliptic is in fact the path of the Earth's orbit around the Sun). The narrow circular band of the heavens that has the line of the ecliptic through its center is called the zodiac.

ELEMENTS The four fundamental substances (fire, earth, air, and water) under which the signs of the zodiac are classified. Fire signs are energetic and enthusiastic; earth signs are practical and stable; air signs are communicative and intellectual; water signs are emotional and imaginative.

EPHEMERIS (Plural, *ephemerides*) An almanac that lists the positions of the Sun, Moon, and planets for each day of the year.

EQUINOXES (From the Latin, meaning "equal night") The two points during the year when the path of the Sun (the ecliptic) crosses the celestial equator, and day and night are of equal length. The vernal equinox (spring) occurs when the Sun enters the sign of Aries; at that point the center of the Sun intersects the celestial equator as the Sun moves from the southern hemisphere into the northern hemisphere. The autumnal equinox (fall) occurs when the Sun enters the sign of Libra; at that point the center of the Sun intersects the celestial equator as the Sun moves from the northern hemisphere into the southern hemisphere.

FEMININE SIGNS The signs of the zodiac belonging to the earth and water triplicities, namely, Taurus, Cancer, Virgo, Scorpio, Capricorn, and Pisces. In astrology, feminine signs are characterized as receptive, magnetic, and possessing strong inner resources.

FIRE One of the four elements (fire, earth, air, and water) under which the signs of the zodiac are classified. Aries, Leo, and Sagittarius are fire signs and comprise the fire triplicity. In astrology, fire signifies energy, aggressiveness, enthusiasm, and impulsiveness.

FIXED One of the three qualities under which the signs of the zodiac are classified. The three qualities are cardinal, fixed, and mutable. Taurus, Leo, Scorpio, and Aquarius are the fixed signs and comprise the fixed quadruplicity. In astrology, the fixed quality signifies persistence, single-mindedness, determination, and resourcefulness.

GEMINI The third sign of the zodiac, which the Sun transits each year from approximately May 21 to June 20. Gemini has as its element air and is mutable in quality. The sign is symbolized by the Twins and ruled by the planet Mercury. Gemini natives are characterized as mentally facile, versatile, clever, and gifted in the ability to communicate.

GEOCENTRIC (From the Greek words *ge*, meaning "earth," and *kentron*, meaning "center") Viewed or measured from the center of the Earth. The concept of Earth as the center of the universe is the classical viewpoint of astrology, which considers the Earth to be the center of human experience and thus studies the positions and movements of celestial bodies as seen from the Earth. Most horoscopes are geocentric, although some modern astrologers also work with heliocentric (Sun-centered) charts. (*See also* Heliocentric.)

GLYPH The written astrological symbol for a planet or a zodiacal sign. The glyphs have symbolic meanings; for example, the circle represents the spiritual world; the half-circle represents the soul; the cross represents the material world.

GRAND CROSS The rarest aspect-pattern in a horoscope, consisting of two pairs of planets in opposition, the four planets involved forming a square aspect to each other. This pattern forms a cross in the birth chart. Combining as it does four squares and two oppositions, the Grand Cross can be a most difficult configuration, often indicating an obsessive, maladjusted personality. However, it also signifies dynamic energy, intensity, and force. A Grand Cross often appears in the charts of self-made men and women.

GRAND TRINE An unusual aspect-pattern in a horoscope, in which three planets are all in trine to each other (i.e., 120° away from each other), forming a grand triangle. Because a Grand Trine by its nature heavily stresses a particular element, for example, fire or water, it tends to indicate an imbalance in the chart. However, a trine is also very favorable, and a Grand Trine signifies enormous creativity or energy, and usually indicates that the native will be blessed with luck or success.

GREAT MONTH *See* Age, Astrological.

GREAT YEAR *See* Age, Astrological.

HELIOCENTRIC (From the Greek words *helios*, meaning "Sun," and *kentron*, meaning "center") Viewed or measured from the center of the Sun. Since the death of the astronomer Nicolaus Copernicus in 1543, humankind's concept of the universe has been heliocentric, i.e., that our solar system has the Sun at its center. The roots of astrology go much farther back in history, to a time when for thousands of years the concept of the universe was geocentric. Because astrology is concerned with celestial movements as they relate to human beings here on Earth and also as seen by human beings on Earth, modern astrology continues to operate within a geocentric framework. However, heliocentric charts are used by many astrologers, usually in combination with geocentric charts, and a number of heliocentric ephemerides are in common use.

HEMISPHERE EMPHASIS The circle of the horoscope is divided into four hemispheres—the top half and bottom half (southern and northern hemispheres), and left half and right half (eastern and western hemispheres). In a birth chart a preponderance of planets in the top hemisphere emphasizes extrovertedness, while a preponderance of planets in the bottom hemisphere emphasizes introvertedness. A preponderance of planets in the left hemisphere emphasizes the native's impact on the world, while a preponderance of planets in the right hemisphere emphasizes the world's impact on the native.

HERMETIC THEORY The theory, arising out of ancient Egyptian philosophical wisdom, that the human being is a miniature version of the cosmos and that everything in nature has its parallel in man. Out of the Hermetic Theory of "man in microcosm" grew a vast body of correspondences surrounding the twelve signs of the zodiac: each sign governs a part of the body, rules over specific plants, herbs, colors, jewels, cities, animals, etc. The Hermetic Theory is also the basis for such divinatory arts as palm reading and physiognomy (facial reading).

HORARY CHART (From the Greek word *hora*, meaning "hour.") A special horoscope cast for the moment in which a specific question is asked, as opposed to a natal chart, which is cast for the moment of birth. The theory behind horary astrology is that there is a sympathy between the cosmos and the human mind; therefore when a question is asked, the positions of the planets at that moment can help to answer the question.

HORIZON In a horoscope, the line that intersects the circle from east to west and divides the circle into a top half and a bottom half. The line of the horizon in a horoscope connects the Ascendant and the Descendant.

HOROSCOPE (From the Greek words *hora*, meaning "hour," and *skopos*, meaning "watcher") A diagram of the heavens, specifically that part of the heavens called the zodiac, that charts the positions of the Sun, Moon, and planets as they appeared at a given moment and in relation to a given place on Earth. The word *horoscope* also refers to the analysis and interpretation of that chart. Nowadays, the term has also come to mean the predictions for the signs that appear in newspapers and magazines, as in one's "daily horoscope."

HOUSES The twelve divisions of a horoscope that represent different categories or areas of life. The twelve Houses of astrology are:

First House of Self
Second House of Money and Possessions
Third House of Communication
Fourth House of Beginnings and Home Life
Fifth House of Pleasure, Creativity, and Sex
Sixth House of Service and Health
Seventh House of Partnership and Marriage
Eighth House of Death and Regeneration
Ninth House of Mental Exploration and Long-Distance
    Travel
Tenth House of Career and Public Standing
Eleventh House of Friends and of Hopes and Wishes
Twelfth House of Secrets, Sorrows, and Self-Undoing

Currently, there is a great deal of discussion among astrologers about Houses, especially about *House division*. While there is little disagreement about the basic concept of Houses, there is some debate about the number of them. For example, the Irish sidereal astrologer Cyril Fagan favored eight Houses instead of twelve. A much more hotly debated subject, however, is House division, and there are at least twenty methods presently in use in the modern astrological world. Among the most popular House systems are the Placidus system, the Equal House system, the Koch system, the Campanus system, the Regiomontanus system, the Morinus system, and the Topocentric system. The House division used in the CD-ROM in this book is the Placidus system.

IMUM COELI (Latin for "lowest part of the heavens") *See* Nadir.

INGRESS The entrance of the Sun, Moon, or any of the planets into a sign of the zodiac.

JUPITER In astrology Jupiter is the planet of good fortune, expansion, abundance, and wisdom. The planet is known as the Greater Fortune (Venus is the Lesser Fortune). Jupiter rules the sign of Sagittarius, and at one time also ruled Pisces. (Pisces is now ruled by the planet Neptune, discovered in 1846.) When Jupiter is prominent in a birth chart, the native tends to be well-liked, cheerful, and successful in his or her career. Jupiter's influence can also incline a person toward extravagance and overconfidence.

KARMA The philosophical concept, originating in the Hindu and Buddhist religions, that a person's past and present deeds determine his or her destiny in this life and in lives yet to come. Karma is not an astrological term, but the doctrine of karma is used in esoteric astrology, a form of astrology and theosophy that stresses spiritual evolution and the unity of the soul with the cosmos.

LATITUDE The distance north or south of the Earth's equator, measured in degrees. Divisions of latitude are depicted on a map by horizontal parallel lines. The equator is 0° latitude; the North Pole is 90° North latitude; the South Pole is 90° South latitude. In order to calculate an exact birth chart, an astrologer must know both the latitude and longitude of the birthplace of the native.

LEO The fifth sign of the zodiac, which the Sun transits each year from approximately July 23 to August 22. Leo has as its element fire and is fixed in quality. The sign is symbolized by the Lion and ruled by the Sun. Leo natives are characterized as exuberant, creative, egocentric, and possessing a talent for showmanship.

LIBRA The seventh sign of the zodiac, which the Sun transits each year from approximately September 23 to October 22. Libra has as its element air and is cardinal in quality. The sign is symbolized by the Scales and ruled by the planet Venus. Libra natives are characterized as peaceable, artistic, socially adept, and able to see both sides of a question.

LONGITUDE The distance east or west on the Earth's surface, measured in degrees from the prime meridian, which is 0° longitude. The prime meridian (also called Greenwich Meridian) is a vertical line running from the North Pole to the South Pole that intersects Greenwich, England. Greenwich, England, is 0° longitude; New York City is 74° West longitude; Tokyo is 140° East longitude. Longitude also represents differences in *time*; each 15° of longitude represents one hour. When it is 12:00 noon in Greenwich, England (known as Greenwich Mean Time), it is 7:00 A.M. in New York City and 9:00 P.M. in Tokyo.

LUMINARIES The Sun and the Moon. In classical astrology, luminary was the more common term for the Sun or the Moon. Nowadays the word *planet* is applied to the Sun and Moon as well as to the planets.

LUNAR MANSIONS Division of the zodiac into twenty-eight (or sometimes twenty-seven) parts, based on the Moon's twenty-eight-day cycle (27.32166 days, to be exact). Lunar mansions are used primarily in the astrology of the Eastern world, e.g., Hindu, Chinese, Arab. Eastern astrology ("Children of the Moon") is based on the lunar cycle, whereas Western astrology ("Children of the Sun") is based on the solar cycle.

LUNAR RETURN CHART A horoscope cast for the moment in which the Moon returns to the exact degree it occupied at the moment of birth. A lunar return chart is used to forecast trends and events in the native's life during the coming month.

LUNATION The moment of conjunction of the Sun and the Moon, in other words, the New Moon. A lunation is also the period between one New Moon and the next, a time span of approximately twenty-nine days. Modern astrologers tend to use the term *lunation* to mean a New Moon, which in a horoscope marks the beginning of a new cycle.

MARS In astrology Mars is the planet of energy, force, sexual desire, and aggression. Mars rules the sign of Aries and is still considered by some astrologers to be the coruler of Scorpio, a sign that it once ruled entirely. (Scorpio is now ruled by the planet Pluto, discovered in 1930, and Mars's rulership of this sign has greatly diminished.) When Mars is prominent in a birth chart, the native tends to be active, enterprising, courageous, and passionate. Mars's influence can also incline a person toward impatience, anger, strife, and accident-proneness.

MASCULINE SIGNS The signs of the zodiac belonging to the fire and air triplicities, namely, Aries, Gemini, Leo, Libra, Sagittarius, and Aquarius. In astrology, masculine signs are characterized as energetic, outer-directed, and strong through action.

MEDICAL ASTROLOGY Astrology applied to questions of health, well-being, nutrition, and susceptibility to certain illnesses and diseases. Down through history astrology has been used as a tool in medicine. The signs of the zodiac and the planets correspond to various parts of the body, also to the illnesses connected with them, to diet needs, and to the glands and hormones. Although modern astrologers reject the notion of practicing medicine, the correlation between astrology and the human body is still a valid guide to maintaining physical well-being.

MEDIUM COELI (Latin for "middle of the heavens") *See* Midheaven.

MERCURY In astrology Mercury is the planet of communication, intelligence, perception, and intellectual energy. Mercury rules the two signs of Gemini and Virgo. When Mercury is prominent in a birth chart, the native tends to be clever, facile in speech, quick, high-strung, and likely to possess a good memory. Mercury's influence can also incline a person toward sarcasm, argumentativeness, coldness, and deceit.

MERIDIAN In a horoscope, the line that intersects the circle from north to south and divides the circle into a left-hand side and a right-hand side. The line of the meridian in a horoscope connects the Nadir and the Midheaven.

MIDHEAVEN (Also known as Medium Coeli, "middle of the heavens"; abbreviated in charts as M.C.) One of the four angles in a horoscope (the four most important points in a chart). The Midheaven, which marks the cusp of the Tenth House, is the point in a birth chart directly opposite the Nadir. The Midheaven represents ambition, ideals, and public image. Planets at or near the Midheaven indicate that the native is likely to make a mark on the outside world.

MODERN PLANETS Uranus, Neptune, and Pluto, referred to as modern because of their relatively recent discovery. Uranus was discovered in 1781, Neptune in 1846, and Pluto in 1930.

MOON In astrology the Moon represents emotions, instincts, sensitivity, and the unconscious. It is often called the feminine principle. The sign that the Moon was transiting at the time of birth, known as the Moon sign, is a most pervasive influence in a birth chart, second only in importance to the Sun sign. The Moon sign signifies the emotional, spontaneous, unconscious, and often hidden part of the personality. In the zodiac, the Moon rules the sign of Cancer.

MUNDANE ASTROLOGY (From the Latin word *mundus*, meaning "the world") The branch of astrology that assesses and forecasts world events, political movements, national occurrences, and cultural trends according to the planetary cycles.

MUTABLE One of the three qualities under which the signs of the zodiac are classified. The three qualities are cardinal, fixed, and mutable. Gemini, Virgo, Sagittarius, and Pisces are the mutable signs and comprise the mutable quadruplicity. In astrology, the mutable quality signifies adaptability, versatility, openness to change, and flexibility.

MUTUAL RECEPTION In a horoscope, a term used to describe the relationship between two planets when each is located in the sign that the other one rules. For example, if in a birth chart the Sun is in Libra and Venus is in Leo, the Sun and Venus are in mutual reception. This "visiting of each other's home" strengthens the power of the two planets, for they work in cooperation with each other.

NADIR (Also known as Imum Coeli, "lowest part of the heavens"; abbreviated in charts as I.C.) One of the four angles in a horoscope (the four most important points in a chart). The Nadir, which marks the cusp of the Fourth House, is the point in a birth chart directly opposite the Midheaven. The Nadir represents a person's beginnings and psychological roots: parents, home life, and what he or she inherits from previous generations. Planets at or near the Nadir indicate the unconscious motivation behind the native's actions.

NATAL CHART *See* Birth Chart.

NEPTUNE In astrology Neptune is the planet of mystery, illusion, imagination, and mysticism. Neptune, discovered in 1846, is the second of our modern planets. It rules the sign of Pisces (which was traditionally ruled by Jupiter). When Neptune is prominent in a birth chart, the native tends to be artistic, visionary and clairvoyant, and interested in spiritual matters. Neptune's influence can also incline a person toward escapism, difficulty in separating fantasy from reality, and psychic problems.

NODES The two points, north and south, where the orbit of the Moon or any of the planets intersects the ecliptic (the path of the Sun). Nodes usually refer to the Moon's nodes, called *lunar nodes*. In classical astrology, the north node (also called ascending node) was known as Caput Draconis, meaning "Dragon's Head," and the south node (also called descending node) was known as Cauda Draconis, meaning "Dragon's Tail." This referred to the imagery of a giant celestial dragon swallowing the Moon during its eclipses. In a birth chart, lunar nodes mark sensitive points, but there is much discussion currently among astrologers as to their exact meaning. Generally, the north node denotes the positive qualities with which you enter this life, and the south node the negative behavior you need to release. Some astrologers feel that the Moon's nodes pertain to relationships—the north node to forming ties and the south node to dissolving them.

OPPOSITION One of the major aspects, in which two or more planets are opposite each other in a horoscope, i.e., separated by 180° (or within 9° either way of 180°). The traditional view of an opposition in a chart is that it is an unharmonious aspect, one that produces tension and conflict. The modern view is that an opposition also brings challenge for growth and achievement, because the native must work through his or her problems and conflicts and thus gain maturity.

ORB (Also known as orb of influence) The slight variation in degrees within which an aspect is considered potent. For example, a trine is an aspect in which planets are 120° apart. An exact trine is 120°; the allowable orb for a trine is 9° either way of 120°. This means that if two planets are as few as 111° apart or as many as 129° apart, the trine is still effective in the horoscope.

ORBIT The path of any heavenly body in its revolution around another heavenly body. In our solar system, the Earth and planets describe orbits around the Sun. The Earth's orbit around the Sun is called the ecliptic. The ecliptic is also known as the path of the Sun around the Earth, but in reality it is the Earth that is orbiting around the Sun.

PART OF FORTUNE (Also known by its Latin name, Pars Fortuna) A point in a horoscope, arrived at by the calculation of an ancient Arabic mathematical formula in which the longitude of the Ascendant is added to the longitude of the Moon, and the longitude of the Sun is subtracted from that sum. The Part of Fortune in a birth chart is still considered by modern astrologers to be indicative of ease and good fortune. The activities of the sign and house in which the Part of Fortune appears are those in which the native finds success.

PISCES The twelfth sign of the zodiac, which the Sun transits each year from approximately February 19 to March 20. Pisces has as its element water and is mutable in quality. The sign is symbolized by Two Fishes and is ruled by the planet Neptune. Pisces natives are characterized as emotional, romantic, impressionable and adaptable, highly imaginative, and intuitive.

PLANET (From the Greek word *planetes*, meaning "wanderer") One of the heavenly bodies (except comets and meteors) that move around the Sun. From ancient times planets have been distinguished by their movement across the face of the fixed stars. In astrology, the word planets also includes the Sun and the Moon (traditionally called luminaries). In classical astrology there were seven *planets*: Sun, Moon, Mercury, Venus, Mars, Jupiter, and Saturn. Modern astrology has added three new planets discovered in the last two centuries: Uranus, Neptune, and Pluto. Each planet rules one (and in some cases two) astrological signs. The science of astrology is based on the premise that the movements of the planets significantly relate to human events, behavior, and personality. A horoscope is a chart of the positions of the planets at a given moment in time.

PLUTO In astrology Pluto is the planet of regenerative forces, of destruction, annihilation, and transformation. Pluto, discovered in 1930, is the third of our modern planets. It rules the sign of Scorpio (which was traditionally ruled by Mars). Pluto spends a great many years transiting each sign of the zodiac, and its influence is more obvious on a whole generation of people than on a single individual. However, when Pluto is prominent in a horoscope, the native's life will show marked reversal or change. Pluto also exhibits its power in a person's need to dominate and control. Its positive influence is seen in great leaders; its negative influence is seen in dictators, mobsters, and murderers.

POLARITY A group of two astrological signs, each sign opposite in the zodiac to the other sign; for example, Aries and Libra are a polarity. Also, the opposite sign in the zodiac; for example, Aquarius is Leo's polarity.

PRECESSION OF THE EQUINOXES The slow, constant shift of the vernal and autumnal equinoxes backward through the signs of the zodiac, caused by the earth's rotational tilt as it spins on its axis. The time span that it takes the vernal equinox to move through one sign, approximately 2,150 years, is known as an Astrological Age. Sidereal astrology is based on the theory that the dates of the Sun's entrance into each zodiacal sign should change along with the earth's shift in position. (*See* Age, Astrological. *See also* Sidereal Astrology.)

PROGRESSED HOROSCOPE A special chart cast for a specific date in the future and used in combination with the native's birth chart to predict and assess future trends and events. The most popular method of progressing a chart is the day-for-a-year formula, in which a horoscope is cast for a date that is as many days following a birth date as the years following a birth date that the person wishes to see.

QUADRANT (From the Latin word q[...] fourth") One of the four quarters of the [...] Each quadrant of the horoscope contains t[...] a birth chart, a preponderance of planets in an[...] four quadrants has specific meanings and interpr[...] depending on which quadrants are heavily populated[...]

QUADRUPLICITY A group of four astrological signs belonging to the same quality. There are three quadruplicities in the zodiac: the cardinal quadruplicity (Aries, Cancer, Libra, Capricorn); the fixed quadruplicity (Taurus, Leo, Scorpio, Aquarius); the mutable quadruplicity (Gemini, Virgo, Sagittarius, Pisces).

QUALITIES The three kinds of energy under which signs of the zodiac are classified. The three qualities are cardinal, fixed, and mutable. Cardinal signs are enterprising, active, initiating. Fixed signs are persistent, determined, and resourceful. Mutable signs are versatile, adaptable, and flexible.

QUINCUNX One of the minor aspects, in which two or more planets in a birth chart are 150° apart (or within 2° either way of 150°). The quincunx was originally classified as mildly adverse; some modern astrologers think it more powerful than at first regarded.

RECTIFICATION The art of correcting a birth chart of unknown or uncertain birth time, using as guideposts major events in the life of the native and/or dominant personality traits that correspond to planetary aspects governing such events and traits.

RETROGRADE The apparent backward motion of a planet traveling through the zodiac. (The Sun and Moon are never retrograde.) In reality, planets in our solar system do

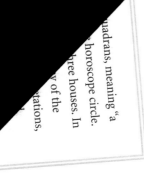

...quadrans, meaning "a horoscope circle. ...ree houses. In ...y of the ...ations,

...hey only seem to do ...n here on earth. Ret-
...to looking through ...ond train that is ...e slowly. The slower-
...backward, although ...al astrology a retro-
...as having a nega-
...ider retrograde ...aving an influence ...n life.

...ING SIGN The sign of the zodiac that was rising on the eastern horizon at the moment of birth. The Rising sign (or Ascendant) characterizes a person's outward approach to life. (*See also* Ascendant.)

RULER (Also known as ruling planet) 1. The planet that has dominion over a specific astrological sign, for example, Mars is the ruler of Aries. In classical astrology rulership of the twelve signs was divided among seven planets. Since the eighteenth century three signs have been reassigned to the three modern planets. The list of rulerships is as follows:

Aries ruled by Mars
Taurus ruled by Venus
Gemini ruled by Mercury
Cancer ruled by the Moon
Leo ruled by the Sun
Virgo ruled by Mercury
Libra ruled by Venus
Scorpio ruled by Pluto (traditionally ruled by Mars)
Sagittarius ruled by Jupiter
Capricorn ruled by Saturn

[handwritten note: Mine are in 12th—Gem, 12th Gem]

Aquarius ruled by Uranus (traditionally ruled by Saturn)
Pisces ruled by Neptune (traditionally ruled by Jupiter)

2. In a birth chart, the planet that rules the Rising sign (Ascendant) is said to be the ruling planet of the chart.

SAGITTARIUS The ninth sign of the zodiac, which the Sun transits each year from approximately November 22 to December 21. Sagittarius has as its element fire and is mutable in quality. The sign is symbolized by the Archer and ruled by the planet Jupiter. Sagittarius natives are characterized as freedom-loving, expansive, seekers of knowledge, and open to new ideas and exploration.

SATURN In astrology Saturn is the planet of discipline, responsibility, restriction, and limitation. The planet has been called the Celestial Taskmaster. Saturn rules the sign of Capricorn, and at one time also ruled Aquarius. (Aquarius is now ruled by the planet Uranus, discovered in 1781.) When Saturn is prominent in a birth chart the native tends to be diligent, determined, reliable, and industrious. Saturn's influence can also incline a person toward pessimism, inflexibility, and selfishness.

SCORPIO The eighth sign of the zodiac, which the Sun transits each year from approximately October 23 to November 21. Scorpio has as its element water and is fixed in quality. The sign is symbolized by the Scorpion and ruled by the planet Pluto. (Some astrologers still consider Scorpio's traditional ruler, Mars, to be its coruler.) Scorpio natives are characterized as sensual and secretive, intensely emotional, imaginative, and possessing psychic ability.

SEMISEXTILE One of the minor aspects, in which two or more planets in a birth chart are 30° apart (or within 2°

either way of 30°). Classified as mildly favorable, much less powerful than a sextile.

SEMISQUARE One of the minor aspects, in which two or more planets in a birth chart are 45° apart (or within 2° either way of 45°). Classified as mildly adverse, less powerful than a square.

SESQUISQUARE (Also known as Sesquiquadrate) One of the minor aspects, in which two or more planets in a birth chart are 135° apart (or within 2° either way of 135°). Classified as mildly adverse, similar in influence to a semisquare.

SEXTILE One of the major aspects, in which two or more planets in a birth chart are 60° apart (or within 6° either way of 60°). Classified by both ancient and modern astrologers as harmonious and favorable. A sextile brings opportunity, but the native must make an effort in order to realize its benefits.

SIDEREAL ASTROLOGY (From the Latin word *sidus*, meaning "star") A school of astrology that bases its zodiac on the actual star groupings, or constellations, intersected by the ecliptic. Because of the Earth's slow, constant tilt as it turns on its axis, the vernal and autumnal equinoxes slowly travel through the constellations of the zodiac—a phenomenon known as the precession of the equinoxes. Siderealists believe that the Sun's entrance into the signs of the zodiac should be based on the precession of the equinoxes, and therefore their zodiac slowly changes along with the Earth's shift in position. Thus, a person born in Aries according to traditional (tropical) astrology, would be currently regarded by siderealists as a native of Pisces.

SIGNS OF THE ZODIAC (Also known as astrological signs) The twelve 30° segments of the zodiac, namely: Aries, Taurus, Gemini, Cancer, Leo, Virgo, Libra, Scorpio, Sagittarius, Capricorn, Aquarius, and Pisces. The signs of the zodiac are based on the band of constellations in the heavens through which the Sun travels on its apparent yearly journey around the earth. Unlike the actual constellations in the sky, the signs are of equal size and marked by definite 30° boundaries.

SOLAR CHART A horoscope in which the Sun sign is also considered to be the Rising sign (Ascendant). This horoscope is used when the birth time is unknown. In a solar chart the Sun sign also becomes the First House, and thus the houses placed around the chart are known as solar houses. For many astrologers a solar chart is a useful horoscope that enables one to look at the overall pattern of a personality and to ascertain general trends, especially when used in combination with a natal chart. (See also Birth Chart.)

SOLAR RETURN CHART A horoscope cast for the moment in which the Sun returns to the exact degree it occupied at the moment of birth. A solar return chart is used to assess and predict trends and events in the native's life during the coming year.

SOLSTICES (From the Latin words *sol*, meaning "Sun" and *sistere*, meaning "to stand still") The two points during the year when the Sun is at its farthest distance from the celestial equator. Upon reaching these points the Sun appears to stand still. The summer solstice occurs when the Sun enters the sign of Cancer, and this is the longest day of the year. The winter solstice occurs when the Sun enters the sign of Capricorn, and this is the shortest day of the year.

SQUARE One of the major aspects, in which two or more planets in a birth chart are 90° apart (or within 9° either way of 90°). Originally classified as malefic, squares are now considered by modern astrologers to be indicative of conflict or challenge that spurs the native to build character.

STATIONARY The apparent unmoving or standing-still position of a planet in orbit just prior to its reversing from direct motion to retrograde motion, or from retrograde motion to direct motion. Like retrograde motion, the stationary position of a planet is an illusion due to the angle of observation from the Earth. In a birth chart, stationary planets are considered very strong in their influence. (*See also* Direct and Retrograde.)

SUCCEDENT (From the Latin word *succedere*, meaning "to follow") The four Houses in a horoscope that immediately follow Angular Houses. Succedent Houses are the Second, Fifth, Eighth, and Eleventh Houses. In a birth chart, planets in any of these houses indicate that the native has strong willpower and fixity of purpose.

SUN In astrology the Sun represents the ego, individuality, the power of self, and the conscious will. The sign that the Sun was transiting at the time of birth, known as the Sun sign, is the most pervasive influence in a birth chart. The Sun sign governs a person's distinctive style and drive to fulfill his or her goals. In many ways the Sun sign determines how the world regards the native. In the zodiac, the Sun rules the sign of Leo.

SUN SIGN ASTROLOGY A term used to describe the form of astrology that concerns itself solely with Sun signs. This is, of course, an oversimplification of the science of as-trology. Daily newspaper horoscopes and many widely-read books are based entirely on Sun signs.

TABLE OF HOUSES A table used in plotting a birth chart that shows the signs and degrees of the Houses to be placed around the horoscope wheel for different latitudes (of birthplace) and birth times. There are various tables of Houses for the different House systems in use.

TAURUS The second sign of the zodiac, which the Sun transits each year from approximately April 20 to May 20. Taurus has as its element earth and is fixed in quality. The sign is symbolized by the Bull and ruled by the planet Venus. Taurus natives are characterized as practical, determined, artistic and loving, stubborn and resistant to change.

TRANSIT (From the Latin word *transitus*, meaning "the act of going across") 1. The passage of the Sun, Moon, or planet through a sign of the zodiac, for example, the transit of Venus through Aries.

2. The passage of the Sun, Moon, or planet through the same position it or another planet occupies in a horoscope. For example, if in a birth chart the Sun were at 15° Aries and next month Jupiter is to be in 15° Aries, this Jupiter transit next month augurs a fortunate financial trend for the native of the chart.

TRINE One of the major aspects, in which two or more planets in a birth chart are 120° apart (or within 9° either way of 120°). A trine is the most beneficial and harmonious aspect, bringing advantage and ease. Many astrologers feel, however, that trines may be conducive to complacency or laziness, because the native does not have to make sufficient effort in order to realize success.

TRIPLICITY A group of three astrological signs all belonging to the same element. There are four triplicities in the zodiac: the fire triplicity (Aries, Leo, Sagittarius); the earth triplicity (Taurus, Virgo, Capricorn); the air triplicity (Gemini, Libra, Aquarius); and the water triplicity (Cancer, Scorpio, Pisces).

T-SQUARE An unusual aspect-pattern in a birth chart that consists of three planets, two of them in opposition to each other and the third halfway between the two (thus forming a square to each of the two planets). A T-square can be a difficult influence in a birth chart, signifying tension, obstruction, and conflict. However, it is an energizing influence that motivates the native to fight and to resolve problems. A T-square appears in many charts of famous men and women.

URANUS In astrology Uranus is the planet of change, originality, upheaval, and revolution. Uranus, discovered in 1781, is the first of our modern planets. It rules the sign of Aquarius (which was traditionally ruled by Saturn). When Uranus is prominent in a birth chart the native tends to be inventive, independent, and of an unconventional turn of mind. Uranus's influence can also incline a person toward eccentricity, rebelliousness, and fanaticism.

VENUS In astrology Venus is the planet of love, affection, art, beauty, esthetics, and pleasure. Venus rules the two signs of Taurus and Libra. When Venus is prominent in a birth chart the native tends to be friendly, flirtatious, and socially adept, and to possess great personal charm. Venus's influence can also incline a person toward fickleness, extravagance and overindulgence, vanity and narcissism.

VIRGO The sixth sign of the zodiac, which the Sun transits each year from approximately August 23 to September 22. Virgo has as its element earth and is mutable in quality. The sign is symbolized by the Virgin and ruled by the planet Mercury. Virgo natives are characterized as industrious, discriminating, logical and analytical, intellectual, and having a tendency to be critical.

WATER One of the four elements (fire, earth, air, and water) under which signs of the zodiac are classified. Cancer, Scorpio, and Pisces are the water signs and comprise the water triplicity. In astrology, water signifies emotion, imagination, sensitivity, and spirituality.

ZODIAC (From the Greek word *zodiakos*, meaning "circle of animals") A narrow band of the heavens circling the Earth that is divided into twelve signs: Aries, Taurus, Gemini, Cancer, Leo, Virgo, Libra, Scorpio, Sagittarius, Capricorn, Aquarius, and Pisces. These signs correspond to the twelve constellations (groups of stars) of the same name that are contained within this narrow band of the zodiac, but the signs and the constellations are not the same. Whereas the constellations are of different sizes, the signs of the zodiac are equal segments of 30° each, forming a complete 360° circle. The center of the zodiac band is marked by the path of the Sun (the ecliptic). The Sun, Moon, and all the planets except Pluto orbit within the circle of the zodiac.

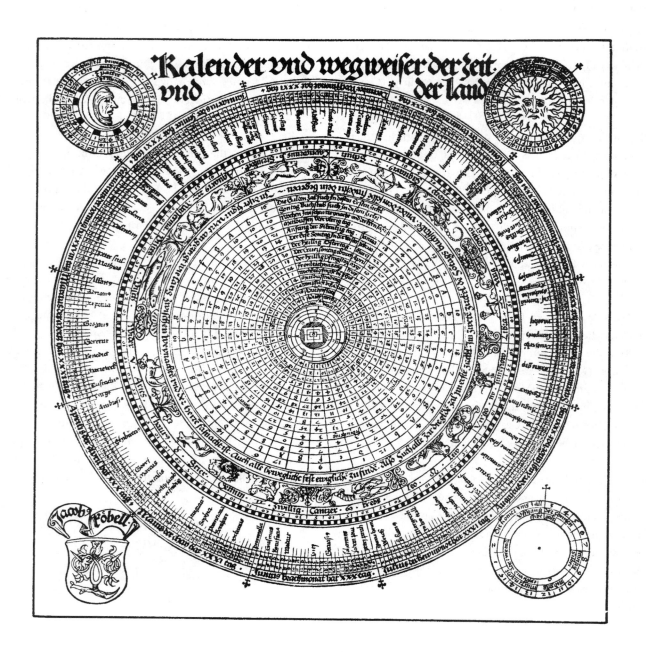

Part Seven

ASTROLOGICAL TABLES FOR THE YEARS 1900–2100

What Is Your Exact Sun Sign?

THE SUN TRAVELS through each sign of the zodiac at approximately the same time every year. The dates on which the Sun enters and leaves each sign are those that you usually see published in books and newspapers. For example, you may read that the Sun is in the sign of Aries each year from March 21 through April 19.

However, these dates are *not* exact. Some years the Sun will enter or leave a sign one or two days before or after the dates you see published. This is because the Sun does not travel at the exact same speed year in and year out. There are slight changes in its forward motion due to the position of the Earth. Also, at certain times of the year the Sun travels faster than at other times (for example, the Sun is traveling four minutes faster per day in early January than in early June).

These variations are minor, but even the difference of a day or two may cause confusion for the thousands of people whose birthdays fall near the beginning or end of a zodiacal sign.*

The following Sun Tables will show you your exact Sun sign. To use these tables, all you need to do is look up the year and month of your birthday. You will see exactly what day of that month the Sun moved into a particular astrological sign.

If your birthday falls earlier in the month than that day, the beginning of your Sun sign is in the previous month. If your birthday falls after the day on which the Sun moved into a new sign, that new sign is your Sun sign.

Example: You were born on August 4, 1970. Find the column marked *1970*, and place a ruler along the line marked *AUG.* You will see that the Sun moved into Virgo on the 23rd of August in 1970. Since you were born on the 4th of August, look at the previous month to find the Sun's position. You will see that the Sun moved into Leo on the 23rd of July and did not move into Virgo until the 23rd of August. Therefore, your Sun sign is Leo.

Example: You were born on October 29, 1980. Find the column marked *1980*, and place a ruler along the line marked *OCT.* You will see that the Sun moved into Scorpio on the 23rd of October in 1980. Since you were born on the 29th of October, your Sun sign is Scorpio.

Example: You were born on January 20, 1963. Find the column marked *1963*, and place a ruler along the line marked *JAN.* You will see that the Sun moved into Aquarius on the 20th of January in 1963. Your Sun sign, therefore, is Aquarius.

*If your birthday falls into this category, you should definitely use the enclosed CD-ROM. It will tell you your *exact* Sun sign (and the exact degree of this sign your Sun is in). You are known as having been "born on the cusp." Read more about yourself and your special qualities in the section on Cusps (beginning on page 159).

Sun Tables 1900–1914

	1900	1901	1902	1903	1904	1905	1906	1907	1908	1909	1910	1911	1912	1913	1914
JAN	20 AQU	20 AQU	20 AQU	21 AQU	21 AQU	20 AQU	20 AQU	21 AQU	21 AQU	20 AQU	20 AQU	20 AQU	20 AQU	20 AQU	20 AQU
FEB	18 PIS	19 PIS	19 PIS	19 PIS	19 PIS	19 PIS	19 PIS	19 PIS	19 PIS	19 PIS	19 PIS	19 PIS	19 PIS	19 PIS	19 PIS
MAR	20 ARI	21 ARI	21 ARI	21 ARI	20 ARI	21 ARI	21 ARI	21 ARI	20 ARI	21 ARI	21 ARI	21 ARI	21 ARI	20 ARI	21 ARI
APR	20 TAU	20 TAU	20 TAU	21 TAU	20 TAU	20 TAU	21 TAU	21 TAU	20 TAU	21 TAU	20 TAU	21 TAU	20 TAU	20 TAU	20 TAU
MAY	21 GEM	21 GEM	21 GEM	22 GEM	21 GEM	21 GEM	21 GEM	21 GEM	22 GEM	21 GEM	21 GEM	21 GEM	22 GEM	21 GEM	21 GEM
JUN	21 CAN	21 CAN	22 CAN	22 CAN	21 CAN	21 CAN	21 CAN	22 CAN	22 CAN	21 CAN	22 CAN	22 CAN	22 CAN	21 CAN	22 CAN
JUL	23 LEO	23 LEO	23 LEO	23 LEO	23 LEO	23 LEO	23 LEO	23 LEO	23 LEO	23 LEO	23 LEO	23 LEO	23 LEO	23 LEO	23 LEO
AUG	23 VIR	23 VIR	23 VIR	24 VIR	23 VIR	23 VIR	23 VIR	23 VIR	24 VIR	23 VIR	23 VIR	23 VIR	24 VIR	23 VIR	23 VIR
SEP	23 LIB	23 LIB	23 LIB	24 LIB	23 LIB	23 LIB	23 LIB	24 LIB	24 LIB	23 LIB	23 LIB	23 LIB	24 LIB	23 LIB	23 LIB
OCT	23 SCO	23 SCO	24 SCO	24 SCO	24 SCO	23 SCO	23 SCO	24 SCO	24 SCO	24 SCO	23 SCO	23 SCO	24 SCO	23 SCO	24 SCO
NOV	22 SAG	22 SAG	23 SAG	23 SAG	22 SAG	22 SAG	22 SAG	23 SAG	23 SAG	22 SAG	22 SAG	22 SAG	23 SAG	22 SAG	22 SAG
DEC	22 CAP	22 CAP	22 CAP	22 CAP	22 CAP	22 CAP	22 CAP	22 CAP	22 CAP	22 CAP	22 CAP	22 CAP	22 CAP	22 CAP	22 CAP

Sun Tables 1915–1929

	1915	1916	1917	1918	1919	1920	1921	1922	1923	1924	1925	1926	1927	1928	1929
JAN	21 AQU	21 AQU	20 AQU	20 AQU	20 AQU	21 AQU	20 AQU	20 AQU	20 AQU	21 AQU	20 AQU	20 AQU	20 AQU	20 AQU	20 AQU
FEB	19 PIS	19 PIS	19 PIS	19 PIS	19 PIS	19 PIS	19 PIS	19 PIS	19 PIS	19 PIS	18 PIS	19 PIS	19 PIS	19 PIS	18 PIS
MAR	21 ARI	20 ARI	21 ARI	21 ARI	21 ARI	20 ARI	20 ARI	21 ARI	21 ARI	20 ARI	20 ARI	21 ARI	21 ARI	20 ARI	20 ARI
APR	21 TAU	20 TAU	20 TAU	20 TAU	20 TAU	20 TAU	20 TAU	20 TAU	20 TAU	20 TAU	20 TAU	20 TAU	20 TAU	20 TAU	20 TAU
MAY	22 GEM	21 GEM	21 GEM	21 GEM	21 GEM	22 GEM	21 GEM	21 GEM	21 GEM	21 GEM	21 GEM	21 GEM	21 GEM	21 GEM	21 GEM
JUN	22 CAN	21 CAN	21 CAN	22 CAN	22 CAN	21 CAN	21 CAN	22 CAN	22 CAN	22 CAN	21 CAN	22 CAN	22 CAN	22 CAN	21 CAN
JUL	23 LEO	23 LEO	23 LEO	23 LEO	23 LEO	23 LEO	23 LEO	23 LEO	23 LEO	22 LEO	23 LEO	23 LEO	23 LEO	22 LEO	23 LEO
AUG	24 VIR	23 VIR	23 VIR	23 VIR	24 VIR	23 VIR	23 VIR	23 VIR	24 VIR	23 VIR	23 VIR	23 VIR	24 VIR	23 VIR	23 VIR
SEP	24 LIB	23 LIB	23 LIB	23 LIB	23 LIB	23 LIB	23 LIB	23 LIB	23 LIB	23 LIB	23 LIB	23 LIB	23 LIB	23 LIB	23 LIB
OCT	24 SCO	23 SCO	23 SCO	24 SCO	24 SCO	23 SCO	23 SCO	23 SCO	24 SCO	23 SCO	23 SCO	24 SCO	24 SCO	23 SCO	23 SCO
NOV	23 SAG	22 SAG	22 SAG	22 SAG	23 SAG	22 SAG	22 SAG	22 SAG	23 SAG	22 SAG	22 SAG	22 SAG	23 SAG	22 SAG	22 SAG
DEC	22 CAP	21 CAP	22 CAP	22 CAP	22 CAP	21 CAP	22 CAP	22 CAP	22 CAP	21 CAP	22 CAP	22 CAP	22 CAP	21 CAP	22 CAP

Sun Tables 1930–1944

	1930	1931	1932	1933	1934	1935	1936	1937	1938	1939	1940	1941	1942	1943	1944
JAN	20 AQU	20 AQU	21 AQU	20 AQU	20 AQU	20 AQU	21 AQU	20 AQU	20 AQU	20 AQU	21 AQU	20 AQU	20 AQU	20 AQU	21 AQU
FEB	19 PIS	19 PIS	19 PIS	18 PIS	19 PIS	19 PIS	19 PIS	18 PIS	19 PIS	19 PIS	19 PIS	18 PIS	19 PIS	19 PIS	19 PIS
MAR	21 ARI	21 ARI	20 ARI	20 ARI	21 ARI	21 ARI	20 ARI	20 ARI	21 ARI	21 ARI	20 ARI	20 ARI	21 ARI	21 ARI	20 ARI
APR	20 TAU	20 TAU	20 TAU	20 TAU	20 TAU	20 TAU	20 TAU	20 TAU	20 TAU	20 TAU	20 TAU	20 TAU	20 TAU	20 TAU	20 TAU
MAY	21 GEM	21 GEM	21 GEM	21 GEM	21 GEM	21 GEM	21 GEM	21 GEM	21 GEM	21 GEM	21 GEM	21 GEM	21 GEM	21 GEM	21 GEM
JUN	21 CAN	22 CAN	21 CAN	21 CAN	21 CAN	21 CAN	22 CAN	21 CAN	21 CAN	21 CAN	21 CAN	21 CAN	21 CAN	22 CAN	21 CAN
JUL	23 LEO	23 LEO	23 LEO	23 LEO	23 LEO	23 LEO	23 LEO	22 LEO	23 LEO	23 LEO	23 LEO	22 LEO	23 LEO	23 LEO	22 LEO
AUG	23 VIR	23 VIR	23 VIR	23 VIR	23 VIR	23 VIR	23 VIR	23 VIR	23 VIR	23 VIR	23 VIR	23 VIR	23 VIR	23 VIR	23 VIR
SEP	23 LIB	23 LIB	23 LIB	23 LIB	23 LIB	23 LIB	23 LIB	23 LIB	23 LIB	23 LIB	23 LIB	23 LIB	23 LIB	23 LIB	23 LIB
OCT	23 SCO	24 SCO	23 SCO	23 SCO	23 SCO	24 SCO	23 SCO	23 SCO	23 SCO	24 SCO	23 SCO	23 SCO	23 SCO	24 SCO	23 SCO
NOV	22 SAG	23 SAG	22 SAG	22 SAG	22 SAG	23 SAG	22 SAG	22 SAG	22 SAG	22 SAG	22 SAG	22 SAG	22 SAG	23 SAG	22 SAG
DEC	22 CAP	22 CAP	21 CAP	22 CAP	22 CAP	22 CAP	21 CAP	22 CAP	22 CAP	22 CAP	21 CAP	22 CAP	22 CAP	22 CAP	21 CAP

Sun Tables 1945–1959

	1945	1946	1947	1948	1949	1950	1951	1952	1953	1954	1955	1956	1957	1958	1959
JAN	20 AQU	20 AQU	20 AQU	20 AQU	20 AQU	20 AQU	20 AQU	20 AQU	20 AQU	20 AQU	20 AQU	20 AQU	20 AQU	20 AQU	20 AQU
FEB	18 PIS	19 PIS	19 PIS	19 PIS	18 PIS	19 PIS	19 PIS	19 PIS	18 PIS	19 PIS	19 PIS	19 PIS	18 PIS	18 PIS	19 PIS
MAR	20 ARI	21 ARI	21 ARI	20 ARI	20 ARI	21 ARI	21 ARI	20 ARI	20 ARI	20 ARI	21 ARI	20 ARI	20 ARI	20 ARI	21 ARI
APR	20 TAU	20 TAU	20 TAU	20 TAU	20 TAU	20 TAU	21 TAU	19 TAU	20 TAU	20 TAU	21 TAU	20 TAU	20 TAU	20 TAU	20 TAU
MAY	21 GEM	21 GEM	21 GEM	20 GEM	21 GEM	21 GEM	21 GEM	20 GEM	21 GEM	21 GEM	21 GEM	20 GEM	21 GEM	21 GEM	21 GEM
JUN	21 CAN	21 CAN	22 CAN	21 CAN	21 CAN	21 CAN	21 CAN	21 CAN	21 CAN	21 CAN	21 CAN	21 CAN	21 CAN	21 CAN	21 CAN
JUL	23 LEO	23 LEO	23 LEO	22 LEO	23 LEO	23 LEO	23 LEO	22 LEO	23 LEO	23 LEO	23 LEO	22 LEO	22 LEO	23 LEO	23 LEO
AUG	23 VIR	23 VIR	23 VIR	23 VIR	23 VIR	23 VIR	23 VIR	23 VIR	23 VIR	23 VIR	23 VIR	23 VIR	23 VIR	23 VIR	23 VIR
SEP	23 LIB	23 LIB	23 LIB	22 LIB	23 LIB	23 LIB	23 LIB	22 LIB	23 LIB	23 LIB	23 LIB	22 LIB	23 LIB	23 LIB	23 LIB
OCT	23 SCO	23 SCO	24 SCO	23 SCO	23 SCO	23 SCO	24 SCO	23 SCO	23 SCO	23 SCO	24 SCO	23 SCO	23 SCO	23 SCO	24 SCO
NOV	22 SAG	22 SAG	22 SAG	22 SAG	22 SAG	22 SAG	22 SAG	22 SAG	22 SAG	22 SAG	22 SAG	22 SAG	22 SAG	22 SAG	22 SAG
DEC	22 CAP	22 CAP	22 CAP	21 CAP	22 CAP	22 CAP	22 CAP	21 CAP	22 CAP	22 CAP	22 CAP	21 CAP	21 CAP	22 CAP	22 CAP

Sun Tables 1960–1974

	1960	1961	1962	1963	1964	1965	1966	1967	1968	1969	1970	1971	1972	1973	1974
JAN	20 AQU	20 AQU	20 AQU	20 AQU	20 AQU	20 AQU	20 AQU	20 AQU	20 AQU	20 AQU	20 AQU	20 AQU	20 AQU	20 AQU	20 AQU
FEB	19 PIS	18 PIS	18 PIS	19 PIS	19 PIS	18 PIS	18 PIS	19 PIS	19 PIS	18 PIS	18 PIS	19 PIS	19 PIS	18 PIS	18 PIS
MAR	20 ARI	20 ARI	20 ARI	21 ARI	20 ARI	20 ARI	20 ARI	21 ARI	20 ARI	20 ARI	20 ARI	21 ARI	20 ARI	20 ARI	20 ARI
APR	19 TAU	20 TAU	20 TAU	20 TAU	19 TAU	20 TAU	20 TAU	20 TAU	19 TAU	20 TAU	20 TAU	20 TAU	19 TAU	20 TAU	20 TAU
MAY	20 GEM	21 GEM	21 GEM	21 GEM	20 GEM	21 GEM	21 GEM	21 GEM	20 GEM	21 GEM	21 GEM	21 GEM	20 GEM	21 GEM	21 GEM
JUN	21 CAN	21 CAN	21 CAN	22 CAN	21 CAN	21 CAN	21 CAN	22 CAN	21 CAN	21 CAN	21 CAN	22 CAN	21 CAN	21 CAN	21 CAN
JUL	22 LEO	22 LEO	22 LEO	23 LEO	22 LEO	22 LEO	23 LEO	23 LEO	22 LEO	22 LEO	23 LEO	23 LEO	22 LEO	22 LEO	23 LEO
AUG	22 VIR	23 VIR	23 VIR	23 VIR	22 VIR	23 VIR	23 VIR	23 VIR	22 VIR	23 VIR	23 VIR	23 VIR	22 VIR	23 VIR	23 VIR
SEP	22 LIB	23 LIB	23 LIB	23 LIB	22 LIB	23 LIB	23 LIB	23 LIB	22 LIB	23 LIB	23 LIB	23 LIB	22 LIB	23 LIB	23 LIB
OCT	23 SCO	23 SCO	23 SCO	23 SCO	23 SCO	23 SCO	23 SCO	23 SCO	23 SCO	23 SCO	23 SCO	23 SCO	23 SCO	23 SCO	23 SCO
NOV	22 SAG	22 SAG	22 SAG	22 SAG	22 SAG	22 SAG	22 SAG	22 SAG	22 SAG	22 SAG	22 SAG	22 SAG	22 SAG	22 SAG	22 SAG
DEC	21 CAP	21 CAP	22 CAP	22 CAP	21 CAP	21 CAP	22 CAP	22 CAP	21 CAP	21 CAP	22 CAP	22 CAP	21 CAP	21 CAP	22 CAP

	1975	1976	1977	1978	1979	1980	1981	1982	1983	1984	1985	1986	1987	1988	1989
JAN	20 AQU	20 AQU	20 AQU	20 AQU	20 AQU	20 AQU	19 AQU	19 AQU	20 AQU	20 AQU	19 AQU	20 AQU	20 AQU	20 AQU	19 AQU
FEB	19 PIS	19 PIS	18 PIS	18 PIS	19 PIS	19 PIS	18 PIS	18 PIS	19 PIS	19 PIS	18 PIS	18 PIS	19 PIS	19 PIS	18 PIS
MAR	21 ARI	20 ARI	20 ARI	20 ARI	21 ARI	20 ARI	20 ARI	20 ARI	21 ARI	20 ARI	20 ARI	20 ARI	21 ARI	20 ARI	20 ARI
APR	20 TAU	19 TAU	20 TAU	20 TAU	20 TAU	19 TAU	20 TAU	20 TAU	20 TAU	19 TAU	20 TAU	20 TAU	20 TAU	19 TAU	19 TAU
MAY	21 GEM	20 GEM	21 GEM	21 GEM	21 GEM	20 GEM	20 GEM	21 GEM	21 GEM	20 GEM	20 GEM	21 GEM	21 GEM	20 GEM	20 GEM
JUN	21 CAN	21 CAN	21 CAN	21 CAN	21 CAN	21 CAN	21 CAN	21 CAN	21 CAN	21 CAN	21 CAN	21 CAN	21 CAN	20 CAN	21 CAN
JUL	23 LEO	22 LEO	22 LEO	23 LEO	23 LEO	22 LEO	22 LEO	22 LEO	23 LEO	23 LEO	22 LEO	22 LEO	23 LEO	22 LEO	22 LEO
AUG	23 VIR	22 VIR	23 VIR	23 VIR	23 VIR	22 VIR	23 VIR	23 VIR	23 VIR	23 VIR	23 VIR	23 VIR	23 VIR	22 VIR	23 VIR
SEP	23 LIB	22 LIB	22 LIB	23 LIB	23 LIB	22 LIB	23 LIB	22 LIB	23 LIB	22 LIB	22 LIB	23 LIB	23 LIB	22 LIB	22 LIB
OCT	23 SCO	23 SCO	23 SCO	23 SCO	23 SCO	23 SCO	23 SCO	23 SCO	23 SCO	23 SCO	23 SCO	23 SCO	23 SCO	23 SCO	23 SCO
NOV	22 SAG	22 SAG	22 SAG	22 SAG	22 SAG	22 SAG	22 SAG	22 SAG	22 SAG	22 SAG	21 SAG	22 SAG	22 SAG	21 SAG	22 SAG
DEC	22 CAP	21 CAP	21 CAP	22 CAP	22 CAP	21 CAP	21 CAP	22 CAP	22 CAP	21 CAP	21 CAP	21 CAP	22 CAP	21 CAP	21 CAP

	1990	1991	1992	1993	1994	1995	1996	1997	1998	1999	2000	2001	2002	2003	2004
JAN	20 AQU	20 AQU	20 AQU	19 AQU	20 AQU	20 AQU	20 AQU	19 AQU	20 AQU	20 AQU	20 AQU	20 AQU	20 AQU	20 AQU	20 AQU
FEB	18 PIS	18 PIS	19 PIS	18 PIS	18 PIS	18 PIS	19 PIS	18 PIS	18 PIS	18 PIS	19 PIS	18 PIS	18 PIS	18 PIS	19 PIS
MAR	20 ARI	20 ARI	20 ARI	20 ARI	20 ARI	20 ARI	20 ARI	20 ARI	20 ARI	20 ARI	20 ARI	20 ARI	20 ARI	20 ARI	20 ARI
APR	20 TAU	20 TAU	19 TAU	19 TAU	20 TAU	20 TAU	19 TAU	19 TAU	20 TAU	20 TAU	19 TAU	19 TAU	20 TAU	20 TAU	19 TAU
MAY	21 GEM	21 GEM	20 GEM	20 GEM	21 GEM	21 GEM	20 GEM	20 GEM	21 GEM	21 GEM	20 GEM	20 GEM	21 GEM	21 GEM	20 GEM
JUN	21 CAN	21 CAN	21 CAN	21 CAN	21 CAN	21 CAN	21 CAN	21 CAN	21 CAN	21 CAN	21 CAN	21 CAN	21 CAN	21 CAN	21 CAN
JUL	22 LEO	23 LEO	22 LEO	22 LEO	22 LEO	23 LEO	22 LEO	22 LEO	22 LEO	23 LEO	22 LEO	22 LEO	22 LEO	23 LEO	22 LEO
AUG	23 VIR	23 VIR	22 VIR	22 VIR	23 VIR	23 VIR	22 VIR	22 VIR	23 VIR	23 VIR	22 VIR	22 VIR	23 VIR	23 VIR	22 VIR
SEP	23 LIB	23 LIB	22 LIB	22 LIB	23 LIB	23 LIB	22 LIB	22 LIB	23 LIB	23 LIB	22 LIB	22 LIB	23 LIB	23 LIB	22 LIB
OCT	23 SCO	23 SCO	22 SCO	23 SCO	23 SCO	23 SCO	22 SCO	23 SCO	23 SCO	23 SCO	22 SCO	23 SCO	23 SCO	23 SCO	22 SCO
NOV	22 SAG	22 SAG	22 SAG	22 SAG	22 SAG	22 SAG	21 SAG	22 SAG	22 SAG	22 SAG	22 SAG	22 SAG	22 SAG	22 SAG	21 SAG
DEC	21 CAP	22 CAP	21 CAP	21 CAP	21 CAP	22 CAP	21 CAP	21 CAP	21 CAP	22 CAP	21 CAP	21 CAP	21 CAP	22 CAP	21 CAP

	2005	2006	2007	2008	2009	2010	2011	2012	2013	2014	2015	2016	2017	2018	2019
JAN	19 AQU	20 AQU	20 AQU	20 AQU	19 AQU	20 AQU	20 AQU	20 AQU	19 AQU	20 AQU	20 AQU	20 AQU	19 AQU	20 AQU	20 AQU
FEB	18 PIS	18 PIS	18 PIS	19 PIS	18 PIS	18 PIS	18 PIS	19 PIS	18 PIS	18 PIS	18 PIS	19 PIS	18 PIS	18 PIS	18 PIS
MAR	20 ARI	20 ARI	20 ARI	20 ARI	20 ARI	20 ARI	20 ARI	20 ARI	20 ARI	20 ARI	20 ARI	20 ARI	20 ARI	20 ARI	20 ARI
APR	19 TAU	20 TAU	20 TAU	19 TAU	19 TAU	20 TAU	20 TAU	19 TAU	19 TAU	20 TAU	20 TAU	19 TAU	19 TAU	20 TAU	20 TAU
MAY	20 GEM	21 GEM	21 GEM	20 GEM	20 GEM	21 GEM	21 GEM	20 GEM	20 GEM	21 GEM	21 GEM	20 GEM	20 GEM	21 GEM	21 GEM
JUN	21 CAN	21 CAN	21 CAN	20 CAN	21 CAN	21 CAN	21 CAN	21 CAN	21 CAN	21 CAN	21 CAN	21 CAN	21 CAN	21 CAN	21 CAN
JUL	22 LEO	22 LEO	23 LEO	22 LEO	22 LEO	22 LEO	23 LEO	22 LEO	22 LEO	22 LEO	22 LEO	22 LEO	22 LEO	22 LEO	22 LEO
AUG	22 VIR	23 VIR	23 VIR	22 VIR	22 VIR	23 VIR	23 VIR	22 VIR	22 VIR	23 VIR	23 VIR	22 VIR	22 VIR	23 VIR	23 VIR
SEP	22 LIB	23 LIB	23 LIB	22 LIB	22 LIB	23 LIB	23 LIB	22 LIB	22 LIB	23 LIB	23 LIB	22 LIB	22 LIB	23 LIB	23 LIB
OCT	23 SCO	23 SCO	23 SCO	22 SCO	23 SCO	23 SCO	23 SCO	22 SCO	23 SCO	23 SCO	23 SCO	22 SCO	23 SCO	23 SCO	23 SCO
NOV	22 SAG	22 SAG	22 SAG	21 SAG	22 SAG	22 SAG	22 SAG	21 SAG	22 SAG	22 SAG	22 SAG	21 SAG	22 SAG	22 SAG	22 SAG
DEC	21 CAP	21 CAP	22 CAP	21 CAP	21 CAP	21 CAP	22 CAP	21 CAP	21 CAP	21 CAP	22 CAP	21 CAP	21 CAP	21 CAP	22 CAP

	2020	2021	2022	2023	2024	2025	2026	2027	2028	2029	2030	2031	2032	2033	2034
JAN	20 AQU	20 AQU	19 AQU	20 AQU	20 AQU	19 AQU	20 AQU	20 AQU	20 AQU	19 AQU	20 AQU	20 AQU	20 AQU	19 AQU	20 AQU
FEB	19 PIS	18 PIS	18 PIS	18 PIS	19 PIS	18 PIS	18 PIS	18 PIS	18 PIS	18 PIS	18 PIS	18 PIS	18 PIS	18 PIS	18 PIS
MAR	19 ARI	20 ARI	20 ARI	20 ARI	19 ARI	20 ARI	20 ARI	20 ARI	20 ARI	20 ARI	20 ARI	20 ARI	20 ARI	19 ARI	20 ARI
APR	19 TAU	19 TAU	20 TAU	20 TAU	19 TAU	19 TAU	20 TAU	20 TAU	19 TAU	19 TAU	20 TAU	20 TAU	19 TAU	19 TAU	20 TAU
MAY	20 GEM	20 GEM	21 GEM	21 GEM	20 GEM	20 GEM	21 GEM	21 GEM	20 GEM	20 GEM	21 GEM	21 GEM	20 GEM	20 GEM	20 GEM
JUN	20 CAN	21 CAN	21 CAN	21 CAN	20 CAN	21 CAN	21 CAN	21 CAN	21 CAN	21 CAN	21 CAN	21 CAN	20 CAN	21 CAN	21 CAN
JUL	22 LEO	22 LEO	22 LEO	23 LEO	22 LEO	22 LEO	22 LEO	22 LEO	22 LEO	22 LEO	22 LEO	22 LEO	22 LEO	22 LEO	22 LEO
AUG	22 VIR	22 VIR	23 VIR	23 VIR	22 VIR	22 VIR	23 VIR	23 VIR	22 VIR	22 VIR	23 VIR	22 VIR	22 VIR	22 VIR	22 VIR
SEP	22 LIB	22 LIB	23 LIB	23 LIB	22 LIB	22 LIB	23 LIB	23 LIB	22 LIB	22 LIB	23 LIB	22 LIB	22 LIB	22 LIB	22 LIB
OCT	22 SCO	23 SCO	23 SCO	23 SCO	22 SCO	23 SCO	23 SCO	23 SCO	22 SCO	23 SCO	23 SCO	23 SCO	22 SCO	23 SCO	23 SCO
NOV	21 SAG	21 SAG	22 SAG	22 SAG	21 SAG	22 SAG	22 SAG	22 SAG	21 SAG	22 SAG	22 SAG	22 SAG	21 SAG	22 SAG	22 SAG
DEC	21 CAP	21 CAP	21 CAP	21 CAP	21 CAP	21 CAP	21 CAP	21 CAP	21 CAP	21 CAP	21 CAP	21 CAP	21 CAP	21 CAP	21 CAP

	2035	2036	2037	2038	2039	2040	2041	2042	2043	2044	2045	2046	2047	2048	2049
JAN	20 AQU	20 AQU	19 AQU	20 AQU	20 AQU	20 AQU	19 AQU	20 AQU	20 AQU	20 AQU	19 AQU	20 AQU	20 AQU	20 AQU	19 AQU
FEB	18 PIS	18 PIS	18 PIS	18 PIS	19 PIS	18 PIS	18 PIS	18 PIS	18 PIS	18 PIS	18 PIS	18 PIS	18 PIS	18 PIS	18 PIS
MAR	20 ARI	20 ARI	19 ARI	20 ARI	20 ARI	20 ARI	20 ARI	20 ARI	20 ARI	19 ARI	20 ARI	20 ARI	20 ARI	19 ARI	20 ARI
APR	20 TAU	19 TAU	19 TAU	19 TAU	20 TAU	19 TAU	19 TAU	19 TAU	20 TAU	19 TAU	19 TAU	19 TAU	20 TAU	19 TAU	19 TAU
MAY	21 GEM	20 GEM	20 GEM	20 GEM	21 GEM	20 GEM	20 GEM	20 GEM	20 GEM	20 GEM	20 GEM	20 GEM	20 GEM	20 GEM	20 GEM
JUN	21 CAN	20 CAN	20 CAN	21 CAN	21 CAN	20 CAN	20 CAN	20 CAN	21 CAN	20 CAN	20 CAN	21 CAN	21 CAN	20 CAN	21 CAN
JUL	22 LEO	22 LEO	22 LEO	22 LEO	22 LEO	22 LEO	22 LEO	22 LEO	22 LEO	22 LEO	21 LEO	22 LEO	22 LEO	22 LEO	21 LEO
AUG	23 VIR	22 VIR	22 VIR	22 VIR	23 VIR	22 VIR	22 VIR	22 VIR	23 VIR	22 VIR	22 VIR	23 VIR	22 VIR	22 VIR	22 VIR
SEP	23 LIB	22 LIB	22 LIB	22 LIB	23 LIB	22 LIB	22 LIB	22 LIB	22 LIB	22 LIB	22 LIB	22 LIB	22 LIB	22 LIB	22 LIB
OCT	23 SCO	22 SCO	22 SCO	23 SCO	23 SCO	22 SCO	22 SCO	23 SCO	23 SCO	22 SCO	22 SCO	23 SCO	23 SCO	22 SCO	22 SCO
NOV	22 SAG	21 SAG	21 SAG	22 SAG	22 SAG	21 SAG	21 SAG	22 SAG	22 SAG	21 SAG	21 SAG	22 SAG	21 SAG	21 SAG	22 SAG
DEC	21 CAP	21 CAP	21 CAP	21 CAP	21 CAP	21 CAP	21 CAP	21 CAP	21 CAP	21 CAP	21 CAP	21 CAP	21 CAP	21 CAP	21 CAP

	2050	2051	2052	2053	2054	2055	2056	2057	2058	2059	2060	2061	2062	2063	2064
JAN	19 AQU	19 AQU	20 AQU	19 AQU	19 AQU	19 AQU	20 AQU	19 AQU	19 AQU	19 AQU	20 AQU	19 AQU	19 AQU	19 AQU	20 AQU
FEB	18 PIS	18 PIS	18 PIS	18 PIS	18 PIS	18 PIS	18 PIS	18 PIS	18 PIS	18 PIS	18 PIS	18 PIS	17 PIS	18 PIS	18 PIS
MAR	20 ARI	20 ARI	19 ARI	19 ARI	20 ARI	20 ARI	19 ARI	19 ARI	20 ARI	20 ARI	20 ARI	19 ARI	19 ARI	20 ARI	19 ARI
APR	19 TAU	19 TAU	19 TAU	19 TAU	19 TAU	19 TAU	19 TAU	19 TAU	19 TAU	19 TAU	19 TAU	19 TAU	19 TAU	19 TAU	19 TAU
MAY	20 GEM	20 GEM	20 GEM	20 GEM	20 GEM	20 GEM	20 GEM	20 GEM	20 GEM	20 GEM	20 GEM	20 GEM	20 GEM	20 GEM	20 GEM
JUN	20 CAN	21 CAN	20 CAN	20 CAN	21 CAN	21 CAN	20 CAN	20 CAN	20 CAN	20 CAN	20 CAN	20 CAN	20 CAN	21 CAN	20 CAN
JUL	22 LEO	22 LEO	21 LEO	22 LEO	22 LEO	22 LEO	21 LEO	22 LEO	22 LEO	22 LEO	21 LEO	22 LEO	22 LEO	22 LEO	21 LEO
AUG	22 VIR	22 VIR	22 VIR	22 VIR	22 VIR	22 VIR	22 VIR	22 VIR	22 VIR	22 VIR	22 VIR	22 VIR	22 VIR	22 VIR	22 VIR
SEP	22 LIB	22 LIB	22 LIB	22 LIB	22 LIB	22 LIB	22 LIB	22 LIB	22 LIB	22 LIB	22 LIB	22 LIB	22 LIB	22 LIB	22 LIB
OCT	23 SCO	23 SCO	22 SCO	22 SCO	23 SCO	23 SCO	22 SCO	22 SCO	22 SCO	22 SCO	23 SCO	22 SCO	22 SCO	23 SCO	22 SCO
NOV	22 SAG	21 SAG	21 SAG	21 SAG	22 SAG	22 SAG	21 SAG	21 SAG	21 SAG	21 SAG	21 SAG	21 SAG	21 SAG	21 SAG	21 SAG
DEC	21 CAP	21 CAP	21 CAP	21 CAP	21 CAP	21 CAP	20 CAP	21 CAP	21 CAP	21 CAP	21 CAP	20 CAP	21 CAP	21 CAP	20 CAP

	2065	2066	2067	2068	2069	2070	2071	2072	2073	2074	2075	2076	2077	2078	2079
JAN	19 AQU	19 AQU	19 AQU	20 AQU	19 AQU	19 AQU	19 AQU	20 AQU	19 AQU	19 AQU	19 AQU	20 AQU	19 AQU	20 AQU	19 AQU
FEB	17 PIS	18 PIS	18 PIS	18 PIS	17 PIS	18 PIS	18 PIS	18 PIS	17 PIS	18 PIS	18 PIS	18 PIS	17 PIS	18 PIS	18 PIS
MAR	19 ARI	20 ARI	20 ARI	19 ARI	19 ARI	20 ARI	20 ARI	19 ARI	19 ARI	20 ARI	20 ARI	19 ARI	19 ARI	20 ARI	20 ARI
APR	19 TAU	19 TAU	19 TAU	19 TAU	19 TAU	19 TAU	19 TAU	19 TAU	19 TAU	19 TAU	19 TAU	19 TAU	19 TAU	19 TAU	19 TAU
MAY	20 GEM	20 GEM	20 GEM	20 GEM	20 GEM	20 GEM	20 GEM	19 GEM	20 GEM	20 GEM	20 GEM	20 GEM	19 GEM	20 GEM	20 GEM
JUN	20 CAN	21 CAN	21 CAN	20 CAN	20 CAN	20 CAN	20 CAN	21 CAN	20 CAN	20 CAN	21 CAN	20 CAN	20 CAN	20 CAN	20 CAN
JUL	22 LEO	22 LEO	22 LEO	21 LEO	22 LEO	22 LEO	22 LEO	22 LEO	22 LEO	21 LEO	22 LEO	21 LEO	21 LEO	21 LEO	22 LEO
AUG	22 VIR	22 VIR	22 VIR	22 VIR	22 VIR	22 VIR	22 VIR	22 VIR	22 VIR	22 VIR	22 VIR	22 VIR	22 VIR	22 VIR	22 VIR
SEP	22 LIB	22 LIB	22 LIB	22 LIB	22 LIB	22 LIB	22 LIB	21 LIB	22 LIB	22 LIB	22 LIB	22 LIB	21 LIB	22 LIB	22 LIB
OCT	22 SCO	22 SCO	23 SCO	22 SCO	22 SCO	22 SCO	23 SCO	22 SCO	22 SCO	22 SCO	22 SCO	23 SCO	22 SCO	22 SCO	23 SCO
NOV	21 SAG	21 SAG	22 SAG	21 SAG	21 SAG	21 SAG	21 SAG	21 SAG	21 SAG	21 SAG	22 SAG	21 SAG	21 SAG	21 SAG	22 SAG
DEC	21 CAP	21 CAP	21 CAP	20 CAP	21 CAP	21 CAP	21 CAP	20 CAP	21 CAP	20 CAP	21 CAP	20 CAP	21 CAP	21 CAP	21 CAP

	2080	2081	2082	2083	2084	2085	2086	2087	2088	2089	2090	2091	2092	2093	2094
JAN	19 AQU	19 AQU	19 AQU	20 AQU	19 AQU	19 AQU	19 AQU	19 AQU	19 AQU	19 AQU	19 AQU	19 AQU	19 AQU	19 AQU	20 AQU
FEB	18 PIS	17 PIS	18 PIS	18 PIS	18 PIS	17 PIS	18 PIS	18 PIS	18 PIS	17 PIS	18 PIS	18 PIS	18 PIS	17 PIS	17 PIS
MAR	19 ARI	19 ARI	20 ARI	20 ARI	19 ARI	19 ARI	19 ARI	20 ARI	19 ARI	19 ARI	19 ARI	20 ARI	19 ARI	19 ARI	19 ARI
APR	19 TAU	19 TAU	19 TAU	19 TAU	18 TAU	19 TAU	19 TAU	19 TAU	18 TAU	19 TAU	19 TAU	19 TAU	18 TAU	19 TAU	19 TAU
MAY	19 GEM	20 GEM	20 GEM	20 GEM	19 GEM	20 GEM	20 GEM	20 GEM	19 GEM	20 GEM	20 GEM	20 GEM	19 GEM	20 GEM	20 GEM
JUN	20 CAN	20 CAN	20 CAN	20 CAN	20 CAN	20 CAN	20 CAN	20 CAN	20 CAN	20 CAN	20 CAN	20 CAN	20 CAN	21 CAN	20 CAN
JUL	21 LEO	21 LEO	22 LEO	22 LEO	21 LEO	21 LEO	22 LEO	22 LEO	21 LEO	21 LEO	22 LEO	22 LEO	21 LEO	21 LEO	21 LEO
AUG	21 VIR	22 VIR	22 VIR	22 VIR	21 VIR	22 VIR	22 VIR	22 VIR	21 VIR	22 VIR	22 VIR	22 VIR	21 VIR	22 VIR	22 VIR
SEP	22 LIB	22 LIB	22 LIB	22 LIB	21 LIB	22 LIB	22 LIB	22 LIB	21 LIB	22 LIB	22 LIB	22 LIB	21 LIB	22 LIB	22 LIB
OCT	22 SCO	22 SCO	22 SCO	23 SCO	22 SCO	22 SCO	22 SCO	23 SCO	22 SCO	22 SCO	22 SCO	22 SCO	22 SCO	22 SCO	22 SCO
NOV	21 SAG	21 SAG	21 SAG	21 SAG	21 SAG	21 SAG	21 SAG	21 SAG	21 SAG	21 SAG	21 SAG	21 SAG	21 SAG	21 SAG	21 SAG
DEC	20 CAP	21 CAP	21 CAP	21 CAP	20 CAP	21 CAP	21 CAP	21 CAP	20 CAP	21 CAP	21 CAP	21 CAP	20 CAP	20 CAP	21 CAP

	2095	2096	2097	2098	2099	2100
JAN	19 AQU	19 AQU	19 AQU	19 AQU	19 AQU	19 AQU
FEB	18 PIS	18 PIS	17 PIS	17 PIS	18 PIS	18 PIS
MAR	20 ARI	19 ARI	19 ARI	19 ARI	20 ARI	20 ARI
APR	19 TAU	18 TAU	19 TAU	19 TAU	19 TAU	19 TAU
MAY	20 GEM	19 GEM	20 GEM	20 GEM	20 GEM	20 GEM
JUN	20 CAN	20 CAN	20 CAN	20 CAN	20 CAN	21 CAN
JUL	22 LEO	21 LEO	21 LEO	22 LEO	22 LEO	22 LEO
AUG	22 VIR	22 VIR	22 VIR	22 VIR	22 VIR	22 VIR
SEP	22 LIB	21 LIB	22 LIB	22 LIB	22 LIB	22 LIB
OCT	22 SCO	22 SCO	22 SCO	22 SCO	22 SCO	23 SCO
NOV	21 SAG	21 SAG	21 SAG	21 SAG	21 SAG	22 SAG
DEC	21 CAP	20 CAP	20 CAP	21 CAP	21 CAP	21 CAP

What Is Your Moon Sign?

THE MOON MOVES very quickly, traveling through all twelve signs of the zodiac approximately every twenty-nine days. This means that the Moon spends, on the average, about two and a half days in each sign.

The following Moon Tables will help you to locate your Moon sign. Find your year of birth, then locate the column for your birthday month. The tables list for your month every date on which the Moon *moved* into a new sign.

Example: You were born September 7, 1962. Find the year *1962* and the column marked *SEP*. You will see that on the 5th of September in 1962 the Moon moved into Sagittarius, and on the 8th of September it moved into Capricorn. Since you were born on the 7th of September, your Moon sign is Sagittarius.

However, if in these Moon tables you see that your birthday falls on a day on which the Moon moved into a new sign, the question is *what time of day* did the Moon change signs. The Moon travels fast, and if it changed signs on your birthday the possibility exists that you were born at an hour when the Moon was in the previous sign. To find out your *exact* Moon sign, you should definitely use the enclosed CD-ROM. It will tell you your exact Moon sign—and the exact degree of this sign your Moon is in.

JAN	FEB	MAR	APR	MAY	JUN	JUL	AUG	SEP	OCT	NOV	DEC
2 AQU	1 PIS	2 ARI	1 TAU	2 CAN	1 LEO	1 VIR	2 SCO	1 SAG	1 CAP	1 PIS	1 ARI
4 PIS	3 ARI	4 TAU	3 GEM	5 LEO	3 VIR	3 LIB	5 SAG	3 CAP	3 AQU	3 ARI	3 TAU
6 ARI	5 TAU	6 GEM	5 CAN	7 VIR	6 LIB	6 SCO	7 CAP	5 AQU	5 PIS	5 TAU	5 GEM
8 TAU	7 GEM	9 CAN	7 LEO	10 LIB	8 SCO	8 SAG	9 AQU	7 PIS	7 ARI	7 GEM	7 CAN
11 GEM	9 CAN	11 LEO	10 VIR	12 SCO	11 SAG	10 CAP	11 PIS	9 ARI	9 TAU	9 CAN	9 LEO
13 CAN	12 LEO	13 VIR	12 LIB	14 SAG	13 CAP	13 AQU	13 ARI	11 TAU	11 GEM	11 LEO	11 VIR
15 LEO	14 VIR	16 LIB	15 SCO	17 CAP	15 AQU	15 PIS	15 TAU	13 GEM	13 CAN	14 VIR	14 LIB
18 VIR	17 LIB	19 SCO	17 SAG	19 AQU	17 PIS	17 ARI	17 GEM	16 CAN	15 LEO	17 LIB	16 SCO
21 LIB	19 SCO	21 SAG	20 CAP	21 PIS	19 ARI	19 TAU	19 CAN	18 LEO	18 VIR	19 SCO	19 SAG
23 SCO	22 SAG	23 CAP	22 AQU	23 ARI	21 TAU	22 GEM	22 LEO	21 VIR	20 LIB	22 SAG	21 CAP
25 SAG	24 CAP	25 AQU	24 PIS	25 TAU	24 GEM	24 CAN	24 VIR	23 LIB	23 SCO	24 CAP	24 AQU
28 CAP	26 AQU	28 PIS	26 ARI	27 GEM	26 CAN	26 LEO	27 LIB	26 SCO	25 SAG	26 AQU	26 PIS
30 AQU	28 PIS	30 ARI	28 TAU	30 CAN	28 LEO	28 VIR	29 SCO	28 SAG	28 CAP	29 PIS	28 ARI
			30 GEM			31 LIB			30 AQU		30 TAU

JAN	FEB	MAR	APR	MAY	JUN	JUL	AUG	SEP	OCT	NOV	DEC
1 GEM	2 LEO	1 LEO	2 LIB	2 SCO	1 SAG	1 CAP	1 PIS	2 TAU	1 GEM	2 LEO	1 VIR
3 CAN	4 VIR	3 VIR	5 SCO	5 SAG	3 CAP	3 AQU	4 ARI	4 GEM	3 CAN	4 VIR	4 LIB
5 LEO	7 LIB	7 LIB	7 SAG	7 CAP	6 AQU	5 PIS	6 TAU	6 CAN	6 LEO	7 LIB	6 SCO
8 VIR	9 SCO	8 SCO	10 CAP	9 AQU	8 PIS	7 ARI	8 GEM	8 LEO	8 VIR	9 SCO	9 SAG
10 LIB	12 SAG	11 SAG	12 AQU	12 PIS	10 ARI	9 TAU	10 CAN	11 VIR	10 LIB	12 SAG	11 CAP
13 SCO	14 CAP	13 CAP	14 PIS	14 ARI	12 TAU	12 GEM	12 LEO	13 LIB	13 SCO	14 CAP	14 AQU
15 SAG	16 AQU	16 AQU	16 ARI	16 TAU	14 GEM	14 CAN	14 VIR	16 SCO	15 SAG	17 AQU	16 PIS
18 CAP	18 PIS	18 PIS	18 TAU	18 GEM	16 CAN	16 LEO	17 LIB	18 SAG	18 CAP	19 PIS	18 ARI
20 AQU	20 ARI	20 ARI	20 GEM	20 CAN	18 LEO	18 VIR	19 SCO	21 CAP	20 AQU	21 ARI	21 TAU
22 PIS	22 TAU	22 TAU	22 CAN	22 LEO	21 VIR	20 LIB	22 SAG	23 AQU	23 PIS	23 TAU	23 GEM
24 ARI	25 GEM	24 GEM	25 LEO	24 VIR	23 LIB	23 SCO	24 CAP	25 PIS	25 ARI	25 GEM	25 CAN
26 TAU	27 CAN	26 CAN	27 VIR	27 LIB	26 SCO	25 SAG	27 AQU	27 ARI	27 TAU	27 CAN	27 LEO
28 GEM		28 LEO	29 LIB	29 SCO	28 SAG	28 CAP	29 PIS	29 TAU	29 GEM	29 LEO	29 VIR
31 CAN		31 VIR				30 AQU	31 ARI		31 CAN		31 LIB

JAN	FEB	MAR	APR	MAY	JUN	JUL	AUG	SEP	OCT	NOV	DEC
3 SCO	1 SAG	1 SAG	2 AQU	2 PIS	3 TAU	2 GEM	2 LEO	1 VIR	3 SCO	2 SAG	1 CAP
5 SAG	4 CAP	3 CAP	4 PIS	4 ARI	5 GEM	4 CAN	4 VIR	3 LIB	5 SAG	4 CAP	4 AQU
8 CAP	6 AQU	6 AQU	7 ARI	6 TAU	7 CAN	6 LEO	7 LIB	5 SCO	8 CAP	7 AQU	6 PIS
10 AQU	9 PIS	8 PIS	9 TAU	8 GEM	9 LEO	8 VIR	9 SCO	8 SAG	10 AQU	9 PIS	9 ARI
12 PIS	11 ARI	10 ARI	11 GEM	10 CAN	11 VIR	11 LIB	12 SAG	10 CAP	13 PIS	11 ARI	11 TAU
15 ARI	13 TAU	12 TAU	13 CAN	12 LEO	13 LIB	13 SCO	14 CAP	13 AQU	15 ARI	13 TAU	13 GEM
17 TAU	15 GEM	14 GEM	15 LEO	14 VIR	15 SCO	15 SAG	17 AQU	15 PIS	17 TAU	16 GEM	15 CAN
19 GEM	17 CAN	17 CAN	17 VIR	17 LIB	18 SAG	18 CAP	19 PIS	18 ARI	19 GEM	18 CAN	17 LEO
21 CAN	19 LEO	19 LEO	20 LIB	19 SCO	20 CAP	20 AQU	21 ARI	20 TAU	21 CAN	20 LEO	19 VIR
23 LEO	22 VIR	21 VIR	22 SCO	22 SAG	23 AQU	23 PIS	23 TAU	22 GEM	23 LEO	22 VIR	21 LIB
25 VIR	24 LIB	23 LIB	24 SAG	24 CAP	25 PIS	25 ARI	26 GEM	24 CAN	25 VIR	24 LIB	24 SCO
27 LIB	26 SCO	26 SCO	27 CAP	27 AQU	28 ARI	27 TAU	28 CAN	26 LEO	28 LIB	26 SCO	26 SAG
30 SCO		28 SAG	29 AQU	29 PIS	30 TAU	29 GEM	30 LEO	28 VIR	30 SCO	29 SAG	29 CAP
		31 CAP		31 ARI		31 CAN		30 LIB			31 AQU

JAN	FEB	MAR	APR	MAY	JUN	JUL	AUG	SEP	OCT	NOV	DEC
3 PIS	1 ARI	3 TAU	1 GEM	1 CAN	1 VIR	1 LIB	1 SAG	3 AQU	3 PIS	1 ARI	1 TAU
5 ARI	4 TAU	5 GEM	3 CAN	3 LEO	3 LIB	3 SCO	4 CAP	5 PIS	5 ARI	4 TAU	3 GEM
7 TAU	6 GEM	7 CAN	5 LEO	5 VIR	6 SCO	6 SAG	6 AQU	8 ARI	7 TAU	6 GEM	5 CAN
9 GEM	8 CAN	9 LEO	8 VIR	7 LIB	8 SAG	8 CAP	9 PIS	10 TAU	10 GEM	8 CAN	7 LEO
11 CAN	10 LEO	11 VIR	10 LIB	9 SCO	10 CAP	10 AQU	11 ARI	12 GEM	12 CAN	10 LEO	9 VIR
13 LEO	12 VIR	13 LIB	12 SCO	12 SAG	13 AQU	13 PIS	14 TAU	15 CAN	14 LEO	12 VIR	12 LIB
15 VIR	14 LIB	16 SCO	14 SAG	14 CAP	15 PIS	15 ARI	16 GEM	17 LEO	16 VIR	14 LIB	14 SCO
18 LIB	16 SCO	18 SAG	17 CAP	17 AQU	18 ARI	18 TAU	18 CAN	19 VIR	18 LIB	17 SCO	16 SAG
20 SCO	19 SAG	20 CAP	19 AQU	19 PIS	20 TAU	20 GEM	20 LEO	21 LIB	20 SCO	19 SAG	19 CAP
22 SAG	21 CAP	23 AQU	22 PIS	22 ARI	22 GEM	22 CAN	22 VIR	23 SCO	22 SAG	21 CAP	21 AQU
25 CAP	24 AQU	25 PIS	24 ARI	24 TAU	24 CAN	24 LEO	24 LIB	25 SAG	25 CAP	24 AQU	24 PIS
27 AQU	26 PIS	28 ARI	26 TAU	26 GEM	26 LEO	26 VIR	26 SCO	27 CAP	27 AQU	26 PIS	26 ARI
30 PIS	28 ARI	30 TAU	29 GEM	28 CAN	28 VIR	28 LIB	29 SAG	29 SAG	30 AQU	29 ARI	28 TAU
				30 LEO		30 SCO	31 CAP				31 GEM

JAN	FEB	MAR	APR	MAY	JUN	JUL	AUG	SEP	OCT	NOV	DEC
2 CAN	2 VIR	1 VIR	1 SCO	1 SAG	2 AQU	2 PIS	3 TAU	2 GEM	1 CAN	2 VIR	1 LIB
4 LEO	4 LIB	3 LIB	3 SAG	3 CAP	4 PIS	4 ARI	5 GEM	4 CAN	3 LEO	4 LIB	3 SCO
6 VIR	6 SCO	5 SCO	6 CAP	5 AQU	7 ARI	7 TAU	8 CAN	6 LEO	5 VIR	6 SCO	5 SAG
8 LIB	9 SAG	7 SAG	8 AQU	8 PIS	9 TAU	9 GEM	10 LEO	8 VIR	7 LIB	8 SAG	8 CAP
10 SCO	11 CAP	9 CAP	11 PIS	10 ARI	12 GEM	11 CAN	12 VIR	10 LIB	9 SCO	10 CAP	10 AQU
12 SAG	14 AQU	12 AQU	13 ARI	13 TAU	14 CAN	13 LEO	14 LIB	12 SCO	12 SAG	12 AQU	12 PIS
15 CAP	16 PIS	14 PIS	16 TAU	15 GEM	16 LEO	16 VIR	16 SCO	14 SAG	14 CAP	15 PIS	15 ARI
17 AQU	19 ARI	17 ARI	18 GEM	17 CAN	18 VIR	17 LIB	18 SAG	16 CAP	16 AQU	18 ARI	17 TAU
20 PIS	21 TAU	19 TAU	20 CAN	20 LEO	20 LIB	19 SCO	20 CAP	19 AQU	19 PIS	20 TAU	20 GEM
22 ARI	23 GEM	22 GEM	22 LEO	22 VIR	22 SCO	22 SAG	23 AQU	21 PIS	21 ARI	22 GEM	22 CAN
25 TAU	26 CAN	24 CAN	24 VIR	24 LIB	24 SAG	24 CAP	25 PIS	24 ARI	24 TAU	25 CAN	24 LEO
27 GEM	28 LEO	26 LEO	27 LIB	26 SCO	27 CAP	26 AQU	28 ARI	26 TAU	26 GEM	27 LEO	26 VIR
29 CAN		28 VIR	29 SCO	28 SAG	29 AQU	29 PIS	30 TAU	29 GEM	28 CAN	29 VIR	28 LIB
31 LEO		30 LIB		30 CAP		31 ARI			31 LEO		31 SCO

JAN	FEB	MAR	APR	MAY	JUN	JUL	AUG	SEP	OCT	NOV	DEC
2 SAG	3 AQU	2 AQU	1 PIS	3 TAU	2 GEM	1 CAN	2 VIR	2 SCO	2 SAG	3 AQU	2 PIS
4 CAP	5 PIS	4 PIS	3 ARI	5 GEM	4 CAN	4 LEO	4 LIB	5 SAG	4 CAP	5 PIS	5 ARI
6 AQU	8 ARI	7 ARI	6 TAU	8 CAN	6 LEO	6 VIR	6 SCO	7 CAP	6 AQU	7 ARI	7 TAU
9 PIS	10 TAU	9 TAU	8 GEM	10 LEO	8 VIR	8 LIB	8 SAG	9 AQU	9 PIS	10 TAU	10 GEM
11 ARI	13 GEM	12 GEM	10 CAN	12 VIR	11 LIB	10 SCO	10 CAP	11 PIS	11 ARI	12 GEM	12 CAN
14 TAU	15 CAN	14 CAN	13 LEO	14 LIB	13 SCO	12 SAG	13 AQU	14 ARI	14 TAU	15 CAN	15 LEO
16 GEM	17 LEO	16 LEO	15 VIR	16 SCO	15 SAG	14 CAP	15 PIS	16 TAU	16 GEM	17 LEO	17 VIR
18 CAN	19 VIR	19 VIR	17 LIB	18 SAG	17 CAP	16 AQU	18 ARI	19 GEM	19 CAN	20 VIR	19 LIB
21 LEO	21 LIB	21 LIB	19 SCO	20 CAP	19 AQU	19 PIS	20 TAU	21 CAN	21 LEO	22 LIB	21 SCO
23 VIR	23 SCO	22 SCO	21 SAG	23 AQU	21 PIS	21 ARI	23 GEM	24 LEO	23 VIR	24 SCO	23 SAG
25 LIB	25 SAG	25 SAG	23 CAP	25 PIS	24 ARI	24 TAU	25 CAN	26 VIR	25 LIB	26 SAG	25 CAP
27 SCO	27 CAP	27 CAP	25 AQU	28 ARI	26 TAU	26 GEM	27 LEO	28 LIB	27 SCO	28 CAP	27 AQU
29 SAG		29 AQU	28 PIS	30 TAU	29 GEM	29 CAN	29 VIR	30 SCO	29 SAG	30 AQU	30 PIS
31 CAP			30 ARI			31 LEO	31 LIB		31 CAP		

JAN	FEB	MAR	APR	MAY	JUN	JUL	AUG	SEP	OCT	NOV	DEC
1 ARI	2 GEM	2 GEM	1 CAN	3 VIR	1 LIB	1 SCO	1 CAP	2 PIS	1 ARI	2 GEM	2 CAN
3 TAU	5 CAN	4 CAN	3 LEO	5 LIB	3 SCO	3 SAG	3 AQU	4 ARI	4 TAU	5 CAN	5 LEO
6 GEM	7 LEO	7 LEO	5 VIR	7 SCO	5 SAG	5 CAP	5 PIS	6 TAU	6 GEM	7 LEO	7 VIR
8 CAN	9 VIR	9 VIR	7 LIB	9 SAG	7 CAP	7 AQU	7 ARI	9 GEM	9 CAN	10 VIR	9 LIB
11 LEO	12 LIB	11 LIB	9 SCO	11 CAP	9 AQU	9 PIS	10 TAU	11 CAN	11 LEO	12 LIB	12 SCO
13 VIR	14 SCO	13 SCO	11 SAG	13 AQU	11 PIS	11 ARI	12 GEM	14 LEO	13 VIR	14 SCO	14 SAG
15 LIB	16 SAG	15 SAG	13 CAP	15 PIS	14 ARI	14 TAU	15 CAN	16 VIR	16 LIB	16 SAG	16 CAP
17 SCO	18 CAP	17 CAP	16 AQU	17 ARI	16 TAU	16 GEM	17 LEO	18 LIB	18 SCO	18 CAP	18 AQU
19 SAG	20 AQU	19 AQU	18 PIS	20 TAU	19 GEM	18 CAN	20 VIR	20 SCO	20 SAG	20 AQU	20 PIS
22 CAP	22 PIS	22 PIS	20 ARI	23 GEM	21 CAN	21 LEO	22 LIB	22 SAG	22 CAP	22 PIS	22 ARI
24 AQU	25 ARI	24 ARI	23 TAU	25 CAN	24 LEO	23 VIR	24 SCO	24 CAP	24 AQU	25 ARI	24 TAU
26 PIS	27 TAU	26 TAU	25 GEM	28 LEO	26 VIR	25 LIB	26 SAG	27 AQU	26 PIS	27 TAU	27 GEM
28 ARI		29 GEM	28 CAN	30 VIR	28 LIB	28 SCO	28 CAP	29 PIS	28 ARI	30 GEM	29 CAN
31 TAU			30 LEO			30 SAG	30 AQU		31 TAU		

JAN	FEB	MAR	APR	MAY	JUN	JUL	AUG	SEP	OCT	NOV	DEC
1 LEO	2 LIB	1 LIB	2 SAG	1 CAP	2 PIS	2 ARI	2 GEM	1 CAN	1 LEO	2 LIB	2 SCO
3 VIR	4 SCO	3 SCO	4 CAP	3 AQU	4 ARI	3 TAU	5 CAN	4 LEO	3 VIR	4 SCO	4 SAG
6 LIB	6 SAG	6 SAG	6 AQU	5 PIS	6 TAU	6 GEM	7 LEO	6 VIR	6 LIB	6 SAG	6 CAP
8 SCO	8 CAP	8 CAP	8 PIS	8 ARI	9 GEM	9 CAN	10 VIR	8 LIB	8 SCO	9 CAP	9 AQU
10 SAG	10 AQU	10 AQU	10 ARI	10 TAU	11 CAN	11 LEO	12 LIB	11 SCO	10 SAG	11 AQU	10 PIS
12 CAP	13 PIS	12 PIS	13 TAU	12 GEM	14 LEO	14 VIR	14 SCO	13 SAG	12 CAP	13 PIS	12 ARI
14 AQU	15 ARI	14 ARI	15 GEM	15 CAN	16 VIR	16 LIB	17 SAG	15 CAP	14 AQU	15 ARI	14 TAU
16 PIS	17 TAU	16 TAU	18 CAN	17 LEO	19 LIB	18 SCO	19 CAP	17 AQU	17 PIS	17 TAU	17 GEM
18 ARI	19 GEM	19 GEM	20 LEO	20 VIR	21 SCO	21 SAG	21 AQU	19 PIS	19 ARI	20 GEM	19 CAN
21 TAU	22 CAN	21 CAN	23 VIR	22 LIB	23 SAG	22 CAP	23 PIS	21 ARI	21 TAU	22 CAN	22 LEO
23 GEM	24 LEO	24 LEO	25 LIB	25 SCO	25 CAP	24 AQU	25 ARI	24 TAU	23 GEM	25 LEO	24 VIR
26 CAN	27 VIR	26 VIR	27 SCO	27 SAG	27 AQU	26 PIS	27 TAU	26 GEM	26 CAN	27 VIR	27 LIB
28 LEO		29 LIB	29 SAG	29 CAP	29 PIS	29 ARI	30 GEM	28 CAN	28 LEO	30 LIB	29 SCO
31 VIR		31 SCO		31 AQU		31 TAU			31 VIR		31 SAG

JAN	FEB	MAR	APR	MAY	JUN	JUL	AUG	SEP	OCT	NOV	DEC
2 CAP	1 AQU	1 PIS	2 TAU	1 GEM	3 LEO	2 VIR	1 LIB	2 SAG	2 CAP	2 PIS	2 ARI
4 AQU	3 PIS	3 ARI	4 GEM	4 CAN	5 VIR	5 LIB	4 SCO	5 CAP	4 AQU	4 ARI	4 TAU
6 PIS	5 ARI	5 TAU	6 CAN	6 LEO	8 LIB	7 SCO	6 SAG	7 AQU	6 PIS	7 TAU	6 GEM
8 ARI	7 TAU	8 GEM	9 LEO	9 VIR	10 SCO	10 SAG	8 CAP	9 PIS	8 ARI	9 GEM	8 CAN
11 TAU	9 GEM	10 CAN	11 VIR	11 LIB	12 SAG	12 CAP	10 AQU	11 ARI	10 TAU	11 CAN	11 LEO
13 GEM	12 CAN	13 LEO	14 LIB	14 SCO	14 CAP	14 AQU	12 PIS	13 TAU	12 GEM	13 LEO	13 VIR
16 CAN	14 LEO	15 VIR	16 SCO	16 SAG	16 AQU	16 PIS	14 ARI	15 GEM	15 CAN	16 VIR	16 LIB
18 LEO	17 VIR	18 LIB	19 SAG	18 CAP	18 PIS	18 ARI	16 TAU	17 CAN	17 LEO	18 LIB	18 SCO
21 VIR	19 LIB	20 SCO	21 CAP	20 AQU	21 ARI	20 TAU	19 GEM	20 LEO	20 VIR	21 SCO	21 SAG
23 LIB	22 SCO	22 SAG	23 AQU	23 PIS	23 TAU	22 GEM	21 CAN	22 VIR	22 LIB	23 SAG	23 CAP
26 SCO	24 SAG	24 CAP	25 PIS	25 ARI	25 GEM	25 CAN	23 LEO	25 LIB	24 SCO	25 CAP	25 AQU
28 SAG	26 CAP	27 AQU	27 ARI	27 TAU	27 CAN	27 LEO	26 VIR	27 SCO	27 SAG	27 AQU	27 PIS
30 CAP	28 AQU	29 PIS	29 TAU	29 GEM	30 LEO	30 VIR	28 LIB	30 SAG	29 CAP	29 PIS	29 ARI
		31 ARI		31 CAN			31 SCO		31 AQU		31 TAU

JAN	FEB	MAR	APR	MAY	JUN	JUL	AUG	SEP	OCT	NOV	DEC
2 GEM	1 CAN	3 LEO	1 VIR	1 LIB	2 SAG	2 CAP	1 AQU	1 ARI	2 GEM	1 CAN	1 LEO
5 CAN	3 LEO	5 VIR	4 LIB	4 SCO	5 CAP	4 AQU	3 PIS	3 TAU	5 CAN	3 LEO	3 VIR
7 LEO	6 VIR	8 LIB	6 SCO	6 SAG	7 AQU	6 PIS	5 ARI	5 GEM	7 LEO	6 VIR	5 LIB
10 VIR	8 LIB	10 SCO	9 SAG	8 CAP	9 PIS	8 ARI	7 TAU	7 CAN	9 VIR	8 LIB	8 SCO
12 LIB	11 SCO	13 SAG	11 CAP	11 AQU	11 ARI	10 TAU	9 GEM	10 LEO	12 LIB	11 SCO	11 SAG
15 SCO	13 SAG	15 CAP	13 AQU	13 PIS	13 TAU	13 GEM	11 CAN	12 VIR	14 SCO	13 SAG	13 CAP
17 SAG	16 CAP	17 AQU	15 PIS	15 ARI	15 GEM	15 CAN	13 LEO	15 LIB	17 SAG	16 CAP	15 AQU
19 CAP	18 AQU	19 PIS	18 ARI	17 TAU	18 CAN	17 LEO	16 VIR	17 SCO	19 CAP	18 AQU	17 PIS
21 AQU	20 PIS	21 ARI	20 TAU	19 GEM	20 LEO	20 VIR	18 LIB	20 SAG	22 AQU	20 PIS	20 ARI
23 PIS	22 ARI	23 TAU	22 GEM	21 CAN	22 VIR	22 LIB	21 SCO	22 CAP	24 PIS	22 ARI	22 TAU
25 ARI	24 TAU	25 GEM	24 CAN	23 LEO	25 LIB	25 SCO	23 SAG	24 AQU	26 ARI	24 TAU	24 GEM
27 TAU	26 GEM	27 CAN	26 LEO	26 VIR	27 SCO	27 SAG	26 CAP	26 PIS	28 TAU	26 GEM	26 CAN
30 GEM	28 CAN	30 LEO	29 VIR	28 LIB	30 SAG	29 CAP	28 AQU	28 ARI	30 GEM	28 CAN	28 LEO
				31 SCO			30 PIS	30 TAU			30 VIR

JAN	FEB	MAR	APR	MAY	JUN	JUL	AUG	SEP	OCT	NOV	DEC
2 LIB	1 SCO	3 SAG	1 CAP	1 AQU	2 ARI	1 TAU	2 CAN	2 VIR	2 LIB	1 SCO	3 CAP
4 SCO	3 SAG	5 CAP	4 AQU	3 PIS	4 TAU	3 GEM	4 LEO	5 LIB	4 SCO	3 SAG	5 AQU
7 SAG	6 CAP	7 AQU	6 PIS	5 ARI	6 GEM	5 CAN	6 VIR	7 SCO	7 SAG	6 CAP	8 PIS
9 CAP	8 AQU	9 PIS	8 ARI	7 TAU	8 CAN	7 LEO	8 LIB	9 CAP	9 CAP	8 AQU	10 ARI
11 AQU	10 PIS	11 ARI	10 TAU	9 GEM	10 LEO	10 VIR	11 SCO	12 CAP	12 AQU	11 PIS	12 TAU
14 PIS	12 ARI	13 TAU	12 GEM	11 CAN	12 VIR	12 LIB	13 SAG	14 AQU	14 PIS	13 ARI	14 GEM
16 ARI	14 TAU	16 GEM	14 CAN	14 LEO	15 LIB	14 SCO	16 CAP	17 PIS	16 ARI	15 TAU	16 CAN
18 TAU	16 GEM	18 CAN	16 LEO	16 VIR	17 SCO	17 SAG	18 AQU	19 ARI	18 TAU	17 GEM	18 LEO
20 GEM	18 CAN	20 LEO	19 VIR	18 LIB	20 SAG	19 CAP	20 PIS	21 TAU	20 GEM	19 CAN	20 VIR
22 CAN	21 LEO	22 VIR	21 LIB	21 SCO	22 CAP	22 AQU	22 ARI	23 GEM	22 CAN	21 LEO	23 LIB
24 LEO	23 VIR	25 LIB	24 SCO	23 SAG	24 AQU	24 PIS	25 TAU	25 CAN	24 LEO	23 VIR	25 SCO
27 VIR	25 LIB	27 SCO	26 SAG	26 CAP	27 PIS	26 ARI	27 GEM	27 LEO	27 VIR	25 LIB	28 SAG
29 LIB	28 SCO	30 SAG	29 CAP	28 AQU	29 ARI	28 TAU	29 CAN	29 VIR	29 LIB	28 SCO	30 CAP
				31 PIS		30 GEM	31 LEO				

JAN	FEB	MAR	APR	MAY	JUN	JUL	AUG	SEP	OCT	NOV	DEC
2 AQU	3 ARI	2 ARI	2 GEM	2 CAN	2 VIR	2 LIB	1 SCO	2 CAP	2 AQU	1 PIS	2 TAU
4 PIS	5 TAU	4 TAU	4 CAN	4 LEO	5 LIB	4 SCO	3 SAG	4 AQU	4 PIS	3 ARI	5 GEM
6 ARI	7 GEM	6 GEM	7 LEO	6 VIR	7 SCO	7 SAG	6 CAP	7 PIS	6 ARI	5 TAU	7 CAN
9 TAU	9 CAN	8 CAN	9 VIR	8 LIB	10 SAG	9 CAP	8 AQU	9 ARI	9 TAU	7 GEM	9 LEO
11 GEM	11 LEO	10 LEO	11 LIB	11 SCO	12 CAP	12 AQU	11 PIS	11 TAU	11 GEM	9 CAN	11 VIR
13 CAN	13 VIR	13 VIR	14 SCO	13 SAG	15 AQU	14 PIS	13 ARI	13 GEM	13 CAN	11 LEO	13 LIB
15 LEO	15 LIB	15 LIB	16 SAG	16 CAP	17 PIS	17 ARI	15 TAU	15 CAN	15 LEO	13 VIR	15 SCO
17 VIR	18 SCO	17 SCO	19 CAP	18 AQU	19 ARI	19 TAU	17 GEM	18 LEO	17 VIR	16 LIB	18 SAG
19 LIB	20 SAG	20 SAG	21 AQU	21 PIS	22 TAU	21 GEM	19 CAN	20 VIR	19 LIB	18 SCO	20 CAP
21 SCO	23 CAP	22 CAP	23 PIS	23 ARI	24 GEM	23 CAN	21 LEO	22 LIB	22 SCO	20 SAG	23 AQU
24 SAG	25 AQU	25 AQU	26 ARI	25 TAU	26 CAN	25 LEO	23 VIR	24 SCO	24 SAG	23 CAP	25 PIS
27 CAP	28 PIS	27 PIS	28 TAU	27 GEM	28 LEO	27 VIR	26 LIB	27 SAG	27 CAP	25 AQU	28 ARI
29 AQU		29 ARI	30 GEM	29 CAN	30 VIR	29 LIB	28 SCO	29 CAP	29 AQU	28 PIS	30 TAU
31 PIS		31 TAU		31 LEO			30 SAG			30 ARI	

1912

JAN	FEB	MAR	APR	MAY	JUN	JUL	AUG	SEP	OCT	NOV	DEC
1 GEM	1 LEO	2 VIR	3 SCO	2 SAG	1 CAP	1 AQU	2 ARI	1 TAU	2 CAN	1 LEO	2 LIB
3 CAN	3 VIR	4 LIB	5 SAG	5 CAP	3 AQU	3 PIS	4 TAU	3 GEM	5 LEO	3 VIR	4 SCO
5 LEO	6 LIB	6 SCO	7 CAP	7 AQU	6 PIS	6 ARI	7 GEM	5 CAN	7 VIR	5 LIB	7 SAG
7 VIR	8 SCO	8 SAG	10 AQU	10 PIS	8 ARI	8 TAU	9 CAN	7 LEO	9 LIB	7 SCO	9 CAP
9 LIB	10 SAG	11 CAP	12 PIS	12 ARI	11 TAU	10 GEM	11 LEO	9 VIR	11 SCO	9 SAG	12 AQU
11 SCO	13 CAP	13 AQU	15 ARI	14 TAU	13 GEM	12 CAN	13 VIR	11 LIB	13 SAG	12 CAP	14 PIS
14 SAG	15 AQU	16 PIS	17 TAU	17 GEM	15 CAN	14 LEO	15 LIB	13 SCO	15 CAP	14 AQU	17 ARI
16 CAP	18 PIS	18 ARI	19 GEM	19 CAN	17 LEO	16 VIR	17 SCO	15 SAG	18 AQU	17 PIS	19 TAU
19 AQU	20 ARI	21 TAU	21 CAN	21 LEO	19 VIR	18 LIB	19 SAG	18 CAP	20 PIS	19 ARI	21 GEM
21 PIS	22 TAU	23 GEM	23 LEO	23 VIR	21 LIB	21 SCO	22 CAP	21 AQU	23 ARI	22 TAU	23 CAN
24 ARI	25 GEM	25 CAN	26 VIR	25 LIB	23 SCO	23 SAG	24 AQU	23 PIS	25 TAU	24 GEM	25 LEO
26 TAU	27 CAN	27 LEO	28 LIB	27 SCO	26 SAG	25 CAP	27 PIS	25 ARI	27 GEM	26 CAN	27 VIR
28 GEM	29 LEO	29 VIR	30 SCO	30 SAG	28 CAP	28 AQU	29 ARI	28 TAU	30 CAN	28 LEO	29 LIB
30 CAN		31 LIB				31 PIS		30 GEM		30 VIR	

1913

JAN	FEB	MAR	APR	MAY	JUN	JUL	AUG	SEP	OCT	NOV	DEC
1 SCO	2 CAP	1 CAP	2 PIS	2 ARI	1 TAU	3 CAN	1 LEO	2 LIB	1 SCO	2 CAP	1 AQU
3 SAG	4 AQU	3 AQU	5 ARI	4 TAU	3 GEM	5 LEO	3 VIR	4 SCO	3 SAG	4 AQU	4 PIS
5 CAP	7 PIS	6 PIS	7 TAU	7 GEM	5 CAN	7 VIR	5 LIB	6 SAG	5 CAP	7 PIS	6 ARI
8 AQU	9 ARI	8 ARI	10 GEM	9 CAN	7 LEO	9 LIB	7 SCO	8 CAP	8 AQU	9 ARI	9 TAU
10 PIS	12 TAU	11 TAU	12 CAN	11 LEO	9 VIR	11 SCO	10 SAG	10 AQU	10 PIS	12 TAU	11 GEM
13 ARI	14 GEM	13 GEM	14 LEO	13 VIR	12 LIB	13 SAG	12 CAP	13 PIS	13 ARI	14 GEM	14 CAN
15 TAU	16 CAN	16 CAN	16 VIR	15 LIB	14 SCO	16 CAP	14 AQU	15 ARI	15 TAU	16 CAN	16 LEO
18 GEM	18 LEO	18 LEO	18 LIB	18 SCO	16 SAG	18 AQU	17 PIS	18 TAU	18 GEM	19 LEO	18 VIR
20 CAN	20 VIR	20 VIR	20 SCO	20 SAG	18 CAP	20 PIS	19 ARI	20 GEM	20 CAN	21 VIR	20 LIB
22 LEO	22 LIB	22 LIB	22 SAG	22 CAP	21 AQU	23 ARI	22 TAU	23 CAN	22 LEO	23 LIB	22 SCO
24 VIR	24 SCO	24 SCO	25 CAP	24 AQU	23 PIS	25 TAU	24 GEM	25 LEO	24 VIR	25 SCO	24 SAG
26 LIB	27 SAG	26 SAG	27 AQU	27 PIS	26 ARI	28 GEM	26 CAN	27 VIR	27 LIB	27 SAG	27 CAP
28 SCO		28 CAP	29 PIS	29 ARI	28 TAU	30 CAN	29 LEO	29 LIB	29 SCO	29 CAP	29 AQU
30 SAG		31 AQU			30 GEM		31 VIR		31 SAG		31 PIS

1914

JAN	FEB	MAR	APR	MAY	JUN	JUL	AUG	SEP	OCT	NOV	DEC
3 ARI	2 TAU	1 TAU	2 CAN	2 LEO	2 LIB	2 SCO	2 CAP	1 AQU	3 ARI	1 TAU	1 GEM
5 TAU	4 GEM	3 GEM	4 LEO	4 VIR	4 SCO	4 SAG	4 AQU	3 PIS	5 TAU	4 GEM	4 CAN
8 GEM	6 CAN	6 CAN	7 VIR	6 LIB	6 SAG	6 CAP	7 PIS	5 ARI	8 GEM	6 CAN	6 LEO
10 CAN	9 LEO	8 LEO	9 LIB	8 SCO	8 CAP	8 AQU	9 ARI	8 TAU	10 CAN	9 LEO	8 VIR
12 LEO	11 VIR	10 VIR	11 SCO	10 SAG	11 AQU	10 PIS	12 TAU	10 GEM	13 LEO	11 VIR	11 LIB
14 VIR	13 LIB	12 LIB	13 SAG	12 CAP	13 PIS	13 ARI	14 GEM	13 CAN	15 VIR	13 LIB	13 SCO
16 LIB	15 SCO	14 SCO	15 CAP	15 AQU	15 ARI	15 TAU	17 CAN	15 LEO	17 LIB	15 SCO	15 SAG
18 SCO	17 SAG	16 SAG	17 AQU	17 PIS	18 TAU	18 GEM	19 LEO	17 VIR	19 SCO	17 SAG	17 CAP
21 SAG	19 CAP	18 CAP	19 PIS	19 ARI	20 GEM	20 CAN	21 VIR	19 LIB	21 SAG	19 CAP	19 AQU
23 CAP	21 AQU	21 AQU	22 ARI	22 TAU	23 CAN	22 LEO	23 LIB	21 SCO	23 CAP	21 AQU	21 PIS
25 AQU	24 PIS	23 PIS	24 TAU	24 GEM	25 LEO	25 VIR	25 SCO	23 SAG	25 AQU	24 PIS	24 ARI
28 PIS	26 ARI	26 ARI	27 GEM	27 CAN	27 VIR	27 LIB	27 SAG	26 CAP	27 PIS	26 ARI	26 TAU
30 ARI		28 TAU	29 CAN	29 LEO	29 LIB	29 SCO	29 CAP	28 AQU	30 ARI	29 TAU	29 GEM
		31 GEM		31 VIR		31 SAG		30 PIS			31 CAN

1915

JAN	FEB	MAR	APR	MAY	JUN	JUL	AUG	SEP	OCT	NOV	DEC
2 LEO	1 VIR	2 LIB	1 SCO	2 CAP	1 AQU	3 ARI	1 TAU	3 CAN	3 LEO	1 VIR	1 LIB
5 VIR	3 LIB	5 SCO	3 SAG	4 AQU	3 PIS	5 TAU	4 GEM	5 LEO	5 VIR	3 LIB	3 SCO
7 LIB	5 SCO	7 SAG	5 CAP	7 PIS	5 ARI	8 GEM	6 CAN	8 VIR	7 LIB	6 SCO	5 SAG
9 SCO	7 SAG	9 CAP	7 AQU	9 ARI	8 TAU	10 CAN	9 LEO	10 LIB	9 SCO	8 SAG	7 CAP
11 SAG	10 CAP	11 AQU	9 PIS	11 TAU	10 GEM	13 LEO	11 VIR	12 SCO	11 SAG	10 CAP	9 AQU
13 CAP	12 AQU	13 PIS	12 ARI	14 GEM	13 CAN	15 VIR	13 LIB	14 SAG	13 CAP	12 AQU	11 PIS
15 AQU	14 PIS	16 ARI	14 TAU	16 CAN	15 LEO	17 LIB	16 SCO	16 CAP	16 AQU	14 PIS	14 ARI
18 PIS	16 ARI	18 TAU	17 GEM	19 LEO	18 VIR	19 SCO	18 SAG	18 AQU	18 PIS	16 ARI	16 TAU
20 ARI	19 TAU	21 GEM	19 CAN	21 VIR	20 LIB	22 SAG	20 CAP	20 PIS	20 ARI	19 TAU	18 GEM
22 TAU	21 GEM	23 CAN	22 LEO	24 LIB	22 SCO	24 CAP	22 AQU	23 ARI	23 TAU	21 GEM	21 CAN
25 GEM	24 CAN	25 LEO	24 VIR	26 SCO	24 SAG	26 AQU	24 PIS	25 TAU	25 GEM	24 CAN	23 LEO
27 CAN	26 LEO	28 VIR	26 LIB	28 SAG	26 CAP	28 PIS	26 ARI	28 GEM	27 CAN	26 LEO	26 VIR
30 LEO	28 VIR	30 LIB	28 SCO	30 CAP	28 AQU	30 ARI	29 TAU	30 CAN	30 LEO	29 VIR	28 LIB
			30 SAG		30 PIS		31 GEM				31 SCO

JAN	FEB	MAR	APR	MAY	JUN	JUL	AUG	SEP	OCT	NOV	DEC
2 SAG	2 AQU	3 PIS	1 ARI	1 TAU	2 CAN	2 LEO	3 LIB	1 SCO	1 SAG	1 AQU	1 PIS
4 CAP	4 PIS	5 ARI	3 TAU	3 GEM	4 LEO	4 VIR	5 SCO	3 SAG	3 CAP	3 PIS	3 ARI
6 AQU	6 ARI	7 TAU	6 GEM	5 CAN	7 VIR	7 LIB	7 SAG	6 CAP	5 AQU	6 ARI	5 TAU
8 PIS	9 TAU	9 GEM	8 CAN	8 LEO	9 LIB	9 SCO	9 CAP	8 AQU	7 PIS	8 TAU	7 GEM
10 ARI	11 GEM	11 CAN	11 LEO	11 VIR	11 SCO	11 SAG	11 AQU	10 PIS	9 ARI	10 GEM	10 CAN
12 TAU	14 CAN	14 LEO	13 VIR	13 LIB	13 SAG	13 CAP	13 PIS	12 ARI	11 TAU	13 CAN	12 LEO
15 GEM	16 LEO	17 VIR	15 LIB	15 SCO	16 CAP	15 AQU	16 ARI	14 TAU	14 GEM	15 LEO	15 VIR
17 CAN	18 VIR	21 SCO	17 SCO	17 SAG	18 AQU	18 PIS	18 TAU	16 GEM	16 CAN	18 VIR	17 LIB
20 LEO	21 LIB	23 SAG	19 SAG	19 CAP	20 PIS	19 ARI	20 GEM	19 CAN	19 LEO	20 LIB	20 SCO
22 VIR	23 SCO	26 CAP	22 CAP	21 AQU	22 ARI	21 TAU	23 CAN	21 LEO	21 VIR	22 SCO	22 SAG
25 LIB	25 SAG	28 AQU	24 AQU	23 PIS	24 TAU	24 GEM	25 LEO	24 VIR	24 LIB	24 SAG	24 CAP
27 SCO	27 CAP	30 PIS	26 PIS	26 ARI	27 GEM	26 CAN	28 VIR	26 LIB	26 SCO	27 CAP	26 AQU
29 SAG	29 AQU		28 ARI	28 TAU	29 CAN	29 LEO	30 LIB	29 SCO	28 SAG	29 AQU	28 PIS
31 CAP				30 GEM		31 VIR			30 CAP		30 ARI

JAN	FEB	MAR	APR	MAY	JUN	JUL	AUG	SEP	OCT	NOV	DEC
1 TAU	2 CAN	2 CAN	3 VIR	3 LIB	2 SCO	1 SAG	2 AQU	2 ARI	2 TAU	2 CAN	2 LEO
4 GEM	5 LEO	4 LEO	5 LIB	5 SCO	4 SAG	3 CAP	4 PIS	4 TAU	4 GEM	5 LEO	5 VIR
6 CAN	7 VIR	7 VIR	8 SCO	7 SAG	6 CAP	5 AQU	6 ARI	6 GEM	6 CAN	7 VIR	7 LIB
9 LEO	10 LIB	9 LIB	10 SAG	10 CAP	8 AQU	7 PIS	8 TAU	9 CAN	9 LEO	10 LIB	10 SCO
11 VIR	12 SCO	12 SCO	12 CAP	12 AQU	10 PIS	9 ARI	10 GEM	11 LEO	11 VIR	12 SCO	12 SAG
14 LIB	15 SAG	14 SAG	15 AQU	14 PIS	12 ARI	12 TAU	13 CAN	14 VIR	14 LIB	15 SAG	14 CAP
16 SCO	17 CAP	16 CAP	17 PIS	16 ARI	14 TAU	14 GEM	15 LEO	16 LIB	16 SCO	17 CAP	16 AQU
18 SAG	19 AQU	18 AQU	19 ARI	18 TAU	17 GEM	16 CAN	18 VIR	19 SCO	18 SAG	19 AQU	19 PIS
20 CAP	21 PIS	20 PIS	21 TAU	20 GEM	19 CAN	19 LEO	20 LIB	21 SAG	21 CAP	21 PIS	21 ARI
22 AQU	23 ARI	22 ARI	23 GEM	23 CAN	21 LEO	21 VIR	23 SCO	23 CAP	23 AQU	23 ARI	23 TAU
24 PIS	25 TAU	24 TAU	25 CAN	25 LEO	24 VIR	24 LIB	25 SAG	26 AQU	25 PIS	25 TAU	25 GEM
26 ARI	27 GEM	27 GEM	28 LEO	28 VIR	27 LIB	26 SCO	27 CAP	28 PIS	27 ARI	28 GEM	27 CAN
29 TAU		29 CAN	30 VIR	30 LIB	29 SCO	29 SAG	29 AQU	30 ARI	29 TAU	30 CAN	30 LEO
31 GEM		31 LEO				31 CAP	31 PIS		31 GEM		

JAN	FEB	MAR	APR	MAY	JUN	JUL	AUG	SEP	OCT	NOV	DEC
1 VIR	2 SCO	2 SCO	3 CAP	2 AQU	1 PIS	2 TAU	1 GEM	1 LEO	1 VIR	2 SCO	2 SAG
4 LIB	5 SAG	4 SAG	5 AQU	4 PIS	3 ARI	4 CAN	3 CAN	3 VIR	3 LIB	5 SAG	4 CAP
6 SCO	7 CAP	7 CAP	7 PIS	7 ARI	5 TAU	6 CAN	5 LEO	6 LIB	6 SCO	7 CAP	7 AQU
8 SAG	9 AQU	9 AQU	9 ARI	9 TAU	7 GEM	9 LEO	7 VIR	9 SCO	9 SAG	10 AQU	9 PIS
11 CAP	11 PIS	11 PIS	11 TAU	11 GEM	9 CAN	11 VIR	10 LIB	11 SAG	11 CAP	12 PIS	11 ARI
13 AQU	13 ARI	13 ARI	13 GEM	13 CAN	11 LEO	14 LIB	12 SCO	13 CAP	13 AQU	14 ARI	13 TAU
15 PIS	15 TAU	15 TAU	15 CAN	15 LEO	14 VIR	16 SCO	14 SAG	15 AQU	15 PIS	16 TAU	15 GEM
17 ARI	17 GEM	17 GEM	18 LEO	17 VIR	16 LIB	19 SAG	17 CAP	18 PIS	18 ARI	18 GEM	17 CAN
19 TAU	20 CAN	19 CAN	20 VIR	20 LIB	19 SCO	21 CAP	20 AQU	20 ARI	20 TAU	20 CAN	20 LEO
21 GEM	22 LEO	21 LEO	23 LIB	22 SCO	21 SAG	23 AQU	22 PIS	22 TAU	22 GEM	22 LEO	22 VIR
24 CAN	25 VIR	24 VIR	25 SCO	25 SAG	24 CAP	25 PIS	24 ARI	24 GEM	24 CAN	25 VIR	24 LIB
26 LEO	27 LIB	26 LIB	28 SAG	27 CAP	26 AQU	27 ARI	26 TAU	26 CAN	26 LEO	27 LIB	27 SCO
28 VIR		29 SCO	30 CAP	30 AQU	28 PIS	29 TAU	28 GEM	29 LEO	28 VIR	30 SCO	29 SAG
31 LIB		31 SAG			30 ARI		30 CAN		31 LIB		

JAN	FEB	MAR	APR	MAY	JUN	JUL	AUG	SEP	OCT	NOV	DEC
1 CAP	2 PIS	1 PIS	1 TAU	1 GEM	1 LEO	1 VIR	2 SCO	1 SAG	1 CAP	2 PIS	2 ARI
3 AQU	4 ARI	3 ARI	3 GEM	3 CAN	3 VIR	4 LIB	5 SAG	3 CAP	3 AQU	4 ARI	4 TAU
5 PIS	6 TAU	5 TAU	6 CAN	5 LEO	6 LIB	6 SCO	7 CAP	6 AQU	6 PIS	6 TAU	6 GEM
7 ARI	8 GEM	7 GEM	8 LEO	7 VIR	9 SCO	8 SAG	10 AQU	8 PIS	8 ARI	8 GEM	8 CAN
10 TAU	10 CAN	9 CAN	10 VIR	10 LIB	11 SAG	11 CAP	12 PIS	10 ARI	10 TAU	10 CAN	10 LEO
12 GEM	12 LEO	12 LEO	13 LIB	12 SCO	14 CAP	13 AQU	14 ARI	12 TAU	12 GEM	12 LEO	12 VIR
14 CAN	15 VIR	14 VIR	15 SCO	15 SAG	16 AQU	16 PIS	16 TAU	15 GEM	14 CAN	15 VIR	14 LIB
16 LEO	17 LIB	16 LIB	18 SAG	17 CAP	18 PIS	18 ARI	18 GEM	17 CAN	16 LEO	17 LIB	17 SCO
18 VIR	20 SCO	19 SCO	20 CAP	20 AQU	21 ARI	20 TAU	20 CAN	19 LEO	18 VIR	19 SCO	19 SAG
21 LIB	22 SAG	21 SAG	23 AQU	22 PIS	23 TAU	22 GEM	23 LEO	21 VIR	21 LIB	22 SAG	22 CAP
23 SCO	25 CAP	24 CAP	25 PIS	24 ARI	25 GEM	24 CAN	25 VIR	23 LIB	23 SCO	25 CAP	24 AQU
26 SAG	27 AQU	26 AQU	27 ARI	26 TAU	27 CAN	26 LEO	27 LIB	26 SCO	26 SAG	27 AQU	27 PIS
28 CAP		28 PIS	29 TAU	28 GEM	29 LEO	28 VIR	30 SCO	28 SAG	28 CAP	29 PIS	29 ARI
30 AQU		30 ARI		30 CAN		31 LIB			31 AQU		31 TAU

1920

JAN	FEB	MAR	APR	MAY	JUN	JUL	AUG	SEP	OCT	NOV	DEC
2 GEM	1 CAN	1 LEO	2 LIB	1 SCO	3 CAP	2 AQU	1 PIS	2 TAU	1 GEM	2 LEO	1 VIR
4 CAN	3 LEO	3 VIR	4 SCO	3 SAG	5 AQU	5 PIS	3 ARI	4 GEM	4 CAN	4 VIR	3 LIB
6 LEO	5 VIR	5 LIB	7 SAG	6 CAP	8 PIS	7 ARI	6 TAU	6 CAN	6 LEO	6 LIB	6 SCO
8 VIR	7 LIB	8 SCO	9 CAP	8 AQU	10 ARI	9 TAU	8 GEM	8 LEO	8 VIR	9 SCO	8 SAG
11 LIB	9 SCO	10 SAG	12 AQU	11 PIS	12 TAU	12 GEM	10 CAN	10 VIR	10 LIB	11 SAG	11 CAP
13 SCO	12 SAG	13 CAP	14 PIS	14 ARI	14 GEM	14 CAN	12 LEO	13 LIB	12 SCO	13 CAP	13 AQU
16 SAG	14 CAP	15 AQU	16 ARI	16 TAU	16 CAN	16 LEO	14 VIR	15 SCO	15 SAG	16 AQU	16 PIS
18 CAP	17 AQU	18 PIS	18 TAU	18 GEM	18 LEO	18 VIR	16 LIB	17 SAG	17 CAP	18 PIS	18 ARI
21 AQU	19 PIS	20 ARI	20 GEM	20 CAN	20 VIR	20 LIB	18 SCO	20 CAP	20 AQU	21 ARI	20 TAU
23 PIS	21 ARI	22 TAU	22 CAN	22 LEO	22 LIB	22 SCO	21 SAG	22 AQU	22 PIS	23 TAU	23 GEM
25 ARI	24 TAU	24 GEM	24 LEO	24 VIR	25 SCO	25 SAG	23 CAP	25 PIS	24 ARI	25 GEM	25 CAN
27 TAU	26 GEM	26 CAN	27 VIR	26 LIB	27 SAG	27 CAP	25 AQU	27 ARI	27 TAU	27 CAN	27 LEO
30 GEM	28 CAN	28 LEO	29 LIB	29 SCO	30 CAP	30 AQU	28 PIS	29 TAU	29 GEM	29 LEO	29 VIR
		30 VIR		31 SAG			31 ARI		31 CAN		31 LIB

1921

JAN	FEB	MAR	APR	MAY	JUN	JUL	AUG	SEP	OCT	NOV	DEC
2 SCO	1 SAG	3 CAP	1 AQU	1 PIS	2 TAU	2 GEM	2 LEO	1 VIR	2 SCO	1 SAG	1 CAP
4 SAG	3 CAP	5 AQU	4 PIS	4 ARI	5 GEM	4 CAN	4 VIR	3 LIB	5 SAG	3 CAP	3 AQU
7 CAP	6 AQU	8 PIS	6 ARI	6 TAU	7 CAN	6 LEO	6 LIB	5 SCO	7 CAP	6 AQU	6 PIS
9 AQU	8 PIS	10 ARI	8 TAU	8 GEM	9 LEO	8 VIR	9 SCO	7 SAG	9 AQU	8 PIS	8 ARI
12 PIS	11 ARI	12 TAU	11 GEM	10 CAN	11 VIR	10 LIB	11 SAG	10 CAP	12 PIS	11 ARI	11 TAU
14 ARI	13 TAU	15 GEM	13 CAN	12 LEO	13 LIB	12 SCO	13 CAP	12 AQU	14 ARI	13 TAU	13 GEM
17 TAU	15 GEM	17 CAN	15 LEO	14 VIR	15 SCO	15 SAG	16 AQU	15 PIS	17 TAU	15 GEM	15 CAN
19 GEM	17 CAN	19 LEO	17 VIR	17 LIB	17 SAG	17 CAP	18 PIS	17 ARI	19 GEM	18 CAN	17 LEO
21 CAN	19 LEO	21 VIR	19 LIB	19 SCO	20 CAP	20 AQU	21 ARI	20 TAU	21 CAN	20 LEO	19 VIR
23 LEO	21 VIR	23 LIB	21 SCO	21 SAG	22 AQU	22 PIS	23 TAU	22 GEM	23 LEO	22 VIR	21 LIB
25 VIR	24 LIB	25 SCO	24 SAG	24 CAP	25 PIS	25 ARI	26 GEM	24 CAN	26 VIR	24 LIB	23 SCO
27 LIB	26 SCO	27 SAG	26 CAP	26 AQU	27 ARI	27 TAU	28 CAN	26 LEO	28 LIB	26 SCO	26 SAG
29 SCO	28 SAG	30 CAP	29 AQU	29 PIS	30 TAU	29 GEM	30 LEO	28 VIR	30 SCO	28 SAG	28 CAP
				31 ARI		31 CAN		30 LIB			30 AQU

1922

JAN	FEB	MAR	APR	MAY	JUN	JUL	AUG	SEP	OCT	NOV	DEC
2 PIS	1 ARI	2 TAU	1 GEM	1 CAN	1 VIR	1 LIB	1 SAG	2 AQU	2 PIS	1 ARI	3 GEM
4 ARI	3 TAU	5 GEM	3 CAN	3 LEO	3 LIB	3 SCO	3 CAP	5 PIS	4 ARI	3 TAU	5 CAN
7 TAU	6 GEM	7 CAN	6 LEO	5 VIR	5 SCO	5 SAG	6 AQU	7 ARI	7 TAU	6 GEM	7 LEO
9 GEM	8 CAN	9 LEO	9 VIR	7 LIB	7 SAG	7 CAP	8 PIS	9 TAU	9 GEM	8 CAN	10 VIR
11 CAN	10 LEO	11 VIR	10 LIB	9 SCO	10 CAP	10 AQU	11 ARI	12 GEM	12 CAN	10 LEO	12 LIB
13 LEO	12 VIR	13 LIB	12 SCO	11 SAG	12 AQU	12 PIS	13 TAU	14 CAN	14 LEO	12 VIR	14 SCO
15 VIR	14 LIB	15 SCO	15 SAG	13 CAP	15 PIS	15 ARI	16 GEM	17 LEO	16 VIR	15 LIB	16 SAG
17 LIB	16 SCO	17 SAG	16 CAP	16 AQU	17 ARI	17 TAU	18 CAN	19 VIR	18 LIB	17 SCO	18 CAP
20 SCO	18 SAG	20 CAP	18 AQU	18 PIS	20 TAU	19 GEM	20 LEO	21 LIB	20 SCO	19 SAG	20 AQU
22 SAG	20 CAP	22 AQU	21 PIS	20 ARI	22 GEM	22 CAN	22 VIR	23 SCO	22 SAG	21 CAP	23 PIS
24 CAP	22 AQU	25 PIS	24 ARI	23 TAU	24 CAN	24 LEO	24 LIB	25 SAG	24 CAP	23 AQU	25 ARI
27 AQU	25 PIS	27 ARI	26 TAU	26 GEM	26 LEO	26 VIR	26 SCO	27 CAP	27 AQU	25 PIS	28 TAU
29 PIS	28 ARI	30 TAU	28 GEM	28 CAN	28 VIR	28 LIB	28 SAG	29 AQU	29 PIS	28 ARI	30 GEM
				30 LEO		30 SCO	31 CAP			30 TAU	

1923

JAN	FEB	MAR	APR	MAY	JUN	JUL	AUG	SEP	OCT	NOV	DEC
2 CAN	2 VIR	2 VIR	2 SCO	2 SAG	2 AQU	2 PIS	1 ARI	2 GEM	2 CAN	1 LEO	2 LIB
4 LEO	4 LIB	4 LIB	4 SAG	4 CAP	4 PIS	4 ARI	3 TAU	4 CAN	4 LEO	3 VIR	4 SCO
6 VIR	6 SCO	6 SCO	6 CAP	6 AQU	6 ARI	7 TAU	6 GEM	7 LEO	6 VIR	5 LIB	6 SAG
8 LIB	8 SAG	8 SAG	8 AQU	8 PIS	9 TAU	9 GEM	8 CAN	9 VIR	8 LIB	7 SCO	8 CAP
10 SCO	11 CAP	10 CAP	11 PIS	11 ARI	12 GEM	12 CAN	10 LEO	11 LIB	10 SCO	9 SAG	10 AQU
12 SAG	13 AQU	12 AQU	13 ARI	13 TAU	14 CAN	14 LEO	13 VIR	13 SCO	12 SAG	11 CAP	13 PIS
14 CAP	15 PIS	15 PIS	16 TAU	16 GEM	17 LEO	16 VIR	15 LIB	15 SAG	15 CAP	13 AQU	15 ARI
17 AQU	18 ARI	17 ARI	18 GEM	18 CAN	19 VIR	18 LIB	17 SCO	17 CAP	17 AQU	15 PIS	18 TAU
19 PIS	20 TAU	20 TAU	21 CAN	21 LEO	21 LIB	21 SCO	19 SAG	19 AQU	19 PIS	18 ARI	20 GEM
22 ARI	23 GEM	22 GEM	23 LEO	23 VIR	23 SCO	23 SAG	21 CAP	22 PIS	22 ARI	20 TAU	23 CAN
24 TAU	25 CAN	25 CAN	25 VIR	25 LIB	25 SAG	25 CAP	23 AQU	24 ARI	24 TAU	23 GEM	25 LEO
27 GEM	28 LEO	27 LEO	28 LIB	27 SCO	27 CAP	27 AQU	26 PIS	27 TAU	27 GEM	25 CAN	27 VIR
29 CAN		29 VIR	30 SCO	29 SAG	29 AQU	30 PIS	28 ARI	29 GEM	29 CAN	28 LEO	30 LIB
31 LEO		31 LIB		31 CAP			30 TAU			30 VIR	

1924

JAN	FEB	MAR	APR	MAY	JUN	JUL	AUG	SEP	OCT	NOV	DEC
1 SCO	1 CAP	2 AQU	2 ARI	2 TAU	1 GEM	1 CAN	2 VIR	3 SCO	2 SAG	2 AQU	2 PIS
3 SAG	3 AQU	4 PIS	5 TAU	5 GEM	3 CAN	3 LEO	4 LIB	5 SAG	4 CAP	5 PIS	4 ARI
5 CAP	5 PIS	6 ARI	7 GEM	7 CAN	6 LEO	6 VIR	6 SCO	7 CAP	6 AQU	7 ARI	7 TAU
7 AQU	8 ARI	9 TAU	10 CAN	10 LEO	8 VIR	8 LIB	8 SAG	9 AQU	8 PIS	9 TAU	9 GEM
9 PIS	10 TAU	11 GEM	12 LEO	12 VIR	11 LIB	10 SCO	10 CAP	11 PIS	11 ARI	12 GEM	12 CAN
11 ARI	13 GEM	14 CAN	15 VIR	14 LIB	13 SCO	12 SAG	13 AQU	13 ARI	13 TAU	14 CAN	14 LEO
14 TAU	15 CAN	16 LEO	17 LIB	16 SCO	15 SAG	14 CAP	15 PIS	16 TAU	16 GEM	17 LEO	17 VIR
16 GEM	18 LEO	18 VIR	19 SCO	18 SAG	17 CAP	16 AQU	17 ARI	18 GEM	18 CAN	19 VIR	19 LIB
19 CAN	20 VIR	20 LIB	21 SAG	20 CAP	19 AQU	18 PIS	19 TAU	21 CAN	21 LEO	22 LIB	21 SCO
21 LEO	22 LIB	23 SCO	23 CAP	22 AQU	21 PIS	21 ARI	22 GEM	23 LEO	23 VIR	24 SCO	23 SAG
24 VIR	24 SCO	25 SAG	25 AQU	25 PIS	23 ARI	23 TAU	24 CAN	26 VIR	25 LIB	26 SAG	25 CAP
26 LIB	26 SAG	27 CAP	27 PIS	27 ARI	26 TAU	25 GEM	27 LEO	28 LIB	27 SCO	28 CAP	27 AQU
28 SCO	28 CAP	29 AQU	30 ARI	29 TAU	28 GEM	28 CAN	29 VIR	30 SCO	29 SAG	30 AQU	29 PIS
30 SAG		31 PIS				30 LEO	31 LIB		31 CAP		31 ARI

1925

JAN	FEB	MAR	APR	MAY	JUN	JUL	AUG	SEP	OCT	NOV	DEC
3 TAU	2 GEM	1 GEM	2 LEO	2 VIR	1 LIB	3 SAG	1 CAP	1 PIS	1 ARI	2 GEM	1 CAN
5 GEM	4 CAN	3 CAN	5 VIR	4 LIB	3 SCO	5 CAP	3 AQU	4 ARI	3 TAU	4 CAN	4 LEO
8 CAN	7 LEO	6 LEO	7 LIB	7 SCO	5 SAG	7 AQU	5 PIS	6 TAU	5 GEM	7 LEO	6 VIR
10 LEO	9 VIR	8 VIR	9 SCO	9 SAG	7 CAP	9 PIS	7 ARI	8 GEM	8 CAN	9 VIR	9 LIB
13 VIR	11 LIB	11 LIB	11 SAG	11 CAP	9 AQU	11 ARI	9 TAU	10 CAN	10 LEO	12 LIB	11 SCO
15 LIB	14 SCO	13 SCO	13 CAP	13 AQU	11 PIS	13 TAU	12 GEM	13 LEO	12 VIR	14 SCO	13 SAG
17 SCO	16 SAG	15 SAG	16 AQU	15 PIS	13 ARI	15 GEM	14 CAN	15 VIR	15 LIB	16 SAG	16 CAP
20 SAG	18 CAP	17 CAP	18 PIS	17 ARI	16 TAU	18 CAN	17 LEO	18 LIB	18 SCO	18 CAP	18 AQU
22 CAP	20 AQU	19 AQU	20 ARI	19 TAU	18 GEM	20 LEO	19 VIR	20 SCO	20 SAG	20 AQU	20 PIS
24 AQU	22 PIS	21 PIS	22 TAU	22 GEM	21 CAN	23 VIR	22 LIB	22 SAG	22 CAP	22 PIS	22 ARI
26 PIS	24 ARI	24 ARI	25 GEM	24 CAN	23 LEO	25 LIB	24 SCO	25 CAP	24 AQU	25 ARI	24 TAU
28 ARI	26 TAU	26 TAU	27 CAN	27 LEO	26 VIR	28 SCO	26 SAG	27 AQU	26 PIS	27 TAU	26 GEM
30 TAU		28 GEM	30 LEO	29 VIR	28 LIB	30 SAG	28 CAP	29 PIS	28 ARI	29 GEM	29 CAN
		31 CAN			30 SCO		30 AQU		30 TAU		31 LEO

1926

JAN	FEB	MAR	APR	MAY	JUN	JUL	AUG	SEP	OCT	NOV	DEC
3 VIR	2 LIB	1 LIB	2 SAG	1 CAP	2 PIS	1 ARI	2 GEM	2 LEO	3 VIR	1 LIB	1 SCO
5 LIB	4 SCO	3 SCO	4 CAP	3 AQU	4 ARI	3 TAU	4 CAN	4 VIR	5 LIB	4 SCO	4 SAG
8 SCO	6 SAG	6 SAG	6 AQU	5 PIS	6 TAU	6 GEM	7 LEO	6 LIB	8 SCO	6 SAG	6 CAP
10 SAG	8 CAP	8 CAP	8 PIS	8 ARI	8 GEM	8 CAN	9 VIR	8 SCO	10 SAG	9 CAP	8 AQU
12 CAP	10 AQU	10 AQU	10 ARI	10 TAU	11 CAN	10 LEO	12 LIB	10 SAG	12 CAP	11 AQU	10 PIS
14 AQU	12 PIS	12 PIS	12 TAU	12 GEM	13 LEO	13 VIR	14 SCO	13 CAP	15 AQU	13 PIS	12 ARI
16 PIS	14 ARI	14 ARI	15 GEM	14 CAN	16 VIR	15 LIB	17 SAG	15 AQU	17 PIS	15 ARI	14 TAU
18 ARI	17 TAU	16 TAU	17 CAN	17 LEO	18 LIB	18 SCO	19 CAP	17 PIS	19 ARI	17 TAU	17 GEM
20 TAU	19 GEM	18 GEM	19 LEO	19 VIR	20 SCO	20 SAG	21 AQU	19 ARI	21 TAU	19 GEM	19 CAN
23 GEM	21 CAN	21 CAN	22 VIR	22 LIB	23 SAG	22 CAP	24 PIS	21 TAU	23 GEM	21 CAN	21 LEO
25 CAN	24 LEO	23 LEO	24 LIB	24 SCO	25 CAP	24 AQU	26 ARI	23 GEM	25 CAN	24 LEO	24 VIR
27 LEO	26 VIR	26 VIR	27 SCO	26 SAG	27 AQU	26 PIS	28 TAU	25 CAN	27 LEO	26 VIR	26 LIB
30 VIR		28 LIB	29 SAG	29 CAP	29 PIS	28 ARI	29 GEM	30 LEO	30 VIR	30 VIR	29 SCO
		30 SCO		31 AQU		31 TAU	31 CAN				31 SAG

1927

JAN	FEB	MAR	APR	MAY	JUN	JUL	AUG	SEP	OCT	NOV	DEC
2 CAP	1 AQU	2 PIS	1 ARI	2 GEM	1 CAN	3 VIR	1 LIB	3 SAG	3 CAP	1 AQU	1 PIS
4 AQU	3 PIS	4 ARI	3 TAU	4 CAN	3 LEO	5 LIB	4 SCO	5 CAP	5 AQU	3 PIS	3 ARI
6 PIS	5 ARI	6 TAU	5 GEM	7 LEO	5 VIR	8 SCO	7 SAG	7 AQU	7 PIS	6 ARI	5 TAU
9 ARI	7 TAU	8 GEM	7 CAN	9 VIR	8 LIB	10 SAG	9 CAP	9 PIS	9 ARI	8 TAU	7 GEM
11 TAU	9 GEM	11 CAN	9 LEO	12 LIB	10 SCO	13 CAP	11 AQU	12 ARI	11 TAU	10 GEM	9 CAN
13 GEM	11 CAN	13 LEO	12 VIR	14 SCO	13 SAG	15 AQU	13 PIS	14 TAU	13 GEM	12 CAN	11 LEO
15 CAN	14 LEO	15 VIR	14 LIB	16 SAG	15 CAP	17 PIS	15 ARI	16 GEM	15 CAN	14 LEO	13 VIR
17 LEO	16 VIR	18 LIB	17 SCO	19 CAP	17 AQU	19 ARI	17 TAU	18 CAN	17 LEO	16 VIR	16 LIB
20 VIR	19 LIB	21 SCO	19 SAG	21 AQU	20 PIS	21 TAU	19 GEM	20 LEO	20 VIR	19 LIB	18 SCO
22 LIB	21 SCO	23 SAG	22 CAP	23 PIS	22 ARI	23 GEM	21 CAN	23 VIR	22 LIB	21 SCO	21 SAG
25 SCO	24 SAG	25 CAP	24 AQU	25 ARI	24 TAU	25 CAN	24 LEO	25 LIB	25 SCO	24 SAG	23 CAP
27 SAG	26 CAP	28 AQU	26 PIS	27 TAU	26 GEM	28 LEO	26 VIR	28 SCO	27 SAG	26 CAP	26 AQU
30 CAP	28 AQU	30 PIS	28 ARI	30 GEM	28 CAN	30 VIR	29 LIB	30 SAG	30 CAP	28 AQU	28 PIS
			30 TAU		30 LEO		31 SCO				30 ARI

1928

JAN	FEB	MAR	APR	MAY	JUN	JUL	AUG	SEP	OCT	NOV	DEC
1 TAU	2 CAN	2 LEO	1 VIR	3 SCO	1 SAG	2 CAP	3 PIS	1 ARI	3 GEM	1 CAN	3 VIR
3 GEM	4 LEO	5 VIR	3 LIB	5 SAG	4 CAP	4 AQU	5 ARI	3 TAU	5 CAN	3 LEO	5 LIB
5 CAN	6 VIR	7 LIB	6 SCO	8 CAP	7 AQU	6 PIS	7 TAU	5 GEM	7 LEO	5 VIR	7 SCO
8 LEO	9 LIB	9 SCO	8 SAG	10 AQU	9 PIS	9 ARI	9 GEM	7 CAN	9 VIR	7 LIB	10 SAG
10 VIR	11 SCO	12 SAG	11 CAP	13 PIS	11 ARI	11 TAU	11 CAN	10 LEO	11 LIB	10 SCO	12 CAP
12 LIB	14 SAG	14 CAP	13 AQU	15 ARI	13 TAU	13 GEM	13 LEO	12 VIR	14 SCO	13 SAG	15 AQU
15 SCO	16 CAP	17 AQU	15 PIS	17 TAU	15 GEM	15 CAN	15 VIR	14 LIB	16 SAG	15 CAP	17 PIS
17 SAG	18 AQU	19 PIS	18 ARI	19 GEM	17 CAN	17 LEO	18 LIB	16 SCO	19 CAP	18 AQU	20 ARI
20 CAP	21 PIS	21 ARI	20 TAU	21 CAN	19 LEO	19 VIR	20 SCO	19 SAG	21 AQU	20 PIS	22 TAU
22 AQU	23 ARI	23 TAU	22 GEM	23 LEO	22 VIR	21 LIB	23 SAG	21 CAP	24 PIS	22 ARI	24 GEM
24 PIS	25 TAU	25 GEM	24 CAN	25 VIR	24 LIB	24 SCO	25 CAP	24 AQU	26 ARI	24 TAU	26 CAN
26 ARI	27 GEM	27 CAN	26 LEO	28 LIB	26 SCO	26 SAG	28 AQU	26 PIS	28 TAU	26 GEM	28 LEO
28 TAU	29 CAN	29 LEO	28 VIR	30 SCO	29 SAG	29 CAP	30 PIS	28 ARI	30 GEM	28 CAN	30 VIR
31 GEM			30 LIB			31 AQU		30 TAU		30 LEO	

1929

JAN	FEB	MAR	APR	MAY	JUN	JUL	AUG	SEP	OCT	NOV	DEC
1 LIB	2 SAG	2 SAG	1 CAP	3 PIS	2 ARI	1 TAU	2 CAN	2 VIR	2 LIB	2 SAG	2 CAP
4 SCO	5 CAP	4 CAP	3 AQU	5 ARI	4 TAU	3 GEM	4 LEO	4 LIB	4 SCO	5 CAP	5 AQU
6 SAG	7 AQU	7 AQU	5 PIS	7 TAU	6 GEM	5 CAN	6 VIR	6 SCO	6 SAG	7 AQU	7 PIS
9 CAP	10 PIS	9 PIS	8 ARI	9 GEM	8 CAN	7 LEO	8 LIB	9 SAG	9 CAP	10 PIS	10 ARI
11 AQU	12 ARI	11 ARI	10 TAU	11 CAN	10 LEO	9 VIR	10 SCO	11 CAP	11 AQU	12 ARI	12 TAU
14 PIS	14 TAU	14 TAU	12 GEM	13 LEO	12 VIR	11 LIB	12 SAG	14 AQU	14 PIS	15 TAU	14 GEM
16 ARI	16 GEM	16 GEM	14 CAN	16 VIR	14 LIB	14 SCO	15 CAP	16 PIS	16 ARI	17 GEM	16 CAN
18 TAU	19 CAN	18 CAN	16 LEO	18 LIB	16 SCO	16 SAG	17 AQU	19 ARI	18 TAU	19 CAN	18 LEO
20 GEM	21 LEO	20 LEO	18 VIR	20 SCO	19 SAG	19 CAP	20 PIS	21 TAU	20 GEM	21 LEO	20 VIR
22 CAN	23 VIR	22 VIR	21 LIB	23 SAG	21 CAP	21 AQU	22 ARI	23 GEM	22 CAN	23 VIR	22 LIB
24 LEO	25 LIB	24 LIB	23 SCO	25 CAP	24 AQU	24 PIS	25 TAU	25 CAN	25 LEO	25 LIB	25 SCO
26 VIR	27 SCO	27 SCO	25 SAG	28 AQU	26 PIS	26 ARI	27 GEM	27 LEO	27 VIR	27 SCO	27 SAG
29 LIB		29 SAG	28 CAP	30 PIS	29 ARI	28 TAU	29 CAN	29 VIR	29 LIB	30 SAG	30 CAP
31 SCO			30 AQU			31 GEM	31 LEO		31 SCO		

1930

JAN	FEB	MAR	APR	MAY	JUN	JUL	AUG	SEP	OCT	NOV	DEC
1 AQU	2 ARI	2 ARI	2 GEM	2 CAN	2 VIR	2 LIB	2 SAG	1 CAP	1 AQU	2 ARI	2 TAU
4 PIS	5 TAU	4 TAU	5 CAN	4 LEO	4 LIB	4 SCO	5 CAP	4 AQU	3 PIS	5 TAU	4 GEM
6 ARI	7 GEM	6 GEM	7 LEO	6 VIR	7 SCO	6 SAG	7 AQU	6 PIS	6 ARI	7 GEM	7 CAN
8 TAU	9 CAN	8 CAN	9 VIR	8 LIB	9 SAG	9 CAP	10 PIS	9 ARI	8 TAU	9 CAN	9 LEO
11 GEM	11 LEO	10 LEO	11 LIB	10 SCO	11 CAP	11 AQU	12 ARI	11 TAU	11 GEM	11 LEO	11 VIR
13 CAN	13 VIR	12 VIR	13 SCO	13 SAG	14 AQU	14 PIS	15 TAU	14 GEM	13 CAN	13 VIR	13 LIB
15 LEO	15 LIB	15 LIB	15 SAG	15 CAP	16 PIS	16 ARI	17 GEM	16 CAN	15 LEO	16 LIB	15 SCO
17 VIR	17 SCO	17 SCO	18 CAP	18 AQU	19 ARI	19 TAU	19 CAN	18 LEO	17 VIR	18 SCO	17 SAG
19 LIB	20 SAG	19 SAG	20 AQU	20 PIS	21 TAU	21 GEM	21 LEO	20 VIR	20 LIB	20 SAG	20 CAP
21 SCO	22 CAP	21 CAP	23 PIS	23 ARI	24 GEM	23 CAN	23 VIR	22 LIB	22 SCO	22 CAP	22 AQU
23 SAG	25 AQU	24 AQU	25 ARI	25 TAU	26 CAN	25 LEO	25 LIB	24 SCO	24 SAG	25 AQU	24 PIS
26 CAP	27 PIS	26 PIS	28 TAU	27 GEM	28 LEO	27 VIR	28 SCO	26 SAG	26 CAP	27 PIS	27 ARI
28 AQU		29 ARI	30 GEM	29 CAN	30 VIR	29 LIB	30 SAG	28 CAP	28 AQU	30 ARI	29 TAU
31 PIS		31 TAU		31 LEO		31 SCO			31 PIS		

1931

JAN	FEB	MAR	APR	MAY	JUN	JUL	AUG	SEP	OCT	NOV	DEC
1 GEM	1 LEO	1 LEO	1 LIB	1 SCO	1 CAP	1 AQU	2 ARI	1 TAU	1 GEM	2 LEO	1 VIR
3 CAN	3 VIR	3 VIR	3 SCO	3 SAG	4 AQU	4 PIS	5 TAU	4 GEM	3 CAN	4 VIR	3 LIB
5 LEO	5 LIB	5 LIB	5 SAG	5 CAP	6 PIS	6 ARI	7 GEM	6 CAN	6 LEO	6 LIB	6 SCO
7 VIR	8 SCO	7 SCO	8 CAP	7 AQU	9 ARI	9 TAU	10 CAN	8 LEO	8 VIR	8 SCO	8 SAG
9 LIB	10 SAG	9 SAG	10 AQU	10 PIS	11 TAU	11 GEM	12 LEO	10 VIR	10 LIB	10 SAG	10 CAP
11 SCO	12 CAP	11 CAP	13 PIS	12 ARI	14 GEM	13 CAN	14 VIR	12 LIB	12 SCO	12 CAP	12 AQU
13 SAG	15 AQU	14 AQU	15 ARI	15 TAU	16 CAN	15 LEO	16 LIB	14 SCO	14 SAG	14 AQU	14 PIS
16 CAP	17 PIS	16 PIS	18 TAU	17 GEM	18 LEO	17 VIR	18 SCO	16 SAG	16 CAP	17 PIS	17 ARI
18 AQU	20 ARI	19 ARI	20 GEM	20 CAN	20 VIR	20 LIB	20 SAG	19 CAP	18 AQU	19 ARI	19 TAU
21 PIS	22 TAU	21 TAU	22 CAN	22 LEO	22 LIB	22 SCO	22 CAP	21 AQU	21 PIS	22 TAU	22 GEM
23 ARI	25 GEM	24 GEM	25 LEO	24 VIR	24 SCO	24 SAG	25 AQU	23 PIS	23 ARI	24 GEM	24 CAN
26 TAU	27 CAN	26 CAN	27 VIR	26 LIB	27 SAG	26 CAP	27 PIS	26 ARI	26 TAU	27 CAN	26 LEO
28 GEM		28 LEO	29 LIB	28 SCO	29 CAP	28 AQU	30 ARI	28 TAU	28 GEM	29 LEO	29 VIR
30 CAN		30 VIR		30 SAG		31 PIS			31 CAN		31 LIB

1932

JAN	FEB	MAR	APR	MAY	JUN	JUL	AUG	SEP	OCT	NOV	DEC
2 SCO	2 CAP	1 CAP	2 PIS	1 ARI	3 GEM	2 CAN	1 LEO	2 LIB	1 SCO	1 CAP	1 AQU
4 SAG	5 AQU	3 AQU	4 ARI	4 TAU	5 CAN	5 LEO	3 VIR	4 SCO	3 SAG	4 AQU	3 PIS
6 CAP	7 PIS	5 PIS	7 TAU	6 GEM	7 LEO	7 VIR	5 LIB	6 SAG	5 CAP	6 PIS	6 ARI
8 AQU	9 ARI	8 ARI	9 GEM	9 CAN	10 VIR	9 LIB	7 SCO	8 CAP	7 AQU	8 ARI	8 TAU
11 PIS	12 TAU	10 TAU	12 CAN	11 LEO	12 LIB	11 SCO	10 SAG	10 AQU	10 PIS	11 TAU	11 GEM
13 ARI	14 GEM	13 GEM	14 LEO	13 VIR	14 SCO	13 SAG	12 CAP	12 PIS	12 ARI	13 GEM	13 CAN
16 TAU	17 CAN	15 CAN	16 VIR	16 LIB	16 SAG	15 CAP	14 AQU	15 ARI	15 TAU	16 CAN	16 LEO
18 GEM	19 LEO	18 LEO	18 LIB	18 SCO	18 CAP	18 AQU	16 PIS	17 TAU	17 GEM	18 LEO	18 VIR
20 CAN	21 VIR	20 VIR	20 SCO	20 SAG	20 AQU	20 PIS	19 ARI	20 GEM	20 CAN	21 VIR	20 LIB
23 LEO	23 LIB	22 LIB	22 SAG	22 CAP	22 PIS	22 ARI	21 TAU	22 CAN	22 LEO	23 LIB	22 SCO
25 VIR	25 SCO	24 SCO	24 CAP	24 AQU	25 ARI	25 TAU	24 GEM	25 LEO	24 VIR	25 SCO	24 SAG
27 LIB	27 SAG	26 SAG	26 AQU	26 PIS	27 TAU	27 GEM	26 CAN	27 VIR	27 LIB	27 SAG	26 CAP
29 SCO		28 CAP	29 PIS	29 ARI	30 GEM	30 CAN	28 LEO	29 LIB	29 SCO	29 CAP	28 AQU
31 SAG		30 AQU		31 TAU			31 VIR		30 SAG		31 PIS

1933

JAN	FEB	MAR	APR	MAY	JUN	JUL	AUG	SEP	OCT	NOV	DEC
2 ARI	1 TAU	3 GEM	1 CAN	1 LEO	2 LIB	2 SCO	2 CAP	2 AQU	2 ARI	1 TAU	1 GEM
4 TAU	3 GEM	5 CAN	4 LEO	4 VIR	4 SCO	4 SAG	4 AQU	3 PIS	5 TAU	3 GEM	3 CAN
7 GEM	6 CAN	8 LEO	6 VIR	6 LIB	6 SAG	6 CAP	6 PIS	5 ARI	7 GEM	6 CAN	6 LEO
9 CAN	8 LEO	10 VIR	8 LIB	8 SCO	8 CAP	8 AQU	8 ARI	7 TAU	9 CAN	8 LEO	8 VIR
12 LEO	10 VIR	12 LIB	10 SCO	10 SAG	10 AQU	10 PIS	11 TAU	10 GEM	12 LEO	11 VIR	11 LIB
14 VIR	13 LIB	14 SCO	12 SAG	12 CAP	12 PIS	12 ARI	13 GEM	12 CAN	14 VIR	13 LIB	13 SCO
16 LIB	15 SCO	16 SAG	14 CAP	14 AQU	15 ARI	14 TAU	16 CAN	14 LEO	17 LIB	15 SCO	15 SAG
19 SCO	17 SAG	18 CAP	17 AQU	16 PIS	17 TAU	17 GEM	18 LEO	17 VIR	19 SCO	17 SAG	17 CAP
21 SAG	19 CAP	20 AQU	19 PIS	19 ARI	20 GEM	20 CAN	21 VIR	19 LIB	21 SAG	19 CAP	19 AQU
23 CAP	21 AQU	23 PIS	21 ARI	21 TAU	22 CAN	22 LEO	23 LIB	21 SCO	23 CAP	21 AQU	21 PIS
25 AQU	23 PIS	25 ARI	24 TAU	23 GEM	25 LEO	24 VIR	25 SCO	23 SAG	25 AQU	23 PIS	23 ARI
27 PIS	26 ARI	27 TAU	26 GEM	26 CAN	27 VIR	27 LIB	27 SAG	25 CAP	27 PIS	26 ARI	25 TAU
29 ARI	28 TAU	30 GEM	29 CAN	29 LEO	30 LIB	29 SCO	29 CAP	28 AQU	30 ARI	28 TAU	28 GEM
				31 VIR		31 SAG		30 PIS			30 CAN

1934

JAN	FEB	MAR	APR	MAY	JUN	JUL	AUG	SEP	OCT	NOV	DEC
2 LEO	1 VIR	2 LIB	1 SCO	2 CAP	1 AQU	2 ARI	1 TAU	2 CAN	2 LEO	1 VIR	3 SCO
4 VIR	3 LIB	5 SCO	3 SAG	5 AQU	3 PIS	5 TAU	3 GEM	4 LEO	4 VIR	3 LIB	5 SAG
7 LIB	5 SCO	7 SAG	5 CAP	7 PIS	5 ARI	7 GEM	6 CAN	6 VIR	7 LIB	5 SCO	7 CAP
9 SCO	8 SAG	9 CAP	7 AQU	9 ARI	7 TAU	9 CAN	8 LEO	9 LIB	9 SCO	8 SAG	9 AQU
11 SAG	10 CAP	11 AQU	9 PIS	11 TAU	10 GEM	12 LEO	11 VIR	12 SCO	11 SAG	10 CAP	11 PIS
13 CAP	12 AQU	13 PIS	11 ARI	13 GEM	12 CAN	15 VIR	13 LIB	14 SAG	14 CAP	12 AQU	13 ARI
15 AQU	14 PIS	15 ARI	14 TAU	16 CAN	15 LEO	17 LIB	16 SCO	16 CAP	16 AQU	14 PIS	16 TAU
17 PIS	16 ARI	17 TAU	16 GEM	18 LEO	17 VIR	19 SCO	18 SAG	18 AQU	18 PIS	16 ARI	18 GEM
19 ARI	18 TAU	20 GEM	19 CAN	21 VIR	20 LIB	22 SAG	20 CAP	20 PIS	20 ARI	18 TAU	20 CAN
22 TAU	20 GEM	22 CAN	21 LEO	23 LIB	22 SCO	24 CAP	22 AQU	23 ARI	22 TAU	21 GEM	23 LEO
24 GEM	23 CAN	25 LEO	24 VIR	26 SCO	24 SAG	26 AQU	24 PIS	25 TAU	24 GEM	23 CAN	25 VIR
27 CAN	25 LEO	27 VIR	26 LIB	28 SAG	26 CAP	28 PIS	26 ARI	27 GEM	27 CAN	25 LEO	28 LIB
29 LEO	28 VIR	30 LIB	28 SCO	30 CAP	28 AQU	30 ARI	28 TAU	29 CAN	29 LEO	28 VIR	30 SCO
			30 SAG		30 PIS		30 GEM			30 LIB	

1935

JAN	FEB	MAR	APR	MAY	JUN	JUL	AUG	SEP	OCT	NOV	DEC
1 SAG	2 AQU	2 AQU	2 ARI	1 TAU	2 CAN	2 LEO	1 VIR	2 SCO	2 SAG	2 AQU	2 PIS
4 CAP	4 PIS	4 PIS	4 TAU	4 GEM	5 LEO	4 VIR	3 LIB	4 SAG	4 CAP	5 PIS	4 ARI
6 AQU	6 ARI	6 ARI	6 GEM	6 CAN	7 VIR	7 LIB	6 SCO	7 CAP	6 AQU	7 ARI	6 TAU
8 PIS	8 TAU	8 TAU	8 CAN	8 LEO	10 LIB	9 SCO	8 SAG	9 AQU	8 PIS	9 TAU	8 GEM
10 ARI	10 GEM	10 GEM	11 LEO	11 VIR	12 SCO	12 SAG	10 CAP	11 PIS	10 ARI	11 GEM	10 CAN
12 TAU	13 CAN	12 CAN	13 VIR	13 LIB	14 SAG	14 CAP	13 AQU	14 ARI	12 TAU	13 CAN	13 LEO
14 GEM	15 LEO	15 LEO	16 LIB	16 SCO	17 CAP	16 AQU	15 PIS	17 TAU	14 GEM	15 LEO	15 VIR
17 CAN	18 VIR	17 VIR	18 SCO	18 SAG	19 AQU	18 PIS	17 ARI	19 GEM	17 CAN	18 VIR	18 LIB
19 LEO	20 LIB	20 LIB	21 SAG	20 CAP	21 PIS	21 ARI	19 TAU	22 CAN	19 LEO	20 LIB	20 SCO
22 VIR	23 SCO	22 SCO	23 CAP	22 AQU	23 ARI	23 TAU	22 GEM	24 LEO	21 VIR	23 SCO	23 SAG
24 LIB	25 SAG	24 SAG	25 AQU	24 PIS	25 TAU	25 GEM	24 CAN	27 VIR	24 LIB	25 SAG	25 CAP
27 SCO	27 CAP	27 CAP	27 PIS	27 ARI	27 GEM	27 CAN	27 LEO	29 LIB	26 SCO	27 CAP	27 AQU
29 SAG		29 AQU	29 ARI	29 TAU	29 CAN	29 LEO	28 VIR		29 SAG	30 AQU	29 PIS
31 CAP		31 PIS		31 GEM			30 LIB		31 CAP		31 ARI

JAN	FEB	MAR	APR	MAY	JUN	JUL	AUG	SEP	OCT	NOV	DEC
2 TAU	1 GEM	1 CAN	2 VIR	2 LIB	1 SCO	1 SAG	2 AQU	2 ARI	2 TAU	2 CAN	2 LEO
5 GEM	3 CAN	4 LEO	5 LIB	5 SCO	3 SAG	3 CAP	4 PIS	4 TAU	4 GEM	4 LEO	4 VIR
7 CAN	5 LEO	6 VIR	7 SCO	7 SAG	6 CAP	5 AQU	6 ARI	6 GEM	6 CAN	7 VIR	6 LIB
9 LEO	8 VIR	9 LIB	9 SAG	9 CAP	8 AQU	8 PIS	8 TAU	8 CAN	8 LEO	9 LIB	9 SCO
11 VIR	10 LIB	11 SCO	12 CAP	12 AQU	10 PIS	10 ARI	10 GEM	11 LEO	10 VIR	12 SCO	11 SAG
14 LIB	13 SCO	14 SAG	15 AQU	14 PIS	12 ARI	12 TAU	12 CAN	13 VIR	13 LIB	14 SAG	14 CAP
16 SCO	15 SAG	16 CAP	17 PIS	16 ARI	14 TAU	14 GEM	15 LEO	16 LIB	15 SCO	17 CAP	16 AQU
19 SAG	18 CAP	18 AQU	19 ARI	18 TAU	16 GEM	16 CAN	17 VIR	18 SCO	18 SAG	19 AQU	19 PIS
21 CAP	20 AQU	20 PIS	21 TAU	20 GEM	19 CAN	18 LEO	19 LIB	21 SAG	20 CAP	21 PIS	21 ARI
23 AQU	22 PIS	22 ARI	23 GEM	22 CAN	21 LEO	21 VIR	22 SCO	23 CAP	23 AQU	24 ARI	23 TAU
25 PIS	24 ARI	24 TAU	25 CAN	24 LEO	23 VIR	23 LIB	24 SAG	25 AQU	25 PIS	26 TAU	25 GEM
27 ARI	26 TAU	26 GEM	27 LEO	27 VIR	26 LIB	26 SCO	26 CAP	28 PIS	27 ARI	28 GEM	27 CAN
30 TAU	28 GEM	28 CAN	30 VIR	29 LIB	28 SCO	28 SAG	28 AQU	30 ARI	29 TAU	30 CAN	29 LEO
		31 LEO				30 CAP	31 PIS		31 GEM		31 VIR

JAN	FEB	MAR	APR	MAY	JUN	JUL	AUG	SEP	OCT	NOV	DEC
3 LIB	2 SCO	1 SCO	2 CAP	2 AQU	1 PIS	2 TAU	1 GEM	1 LEO	1 VIR	2 SCO	1 SAG
5 SCO	4 SAG	3 SAG	5 AQU	4 PIS	3 ARI	4 GEM	3 CAN	3 VIR	3 LIB	4 SAG	4 CAP
8 SAG	7 CAP	6 CAP	7 PIS	7 ARI	5 TAU	6 CAN	5 LEO	6 LIB	5 SCO	7 CAP	6 AQU
10 CAP	9 AQU	8 AQU	9 ARI	9 TAU	7 GEM	8 LEO	7 VIR	8 SCO	8 SAG	9 AQU	9 PIS
13 AQU	11 PIS	11 PIS	11 TAU	11 GEM	9 CAN	11 VIR	9 LIB	10 SAG	10 CAP	12 PIS	11 ARI
15 PIS	13 ARI	13 ARI	13 GEM	13 CAN	11 LEO	13 LIB	12 SCO	13 CAP	13 AQU	14 ARI	13 TAU
17 ARI	15 TAU	15 TAU	15 CAN	15 LEO	13 VIR	15 SCO	14 SAG	15 AQU	15 PIS	16 TAU	15 GEM
19 TAU	18 GEM	17 GEM	17 LEO	17 VIR	16 LIB	18 SAG	17 CAP	18 PIS	17 ARI	18 GEM	17 CAN
21 GEM	20 CAN	19 CAN	20 VIR	19 LIB	18 SCO	20 CAP	19 AQU	20 ARI	19 TAU	20 CAN	19 LEO
23 CAN	22 LEO	21 LEO	22 LIB	22 SCO	21 SAG	23 AQU	21 PIS	22 TAU	22 GEM	22 LEO	21 VIR
26 LEO	24 VIR	23 VIR	25 SCO	24 SAG	23 CAP	25 PIS	24 ARI	24 GEM	24 CAN	24 VIR	24 LIB
28 VIR	26 LIB	26 LIB	27 SAG	27 CAP	26 AQU	27 ARI	26 TAU	26 CAN	26 LEO	26 LIB	26 SCO
30 LIB		28 SCO	30 CAP	29 AQU	28 PIS	30 TAU	28 GEM	28 LEO	28 VIR	29 SCO	29 SAG
		31 SAG			30 ARI		30 CAN		30 LIB		31 CAP

JAN	FEB	MAR	APR	MAY	JUN	JUL	AUG	SEP	OCT	NOV	DEC
3 AQU	1 PIS	1 PIS	1 TAU	1 GEM	1 LEO	1 VIR	2 SCO	3 CAP	3 AQU	2 PIS	1 ARI
5 PIS	4 ARI	3 ARI	4 GEM	3 CAN	3 VIR	3 LIB	4 SAG	5 AQU	5 PIS	4 ARI	4 TAU
7 ARI	6 TAU	5 TAU	6 CAN	5 LEO	6 LIB	5 SCO	7 CAP	8 PIS	8 ARI	6 TAU	6 GEM
10 TAU	8 GEM	7 GEM	8 LEO	7 VIR	8 SCO	8 SAG	9 AQU	10 ARI	10 TAU	8 GEM	8 CAN
12 GEM	10 CAN	9 CAN	10 VIR	9 LIB	10 SAG	10 CAP	12 PIS	12 TAU	12 GEM	10 CAN	10 LEO
14 CAN	12 LEO	12 LEO	12 LIB	12 SCO	13 CAP	13 AQU	14 ARI	15 GEM	14 CAN	12 LEO	12 VIR
16 LEO	14 VIR	14 VIR	15 SCO	14 SAG	16 AQU	15 PIS	16 TAU	17 CAN	16 LEO	15 VIR	14 LIB
18 VIR	16 LIB	16 LIB	17 SAG	17 CAP	18 PIS	18 ARI	18 GEM	19 LEO	18 VIR	17 LIB	16 SCO
20 LIB	19 SCO	18 SCO	19 CAP	19 AQU	20 ARI	20 TAU	21 CAN	21 VIR	20 LIB	19 SCO	19 SAG
22 SCO	21 SAG	21 SAG	22 AQU	22 PIS	23 TAU	22 GEM	23 LEO	23 LIB	23 SCO	21 SAG	21 CAP
25 SAG	24 CAP	23 CAP	24 PIS	24 ARI	25 GEM	24 CAN	25 VIR	25 SCO	25 SAG	24 CAP	24 AQU
27 CAP	26 AQU	26 AQU	27 ARI	26 TAU	27 CAN	26 LEO	27 LIB	28 SAG	27 CAP	26 AQU	26 PIS
30 AQU		28 PIS	29 TAU	28 GEM	29 LEO	28 VIR	29 SCO	30 CAP	30 AQU	29 PIS	29 ARI
		30 ARI		30 CAN		30 LIB	31 SAG				31 TAU

JAN	FEB	MAR	APR	MAY	JUN	JUL	AUG	SEP	OCT	NOV	DEC
2 GEM	1 CAN	2 LEO	3 LIB	2 SCO	1 SAG	3 AQU	1 PIS	3 TAU	2 GEM	1 CAN	2 VIR
4 CAN	3 LEO	4 VIR	5 SCO	4 SAG	3 CAP	5 PIS	4 ARI	5 GEM	5 CAN	3 LEO	5 LIB
6 LEO	5 VIR	6 LIB	7 SAG	7 CAP	5 AQU	8 ARI	6 TAU	7 CAN	7 LEO	5 VIR	7 SCO
8 VIR	7 LIB	8 SCO	9 CAP	9 AQU	8 PIS	10 TAU	9 GEM	9 LEO	9 VIR	7 LIB	9 SAG
10 LIB	9 SCO	10 SAG	12 AQU	12 PIS	10 ARI	12 GEM	11 CAN	11 VIR	11 LIB	9 SCO	11 CAP
12 SCO	11 SAG	13 CAP	14 PIS	14 ARI	13 TAU	15 CAN	13 LEO	13 LIB	13 SCO	11 SAG	13 AQU
15 SAG	14 CAP	15 AQU	17 ARI	16 TAU	15 GEM	17 LEO	15 VIR	15 SCO	15 SAG	14 CAP	16 PIS
17 CAP	16 AQU	18 PIS	19 TAU	19 GEM	17 CAN	19 VIR	17 LIB	18 SAG	17 CAP	16 AQU	19 ARI
20 AQU	19 PIS	20 ARI	21 GEM	21 CAN	19 LEO	21 LIB	19 SCO	20 CAP	20 AQU	19 PIS	21 TAU
22 PIS	21 ARI	23 TAU	24 CAN	23 LEO	21 VIR	23 SCO	21 SAG	22 AQU	22 PIS	21 ARI	23 GEM
25 ARI	24 TAU	25 GEM	26 LEO	25 VIR	23 LIB	25 SAG	24 CAP	25 PIS	25 ARI	24 TAU	26 CAN
27 TAU	26 GEM	27 CAN	28 VIR	27 LIB	26 SCO	27 CAP	26 AQU	28 ARI	27 TAU	26 GEM	28 LEO
30 GEM	28 CAN	29 LEO	30 LIB	29 SCO	28 SAG	30 AQU	29 PIS	30 TAU	30 GEM	28 CAN	30 VIR
		31 VIR			30 CAP		31 ARI				

JAN	FEB	MAR	APR	MAY	JUN	JUL	AUG	SEP	OCT	NOV	DEC
1 LIB	1 SAG	2 CAP	1 AQU	3 ARI	2 TAU	2 GEM	2 LEO	1 VIR	2 SCO	1 SAG	2 AQU
3 SCO	4 CAP	4 AQU	3 PIS	5 TAU	4 GEM	4 CAN	4 VIR	3 LIB	4 SAG	3 CAP	5 PIS
5 SAG	6 AQU	7 PIS	6 ARI	8 GEM	6 CAN	6 LEO	6 LIB	5 SCO	6 CAP	5 AQU	7 ARI
7 CAP	9 PIS	9 ARI	8 TAU	10 CAN	9 LEO	9 VIR	9 SCO	7 SAG	9 AQU	7 PIS	10 TAU
10 AQU	11 ARI	12 TAU	11 GEM	12 LEO	11 VIR	10 LIB	11 SAG	9 CAP	11 PIS	10 ARI	12 GEM
12 PIS	14 TAU	14 GEM	13 CAN	15 VIR	13 LIB	12 SCO	13 CAP	11 AQU	14 ARI	13 TAU	15 CAN
15 ARI	16 GEM	17 CAN	15 LEO	17 LIB	15 SCO	14 SAG	15 AQU	14 PIS	16 TAU	15 GEM	17 LEO
17 TAU	18 CAN	19 LEO	17 VIR	19 SCO	17 SAG	17 CAP	18 PIS	16 ARI	19 GEM	17 CAN	19 VIR
20 GEM	20 LEO	21 VIR	19 LIB	21 SAG	19 CAP	19 AQU	20 ARI	19 TAU	21 CAN	20 LEO	21 LIB
22 CAN	22 VIR	23 LIB	21 SCO	23 CAP	22 AQU	21 PIS	23 TAU	21 GEM	23 LEO	22 VIR	23 SCO
24 LEO	24 LIB	25 SCO	23 SAG	25 AQU	24 PIS	24 ARI	25 GEM	24 CAN	26 VIR	24 LIB	26 SAG
26 VIR	26 SCO	27 SAG	25 CAP	28 PIS	27 ARI	26 TAU	28 CAN	26 LEO	28 LIB	26 SCO	28 CAP
28 LIB	29 SAG	29 CAP	28 AQU	30 ARI	29 TAU	29 GEM	30 LEO	28 VIR	30 SCO	28 SAG	30 AQU
30 SCO			30 PIS			31 CAN		30 LIB		30 CAP	

JAN	FEB	MAR	APR	MAY	JUN	JUL	AUG	SEP	OCT	NOV	DEC
1 PIS	2 TAU	2 TAU	1 GEM	3 LEO	1 VIR	1 LIB	1 SAG	2 AQU	1 PIS	2 TAU	2 GEM
4 ARI	5 GEM	4 GEM	3 CAN	5 VIR	4 LIB	3 SCO	3 CAP	4 PIS	4 ARI	5 GEM	5 CAN
6 TAU	7 CAN	7 CAN	5 LEO	7 LIB	6 SCO	5 SAG	5 AQU	6 ARI	6 TAU	7 CAN	7 LEO
9 GEM	10 LEO	9 LEO	8 VIR	9 SCO	8 SAG	7 CAP	7 PIS	9 TAU	9 GEM	10 LEO	10 VIR
11 CAN	12 VIR	11 VIR	10 LIB	11 SAG	10 CAP	9 AQU	10 ARI	11 GEM	11 CAN	12 VIR	12 LIB
13 LEO	14 LIB	13 LIB	12 SCO	13 CAP	12 AQU	11 PIS	13 TAU	14 CAN	14 LEO	15 LIB	14 SCO
15 VIR	16 SCO	15 SCO	14 SAG	15 AQU	14 PIS	14 ARI	15 GEM	16 LEO	16 VIR	17 SCO	16 SAG
18 LIB	18 SAG	17 SAG	16 CAP	18 PIS	16 ARI	16 TAU	18 CAN	19 VIR	18 LIB	19 SAG	18 CAP
20 SCO	20 CAP	19 CAP	18 AQU	20 ARI	19 TAU	19 GEM	20 LEO	21 LIB	20 SCO	21 CAP	20 AQU
22 SAG	23 AQU	22 AQU	20 PIS	23 TAU	21 GEM	21 CAN	22 VIR	23 SCO	22 SAG	23 AQU	22 PIS
24 CAP	25 PIS	24 PIS	23 ARI	25 GEM	24 CAN	24 LEO	24 LIB	25 SAG	24 CAP	25 PIS	24 ARI
26 AQU	27 ARI	27 ARI	25 TAU	28 CAN	26 LEO	26 VIR	26 SCO	27 CAP	26 AQU	27 ARI	27 TAU
29 PIS		29 TAU	28 GEM	30 LEO	29 VIR	28 LIB	28 SAG	29 AQU	29 PIS	30 TAU	29 GEM
31 ARI			30 CAN			30 SCO	31 CAP		31 ARI		

JAN	FEB	MAR	APR	MAY	JUN	JUL	AUG	SEP	OCT	NOV	DEC
1 CAN	2 VIR	1 VIR	2 SCO	2 SAG	2 AQU	1 PIS	2 TAU	1 GEM	1 CAN	2 VIR	2 LIB
3 LEO	4 LIB	4 LIB	4 SAG	4 CAP	4 PIS	4 ARI	5 GEM	4 CAN	4 LEO	5 LIB	4 SCO
6 VIR	7 SCO	6 SCO	6 CAP	6 AQU	6 ARI	6 TAU	7 CAN	6 LEO	6 VIR	7 SCO	6 SAG
8 LIB	9 SAG	8 SAG	8 AQU	8 PIS	9 TAU	9 GEM	10 LEO	9 VIR	8 LIB	9 SAG	8 CAP
10 SCO	11 CAP	10 CAP	11 PIS	10 ARI	11 GEM	11 CAN	12 VIR	11 LIB	10 SCO	11 CAP	10 AQU
12 SAG	13 AQU	12 AQU	13 ARI	13 TAU	14 CAN	14 LEO	15 LIB	13 SCO	13 SAG	13 AQU	12 PIS
14 CAP	15 PIS	14 PIS	15 TAU	15 GEM	16 LEO	16 VIR	17 SCO	15 SAG	15 CAP	15 PIS	15 ARI
16 AQU	17 ARI	17 ARI	18 GEM	18 CAN	19 VIR	18 LIB	19 SAG	17 CAP	17 AQU	17 ARI	17 TAU
19 PIS	20 TAU	19 TAU	20 CAN	20 LEO	21 LIB	21 SCO	21 CAP	20 AQU	19 PIS	20 TAU	19 GEM
21 ARI	22 GEM	21 GEM	23 LEO	23 VIR	23 SCO	23 SAG	23 AQU	22 PIS	21 ARI	22 GEM	22 CAN
23 TAU	25 CAN	24 CAN	25 VIR	25 LIB	25 SAG	25 CAP	25 PIS	24 ARI	23 TAU	25 CAN	24 LEO
26 GEM	27 LEO	26 LEO	27 LIB	27 SCO	27 CAP	27 AQU	27 ARI	26 TAU	26 GEM	27 LEO	27 VIR
28 CAN		29 VIR	30 SCO	29 SAG	29 AQU	29 PIS	30 TAU	29 GEM	28 CAN	30 VIR	29 LIB
31 LEO		31 LIB		31 CAP		31 ARI			31 LEO		

JAN	FEB	MAR	APR	MAY	JUN	JUL	AUG	SEP	OCT	NOV	DEC
1 SCO	1 CAP	1 CAP	1 PIS	3 TAU	1 GEM	1 CAN	2 VIR	1 LIB	1 SCO	1 CAP	1 AQU
3 SAG	3 AQU	3 AQU	3 ARI	5 GEM	4 CAN	4 LEO	5 LIB	3 SCO	3 SAG	4 AQU	3 PIS
5 CAP	5 PIS	5 PIS	5 TAU	7 CAN	6 LEO	6 VIR	7 SCO	6 SAG	5 CAP	6 PIS	5 ARI
7 AQU	7 ARI	7 ARI	8 GEM	10 LEO	9 VIR	9 LIB	10 SAG	8 CAP	7 AQU	8 ARI	7 TAU
9 PIS	10 TAU	9 TAU	10 CAN	12 VIR	11 LIB	11 SCO	12 CAP	10 AQU	9 PIS	10 TAU	10 GEM
11 ARI	12 GEM	11 GEM	13 LEO	15 LIB	14 SCO	13 SAG	14 AQU	12 PIS	12 ARI	12 GEM	12 CAN
13 TAU	14 CAN	14 CAN	15 VIR	17 SCO	16 SAG	15 CAP	16 PIS	14 ARI	14 TAU	15 CAN	14 LEO
16 GEM	17 LEO	16 LEO	18 LIB	19 SAG	18 CAP	17 AQU	18 ARI	16 TAU	16 GEM	17 LEO	17 VIR
18 CAN	19 VIR	19 VIR	20 SCO	21 CAP	20 AQU	19 PIS	20 TAU	18 GEM	18 CAN	20 VIR	19 LIB
21 LEO	22 LIB	21 LIB	22 SAG	23 AQU	22 PIS	21 ARI	22 GEM	21 CAN	21 LEO	22 LIB	22 SCO
23 VIR	24 SCO	23 SCO	24 CAP	26 PIS	24 ARI	23 TAU	25 CAN	23 LEO	23 VIR	24 SCO	24 SAG
26 LIB	26 SAG	26 SAG	26 AQU	28 ARI	26 TAU	26 GEM	27 LEO	26 VIR	26 LIB	27 SAG	26 CAP
28 SCO		28 CAP	28 PIS	30 TAU	29 GEM	28 CAN	30 VIR	28 LIB	28 SCO	29 CAP	28 AQU
30 SAG		30 AQU	30 ARI			31 LEO			30 SAG		30 PIS

1944

JAN	FEB	MAR	APR	MAY	JUN	JUL	AUG	SEP	OCT	NOV	DEC
1 ARI	2 GEM	3 CAN	1 LEO	1 VIR	3 SCO	2 SAG	1 CAP	1 PIS	1 ARI	1 GEM	1 CAN
3 TAU	4 CAN	5 LEO	4 VIR	4 LIB	5 SAG	4 CAP	3 AQU	3 ARI	3 TAU	4 CAN	3 LEO
6 GEM	7 LEO	8 VIR	6 LIB	6 SCO	7 CAP	7 AQU	5 PIS	5 TAU	5 GEM	6 LEO	6 VIR
8 CAN	9 VIR	10 LIB	9 SCO	9 SAG	9 AQU	9 PIS	7 ARI	7 GEM	8 CAN	8 VIR	8 LIB
11 LEO	12 LIB	13 SCO	11 SAG	11 CAP	11 PIS	11 ARI	9 TAU	10 CAN	10 LEO	11 LIB	11 SCO
13 VIR	14 SCO	15 SAG	14 CAP	13 AQU	13 ARI	13 TAU	11 GEM	12 LEO	12 VIR	13 SCO	13 SAG
16 LIB	17 SAG	17 CAP	16 AQU	16 PIS	15 TAU	15 GEM	14 CAN	15 VIR	15 LIB	15 SAG	15 CAP
18 SCO	19 CAP	19 AQU	18 PIS	18 ARI	18 GEM	17 CAN	16 LEO	17 LIB	17 SCO	18 CAP	18 AQU
20 SAG	21 AQU	22 PIS	20 ARI	20 TAU	20 CAN	20 LEO	19 VIR	20 SCO	19 SAG	20 AQU	20 PIS
23 CAP	23 PIS	24 ARI	22 TAU	22 GEM	22 LEO	22 VIR	21 LIB	22 SAG	22 CAP	23 PIS	22 ARI
25 AQU	25 ARI	26 TAU	24 GEM	24 CAN	25 VIR	25 LIB	24 SCO	25 CAP	24 AQU	25 ARI	24 TAU
27 PIS	27 TAU	28 GEM	26 CAN	26 LEO	27 LIB	27 SCO	26 SAG	27 AQU	27 PIS	27 TAU	26 GEM
29 ARI	29 GEM	30 CAN	29 LEO	29 VIR	29 SCO	30 SAG	28 CAP	29 PIS	29 ARI	29 GEM	28 CAN
31 TAU				31 LIB			30 AQU		31 TAU		31 LEO

1945

JAN	FEB	MAR	APR	MAY	JUN	JUL	AUG	SEP	OCT	NOV	DEC
2 VIR	1 LIB	3 SCO	1 SAG	1 CAP	2 PIS	1 ARI	2 GEM	2 LEO	2 VIR	1 LIB	3 SAG
4 LIB	3 SCO	5 SAG	4 CAP	3 AQU	4 ARI	3 TAU	4 CAN	5 VIR	4 LIB	3 SCO	6 CAP
7 SCO	6 SAG	8 CAP	6 AQU	6 PIS	6 TAU	6 GEM	6 LEO	7 LIB	7 SCO	6 SAG	8 AQU
9 SAG	8 CAP	10 AQU	8 PIS	8 ARI	8 GEM	8 CAN	8 VIR	10 SCO	9 SAG	8 CAP	10 PIS
12 CAP	10 AQU	12 PIS	10 ARI	10 TAU	10 CAN	10 LEO	11 LIB	12 SAG	12 CAP	11 AQU	12 ARI
14 AQU	12 PIS	14 ARI	12 TAU	12 GEM	12 LEO	12 VIR	13 SCO	15 CAP	14 AQU	13 PIS	15 TAU
16 PIS	14 ARI	16 TAU	14 GEM	14 CAN	15 VIR	15 LIB	16 SAG	17 AQU	17 PIS	15 ARI	17 GEM
18 ARI	16 TAU	18 GEM	16 CAN	16 LEO	17 LIB	17 SCO	18 CAP	19 PIS	19 ARI	17 TAU	19 CAN
20 TAU	19 GEM	20 CAN	19 LEO	18 VIR	20 SCO	20 SAG	21 AQU	21 ARI	21 TAU	19 GEM	21 LEO
22 GEM	21 CAN	22 LEO	21 VIR	20 LIB	22 SAG	22 CAP	23 PIS	23 TAU	23 GEM	21 CAN	23 VIR
25 CAN	23 LEO	25 VIR	24 LIB	23 SCO	25 CAP	24 AQU	25 ARI	25 GEM	25 CAN	23 LEO	25 LIB
27 LEO	26 VIR	27 LIB	26 SCO	26 SAG	27 AQU	26 PIS	27 TAU	27 CAN	27 LEO	26 VIR	28 SCO
29 VIR	28 LIB	30 SCO	29 SAG	28 CAP	29 PIS	29 ARI	29 GEM	30 LEO	29 VIR	28 LIB	30 SAG
				31 AQU		31 TAU	31 CAN			30 SCO	

1946

JAN	FEB	MAR	APR	MAY	JUN	JUL	AUG	SEP	OCT	NOV	DEC
2 CAP	1 AQU	2 PIS	1 ARI	2 GEM	1 CAN	2 VIR	1 LIB	2 SAG	2 CAP	1 AQU	3 ARI
4 AQU	3 PIS	4 ARI	3 TAU	4 CAN	3 LEO	4 LIB	3 SCO	5 CAP	4 AQU	3 PIS	5 TAU
6 PIS	5 ARI	6 TAU	5 GEM	6 LEO	5 VIR	7 SCO	6 SAG	7 AQU	7 PIS	5 ARI	7 GEM
9 ARI	7 TAU	8 GEM	7 CAN	9 VIR	7 LIB	9 SAG	8 CAP	9 PIS	9 ARI	7 TAU	9 CAN
11 TAU	9 GEM	11 CAN	9 LEO	11 LIB	10 SCO	12 CAP	11 AQU	12 ARI	11 TAU	10 GEM	11 LEO
13 GEM	11 CAN	13 LEO	11 VIR	13 SCO	12 SAG	14 AQU	13 PIS	14 TAU	13 GEM	12 CAN	13 VIR
15 CAN	13 LEO	15 VIR	14 LIB	16 SAG	15 CAP	17 PIS	15 ARI	16 GEM	15 CAN	14 LEO	15 LIB
17 LEO	16 VIR	17 LIB	16 SCO	18 CAP	17 AQU	19 ARI	17 TAU	18 CAN	17 LEO	16 VIR	18 SCO
19 VIR	18 LIB	20 SCO	19 SAG	21 AQU	20 PIS	21 TAU	20 GEM	20 LEO	20 VIR	18 LIB	20 SAG
22 LIB	20 SCO	22 SAG	21 CAP	23 PIS	22 ARI	23 GEM	22 CAN	22 VIR	22 LIB	20 SCO	23 CAP
24 SCO	23 SAG	25 CAP	24 AQU	26 ARI	24 TAU	25 CAN	24 LEO	25 LIB	24 SCO	23 SAG	25 AQU
27 SAG	26 CAP	27 AQU	26 PIS	28 TAU	26 GEM	27 LEO	26 VIR	27 SCO	27 SAG	25 CAP	28 PIS
29 CAP	28 AQU	30 PIS	28 ARI	30 GEM	28 CAN	30 VIR	28 LIB	29 SAG	29 CAP	28 AQU	30 ARI
			30 TAU		30 LEO		31 SCO			30 PIS	

1947

JAN	FEB	MAR	APR	MAY	JUN	JUL	AUG	SEP	OCT	NOV	DEC
1 TAU	2 CAN	1 CAN	2 VIR	1 LIB	2 SAG	2 CAP	1 AQU	2 ARI	1 TAU	2 CAN	1 LEO
3 GEM	4 LEO	3 LEO	4 LIB	3 SCO	5 CAP	4 AQU	3 PIS	4 TAU	4 GEM	4 LEO	3 VIR
5 CAN	6 VIR	5 VIR	6 SCO	6 SAG	7 AQU	7 PIS	6 ARI	6 GEM	6 CAN	6 VIR	6 LIB
7 LEO	8 LIB	7 LIB	8 SAG	8 CAP	10 PIS	9 ARI	8 TAU	9 CAN	8 LEO	8 LIB	8 SCO
9 VIR	10 SCO	10 SCO	11 CAP	11 AQU	12 ARI	12 TAU	10 GEM	11 LEO	10 VIR	11 SCO	10 SAG
12 LIB	13 SAG	12 SAG	13 AQU	13 PIS	14 TAU	14 GEM	12 CAN	13 VIR	13 LIB	13 SAG	13 CAP
14 SCO	15 CAP	15 CAP	16 PIS	16 ARI	16 GEM	16 CAN	14 LEO	15 LIB	15 SCO	15 CAP	15 AQU
16 SAG	18 AQU	17 AQU	18 ARI	18 TAU	18 CAN	18 LEO	16 VIR	17 SCO	17 SAG	18 AQU	18 PIS
19 CAP	20 PIS	20 PIS	20 TAU	20 GEM	20 LEO	20 VIR	18 LIB	19 SAG	19 CAP	20 PIS	20 ARI
22 AQU	23 ARI	22 ARI	23 GEM	22 CAN	22 VIR	22 LIB	20 SCO	22 CAP	22 AQU	23 ARI	23 TAU
24 PIS	25 TAU	24 TAU	25 CAN	24 LEO	25 LIB	24 SCO	23 SAG	24 AQU	24 PIS	25 TAU	25 GEM
26 ARI	27 GEM	26 GEM	27 LEO	26 VIR	27 SCO	27 SAG	25 CAP	27 PIS	26 ARI	27 GEM	27 CAN
29 TAU		28 CAN	29 VIR	28 LIB	29 SAG	29 CAP	28 AQU	29 ARI	29 TAU	29 CAN	29 LEO
31 GEM		31 LEO		31 SCO			30 PIS		31 GEM		31 VIR

1948

JAN	FEB	MAR	APR	MAY	JUN	JUL	AUG	SEP	OCT	NOV	DEC
2 LIB	3 SAG	1 SAG	2 AQU	2 PIS	1 TAU	1 TAU	2 CAN	2 VIR	1 LIB	2 SAG	2 CAP
4 SCO	5 CAP	3 CAP	5 PIS	5 ARI	3 GEM	3 GEM	4 LEO	4 LIB	3 SCO	4 CAP	4 AQU
6 SAG	8 AQU	6 AQU	7 ARI	7 TAU	6 CAN	5 CAN	6 VIR	6 SCO	5 SAG	7 AQU	6 PIS
9 CAP	10 PIS	8 PIS	10 TAU	9 GEM	8 LEO	7 LEO	8 LIB	8 SAG	8 CAP	9 PIS	9 ARI
11 AQU	13 ARI	11 ARI	12 GEM	11 CAN	10 VIR	9 VIR	10 SCO	11 CAP	10 AQU	12 ARI	12 TAU
14 PIS	15 TAU	13 TAU	14 CAN	14 LEO	12 LIB	11 LIB	12 SAG	13 AQU	13 PIS	14 TAU	14 GEM
16 ARI	17 GEM	16 GEM	16 LEO	16 VIR	14 SCO	13 SCO	14 CAP	15 PIS	15 ARI	17 GEM	16 CAN
19 TAU	20 CAN	18 CAN	18 VIR	18 LIB	16 SAG	16 SAG	17 AQU	18 ARI	18 TAU	19 CAN	18 LEO
21 GEM	22 LEO	20 LEO	21 LIB	20 SCO	18 CAP	18 CAP	19 PIS	21 TAU	20 GEM	21 LEO	20 VIR
23 CAN	24 VIR	22 VIR	23 SCO	22 SAG	21 AQU	21 AQU	21 ARI	23 GEM	23 CAN	23 VIR	22 LIB
25 LEO	26 LIB	24 LIB	25 SAG	25 CAP	23 PIS	23 PIS	23 TAU	25 CAN	25 LEO	25 LIB	25 SCO
27 VIR	28 SCO	26 SCO	27 CAP	27 AQU	26 ARI	26 ARI	26 GEM	27 LEO	27 VIR	27 SCO	27 SAG
29 LIB		28 SAG	30 AQU	29 PIS	28 TAU	28 TAU	29 CAN	29 VIR	29 LIB	29 SAG	29 CAP
31 SCO		31 CAP				30 GEM	31 LEO		31 SCO		31 AQU

1949

JAN	FEB	MAR	APR	MAY	JUN	JUL	AUG	SEP	OCT	NOV	DEC
3 PIS	2 ARI	1 ARI	2 GEM	2 CAN	2 VIR	2 LIB	2 SAG	1 CAP	3 PIS	2 ARI	1 TAU
5 ARI	4 TAU	3 TAU	5 CAN	4 LEO	5 LIB	4 SCO	5 CAP	3 AQU	5 ARI	4 TAU	4 GEM
8 TAU	7 GEM	6 GEM	7 LEO	6 VIR	7 SCO	6 SAG	7 AQU	6 PIS	8 TAU	7 GEM	6 CAN
10 GEM	9 CAN	8 CAN	9 VIR	8 LIB	9 SAG	8 CAP	9 PIS	8 ARI	10 GEM	9 CAN	9 LEO
12 CAN	11 LEO	10 LEO	11 LIB	10 SCO	11 CAP	11 AQU	11 ARI	10 TAU	13 CAN	11 LEO	11 VIR
15 LEO	13 VIR	13 VIR	13 SCO	12 SAG	13 AQU	13 PIS	14 TAU	13 GEM	15 LEO	14 VIR	13 LIB
17 VIR	15 LIB	14 LIB	15 SAG	15 CAP	16 PIS	15 ARI	16 GEM	15 CAN	17 VIR	16 LIB	15 SCO
19 LIB	17 SCO	16 SCO	17 CAP	17 AQU	18 ARI	18 TAU	19 CAN	18 LEO	19 LIB	18 SCO	17 SAG
21 SCO	19 SAG	19 SAG	19 AQU	19 PIS	21 TAU	20 GEM	21 LEO	20 VIR	21 SCO	20 SAG	19 CAP
23 SAG	22 CAP	21 CAP	22 PIS	22 ARI	23 GEM	23 CAN	23 VIR	22 LIB	23 SAG	22 CAP	21 AQU
25 CAP	24 AQU	23 AQU	24 ARI	24 TAU	25 CAN	25 LEO	25 LIB	24 SCO	25 CAP	24 AQU	24 PIS
28 AQU	26 PIS	26 PIS	27 TAU	27 GEM	28 LEO	27 VIR	27 SCO	26 SAG	28 AQU	26 PIS	26 ARI
30 PIS		28 ARI	29 GEM	29 CAN	30 VIR	29 LIB	30 SAG	28 CAP	30 PIS	29 ARI	29 TAU
		31 TAU		31 LEO		31 SCO		30 AQU			31 GEM

1950

JAN	FEB	MAR	APR	MAY	JUN	JUL	AUG	SEP	OCT	NOV	DEC
3 CAN	1 LEO	1 LEO	1 LIB	1 SCO	1 CAP	1 AQU	1 ARI	3 GEM	3 CAN	2 LEO	1 VIR
5 LEO	3 VIR	3 VIR	3 SCO	3 SAG	3 AQU	3 PIS	4 TAU	5 CAN	5 LEO	4 VIR	3 LIB
7 VIR	6 LIB	5 LIB	5 SAG	5 CAP	5 PIS	5 ARI	7 GEM	8 LEO	7 VIR	6 LIB	6 SCO
9 LIB	8 SCO	7 SCO	7 CAP	7 AQU	8 ARI	8 TAU	9 CAN	10 VIR	10 LIB	8 SCO	8 SAG
11 SCO	10 SAG	9 SAG	10 AQU	9 PIS	10 TAU	10 GEM	11 LEO	12 LIB	12 SCO	10 SAG	10 CAP
14 SAG	12 CAP	11 CAP	12 PIS	12 ARI	13 GEM	13 CAN	14 VIR	14 SCO	14 SAG	12 CAP	12 AQU
16 CAP	14 AQU	13 AQU	14 ARI	14 TAU	15 CAN	15 LEO	16 LIB	16 SAG	16 CAP	14 AQU	14 PIS
18 AQU	16 PIS	16 PIS	17 TAU	17 GEM	18 LEO	17 VIR	18 SCO	18 CAP	18 AQU	16 PIS	16 ARI
20 PIS	19 ARI	18 ARI	19 GEM	19 CAN	20 VIR	20 LIB	20 SAG	21 AQU	20 PIS	19 ARI	19 TAU
22 ARI	21 TAU	21 TAU	22 CAN	22 LEO	22 LIB	22 SCO	22 CAP	23 PIS	23 ARI	21 TAU	21 GEM
25 TAU	24 GEM	23 GEM	24 LEO	24 VIR	25 SCO	24 SAG	24 AQU	25 ARI	25 TAU	24 GEM	24 CAN
28 GEM	26 CAN	26 CAN	27 VIR	26 LIB	27 SAG	26 CAP	27 PIS	28 TAU	28 GEM	26 CAN	26 LEO
30 CAN		28 LEO	29 LIB	28 SCO	29 CAP	28 AQU	29 ARI	30 GEM	30 CAN	29 LEO	28 VIR
		30 VIR		30 SAG		30 PIS	31 TAU				31 LIB

1951

JAN	FEB	MAR	APR	MAY	JUN	JUL	AUG	SEP	OCT	NOV	DEC
2 SCO	2 CAP	2 CAP	2 PIS	2 ARI	3 GEM	3 CAN	1 LEO	3 LIB	2 SCO	1 SAG	2 AQU
4 SAG	4 AQU	4 AQU	5 ARI	4 TAU	5 CAN	5 LEO	4 VIR	5 SCO	4 SAG	3 CAP	4 PIS
6 CAP	7 PIS	6 PIS	7 TAU	7 GEM	8 LEO	8 VIR	6 LIB	7 SAG	6 CAP	5 AQU	6 ARI
8 AQU	9 ARI	8 ARI	9 GEM	9 CAN	10 VIR	10 LIB	9 SCO	9 CAP	8 AQU	7 PIS	9 TAU
10 PIS	11 TAU	11 TAU	12 CAN	12 LEO	13 LIB	12 SCO	11 SAG	11 AQU	11 PIS	9 ARI	11 GEM
12 ARI	14 GEM	13 GEM	14 LEO	14 VIR	15 SCO	14 SAG	13 CAP	13 PIS	13 ARI	11 TAU	13 CAN
15 TAU	16 CAN	16 CAN	17 VIR	16 LIB	17 SAG	16 CAP	15 AQU	15 ARI	15 TAU	14 GEM	16 LEO
17 GEM	19 LEO	18 LEO	19 LIB	19 SCO	19 CAP	18 AQU	17 PIS	18 TAU	17 GEM	16 CAN	19 VIR
20 CAN	21 VIR	20 VIR	21 SCO	21 SAG	21 AQU	20 PIS	19 ARI	20 GEM	20 CAN	19 LEO	21 LIB
22 LEO	23 LIB	23 LIB	23 SAG	23 CAP	23 PIS	23 ARI	21 TAU	23 CAN	22 LEO	21 VIR	23 SCO
25 VIR	25 SCO	25 SCO	25 CAP	25 AQU	25 ARI	25 TAU	24 GEM	25 LEO	25 VIR	24 LIB	25 SAG
27 LIB	28 SAG	27 SAG	27 AQU	27 PIS	28 TAU	27 GEM	26 CAN	28 VIR	27 LIB	26 SCO	27 CAP
29 SCO		29 CAP	29 PIS	29 ARI	30 GEM	30 CAN	29 LEO	30 LIB	29 SCO	28 SAG	29 AQU
31 SAG		31 AQU		31 TAU			31 VIR			30 CAP	31 PIS

JAN	FEB	MAR	APR	MAY	JUN	JUL	AUG	SEP	OCT	NOV	DEC
3 ARI	1 TAU	2 GEM	1 CAN	3 VIR	2 LIB	2 SCO	2 CAP	1 AQU	2 ARI	1 TAU	2 CAN
5 TAU	3 GEM	4 CAN	3 LEO	5 LIB	4 SCO	4 SAG	4 AQU	3 PIS	4 TAU	3 GEM	5 LEO
7 GEM	6 CAN	7 LEO	6 VIR	8 SCO	6 SAG	6 CAP	6 PIS	5 ARI	6 GEM	5 CAN	7 VIR
10 CAN	9 LEO	9 VIR	8 LIB	10 SAG	8 CAP	8 AQU	8 ARI	7 TAU	9 CAN	7 LEO	10 LIB
12 LEO	11 VIR	12 LIB	10 SCO	12 CAP	10 AQU	10 PIS	10 TAU	9 GEM	11 LEO	10 VIR	12 SCO
15 VIR	14 LIB	14 SCO	13 SAG	14 AQU	12 PIS	12 ARI	13 GEM	11 CAN	14 VIR	13 LIB	15 SAG
17 LIB	16 SCO	16 SAG	15 CAP	16 PIS	15 ARI	14 TAU	15 CAN	14 LEO	16 LIB	15 SCO	17 CAP
20 SCO	18 SAG	19 CAP	17 AQU	18 ARI	17 TAU	16 GEM	18 LEO	16 VIR	19 SCO	17 SAG	19 AQU
22 SAG	20 CAP	21 AQU	19 PIS	21 TAU	19 GEM	19 CAN	20 VIR	19 LIB	21 SAG	19 CAP	21 PIS
24 CAP	22 AQU	23 PIS	21 ARI	23 GEM	22 CAN	21 LEO	23 LIB	21 SCO	23 CAP	21 AQU	23 ARI
26 AQU	24 PIS	25 ARI	23 TAU	25 CAN	24 LEO	24 VIR	25 SCO	23 CAP	25 AQU	24 PIS	25 TAU
28 PIS	26 ARI	27 TAU	26 GEM	28 LEO	26 VIR	26 LIB	27 SAG	25 AQU	27 PIS	26 ARI	27 GEM
30 ARI	29 TAU	29 GEM	28 CAN	30 VIR	29 LIB	29 SCO	30 CAP	27 PIS	29 ARI	28 TAU	30 CAN
			30 LEO			31 SAG		30 PIS		30 GEM	

JAN	FEB	MAR	APR	MAY	JUN	JUL	AUG	SEP	OCT	NOV	DEC
1 LEO	3 LIB	2 LIB	1 SCO	2 CAP	1 AQU	2 ARI	1 TAU	1 CAN	1 LEO	2 LIB	2 SCO
4 VIR	5 SCO	4 SCO	3 SAG	5 AQU	3 PIS	5 TAU	3 GEM	4 LEO	4 VIR	5 SCO	5 SAG
6 LIB	7 SAG	7 SAG	5 CAP	7 PIS	5 ARI	7 GEM	5 CAN	6 VIR	6 LIB	7 SAG	7 CAP
9 SCO	10 CAP	9 CAP	7 AQU	9 ARI	7 TAU	9 CAN	8 LEO	9 LIB	9 SCO	10 CAP	9 AQU
11 SAG	12 AQU	11 AQU	10 PIS	11 TAU	9 GEM	11 LEO	10 VIR	11 SCO	11 SAG	12 AQU	11 PIS
13 CAP	14 PIS	13 PIS	12 ARI	13 GEM	12 CAN	14 VIR	13 LIB	14 SAG	13 CAP	14 PIS	14 ARI
15 AQU	16 ARI	15 ARI	14 TAU	15 CAN	14 LEO	16 LIB	15 SCO	16 CAP	16 AQU	16 ARI	16 TAU
17 PIS	18 TAU	17 TAU	16 GEM	18 LEO	16 VIR	19 SCO	18 SAG	18 AQU	18 PIS	18 TAU	18 GEM
19 ARI	20 GEM	19 GEM	18 CAN	20 VIR	19 LIB	21 SAG	20 CAP	21 PIS	20 ARI	20 GEM	20 CAN
21 TAU	22 CAN	22 CAN	20 LEO	23 LIB	21 SCO	23 CAP	22 AQU	22 ARI	22 TAU	22 CAN	22 LEO
24 GEM	25 LEO	24 LEO	23 VIR	25 SCO	24 SAG	26 AQU	24 PIS	24 TAU	24 GEM	25 LEO	25 VIR
26 CAN	27 VIR	27 VIR	25 LIB	27 SAG	26 CAP	28 PIS	26 ARI	27 GEM	26 CAN	27 VIR	27 LIB
28 LEO		29 LIB	28 SCO	30 CAP	28 AQU	30 ARI	28 TAU	29 CAN	28 LEO	30 LIB	30 SCO
31 VIR			30 SAG		30 PIS		30 GEM		31 VIR		

JAN	FEB	MAR	APR	MAY	JUN	JUL	AUG	SEP	OCT	NOV	DEC
1 SAG	2 AQU	1 AQU	2 ARI	1 TAU	2 CAN	1 LEO	2 LIB	1 SCO	1 SAG	2 AQU	2 PIS
3 CAP	4 PIS	3 PIS	4 TAU	3 GEM	4 LEO	4 VIR	5 SCO	3 SAG	4 CAP	5 PIS	4 ARI
6 AQU	6 ARI	5 ARI	6 GEM	5 CAN	6 VIR	6 LIB	7 SAG	6 CAP	6 AQU	7 ARI	6 TAU
8 PIS	8 TAU	7 TAU	8 CAN	8 LEO	9 LIB	9 SCO	10 CAP	9 AQU	8 PIS	9 TAU	8 GEM
10 ARI	10 GEM	10 GEM	10 LEO	10 VIR	11 SCO	11 SAG	12 AQU	11 PIS	10 ARI	11 GEM	10 CAN
12 TAU	13 CAN	12 CAN	13 VIR	12 LIB	14 SAG	14 CAP	14 PIS	13 ARI	12 TAU	13 CAN	12 LEO
14 GEM	15 LEO	14 LEO	15 LIB	15 SCO	16 CAP	16 AQU	16 ARI	15 TAU	14 GEM	15 LEO	14 VIR
16 CAN	17 VIR	16 VIR	18 SCO	17 SAG	19 AQU	18 PIS	18 TAU	17 GEM	16 CAN	17 VIR	17 LIB
19 LEO	20 LIB	19 LIB	20 SAG	20 CAP	21 PIS	20 ARI	21 GEM	19 CAN	19 LEO	20 LIB	19 SCO
21 VIR	22 SCO	21 SCO	23 CAP	22 AQU	23 ARI	23 TAU	23 CAN	21 LEO	21 VIR	22 SCO	22 SAG
23 LIB	25 SAG	24 SAG	25 AQU	25 PIS	25 TAU	24 GEM	25 LEO	24 VIR	24 LIB	25 SAG	24 CAP
26 SCO	27 CAP	26 CAP	27 PIS	27 ARI	27 GEM	27 CAN	27 VIR	26 LIB	26 SCO	27 CAP	27 AQU
28 SAG		29 AQU	29 ARI	29 TAU	29 CAN	29 LEO	30 LIB	29 SCO	28 SAG	30 AQU	29 PIS
31 CAP		31 PIS		31 GEM		31 VIR			31 CAP		31 ARI

JAN	FEB	MAR	APR	MAY	JUN	JUL	AUG	SEP	OCT	NOV	DEC
3 TAU	1 GEM	2 CAN	1 LEO	2 LIB	1 SCO	1 SAG	2 AQU	1 PIS	1 ARI	1 GEM	1 CAN
5 GEM	3 CAN	4 LEO	3 VIR	5 SCO	3 SAG	3 CAP	5 PIS	3 ARI	3 TAU	3 CAN	3 LEO
7 CAN	5 LEO	7 VIR	5 LIB	7 SAG	6 CAP	6 AQU	7 ARI	5 TAU	5 GEM	5 LEO	5 VIR
9 LEO	7 VIR	9 LIB	8 SCO	10 CAP	9 AQU	8 PIS	9 TAU	7 GEM	7 CAN	7 VIR	7 LIB
11 VIR	10 LIB	11 SCO	10 SAG	12 AQU	11 PIS	11 ARI	11 GEM	10 CAN	9 LEO	10 LIB	9 SCO
13 LIB	12 SCO	14 SAG	13 CAP	15 PIS	13 ARI	13 TAU	13 CAN	12 LEO	11 VIR	12 SCO	12 SAG
16 SCO	15 SAG	16 CAP	15 AQU	17 ARI	16 TAU	15 GEM	15 LEO	14 VIR	13 LIB	15 SAG	14 CAP
18 SAG	17 CAP	19 AQU	18 PIS	19 TAU	18 GEM	17 CAN	18 VIR	16 LIB	16 SCO	17 CAP	17 AQU
21 CAP	19 AQU	21 PIS	20 ARI	21 GEM	20 CAN	19 LEO	20 LIB	18 SCO	18 SAG	20 AQU	19 PIS
23 AQU	22 PIS	23 ARI	22 TAU	23 CAN	22 LEO	21 VIR	22 SCO	21 SAG	21 CAP	22 PIS	22 ARI
25 PIS	24 ARI	25 TAU	24 GEM	25 LEO	24 VIR	23 LIB	25 SAG	23 CAP	23 AQU	24 ARI	24 TAU
28 ARI	26 TAU	27 GEM	26 CAN	27 VIR	26 LIB	26 SCO	27 CAP	26 AQU	26 PIS	27 TAU	26 GEM
30 TAU	28 GEM	29 CAN	28 LEO	30 LIB	28 SCO	28 SAG	30 AQU	28 PIS	28 ARI	29 GEM	28 CAN
			30 VIR			31 CAP			30 TAU		30 LEO

1956

JAN: 1 VIR, 3 LIB, 6 SCO, 8 SAG, 11 CAP, 13 AQU, 16 PIS, 18 ARI, 20 TAU, 22 GEM, 24 CAN, 26 LEO, 28 VIR, 31 LIB
FEB: 2 SCO, 4 SAG, 7 CAP, 9 AQU, 12 PIS, 14 ARI, 16 TAU, 19 GEM, 21 CAN, 23 LEO, 25 VIR, 27 LIB, 29 SCO
MAR: 3 SAG, 5 CAP, 8 AQU, 10 PIS, 12 ARI, 15 TAU, 17 GEM, 19 CAN, 21 LEO, 23 VIR, 25 LIB, 28 SCO, 30 SAG
APR: 1 CAP, 4 AQU, 6 PIS, 9 ARI, 11 TAU, 13 GEM, 15 CAN, 17 LEO, 20 VIR, 22 LIB, 24 SCO, 26 SAG, 29 CAP
MAY: 1 AQU, 4 PIS, 6 ARI, 8 TAU, 11 GEM, 13 CAN, 15 LEO, 17 VIR, 19 LIB, 21 SCO, 24 SAG, 26 CAP, 29 AQU, 31 PIS
JUN: 3 ARI, 5 TAU, 7 GEM, 9 CAN, 11 LEO, 13 VIR, 15 LIB, 18 SCO, 20 SAG, 22 CAP, 25 AQU, 27 PIS, 29 ARI
JUL: 2 TAU, 4 GEM, 6 CAN, 8 LEO, 10 VIR, 12 LIB, 15 SCO, 17 SAG, 20 CAP, 22 AQU, 25 PIS, 27 ARI, 30 TAU
AUG: 1 GEM, 3 CAN, 5 LEO, 7 VIR, 9 LIB, 11 SCO, 13 SAG, 16 CAP, 18 AQU, 21 PIS, 23 ARI, 26 TAU, 28 GEM, 30 CAN
SEP: 1 LEO, 3 VIR, 5 LIB, 7 SCO, 10 SAG, 12 CAP, 15 AQU, 17 PIS, 20 ARI, 22 TAU, 24 GEM, 26 CAN, 29 LEO
OCT: 1 VIR, 3 LIB, 5 SCO, 7 SAG, 10 CAP, 12 AQU, 15 PIS, 17 ARI, 19 TAU, 22 GEM, 24 CAN, 26 LEO, 28 VIR, 30 LIB
NOV: 1 SCO, 3 SAG, 6 CAP, 8 AQU, 11 PIS, 13 ARI, 16 TAU, 18 GEM, 20 CAN, 22 LEO, 24 VIR, 26 LIB, 29 SCO
DEC: 1 SAG, 3 CAP, 6 AQU, 8 PIS, 11 ARI, 13 TAU, 15 GEM, 17 CAN, 19 LEO, 21 VIR, 23 LIB, 26 SCO, 28 SAG, 31 CAP

1957

JAN: 2 AQU, 5 PIS, 7 ARI, 9 TAU, 12 GEM, 14 CAN, 16 LEO, 18 VIR, 20 LIB, 22 SCO, 24 SAG, 27 CAP, 29 AQU
FEB: 1 PIS, 3 ARI, 6 TAU, 8 GEM, 10 CAN, 12 LEO, 14 VIR, 16 LIB, 18 SCO, 21 SAG, 23 CAP, 26 AQU, 28 PIS
MAR: 3 ARI, 5 TAU, 7 GEM, 10 CAN, 12 LEO, 14 VIR, 16 LIB, 18 SCO, 20 SAG, 22 CAP, 25 AQU, 27 PIS, 30 ARI
APR: 1 TAU, 4 GEM, 6 CAN, 8 LEO, 10 VIR, 12 LIB, 14 SCO, 16 SAG, 19 CAP, 21 AQU, 24 PIS, 26 ARI, 29 TAU
MAY: 1 GEM, 3 CAN, 5 LEO, 7 VIR, 9 LIB, 12 SCO, 14 SAG, 16 CAP, 18 AQU, 21 PIS, 23 ARI, 26 TAU, 28 GEM, 30 CAN
JUN: 1 LEO, 4 VIR, 6 LIB, 8 SCO, 10 SAG, 12 CAP, 15 AQU, 17 PIS, 20 ARI, 22 TAU, 25 GEM, 27 CAN, 29 LEO
JUL: 1 VIR, 3 LIB, 5 SCO, 7 SAG, 10 CAP, 12 AQU, 15 PIS, 17 ARI, 20 TAU, 22 GEM, 25 CAN, 26 LEO, 28 VIR, 30 LIB
AUG: 1 SCO, 3 SAG, 6 CAP, 8 AQU, 11 PIS, 13 ARI, 16 TAU, 18 GEM, 21 CAN, 23 LEO, 25 VIR, 27 LIB, 29 SCO, 31 SAG
SEP: 2 CAP, 4 AQU, 7 PIS, 10 ARI, 12 TAU, 15 GEM, 17 CAN, 19 LEO, 21 VIR, 23 LIB, 25 SCO, 27 SAG, 29 CAP
OCT: 2 AQU, 4 PIS, 7 ARI, 9 TAU, 12 GEM, 14 CAN, 16 LEO, 18 VIR, 21 LIB, 23 SCO, 25 SAG, 27 CAP, 29 AQU
NOV: 1 PIS, 3 ARI, 6 TAU, 8 GEM, 10 CAN, 13 LEO, 15 VIR, 17 LIB, 19 SCO, 21 SAG, 23 CAP, 26 AQU, 28 PIS
DEC: 1 ARI, 3 TAU, 5 GEM, 8 CAN, 10 LEO, 12 VIR, 14 LIB, 16 SCO, 18 SAG, 21 CAP, 23 AQU, 25 PIS, 28 ARI, 30 TAU

1958

JAN: 2 GEM, 4 CAN, 6 LEO, 8 VIR, 10 LIB, 12 SCO, 15 SAG, 17 CAP, 19 AQU, 22 PIS, 24 ARI, 27 TAU, 29 GEM, 31 CAN
FEB: 3 LEO, 5 VIR, 7 LIB, 9 SCO, 11 SAG, 13 CAP, 16 AQU, 18 PIS, 21 ARI, 23 TAU, 26 GEM, 28 CAN
MAR: 2 LEO, 4 VIR, 6 LIB, 8 SCO, 10 SAG, 12 CAP, 15 AQU, 17 PIS, 20 ARI, 22 TAU, 25 GEM, 27 CAN, 29 LEO
APR: 1 VIR, 3 LIB, 5 SCO, 7 SAG, 9 CAP, 11 AQU, 13 PIS, 16 ARI, 19 TAU, 21 GEM, 23 CAN, 26 LEO, 28 VIR, 30 LIB
MAY: 2 SCO, 4 SAG, 6 CAP, 8 AQU, 11 PIS, 13 ARI, 16 TAU, 18 GEM, 21 CAN, 23 LEO, 25 VIR, 27 LIB, 29 SCO, 31 SAG
JUN: 3 CAP, 5 AQU, 7 PIS, 10 ARI, 12 TAU, 15 GEM, 17 CAN, 19 LEO, 21 VIR, 23 LIB, 26 SCO, 28 SAG, 30 CAP
JUL: 2 AQU, 4 PIS, 7 ARI, 9 TAU, 12 GEM, 14 CAN, 17 LEO, 19 VIR, 21 LIB, 23 SCO, 25 SAG, 27 CAP, 29 AQU
AUG: 1 PIS, 3 ARI, 6 TAU, 8 GEM, 11 CAN, 13 LEO, 15 VIR, 17 LIB, 19 SCO, 21 SAG, 23 CAP, 26 AQU, 28 PIS, 31 ARI
SEP: 2 TAU, 5 GEM, 7 CAN, 9 LEO, 11 VIR, 13 LIB, 15 SCO, 18 SAG, 20 CAP, 22 AQU, 24 PIS, 27 ARI, 29 TAU
OCT: 2 GEM, 4 CAN, 7 LEO, 9 VIR, 11 LIB, 13 SCO, 15 SAG, 17 CAP, 19 AQU, 22 PIS, 24 ARI, 27 TAU, 29 GEM
NOV: 1 CAN, 3 LEO, 5 VIR, 7 LIB, 9 SCO, 11 SAG, 13 CAP, 16 AQU, 18 PIS, 20 ARI, 23 TAU, 25 GEM, 28 CAN
DEC: 3 VIR, 5 LIB, 7 SCO, 9 SAG, 11 CAP, 13 AQU, 15 PIS, 18 ARI, 20 TAU, 23 GEM, 25 CAN, 27 LEO, 30 VIR

1959

JAN: 1 LIB, 3 SCO, 5 SAG, 7 CAP, 9 AQU, 12 PIS, 14 ARI, 17 TAU, 19 GEM, 21 CAN, 24 LEO, 26 VIR, 28 LIB, 30 SCO
FEB: 1 SAG, 4 CAP, 6 AQU, 8 PIS, 10 ARI, 13 TAU, 15 GEM, 18 CAN, 20 LEO, 22 VIR, 24 LIB, 27 SCO
MAR: 1 SAG, 3 CAP, 5 AQU, 7 PIS, 10 ARI, 12 TAU, 15 GEM, 17 CAN, 20 LEO, 22 VIR, 24 LIB, 26 SCO, 28 SAG, 30 CAP
APR: 1 AQU, 4 PIS, 6 ARI, 8 TAU, 11 GEM, 14 CAN, 16 LEO, 18 VIR, 20 LIB, 22 SCO, 24 SAG, 26 CAP, 28 AQU
MAY: 1 PIS, 3 ARI, 6 TAU, 8 GEM, 11 CAN, 13 LEO, 16 VIR, 18 LIB, 20 SCO, 22 SAG, 24 CAP, 26 AQU, 28 PIS, 30 ARI
JUN: 2 TAU, 5 GEM, 7 CAN, 9 LEO, 12 VIR, 14 LIB, 16 SCO, 18 SAG, 20 CAP, 22 AQU, 24 PIS, 27 ARI, 29 TAU
JUL: 2 GEM, 4 CAN, 7 LEO, 9 VIR, 11 LIB, 13 SCO, 16 SAG, 18 CAP, 20 AQU, 22 PIS, 24 ARI, 27 TAU, 29 GEM
AUG: 1 CAN, 3 LEO, 5 VIR, 8 LIB, 10 SCO, 12 SAG, 14 CAP, 16 AQU, 18 PIS, 20 ARI, 23 TAU, 25 GEM, 28 CAN, 30 LEO
SEP: 2 VIR, 4 LIB, 6 SCO, 8 SAG, 10 CAP, 12 AQU, 15 PIS, 17 ARI, 19 TAU, 22 GEM, 24 CAN, 27 LEO, 29 VIR
OCT: 1 LIB, 3 SCO, 5 SAG, 7 CAP, 10 AQU, 12 PIS, 14 ARI, 17 TAU, 19 GEM, 22 CAN, 24 LEO, 26 VIR, 29 LIB, 31 SCO
NOV: 2 SAG, 4 CAP, 6 AQU, 8 PIS, 10 ARI, 13 TAU, 15 GEM, 18 CAN, 20 LEO, 23 VIR, 25 LIB, 27 SCO, 29 SAG
DEC: 1 CAP, 3 AQU, 5 PIS, 8 ARI, 10 TAU, 13 GEM, 15 CAN, 18 LEO, 20 VIR, 22 LIB, 25 SCO, 27 SAG, 29 CAP, 31 AQU

JAN	FEB	MAR	APR	MAY	JUN	JUL	AUG	SEP	OCT	NOV	DEC
2 PIS	3 TAU	1 TAU	2 CAN	2 LEO	1 VIR	1 LIB	1 SAG	2 AQU	1 PIS	2 TAU	2 GEM
4 ARI	5 GEM	4 GEM	5 LEO	5 VIR	3 LIB	3 SCO	3 CAP	4 PIS	3 ARI	4 GEM	4 CAN
6 TAU	8 CAN	6 CAN	7 VIR	7 LIB	6 SCO	5 SAG	5 AQU	6 ARI	6 TAU	7 CAN	7 LEO
9 GEM	10 LEO	9 LEO	10 LIB	9 SCO	8 SAG	7 CAP	7 PIS	8 TAU	8 GEM	9 LEO	9 VIR
11 CAN	13 VIR	11 VIR	13 SCO	11 SAG	10 CAP	9 AQU	10 ARI	11 GEM	10 CAN	12 VIR	12 LIB
14 LEO	15 LIB	13 LIB	14 SAG	13 CAP	12 AQU	11 PIS	12 TAU	13 CAN	13 LEO	14 LIB	14 SCO
16 VIR	17 SCO	15 SCO	16 CAP	15 AQU	14 PIS	13 ARI	14 GEM	16 LEO	15 VIR	16 SCO	16 SAG
19 LIB	19 SAG	17 SAG	18 AQU	17 PIS	16 ARI	15 TAU	17 CAN	18 VIR	18 LIB	19 SAG	18 CAP
21 SCO	21 CAP	20 CAP	20 PIS	20 ARI	18 TAU	18 GEM	19 LEO	20 LIB	20 SCO	21 CAP	20 AQU
23 SAG	23 AQU	22 AQU	22 ARI	22 TAU	21 GEM	20 CAN	22 VIR	23 SCO	22 SAG	23 AQU	22 PIS
25 CAP	26 PIS	24 PIS	25 TAU	24 GEM	23 CAN	23 LEO	24 LIB	25 SAG	24 CAP	25 PIS	24 ARI
27 AQU	28 ARI	26 ARI	27 GEM	26 CAN	26 LEO	25 VIR	26 SCO	27 CAP	26 AQU	27 ARI	26 TAU
29 PIS		28 TAU	30 CAN	29 LEO	28 VIR	28 LIB	28 SAG	29 AQU	28 PIS	29 TAU	29 GEM
31 ARI		31 GEM				30 SCO	31 CAP		31 ARI		31 CAN

JAN	FEB	MAR	APR	MAY	JUN	JUL	AUG	SEP	OCT	NOV	DEC
3 LEO	2 VIR	1 VIR	2 SCO	2 SAG	2 AQU	1 PIS	2 TAU	1 GEM	3 LEO	2 VIR	1 LIB
5 VIR	4 LIB	3 LIB	4 SAG	4 CAP	4 PIS	4 ARI	4 GEM	3 CAN	5 VIR	4 LIB	4 SCO
8 LIB	6 SCO	6 SCO	6 CAP	6 AQU	6 ARI	6 TAU	7 CAN	5 LEO	8 LIB	6 SCO	6 SAG
10 SCO	9 SAG	8 SAG	9 AQU	8 PIS	8 TAU	8 GEM	9 LEO	8 VIR	10 SCO	9 SAG	8 CAP
12 SAG	11 CAP	10 CAP	11 PIS	11 ARI	11 GEM	10 CAN	12 VIR	10 LIB	13 SAG	11 CAP	10 AQU
14 CAP	13 AQU	12 AQU	13 ARI	13 TAU	13 CAN	13 LEO	14 LIB	13 SCO	15 CAP	13 AQU	13 PIS
16 AQU	15 PIS	14 PIS	15 TAU	15 GEM	16 LEO	15 VIR	17 SCO	15 SAG	17 AQU	15 PIS	15 ARI
18 PIS	17 ARI	16 ARI	17 GEM	17 CAN	18 VIR	18 LIB	19 SAG	18 CAP	19 PIS	17 ARI	17 TAU
20 ARI	19 TAU	18 TAU	19 CAN	19 LEO	21 LIB	20 SCO	21 CAP	20 AQU	21 ARI	20 TAU	19 GEM
23 TAU	21 GEM	21 GEM	22 LEO	22 VIR	23 SCO	23 SAG	23 AQU	22 PIS	23 TAU	22 GEM	21 CAN
25 GEM	24 CAN	23 CAN	25 VIR	24 LIB	25 SAG	25 CAP	25 PIS	24 ARI	25 GEM	24 CAN	24 LEO
28 CAN	26 LEO	26 LEO	27 LIB	27 SCO	27 CAP	27 AQU	27 ARI	26 TAU	28 CAN	26 LEO	26 VIR
30 LEO		28 VIR	29 SCO	29 SAG	29 AQU	29 PIS	29 TAU	28 GEM	30 LEO	29 VIR	29 LIB
		31 LIB		31 CAP		31 ARI		30 CAN			31 SCO

JAN	FEB	MAR	APR	MAY	JUN	JUL	AUG	SEP	OCT	NOV	DEC
3 SAG	1 CAP	1 CAP	1 PIS	1 ARI	1 GEM	1 CAN	2 VIR	3 SCO	3 SAG	1 CAP	1 AQU
5 CAP	3 AQU	3 AQU	3 ARI	3 TAU	3 CAN	3 LEO	4 LIB	5 SAG	5 CAP	4 AQU	3 PIS
7 AQU	5 PIS	5 PIS	5 TAU	5 GEM	6 LEO	5 VIR	7 SCO	8 CAP	7 AQU	6 PIS	5 ARI
9 PIS	7 ARI	7 ARI	7 GEM	7 CAN	8 VIR	8 LIB	9 SAG	10 AQU	10 PIS	8 ARI	7 TAU
11 ARI	9 TAU	9 TAU	9 CAN	10 LEO	10 LIB	10 SCO	11 CAP	12 PIS	12 ARI	10 TAU	9 GEM
13 TAU	12 GEM	11 GEM	12 LEO	12 VIR	13 SCO	13 SAG	14 AQU	14 ARI	14 TAU	12 GEM	11 CAN
15 GEM	14 CAN	13 CAN	14 VIR	14 LIB	15 SAG	15 CAP	16 PIS	16 TAU	16 GEM	14 CAN	14 LEO
18 CAN	16 LEO	16 LEO	17 LIB	17 SCO	18 CAP	17 AQU	18 ARI	18 GEM	18 CAN	16 LEO	16 VIR
20 LEO	19 VIR	18 VIR	19 SCO	19 SAG	20 AQU	19 PIS	20 TAU	20 CAN	20 LEO	19 VIR	19 LIB
23 VIR	21 LIB	21 LIB	22 SAG	22 CAP	22 PIS	21 ARI	22 GEM	23 LEO	22 VIR	21 LIB	21 SCO
25 LIB	24 SCO	23 SCO	24 CAP	24 AQU	24 ARI	23 TAU	24 CAN	25 VIR	25 LIB	24 SCO	24 SAG
28 SCO	26 SAG	26 SAG	26 AQU	26 PIS	26 TAU	26 GEM	26 LEO	28 LIB	27 SCO	26 SAG	26 CAP
30 SAG		28 CAP	28 PIS	28 ARI	28 GEM	28 CAN	29 VIR	30 SCO	30 SAG	29 CAP	28 AQU
		30 AQU		30 TAU		30 LEO	31 LIB				30 PIS

JAN	FEB	MAR	APR	MAY	JUN	JUL	AUG	SEP	OCT	NOV	DEC
1 ARI	2 GEM	1 GEM	2 LEO	2 VIR	3 SCO	3 SAG	1 CAP	2 PIS	2 ARI	2 GEM	2 CAN
4 TAU	4 CAN	3 CAN	4 VIR	4 LIB	5 SAG	5 CAP	5 AQU	4 ARI	4 TAU	4 CAN	4 LEO
6 GEM	6 LEO	6 LEO	7 LIB	7 SCO	8 CAP	7 AQU	8 ARI	7 TAU	6 GEM	6 LEO	6 VIR
8 CAN	9 VIR	8 VIR	9 SCO	9 SAG	10 AQU	10 PIS	10 TAU	9 GEM	8 CAN	9 VIR	8 LIB
10 LEO	11 LIB	11 LIB	12 SAG	12 CAP	12 PIS	12 ARI	12 GEM	11 CAN	10 LEO	11 LIB	11 SCO
12 VIR	14 SCO	13 SCO	14 CAP	14 AQU	15 ARI	14 TAU	14 CAN	13 LEO	12 VIR	14 SCO	13 SAG
15 LIB	16 SAG	16 SAG	17 AQU	16 PIS	17 TAU	16 GEM	17 LEO	15 VIR	15 LIB	16 SAG	16 CAP
17 SCO	19 CAP	18 CAP	19 PIS	18 ARI	19 GEM	18 CAN	19 VIR	18 LIB	17 SCO	19 CAP	18 AQU
20 SAG	21 AQU	20 AQU	21 ARI	20 TAU	21 CAN	20 LEO	21 LIB	20 SCO	20 SAG	21 AQU	21 PIS
22 CAP	23 PIS	23 PIS	23 TAU	22 GEM	23 LEO	23 VIR	24 SCO	23 SAG	22 CAP	24 PIS	23 ARI
25 AQU	25 ARI	25 ARI	25 GEM	24 CAN	25 VIR	25 LIB	26 SAG	25 CAP	25 AQU	26 ARI	25 TAU
27 PIS	27 TAU	26 TAU	27 CAN	27 LEO	28 LIB	27 SCO	29 CAP	28 AQU	27 PIS	28 TAU	27 GEM
29 ARI		29 GEM	29 LEO	29 VIR	30 SCO	30 SAG	31 AQU	30 PIS	29 ARI	30 GEM	29 CAN
31 TAU		31 CAN		31 LIB					31 TAU		31 LEO

JAN	FEB	MAR	APR	MAY	JUN	JUL	AUG	SEP	OCT	NOV	DEC
2 VIR	1 LIB	2 SCO	1 SAG	1 CAP	2 PIS	1 ARI	2 GEM	2 LEO	2 VIR	3 SCO	2 SAG
5 LIB	4 SCO	4 SAG	3 CAP	3 AQU	4 ARI	4 TAU	4 CAN	5 VIR	4 LIB	5 SAG	5 CAP
7 SCO	6 SAG	7 CAP	6 AQU	5 PIS	6 TAU	6 GEM	6 LEO	7 LIB	6 SCO	8 CAP	7 AQU
10 SAG	9 CAP	9 AQU	8 PIS	8 ARI	8 GEM	8 CAN	8 VIR	9 SCO	9 SAG	10 AQU	10 PIS
12 CAP	11 AQU	12 PIS	10 ARI	10 TAU	10 CAN	10 LEO	10 LIB	11 SAG	11 CAP	13 PIS	12 ARI
15 AQU	13 PIS	14 ARI	12 TAU	12 GEM	12 LEO	12 VIR	13 SCO	14 CAP	14 AQU	15 ARI	15 TAU
17 PIS	16 ARI	16 TAU	14 GEM	14 CAN	14 VIR	14 LIB	15 SAG	16 AQU	16 PIS	17 TAU	17 GEM
19 ARI	18 TAU	18 GEM	16 CAN	16 LEO	17 LIB	17 SCO	18 CAP	19 PIS	19 ARI	19 GEM	19 CAN
21 TAU	20 GEM	20 CAN	19 LEO	18 VIR	19 SCO	19 SAG	20 AQU	21 ARI	21 TAU	21 CAN	21 LEO
24 GEM	22 CAN	22 VIR	21 VIR	20 LIB	22 SAG	21 CAP	23 PIS	23 TAU	23 GEM	23 LEO	23 VIR
26 CAN	24 LEO	25 VIR	23 LIB	23 SCO	24 CAP	24 AQU	25 ARI	25 GEM	25 CAN	25 VIR	25 LIB
28 LEO	26 VIR	27 LIB	26 SCO	25 SAG	27 AQU	26 PIS	27 TAU	28 CAN	27 LEO	27 LIB	27 SCO
30 VIR	28 LIB	29 SCO	28 SAG	28 CAP	29 PIS	29 ARI	29 GEM	30 LEO	30 VIR	30 SCO	30 SAG
				30 AQU		31 TAU	31 CAN		31 LIB		

JAN	FEB	MAR	APR	MAY	JUN	JUL	AUG	SEP	OCT	NOV	DEC
1 CAP	2 PIS	2 PIS	3 TAU	2 GEM	1 CAN	2 VIR	3 SCO	1 SAG	1 CAP	2 PIS	2 ARI
4 AQU	5 ARI	4 ARI	5 GEM	4 CAN	3 LEO	4 LIB	5 SAG	4 CAP	4 AQU	5 ARI	5 TAU
6 PIS	7 TAU	6 TAU	7 CAN	6 LEO	5 VIR	6 SCO	7 CAP	6 AQU	6 PIS	7 TAU	7 GEM
9 ARI	9 GEM	9 GEM	9 LEO	8 VIR	7 LIB	9 SAG	10 AQU	9 PIS	9 ARI	9 GEM	9 CAN
11 TAU	11 CAN	11 CAN	11 VIR	11 LIB	9 SCO	11 CAP	13 PIS	11 ARI	11 TAU	12 CAN	11 LEO
13 GEM	13 LEO	13 LEO	13 LIB	13 SCO	12 SAG	14 AQU	15 ARI	14 TAU	13 GEM	14 LEO	13 VIR
15 CAN	16 VIR	15 VIR	15 SCO	15 SAG	14 CAP	16 PIS	17 TAU	16 GEM	15 CAN	16 VIR	15 LIB
17 LEO	18 LIB	17 LIB	18 SAG	18 CAP	16 AQU	19 ARI	19 GEM	18 CAN	17 LEO	18 LIB	17 SCO
19 VIR	20 SCO	19 SCO	20 CAP	20 AQU	19 PIS	21 TAU	21 CAN	20 LEO	20 VIR	20 SCO	20 SAG
21 LIB	22 SAG	22 SAG	23 AQU	23 PIS	21 ARI	23 GEM	23 LEO	22 VIR	22 LIB	22 SAG	22 CAP
23 SCO	25 CAP	24 CAP	25 PIS	25 ARI	24 TAU	25 CAN	26 VIR	24 LIB	24 SCO	25 CAP	25 AQU
26 SAG	27 AQU	27 AQU	28 ARI	27 TAU	26 GEM	27 LEO	28 LIB	26 SCO	26 SAG	27 AQU	27 PIS
28 CAP		29 PIS	30 TAU	30 GEM	28 CAN	29 VIR	30 SCO	29 SAG	28 CAP	30 PIS	30 ARI
31 AQU		31 ARI			30 LEO	31 LIB			31 AQU		

JAN	FEB	MAR	APR	MAY	JUN	JUL	AUG	SEP	OCT	NOV	DEC
1 TAU	2 CAN	1 CAN	2 VIR	1 LIB	2 SAG	1 CAP	2 PIS	1 ARI	1 TAU	2 CAN	2 LEO
3 GEM	4 LEO	3 LEO	4 LIB	3 SCO	4 CAP	4 AQU	4 ARI	4 TAU	3 GEM	4 LEO	4 VIR
5 CAN	6 VIR	5 VIR	6 SCO	5 SAG	6 AQU	6 PIS	6 TAU	6 GEM	6 CAN	6 VIR	6 LIB
7 LEO	7 LIB	7 LIB	8 SAG	8 CAP	9 PIS	9 ARI	9 GEM	9 CAN	8 LEO	8 LIB	8 SCO
9 VIR	10 SCO	9 SCO	10 CAP	10 AQU	11 ARI	11 TAU	11 CAN	11 LEO	10 VIR	11 SCO	10 SAG
11 LIB	12 SAG	12 SAG	13 AQU	12 PIS	14 TAU	14 GEM	14 LEO	13 VIR	12 LIB	13 SAG	12 CAP
14 SCO	15 CAP	14 CAP	15 PIS	15 ARI	16 GEM	16 CAN	16 VIR	15 LIB	14 SCO	15 CAP	14 AQU
16 SAG	17 AQU	16 AQU	18 ARI	17 TAU	18 CAN	18 LEO	18 LIB	17 SCO	16 SAG	17 AQU	17 PIS
18 CAP	20 PIS	19 PIS	20 TAU	20 GEM	20 LEO	20 VIR	20 SCO	19 SAG	18 CAP	20 PIS	19 ARI
21 AQU	22 ARI	21 ARI	22 GEM	22 CAN	23 VIR	23 LIB	22 SAG	21 CAP	21 AQU	22 ARI	22 TAU
23 PIS	25 TAU	24 TAU	25 CAN	24 LEO	25 LIB	24 SCO	25 CAP	23 AQU	23 PIS	25 TAU	24 GEM
26 ARI	27 GEM	26 GEM	27 LEO	26 VIR	27 SCO	26 SAG	27 AQU	26 PIS	26 ARI	27 GEM	27 CAN
28 TAU		29 CAN	29 VIR	28 LIB	29 SAG	29 CAP	30 PIS	28 ARI	28 TAU	29 CAN	29 LEO
31 GEM		31 LEO		31 SCO		31 AQU			31 GEM		31 VIR

JAN	FEB	MAR	APR	MAY	JUN	JUL	AUG	SEP	OCT	NOV	DEC
2 LIB	3 SAG	2 SAG	3 AQU	2 PIS	1 ARI	1 TAU	2 CAN	1 LEO	2 LIB	1 SCO	2 CAP
4 SCO	5 CAP	4 CAP	5 PIS	5 ARI	4 TAU	4 GEM	4 LEO	3 VIR	4 SCO	3 SAG	4 AQU
6 SAG	7 AQU	6 AQU	8 ARI	7 TAU	6 GEM	6 CAN	6 VIR	5 LIB	6 SAG	5 CAP	7 PIS
9 CAP	10 PIS	9 PIS	10 TAU	10 GEM	9 CAN	8 LEO	9 LIB	7 SCO	9 CAP	7 AQU	9 ARI
11 AQU	12 ARI	11 ARI	13 GEM	12 CAN	11 LEO	10 VIR	11 SCO	9 SAG	11 AQU	9 PIS	12 TAU
13 PIS	15 TAU	14 TAU	15 CAN	15 LEO	13 VIR	12 LIB	13 SAG	11 CAP	13 PIS	12 ARI	14 GEM
16 ARI	17 GEM	16 GEM	17 LEO	17 VIR	15 LIB	15 SCO	15 CAP	14 AQU	16 ARI	14 TAU	17 CAN
18 TAU	19 CAN	19 CAN	20 VIR	19 LIB	17 SCO	17 SAG	17 AQU	16 PIS	18 TAU	17 GEM	19 LEO
21 GEM	22 LEO	21 LEO	22 LIB	21 SCO	19 SAG	19 CAP	20 PIS	18 ARI	21 GEM	19 CAN	21 VIR
23 CAN	24 VIR	23 VIR	24 SCO	23 SAG	21 CAP	22 AQU	22 ARI	21 TAU	23 CAN	22 LEO	24 LIB
25 LEO	26 LIB	25 LIB	26 SAG	25 CAP	24 AQU	23 PIS	25 TAU	23 GEM	26 LEO	24 VIR	26 SCO
27 VIR	28 SCO	27 SCO	28 CAP	27 AQU	26 PIS	26 ARI	27 GEM	26 CAN	28 VIR	26 LIB	28 SAG
29 LIB		29 SAG	30 AQU	30 PIS	28 ARI	28 TAU	30 CAN	28 LEO	30 LIB	28 SCO	30 CAP
31 SCO		31 CAP				31 GEM		30 VIR		30 SAG	

1968

JAN	FEB	MAR	APR	MAY	JUN	JUL	AUG	SEP	OCT	NOV	DEC
1 AQU	2 ARI	3 TAU	2 GEM	1 CAN	2 VIR	2 LIB	3 SAG	1 CAP	2 PIS	1 ARI	1 TAU
3 PIS	4 TAU	5 GEM	4 CAN	4 LEO	5 LIB	4 SCO	5 CAP	3 AQU	5 ARI	3 TAU	3 GEM
6 ARI	7 GEM	8 CAN	7 LEO	6 VIR	7 SCO	6 SAG	7 AQU	5 PIS	7 TAU	6 GEM	6 CAN
8 TAU	9 CAN	10 LEO	9 VIR	8 LIB	9 SAG	8 CAP	9 PIS	7 ARI	10 GEM	8 CAN	8 LEO
11 GEM	12 LEO	12 VIR	11 LIB	10 SCO	11 CAP	10 AQU	11 ARI	10 TAU	12 CAN	11 LEO	11 VIR
13 CAN	14 VIR	14 LIB	13 SCO	12 SAG	13 AQU	12 PIS	13 TAU	12 GEM	15 LEO	13 VIR	13 LIB
15 LEO	16 LIB	17 SCO	15 SAG	14 CAP	15 PIS	15 ARI	16 GEM	15 CAN	17 VIR	16 LIB	15 SCO
18 VIR	18 SCO	19 SAG	17 CAP	16 AQU	17 ARI	17 TAU	18 CAN	17 LEO	19 LIB	18 SCO	17 SAG
20 LIB	20 SAG	21 CAP	19 AQU	19 PIS	20 TAU	20 GEM	21 LEO	20 VIR	21 SCO	20 SAG	19 CAP
22 SCO	22 CAP	23 AQU	21 PIS	21 ARI	22 GEM	22 CAN	23 VIR	22 LIB	23 SAG	22 CAP	21 AQU
24 SAG	25 AQU	25 PIS	24 ARI	24 TAU	25 CAN	25 LEO	25 LIB	24 SCO	25 CAP	24 AQU	23 PIS
26 CAP	27 PIS	28 ARI	26 TAU	26 GEM	27 LEO	27 VIR	28 SCO	26 SAG	27 AQU	26 PIS	26 ARI
28 AQU	29 ARI	30 TAU	29 GEM	29 CAN	30 VIR	29 LIB	30 SAG	28 CAP	30 PIS	28 ARI	28 TAU
31 PIS				31 LEO		31 SCO		30 AQU			30 GEM

1969

JAN	FEB	MAR	APR	MAY	JUN	JUL	AUG	SEP	OCT	NOV	DEC
2 CAN	1 LEO	2 VIR	1 LIB	1 SCO	1 CAP	1 AQU	1 ARI	2 GEM	2 CAN	1 LEO	1 VIR
4 LEO	3 VIR	5 LIB	3 SCO	3 SAG	3 AQU	3 PIS	3 TAU	5 CAN	4 LEO	3 VIR	3 LIB
7 VIR	6 LIB	7 SCO	5 SAG	5 CAP	5 PIS	5 ARI	6 GEM	7 LEO	7 VIR	6 LIB	5 SCO
9 LIB	8 SCO	9 SAG	8 CAP	7 AQU	7 ARI	7 TAU	8 CAN	10 VIR	9 LIB	8 SCO	8 SAG
12 SCO	10 SAG	11 CAP	10 AQU	9 PIS	10 TAU	10 GEM	11 LEO	12 LIB	12 SCO	10 SAG	10 CAP
14 SAG	12 CAP	13 AQU	12 PIS	11 ARI	12 GEM	12 CAN	13 VIR	14 SCO	14 SAG	12 CAP	12 AQU
16 CAP	14 AQU	16 PIS	14 ARI	14 TAU	15 CAN	15 LEO	16 LIB	17 SAG	16 CAP	14 AQU	14 PIS
18 AQU	16 PIS	18 ARI	16 TAU	16 GEM	17 LEO	17 VIR	18 SCO	19 CAP	18 AQU	16 PIS	16 ARI
20 PIS	18 ARI	20 TAU	19 GEM	19 CAN	20 VIR	20 LIB	20 SAG	21 AQU	20 PIS	19 ARI	18 TAU
22 ARI	21 TAU	22 GEM	21 CAN	21 LEO	22 LIB	22 SCO	22 CAP	23 PIS	22 ARI	21 TAU	20 GEM
24 TAU	23 GEM	25 CAN	24 LEO	24 VIR	24 SCO	24 SAG	24 AQU	25 ARI	25 TAU	23 GEM	23 CAN
27 GEM	26 CAN	27 LEO	26 VIR	26 LIB	26 SAG	26 CAP	26 PIS	27 TAU	27 GEM	26 CAN	25 LEO
29 CAN	28 LEO	30 VIR	29 LIB	28 SCO	29 CAP	28 AQU	28 ARI	29 GEM	29 CAN	28 LEO	28 VIR
				30 SAG		30 PIS	31 TAU				30 LIB

1970

JAN	FEB	MAR	APR	MAY	JUN	JUL	AUG	SEP	OCT	NOV	DEC
2 SCO	2 CAP	2 CAP	2 PIS	2 ARI	2 GEM	2 CAN	1 LEO	2 LIB	2 SCO	3 CAP	2 AQU
4 SAG	4 AQU	4 AQU	4 ARI	4 TAU	5 CAN	4 LEO	3 VIR	5 SCO	4 SAG	5 AQU	4 PIS
6 CAP	6 PIS	6 PIS	6 TAU	6 GEM	7 LEO	7 VIR	6 LIB	7 SAG	6 CAP	7 PIS	6 ARI
8 AQU	8 ARI	8 ARI	9 GEM	8 CAN	10 VIR	10 LIB	8 SCO	9 CAP	9 AQU	9 ARI	8 TAU
10 PIS	11 TAU	10 TAU	11 CAN	11 LEO	12 LIB	12 SCO	11 SAG	11 AQU	11 PIS	11 TAU	11 GEM
12 ARI	13 GEM	12 GEM	14 LEO	13 VIR	15 SCO	14 SAG	13 CAP	13 PIS	13 ARI	13 GEM	13 CAN
14 TAU	15 CAN	15 CAN	16 VIR	16 LIB	17 SAG	16 CAP	15 AQU	15 ARI	15 TAU	16 CAN	15 LEO
17 GEM	18 LEO	17 LEO	19 LIB	18 SCO	19 CAP	18 AQU	17 PIS	17 TAU	17 GEM	18 LEO	18 VIR
19 CAN	20 VIR	20 VIR	21 SCO	20 SAG	21 AQU	20 PIS	19 ARI	19 GEM	19 CAN	20 VIR	20 LIB
22 LEO	23 LIB	22 LIB	23 SAG	23 CAP	23 PIS	22 ARI	21 TAU	22 CAN	22 LEO	23 LIB	23 SCO
24 VIR	25 SCO	25 SCO	25 CAP	25 AQU	25 ARI	25 TAU	23 GEM	24 LEO	24 VIR	25 SCO	25 SAG
27 LIB	28 SAG	27 SAG	27 AQU	27 PIS	27 TAU	27 GEM	25 CAN	27 VIR	27 LIB	28 SAG	27 CAP
29 SCO		29 CAP	30 PIS	29 ARI	29 GEM	29 CAN	28 LEO	29 LIB	29 SCO	30 CAP	29 AQU
31 SAG		31 AQU		31 TAU			31 VIR		31 SAG		31 PIS

1971

JAN	FEB	MAR	APR	MAY	JUN	JUL	AUG	SEP	OCT	NOV	DEC
3 ARI	1 TAU	2 GEM	1 CAN	1 LEO	2 LIB	2 SCO	1 SAG	2 AQU	1 PIS	2 TAU	1 GEM
5 TAU	3 GEM	5 CAN	3 LEO	3 VIR	5 SCO	4 SAG	3 CAP	4 PIS	3 ARI	4 GEM	3 CAN
7 GEM	5 CAN	7 LEO	6 VIR	6 LIB	7 SAG	6 CAP	5 AQU	6 ARI	5 TAU	6 CAN	5 LEO
9 CAN	8 LEO	10 VIR	8 LIB	8 SCO	9 CAP	9 AQU	7 PIS	8 TAU	7 GEM	8 LEO	8 VIR
12 LEO	10 VIR	12 LIB	11 SCO	11 SAG	11 AQU	11 PIS	9 ARI	10 GEM	9 CAN	11 VIR	10 LIB
14 VIR	13 LIB	15 SCO	13 SAG	13 CAP	14 PIS	13 ARI	11 TAU	12 CAN	12 LEO	13 LIB	13 SCO
17 LIB	15 SCO	17 SAG	16 CAP	15 AQU	16 ARI	15 TAU	13 GEM	14 LEO	14 VIR	15 SCO	15 SAG
19 SCO	18 SAG	20 CAP	18 AQU	17 PIS	18 TAU	17 GEM	16 CAN	17 VIR	16 LIB	18 SAG	17 CAP
22 SAG	20 CAP	22 AQU	20 PIS	20 ARI	20 GEM	19 CAN	18 LEO	19 LIB	19 SCO	20 CAP	20 AQU
24 CAP	22 AQU	24 PIS	22 ARI	22 TAU	22 CAN	22 LEO	20 VIR	22 SCO	22 SAG	23 AQU	22 PIS
26 AQU	24 PIS	26 ARI	24 TAU	24 GEM	24 LEO	24 VIR	23 LIB	24 SAG	24 CAP	25 PIS	24 ARI
28 PIS	26 ARI	28 TAU	26 GEM	26 CAN	27 VIR	27 LIB	26 SCO	27 CAP	26 AQU	27 ARI	26 TAU
30 ARI	28 TAU	30 GEM	28 CAN	28 LEO	29 LIB	29 SCO	28 SAG	29 AQU	28 PIS	29 TAU	28 GEM
				30 VIR			30 CAP		31 ARI		30 CAN

1972

JAN	FEB	MAR	APR	MAY	JUN	JUL	AUG	SEP	OCT	NOV	DEC
2 LEO	3 LIB	1 LIB	2 SAG	2 CAP	1 AQU	3 ARI	1 TAU	1 CAN	1 LEO	2 LIB	1 SCO
4 VIR	5 SCO	4 SCO	5 CAP	5 AQU	3 PIS	5 TAU	3 GEM	4 LEO	3 VIR	4 SCO	4 SAG
6 LIB	8 SAG	6 SAG	7 AQU	7 PIS	5 ARI	7 GEM	5 CAN	6 VIR	5 LIB	7 SAG	7 CAP
9 SCO	10 CAP	9 CAP	9 PIS	9 ARI	7 TAU	9 CAN	7 LEO	8 LIB	8 SCO	9 CAP	9 AQU
11 SAG	12 AQU	11 AQU	11 ARI	11 TAU	9 GEM	11 LEO	10 VIR	11 SCO	10 SAG	12 AQU	11 PIS
14 CAP	15 PIS	13 PIS	14 TAU	13 GEM	11 CAN	13 VIR	12 LIB	13 SAG	13 CAP	14 PIS	14 ARI
16 AQU	17 ARI	15 ARI	16 GEM	15 CAN	14 LEO	15 LIB	14 SCO	16 CAP	15 AQU	16 ARI	16 TAU
18 PIS	19 TAU	17 TAU	18 CAN	17 LEO	16 VIR	18 SCO	17 SAG	18 AQU	18 PIS	18 TAU	18 GEM
20 ARI	21 GEM	19 GEM	20 LEO	19 VIR	18 LIB	20 SAG	19 CAP	20 PIS	20 ARI	20 GEM	20 CAN
23 TAU	23 CAN	21 CAN	22 VIR	22 LIB	21 SCO	23 CAP	22 AQU	22 ARI	22 TAU	22 CAN	22 LEO
25 GEM	25 LEO	24 LEO	25 LIB	24 SCO	23 SAG	25 AQU	24 PIS	24 TAU	24 GEM	24 LEO	24 VIR
27 CAN	28 VIR	26 VIR	27 SCO	27 SAG	26 CAP	28 PIS	26 ARI	27 GEM	26 CAN	27 VIR	26 LIB
29 LEO		28 LIB	30 SAG	29 CAP	28 AQU	30 ARI	28 TAU	29 CAN	28 LEO	29 LIB	29 SCO
31 VIR		31 SCO			30 PIS		30 GEM		30 VIR		31 SAG

1973

JAN	FEB	MAR	APR	MAY	JUN	JUL	AUG	SEP	OCT	NOV	DEC
3 CAP	2 AQU	1 AQU	2 ARI	1 TAU	2 CAN	1 LEO	2 LIB	1 SCO	3 CAP	2 AQU	1 PIS
5 AQU	4 PIS	3 PIS	4 TAU	3 GEM	4 LEO	3 VIR	4 SCO	3 SAG	5 AQU	4 PIS	4 ARI
8 PIS	6 ARI	5 ARI	6 GEM	5 CAN	6 VIR	6 LIB	7 SAG	5 CAP	8 PIS	6 ARI	6 TAU
10 ARI	8 TAU	8 TAU	8 CAN	7 LEO	8 LIB	8 SCO	9 CAP	8 AQU	10 ARI	9 TAU	8 GEM
12 TAU	10 GEM	10 GEM	10 LEO	9 VIR	11 SCO	10 SAG	12 AQU	10 PIS	12 TAU	11 GEM	10 CAN
14 GEM	13 CAN	12 CAN	12 VIR	12 LIB	13 SAG	13 CAP	14 PIS	13 ARI	14 GEM	13 CAN	12 LEO
16 CAN	15 LEO	14 LEO	15 LIB	14 SCO	16 CAP	15 AQU	16 ARI	15 TAU	16 CAN	15 LEO	14 VIR
18 LEO	17 VIR	16 VIR	17 SCO	17 SAG	18 AQU	18 PIS	19 TAU	17 GEM	19 LEO	17 VIR	16 LIB
20 VIR	19 LIB	18 LIB	20 SAG	19 CAP	21 PIS	20 ARI	21 GEM	19 CAN	21 VIR	19 LIB	19 SCO
23 LIB	21 SCO	21 SCO	22 CAP	22 AQU	23 ARI	22 TAU	23 CAN	21 LEO	23 LIB	22 SCO	21 SAG
25 SCO	24 SAG	23 SAG	25 AQU	24 PIS	25 TAU	25 GEM	25 LEO	23 VIR	25 SCO	24 SAG	24 CAP
28 SAG	26 CAP	26 CAP	27 PIS	27 ARI	27 GEM	27 CAN	27 VIR	26 LIB	28 SAG	26 CAP	26 AQU
30 CAP		28 AQU	29 ARI	29 TAU	29 CAN	29 LEO	29 LIB	28 SCO	30 CAP	29 AQU	29 PIS
		31 PIS		31 GEM		31 VIR		30 SAG			31 ARI

1974

JAN	FEB	MAR	APR	MAY	JUN	JUL	AUG	SEP	OCT	NOV	DEC
2 TAU	1 GEM	2 CAN	1 LEO	2 LIB	1 SCO	3 CAP	2 AQU	3 ARI	2 TAU	1 GEM	1 CAN
5 GEM	3 CAN	4 LEO	3 VIR	4 SCO	3 SAG	5 AQU	4 PIS	5 TAU	5 GEM	3 CAN	3 LEO
7 CAN	5 LEO	7 VIR	5 LIB	7 SAG	6 CAP	8 PIS	7 ARI	8 GEM	7 CAN	5 LEO	5 VIR
9 LEO	7 VIR	9 LIB	7 SCO	9 CAP	8 AQU	10 ARI	9 TAU	11 CAN	9 LEO	8 VIR	7 LIB
11 VIR	9 LIB	11 SCO	9 SAG	12 AQU	11 PIS	13 TAU	11 GEM	13 LEO	11 VIR	10 LIB	9 SCO
13 LIB	11 SCO	13 SAG	12 CAP	14 PIS	13 ARI	15 GEM	13 CAN	15 VIR	13 LIB	12 SCO	11 SAG
15 SCO	14 SAG	16 CAP	14 AQU	17 ARI	15 TAU	17 CAN	15 LEO	17 LIB	15 SCO	14 SAG	14 CAP
17 SAG	16 CAP	18 AQU	17 PIS	19 TAU	18 GEM	19 LEO	17 VIR	19 SCO	18 SAG	16 CAP	16 AQU
20 CAP	19 AQU	21 PIS	19 ARI	21 GEM	20 CAN	21 VIR	19 LIB	20 SAG	20 CAP	19 AQU	19 PIS
22 AQU	21 PIS	23 ARI	22 TAU	23 CAN	22 LEO	23 LIB	22 SCO	23 CAP	22 AQU	21 PIS	21 ARI
25 PIS	24 ARI	25 TAU	24 GEM	25 LEO	24 VIR	25 SCO	24 SAG	25 AQU	25 PIS	24 ARI	24 TAU
27 ARI	26 TAU	27 GEM	26 CAN	27 VIR	26 LIB	28 SAG	26 CAP	28 PIS	27 ARI	26 TAU	26 GEM
30 TAU	28 GEM	30 CAN	28 LEO	30 LIB	28 SCO	30 CAP	29 AQU	30 ARI	30 TAU	28 GEM	28 CAN
			30 VIR		30 SAG		31 PIS				30 LEO

1975

JAN	FEB	MAR	APR	MAY	JUN	JUL	AUG	SEP	OCT	NOV	DEC
1 VIR	2 SCO	1 SCO	2 CAP	2 AQU	3 ARI	3 TAU	1 GEM	2 LEO	2 VIR	2 SCO	2 SAG
3 LIB	4 SAG	3 SAG	4 AQU	4 PIS	5 TAU	5 GEM	4 CAN	4 VIR	4 LIB	4 SAG	4 CAP
5 SCO	6 CAP	5 CAP	7 PIS	7 ARI	7 GEM	7 CAN	6 LEO	6 LIB	6 SCO	6 CAP	6 AQU
8 SAG	9 AQU	8 AQU	9 ARI	9 TAU	10 CAN	9 LEO	8 VIR	8 SCO	8 SAG	9 AQU	8 PIS
10 CAP	11 PIS	10 PIS	12 TAU	11 GEM	12 LEO	11 VIR	10 LIB	10 SAG	10 CAP	11 PIS	11 ARI
12 AQU	14 ARI	13 ARI	14 GEM	14 CAN	14 VIR	14 LIB	12 SCO	13 CAP	12 AQU	14 ARI	13 TAU
15 PIS	16 TAU	15 TAU	16 CAN	16 LEO	16 LIB	16 SCO	14 SAG	15 AQU	15 PIS	16 TAU	16 GEM
17 ARI	19 GEM	18 GEM	19 LEO	18 VIR	18 SCO	18 SAG	16 CAP	18 PIS	17 ARI	19 GEM	18 CAN
20 TAU	21 CAN	20 CAN	21 VIR	20 LIB	21 SAG	20 CAP	19 AQU	20 ARI	20 TAU	21 CAN	20 LEO
22 GEM	23 LEO	22 LEO	23 LIB	22 SCO	23 CAP	23 AQU	21 PIS	23 TAU	22 GEM	23 LEO	23 VIR
24 CAN	25 VIR	24 VIR	25 SCO	24 SAG	25 AQU	25 PIS	24 ARI	25 GEM	25 CAN	25 VIR	25 LIB
26 LEO	27 LIB	26 LIB	27 SAG	27 CAP	28 PIS	28 ARI	26 TAU	27 CAN	27 LEO	27 LIB	27 SCO
28 VIR		28 SCO	29 CAP	29 AQU	30 ARI	30 TAU	29 GEM	29 LEO	29 VIR	30 SCO	29 SAG
30 LIB		30 SAG		31 PIS			31 CAN		31 LIB		31 CAP

1976

JAN	FEB	MAR	APR	MAY	JUN	JUL	AUG	SEP	OCT	NOV	DEC
2 AQU	1 PIS	2 ARI	1 TAU	3 CAN	1 LEO	1 VIR	1 SCO	2 CAP	1 AQU	2 ARI	2 TAU
5 PIS	4 ARI	4 TAU	3 GEM	5 LEO	4 VIR	3 LIB	3 SAG	4 AQU	4 PIS	5 TAU	5 GEM
7 ARI	6 TAU	7 GEM	6 CAN	7 VIR	6 LIB	5 SCO	5 CAP	7 PIS	6 ARI	8 GEM	7 CAN
10 TAU	9 GEM	9 CAN	8 LEO	10 LIB	8 SCO	7 SAG	8 AQU	9 ARI	9 TAU	10 CAN	10 LEO
12 GEM	11 CAN	12 LEO	10 VIR	12 SCO	10 SAG	9 CAP	10 PIS	11 TAU	11 GEM	12 LEO	12 VIR
15 CAN	13 LEO	14 VIR	12 LIB	14 SAG	12 CAP	12 AQU	13 ARI	14 GEM	14 CAN	15 VIR	14 LIB
17 LEO	15 VIR	16 LIB	14 SCO	16 CAP	14 AQU	14 PIS	15 TAU	17 CAN	16 LEO	17 LIB	16 SCO
19 VIR	17 LIB	18 SCO	16 SAG	18 AQU	16 PIS	17 ARI	18 GEM	19 LEO	18 VIR	19 SCO	18 SAG
21 LIB	19 SCO	20 SAG	18 CAP	20 PIS	19 ARI	19 TAU	20 CAN	21 VIR	21 LIB	21 SAG	20 CAP
23 SCO	21 SAG	22 CAP	20 AQU	23 ARI	22 TAU	21 GEM	22 LEO	23 LIB	23 SCO	23 CAP	22 AQU
25 SAG	24 CAP	24 AQU	23 PIS	25 TAU	24 GEM	24 CAN	25 VIR	25 SCO	24 SAG	25 AQU	25 PIS
27 CAP	26 AQU	27 PIS	25 ARI	28 GEM	26 CAN	26 LEO	27 LIB	27 SAG	27 CAP	27 PIS	27 ARI
30 AQU	28 PIS	29 ARI	28 TAU	30 CAN	29 LEO	28 VIR	29 SCO	29 CAP	29 AQU	30 ARI	30 TAU
			30 GEM			30 LIB	31 SAG		31 PIS		

1977

JAN	FEB	MAR	APR	MAY	JUN	JUL	AUG	SEP	OCT	NOV	DEC
1 GEM	2 LEO	2 LEO	2 LIB	2 SCO	2 CAP	2 AQU	3 ARI	1 TAU	1 GEM	3 LEO	2 VIR
4 CAN	5 VIR	4 VIR	5 SCO	4 SAG	4 AQU	4 PIS	5 TAU	4 GEM	4 CAN	5 VIR	5 LIB
6 LEO	7 LIB	6 LIB	7 SAG	6 CAP	7 PIS	7 ARI	7 GEM	6 CAN	6 LEO	7 LIB	7 SCO
8 VIR	9 SCO	8 SCO	9 CAP	8 AQU	9 ARI	9 TAU	10 CAN	9 LEO	9 VIR	9 SCO	9 SAG
10 LIB	11 SAG	10 SAG	11 AQU	10 PIS	11 TAU	11 GEM	12 LEO	11 VIR	11 LIB	11 SAG	11 CAP
13 SCO	13 CAP	12 CAP	13 PIS	13 ARI	14 GEM	14 CAN	15 VIR	13 LIB	13 SCO	13 CAP	13 AQU
15 SAG	15 AQU	15 AQU	15 ARI	15 TAU	16 CAN	16 LEO	17 LIB	16 SCO	15 SAG	15 AQU	15 PIS
17 CAP	17 PIS	17 PIS	18 TAU	18 GEM	19 LEO	19 VIR	19 SCO	18 SAG	17 CAP	18 PIS	17 ARI
19 AQU	20 ARI	19 ARI	20 GEM	20 CAN	21 VIR	21 LIB	21 SAG	20 CAP	19 AQU	20 ARI	19 TAU
21 PIS	22 TAU	22 TAU	23 CAN	23 LEO	23 LIB	23 SCO	24 CAP	22 AQU	21 PIS	22 TAU	22 GEM
23 ARI	25 GEM	24 GEM	25 LEO	25 VIR	26 SCO	25 SAG	26 AQU	24 PIS	24 ARI	25 GEM	25 CAN
26 TAU	27 CAN	27 CAN	28 VIR	27 LIB	28 SAG	27 CAP	28 PIS	26 ARI	26 TAU	27 CAN	27 LEO
28 GEM		29 LEO	30 LIB	29 SCO	30 CAP	29 AQU	30 ARI	29 TAU	28 GEM	30 LEO	30 VIR
31 CAN		31 VIR		31 SAG		31 PIS			31 CAN		

1978

JAN	FEB	MAR	APR	MAY	JUN	JUL	AUG	SEP	OCT	NOV	DEC
1 LIB	2 SAG	1 SAG	1 AQU	1 PIS	1 TAU	1 GEM	2 LEO	1 VIR	1 LIB	2 SAG	1 CAP
3 SCO	4 CAP	3 CAP	3 PIS	3 ARI	4 GEM	4 CAN	5 VIR	4 LIB	3 SCO	4 CAP	3 AQU
5 SAG	6 AQU	5 AQU	6 ARI	5 TAU	6 CAN	6 LEO	7 LIB	6 SCO	5 SAG	6 AQU	5 PIS
7 CAP	8 PIS	7 PIS	8 TAU	8 GEM	9 LEO	9 VIR	10 SCO	8 SAG	8 CAP	8 PIS	7 ARI
9 AQU	10 ARI	9 ARI	10 GEM	10 CAN	11 VIR	11 LIB	12 SAG	10 CAP	10 AQU	10 ARI	10 TAU
11 PIS	12 TAU	12 TAU	13 CAN	13 LEO	14 LIB	13 SCO	14 CAP	12 AQU	12 PIS	12 TAU	12 GEM
13 ARI	15 GEM	14 GEM	15 LEO	15 VIR	16 SCO	16 SAG	16 AQU	14 PIS	14 ARI	15 GEM	14 CAN
16 TAU	17 CAN	16 CAN	18 VIR	17 LIB	18 SAG	18 CAP	18 PIS	17 ARI	16 TAU	17 CAN	17 LEO
18 GEM	20 LEO	19 LEO	20 LIB	20 SCO	20 CAP	20 AQU	20 ARI	19 TAU	18 GEM	20 LEO	19 VIR
21 CAN	22 VIR	21 VIR	22 SCO	22 SAG	22 AQU	22 PIS	22 TAU	21 GEM	21 CAN	22 VIR	22 LIB
23 LEO	24 LIB	24 LIB	24 SAG	24 CAP	24 PIS	24 ARI	25 GEM	23 CAN	23 LEO	25 LIB	24 SCO
26 VIR	27 SCO	26 SCO	26 CAP	26 AQU	26 ARI	26 TAU	27 CAN	26 LEO	26 VIR	27 SCO	27 SAG
28 LIB		28 SAG	29 AQU	28 PIS	29 TAU	28 GEM	30 LEO	28 VIR	28 LIB	29 SAG	29 CAP
30 SCO		30 CAP		30 ARI		31 CAN			31 SCO		31 AQU

1979

JAN	FEB	MAR	APR	MAY	JUN	JUL	AUG	SEP	OCT	NOV	DEC
2 PIS	2 TAU	2 TAU	3 CAN	2 LEO	1 VIR	1 LIB	2 SAG	1 CAP	2 PIS	1 ARI	2 GEM
4 ARI	5 GEM	4 GEM	5 LEO	5 VIR	4 LIB	4 SCO	4 CAP	3 AQU	4 ARI	3 TAU	4 CAN
6 TAU	7 CAN	6 CAN	8 VIR	7 LIB	6 SCO	6 SAG	6 AQU	5 PIS	6 TAU	5 GEM	7 LEO
8 GEM	9 LEO	9 LEO	10 LIB	10 SCO	8 SAG	8 CAP	8 PIS	7 ARI	8 GEM	7 CAN	9 VIR
11 CAN	12 VIR	11 VIR	12 SCO	12 SAG	11 CAP	10 AQU	10 ARI	9 TAU	11 CAN	9 LEO	12 LIB
13 LEO	15 LIB	14 LIB	15 SAG	14 CAP	13 AQU	12 PIS	13 TAU	11 GEM	13 LEO	12 VIR	14 SCO
16 VIR	17 SCO	16 SCO	17 CAP	16 AQU	15 PIS	14 ARI	15 GEM	13 CAN	16 VIR	14 LIB	17 SAG
18 LIB	19 SAG	19 SAG	19 AQU	18 PIS	17 ARI	16 TAU	17 CAN	16 LEO	18 LIB	17 SCO	19 CAP
21 SCO	21 CAP	21 CAP	21 PIS	21 ARI	19 TAU	18 GEM	20 LEO	18 VIR	21 SCO	19 SAG	21 AQU
23 SAG	24 AQU	23 AQU	23 ARI	23 TAU	21 GEM	21 CAN	22 VIR	21 LIB	23 SAG	22 CAP	23 PIS
25 CAP	25 PIS	25 PIS	25 TAU	25 GEM	24 CAN	23 LEO	25 LIB	23 SCO	25 CAP	24 AQU	25 ARI
27 AQU	27 ARI	27 ARI	28 GEM	27 CAN	26 LEO	26 VIR	27 SCO	26 SAG	28 AQU	26 PIS	27 TAU
29 PIS		29 TAU	30 CAN	30 LEO	29 VIR	28 LIB	30 SAG	28 CAP	30 PIS	28 ARI	30 GEM
31 ARI		31 GEM				31 SCO		30 AQU		30 TAU	

1980

JAN	FEB	MAR	APR	MAY	JUN	JUL	AUG	SEP	OCT	NOV	DEC
1 CAN	2 VIR	3 LIB	2 SCO	1 SAG	2 AQU	2 PIS	2 TAU	3 CAN	2 LEO	1 VIR	1 LIB
3 LEO	4 LIB	5 SCO	4 SAG	4 CAP	4 PIS	4 ARI	4 GEM	5 LEO	5 VIR	3 LIB	3 SCO
6 VIR	7 SCO	8 SAG	6 CAP	6 AQU	6 ARI	6 TAU	6 CAN	7 VIR	7 LIB	6 SCO	6 SAG
8 LIB	9 SAG	10 CAP	9 AQU	8 PIS	8 TAU	9 GEM	9 LEO	10 LIB	10 SCO	8 SAG	8 CAP
11 SCO	12 CAP	12 AQU	11 PIS	10 ARI	11 GEM	11 CAN	11 VIR	12 SCO	12 SAG	11 CAP	10 AQU
13 SAG	14 AQU	14 PIS	13 ARI	12 TAU	13 CAN	13 LEO	14 LIB	15 SAG	15 CAP	13 AQU	13 PIS
15 CAP	16 PIS	16 ARI	15 TAU	14 GEM	15 LEO	15 VIR	16 SCO	17 CAP	17 AQU	15 PIS	15 ARI
17 AQU	18 ARI	18 TAU	17 GEM	16 CAN	17 VIR	17 LIB	19 SAG	20 AQU	19 PIS	18 ARI	17 TAU
19 PIS	20 TAU	20 GEM	19 CAN	19 LEO	20 LIB	20 SCO	21 CAP	22 PIS	21 ARI	20 TAU	19 GEM
21 ARI	22 GEM	23 CAN	21 LEO	21 VIR	22 SCO	22 SAG	23 AQU	24 ARI	23 TAU	22 GEM	21 CAN
24 TAU	24 CAN	25 LEO	24 VIR	24 LIB	25 SAG	25 CAP	25 PIS	26 TAU	25 GEM	24 CAN	23 LEO
26 GEM	27 LEO	27 VIR	26 LIB	26 SCO	27 CAP	27 AQU	27 ARI	28 GEM	27 CAN	26 LEO	25 VIR
28 CAN	29 VIR	30 LIB	29 SCO	29 SAG	29 AQU	29 PIS	29 TAU	30 CAN	29 LEO	28 VIR	28 LIB
30 LEO				31 CAP		31 ARI	31 GEM				30 SCO

1981

JAN	FEB	MAR	APR	MAY	JUN	JUL	AUG	SEP	OCT	NOV	DEC
2 SAG	1 CAP	2 AQU	1 PIS	1 ARI	1 GEM	2 LEO	1 VIR	2 SCO	2 SAG	1 CAP	1 AQU
4 CAP	3 AQU	5 PIS	3 ARI	3 TAU	3 CAN	4 VIR	3 LIB	5 SAG	5 CAP	3 AQU	3 PIS
7 AQU	5 PIS	7 ARI	5 TAU	5 GEM	5 LEO	7 LIB	6 SCO	7 CAP	7 AQU	6 PIS	5 ARI
9 PIS	7 ARI	9 TAU	7 GEM	7 CAN	7 VIR	10 SCO	8 SAG	10 AQU	9 PIS	8 ARI	7 TAU
11 ARI	9 TAU	11 GEM	9 CAN	9 LEO	10 LIB	12 SAG	11 CAP	12 PIS	11 ARI	10 TAU	9 GEM
13 TAU	12 GEM	13 CAN	11 LEO	11 VIR	12 SCO	15 CAP	13 AQU	14 ARI	13 TAU	12 GEM	11 CAN
15 GEM	14 CAN	15 LEO	14 VIR	13 LIB	15 SAG	17 AQU	16 PIS	16 TAU	15 GEM	14 CAN	13 LEO
17 CAN	16 LEO	18 VIR	16 LIB	16 SCO	17 CAP	19 PIS	18 ARI	18 GEM	18 CAN	16 LEO	16 VIR
20 LEO	18 VIR	20 LIB	19 SCO	18 SAG	20 AQU	21 ARI	20 TAU	20 CAN	20 LEO	18 VIR	18 LIB
22 VIR	21 LIB	22 SCO	21 SAG	21 CAP	22 PIS	24 TAU	22 GEM	22 LEO	22 VIR	21 LIB	20 SCO
24 LIB	23 SCO	25 SAG	24 CAP	23 AQU	24 ARI	26 GEM	24 CAN	25 VIR	24 LIB	23 SCO	23 SAG
27 SCO	26 SAG	27 CAP	26 AQU	26 PIS	26 TAU	28 CAN	26 LEO	27 LIB	27 SCO	26 SAG	25 CAP
29 SAG	28 CAP	30 AQU	28 PIS	28 ARI	28 GEM	30 LEO	28 VIR	29 SCO	29 SAG	28 CAP	28 AQU
				30 TAU	30 CAN		31 LIB				30 PIS

1982

JAN	FEB	MAR	APR	MAY	JUN	JUL	AUG	SEP	OCT	NOV	DEC
2 ARI	2 GEM	1 GEM	2 LEO	1 VIR	2 SCO	2 SAG	1 CAP	2 PIS	2 ARI	2 GEM	2 CAN
4 TAU	4 CAN	3 CAN	4 VIR	4 LIB	5 SAG	4 CAP	3 AQU	4 ARI	4 TAU	4 CAN	4 LEO
6 GEM	6 LEO	6 LEO	6 LIB	6 SCO	7 CAP	7 AQU	6 PIS	7 TAU	6 GEM	6 LEO	6 VIR
8 CAN	8 VIR	8 VIR	9 SCO	8 SAG	10 AQU	9 PIS	8 ARI	9 GEM	8 CAN	9 VIR	8 LIB
10 LEO	11 LIB	10 LIB	11 SAG	11 CAP	12 PIS	11 ARI	10 TAU	11 CAN	10 LEO	11 LIB	10 SCO
12 VIR	13 SCO	12 SCO	14 CAP	13 AQU	15 ARI	14 TAU	13 GEM	13 LEO	12 VIR	13 SCO	13 SAG
14 LIB	15 SAG	15 SAG	16 AQU	16 PIS	17 TAU	16 GEM	15 CAN	15 VIR	15 LIB	15 SAG	15 CAP
17 SCO	18 CAP	17 CAP	19 PIS	18 ARI	19 GEM	18 CAN	17 LEO	17 LIB	17 SCO	18 CAP	18 AQU
19 SAG	20 AQU	20 AQU	21 ARI	20 TAU	21 CAN	20 LEO	19 VIR	19 SCO	19 SAG	21 AQU	20 PIS
22 CAP	23 PIS	22 PIS	23 TAU	22 GEM	23 LEO	22 VIR	21 LIB	22 SAG	22 CAP	23 PIS	23 ARI
24 AQU	25 ARI	24 ARI	25 GEM	24 CAN	25 VIR	24 LIB	23 SCO	24 CAP	24 AQU	25 ARI	25 TAU
26 PIS	27 TAU	27 TAU	27 CAN	26 LEO	27 LIB	27 SCO	25 SAG	27 AQU	27 PIS	28 TAU	27 GEM
29 ARI		29 GEM	29 LEO	29 VIR	29 SCO	29 SAG	28 CAP	29 PIS	29 ARI	30 GEM	29 CAN
31 TAU		31 CAN		31 LIB			31 AQU		31 TAU		31 LEO

1983

JAN	FEB	MAR	APR	MAY	JUN	JUL	AUG	SEP	OCT	NOV	DEC
2 VIR	1 LIB	2 SCO	1 SAG	1 CAP	2 PIS	2 ARI	1 TAU	1 CAN	1 LEO	1 LIB	1 SCO
4 LIB	3 SCO	5 SAG	3 CAP	3 AQU	5 ARI	4 TAU	3 GEM	3 LEO	3 VIR	3 SCO	3 SAG
7 SCO	5 SAG	7 CAP	6 AQU	6 PIS	7 TAU	7 GEM	5 CAN	5 VIR	5 LIB	5 SAG	5 CAP
9 SAG	8 CAP	10 AQU	8 PIS	8 ARI	9 GEM	9 CAN	7 LEO	7 LIB	7 SCO	8 CAP	8 AQU
12 CAP	10 AQU	12 PIS	11 ARI	11 TAU	11 CAN	11 LEO	9 VIR	10 SCO	10 SAG	10 AQU	10 PIS
14 AQU	13 PIS	15 ARI	13 TAU	13 GEM	13 LEO	13 VIR	11 LIB	12 SAG	12 CAP	13 PIS	13 ARI
17 PIS	15 ARI	17 TAU	15 GEM	15 CAN	15 VIR	15 LIB	13 SCO	14 CAP	14 AQU	15 ARI	15 TAU
19 ARI	18 TAU	19 GEM	18 CAN	17 LEO	17 LIB	17 SCO	15 SAG	17 AQU	16 PIS	18 TAU	17 GEM
21 TAU	20 GEM	21 CAN	20 LEO	19 VIR	20 SCO	19 SAG	18 CAP	19 PIS	19 ARI	20 GEM	20 CAN
24 GEM	22 CAN	23 LEO	22 VIR	21 LIB	22 SAG	22 CAP	20 AQU	22 ARI	21 TAU	22 CAN	22 LEO
26 CAN	24 LEO	26 VIR	24 LIB	23 SCO	24 CAP	24 AQU	23 PIS	24 TAU	24 GEM	24 LEO	24 VIR
28 LEO	26 VIR	28 LIB	26 SCO	26 SAG	27 AQU	27 PIS	25 ARI	26 GEM	26 CAN	26 VIR	26 LIB
30 VIR	28 LIB	30 SCO	28 SAG	28 CAP	29 PIS	29 ARI	28 TAU	29 CAN	28 LEO	29 LIB	28 SCO
				31 AQU			30 GEM		30 VIR		30 SAG

JAN	FEB	MAR	APR	MAY	JUN	JUL	AUG	SEP	OCT	NOV	DEC
2 CAP	3 PIS	1 PIS	2 TAU	2 GEM	1 CAN	2 VIR	3 SCO	1 SAG	1 CAP	2 PIS	1 ARI
4 AQU	5 ARI	4 ARI	5 GEM	4 CAN	3 LEO	4 LIB	5 SAG	3 CAP	3 AQU	4 ARI	4 TAU
6 PIS	8 TAU	6 TAU	7 CAN	6 LEO	5 VIR	6 SCO	7 CAP	6 AQU	5 PIS	7 TAU	6 GEM
9 ARI	10 GEM	8 GEM	9 LEO	9 VIR	7 LIB	9 SAG	9 AQU	8 PIS	8 ARI	9 GEM	9 CAN
11 TAU	12 CAN	11 CAN	11 VIR	11 LIB	9 SCO	11 CAP	12 PIS	11 ARI	10 TAU	12 CAN	11 LEO
14 GEM	15 LEO	13 LEO	13 LIB	13 SCO	11 SAG	13 AQU	14 ARI	13 TAU	13 GEM	14 LEO	13 VIR
16 CAN	16 VIR	15 VIR	15 SCO	15 SAG	13 CAP	16 PIS	17 TAU	16 GEM	15 CAN	16 VIR	15 LIB
18 LEO	18 LIB	17 LIB	17 SAG	17 CAP	16 AQU	18 ARI	19 GEM	18 CAN	18 LEO	18 LIB	17 SCO
20 VIR	20 SCO	19 SCO	19 CAP	19 AQU	18 PIS	21 TAU	22 CAN	20 LEO	20 VIR	20 SCO	20 SAG
22 LIB	23 SAG	21 SAG	22 AQU	22 PIS	21 ARI	23 GEM	24 LEO	22 VIR	22 LIB	22 SAG	22 CAP
24 SCO	25 CAP	23 CAP	25 PIS	24 ARI	23 TAU	25 CAN	26 VIR	24 LIB	24 SCO	24 CAP	24 AQU
26 SAG	28 AQU	26 AQU	27 ARI	27 TAU	26 GEM	27 LEO	28 LIB	26 SCO	26 SAG	27 AQU	26 PIS
29 CAP		28 PIS	30 TAU	29 GEM	28 CAN	29 VIR	30 SCO	28 SAG	28 CAP	29 PIS	29 ARI
31 AQU		31 ARI			30 LEO	31 LIB			30 AQU		31 TAU

JAN	FEB	MAR	APR	MAY	JUN	JUL	AUG	SEP	OCT	NOV	DEC
3 GEM	2 CAN	1 CAN	2 VIR	1 LIB	2 SAG	1 CAP	2 PIS	1 ARI	3 GEM	2 CAN	1 LEO
5 CAN	4 LEO	3 LEO	4 LIB	3 SCO	4 CAP	3 AQU	4 ARI	3 TAU	5 CAN	4 LEO	4 VIR
7 LEO	6 VIR	5 VIR	6 SCO	5 SAG	6 AQU	5 PIS	7 TAU	6 GEM	8 LEO	6 VIR	6 LIB
9 VIR	8 LIB	7 LIB	8 SAG	7 CAP	8 PIS	8 ARI	9 GEM	8 CAN	10 VIR	9 LIB	8 SCO
12 LIB	10 SCO	9 SCO	10 CAP	9 AQU	11 ARI	10 TAU	12 CAN	10 LEO	12 LIB	11 SCO	10 SAG
14 SCO	12 SAG	11 SAG	12 AQU	12 PIS	13 TAU	13 GEM	14 LEO	13 VIR	14 SCO	13 SAG	12 CAP
16 SAG	14 CAP	14 CAP	14 PIS	14 ARI	16 GEM	15 CAN	16 VIR	15 LIB	16 SAG	15 CAP	14 AQU
18 CAP	17 AQU	16 AQU	17 ARI	16 TAU	18 CAN	18 LEO	18 LIB	17 SCO	18 CAP	17 AQU	16 PIS
20 AQU	19 PIS	18 PIS	20 TAU	19 GEM	20 LEO	20 VIR	20 SCO	19 SAG	20 AQU	19 PIS	19 ARI
23 PIS	21 ARI	21 ARI	22 GEM	22 CAN	23 VIR	22 LIB	22 SAG	21 CAP	23 PIS	21 ARI	21 TAU
25 ARI	24 TAU	23 TAU	25 CAN	24 LEO	25 LIB	24 SCO	25 CAP	23 AQU	25 ARI	24 TAU	24 GEM
28 TAU	27 GEM	26 GEM	27 LEO	26 VIR	27 SCO	26 SAG	27 AQU	25 PIS	28 TAU	26 GEM	26 CAN
30 GEM		28 CAN	29 VIR	29 LIB	29 SAG	28 CAP	29 PIS	28 ARI	30 GEM	29 CAN	29 LEO
		31 LEO		31 SCO		31 AQU		30 TAU			31 VIR

JAN	FEB	MAR	APR	MAY	JUN	JUL	AUG	SEP	OCT	NOV	DEC
2 LIB	1 SCO	2 SAG	2 AQU	2 PIS	3 TAU	3 GEM	2 CAN	3 VIR	2 LIB	1 SCO	2 CAP
4 SCO	3 SAG	4 CAP	5 PIS	4 ARI	5 GEM	5 CAN	4 LEO	5 LIB	4 SCO	3 SAG	4 AQU
6 SAG	5 CAP	6 AQU	7 ARI	7 TAU	8 CAN	8 LEO	6 VIR	7 SCO	7 SAG	5 CAP	6 PIS
8 CAP	7 AQU	8 PIS	9 TAU	9 GEM	11 LEO	10 VIR	9 LIB	9 SAG	9 CAP	7 AQU	9 ARI
11 AQU	9 PIS	11 ARI	12 GEM	12 CAN	13 VIR	12 LIB	11 SCO	11 CAP	11 AQU	9 PIS	11 TAU
13 PIS	11 ARI	13 TAU	14 CAN	14 LEO	15 LIB	15 SCO	13 SAG	14 AQU	13 PIS	11 ARI	14 GEM
15 ARI	14 TAU	16 GEM	17 LEO	17 VIR	17 SCO	17 SAG	15 CAP	16 PIS	15 ARI	14 TAU	16 CAN
17 TAU	16 GEM	18 CAN	19 VIR	19 LIB	19 SAG	19 CAP	17 AQU	18 ARI	18 TAU	16 GEM	19 LEO
20 GEM	19 CAN	21 LEO	21 LIB	21 SCO	21 CAP	21 AQU	19 PIS	20 TAU	20 GEM	19 CAN	21 VIR
22 CAN	21 LEO	23 VIR	24 SCO	23 SAG	23 AQU	23 PIS	22 ARI	23 GEM	23 CAN	21 LEO	24 LIB
25 LEO	23 VIR	25 LIB	26 SAG	25 CAP	26 PIS	26 ARI	24 TAU	25 CAN	25 LEO	24 VIR	26 SCO
27 VIR	26 LIB	27 SCO	28 CAP	27 AQU	28 ARI	28 TAU	26 GEM	28 LEO	27 VIR	26 LIB	28 SAG
29 LIB	28 SCO	29 SAG	30 AQU	29 PIS	30 TAU	30 GEM	29 CAN	30 VIR	30 LIB	28 SCO	30 CAP
		31 CAP		31 ARI			31 LEO			30 SAG	

JAN	FEB	MAR	APR	MAY	JUN	JUL	AUG	SEP	OCT	NOV	DEC
1 AQU	1 ARI	1 ARI	2 GEM	2 CAN	3 VIR	3 LIB	1 SCO	2 CAP	1 AQU	2 ARI	1 TAU
3 PIS	4 TAU	3 TAU	4 CAN	4 LEO	5 LIB	5 SCO	4 SAG	4 AQU	3 PIS	4 TAU	4 GEM
5 ARI	6 GEM	5 GEM	7 LEO	7 VIR	8 SCO	7 SAG	6 CAP	6 PIS	6 ARI	6 GEM	6 CAN
7 TAU	9 CAN	8 CAN	9 VIR	9 LIB	10 SAG	9 CAP	8 AQU	8 ARI	8 TAU	9 CAN	8 LEO
10 GEM	11 LEO	10 LEO	12 LIB	11 SCO	12 CAP	11 AQU	10 PIS	10 TAU	10 GEM	11 LEO	11 VIR
12 CAN	14 VIR	13 VIR	14 SCO	13 SAG	14 AQU	13 PIS	12 ARI	13 GEM	12 CAN	14 VIR	14 LIB
15 LEO	16 LIB	15 LIB	16 SAG	15 CAP	16 PIS	15 ARI	14 TAU	15 CAN	15 LEO	16 LIB	16 SCO
17 VIR	18 SCO	18 SCO	18 CAP	17 AQU	18 ARI	18 TAU	16 GEM	17 LEO	17 VIR	18 SCO	18 SAG
20 LIB	21 SAG	20 SAG	20 AQU	20 PIS	20 TAU	20 GEM	19 CAN	20 VIR	20 LIB	21 SAG	20 CAP
22 SCO	23 CAP	22 CAP	22 PIS	22 ARI	23 GEM	22 CAN	21 LEO	22 LIB	22 SCO	23 CAP	22 AQU
24 SAG	25 AQU	24 AQU	25 ARI	24 TAU	25 CAN	25 LEO	24 VIR	25 SCO	24 SAG	25 AQU	24 PIS
26 CAP	27 PIS	26 PIS	27 TAU	26 GEM	28 LEO	27 VIR	26 LIB	27 SAG	26 CAP	27 PIS	26 ARI
28 AQU		28 ARI	29 GEM	29 CAN	30 VIR	30 LIB	29 SCO	29 CAP	29 AQU	29 ARI	29 TAU
30 PIS		30 TAU		31 LEO			31 SAG		31 PIS		31 GEM

1988

JAN	FEB	MAR	APR	MAY	JUN	JUL	AUG	SEP	OCT	NOV	DEC
2 CAN	1 LEO	2 VIR	1 LIB	3 SAG	1 CAP	1 AQU	1 ARI	2 GEM	1 CAN	2 VIR	2 LIB
5 LEO	4 VIR	4 LIB	3 SCO	5 CAP	3 AQU	3 PIS	3 TAU	4 CAN	4 LEO	5 LIB	5 SCO
7 VIR	6 LIB	7 SCO	5 SAG	7 AQU	5 PIS	5 ARI	5 GEM	6 LEO	6 VIR	7 SCO	7 SAG
10 LIB	9 SCO	9 SAG	8 CAP	9 PIS	8 ARI	7 TAU	8 CAN	9 VIR	9 LIB	10 SAG	9 CAP
12 SCO	11 SAG	11 CAP	10 AQU	11 ARI	10 TAU	9 GEM	10 LEO	11 LIB	11 SCO	12 CAP	12 AQU
15 SAG	13 CAP	14 AQU	12 PIS	13 TAU	12 GEM	11 CAN	13 VIR	14 SCO	14 SAG	14 AQU	14 PIS
17 CAP	15 AQU	16 PIS	14 ARI	16 GEM	14 CAN	14 LEO	15 LIB	16 SAG	16 CAP	17 PIS	16 ARI
19 AQU	17 PIS	18 ARI	16 TAU	18 CAN	17 LEO	16 VIR	18 SCO	19 CAP	18 AQU	19 ARI	18 TAU
21 PIS	19 ARI	20 TAU	18 GEM	20 LEO	19 VIR	19 LIB	20 SAG	21 AQU	20 PIS	21 TAU	20 GEM
23 ARI	21 TAU	22 GEM	20 CAN	23 VIR	22 LIB	21 SCO	22 CAP	23 PIS	22 ARI	23 GEM	22 CAN
25 TAU	23 GEM	24 CAN	23 LEO	25 LIB	24 SCO	24 SAG	24 AQU	25 ARI	24 TAU	25 CAN	25 LEO
27 GEM	26 CAN	27 LEO	25 VIR	28 SCO	26 SAG	26 CAP	26 PIS	27 TAU	26 GEM	27 LEO	27 VIR
30 CAN	28 LEO	29 VIR	28 LIB	30 SAG	29 CAP	28 AQU	28 ARI	29 GEM	29 CAN	29 VIR	30 LIB
			30 SCO			30 PIS	30 TAU		31 LEO		

1989

JAN	FEB	MAR	APR	MAY	JUN	JUL	AUG	SEP	OCT	NOV	DEC
1 SCO	2 CAP	2 CAP	2 PIS	2 ARI	2 GEM	2 CAN	3 VIR	1 LIB	1 SCO	2 CAP	2 AQU
4 SAG	4 AQU	4 AQU	4 ARI	4 TAU	4 CAN	4 LEO	5 LIB	4 SCO	4 SAG	5 AQU	4 PIS
6 CAP	6 PIS	6 PIS	6 TAU	6 GEM	6 LEO	6 VIR	8 SCO	6 SAG	6 CAP	7 PIS	7 ARI
8 AQU	8 ARI	8 ARI	8 GEM	8 CAN	9 VIR	9 LIB	10 SAG	9 CAP	9 AQU	9 ARI	9 TAU
10 PIS	11 TAU	10 TAU	10 CAN	10 LEO	11 LIB	11 SCO	12 CAP	11 AQU	11 PIS	11 TAU	11 GEM
12 ARI	13 GEM	12 GEM	13 LEO	13 VIR	14 SCO	14 SAG	15 AQU	13 PIS	13 ARI	13 GEM	13 CAN
14 TAU	15 CAN	14 CAN	15 VIR	15 LIB	16 SAG	16 CAP	17 PIS	15 ARI	15 TAU	15 CAN	15 LEO
16 GEM	17 LEO	17 LEO	18 LIB	18 SCO	19 CAP	18 AQU	19 ARI	17 TAU	17 GEM	17 LEO	17 VIR
19 CAN	20 VIR	19 VIR	20 SCO	20 SAG	21 AQU	20 PIS	21 TAU	19 GEM	19 CAN	20 VIR	19 LIB
21 LEO	22 LIB	22 LIB	23 SAG	22 CAP	23 PIS	23 ARI	23 GEM	21 CAN	21 LEO	22 LIB	22 SCO
23 VIR	25 SCO	24 SCO	25 CAP	25 AQU	25 ARI	25 TAU	25 CAN	24 LEO	23 VIR	25 SCO	24 SAG
26 LIB	27 SAG	27 SAG	28 AQU	27 PIS	27 TAU	27 GEM	28 LEO	26 VIR	26 LIB	27 SAG	27 CAP
29 SCO		29 CAP	30 PIS	29 ARI	30 GEM	29 CAN	30 VIR	29 LIB	28 SCO	30 CAP	29 AQU
31 SAG		31 AQU		31 TAU		31 LEO			31 SAG		

1990

JAN	FEB	MAR	APR	MAY	JUN	JUL	AUG	SEP	OCT	NOV	DEC
1 PIS	1 TAU	2 GEM	1 CAN	3 VIR	1 LIB	1 SCO	2 CAP	1 AQU	1 PIS	2 TAU	1 GEM
3 ARI	3 GEM	5 CAN	3 LEO	5 LIB	4 SCO	4 SAG	5 AQU	3 PIS	3 ARI	4 GEM	3 CAN
5 TAU	5 CAN	7 LEO	5 VIR	8 SCO	6 SAG	6 CAP	7 PIS	6 ARI	5 TAU	6 CAN	5 LEO
7 GEM	8 LEO	9 VIR	8 LIB	10 SAG	9 CAP	9 AQU	9 ARI	8 TAU	7 GEM	8 LEO	7 VIR
9 CAN	10 VIR	12 LIB	10 SCO	13 CAP	11 AQU	11 PIS	11 TAU	10 GEM	9 CAN	10 VIR	9 LIB
11 LEO	12 LIB	14 SCO	13 SAG	15 AQU	14 PIS	13 ARI	14 GEM	12 CAN	11 LEO	12 LIB	12 SCO
13 VIR	15 SCO	16 SAG	15 CAP	17 PIS	16 ARI	15 TAU	16 CAN	14 LEO	14 VIR	15 SCO	14 SAG
16 LIB	17 SAG	19 CAP	18 AQU	20 ARI	18 TAU	17 GEM	18 LEO	16 VIR	16 LIB	17 SAG	17 CAP
18 SCO	20 CAP	21 AQU	20 PIS	22 TAU	20 GEM	19 CAN	20 VIR	19 LIB	18 SCO	20 CAP	19 AQU
21 SAG	22 AQU	24 PIS	22 ARI	24 GEM	22 CAN	21 LEO	22 LIB	21 SCO	21 SAG	22 AQU	22 PIS
23 CAP	24 PIS	26 ARI	24 TAU	26 CAN	24 LEO	24 VIR	25 SCO	24 SAG	23 CAP	25 PIS	24 ARI
26 AQU	26 ARI	28 TAU	26 GEM	28 LEO	26 VIR	26 LIB	27 SAG	26 CAP	26 AQU	27 ARI	26 TAU
28 PIS	28 TAU	30 GEM	28 CAN	30 VIR	29 LIB	28 SCO	30 CAP	29 AQU	28 PIS	29 TAU	28 GEM
30 ARI			30 LEO			31 SAG			30 ARI		30 CAN

1991

JAN	FEB	MAR	APR	MAY	JUN	JUL	AUG	SEP	OCT	NOV	DEC
1 LEO	2 LIB	2 LIB	3 SAG	2 CAP	1 AQU	1 PIS	2 TAU	3 CAN	2 LEO	2 LIB	2 SCO
3 VIR	4 SCO	4 SCO	5 CAP	5 AQU	4 PIS	4 ARI	4 GEM	5 LEO	4 VIR	5 SCO	4 SAG
6 LIB	7 SAG	6 SAG	8 AQU	7 PIS	6 ARI	6 TAU	6 CAN	7 VIR	6 LIB	7 SAG	7 CAP
8 SCO	9 CAP	9 CAP	10 PIS	10 ARI	8 TAU	8 GEM	8 LEO	9 LIB	8 SCO	10 CAP	9 AQU
11 SAG	12 AQU	12 AQU	12 ARI	12 TAU	10 GEM	10 CAN	10 VIR	11 SCO	11 SAG	12 AQU	12 PIS
13 CAP	14 PIS	14 PIS	14 TAU	14 GEM	12 CAN	12 LEO	12 LIB	13 SAG	13 CAP	15 PIS	14 ARI
16 AQU	17 ARI	16 ARI	17 GEM	16 CAN	14 LEO	14 VIR	15 SCO	16 CAP	16 AQU	17 ARI	17 TAU
18 PIS	19 TAU	18 TAU	19 CAN	18 LEO	16 VIR	16 LIB	17 SAG	18 AQU	18 PIS	19 TAU	19 GEM
20 ARI	21 GEM	20 GEM	21 LEO	20 VIR	19 LIB	18 SCO	20 CAP	21 PIS	21 ARI	21 GEM	21 CAN
23 TAU	23 CAN	22 CAN	23 VIR	22 LIB	21 SCO	21 SAG	22 AQU	23 ARI	23 TAU	23 CAN	23 LEO
25 GEM	25 LEO	25 LEO	25 LIB	25 SCO	23 SAG	23 CAP	25 PIS	25 TAU	25 GEM	25 LEO	25 VIR
27 CAN	27 VIR	27 VIR	28 SCO	27 SAG	26 CAP	26 AQU	27 ARI	28 GEM	27 CAN	28 VIR	27 LIB
29 LEO		29 LIB	30 SAG	30 CAP	29 AQU	28 PIS	29 TAU	30 CAN	29 LEO	30 LIB	29 SCO
31 VIR		31 SCO				31 ARI	31 GEM		31 VIR		

1992

JAN	FEB	MAR	APR	MAY	JUN	JUL	AUG	SEP	OCT	NOV	DEC
1 SAG	2 AQU	3 PIS	1 ARI	1 TAU	2 CAN	1 LEO	2 LIB	2 SAG	2 CAP	1 AQU	1 PIS
3 CAP	4 PIS	5 ARI	4 TAU	3 GEM	4 LEO	3 VIR	4 SCO	5 CAP	4 AQU	3 PIS	3 ARI
6 AQU	7 ARI	8 TAU	6 GEM	5 CAN	6 VIR	5 LIB	6 SAG	7 AQU	7 PIS	6 ARI	6 TAU
8 PIS	9 TAU	10 GEM	8 CAN	8 LEO	8 LIB	7 SCO	8 CAP	10 PIS	10 ARI	8 TAU	8 GEM
11 ARI	12 GEM	12 CAN	10 LEO	10 VIR	10 SCO	10 SAG	11 AQU	12 ARI	12 TAU	11 GEM	10 CAN
13 TAU	14 CAN	14 LEO	12 VIR	12 LIB	13 SAG	12 CAP	13 PIS	15 TAU	14 GEM	13 CAN	12 LEO
15 GEM	16 LEO	16 VIR	15 LIB	14 SCO	15 CAP	15 AQU	16 ARI	17 GEM	17 CAN	15 LEO	14 VIR
17 CAN	18 VIR	18 LIB	17 SCO	16 SAG	17 AQU	17 PIS	18 TAU	19 CAN	19 LEO	17 VIR	16 LIB
19 LEO	20 LIB	20 SCO	19 SAG	19 CAP	20 PIS	20 ARI	21 GEM	21 LEO	21 VIR	19 LIB	19 SCO
21 VIR	22 SCO	23 SAG	21 CAP	21 AQU	22 ARI	22 TAU	23 CAN	24 VIR	23 LIB	21 SCO	21 SAG
23 LIB	24 SAG	25 CAP	24 AQU	24 PIS	25 TAU	24 GEM	25 LEO	25 LIB	25 SCO	24 SAG	23 CAP
25 SCO	27 CAP	27 AQU	26 PIS	26 ARI	27 GEM	27 CAN	27 VIR	28 SCO	27 SAG	26 CAP	26 AQU
28 SAG	29 AQU	30 PIS	29 ARI	28 TAU	29 CAN	29 LEO	29 LIB	30 SAG	29 CAP	28 AQU	28 PIS
30 CAP				31 GEM		31 VIR	31 SCO				31 ARI

1993

JAN	FEB	MAR	APR	MAY	JUN	JUL	AUG	SEP	OCT	NOV	DEC
2 TAU	1 GEM	2 CAN	1 LEO	2 LIB	1 SCO	2 CAP	1 AQU	2 ARI	2 TAU	1 GEM	3 LEO
4 GEM	3 CAN	5 LEO	3 VIR	4 SCO	3 SAG	5 AQU	3 PIS	5 TAU	4 GEM	3 CAN	5 VIR
7 CAN	5 LEO	7 VIR	5 LIB	6 SAG	5 CAP	7 PIS	6 ARI	7 GEM	7 CAN	5 LEO	7 LIB
9 LEO	7 VIR	8 LIB	7 SCO	9 CAP	7 AQU	10 ARI	8 TAU	10 CAN	9 LEO	8 VIR	9 SCO
11 VIR	9 LIB	10 SCO	9 SAG	11 AQU	10 PIS	12 TAU	11 GEM	12 LEO	11 VIR	10 LIB	11 SAG
13 LIB	11 SCO	13 SAG	11 CAP	13 PIS	12 ARI	15 GEM	13 CAN	14 VIR	13 LIB	12 SCO	13 CAP
15 SCO	13 SAG	15 CAP	14 AQU	16 ARI	15 TAU	17 CAN	15 LEO	16 LIB	15 SCO	14 SAG	15 AQU
17 SAG	16 CAP	17 AQU	16 PIS	18 TAU	17 GEM	19 LEO	17 VIR	18 SCO	17 SAG	16 CAP	18 PIS
19 CAP	18 AQU	20 PIS	19 ARI	21 GEM	19 CAN	21 VIR	19 LIB	20 SAG	19 CAP	18 AQU	20 ARI
22 AQU	21 PIS	22 ARI	21 TAU	23 CAN	22 LEO	23 LIB	21 SCO	22 CAP	22 AQU	20 PIS	23 TAU
24 PIS	23 ARI	25 TAU	24 GEM	25 LEO	24 VIR	25 SCO	24 SAG	24 AQU	24 PIS	23 ARI	25 GEM
27 ARI	26 TAU	27 GEM	26 CAN	28 VIR	26 LIB	27 SAG	26 CAP	27 PIS	27 ARI	26 TAU	28 CAN
29 TAU	28 GEM	30 CAN	28 LEO	30 LIB	28 SCO	30 CAP	28 AQU	29 ARI	29 TAU	28 GEM	30 LEO
			30 VIR		30 SAG		31 PIS			30 CAN	

1994

JAN	FEB	MAR	APR	MAY	JUN	JUL	AUG	SEP	OCT	NOV	DEC
1 VIR	2 SCO	1 SCO	1 CAP	1 AQU	2 ARI	2 TAU	1 GEM	2 LEO	2 VIR	2 SCO	2 SAG
3 LIB	4 SAG	3 SAG	4 AQU	3 PIS	5 TAU	5 GEM	3 CAN	4 VIR	4 LIB	4 SAG	4 CAP
5 SCO	6 CAP	5 CAP	6 PIS	6 ARI	7 GEM	7 CAN	6 LEO	6 LIB	6 SCO	6 CAP	6 AQU
8 SAG	8 AQU	7 AQU	9 ARI	8 TAU	10 CAN	9 LEO	8 VIR	8 SCO	8 SAG	8 AQU	8 PIS
10 CAP	11 PIS	10 PIS	11 TAU	11 GEM	12 LEO	11 VIR	10 LIB	10 SAG	10 CAP	11 PIS	10 ARI
12 AQU	13 ARI	12 ARI	14 GEM	13 CAN	14 VIR	14 LIB	12 SCO	13 CAP	12 AQU	13 ARI	13 TAU
14 PIS	16 TAU	15 TAU	16 CAN	16 LEO	16 LIB	16 SCO	14 SAG	15 AQU	14 PIS	15 TAU	15 GEM
17 ARI	18 GEM	17 GEM	18 LEO	18 VIR	19 SCO	18 SAG	16 CAP	17 PIS	17 ARI	18 GEM	18 CAN
19 TAU	20 CAN	20 CAN	21 VIR	20 LIB	21 SAG	20 CAP	18 AQU	19 ARI	19 TAU	20 CAN	20 LEO
22 GEM	23 LEO	22 LEO	23 LIB	22 SCO	23 CAP	23 AQU	21 PIS	22 TAU	22 GEM	23 LEO	23 VIR
24 CAN	25 VIR	24 VIR	25 SCO	24 SAG	25 AQU	25 PIS	23 ARI	24 GEM	24 CAN	25 VIR	25 LIB
26 LEO	27 LIB	26 LIB	27 SAG	26 CAP	27 PIS	27 ARI	26 TAU	27 CAN	27 LEO	28 LIB	27 SCO
28 VIR		28 SCO	29 CAP	28 AQU	29 ARI	29 TAU	28 GEM	29 LEO	29 VIR	30 SCO	29 SAG
31 LIB		30 SAG		31 PIS			31 CAN		31 LIB		31 CAP

1995

JAN	FEB	MAR	APR	MAY	JUN	JUL	AUG	SEP	OCT	NOV	DEC
2 AQU	1 PIS	2 ARI	1 TAU	1 GEM	2 LEO	2 VIR	3 SCO	1 SAG	2 AQU	1 PIS	3 TAU
4 PIS	3 ARI	5 TAU	3 GEM	3 CAN	4 VIR	5 LIB	5 SAG	3 CAP	5 PIS	3 ARI	5 GEM
6 ARI	5 TAU	7 GEM	6 CAN	6 LEO	7 LIB	7 SCO	7 CAP	5 AQU	7 ARI	5 TAU	8 CAN
9 TAU	8 GEM	10 CAN	9 LEO	8 VIR	9 SCO	9 SAG	9 AQU	7 PIS	9 TAU	8 GEM	10 LEO
11 GEM	10 CAN	12 LEO	11 VIR	10 LIB	11 SAG	11 CAP	11 PIS	9 ARI	12 GEM	10 CAN	13 VIR
14 CAN	13 LEO	14 VIR	13 LIB	13 SCO	13 CAP	13 AQU	13 ARI	12 TAU	14 CAN	13 LEO	15 LIB
16 LEO	15 VIR	17 LIB	15 SCO	15 SAG	15 AQU	15 PIS	15 TAU	14 GEM	17 LEO	15 VIR	17 SCO
19 VIR	17 LIB	19 SCO	17 SAG	17 CAP	17 PIS	17 ARI	18 GEM	17 CAN	19 VIR	18 LIB	19 SAG
21 LIB	19 SCO	21 SAG	19 CAP	19 AQU	19 ARI	19 TAU	20 CAN	19 LEO	21 LIB	20 SCO	21 CAP
23 SCO	22 SAG	23 CAP	21 AQU	21 PIS	22 TAU	22 GEM	23 LEO	22 VIR	23 SCO	22 SAG	23 AQU
25 SAG	24 CAP	25 AQU	24 PIS	23 ARI	24 GEM	24 CAN	25 VIR	24 LIB	26 SAG	24 CAP	25 PIS
27 CAP	26 AQU	27 PIS	26 ARI	26 TAU	27 CAN	27 LEO	28 LIB	26 SCO	28 CAP	26 AQU	28 ARI
30 AQU	28 PIS	30 ARI	28 TAU	28 GEM	29 LEO	29 VIR	30 SCO	28 SAG	30 AQU	28 PIS	30 TAU
				31 CAN		31 LIB		30 CAP		30 ARI	

JAN	FEB	MAR	APR	MAY	JUN	JUL	AUG	SEP	OCT	NOV	DEC
1 GEM	3 LEO	1 LEO	2 LIB	2 SCO	2 CAP	2 AQU	2 ARI	1 TAU	3 CAN	2 LEO	2 VIR
4 CAN	5 VIR	3 VIR	4 SCO	4 SAG	4 AQU	4 PIS	4 TAU	3 GEM	5 LEO	4 VIR	4 LIB
6 LEO	8 LIB	6 LIB	7 SAG	6 CAP	6 PIS	6 ARI	7 GEM	6 CAN	8 VIR	7 LIB	6 SCO
9 VIR	10 SCO	8 SCO	9 CAP	8 AQU	9 ARI	8 TAU	9 CAN	8 LEO	10 LIB	9 SCO	9 SAG
11 LIB	12 SAG	10 SAG	11 AQU	10 PIS	11 TAU	11 GEM	12 LEO	11 VIR	13 SCO	11 SAG	11 CAP
14 SCO	14 CAP	13 CAP	13 PIS	12 ARI	13 GEM	13 CAN	14 VIR	13 LIB	15 SAG	13 CAP	13 AQU
16 SAG	16 AQU	15 AQU	15 ARI	15 TAU	16 CAN	16 LEO	17 LIB	15 SCO	17 CAP	16 AQU	15 PIS
18 CAP	18 PIS	17 PIS	17 TAU	17 GEM	18 LEO	18 VIR	19 SCO	17 CAP	19 AQU	18 PIS	17 ARI
20 AQU	20 ARI	19 ARI	20 GEM	19 CAN	21 VIR	21 LIB	21 SAG	18 SAG	21 PIS	20 ARI	19 TAU
22 PIS	23 TAU	21 TAU	22 CAN	22 LEO	23 LIB	23 SCO	24 CAP	20 CAP	23 ARI	22 TAU	22 GEM
24 ARI	25 GEM	23 GEM	25 LEO	24 VIR	26 SCO	25 SAG	26 AQU	22 AQU	26 TAU	24 GEM	24 CAN
26 TAU	27 CAN	26 CAN	27 VIR	27 LIB	28 SAG	27 CAP	28 PIS	24 PIS	28 GEM	27 CAN	26 LEO
29 GEM		28 LEO	30 LIB	29 SCO	30 CAP	29 AQU	30 ARI	26 ARI		29 LEO	29 VIR
31 CAN		31 VIR		31 SAG		31 PIS		28 TAU			31 LIB
								30 GEM			

JAN	FEB	MAR	APR	MAY	JUN	JUL	AUG	SEP	OCT	NOV	DEC
3 SCO	1 SAG	1 SAG	1 AQU	1 PIS	1 TAU	1 GEM	2 LEO	3 LIB	3 SCO	1 SAG	1 CAP
5 SAG	4 CAP	3 CAP	4 PIS	3 ARI	3 GEM	3 CAN	4 VIR	6 SCO	5 SAG	4 CAP	3 AQU
7 CAP	6 AQU	6 AQU	6 ARI	5 TAU	6 CAN	5 LEO	7 LIB	8 SAG	8 CAP	6 AQU	5 PIS
9 AQU	8 PIS	7 PIS	8 TAU	7 GEM	8 LEO	8 VIR	9 SCO	10 CAP	10 AQU	8 PIS	8 ARI
11 PIS	10 ARI	9 ARI	10 GEM	9 CAN	11 VIR	10 LIB	12 SAG	12 AQU	12 PIS	10 ARI	10 TAU
13 ARI	12 TAU	11 TAU	12 CAN	12 LEO	13 LIB	13 SCO	14 CAP	14 PIS	14 ARI	12 TAU	12 GEM
15 TAU	14 GEM	13 GEM	14 LEO	14 VIR	16 SCO	15 SAG	16 AQU	16 ARI	16 TAU	14 GEM	14 CAN
18 GEM	16 CAN	16 CAN	17 VIR	17 LIB	18 SAG	18 CAP	18 PIS	18 TAU	18 GEM	17 CAN	16 LEO
20 CAN	19 LEO	18 LEO	19 LIB	19 SCO	20 CAP	20 AQU	20 ARI	21 GEM	20 CAN	19 LEO	19 VIR
23 LEO	21 VIR	21 VIR	22 SCO	22 SAG	22 AQU	22 PIS	22 TAU	23 CAN	23 LEO	21 VIR	21 LIB
25 VIR	24 LIB	23 LIB	24 SAG	24 CAP	24 PIS	24 ARI	24 GEM	25 LEO	25 VIR	24 LIB	24 SCO
28 LIB	26 SCO	26 SCO	27 CAP	26 AQU	26 ARI	26 TAU	27 CAN	28 VIR	28 LIB	26 SCO	26 SAG
30 SCO		28 SAG	29 AQU	28 PIS	29 TAU	28 GEM	30 LEO	30 LIB	30 SCO	29 SAG	28 CAP
		30 CAP		30 ARI		30 CAN					31 AQU

JAN	FEB	MAR	APR	MAY	JUN	JUL	AUG	SEP	OCT	NOV	DEC
2 PIS	2 TAU	2 TAU	2 CAN	2 LEO	3 LIB	3 SCO	2 SAG	3 AQU	2 PIS	1 ARI	2 GEM
4 ARI	4 GEM	4 GEM	4 LEO	4 VIR	5 SCO	5 SAG	4 CAP	5 PIS	4 ARI	3 TAU	4 CAN
6 TAU	7 CAN	6 CAN	7 VIR	7 LIB	8 SAG	8 CAP	6 AQU	7 ARI	6 TAU	5 GEM	6 LEO
8 GEM	9 LEO	8 LEO	9 LIB	9 SCO	10 CAP	10 AQU	8 PIS	9 TAU	8 GEM	7 CAN	9 VIR
10 CAN	11 VIR	11 VIR	12 SCO	12 SAG	13 AQU	12 PIS	11 ARI	11 GEM	10 CAN	9 LEO	11 LIB
13 LEO	14 LIB	13 LIB	14 SAG	14 CAP	15 PIS	14 ARI	13 TAU	13 CAN	13 LEO	11 VIR	13 SCO
15 VIR	16 SCO	16 SCO	17 CAP	16 AQU	17 ARI	16 TAU	15 GEM	15 LEO	15 VIR	14 LIB	16 SAG
18 LIB	19 SAG	18 SAG	19 AQU	19 PIS	19 TAU	18 GEM	17 CAN	18 VIR	17 LIB	16 SCO	18 CAP
20 SCO	21 CAP	21 CAP	21 PIS	21 ARI	21 GEM	21 CAN	19 LEO	20 LIB	20 SCO	19 SAG	21 AQU
23 SAG	23 AQU	23 AQU	23 ARI	23 TAU	23 CAN	23 LEO	21 VIR	23 SCO	23 SAG	21 CAP	23 PIS
25 CAP	25 PIS	25 PIS	25 TAU	25 GEM	25 LEO	25 VIR	24 LIB	25 SAG	25 CAP	24 AQU	25 ARI
27 AQU	27 ARI	27 ARI	27 GEM	27 CAN	28 VIR	28 LIB	26 SCO	28 CAP	27 AQU	26 PIS	28 TAU
29 PIS		29 TAU	29 CAN	29 LEO	30 LIB	30 SCO	29 SAG	30 AQU	30 PIS	28 ARI	30 GEM
31 ARI		31 GEM		31 VIR			31 CAP			30 TAU	

JAN	FEB	MAR	APR	MAY	JUN	JUL	AUG	SEP	OCT	NOV	DEC
1 CAN	1 VIR	1 VIR	2 SCO	2 SAG	3 AQU	2 PIS	1 ARI	2 GEM	1 CAN	1 VIR	1 LIB
3 LEO	4 LIB	3 LIB	4 SAG	4 CAP	5 PIS	5 ARI	3 TAU	4 CAN	3 LEO	4 LIB	3 SCO
5 VIR	6 SCO	6 SCO	7 CAP	7 AQU	7 ARI	7 TAU	5 GEM	6 LEO	5 VIR	6 SCO	6 SAG
7 LIB	9 SAG	8 SAG	9 AQU	9 PIS	10 TAU	9 GEM	7 CAN	8 VIR	8 LIB	9 SAG	8 CAP
10 SCO	11 CAP	11 CAP	12 PIS	11 ARI	12 GEM	11 CAN	9 LEO	10 LIB	10 SCO	11 CAP	11 AQU
12 SAG	14 AQU	13 AQU	14 ARI	13 TAU	14 CAN	13 LEO	12 VIR	13 SCO	12 SAG	14 AQU	13 PIS
15 CAP	16 PIS	15 PIS	16 TAU	15 GEM	16 LEO	15 VIR	14 LIB	15 SAG	15 CAP	16 PIS	16 ARI
17 AQU	18 ARI	17 ARI	18 GEM	17 CAN	18 VIR	17 LIB	16 SCO	18 CAP	17 AQU	18 ARI	18 TAU
19 PIS	20 TAU	19 TAU	20 CAN	19 LEO	20 LIB	20 SCO	19 SAG	20 AQU	20 PIS	21 TAU	20 GEM
22 ARI	22 GEM	21 GEM	22 LEO	21 VIR	23 SCO	22 SAG	21 CAP	22 PIS	22 ARI	23 GEM	22 CAN
24 TAU	24 CAN	23 CAN	24 VIR	24 LIB	25 SAG	25 CAP	24 AQU	25 ARI	24 TAU	25 CAN	24 LEO
26 GEM	26 LEO	26 LEO	27 LIB	26 SCO	28 CAP	27 AQU	26 PIS	27 TAU	26 GEM	27 LEO	26 VIR
28 CAN		28 VIR	29 SCO	29 SAG	30 AQU	30 PIS	28 ARI	29 GEM	28 CAN	29 VIR	28 LIB
30 LEO		30 LIB		31 CAP			30 TAU		30 LEO		31 SCO

2000

JAN	FEB	MAR	APR	MAY	JUN	JUL	AUG	SEP	OCT	NOV	DEC
2 SAG	1 CAP	2 AQU	1 PIS	2 TAU	1 GEM	2 LEO	1 VIR	2 SCO	1 SAG	3 AQU	2 PIS
5 CAP	4 AQU	4 PIS	3 ARI	5 GEM	3 CAN	4 VIR	3 LIB	4 SAG	4 CAP	5 PIS	5 ARI
7 AQU	6 PIS	7 ARI	5 TAU	7 CAN	5 LEO	6 LIB	5 SCO	6 CAP	6 AQU	8 ARI	7 TAU
10 PIS	8 ARI	9 TAU	7 GEM	9 LEO	7 VIR	9 SCO	8 SAG	9 AQU	9 PIS	10 TAU	9 GEM
12 ARI	11 TAU	11 GEM	9 CAN	11 VIR	9 LIB	11 SAG	10 CAP	11 PIS	11 ARI	12 GEM	11 CAN
14 TAU	13 GEM	13 CAN	11 LEO	13 LIB	12 SCO	14 CAP	13 AQU	13 ARI	13 TAU	14 CAN	13 LEO
16 GEM	15 CAN	15 LEO	14 VIR	15 SCO	14 SAG	16 AQU	15 PIS	16 TAU	16 GEM	16 LEO	15 VIR
18 CAN	17 LEO	17 VIR	16 LIB	18 SAG	17 CAP	19 PIS	18 ARI	18 GEM	18 CAN	18 VIR	18 LIB
20 LEO	19 VIR	19 LIB	18 SCO	20 CAP	19 AQU	21 ARI	20 TAU	20 CAN	20 LEO	20 LIB	20 SCO
23 VIR	21 LIB	22 SCO	20 SAG	23 AQU	22 PIS	24 TAU	22 GEM	23 LEO	22 VIR	23 SCO	22 SAG
25 LIB	23 SCO	24 SAG	23 CAP	25 PIS	24 ARI	26 GEM	24 CAN	25 VIR	25 LIB	25 SAG	25 CAP
27 SCO	26 SAG	27 CAP	26 AQU	28 ARI	26 TAU	28 CAN	26 LEO	27 LIB	27 SCO	27 CAP	27 AQU
29 SAG	28 CAP	29 AQU	28 PIS	30 TAU	28 GEM	30 LEO	28 VIR	29 SCO	29 SAG	29 AQU	30 PIS
			30 ARI		30 CAN		30 LIB		31 CAP		

2001

JAN	FEB	MAR	APR	MAY	JUN	JUL	AUG	SEP	OCT	NOV	DEC
1 ARI	2 GEM	1 GEM	2 LEO	1 VIR	2 SCO	1 SAG	3 AQU	1 PIS	1 ARI	2 GEM	2 CAN
4 TAU	4 CAN	4 CAN	4 VIR	3 LIB	4 SAG	4 CAP	5 PIS	4 ARI	4 TAU	4 CAN	4 LEO
6 GEM	6 LEO	6 LEO	6 LIB	6 SCO	6 CAP	6 AQU	8 ARI	6 TAU	6 GEM	7 LEO	6 VIR
8 CAN	8 VIR	8 VIR	8 SCO	8 SAG	9 AQU	9 PIS	10 TAU	9 GEM	8 CAN	9 VIR	8 LIB
10 LEO	10 LIB	10 LIB	10 SAG	10 CAP	11 PIS	11 ARI	12 GEM	11 CAN	11 LEO	11 LIB	10 SCO
12 VIR	12 SCO	12 SCO	13 CAP	12 AQU	14 ARI	14 TAU	15 CAN	13 LEO	13 VIR	13 SCO	12 SAG
14 LIB	15 SAG	14 SAG	15 AQU	15 PIS	16 TAU	16 GEM	17 LEO	15 VIR	15 LIB	15 SAG	15 CAP
16 SCO	17 CAP	16 CAP	18 PIS	18 ARI	19 GEM	18 CAN	19 VIR	17 LIB	17 SCO	17 CAP	17 AQU
18 SAG	20 AQU	19 AQU	20 ARI	20 TAU	21 CAN	20 LEO	21 LIB	19 SCO	19 SAG	20 AQU	20 PIS
21 CAP	22 PIS	22 PIS	23 TAU	22 GEM	23 LEO	22 VIR	23 SCO	21 SAG	21 CAP	22 PIS	22 ARI
23 AQU	25 ARI	24 ARI	25 GEM	24 CAN	25 VIR	24 LIB	25 SAG	24 CAP	23 AQU	25 ARI	25 TAU
26 PIS	27 TAU	26 TAU	27 CAN	27 LEO	27 LIB	26 SCO	27 CAP	26 AQU	26 PIS	27 TAU	27 GEM
28 ARI		29 GEM	29 LEO	29 VIR	29 SCO	29 SAG	30 AQU	29 PIS	28 ARI	30 GEM	29 CAN
31 TAU		31 CAN		31 LIB		31 CAP			31 TAU		31 LEO

2002

JAN	FEB	MAR	APR	MAY	JUN	JUL	AUG	SEP	OCT	NOV	DEC
2 VIR	1 LIB	2 SCO	1 SAG	2 AQU	1 PIS	1 ARI	2 GEM	1 CAN	1 LEO	1 LIB	1 SCO
4 LIB	3 SCO	4 SAG	3 CAP	5 PIS	4 ARI	4 TAU	5 CAN	3 LEO	3 VIR	3 SCO	3 SAG
6 SCO	5 SAG	6 CAP	5 AQU	7 ARI	6 TAU	6 GEM	7 LEO	5 VIR	5 LIB	5 SAG	5 CAP
9 SAG	7 CAP	9 AQU	8 PIS	10 TAU	9 GEM	8 CAN	9 VIR	7 LIB	7 SCO	7 CAP	7 AQU
11 CAP	10 AQU	11 PIS	10 ARI	12 GEM	11 CAN	11 LEO	11 LIB	9 SCO	9 SAG	10 AQU	9 PIS
13 AQU	12 PIS	14 ARI	13 TAU	15 CAN	13 LEO	13 VIR	13 SCO	12 SAG	11 CAP	12 PIS	12 ARI
16 PIS	15 ARI	16 TAU	15 GEM	17 LEO	15 VIR	15 LIB	15 SAG	14 CAP	13 AQU	15 ARI	14 TAU
18 ARI	17 TAU	19 GEM	18 CAN	19 VIR	18 LIB	17 SCO	18 CAP	16 AQU	16 PIS	17 TAU	17 GEM
21 TAU	20 GEM	21 CAN	20 LEO	21 LIB	20 SCO	19 SAG	20 AQU	19 PIS	18 ARI	20 GEM	19 CAN
23 GEM	22 CAN	24 LEO	22 VIR	23 SCO	22 SAG	21 CAP	22 PIS	21 ARI	21 TAU	22 CAN	22 LEO
26 CAN	24 LEO	26 VIR	24 LIB	25 SAG	24 CAP	24 AQU	25 ARI	24 TAU	23 GEM	24 LEO	24 VIR
28 LEO	26 VIR	28 LIB	26 SCO	28 CAP	26 AQU	26 PIS	27 TAU	26 GEM	26 CAN	27 VIR	26 LIB
30 VIR	28 LIB	30 SCO	28 SAG	30 AQU	29 PIS	28 ARI	30 GEM	29 CAN	28 LEO	29 LIB	28 SCO
			30 CAP			31 TAU			30 VIR		30 SAG

2003

JAN	FEB	MAR	APR	MAY	JUN	JUL	AUG	SEP	OCT	NOV	DEC
1 CAP	2 PIS	1 PIS	3 TAU	2 GEM	1 CAN	1 LEO	2 LIB	2 SAG	1 CAP	2 PIS	2 ARI
3 AQU	5 ARI	4 ARI	5 GEM	5 CAN	4 LEO	3 VIR	4 SCO	4 CAP	4 AQU	5 ARI	4 TAU
6 PIS	7 TAU	6 TAU	8 CAN	7 LEO	6 VIR	5 LIB	6 SAG	6 AQU	6 PIS	7 TAU	7 GEM
8 ARI	10 GEM	9 GEM	10 LEO	10 VIR	8 LIB	7 SCO	8 CAP	9 PIS	8 ARI	10 GEM	9 CAN
11 TAU	12 CAN	11 CAN	12 VIR	12 LIB	10 SCO	10 SAG	10 AQU	11 ARI	11 TAU	12 CAN	12 LEO
13 GEM	14 LEO	14 LEO	14 LIB	14 SCO	12 SAG	12 CAP	12 PIS	13 TAU	13 GEM	15 LEO	14 VIR
16 CAN	16 VIR	16 VIR	16 SCO	16 SAG	14 CAP	14 AQU	15 ARI	16 GEM	16 CAN	17 VIR	16 LIB
18 LEO	18 LIB	18 LIB	18 SAG	18 CAP	16 AQU	16 PIS	17 TAU	18 CAN	18 LEO	19 LIB	19 SCO
20 VIR	21 SCO	20 SCO	20 CAP	20 AQU	19 PIS	18 ARI	20 GEM	21 LEO	21 VIR	21 SCO	21 SAG
22 LIB	23 SAG	22 SAG	23 AQU	22 PIS	21 ARI	21 TAU	22 CAN	23 VIR	23 LIB	23 SAG	23 CAP
24 SCO	25 CAP	24 CAP	25 PIS	25 ARI	23 TAU	23 GEM	24 LEO	25 LIB	25 SCO	25 CAP	25 AQU
26 SAG	27 AQU	26 AQU	27 ARI	27 TAU	26 GEM	26 CAN	27 VIR	27 SCO	27 SAG	27 AQU	27 PIS
29 CAP		29 PIS	30 TAU	30 GEM	28 CAN	28 LEO	29 LIB	29 SAG	29 CAP	29 PIS	29 ARI
31 AQU		31 ARI				30 VIR	31 SCO		31 AQU		

JAN	FEB	MAR	APR	MAY	JUN	JUL	AUG	SEP	OCT	NOV	DEC
1 TAU	2 CAN	3 LEO	1 VIR	1 LIB	2 SAG	1 CAP	1 PIS	2 TAU	2 GEM	1 CAN	1 LEO
3 GEM	4 LEO	5 VIR	4 LIB	3 SCO	4 CAP	3 AQU	4 ARI	5 GEM	5 CAN	3 LEO	3 VIR
6 CAN	7 VIR	7 LIB	6 SCO	5 SAG	6 AQU	5 PIS	6 TAU	7 CAN	7 LEO	6 VIR	6 LIB
8 LEO	9 LIB	9 SCO	8 SAG	7 CAP	8 PIS	7 ARI	8 GEM	10 LEO	10 VIR	8 LIB	8 SCO
10 VIR	11 SCO	11 SAG	10 CAP	9 AQU	10 ARI	10 TAU	11 CAN	12 VIR	12 LIB	10 SCO	10 SAG
13 LIB	13 SAG	14 CAP	12 AQU	11 PIS	12 TAU	12 GEM	13 LEO	14 LIB	14 SCO	13 SAG	12 CAP
15 SCO	15 CAP	16 AQU	14 PIS	14 ARI	15 GEM	15 CAN	16 VIR	17 SCO	16 SAG	15 CAP	14 AQU
17 SAG	17 AQU	18 PIS	16 ARI	16 TAU	17 CAN	17 LEO	18 LIB	19 SAG	18 CAP	17 AQU	16 PIS
19 CAP	20 PIS	20 ARI	19 TAU	19 GEM	20 LEO	20 VIR	20 SCO	21 CAP	20 AQU	19 PIS	18 ARI
21 AQU	22 ARI	23 TAU	21 GEM	21 CAN	22 VIR	22 LIB	23 SAG	23 AQU	23 PIS	21 ARI	21 TAU
23 PIS	24 TAU	25 GEM	24 CAN	24 LEO	24 LIB	24 SCO	25 CAP	25 PIS	25 ARI	23 TAU	23 GEM
25 ARI	27 GEM	28 CAN	26 LEO	26 VIR	25 SCO	26 SAG	27 AQU	27 ARI	27 TAU	26 GEM	25 CAN
28 TAU	29 CAN	30 LEO	29 VIR	28 LIB	27 SCO	28 CAP	29 PIS	29 PIS	30 GEM	28 CAN	28 LEO
30 GEM				31 SCO	29 SAG	30 AQU	31 ARI				31 VIR

JAN	FEB	MAR	APR	MAY	JUN	JUL	AUG	SEP	OCT	NOV	DEC
2 LIB	1 SCO	2 SAG	3 AQU	2 PIS	3 TAU	2 GEM	1 CAN	2 VIR	2 LIB	1 SCO	2 CAP
4 SCO	3 SAG	4 CAP	5 PIS	4 ARI	5 GEM	5 CAN	3 LEO	5 LIB	4 SCO	3 SAG	4 AQU
6 SAG	5 CAP	6 AQU	7 ARI	6 TAU	7 CAN	7 LEO	6 VIR	7 SCO	7 SAG	5 CAP	7 PIS
8 CAP	7 AQU	8 PIS	9 TAU	9 GEM	10 LEO	10 VIR	8 LIB	9 SAG	9 CAP	7 AQU	9 ARI
10 AQU	9 PIS	10 ARI	11 GEM	11 CAN	12 VIR	12 LIB	11 SCO	12 CAP	11 AQU	9 PIS	11 TAU
12 PIS	11 ARI	13 TAU	14 CAN	14 LEO	15 LIB	15 SCO	13 SAG	14 AQU	13 PIS	11 ARI	13 GEM
15 ARI	13 TAU	15 GEM	16 LEO	16 VIR	17 SCO	17 SAG	15 CAP	16 PIS	15 ARI	14 TAU	15 CAN
17 TAU	16 GEM	17 CAN	19 VIR	18 LIB	19 SAG	19 CAP	17 AQU	18 ARI	17 TAU	16 GEM	18 LEO
19 GEM	18 CAN	20 LEO	21 LIB	21 SCO	21 CAP	21 AQU	19 PIS	20 TAU	19 GEM	18 CAN	20 VIR
22 CAN	21 LEO	22 VIR	23 SCO	23 SAG	23 AQU	23 PIS	21 ARI	22 GEM	22 CAN	21 LEO	23 LIB
24 LEO	23 VIR	25 LIB	26 SAG	25 CAP	25 PIS	25 ARI	23 TAU	24 CAN	24 LEO	23 VIR	25 SCO
27 VIR	25 LIB	27 SCO	28 CAP	27 AQU	28 ARI	27 TAU	26 GEM	27 LEO	27 VIR	26 LIB	28 SAG
29 LIB	28 SCO	29 SAG	30 AQU	29 PIS	30 TAU	29 GEM	28 CAN	29 VIR	29 LIB	28 SCO	30 CAP
		31 CAP		31 ARI			31 LEO			30 SAG	

JAN	FEB	MAR	APR	MAY	JUN	JUL	AUG	SEP	OCT	NOV	DEC
1 AQU	1 ARI	1 ARI	1 GEM	1 CAN	2 VIR	2 LIB	1 SCO	2 CAP	1 AQU	2 ARI	1 TAU
3 PIS	3 TAU	3 TAU	4 CAN	3 LEO	5 LIB	5 SCO	3 SAG	4 AQU	4 PIS	4 TAU	3 GEM
5 ARI	6 GEM	5 GEM	6 LEO	6 VIR	7 SCO	7 SAG	6 CAP	6 PIS	6 ARI	6 GEM	6 CAN
7 TAU	8 CAN	7 CAN	8 VIR	8 LIB	9 SAG	9 CAP	8 AQU	8 ARI	8 TAU	8 CAN	8 LEO
9 GEM	10 LEO	10 LEO	11 LIB	11 SCO	12 CAP	11 AQU	10 PIS	10 TAU	10 GEM	11 LEO	10 VIR
12 CAN	13 VIR	12 VIR	14 SCO	13 SAG	14 AQU	13 PIS	12 ARI	12 GEM	12 CAN	13 VIR	13 LIB
14 LEO	16 LIB	15 LIB	16 SAG	15 CAP	16 PIS	15 ARI	14 TAU	14 CAN	14 LEO	15 LIB	15 SCO
17 VIR	18 SCO	17 SCO	18 CAP	18 AQU	18 ARI	17 TAU	16 GEM	17 LEO	17 VIR	18 SCO	18 SAG
19 LIB	20 SAG	20 SAG	20 AQU	20 PIS	20 TAU	20 GEM	18 CAN	19 VIR	19 LIB	20 SAG	20 CAP
22 SCO	23 CAP	22 CAP	22 PIS	22 ARI	22 GEM	22 CAN	21 LEO	22 LIB	22 SCO	23 CAP	22 AQU
24 SAG	25 AQU	24 AQU	25 ARI	24 TAU	25 CAN	24 LEO	23 VIR	24 SCO	24 SAG	25 AQU	24 PIS
26 CAP	27 PIS	26 PIS	27 TAU	26 GEM	27 LEO	27 VIR	26 LIB	27 SAG	26 CAP	27 PIS	27 ARI
28 AQU		28 ARI	29 GEM	28 CAN	29 VIR	29 LIB	28 SCO	29 CAP	29 AQU	29 ARI	29 TAU
30 PIS		30 TAU		31 LEO			31 SAG		31 PIS		31 GEM

JAN	FEB	MAR	APR	MAY	JUN	JUL	AUG	SEP	OCT	NOV	DEC
2 CAN	1 LEO	2 VIR	1 LIB	1 SCO	2 CAP	2 AQU	2 ARI	1 TAU	2 CAN	3 VIR	3 LIB
4 LEO	3 VIR	5 LIB	3 SCO	3 SAG	4 AQU	4 PIS	4 TAU	3 GEM	4 LEO	5 LIB	5 SCO
7 VIR	5 LIB	7 SCO	6 SAG	6 CAP	7 PIS	6 ARI	6 GEM	5 CAN	7 VIR	8 SCO	8 SAG
9 LIB	8 SCO	10 SAG	8 CAP	8 AQU	9 ARI	8 TAU	9 CAN	7 LEO	9 LIB	10 SAG	10 CAP
12 SCO	10 SAG	12 CAP	11 AQU	10 PIS	11 TAU	10 GEM	11 LEO	9 VIR	12 SCO	13 CAP	13 AQU
14 SAG	13 CAP	14 AQU	13 PIS	12 ARI	13 GEM	12 CAN	13 VIR	12 LIB	14 SAG	15 AQU	15 PIS
16 CAP	15 AQU	17 PIS	15 ARI	14 TAU	15 CAN	14 LEO	15 LIB	14 SCO	17 CAP	18 PIS	17 ARI
19 AQU	17 PIS	19 ARI	17 TAU	16 GEM	17 LEO	17 VIR	18 SCO	17 SAG	19 AQU	20 ARI	19 TAU
21 PIS	19 ARI	21 TAU	19 GEM	18 CAN	19 VIR	19 LIB	20 SAG	19 CAP	21 PIS	22 TAU	21 GEM
23 ARI	21 TAU	23 GEM	21 CAN	21 LEO	22 LIB	22 SCO	23 CAP	21 AQU	23 ARI	24 GEM	23 CAN
25 TAU	23 GEM	25 CAN	23 LEO	23 VIR	24 SCO	24 SAG	25 AQU	24 PIS	25 TAU	26 CAN	25 LEO
27 GEM	25 CAN	27 LEO	26 VIR	25 LIB	27 SAG	27 CAP	27 PIS	26 ARI	27 GEM	28 LEO	27 VIR
29 CAN	28 LEO	29 VIR	28 LIB	28 SCO	29 CAP	29 AQU	29 ARI	28 TAU	30 GEM	30 VIR	30 LIB
				31 SAG		31 PIS		30 GEM	31 LEO		

JAN	FEB	MAR	APR	MAY	JUN	JUL	AUG	SEP	OCT	NOV	DEC
1 SCO	3 CAP	1 CAP	2 PIS	2 ARI	2 GEM	2 CAN	2 VIR	1 LIB	3 SAG	2 CAP	2 AQU
4 SAG	5 AQU	3 AQU	4 ARI	4 TAU	4 CAN	4 LEO	4 LIB	3 SCO	5 CAP	4 AQU	4 PIS
6 CAP	7 PIS	6 PIS	6 TAU	6 GEM	6 LEO	6 VIR	7 SCO	6 SAG	8 AQU	7 PIS	6 ARI
9 AQU	10 ARI	8 ARI	8 GEM	8 CAN	8 VIR	8 LIB	9 SAG	8 CAP	10 PIS	9 ARI	9 TAU
11 PIS	12 TAU	10 TAU	10 CAN	10 LEO	10 LIB	10 SCO	12 CAP	11 AQU	13 ARI	11 TAU	11 GEM
13 ARI	14 GEM	12 GEM	13 LEO	12 VIR	13 SCO	13 SAG	14 AQU	13 PIS	15 TAU	13 GEM	13 CAN
15 TAU	16 CAN	14 CAN	15 VIR	14 LIB	15 SAG	15 CAP	17 PIS	15 ARI	17 GEM	15 CAN	15 LEO
18 GEM	18 LEO	16 LEO	17 LIB	17 SCO	18 CAP	18 AQU	19 ARI	17 TAU	19 CAN	17 LEO	17 VIR
20 CAN	20 VIR	19 VIR	20 SCO	19 SAG	21 AQU	20 PIS	21 TAU	19 GEM	21 LEO	19 VIR	19 LIB
22 LEO	23 LIB	21 LIB	22 SAG	22 CAP	23 PIS	23 ARI	23 GEM	22 CAN	23 VIR	22 LIB	21 SCO
24 VIR	25 SCO	23 SCO	25 CAP	24 AQU	25 ARI	25 TAU	25 CAN	24 LEO	25 LIB	24 SCO	24 SAG
26 LIB	28 SAG	26 SAG	27 AQU	27 PIS	28 TAU	27 GEM	27 LEO	26 VIR	28 SCO	27 SAG	26 CAP
29 SCO		28 CAP	30 PIS	29 ARI	30 GEM	29 CAN	30 VIR	28 LIB	30 SAG	29 CAP	29 AQU
31 SAG		31 AQU		31 TAU		31 LEO		30 SCO			31 PIS

JAN	FEB	MAR	APR	MAY	JUN	JUL	AUG	SEP	OCT	NOV	DEC
3 ARI	1 TAU	3 GEM	1 CAN	2 VIR	1 LIB	3 SAG	2 CAP	3 PIS	3 ARI	1 TAU	1 GEM
5 TAU	3 GEM	5 CAN	3 LEO	5 LIB	3 SCO	5 CAP	4 AQU	5 ARI	5 TAU	3 GEM	3 CAN
7 GEM	5 CAN	7 LEO	5 VIR	7 SCO	6 SAG	8 AQU	7 PIS	8 TAU	7 GEM	6 CAN	5 LEO
9 CAN	7 LEO	9 VIR	7 LIB	9 SAG	8 CAP	10 PIS	9 ARI	10 GEM	9 CAN	8 LEO	7 VIR
11 LEO	10 VIR	11 LIB	10 SCO	12 CAP	11 AQU	13 ARI	11 TAU	12 CAN	12 LEO	10 VIR	9 LIB
13 VIR	12 LIB	13 SAG	12 SAG	15 AQU	13 PIS	15 TAU	14 GEM	14 LEO	14 VIR	12 LIB	11 SCO
15 LIB	14 SCO	16 SAG	15 CAP	17 PIS	16 ARI	17 GEM	16 CAN	16 VIR	16 LIB	14 SCO	14 SAG
18 SCO	16 SAG	18 CAP	17 AQU	19 ARI	18 TAU	19 CAN	18 LEO	18 LIB	18 SCO	17 SAG	16 CAP
20 SAG	19 CAP	21 AQU	20 PIS	21 TAU	20 GEM	21 LEO	20 VIR	20 SCO	20 SAG	19 CAP	19 AQU
23 CAP	21 AQU	23 PIS	22 ARI	24 GEM	22 CAN	23 VIR	22 LIB	23 SAG	23 CAP	21 AQU	21 PIS
25 AQU	24 PIS	26 ARI	24 TAU	26 CAN	24 LEO	26 LIB	24 SCO	25 CAP	25 AQU	24 PIS	24 ARI
28 PIS	26 ARI	28 TAU	26 GEM	28 LEO	26 VIR	28 SCO	26 SAG	28 AQU	28 PIS	26 ARI	26 TAU
30 ARI	28 TAU	30 GEM	28 CAN	30 VIR	28 LIB	30 SAG	29 CAP	30 PIS	30 ARI	29 TAU	28 GEM
			30 LEO		30 SCO		31 AQU				30 CAN

JAN	FEB	MAR	APR	MAY	JUN	JUL	AUG	SEP	OCT	NOV	DEC
1 LEO	2 LIB	1 LIB	2 SAG	2 CAP	1 AQU	3 ARI	2 TAU	3 CAN	2 LEO	3 LIB	2 SCO
3 VIR	4 SCO	3 SCO	4 CAP	4 AQU	3 PIS	5 TAU	4 GEM	5 LEO	4 VIR	5 SCO	4 SAG
5 LIB	6 SAG	6 SAG	7 AQU	7 PIS	6 ARI	8 GEM	6 CAN	7 VIR	6 LIB	7 SAG	6 CAP
8 SCO	9 CAP	8 CAP	9 PIS	9 ARI	8 TAU	10 CAN	8 LEO	9 LIB	8 SCO	9 CAP	9 AQU
10 SAG	11 AQU	11 AQU	12 ARI	12 TAU	10 GEM	12 LEO	10 VIR	11 SCO	10 SAG	11 AQU	11 PIS
12 CAP	14 PIS	13 PIS	14 TAU	14 GEM	12 CAN	14 VIR	12 LIB	13 SAG	12 CAP	14 PIS	14 ARI
15 AQU	16 ARI	16 ARI	17 GEM	16 CAN	14 LEO	16 LIB	14 SCO	15 CAP	15 AQU	16 ARI	16 TAU
18 PIS	19 TAU	18 TAU	19 CAN	18 LEO	17 VIR	18 SCO	17 SAG	18 AQU	17 PIS	19 TAU	18 GEM
20 ARI	21 GEM	20 GEM	21 LEO	20 VIR	19 LIB	20 SAG	19 CAP	20 PIS	20 ARI	21 GEM	21 CAN
22 TAU	23 CAN	23 CAN	23 VIR	22 LIB	21 SCO	23 CAP	21 AQU	23 ARI	22 TAU	23 CAN	23 LEO
25 GEM	25 LEO	25 LEO	25 LIB	25 SCO	23 SAG	25 AQU	24 PIS	25 TAU	25 GEM	26 LEO	25 VIR
27 CAN	27 VIR	27 VIR	27 SCO	27 SAG	25 CAP	28 PIS	26 ARI	28 GEM	27 CAN	28 VIR	27 LIB
29 LEO		29 LIB	29 SAG	29 CAP	28 AQU	30 ARI	29 TAU	30 CAN	29 LEO	30 LIB	29 SCO
31 VIR		31 SCO			30 PIS		31 GEM		31 VIR		31 SAG

JAN	FEB	MAR	APR	MAY	JUN	JUL	AUG	SEP	OCT	NOV	DEC
3 CAP	1 AQU	1 AQU	2 ARI	2 TAU	3 CAN	2 LEO	1 VIR	1 SCO	3 CAP	1 AQU	1 PIS
5 AQU	4 PIS	3 PIS	4 TAU	4 GEM	5 LEO	4 VIR	3 LIB	3 SAG	5 AQU	4 PIS	3 ARI
7 PIS	6 ARI	6 ARI	7 GEM	6 CAN	7 VIR	6 LIB	5 SCO	5 CAP	7 PIS	6 ARI	6 TAU
10 ARI	9 TAU	8 TAU	9 CAN	9 LEO	9 LIB	9 SCO	7 SAG	8 AQU	10 ARI	9 TAU	8 GEM
12 TAU	11 GEM	11 GEM	11 LEO	11 VIR	11 SCO	11 SAG	9 CAP	10 PIS	12 TAU	11 GEM	11 CAN
15 GEM	14 CAN	13 CAN	14 VIR	13 LIB	13 SAG	13 CAP	11 AQU	13 ARI	15 GEM	14 CAN	13 LEO
17 CAN	16 LEO	15 LEO	16 LIB	15 SCO	16 CAP	15 AQU	14 PIS	15 TAU	17 CAN	16 LEO	15 VIR
19 LEO	18 VIR	17 VIR	18 SCO	17 SAG	18 AQU	18 PIS	16 ARI	18 GEM	20 LEO	18 VIR	18 LIB
21 VIR	20 LIB	19 LIB	20 SAG	19 CAP	20 PIS	20 ARI	19 TAU	20 CAN	22 VIR	20 LIB	20 SCO
23 LIB	22 SCO	21 SCO	22 CAP	21 AQU	23 ARI	22 TAU	21 GEM	22 LEO	24 LIB	22 SCO	22 SAG
25 SCO	24 SAG	23 SAG	24 AQU	24 PIS	25 TAU	25 GEM	24 CAN	24 VIR	26 SCO	24 SAG	24 CAP
28 SAG	26 CAP	25 CAP	26 PIS	26 ARI	28 GEM	27 CAN	26 LEO	26 LIB	28 SAG	26 CAP	26 AQU
30 CAP		28 AQU	29 ARI	29 TAU	30 CAN	30 LEO	28 VIR	28 SCO	30 CAP	29 AQU	28 PIS
		30 PIS		31 GEM			30 LIB	30 SAG			31 ARI

2012

JAN	FEB	MAR	APR	MAY	JUN	JUL	AUG	SEP	OCT	NOV	DEC
2 TAU	1 GEM	2 CAN	1 LEO	2 LIB	1 SCO	1 CAP	1 AQU	2 ARI	1 TAU	3 CAN	2 LEO
5 GEM	4 CAN	4 LEO	3 VIR	4 SCO	3 SAG	4 AQU	3 PIS	4 TAU	4 GEM	5 LEO	5 VIR
7 CAN	6 LEO	6 VIR	5 LIB	6 SAG	5 CAP	6 PIS	5 ARI	6 GEM	6 CAN	7 VIR	7 LIB
9 LEO	8 VIR	8 LIB	7 SCO	8 CAP	7 AQU	9 ARI	8 TAU	9 CAN	9 LEO	10 LIB	9 SCO
12 VIR	10 LIB	11 SCO	9 SAG	11 AQU	9 PIS	11 TAU	10 GEM	11 LEO	11 VIR	12 SCO	11 SAG
14 LIB	12 SCO	13 SAG	11 CAP	13 PIS	11 ARI	13 GEM	13 CAN	14 VIR	13 LIB	14 SAG	13 CAP
16 SCO	14 SAG	15 CAP	13 AQU	15 ARI	14 TAU	16 CAN	15 LEO	16 LIB	15 SCO	16 CAP	15 AQU
18 SAG	17 CAP	17 AQU	16 PIS	18 TAU	17 GEM	19 LEO	17 VIR	18 SCO	17 SAG	18 AQU	17 PIS
20 CAP	19 AQU	19 PIS	18 ARI	20 GEM	19 CAN	21 VIR	19 LIB	20 SAG	19 CAP	20 PIS	20 ARI
22 AQU	21 PIS	22 ARI	20 TAU	23 CAN	21 LEO	23 LIB	22 SCO	22 CAP	22 AQU	22 ARI	22 TAU
25 PIS	23 ARI	24 TAU	23 GEM	25 LEO	24 VIR	25 SCO	24 SAG	24 AQU	24 PIS	25 TAU	25 GEM
27 ARI	26 TAU	27 GEM	26 CAN	28 VIR	26 LIB	28 SAG	26 CAP	27 PIS	26 ARI	27 GEM	27 CAN
30 TAU	28 GEM	29 CAN	28 LEO	30 LIB	28 SCO	30 CAP	28 AQU	29 ARI	29 TAU	30 CAN	30 LEO
			30 VIR		30 SAG		30 PIS		31 GEM		

2013

JAN	FEB	MAR	APR	MAY	JUN	JUL	AUG	SEP	OCT	NOV	DEC
1 VIR	2 SCO	1 SCO	2 CAP	1 AQU	2 ARI	1 TAU	2 CAN	1 LEO	1 VIR	2 SCO	2 SAG
3 LIB	4 SAG	3 SAG	4 AQU	3 PIS	4 TAU	4 GEM	5 LEO	4 VIR	3 LIB	4 SAG	4 CAP
6 SCO	6 CAP	6 CAP	6 PIS	5 ARI	6 GEM	7 CAN	7 VIR	6 LIB	6 SCO	6 CAP	6 AQU
8 SAG	8 AQU	7 AQU	8 ARI	8 TAU	9 CAN	9 LEO	10 LIB	8 SAG	8 SAG	8 AQU	8 PIS
10 CAP	10 PIS	10 PIS	10 TAU	10 GEM	11 LEO	12 SCO	12 SCO	11 SAG	10 CAP	10 PIS	10 ARI
12 AQU	12 ARI	12 ARI	13 GEM	13 CAN	14 VIR	14 LIB	14 SAG	13 CAP	12 AQU	12 ARI	12 TAU
14 PIS	15 TAU	14 TAU	15 CAN	15 LEO	16 LIB	16 SCO	16 CAP	15 AQU	14 PIS	15 TAU	15 GEM
16 ARI	17 GEM	17 GEM	18 LEO	18 VIR	19 SCO	18 SAG	18 AQU	17 PIS	16 ARI	17 GEM	17 CAN
18 TAU	20 CAN	19 CAN	20 VIR	20 LIB	21 SAG	20 CAP	20 PIS	19 ARI	19 TAU	20 CAN	20 LEO
21 GEM	22 LEO	22 LEO	23 LIB	22 SCO	23 CAP	23 AQU	23 ARI	21 TAU	21 GEM	22 LEO	22 VIR
23 CAN	25 VIR	24 VIR	25 SCO	24 SAG	25 AQU	24 PIS	25 TAU	24 GEM	23 CAN	25 VIR	25 LIB
26 LEO	27 LIB	26 LIB	27 SAG	26 CAP	27 PIS	27 ARI	27 GEM	26 CAN	26 LEO	27 LIB	27 SCO
28 VIR		28 SCO	29 CAP	28 AQU	29 ARI	28 TAU	30 CAN	29 LEO	28 VIR	29 SCO	29 SAG
31 LIB		30 SAG		30 PIS		31 GEM			31 LIB		31 CAP

2014

JAN	FEB	MAR	APR	MAY	JUN	JUL	AUG	SEP	OCT	NOV	DEC
2 AQU	2 ARI	2 ARI	1 TAU	3 CAN	1 LEO	1 VIR	2 SCO	1 SAG	3 AQU	1 PIS	3 TAU
4 PIS	5 TAU	4 TAU	3 GEM	5 LEO	4 VIR	4 LIB	5 SAG	3 CAP	5 PIS	3 ARI	5 GEM
6 ARI	7 GEM	6 GEM	5 CAN	8 VIR	6 LIB	6 SCO	7 CAP	5 AQU	7 ARI	5 TAU	7 CAN
8 TAU	10 CAN	9 CAN	8 LEO	10 LIB	9 SCO	9 SAG	9 AQU	7 PIS	9 TAU	7 GEM	9 LEO
11 GEM	12 LEO	11 LEO	10 VIR	12 SCO	11 SAG	11 CAP	11 PIS	9 ARI	11 GEM	10 CAN	12 VIR
13 CAN	15 VIR	14 VIR	13 LIB	15 SAG	13 CAP	13 AQU	13 ARI	11 TAU	13 CAN	12 LEO	14 LIB
16 LEO	17 LIB	16 LIB	15 SCO	17 CAP	15 AQU	14 PIS	15 TAU	14 GEM	16 LEO	15 VIR	17 SCO
18 VIR	19 SCO	19 SCO	17 SAG	19 AQU	17 PIS	16 ARI	18 GEM	16 CAN	18 VIR	17 LIB	19 SAG
21 LIB	22 SAG	21 SAG	19 CAP	21 PIS	19 ARI	19 TAU	20 CAN	18 LEO	21 LIB	20 SCO	21 CAP
23 SCO	24 CAP	23 CAP	21 AQU	23 ARI	21 TAU	21 GEM	22 LEO	21 VIR	23 SCO	22 SAG	23 AQU
25 SAG	26 AQU	25 AQU	24 PIS	25 TAU	24 GEM	24 CAN	25 VIR	23 LIB	25 SAG	24 CAP	25 PIS
28 CAP	28 PIS	27 PIS	26 ARI	27 GEM	26 CAN	26 LEO	27 LIB	26 SCO	28 CAP	26 AQU	28 ARI
29 AQU		29 ARI	28 TAU	30 CAN	29 LEO	28 VIR	30 SCO	28 SAG	30 AQU	28 PIS	30 TAU
31 PIS			30 GEM			31 LIB		30 CAP		30 ARI	

2015

JAN	FEB	MAR	APR	MAY	JUN	JUL	AUG	SEP	OCT	NOV	DEC
1 GEM	2 LEO	1 LEO	3 LIB	2 SCO	1 SAG	1 CAP	1 PIS	2 TAU	1 GEM	2 LEO	2 VIR
3 CAN	5 VIR	4 VIR	5 SCO	5 SAG	3 CAP	3 AQU	3 ARI	4 GEM	3 CAN	4 VIR	4 LIB
6 LEO	7 LIB	6 LIB	8 SAG	7 CAP	6 AQU	5 PIS	5 TAU	6 CAN	6 LEO	7 LIB	7 SCO
8 VIR	10 SCO	9 SCO	10 CAP	9 AQU	8 PIS	7 ARI	8 GEM	8 LEO	8 VIR	9 SCO	9 SAG
11 LIB	12 SAG	11 SAG	12 AQU	11 PIS	10 ARI	9 TAU	10 CAN	11 VIR	11 LIB	12 SAG	12 CAP
13 SCO	14 CAP	14 CAP	14 PIS	14 ARI	12 TAU	11 GEM	12 LEO	13 LIB	13 SCO	14 CAP	14 AQU
16 SAG	16 AQU	16 AQU	16 ARI	16 TAU	14 GEM	14 CAN	15 VIR	16 SCO	16 SAG	17 AQU	16 PIS
18 CAP	18 PIS	18 PIS	18 TAU	18 GEM	16 CAN	16 LEO	17 LIB	18 SAG	18 CAP	19 PIS	18 ARI
20 AQU	20 ARI	20 ARI	20 GEM	20 CAN	19 LEO	19 VIR	20 SCO	21 CAP	20 AQU	21 ARI	20 TAU
22 PIS	22 TAU	22 TAU	22 CAN	22 LEO	21 VIR	21 LIB	22 SAG	23 AQU	23 PIS	23 TAU	22 GEM
24 ARI	24 GEM	24 GEM	25 LEO	25 VIR	24 LIB	23 SCO	24 CAP	25 PIS	25 ARI	25 GEM	25 CAN
26 TAU	27 CAN	26 CAN	27 VIR	27 LIB	26 SCO	26 SAG	27 AQU	27 ARI	27 TAU	27 CAN	27 LEO
28 GEM		29 LEO	30 LIB	30 SCO	28 SAG	28 CAP	29 PIS	29 TAU	29 GEM	29 LEO	29 VIR
31 CAN		31 VIR				30 AQU	31 ARI		31 CAN		

JAN	FEB	MAR	APR	MAY	JUN	JUL	AUG	SEP	OCT	NOV	DEC
1 LIB	2 SAG	3 CAP	1 AQU	1 PIS	1 TAU	1 GEM	1 LEO	2 LIB	2 SCO	1 SAG	1 CAP
3 SCO	4 CAP	5 AQU	4 PIS	3 ARI	3 GEM	3 CAN	4 VIR	5 SCO	5 SAG	3 CAP	3 AQU
6 SAG	7 AQU	7 PIS	6 ARI	5 TAU	5 CAN	5 LEO	6 LIB	7 SAG	7 CAP	6 AQU	5 PIS
8 CAP	9 PIS	9 ARI	8 TAU	7 GEM	8 LEO	7 VIR	8 SCO	10 CAP	10 AQU	8 PIS	8 ARI
10 AQU	11 ARI	11 TAU	10 GEM	9 CAN	10 VIR	10 LIB	11 SAG	12 AQU	12 PIS	10 ARI	10 TAU
12 PIS	13 TAU	13 GEM	12 CAN	11 LEO	12 LIB	12 SCO	13 CAP	14 PIS	14 ARI	12 TAU	12 GEM
14 ARI	15 GEM	15 CAN	14 LEO	14 VIR	15 SCO	15 SAG	16 AQU	16 ARI	16 TAU	14 GEM	14 CAN
17 TAU	17 CAN	18 LEO	16 VIR	16 LIB	17 SAG	17 CAP	18 PIS	18 TAU	18 GEM	16 CAN	16 LEO
19 GEM	19 LEO	20 VIR	19 LIB	19 SCO	20 CAP	19 AQU	20 ARI	21 GEM	20 CAN	18 LEO	18 VIR
21 CAN	22 VIR	23 LIB	21 SCO	21 SAG	22 AQU	22 PIS	22 TAU	23 CAN	22 LEO	21 VIR	20 LIB
23 LEO	24 LIB	25 SCO	24 SAG	24 CAP	24 PIS	24 ARI	24 GEM	25 LEO	24 VIR	23 LIB	23 SCO
25 VIR	27 SCO	28 SAG	26 CAP	26 AQU	26 ARI	26 TAU	26 CAN	27 VIR	27 LIB	26 SCO	25 SAG
28 LIB	29 SAG	30 CAP	29 AQU	28 PIS	29 TAU	28 GEM	28 LEO	29 LIB	30 SCO	28 SAG	28 CAP
30 SCO				30 ARI		30 CAN	31 VIR				30 AQU

JAN	FEB	MAR	APR	MAY	JUN	JUL	AUG	SEP	OCT	NOV	DEC
2 PIS	2 TAU	2 TAU	2 CAN	1 LEO	2 LIB	2 SCO	1 SAG	2 AQU	2 PIS	1 ARI	2 GEM
4 ARI	4 GEM	4 GEM	4 LEO	4 VIR	5 SCO	5 SAG	3 CAP	5 PIS	4 ARI	3 TAU	4 CAN
6 TAU	7 CAN	6 CAN	6 VIR	6 LIB	7 SAG	7 CAP	6 AQU	7 ARI	6 TAU	5 GEM	6 LEO
8 GEM	9 LEO	8 LEO	9 LIB	9 SCO	10 CAP	10 AQU	8 PIS	9 TAU	8 GEM	7 CAN	8 VIR
10 CAN	11 VIR	11 VIR	11 SCO	11 SAG	12 AQU	12 PIS	11 ARI	11 GEM	10 CAN	9 LEO	11 LIB
12 LEO	13 LIB	13 LIB	14 SAG	14 CAP	15 PIS	14 ARI	13 TAU	13 CAN	13 LEO	11 VIR	13 SCO
14 VIR	16 SCO	15 SCO	16 CAP	16 AQU	17 ARI	17 TAU	15 GEM	15 LEO	15 VIR	13 LIB	15 SAG
17 LIB	18 SAG	17 SAG	19 AQU	18 PIS	19 TAU	19 GEM	17 CAN	17 VIR	17 LIB	16 SCO	18 CAP
19 SCO	21 CAP	20 CAP	21 PIS	21 ARI	21 GEM	21 CAN	19 LEO	20 LIB	19 SCO	18 SAG	20 AQU
22 SAG	23 AQU	22 AQU	23 ARI	23 TAU	23 CAN	23 LEO	21 VIR	22 SCO	22 SAG	21 CAP	23 PIS
24 CAP	25 PIS	25 PIS	25 TAU	25 GEM	25 LEO	25 VIR	23 LIB	24 SAG	24 CAP	23 AQU	25 ARI
27 AQU	27 ARI	27 ARI	27 GEM	27 CAN	27 VIR	27 LIB	26 SCO	27 CAP	27 AQU	26 PIS	28 TAU
29 PIS		29 TAU	29 CAN	29 LEO	29 LIB	30 SCO	28 SAG	29 AQU	29 PIS	28 ARI	30 GEM
31 ARI		31 GEM		31 VIR			31 CAP			30 TAU	

JAN	FEB	MAR	APR	MAY	JUN	JUL	AUG	SEP	OCT	NOV	DEC
1 CAN	1 VIR	1 VIR	1 SCO	1 SAG	2 AQU	2 PIS	1 ARI	2 GEM	1 CAN	2 VIR	1 LIB
3 LEO	3 LIB	3 LIB	4 SAG	3 CAP	5 PIS	4 ARI	3 TAU	4 CAN	3 LEO	4 LIB	3 SCO
5 VIR	5 SCO	5 SCO	6 CAP	6 AQU	7 ARI	7 TAU	5 GEM	6 LEO	5 VIR	6 SCO	5 SAG
7 LIB	8 SAG	7 SAG	9 AQU	8 PIS	9 TAU	9 GEM	7 CAN	8 VIR	7 LIB	8 SAG	8 CAP
9 SCO	10 CAP	10 CAP	11 PIS	11 ARI	12 GEM	11 CAN	9 LEO	10 LIB	9 SCO	10 CAP	10 AQU
12 SAG	13 AQU	12 AQU	13 ARI	13 TAU	14 CAN	13 LEO	11 VIR	12 SCO	12 SAG	13 AQU	13 PIS
14 CAP	15 PIS	15 PIS	16 TAU	15 GEM	16 LEO	15 VIR	13 LIB	14 SAG	14 CAP	15 PIS	15 ARI
17 AQU	18 ARI	17 ARI	18 GEM	17 CAN	18 VIR	17 LIB	16 SCO	17 CAP	17 AQU	18 ARI	18 TAU
19 PIS	20 TAU	19 TAU	20 CAN	19 LEO	20 LIB	19 SCO	18 SAG	19 AQU	19 PIS	20 TAU	20 GEM
22 ARI	22 GEM	22 GEM	22 LEO	21 VIR	22 SCO	22 SAG	20 CAP	22 PIS	22 ARI	22 GEM	22 CAN
24 TAU	24 CAN	24 CAN	24 VIR	24 LIB	25 SAG	24 CAP	23 AQU	24 ARI	24 TAU	25 CAN	24 LEO
26 GEM	26 LEO	26 LEO	26 LIB	26 SCO	27 CAP	27 AQU	26 PIS	27 TAU	26 GEM	27 LEO	26 VIR
28 CAN		28 VIR	29 SCO	28 SAG	29 AQU	29 PIS	28 ARI	29 GEM	28 CAN	29 VIR	28 LIB
30 LEO		30 LIB		31 CAP			30 TAU		30 LEO		30 SCO

JAN	FEB	MAR	APR	MAY	JUN	JUL	AUG	SEP	OCT	NOV	DEC
2 SAG	3 AQU	2 AQU	1 PIS	1 ARI	2 GEM	1 CAN	2 VIR	2 SCO	2 SAG	3 AQU	3 PIS
4 CAP	5 PIS	5 PIS	3 ARI	3 TAU	4 CAN	3 LEO	4 LIB	4 SAG	4 CAP	5 PIS	5 ARI
7 AQU	8 ARI	7 ARI	6 TAU	5 GEM	6 LEO	5 VIR	6 SCO	7 CAP	6 AQU	8 ARI	8 TAU
9 PIS	10 TAU	10 TAU	8 GEM	8 CAN	8 VIR	8 LIB	8 SAG	9 AQU	9 PIS	10 TAU	10 GEM
12 ARI	13 GEM	12 GEM	10 CAN	10 LEO	10 LIB	10 SCO	10 CAP	12 PIS	12 ARI	13 GEM	12 CAN
14 TAU	15 CAN	14 CAN	13 LEO	12 VIR	12 SCO	12 SAG	13 AQU	14 ARI	14 TAU	15 CAN	14 LEO
16 GEM	17 LEO	16 LEO	15 VIR	14 LIB	15 SAG	14 CAP	15 PIS	17 TAU	16 GEM	17 LEO	17 VIR
18 CAN	19 VIR	18 VIR	17 LIB	16 SCO	17 CAP	17 AQU	18 ARI	19 GEM	19 CAN	19 VIR	19 LIB
20 LEO	21 LIB	20 LIB	19 SCO	18 SAG	19 AQU	19 PIS	20 TAU	21 CAN	21 LEO	21 LIB	21 SCO
22 VIR	23 SCO	22 SCO	21 SAG	21 CAP	22 PIS	22 ARI	23 GEM	23 LEO	24 VIR	24 SCO	23 SAG
24 LIB	25 SAG	25 SAG	23 CAP	23 AQU	24 ARI	24 TAU	25 CAN	25 VIR	26 LIB	26 SAG	25 CAP
27 SCO	28 CAP	27 CAP	26 AQU	26 PIS	27 TAU	27 GEM	27 LEO	28 LIB	28 SCO	28 CAP	28 AQU
29 SAG		29 AQU	28 PIS	28 ARI	29 GEM	29 CAN	29 VIR	30 SCO	31 CAP	30 AQU	30 PIS
31 CAP				30 TAU		31 LEO	31 LIB				

2020

JAN	FEB	MAR	APR	MAY	JUN	JUL	AUG	SEP	OCT	NOV	DEC
1 ARI	3 GEM	1 GEM	2 LEO	2 VIR	2 SCO	1 SAG	2 AQU	1 PIS	3 TAU	2 GEM	1 CAN
4 TAU	5 CAN	3 CAN	4 VIR	4 LIB	4 SAG	3 CAP	4 PIS	3 ARI	5 GEM	4 CAN	4 LEO
6 GEM	7 LEO	6 LEO	6 LIB	6 SCO	6 CAP	6 AQU	7 ARI	7 TAU	8 CAN	7 LEO	6 VIR
9 CAN	9 VIR	8 VIR	8 SCO	8 SAG	8 AQU	8 PIS	9 TAU	8 GEM	10 LEO	9 VIR	8 LIB
11 LEO	11 LIB	10 LIB	10 SAG	10 CAP	11 PIS	11 ARI	12 GEM	11 CAN	12 VIR	11 LIB	10 SCO
13 VIR	13 SCO	12 SCO	12 CAP	12 AQU	13 ARI	13 TAU	14 CAN	13 LEO	15 LIB	13 SCO	12 SAG
15 LIB	15 SAG	14 SAG	15 AQU	14 PIS	16 TAU	16 GEM	17 LEO	15 VIR	17 SCO	15 SAG	14 CAP
17 SCO	18 CAP	16 CAP	17 PIS	17 ARI	18 GEM	18 CAN	19 VIR	17 LIB	18 SAG	17 CAP	17 AQU
19 SAG	20 AQU	18 AQU	20 ARI	19 TAU	21 CAN	20 LEO	21 LIB	19 SCO	21 CAP	19 AQU	19 PIS
22 CAP	23 PIS	21 PIS	22 TAU	22 GEM	23 LEO	22 VIR	23 SCO	21 SAG	23 AQU	21 PIS	21 ARI
24 AQU	25 ARI	23 ARI	25 GEM	24 CAN	25 VIR	25 LIB	25 SAG	23 AQU	25 PIS	24 ARI	24 TAU
26 PIS	28 TAU	26 TAU	27 CAN	27 LEO	27 LIB	26 SCO	27 CAP	25 PIS	28 ARI	26 TAU	26 GEM
29 ARI		28 GEM	29 LEO	29 VIR	29 SCO	29 SAG	29 AQU	28 PIS	30 TAU	29 GEM	29 CAN
31 TAU		31 CAN		31 LIB		31 CAP		30 ARI			31 LEO

2021

JAN	FEB	MAR	APR	MAY	JUN	JUL	AUG	SEP	OCT	NOV	DEC
2 VIR	1 LIB	2 SCO	1 SAG	2 AQU	1 PIS	3 TAU	2 GEM	1 CAN	3 VIR	1 LIB	1 SCO
5 LIB	3 SCO	4 SAG	3 CAP	4 PIS	3 ARI	5 GEM	4 CAN	3 LEO	5 LIB	3 SCO	3 SAG
7 SCO	5 SAG	6 CAP	5 AQU	7 ARI	6 TAU	8 CAN	7 LEO	5 VIR	7 SCO	5 SAG	5 CAP
9 SAG	7 CAP	9 AQU	7 PIS	9 TAU	8 GEM	10 LEO	9 VIR	7 LIB	9 SAG	7 CAP	7 AQU
11 CAP	9 AQU	11 PIS	10 ARI	12 GEM	11 CAN	13 VIR	11 LIB	10 SCO	11 CAP	9 AQU	9 PIS
13 AQU	12 PIS	13 ARI	12 TAU	14 CAN	13 LEO	15 LIB	13 SCO	12 SAG	13 AQU	12 PIS	11 ARI
15 PIS	14 ARI	16 TAU	15 GEM	17 LEO	15 VIR	17 SCO	15 SAG	14 CAP	15 PIS	14 ARI	14 TAU
18 ARI	16 TAU	18 GEM	17 CAN	19 VIR	18 LIB	19 SAG	18 CAP	16 AQU	18 ARI	16 TAU	16 GEM
20 TAU	19 GEM	21 CAN	20 LEO	21 LIB	20 SCO	21 CAP	20 AQU	18 PIS	20 TAU	19 GEM	19 CAN
23 GEM	21 CAN	23 LEO	22 VIR	23 SCO	22 SAG	23 AQU	22 PIS	20 ARI	23 GEM	21 CAN	21 LEO
25 CAN	24 LEO	25 VIR	24 LIB	25 SAG	24 CAP	25 PIS	24 ARI	23 TAU	25 CAN	24 LEO	24 VIR
27 LEO	26 VIR	28 LIB	26 SCO	27 CAP	26 AQU	28 ARI	26 TAU	25 GEM	28 LEO	26 VIR	26 LIB
30 VIR	28 LIB	30 SCO	28 SAG	29 AQU	28 PIS	30 TAU	29 GEM	28 CAN	30 VIR	29 LIB	28 SCO
			30 CAP		30 ARI			30 LEO			30 SAG

2022

JAN	FEB	MAR	APR	MAY	JUN	JUL	AUG	SEP	OCT	NOV	DEC
1 CAP	2 PIS	1 PIS	2 TAU	2 GEM	1 CAN	3 VIR	1 LIB	2 SAG	2 CAP	2 PIS	1 ARI
3 AQU	4 ARI	3 ARI	4 GEM	4 CAN	3 LEO	5 LIB	4 SCO	4 CAP	4 AQU	4 ARI	4 TAU
5 PIS	6 TAU	6 TAU	7 CAN	7 LEO	6 VIR	8 SCO	6 SAG	6 AQU	6 PIS	7 TAU	6 GEM
8 ARI	9 GEM	8 GEM	9 LEO	9 VIR	8 LIB	10 SAG	8 CAP	8 PIS	8 ARI	9 GEM	9 CAN
10 TAU	11 CAN	11 CAN	12 VIR	12 LIB	10 SCO	12 CAP	10 AQU	11 ARI	10 TAU	11 CAN	11 LEO
12 GEM	14 LEO	13 LEO	14 LIB	14 SCO	12 SAG	14 AQU	12 PIS	13 TAU	13 GEM	14 LEO	14 VIR
15 CAN	16 VIR	15 VIR	16 SCO	16 SAG	14 CAP	16 PIS	14 ARI	15 GEM	15 CAN	16 VIR	16 LIB
17 LEO	18 LIB	18 LIB	18 SAG	18 CAP	16 AQU	18 ARI	16 TAU	18 CAN	17 LEO	19 LIB	18 SCO
20 VIR	21 SCO	20 SCO	20 CAP	20 AQU	18 PIS	20 TAU	19 GEM	20 LEO	20 VIR	21 SCO	21 SAG
22 LIB	23 SAG	22 SAG	23 AQU	22 PIS	20 ARI	23 GEM	21 CAN	23 VIR	22 LIB	23 SAG	23 CAP
24 SCO	25 CAP	24 CAP	25 PIS	24 ARI	23 TAU	25 CAN	24 LEO	25 LIB	25 SCO	25 CAP	25 AQU
27 SAG	27 AQU	26 AQU	27 ARI	27 TAU	25 GEM	28 LEO	26 VIR	27 SCO	27 SAG	27 AQU	27 PIS
29 CAP		28 PIS	29 TAU	29 GEM	28 CAN	30 VIR	29 LIB	29 SAG	29 CAP	29 PIS	29 ARI
31 AQU		31 ARI			30 LEO		31 SCO		31 AQU		31 TAU

2023

JAN	FEB	MAR	APR	MAY	JUN	JUL	AUG	SEP	OCT	NOV	DEC
2 GEM	1 CAN	3 LEO	2 VIR	2 LIB	3 SAG	2 CAP	2 PIS	1 ARI	3 GEM	1 CAN	1 LEO
5 CAN	4 LEO	5 VIR	4 LIB	4 SCO	5 CAP	4 AQU	4 ARI	3 TAU	5 CAN	4 LEO	3 VIR
7 LEO	6 VIR	8 LIB	7 SCO	6 SAG	7 AQU	6 PIS	6 TAU	5 GEM	7 LEO	6 VIR	6 LIB
10 VIR	9 LIB	10 SCO	9 SAG	8 CAP	9 PIS	8 ARI	9 GEM	8 CAN	10 VIR	9 LIB	8 SCO
12 LIB	11 SCO	13 SAG	11 CAP	10 AQU	11 ARI	10 TAU	11 CAN	10 LEO	12 LIB	11 SCO	11 SAG
15 SCO	13 SAG	15 CAP	13 AQU	12 PIS	13 TAU	13 GEM	14 LEO	13 VIR	15 SCO	13 SAG	13 CAP
17 SAG	16 CAP	17 AQU	15 PIS	15 ARI	15 GEM	15 CAN	16 VIR	15 LIB	17 SAG	16 CAP	15 AQU
19 CAP	18 AQU	19 PIS	17 ARI	17 TAU	18 CAN	18 LEO	19 LIB	17 SCO	19 CAP	18 AQU	17 PIS
21 AQU	20 PIS	21 ARI	19 TAU	19 GEM	20 LEO	20 VIR	21 SCO	20 SAG	22 AQU	20 PIS	19 ARI
23 PIS	22 ARI	23 TAU	22 GEM	21 CAN	23 VIR	23 LIB	24 SAG	22 CAP	24 PIS	22 ARI	21 TAU
25 ARI	24 TAU	25 GEM	24 CAN	24 LEO	25 LIB	25 SCO	26 CAP	24 AQU	26 ARI	24 TAU	24 GEM
27 TAU	26 GEM	28 CAN	27 LEO	26 VIR	28 SCO	27 SAG	28 AQU	26 PIS	28 TAU	26 GEM	26 CAN
30 GEM	28 CAN	30 LEO	29 VIR	29 LIB	30 SAG	29 CAP	30 PIS	28 ARI	30 TAU	29 CAN	28 LEO
				31 SCO		31 AQU		30 TAU			31 VIR

2024

JAN	FEB	MAR	APR	MAY	JUN	JUL	AUG	SEP	OCT	NOV	DEC
2 LIB	1 SCO	2 SAG	3 AQU	2 PIS	3 TAU	2 GEM	3 LEO	1 VIR	1 LIB	3 SAG	2 CAP
5 SCO	4 SAG	4 CAP	5 PIS	5 ARI	5 GEM	4 CAN	5 VIR	4 LIB	4 SCO	5 CAP	4 AQU
7 SAG	6 CAP	6 AQU	7 ARI	6 TAU	7 CAN	6 LEO	8 LIB	7 SCO	6 SAG	7 AQU	7 PIS
9 CAP	8 AQU	8 PIS	9 TAU	8 GEM	9 LEO	9 VIR	10 SCO	9 SAG	9 CAP	9 PIS	9 ARI
11 AQU	10 PIS	10 ARI	11 GEM	10 CAN	12 VIR	11 LIB	13 SAG	11 CAP	11 AQU	12 ARI	11 TAU
13 PIS	12 ARI	12 TAU	13 CAN	13 LEO	14 LIB	14 SCO	15 CAP	14 AQU	13 PIS	14 TAU	13 GEM
15 ARI	14 TAU	14 GEM	15 LEO	15 VIR	17 SCO	16 SAG	17 AQU	16 PIS	15 ARI	16 GEM	15 CAN
18 TAU	17 GEM	17 CAN	18 VIR	18 LIB	19 SAG	19 CAP	19 PIS	19 ARI	17 TAU	18 CAN	17 LEO
20 GEM	18 CAN	19 LEO	20 LIB	20 SCO	21 CAP	21 AQU	21 ARI	21 TAU	19 GEM	20 LEO	20 VIR
22 CAN	21 LEO	22 VIR	23 SCO	23 SAG	23 AQU	23 PIS	23 TAU	23 GEM	21 CAN	22 VIR	22 LIB
25 LEO	23 VIR	24 LIB	25 SAG	25 CAP	26 PIS	25 ARI	25 GEM	24 CAN	24 LEO	25 LIB	25 SCO
27 VIR	26 LIB	27 SCO	28 CAP	27 AQU	28 ARI	27 TAU	28 CAN	26 LEO	26 VIR	27 SCO	27 SAG
30 LIB	28 SCO	29 SAG	30 AQU	29 PIS	30 TAU	30 GEM	30 LEO	29 VIR	28 LIB	30 SAG	29 CAP
		31 CAP		31 ARI		31 CAN			31 SCO		

2025

JAN	FEB	MAR	APR	MAY	JUN	JUL	AUG	SEP	OCT	NOV	DEC
1 AQU	1 ARI	1 ARI	1 GEM	1 CAN	1 VIR	1 LIB	3 SAG	1 CAP	1 AQU	2 ARI	1 TAU
3 PIS	3 TAU	3 TAU	3 CAN	3 LEO	4 LIB	4 SCO	5 CAP	4 AQU	3 PIS	4 TAU	3 GEM
5 ARI	6 GEM	5 GEM	5 LEO	5 VIR	5 SCO	6 SAG	7 AQU	6 PIS	5 ARI	6 GEM	5 CAN
7 TAU	8 CAN	7 CAN	8 VIR	8 LIB	9 SAG	9 CAP	10 PIS	8 ARI	8 TAU	8 CAN	7 LEO
9 GEM	10 LEO	9 LEO	10 LIB	10 SCO	11 CAP	11 AQU	12 ARI	10 TAU	10 GEM	10 LEO	9 VIR
11 CAN	12 VIR	12 VIR	13 SCO	13 SAG	14 AQU	13 PIS	14 TAU	12 GEM	12 CAN	12 VIR	12 LIB
14 LEO	15 LIB	14 LIB	15 SAG	15 CAP	16 PIS	15 ARI	16 GEM	14 CAN	14 LEO	15 LIB	14 SCO
16 VIR	17 SCO	17 SCO	18 CAP	18 AQU	18 ARI	18 TAU	18 CAN	17 LEO	16 VIR	17 SCO	17 SAG
18 LIB	20 SAG	19 SAG	20 AQU	20 PIS	20 TAU	20 GEM	20 LEO	19 VIR	18 LIB	20 SAG	19 CAP
21 SCO	22 CAP	22 CAP	23 PIS	22 ARI	22 GEM	22 CAN	23 VIR	21 LIB	21 SCO	22 CAP	22 AQU
23 SAG	25 AQU	24 AQU	25 ARI	24 TAU	24 CAN	24 LEO	25 LIB	24 SCO	23 SAG	25 AQU	24 PIS
26 CAP	27 PIS	26 PIS	27 TAU	26 GEM	26 LEO	26 VIR	27 SCO	26 SAG	26 CAP	27 PIS	27 ARI
28 AQU		28 ARI	29 GEM	28 CAN	29 VIR	29 LIB	29 SAG	29 CAP	28 AQU	29 ARI	29 TAU
30 PIS		30 TAU		30 LEO		31 SCO	30 SAG		31 PIS		31 GEM

2026

JAN	FEB	MAR	APR	MAY	JUN	JUL	AUG	SEP	OCT	NOV	DEC
2 CAN	2 VIR	2 VIR	3 SCO	3 SAG	1 CAP	1 AQU	2 ARI	1 TAU	2 CAN	3 VIR	2 LIB
4 LEO	5 LIB	4 LIB	5 SAG	5 CAP	4 AQU	4 PIS	4 TAU	3 GEM	4 LEO	5 LIB	4 SCO
6 VIR	7 SCO	6 SCO	8 CAP	8 AQU	6 PIS	6 ARI	7 GEM	5 CAN	6 VIR	7 SCO	7 SAG
8 LIB	10 SAG	9 SAG	10 AQU	10 PIS	9 ARI	8 TAU	9 CAN	7 LEO	9 LIB	10 SAG	9 CAP
11 SCO	12 CAP	11 CAP	13 PIS	12 ARI	11 TAU	10 GEM	11 LEO	9 VIR	11 SCO	12 CAP	12 AQU
13 SAG	15 AQU	14 AQU	15 ARI	14 TAU	13 GEM	12 CAN	13 VIR	11 LIB	13 SAG	15 AQU	14 PIS
16 CAP	17 PIS	16 PIS	17 TAU	16 GEM	15 CAN	14 LEO	15 LIB	14 SCO	16 CAP	17 PIS	17 ARI
18 AQU	19 ARI	18 ARI	19 GEM	18 CAN	17 LEO	16 VIR	17 SCO	16 SAG	18 AQU	20 ARI	19 TAU
21 PIS	21 TAU	21 TAU	21 CAN	20 LEO	19 VIR	18 LIB	20 SAG	18 CAP	21 PIS	22 TAU	21 GEM
23 ARI	23 GEM	23 GEM	23 LEO	23 VIR	21 LIB	21 SCO	22 CAP	21 AQU	23 ARI	24 GEM	23 CAN
25 TAU	26 CAN	25 CAN	25 VIR	25 LIB	24 SCO	23 SAG	25 AQU	23 PIS	25 TAU	26 CAN	25 LEO
27 GEM	28 LEO	27 LEO	28 LIB	28 SCO	26 SAG	26 CAP	27 PIS	26 ARI	27 GEM	28 LEO	27 VIR
29 CAN		29 VIR	30 SCO	30 SAG	29 CAP	28 AQU	29 ARI	28 TAU	29 CAN	30 VIR	29 LIB
31 LEO		31 LIB				31 PIS		30 GEM	31 LEO		

2027

JAN	FEB	MAR	APR	MAY	JUN	JUL	AUG	SEP	OCT	NOV	DEC
1 SCO	2 CAP	1 CAP	3 PIS	2 ARI	1 TAU	1 GEM	1 LEO	2 LIB	1 SCO	2 CAP	2 AQU
3 SAG	4 AQU	4 AQU	5 ARI	5 TAU	3 GEM	3 CAN	3 VIR	4 SCO	3 SAG	4 AQU	4 PIS
6 CAP	7 PIS	6 PIS	7 TAU	7 GEM	5 CAN	5 LEO	5 LIB	6 SAG	6 CAP	7 PIS	7 ARI
8 AQU	9 ARI	9 ARI	9 GEM	9 CAN	7 LEO	7 VIR	7 SCO	8 CAP	8 AQU	9 ARI	9 TAU
11 PIS	12 TAU	11 TAU	12 CAN	11 LEO	9 VIR	9 LIB	10 SAG	11 AQU	11 PIS	12 TAU	11 GEM
13 ARI	14 GEM	13 GEM	14 LEO	13 VIR	11 LIB	11 SCO	12 CAP	13 PIS	13 ARI	14 GEM	14 CAN
15 TAU	16 CAN	15 CAN	16 VIR	15 LIB	14 SCO	13 SAG	15 AQU	16 ARI	15 TAU	16 CAN	16 LEO
18 GEM	18 LEO	17 LEO	18 LIB	17 SCO	16 SAG	16 CAP	17 PIS	18 TAU	18 GEM	18 LEO	18 VIR
20 CAN	20 VIR	20 VIR	20 SCO	20 SAG	19 CAP	18 AQU	20 ARI	21 GEM	20 CAN	20 VIR	20 LIB
22 LEO	22 LIB	22 LIB	22 SAG	22 CAP	21 AQU	21 PIS	22 TAU	23 CAN	22 LEO	23 LIB	22 SCO
24 VIR	24 SCO	24 SCO	25 CAP	25 AQU	24 PIS	23 ARI	24 GEM	25 LEO	25 VIR	25 SCO	24 SAG
26 LIB	27 SAG	26 SAG	27 AQU	27 PIS	26 ARI	26 TAU	26 CAN	27 VIR	26 LIB	27 SAG	27 CAP
28 SCO		29 CAP	30 PIS	30 ARI	28 TAU	28 GEM	28 LEO	29 LIB	28 SCO	29 CAP	29 AQU
30 SAG		31 AQU				30 CAN	30 VIR		31 SAG		

2028

```
JAN       FEB       MAR       APR       MAY       JUN
 1 PIS     2 TAU     3 GEM     1 CAN     1 LEO     1 LIB
 3 ARI     4 GEM     5 CAN     3 LEO     3 VIR     3 SCO
 6 TAU     6 CAN     7 LEO     5 VIR     5 LIB     5 SAG
 8 GEM     9 LEO     9 VIR     7 LIB     7 SCO     8 CAP
10 CAN    10 VIR    11 LIB     9 SCO     9 SAG    10 AQU
12 LEO    12 LIB    13 SCO    12 SAG    11 CAP    12 PIS
14 VIR    15 SCO    15 SAG    14 CAP    14 AQU    15 ARI
16 LIB    17 SAG    17 CAP    16 AQU    16 PIS    17 TAU
18 SCO    19 CAP    20 AQU    19 PIS    19 ARI    20 GEM
21 SAG    22 AQU    22 PIS    21 ARI    21 TAU    22 CAN
23 CAP    24 PIS    25 ARI    24 TAU    23 GEM    24 LEO
25 AQU    27 ARI    27 TAU    26 GEM    26 CAN    26 VIR
28 PIS    29 TAU    30 GEM    28 CAN    28 LEO    28 LIB
30 ARI                                 30 VIR    30 SCO

JUL       AUG       SEP       OCT       NOV       DEC
 3 SAG     1 CAP     2 PIS     2 ARI     1 TAU     1 GEM
 5 CAP     4 AQU     5 ARI     5 TAU     3 GEM     3 CAN
 7 AQU     6 PIS     7 TAU     7 GEM     6 CAN     5 LEO
10 PIS     9 ARI    10 GEM     9 CAN     8 LEO     7 VIR
12 ARI    11 TAU    12 CAN    12 LEO    10 VIR     9 LIB
15 GEM    13 GEM    14 LEO    14 VIR    12 LIB    11 SCO
17 CAN    16 CAN    16 VIR    16 LIB    14 SCO    14 SAG
19 LEO    18 LEO    18 LIB    18 SCO    16 SAG    16 CAP
21 VIR    20 VIR    20 SCO    20 SAG    18 CAP    18 AQU
23 LIB    22 LIB    22 SAG    22 CAP    21 AQU    20 PIS
26 SCO    24 SCO    25 CAP    24 AQU    23 PIS    23 ARI
28 SCO    26 SAG    28 AQU    27 PIS    26 ARI    25 TAU
30 SAG    28 CAP    30 PIS    30 ARI    28 TAU    28 GEM
          31 AQU                                  30 CAN
```

2029

```
JAN       FEB       MAR       APR       MAY       JUN
 1 LEO     2 LIB     1 LIB     2 SAG     1 CAP     2 PIS
 4 VIR     4 SCO     3 SCO     4 CAP     4 AQU     5 ARI
 6 LIB     6 SAG     6 SAG     6 AQU     6 PIS     7 TAU
 8 SCO     8 CAP     8 CAP     9 PIS     8 ARI    10 GEM
10 SAG    11 AQU    10 AQU    11 ARI    11 TAU    12 CAN
12 CAP    13 PIS    12 PIS    14 TAU    13 GEM    14 LEO
14 AQU    16 ARI    15 ARI    16 GEM    16 CAN    17 VIR
17 PIS    18 TAU    17 TAU    19 CAN    18 LEO    19 LIB
19 ARI    21 GEM    20 GEM    21 LEO    20 VIR    21 SCO
22 TAU    23 CAN    22 CAN    23 VIR    23 LIB    23 SAG
24 GEM    25 LEO    25 LEO    25 LIB    25 SCO    25 CAP
27 CAN    27 VIR    27 VIR    27 SCO    27 SAG    27 AQU
29 LEO              29 LIB    29 SAG    29 CAP    30 PIS
31 VIR              31 SCO              31 AQU

JUL       AUG       SEP       OCT       NOV       DEC
 2 ARI     1 TAU     2 CAN     2 LEO     3 LIB     2 SCO
 5 TAU     3 GEM     4 LEO     4 VIR     5 SCO     4 SAG
 7 GEM     6 CAN     7 VIR     6 LIB     7 SAG     6 CAP
 9 CAN     8 LEO     9 LIB     8 SCO     9 CAP     8 AQU
12 LEO    10 VIR    11 SCO    10 SAG    11 AQU    10 PIS
14 VIR    12 LIB    13 SAG    12 CAP    13 PIS    13 ARI
16 LIB    14 SCO    15 CAP    14 AQU    15 ARI    15 TAU
19 SCO    16 SAG    17 AQU    17 PIS    18 TAU    18 GEM
21 SAG    19 CAP    20 PIS    19 ARI    21 GEM    20 CAN
23 CAP    21 AQU    22 ARI    22 TAU    23 CAN    23 LEO
25 AQU    23 PIS    24 TAU    24 GEM    25 LEO    25 VIR
27 PIS    26 ARI    27 GEM    27 CAN    28 VIR    27 LIB
29 ARI    28 TAU    30 CAN    29 LEO    30 LIB    29 SCO
          31 GEM              31 VIR              31 SAG
```

2030

```
JAN       FEB       MAR       APR       MAY       JUN
 2 CAP     1 AQU     3 PIS     1 ARI     1 TAU     2 CAN
 5 AQU     3 PIS     5 ARI     4 TAU     3 GEM     5 LEO
 7 PIS     5 ARI     7 TAU     6 GEM     6 CAN     7 VIR
 9 ARI     8 TAU    10 GEM     9 CAN     8 LEO     9 LIB
12 TAU    10 GEM    12 CAN    11 LEO    11 VIR    11 SCO
14 GEM    13 CAN    15 LEO    13 VIR    13 LIB    13 SAG
17 CAN    15 LEO    17 VIR    16 LIB    15 SCO    15 CAP
19 LEO    18 VIR    19 LIB    18 SCO    17 SAG    17 AQU
21 VIR    20 LIB    21 SCO    20 SAG    19 CAP    20 PIS
23 LIB    22 SCO    23 SAG    22 CAP    21 AQU    22 ARI
26 SCO    24 SAG    25 CAP    24 AQU    23 PIS    24 TAU
28 SAG    26 CAP    27 AQU    26 PIS    26 ARI    27 GEM
30 CAP    28 AQU    30 PIS    28 ARI    28 TAU    29 CAN
                                        31 GEM

JUL       AUG       SEP       OCT       NOV       DEC
 2 LEO     1 VIR     1 SCO     1 SAG     1 AQU     1 PIS
 4 VIR     3 LIB     3 SAG     3 CAP     3 PIS     3 ARI
 7 LIB     5 SCO     5 CAP     5 AQU     6 ARI     5 TAU
 9 SCO     7 SAG     7 AQU     7 PIS     8 TAU     8 GEM
11 SAG     9 CAP    10 PIS     9 ARI    10 GEM    10 CAN
13 CAP    11 AQU    12 ARI    12 TAU    13 CAN    13 LEO
15 AQU    13 PIS    14 TAU    14 GEM    16 LEO    15 VIR
17 PIS    15 ARI    17 GEM    17 CAN    18 VIR    18 LIB
19 ARI    18 TAU    19 CAN    19 LEO    20 LIB    20 SCO
22 TAU    20 GEM    22 LEO    22 VIR    22 SCO    22 SAG
24 GEM    22 CAN    24 VIR    24 LIB    24 SAG    24 CAP
27 CAN    25 LEO    26 LIB    26 SCO    26 CAP    26 AQU
29 LEO    27 VIR    28 SCO    28 SAG    28 AQU    28 PIS
          30 LIB              30 CAP              30 ARI
```

2031

```
JAN       FEB       MAR       APR       MAY       JUN
 1 TAU     3 CAN     2 CAN     1 LEO     1 VIR     2 SCO
 4 GEM     5 LEO     5 LEO     3 VIR     3 LIB     4 SAG
 7 CAN     8 VIR     7 VIR     6 LIB     5 SCO     6 CAP
 9 LEO    10 LIB     9 LIB     8 SCO     7 SAG     8 AQU
11 VIR    12 SCO    12 SCO    10 SAG     9 CAP    10 PIS
14 LIB    15 SAG    14 SAG    12 CAP    11 AQU    12 ARI
16 SCO    17 CAP    16 CAP    14 AQU    14 PIS    14 TAU
18 SAG    19 AQU    18 AQU    16 PIS    16 ARI    17 GEM
20 CAP    21 PIS    20 PIS    19 ARI    18 TAU    19 CAN
22 AQU    23 ARI    22 ARI    21 TAU    21 GEM    22 LEO
24 PIS    25 TAU    25 TAU    23 GEM    23 CAN    24 VIR
26 ARI    28 GEM    27 GEM    26 CAN    26 LEO    27 LIB
29 TAU              29 CAN    28 LEO    28 VIR    29 SCO
31 GEM                                  31 LIB

JUL       AUG       SEP       OCT       NOV       DEC
 1 SAG     2 AQU     2 ARI     2 TAU     3 CAN     3 LEO
 3 CAP     4 PIS     4 TAU     4 GEM     5 LEO     5 VIR
 5 AQU     6 ARI     6 GEM     6 CAN     8 VIR     8 LIB
 7 PIS     9 TAU     9 CAN     9 LEO    10 LIB    10 SCO
10 ARI    11 GEM    11 LEO    12 VIR    13 SCO    12 SAG
12 TAU    13 CAN    14 VIR    14 LIB    15 SAG    14 CAP
14 GEM    15 LEO    17 LIB    17 SCO    17 CAP    16 AQU
17 CAN    18 VIR    19 SCO    18 SAG    19 AQU    18 PIS
19 LEO    20 LIB    21 SAG    21 CAP    21 PIS    20 ARI
22 VIR    23 SCO    23 CAP    23 AQU    23 ARI    23 TAU
24 LIB    25 SAG    25 AQU    25 PIS    25 TAU    25 GEM
26 SCO    27 CAP    27 PIS    27 ARI    28 GEM    27 CAN
29 SAG    29 AQU    30 ARI    29 TAU    30 CAN    30 LEO
31 CAP    31 PIS              31 GEM
```

2032

JAN	FEB	MAR	APR	MAY	JUN	JUL	AUG	SEP	OCT	NOV	DEC
1 VIR	3 SCO	1 SCO	2 CAP	1 AQU	2 ARI	1 TAU	2 CAN	1 LEO	3 LIB	2 SCO	1 SAG
4 LIB	5 SAG	3 SAG	4 AQU	3 PIS	4 TAU	3 GEM	4 LEO	3 VIR	5 SCO	4 SAG	4 CAP
6 SCO	7 CAP	5 CAP	6 PIS	5 ARI	6 GEM	6 CAN	7 VIR	6 LIB	8 SAG	6 CAP	6 AQU
9 SAG	9 AQU	8 AQU	8 ARI	7 TAU	8 CAN	8 LEO	9 LIB	8 SCO	10 CAP	8 AQU	8 PIS
11 CAP	11 PIS	10 PIS	10 TAU	10 GEM	11 LEO	11 VIR	12 SCO	11 SAG	12 AQU	11 PIS	10 ARI
13 AQU	13 ARI	12 ARI	12 GEM	12 CAN	13 VIR	13 LIB	14 SAG	13 CAP	14 PIS	13 ARI	12 TAU
15 PIS	15 TAU	14 TAU	15 CAN	14 LEO	16 LIB	16 SCO	16 CAP	15 AQU	16 ARI	15 TAU	14 GEM
17 ARI	18 GEM	16 GEM	17 LEO	17 VIR	18 SCO	18 SAG	18 AQU	17 PIS	18 TAU	17 GEM	17 CAN
19 TAU	20 CAN	18 CAN	20 VIR	19 LIB	20 SAG	20 CAP	20 PIS	19 ARI	20 GEM	19 CAN	19 LEO
21 GEM	22 LEO	21 LEO	22 LIB	22 SCO	23 CAP	22 AQU	22 ARI	21 TAU	23 CAN	21 LEO	21 VIR
24 CAN	25 VIR	23 VIR	24 SCO	24 SAG	25 AQU	24 PIS	25 TAU	23 GEM	25 LEO	24 VIR	24 LIB
26 LEO	27 LIB	26 LIB	27 SAG	26 CAP	27 PIS	26 ARI	27 GEM	25 CAN	28 VIR	27 LIB	26 SCO
29 VIR		28 SCO	29 CAP	28 AQU	29 ARI	28 TAU	29 CAN	28 LEO	30 LIB	29 SCO	29 SAG
31 LIB		30 SAG		30 PIS		30 GEM					31 CAP

2033

JAN	FEB	MAR	APR	MAY	JUN	JUL	AUG	SEP	OCT	NOV	DEC
2 AQU	2 ARI	2 ARI	2 GEM	2 CAN	1 LEO	3 LIB	2 SCO	1 SAG	3 AQU	1 PIS	1 ARI
4 PIS	5 TAU	4 TAU	5 CAN	4 LEO	3 VIR	5 SCO	4 SAG	3 CAP	5 PIS	3 ARI	3 TAU
6 ARI	7 GEM	6 GEM	7 LEO	7 VIR	6 LIB	8 SAG	7 CAP	5 AQU	7 ARI	5 TAU	5 GEM
8 TAU	9 CAN	8 CAN	9 VIR	9 LIB	8 SCO	10 CAP	9 AQU	7 PIS	9 TAU	7 GEM	7 CAN
11 GEM	11 LEO	11 LEO	12 LIB	12 SCO	11 SAG	12 AQU	11 PIS	9 ARI	11 GEM	9 CAN	9 LEO
13 CAN	14 VIR	13 VIR	15 SCO	14 SAG	13 CAP	14 PIS	13 ARI	11 TAU	13 CAN	11 LEO	11 VIR
15 LEO	16 LIB	16 LIB	17 SAG	17 CAP	15 AQU	17 ARI	15 TAU	13 GEM	15 LEO	14 VIR	14 LIB
18 VIR	19 SCO	18 SCO	19 CAP	19 AQU	17 PIS	19 TAU	17 GEM	16 CAN	18 VIR	16 LIB	16 SCO
20 LIB	21 SAG	21 SAG	22 AQU	21 PIS	19 ARI	21 GEM	19 CAN	18 LEO	20 LIB	19 SCO	19 SAG
23 SCO	24 CAP	23 CAP	24 PIS	23 ARI	21 TAU	23 CAN	22 LEO	20 VIR	23 SCO	21 SAG	21 CAP
25 SAG	26 AQU	25 AQU	26 ARI	25 TAU	24 GEM	25 LEO	24 VIR	23 LIB	25 SAG	24 CAP	23 AQU
27 CAP	28 PIS	27 PIS	28 TAU	27 GEM	26 CAN	28 VIR	27 LIB	25 SCO	28 CAP	26 AQU	26 PIS
29 AQU		29 ARI	30 GEM	29 CAN	28 LEO	30 LIB	29 SCO	28 SAG	30 AQU	28 PIS	28 ARI
31 PIS		31 TAU			30 VIR			30 CAP			30 TAU

2034

JAN	FEB	MAR	APR	MAY	JUN	JUL	AUG	SEP	OCT	NOV	DEC
1 GEM	2 LEO	1 LEO	2 LIB	2 SCO	3 CAP	3 AQU	1 PIS	2 TAU	1 GEM	2 LEO	1 VIR
3 CAN	4 VIR	3 VIR	4 SCO	4 SAG	5 AQU	5 PIS	3 ARI	4 GEM	3 CAN	4 VIR	4 LIB
5 LEO	6 LIB	6 LIB	7 SAG	7 CAP	8 PIS	7 ARI	6 TAU	6 CAN	5 LEO	6 LIB	6 SCO
8 VIR	9 SCO	8 SCO	9 CAP	9 AQU	10 ARI	9 TAU	8 GEM	8 LEO	8 VIR	9 SCO	9 SAG
10 LIB	11 SAG	11 SAG	12 AQU	11 PIS	12 TAU	11 GEM	10 CAN	10 VIR	10 LIB	11 SAG	11 CAP
12 SCO	14 CAP	13 CAP	14 PIS	14 ARI	14 GEM	13 CAN	12 LEO	13 LIB	13 SCO	14 CAP	14 AQU
15 SAG	16 AQU	15 AQU	16 ARI	16 TAU	16 CAN	16 LEO	14 VIR	15 SCO	15 SAG	16 AQU	16 PIS
17 CAP	18 PIS	18 PIS	18 TAU	18 GEM	18 LEO	18 VIR	16 LIB	18 SAG	18 CAP	19 PIS	18 ARI
20 AQU	20 ARI	20 ARI	20 GEM	20 CAN	20 VIR	20 LIB	19 SCO	20 CAP	20 AQU	21 ARI	20 TAU
22 PIS	22 TAU	22 TAU	22 CAN	22 LEO	23 LIB	23 SCO	21 SAG	23 AQU	23 PIS	23 TAU	22 GEM
24 ARI	24 GEM	24 GEM	24 LEO	24 VIR	25 SCO	25 SAG	24 CAP	25 PIS	25 ARI	25 GEM	24 CAN
26 TAU	27 CAN	26 CAN	27 VIR	26 LIB	28 SAG	28 CAP	26 AQU	27 ARI	27 TAU	27 CAN	26 LEO
28 GEM		28 LEO	29 LIB	29 SCO	30 CAP	30 AQU	29 PIS	29 TAU	29 GEM	29 LEO	29 VIR
30 CAN		30 VIR		31 SAG			31 ARI		31 CAN		31 LIB

2035

JAN	FEB	MAR	APR	MAY	JUN	JUL	AUG	SEP	OCT	NOV	DEC
2 SCO	1 SAG	3 CAP	2 AQU	2 PIS	2 TAU	2 GEM	2 LEO	1 VIR	2 SCO	1 SAG	1 CAP
5 SAG	4 CAP	5 AQU	4 PIS	4 ARI	4 GEM	4 CAN	4 VIR	3 LIB	5 SAG	4 CAP	4 AQU
7 CAP	6 AQU	8 PIS	6 ARI	6 TAU	6 CAN	6 LEO	6 LIB	5 SCO	7 CAP	6 AQU	6 PIS
10 AQU	8 PIS	10 ARI	8 TAU	8 GEM	8 LEO	8 VIR	9 SCO	8 SAG	10 AQU	9 PIS	8 ARI
12 PIS	11 ARI	12 TAU	11 GEM	10 CAN	10 VIR	10 LIB	11 SAG	10 CAP	12 PIS	11 ARI	11 TAU
15 ARI	13 TAU	14 GEM	13 CAN	12 LEO	13 LIB	12 SCO	14 CAP	13 AQU	15 ARI	13 TAU	13 GEM
17 TAU	15 GEM	16 CAN	15 LEO	14 VIR	15 SCO	15 SAG	16 AQU	15 PIS	17 TAU	15 GEM	15 CAN
19 GEM	17 CAN	19 LEO	17 VIR	17 LIB	18 SAG	17 CAP	19 PIS	17 ARI	19 GEM	17 CAN	17 LEO
21 CAN	19 LEO	21 VIR	19 LIB	19 SCO	20 CAP	20 AQU	21 ARI	20 TAU	21 CAN	19 LEO	19 VIR
23 LEO	21 VIR	23 LIB	22 SCO	21 SAG	23 AQU	22 PIS	23 TAU	22 GEM	23 LEO	22 VIR	21 LIB
25 VIR	24 LIB	25 SCO	24 SAG	24 CAP	25 PIS	25 ARI	25 GEM	24 CAN	25 VIR	24 LIB	23 SCO
27 LIB	26 SCO	28 SAG	27 CAP	26 AQU	28 ARI	27 TAU	28 CAN	26 LEO	28 LIB	26 SCO	26 SAG
30 SCO	28 SAG	30 CAP	29 AQU	29 PIS	30 TAU	29 GEM	30 LEO	28 VIR	30 SCO	29 SAG	28 CAP
				31 ARI		31 CAN		30 LIB			31 AQU

JAN	FEB	MAR	APR	MAY	JUN	JUL	AUG	SEP	OCT	NOV	DEC
2 PIS	1 ARI	2 TAU	2 CAN	2 LEO	2 LIB	2 SCO	3 CAP	1 AQU	1 PIS	2 TAU	2 GEM
5 ARI	3 TAU	4 GEM	4 LEO	4 VIR	4 SCO	4 SAG	5 AQU	4 PIS	4 ARI	5 GEM	4 CAN
7 TAU	6 GEM	6 CAN	6 VIR	6 LIB	7 SAG	7 CAP	8 PIS	6 ARI	6 TAU	7 CAN	6 LEO
9 GEM	8 CAN	8 LEO	9 LIB	8 SCO	9 CAP	9 AQU	10 ARI	9 TAU	8 GEM	9 LEO	8 VIR
11 CAN	10 LEO	10 VIR	11 SCO	10 SAG	12 AQU	11 PIS	13 TAU	11 GEM	11 CAN	11 VIR	10 LIB
13 LEO	12 VIR	12 LIB	13 SAG	13 CAP	14 PIS	14 ARI	15 GEM	13 CAN	13 LEO	13 LIB	13 SCO
15 VIR	14 LIB	14 SCO	15 CAP	15 AQU	17 ARI	16 TAU	17 CAN	15 LEO	15 VIR	15 SCO	15 SAG
17 LIB	16 SCO	17 SAG	18 AQU	18 PIS	19 TAU	19 GEM	19 LEO	18 VIR	17 LIB	18 SAG	17 CAP
20 SCO	18 SAG	19 CAP	20 PIS	20 ARI	21 GEM	21 CAN	21 VIR	20 LIB	19 SCO	20 CAP	20 AQU
22 SAG	21 CAP	22 AQU	23 ARI	23 TAU	23 CAN	23 LEO	23 LIB	22 SCO	21 SAG	22 AQU	22 PIS
25 CAP	23 AQU	24 PIS	25 TAU	25 GEM	25 LEO	25 VIR	25 SCO	24 SAG	24 CAP	25 PIS	25 ARI
27 AQU	26 PIS	27 ARI	27 GEM	27 CAN	27 VIR	27 LIB	27 SAG	26 CAP	26 AQU	27 ARI	27 TAU
30 PIS	28 ARI	29 TAU	29 CAN	29 LEO	29 LIB	29 SCO	30 CAP	29 AQU	29 PIS	30 TAU	29 GEM
		31 GEM		31 VIR		31 SAG			31 ARI		

JAN	FEB	MAR	APR	MAY	JUN	JUL	AUG	SEP	OCT	NOV	DEC
1 CAN	1 VIR	1 VIR	1 SCO	3 CAP	1 AQU	1 PIS	3 TAU	1 GEM	1 CAN	2 VIR	1 LIB
3 LEO	3 LIB	3 LIB	3 SAG	5 AQU	4 PIS	4 ARI	5 GEM	4 CAN	3 LEO	4 LIB	3 SCO
5 VIR	5 SCO	5 SCO	5 CAP	8 PIS	6 ARI	6 TAU	7 CAN	6 LEO	5 VIR	6 SCO	5 SAG
7 LIB	7 SAG	7 SAG	8 AQU	10 ARI	9 TAU	9 GEM	9 LEO	8 VIR	7 LIB	8 SAG	7 CAP
9 SCO	10 CAP	9 CAP	10 PIS	13 TAU	11 GEM	11 CAN	11 VIR	10 LIB	9 SCO	10 CAP	10 AQU
11 SAG	12 AQU	11 AQU	13 ARI	15 GEM	14 CAN	13 LEO	13 LIB	12 SCO	11 SAG	12 AQU	12 PIS
14 CAP	15 PIS	14 PIS	15 TAU	17 CAN	16 LEO	15 VIR	15 SCO	14 SAG	14 CAP	15 PIS	15 ARI
16 AQU	17 ARI	17 ARI	18 GEM	19 LEO	18 VIR	17 LIB	18 SAG	16 CAP	16 AQU	17 ARI	17 TAU
18 PIS	20 TAU	19 TAU	20 CAN	22 VIR	20 LIB	19 SCO	20 CAP	19 AQU	18 PIS	20 TAU	19 GEM
21 ARI	22 GEM	21 GEM	22 LEO	24 LIB	22 SCO	22 SAG	22 AQU	21 PIS	21 ARI	22 GEM	22 CAN
24 TAU	24 CAN	24 CAN	24 VIR	26 SCO	24 SAG	24 CAP	25 PIS	24 ARI	23 TAU	24 CAN	24 LEO
26 GEM	27 LEO	26 LEO	26 LIB	28 SAG	26 CAP	26 AQU	27 ARI	26 TAU	26 GEM	27 LEO	26 VIR
28 CAN		28 VIR	28 SCO	30 CAP	29 AQU	29 PIS	30 TAU	29 GEM	28 CAN	29 VIR	28 LIB
30 LEO		30 LIB	30 SAG			31 ARI			31 LEO		30 SCO

JAN	FEB	MAR	APR	MAY	JUN	JUL	AUG	SEP	OCT	NOV	DEC
2 SAG	2 AQU	2 AQU	3 ARI	3 TAU	1 GEM	1 CAN	2 VIR	2 SCO	2 SAG	2 AQU	2 PIS
4 CAP	5 PIS	4 PIS	5 TAU	5 GEM	4 CAN	3 LEO	4 LIB	4 SAG	4 CAP	5 PIS	4 ARI
6 AQU	7 ARI	6 ARI	8 GEM	7 CAN	6 LEO	6 VIR	6 SCO	7 CAP	6 AQU	7 ARI	7 TAU
8 PIS	10 TAU	9 TAU	10 CAN	10 LEO	8 VIR	8 LIB	8 SAG	9 AQU	8 PIS	10 TAU	9 GEM
11 ARI	12 GEM	12 GEM	13 LEO	12 VIR	10 LIB	10 SCO	10 CAP	11 PIS	11 ARI	12 GEM	12 CAN
13 TAU	15 CAN	14 CAN	15 VIR	14 LIB	13 SCO	12 SAG	13 AQU	14 ARI	13 TAU	15 CAN	14 LEO
16 GEM	17 LEO	16 LEO	17 LIB	16 SCO	15 SAG	14 CAP	15 PIS	16 TAU	16 GEM	17 LEO	16 VIR
18 CAN	19 VIR	18 VIR	19 SCO	18 SAG	17 CAP	16 AQU	17 ARI	19 GEM	18 CAN	19 VIR	19 LIB
20 LEO	21 LIB	20 LIB	21 SAG	20 CAP	19 AQU	19 PIS	20 TAU	21 CAN	21 LEO	22 LIB	21 SCO
22 VIR	23 SCO	23 SCO	23 CAP	22 AQU	21 PIS	21 ARI	22 GEM	23 LEO	23 VIR	24 SCO	23 SAG
25 LIB	25 SAG	25 SAG	25 AQU	25 PIS	24 ARI	23 TAU	25 CAN	26 VIR	25 LIB	26 SAG	25 CAP
27 SCO	27 CAP	26 CAP	27 PIS	27 ARI	26 TAU	26 GEM	27 LEO	28 LIB	27 SCO	28 CAP	27 AQU
29 SAG		29 AQU	30 ARI	30 TAU	29 GEM	28 CAN	29 VIR	30 SCO	29 SAG	30 AQU	29 PIS
31 CAP		31 PIS				31 LEO	31 LIB		31 CAP		

JAN	FEB	MAR	APR	MAY	JUN	JUL	AUG	SEP	OCT	NOV	DEC
1 ARI	2 GEM	1 GEM	3 LEO	2 VIR	1 LIB	2 SAG	1 CAP	1 PIS	1 ARI	2 GEM	2 CAN
3 TAU	5 CAN	4 CAN	5 VIR	5 LIB	3 SCO	4 CAP	3 AQU	4 ARI	3 TAU	5 CAN	4 LEO
6 GEM	7 LEO	6 LEO	7 LIB	7 SCO	5 SAG	6 AQU	5 PIS	7 TAU	6 GEM	7 LEO	7 VIR
8 CAN	9 VIR	9 VIR	9 SCO	9 SAG	7 CAP	9 PIS	7 ARI	9 GEM	8 CAN	10 VIR	9 LIB
11 LEO	11 LIB	11 LIB	11 SAG	11 CAP	9 AQU	11 ARI	10 TAU	11 CAN	11 LEO	12 LIB	11 SCO
13 VIR	13 SCO	13 SCO	13 CAP	13 AQU	11 PIS	13 TAU	12 GEM	13 LEO	13 VIR	14 SCO	13 SAG
15 LIB	16 SAG	15 SAG	15 AQU	15 PIS	13 ARI	16 GEM	15 CAN	16 VIR	15 LIB	16 SAG	15 CAP
17 SCO	18 CAP	17 CAP	18 PIS	17 ARI	16 TAU	18 CAN	17 LEO	18 LIB	17 SCO	18 CAP	17 AQU
19 SAG	20 AQU	19 AQU	20 ARI	20 TAU	18 GEM	21 LEO	19 VIR	20 SCO	20 SAG	20 AQU	19 PIS
21 CAP	22 PIS	21 PIS	22 TAU	22 GEM	21 CAN	23 VIR	21 LIB	22 SAG	22 CAP	22 PIS	22 ARI
24 AQU	24 ARI	24 ARI	25 GEM	25 CAN	23 LEO	25 LIB	24 SCO	24 CAP	24 AQU	24 ARI	24 TAU
26 PIS	27 TAU	26 TAU	27 CAN	27 LEO	26 VIR	28 SCO	26 SAG	26 AQU	26 PIS	27 TAU	27 GEM
28 ARI		29 GEM	30 LEO	30 VIR	28 LIB	30 SAG	28 CAP	29 PIS	28 ARI	29 GEM	29 CAN
30 TAU		31 CAN			30 SCO		30 AQU		31 TAU		

2040

JAN	FEB	MAR	APR	MAY	JUN	JUL	AUG	SEP	OCT	NOV	DEC
1 LEO	2 LIB	2 SCO	1 SAG	2 AQU	1 PIS	2 TAU	1 GEM	2 LEO	2 VIR	1 LIB	1 SCO
3 VIR	4 SCO	4 SAG	3 CAP	4 PIS	3 ARI	5 GEM	3 CAN	5 VIR	4 LIB	3 SCO	3 SAG
5 LIB	6 SAG	7 CAP	5 AQU	6 ARI	5 TAU	7 CAN	6 LEO	7 LIB	7 SCO	5 SAG	5 CAP
8 SCO	8 CAP	9 AQU	7 PIS	9 TAU	7 GEM	10 LEO	8 VIR	9 SCO	9 SAG	7 CAP	7 AQU
10 SAG	10 AQU	11 PIS	9 ARI	11 GEM	10 CAN	12 VIR	11 LIB	12 SAG	11 CAP	10 AQU	9 PIS
12 CAP	12 PIS	13 ARI	11 TAU	14 CAN	12 LEO	15 LIB	13 SCO	14 CAP	13 AQU	12 PIS	11 ARI
14 AQU	14 ARI	15 TAU	14 GEM	16 LEO	15 VIR	17 SCO	16 SAG	16 AQU	15 PIS	14 ARI	13 TAU
16 PIS	17 TAU	17 GEM	16 CAN	19 VIR	17 LIB	19 SAG	18 CAP	18 PIS	17 ARI	16 TAU	16 GEM
18 ARI	19 GEM	20 CAN	19 LEO	21 LIB	20 SCO	21 CAP	20 AQU	20 ARI	20 TAU	18 GEM	18 CAN
20 TAU	22 CAN	23 LEO	21 VIR	23 SCO	22 SAG	23 AQU	22 PIS	23 TAU	22 GEM	21 CAN	21 LEO
23 GEM	24 LEO	25 VIR	24 LIB	25 SAG	24 CAP	25 PIS	24 ARI	25 GEM	24 CAN	23 LEO	23 VIR
25 CAN	27 VIR	27 LIB	26 SCO	27 CAP	26 AQU	27 ARI	26 TAU	27 CAN	27 LEO	26 VIR	26 LIB
28 LEO	29 LIB	30 SCO	28 SAG	29 AQU	28 PIS	30 TAU	28 GEM	30 LEO	30 VIR	28 LIB	28 SCO
30 VIR			30 CAP		30 ARI		31 CAN				30 SAG

2041

JAN	FEB	MAR	APR	MAY	JUN	JUL	AUG	SEP	OCT	NOV	DEC
1 CAP	2 PIS	1 PIS	2 TAU	1 GEM	2 LEO	2 VIR	1 LIB	2 SAG	2 CAP	2 PIS	2 ARI
3 AQU	4 ARI	3 ARI	4 GEM	4 CAN	5 VIR	5 LIB	3 SCO	4 CAP	4 AQU	4 ARI	4 TAU
5 PIS	6 TAU	5 TAU	6 CAN	6 LEO	7 LIB	7 SCO	6 SAG	7 AQU	6 PIS	6 TAU	6 GEM
7 ARI	8 GEM	7 GEM	9 LEO	9 VIR	10 SCO	9 SAG	8 CAP	9 PIS	8 ARI	8 GEM	8 CAN
10 TAU	11 CAN	10 CAN	11 VIR	11 LIB	12 SAG	12 CAP	10 AQU	11 ARI	10 TAU	11 CAN	10 LEO
12 GEM	13 LEO	12 LEO	14 LIB	13 SCO	14 CAP	14 AQU	12 PIS	13 TAU	12 GEM	13 LEO	13 VIR
14 CAN	16 VIR	15 VIR	16 SCO	16 SAG	16 AQU	16 PIS	14 ARI	15 GEM	14 CAN	15 VIR	15 LIB
17 LEO	18 LIB	17 LIB	18 SAG	18 CAP	18 PIS	18 ARI	16 TAU	17 CAN	17 LEO	18 LIB	18 SCO
19 VIR	21 SCO	20 SCO	21 CAP	20 AQU	20 ARI	20 TAU	18 GEM	19 LEO	19 VIR	21 SCO	20 SAG
22 LIB	23 SAG	22 SAG	23 AQU	22 PIS	22 TAU	22 GEM	21 CAN	22 VIR	22 LIB	23 SAG	22 CAP
24 SCO	25 CAP	24 CAP	25 PIS	24 ARI	25 GEM	24 CAN	23 LEO	24 LIB	24 SCO	25 CAP	25 AQU
27 SAG	27 AQU	26 AQU	27 ARI	26 TAU	27 CAN	27 LEO	26 VIR	27 SCO	27 SAG	27 AQU	27 PIS
29 CAP		29 PIS	29 TAU	29 GEM	29 LEO	29 VIR	28 LIB	29 SAG	29 CAP	29 PIS	29 ARI
31 AQU		31 ARI		31 CAN			31 SCO		31 AQU		31 TAU

2042

JAN	FEB	MAR	APR	MAY	JUN	JUL	AUG	SEP	OCT	NOV	DEC
2 GEM	1 CAN	2 LEO	1 VIR	1 LIB	2 SAG	2 CAP	2 PIS	1 ARI	2 GEM	1 CAN	3 VIR
4 CAN	3 LEO	5 VIR	4 LIB	3 SCO	5 CAP	4 AQU	5 ARI	3 TAU	4 CAN	3 LEO	5 LIB
7 LEO	5 VIR	7 LIB	6 SCO	6 SAG	7 AQU	6 PIS	7 TAU	5 GEM	7 LEO	5 VIR	8 SCO
9 VIR	8 LIB	10 SCO	9 SAG	8 CAP	9 PIS	8 ARI	9 GEM	7 CAN	9 VIR	8 LIB	10 SAG
12 LIB	11 SCO	12 SAG	11 CAP	10 AQU	11 ARI	10 TAU	11 CAN	9 LEO	12 LIB	10 SCO	13 CAP
14 SCO	13 SAG	15 CAP	13 AQU	13 PIS	13 TAU	13 GEM	13 LEO	12 VIR	14 SCO	13 SAG	15 AQU
17 SAG	15 CAP	17 AQU	15 PIS	15 ARI	15 GEM	15 CAN	16 VIR	14 LIB	16 SAG	15 CAP	17 PIS
19 CAP	17 AQU	19 PIS	17 ARI	17 TAU	17 CAN	17 LEO	18 LIB	17 SCO	19 CAP	18 AQU	19 ARI
21 AQU	19 PIS	21 ARI	19 TAU	19 GEM	20 LEO	19 VIR	21 SCO	19 SAG	22 AQU	20 PIS	22 TAU
23 PIS	21 ARI	23 TAU	21 GEM	21 CAN	22 VIR	22 LIB	23 SAG	22 CAP	24 PIS	22 ARI	24 GEM
25 ARI	24 TAU	25 GEM	23 CAN	23 LEO	24 LIB	24 SCO	26 CAP	24 AQU	26 ARI	24 TAU	26 CAN
27 TAU	26 GEM	27 CAN	26 LEO	26 VIR	27 SCO	27 SAG	28 AQU	26 PIS	28 TAU	26 GEM	28 LEO
29 GEM	28 CAN	30 LEO	28 VIR	28 LIB	29 SAG	29 CAP	30 PIS	28 ARI	30 GEM	28 CAN	30 VIR
				31 SCO		31 AQU		30 TAU		30 LEO	

2043

JAN	FEB	MAR	APR	MAY	JUN	JUL	AUG	SEP	OCT	NOV	DEC
1 LIB	3 SAG	2 SAG	1 CAP	1 AQU	2 ARI	1 TAU	1 CAN	2 VIR	2 LIB	3 SAG	3 CAP
4 SCO	5 CAP	5 CAP	3 AQU	3 PIS	4 TAU	3 GEM	3 LEO	4 LIB	4 SCO	5 CAP	5 AQU
7 SAG	8 AQU	7 AQU	6 PIS	5 ARI	6 GEM	5 CAN	6 VIR	7 SCO	7 SAG	8 AQU	8 PIS
9 CAP	10 PIS	9 PIS	8 ARI	7 TAU	8 CAN	7 LEO	8 LIB	9 SAG	9 CAP	10 PIS	10 ARI
11 AQU	12 ARI	11 ARI	10 TAU	9 GEM	10 LEO	9 VIR	10 SCO	12 CAP	12 AQU	13 ARI	12 TAU
13 PIS	14 TAU	13 TAU	12 GEM	11 CAN	12 VIR	12 LIB	13 SAG	14 AQU	14 PIS	15 TAU	14 GEM
16 ARI	16 GEM	15 GEM	14 CAN	13 LEO	15 LIB	14 SCO	15 CAP	16 PIS	16 ARI	17 GEM	16 CAN
18 TAU	18 CAN	18 CAN	16 LEO	16 VIR	17 SCO	17 SAG	18 AQU	19 ARI	18 TAU	19 CAN	18 LEO
20 GEM	21 LEO	20 LEO	18 VIR	18 LIB	19 SAG	19 CAP	20 PIS	21 TAU	20 GEM	21 LEO	20 VIR
22 CAN	23 VIR	22 VIR	21 LIB	21 SCO	22 CAP	21 AQU	22 ARI	23 GEM	23 CAN	23 VIR	22 LIB
24 LEO	25 LIB	24 LIB	23 SCO	23 SAG	24 AQU	24 PIS	24 TAU	25 CAN	25 LEO	25 LIB	25 SCO
26 VIR	28 SCO	27 SCO	26 SAG	26 CAP	27 PIS	26 ARI	27 GEM	27 LEO	27 VIR	28 SCO	27 SAG
29 LIB		30 SAG	28 CAP	28 AQU	29 ARI	28 TAU	29 CAN	29 VIR	29 LIB	30 SAG	30 CAP
31 SCO				30 PIS		30 GEM	31 LEO		31 SCO		

2044

JAN	FEB	MAR	APR	MAY	JUN	JUL	AUG	SEP	OCT	NOV	DEC
1 AQU	2 ARI	1 ARI	1 GEM	1 CAN	1 VIR	1 LIB	2 SAG	1 CAP	3 PIS	2 ARI	1 TAU
4 PIS	5 TAU	3 TAU	3 CAN	3 LEO	3 LIB	3 SCO	4 CAP	4 AQU	5 ARI	4 TAU	3 GEM
6 ARI	7 GEM	5 GEM	5 LEO	5 VIR	6 SCO	5 SAG	7 AQU	6 PIS	7 TAU	6 GEM	5 CAN
8 TAU	9 CAN	7 CAN	8 VIR	7 LIB	8 SAG	8 CAP	9 PIS	8 ARI	10 GEM	8 CAN	7 LEO
10 GEM	11 LEO	9 LEO	10 LIB	10 SCO	11 CAP	11 AQU	12 ARI	10 TAU	12 CAN	10 LEO	9 VIR
12 CAN	13 VIR	11 VIR	12 SCO	12 SAG	13 AQU	13 PIS	14 TAU	12 GEM	14 LEO	12 VIR	11 LIB
14 LEO	15 LIB	14 LIB	15 SAG	14 CAP	16 PIS	15 ARI	16 GEM	14 CAN	16 VIR	14 LIB	14 SCO
17 VIR	18 SCO	16 SCO	17 CAP	17 AQU	18 ARI	18 TAU	18 CAN	17 LEO	18 LIB	17 SCO	16 SAG
19 LIB	20 SAG	18 SAG	20 AQU	19 PIS	20 TAU	20 GEM	20 LEO	19 VIR	20 SCO	19 SAG	19 CAP
21 SCO	23 CAP	21 CAP	22 PIS	22 ARI	22 GEM	22 CAN	22 VIR	21 LIB	23 SAG	22 CAP	21 AQU
24 SAG	25 AQU	23 AQU	24 ARI	24 TAU	24 CAN	24 LEO	24 LIB	23 SCO	25 CAP	24 AQU	24 PIS
26 CAP	27 PIS	26 PIS	27 TAU	26 GEM	26 LEO	26 VIR	26 SCO	25 SAG	28 AQU	27 PIS	26 ARI
29 AQU		28 ARI	29 GEM	28 CAN	28 VIR	28 LIB	29 SAG	28 CAP	30 PIS	29 ARI	29 TAU
31 PIS		30 TAU		30 LEO		30 SCO		30 AQU			31 GEM

2045

JAN	FEB	MAR	APR	MAY	JUN	JUL	AUG	SEP	OCT	NOV	DEC
2 CAN	2 VIR	2 VIR	2 SCO	2 SAG	1 CAP	3 PIS	2 ARI	3 GEM	2 CAN	1 LEO	2 LIB
4 LEO	4 LIB	4 LIB	5 SAG	4 CAP	3 AQU	5 ARI	4 TAU	5 CAN	4 LEO	3 VIR	4 SCO
6 VIR	7 SCO	6 SCO	7 CAP	7 AQU	6 PIS	8 TAU	7 GEM	7 LEO	7 VIR	5 LIB	7 SAG
8 LIB	9 SAG	8 SAG	9 AQU	9 PIS	8 ARI	10 GEM	9 CAN	9 VIR	9 LIB	7 SCO	9 CAP
10 SCO	11 CAP	11 CAP	12 PIS	12 ARI	11 TAU	12 CAN	11 LEO	11 LIB	11 SCO	9 SAG	11 AQU
13 SAG	14 AQU	13 AQU	14 ARI	14 TAU	13 GEM	14 LEO	13 VIR	13 SCO	13 SAG	11 CAP	14 PIS
15 CAP	16 PIS	16 PIS	17 TAU	16 GEM	15 CAN	16 VIR	15 LIB	15 SAG	15 CAP	14 AQU	16 ARI
18 AQU	19 ARI	18 ARI	19 GEM	18 CAN	17 LEO	18 LIB	17 SCO	18 CAP	18 AQU	16 PIS	19 TAU
20 PIS	21 TAU	20 TAU	21 CAN	21 LEO	19 VIR	20 SCO	19 SAG	20 AQU	20 PIS	19 ARI	21 GEM
23 ARI	24 GEM	23 GEM	23 LEO	23 VIR	21 LIB	23 SAG	22 CAP	23 PIS	23 ARI	21 TAU	23 CAN
25 TAU	26 CAN	25 CAN	25 VIR	25 LIB	23 SCO	25 CAP	24 AQU	25 ARI	25 TAU	24 GEM	25 LEO
27 GEM	28 LEO	27 LEO	28 LIB	27 SCO	26 SAG	28 AQU	26 PIS	28 TAU	28 GEM	26 CAN	27 VIR
29 CAN		29 VIR	30 SCO	29 SAG	28 CAP	30 PIS	29 ARI	30 GEM	30 CAN	28 LEO	29 LIB
31 LEO		31 LIB			30 AQU		31 TAU			30 VIR	

2046

JAN	FEB	MAR	APR	MAY	JUN	JUL	AUG	SEP	OCT	NOV	DEC
1 SCO	1 CAP	1 CAP	2 PIS	2 ARI	3 GEM	2 CAN	1 LEO	1 LIB	1 SCO	1 CAP	1 AQU
3 SAG	4 AQU	3 AQU	4 ARI	4 TAU	5 CAN	5 LEO	3 VIR	3 SCO	3 SAG	4 AQU	4 PIS
5 CAP	6 PIS	6 PIS	7 TAU	7 GEM	7 LEO	7 VIR	5 LIB	6 SAG	5 CAP	6 PIS	6 ARI
8 AQU	9 ARI	8 ARI	9 GEM	9 CAN	9 VIR	9 LIB	7 SCO	8 CAP	7 AQU	9 ARI	9 TAU
10 PIS	11 TAU	11 TAU	12 CAN	11 LEO	12 LIB	11 SCO	9 SAG	10 AQU	10 PIS	11 TAU	11 GEM
13 ARI	14 GEM	13 GEM	14 LEO	13 VIR	14 SCO	13 SAG	12 CAP	13 PIS	12 ARI	14 GEM	13 CAN
15 TAU	16 CAN	15 CAN	16 VIR	15 LIB	16 SAG	15 CAP	14 AQU	15 ARI	15 TAU	16 CAN	16 LEO
17 GEM	18 LEO	18 LEO	18 LIB	17 SCO	18 CAP	18 AQU	16 PIS	18 TAU	17 GEM	18 LEO	18 VIR
20 CAN	20 VIR	20 VIR	20 SCO	19 SAG	20 AQU	20 PIS	19 ARI	20 GEM	20 CAN	21 VIR	20 LIB
22 LEO	22 LIB	22 LIB	22 SAG	22 CAP	23 PIS	23 ARI	21 TAU	23 CAN	22 LEO	23 LIB	22 SCO
24 VIR	24 SCO	24 SCO	24 CAP	24 AQU	25 ARI	25 TAU	24 GEM	25 LEO	24 VIR	25 SCO	24 SAG
26 LIB	26 SAG	26 SAG	27 AQU	26 PIS	28 TAU	28 GEM	26 CAN	27 VIR	26 LIB	27 SAG	26 CAP
28 SCO		28 CAP	29 PIS	29 ARI	30 GEM	30 CAN	28 LEO	29 LIB	28 SCO	29 CAP	29 AQU
30 SAG		30 AQU		31 TAU			30 VIR		30 SAG		31 PIS

2047

JAN	FEB	MAR	APR	MAY	JUN	JUL	AUG	SEP	OCT	NOV	DEC
2 ARI	1 TAU	1 TAU	2 CAN	1 LEO	2 LIB	2 SCO	2 CAP	3 PIS	2 ARI	1 TAU	1 GEM
5 TAU	4 GEM	3 GEM	4 LEO	4 VIR	4 SCO	4 SAG	4 AQU	5 ARI	5 TAU	4 GEM	3 CAN
7 GEM	6 CAN	6 CAN	6 VIR	6 LIB	6 SAG	6 CAP	6 PIS	8 TAU	7 GEM	6 CAN	6 LEO
10 CAN	8 LEO	8 LEO	8 LIB	8 SCO	8 CAP	8 AQU	9 ARI	10 GEM	10 CAN	9 LEO	8 VIR
12 LEO	10 VIR	10 VIR	10 SCO	10 SAG	10 AQU	10 PIS	11 TAU	13 CAN	12 LEO	11 VIR	11 LIB
14 VIR	13 LIB	12 LIB	12 SAG	12 CAP	13 PIS	12 ARI	14 GEM	15 LEO	15 VIR	13 LIB	13 SCO
16 LIB	15 SCO	14 SCO	14 CAP	14 AQU	15 ARI	15 TAU	16 CAN	17 VIR	17 LIB	15 SCO	15 SAG
18 SCO	17 SAG	16 SAG	17 AQU	16 PIS	18 TAU	17 GEM	19 LEO	19 LIB	19 SCO	17 SAG	17 CAP
20 SAG	19 CAP	18 CAP	19 PIS	19 ARI	20 GEM	20 CAN	21 VIR	21 SCO	21 SAG	19 CAP	19 AQU
23 CAP	21 AQU	20 AQU	22 ARI	21 TAU	23 CAN	22 LEO	23 LIB	23 SAG	23 CAP	21 AQU	21 PIS
25 AQU	24 PIS	23 PIS	24 TAU	24 GEM	25 LEO	24 VIR	25 SCO	25 CAP	25 AQU	23 PIS	23 ARI
27 PIS	26 ARI	25 ARI	27 GEM	26 CAN	27 VIR	27 LIB	27 SAG	28 AQU	28 PIS	26 ARI	26 TAU
30 ARI		28 TAU	29 CAN	29 LEO	29 LIB	29 SCO	29 CAP	30 PIS	30 ARI	28 TAU	28 GEM
		30 GEM		31 VIR		31 SAG	31 AQU				31 CAN

2048

JAN	FEB	MAR	APR	MAY	JUN	JUL	AUG	SEP	OCT	NOV	DEC
2 LEO	1 VIR	1 LIB	2 SAG	1 CAP	2 PIS	1 ARI	1 CAN	1 LEO	1 LEO	2 LIB	2 SCO
5 VIR	3 LIB	3 SCO	4 CAP	3 AQU	4 ARI	4 TAU	5 CAN	4 VIR	3 VIR	4 SCO	4 SAG
7 LIB	5 SCO	6 SAG	6 AQU	5 PIS	7 TAU	6 GEM	8 LEO	6 LIB	6 LIB	7 SAG	6 CAP
9 SCO	7 SAG	8 CAP	8 PIS	8 ARI	9 GEM	9 CAN	10 VIR	9 SCO	8 SCO	9 CAP	8 AQU
11 SAG	9 CAP	10 AQU	11 ARI	10 TAU	12 CAN	11 LEO	12 LIB	11 SAG	10 SAG	11 AQU	10 PIS
13 CAP	12 AQU	12 PIS	13 TAU	13 GEM	14 LEO	14 VIR	15 SCO	13 CAP	12 CAP	13 PIS	12 ARI
15 AQU	14 PIS	14 ARI	16 GEM	15 CAN	17 VIR	16 LIB	17 SAG	15 AQU	14 AQU	15 ARI	15 TAU
17 PIS	16 ARI	16 TAU	18 CAN	18 LEO	19 LIB	18 SCO	19 CAP	17 PIS	17 PIS	17 TAU	17 GEM
20 ARI	18 TAU	19 GEM	21 LEO	20 VIR	21 SCO	20 SAG	21 AQU	19 ARI	19 ARI	20 GEM	20 CAN
22 TAU	21 GEM	22 CAN	23 VIR	23 LIB	23 SAG	22 CAP	23 PIS	22 TAU	21 TAU	22 CAN	22 LEO
25 GEM	23 CAN	24 LEO	25 LIB	25 SCO	25 CAP	24 AQU	25 ARI	24 GEM	24 GEM	25 LEO	25 VIR
27 CAN	26 LEO	27 VIR	27 SCO	27 SAG	27 AQU	27 PIS	27 TAU	26 CAN	26 CAN	27 VIR	27 LIB
29 LEO	28 VIR	29 LIB	29 SAG	29 CAP	29 PIS	29 ARI	30 GEM	29 CAN	29 LEO	30 LIB	29 SCO
		31 SCO		31 AQU		31 TAU			31 VIR		31 SAG

2049

JAN	FEB	MAR	APR	MAY	JUN	JUL	AUG	SEP	OCT	NOV	DEC
2 CAP	1 AQU	2 PIS	1 ARI	3 GEM	1 CAN	1 LEO	3 LIB	1 SCO	1 SAG	1 AQU	1 PIS
4 AQU	3 PIS	4 ARI	3 TAU	5 CAN	4 LEO	4 VIR	5 SCO	3 SAG	3 CAP	3 PIS	3 ARI
6 PIS	5 ARI	7 TAU	5 GEM	8 LEO	7 VIR	6 LIB	7 SAG	5 CAP	5 AQU	5 ARI	5 TAU
9 ARI	7 TAU	9 GEM	8 CAN	10 VIR	9 LIB	9 SCO	9 CAP	8 AQU	7 PIS	8 TAU	7 GEM
11 TAU	10 GEM	12 CAN	10 LEO	13 LIB	11 SCO	11 SAG	11 AQU	10 PIS	9 ARI	10 GEM	10 CAN
13 GEM	12 CAN	14 LEO	13 VIR	15 SCO	13 SAG	13 CAP	13 PIS	12 ARI	11 TAU	12 CAN	12 LEO
16 CAN	15 LEO	17 VIR	15 LIB	17 SAG	15 CAP	15 AQU	15 ARI	14 TAU	13 GEM	15 LEO	15 VIR
18 LEO	17 VIR	19 LIB	17 SCO	19 CAP	17 AQU	17 PIS	17 TAU	16 GEM	16 CAN	17 VIR	17 LIB
21 VIR	20 LIB	21 SCO	19 SAG	21 AQU	19 PIS	19 ARI	20 GEM	19 CAN	18 LEO	20 LIB	19 SCO
23 LIB	22 SCO	23 SAG	22 CAP	23 PIS	22 ARI	21 TAU	22 CAN	21 LEO	21 VIR	22 SCO	22 SAG
26 SCO	24 SAG	25 CAP	24 AQU	25 ARI	24 TAU	23 GEM	25 LEO	24 VIR	23 LIB	24 SAG	24 CAP
28 SAG	26 CAP	28 AQU	26 PIS	28 TAU	26 GEM	26 CAN	27 VIR	26 LIB	26 SCO	26 CAP	26 AQU
30 CAP	28 AQU	30 PIS	28 ARI	30 GEM	29 CAN	29 LEO	30 LIB	28 SCO	28 SAG	28 AQU	28 PIS
			30 TAU			31 VIR			30 CAP		30 ARI

2050

JAN	FEB	MAR	APR	MAY	JUN	JUL	AUG	SEP	OCT	NOV	DEC
1 TAU	2 CAN	1 CAN	3 VIR	3 LIB	1 SCO	1 SAG	2 AQU	2 ARI	2 TAU	2 CAN	2 LEO
3 GEM	5 LEO	4 LEO	5 LIB	5 SCO	4 SAG	3 CAP	4 PIS	4 TAU	4 GEM	5 LEO	4 VIR
6 CAN	7 VIR	6 VIR	8 SCO	7 SAG	6 CAP	5 AQU	6 ARI	6 GEM	6 CAN	7 VIR	7 LIB
8 LEO	10 LIB	9 LIB	10 SAG	9 CAP	8 AQU	7 PIS	8 TAU	9 CAN	8 LEO	10 LIB	9 SCO
11 VIR	12 SCO	11 SCO	12 CAP	12 AQU	10 PIS	9 ARI	10 GEM	11 LEO	11 VIR	12 SCO	12 SAG
13 LIB	14 SAG	14 SAG	14 AQU	14 PIS	12 ARI	11 TAU	12 CAN	13 VIR	13 LIB	14 SAG	14 CAP
16 SCO	17 CAP	16 CAP	17 PIS	16 ARI	14 TAU	14 GEM	15 LEO	16 LIB	16 SCO	17 CAP	16 AQU
18 SAG	19 AQU	18 AQU	19 ARI	18 TAU	16 GEM	16 CAN	17 VIR	19 SCO	18 SAG	19 AQU	18 PIS
20 CAP	21 PIS	20 PIS	21 TAU	20 GEM	19 CAN	18 LEO	20 LIB	21 SAG	21 CAP	21 PIS	21 ARI
22 AQU	23 ARI	22 ARI	23 GEM	22 CAN	21 LEO	21 VIR	22 SCO	23 CAP	23 AQU	23 ARI	23 TAU
24 PIS	25 TAU	24 TAU	25 CAN	25 LEO	24 VIR	23 LIB	25 SAG	25 AQU	25 PIS	25 TAU	25 GEM
26 ARI	27 GEM	26 GEM	27 LEO	27 VIR	26 LIB	26 SCO	27 CAP	28 PIS	27 ARI	27 GEM	27 CAN
28 TAU		29 CAN	30 VIR	30 LIB	29 SCO	28 SAG	29 AQU	30 ARI	29 TAU	30 CAN	29 LEO
31 GEM		31 LEO				31 CAP	31 PIS		31 GEM		

2051

JAN	FEB	MAR	APR	MAY	JUN	JUL	AUG	SEP	OCT	NOV	DEC
1 VIR	2 SCO	1 SCO	3 CAP	2 AQU	1 PIS	2 TAU	3 CAN	1 LEO	1 VIR	2 SCO	2 SAG
3 LIB	5 SAG	4 SAG	5 AQU	4 PIS	3 ARI	4 GEM	5 LEO	3 VIR	3 LIB	5 SAG	4 CAP
6 SCO	7 CAP	6 CAP	7 PIS	6 ARI	5 TAU	6 CAN	7 VIR	6 LIB	6 SCO	7 CAP	7 AQU
8 SAG	9 AQU	8 AQU	9 ARI	8 TAU	7 GEM	9 LEO	9 LIB	8 SCO	8 SAG	9 AQU	9 PIS
10 CAP	11 PIS	11 PIS	11 TAU	10 GEM	9 CAN	11 VIR	12 SCO	11 SAG	11 CAP	12 PIS	11 ARI
13 AQU	13 ARI	13 ARI	13 GEM	13 CAN	11 LEO	13 LIB	15 SAG	13 CAP	13 AQU	14 ARI	13 TAU
15 PIS	15 TAU	15 TAU	15 CAN	15 LEO	13 VIR	16 SCO	17 CAP	15 AQU	15 PIS	16 TAU	15 GEM
17 ARI	17 GEM	17 GEM	17 LEO	17 VIR	16 LIB	18 SAG	19 AQU	18 PIS	17 ARI	18 GEM	17 CAN
19 TAU	20 CAN	19 CAN	20 VIR	20 LIB	18 SCO	21 CAP	21 PIS	20 ARI	19 TAU	20 CAN	19 LEO
21 GEM	22 LEO	21 LEO	22 LIB	22 SCO	21 SAG	23 AQU	23 ARI	22 TAU	21 GEM	22 LEO	22 VIR
23 CAN	24 VIR	24 VIR	25 SCO	25 SAG	23 CAP	25 PIS	26 TAU	24 GEM	23 CAN	24 VIR	24 LIB
26 LEO	27 LIB	26 LIB	27 SAG	27 CAP	26 AQU	27 ARI	28 GEM	26 CAN	26 LEO	27 LIB	27 SCO
28 VIR		29 SCO	30 CAP	29 AQU	28 PIS	29 TAU	30 CAN	28 LEO	28 VIR	29 SCO	29 SAG
31 LIB		31 SAG			30 ARI	31 GEM			30 LIB		

JAN	FEB	MAR	APR	MAY	JUN	JUL	AUG	SEP	OCT	NOV	DEC
1 CAP	1 PIS	2 ARI	2 GEM	2 CAN	2 VIR	2 LIB	1 SCO	2 CAP	2 AQU	1 PIS	3 TAU
3 AQU	4 ARI	4 TAU	4 CAN	4 LEO	5 LIB	5 SCO	3 SAG	5 AQU	4 PIS	3 ARI	5 GEM
5 PIS	6 TAU	6 GEM	7 LEO	6 VIR	7 SCO	7 SAG	6 CAP	7 PIS	7 ARI	5 TAU	7 CAN
7 ARI	8 GEM	8 CAN	9 VIR	9 LIB	10 SAG	10 CAP	8 AQU	9 ARI	9 TAU	7 GEM	9 LEO
9 TAU	10 CAN	10 LEO	11 LIB	11 SCO	12 CAP	12 AQU	11 PIS	11 TAU	11 GEM	9 CAN	11 VIR
12 GEM	12 LEO	13 VIR	14 SCO	14 SAG	15 AQU	14 PIS	13 ARI	13 GEM	13 CAN	11 LEO	13 LIB
14 CAN	14 VIR	15 LIB	16 SAG	16 CAP	17 PIS	17 ARI	15 TAU	15 CAN	15 LEO	13 VIR	15 SCO
16 LEO	17 LIB	18 SCO	19 CAP	19 AQU	19 ARI	19 TAU	17 GEM	18 LEO	17 VIR	16 LIB	18 SAG
18 VIR	19 SCO	20 SAG	21 AQU	21 PIS	22 TAU	21 GEM	19 CAN	20 VIR	20 LIB	18 SCO	20 CAP
20 LIB	22 SAG	23 CAP	23 PIS	23 ARI	24 GEM	23 CAN	21 LEO	22 LIB	22 SCO	21 SAG	23 AQU
23 SCO	24 CAP	25 AQU	26 ARI	25 TAU	26 CAN	25 LEO	24 VIR	25 SCO	24 SAG	23 CAP	25 PIS
25 SAG	27 AQU	27 PIS	28 TAU	27 GEM	28 LEO	27 VIR	26 LIB	27 SAG	27 CAP	26 AQU	28 ARI
28 CAP	29 PIS	29 ARI	30 GEM	29 CAN	30 VIR	30 LIB	28 SCO	30 CAP	29 AQU	28 PIS	30 TAU
30 AQU		31 TAU		31 LEO			31 SAG			30 ARI	

JAN	FEB	MAR	APR	MAY	JUN	JUL	AUG	SEP	OCT	NOV	DEC
1 GEM	1 LEO	1 LEO	1 LIB	1 SCO	2 CAP	2 AQU	1 PIS	2 TAU	1 GEM	2 LEO	1 VIR
3 CAN	4 VIR	3 VIR	4 SCO	4 SAG	5 AQU	5 PIS	3 ARI	4 GEM	3 CAN	4 VIR	3 LIB
5 LEO	6 LIB	5 LIB	6 SAG	6 CAP	7 PIS	7 ARI	6 TAU	6 CAN	6 LEO	6 LIB	6 SCO
7 VIR	8 SCO	7 SCO	9 CAP	9 AQU	10 ARI	9 TAU	8 GEM	8 LEO	8 VIR	8 SCO	8 SAG
9 LIB	11 SAG	10 SAG	11 AQU	11 PIS	12 TAU	11 GEM	10 CAN	10 VIR	10 LIB	11 SAG	10 CAP
12 SCO	13 CAP	12 CAP	14 PIS	13 ARI	14 GEM	13 CAN	12 LEO	12 LIB	12 SCO	13 CAP	13 AQU
14 SAG	16 AQU	15 AQU	16 ARI	16 TAU	16 CAN	15 LEO	14 VIR	15 SCO	14 SAG	16 AQU	15 PIS
17 CAP	18 PIS	17 PIS	18 TAU	18 GEM	18 LEO	17 VIR	16 LIB	17 SAG	17 CAP	18 PIS	18 ARI
19 AQU	20 ARI	20 ARI	20 GEM	20 CAN	20 VIR	20 LIB	18 SCO	19 CAP	19 AQU	21 ARI	20 TAU
22 PIS	22 TAU	22 TAU	22 CAN	22 LEO	22 LIB	22 SCO	21 SAG	22 AQU	22 PIS	23 TAU	22 GEM
24 ARI	25 GEM	24 GEM	24 LEO	24 VIR	25 SCO	24 SAG	23 CAP	24 PIS	24 ARI	25 GEM	24 CAN
26 TAU	27 CAN	26 CAN	27 VIR	26 LIB	27 SAG	27 CAP	26 AQU	27 ARI	26 TAU	27 CAN	26 LEO
28 GEM		28 LEO	29 LIB	28 SCO	30 CAP	29 AQU	28 PIS	29 TAU	29 GEM	29 LEO	28 VIR
30 CAN		30 VIR		31 SAG			30 ARI		31 CAN		31 LIB

JAN	FEB	MAR	APR	MAY	JUN	JUL	AUG	SEP	OCT	NOV	DEC
2 SCO	3 CAP	2 CAP	1 AQU	1 PIS	2 TAU	2 GEM	2 LEO	1 VIR	2 SCO	1 SAG	3 AQU
4 SAG	5 AQU	5 AQU	4 PIS	3 ARI	4 GEM	4 CAN	4 VIR	3 LIB	4 SAG	3 CAP	5 PIS
7 CAP	8 PIS	7 PIS	6 ARI	6 TAU	6 CAN	6 LEO	6 LIB	5 SCO	7 CAP	5 AQU	8 ARI
9 AQU	10 ARI	10 ARI	8 TAU	8 GEM	8 LEO	8 VIR	9 SCO	7 SAG	9 AQU	8 PIS	10 TAU
12 PIS	13 TAU	12 TAU	11 GEM	10 CAN	11 VIR	10 LIB	11 SAG	9 CAP	12 PIS	10 ARI	13 GEM
14 ARI	15 GEM	14 GEM	13 CAN	12 LEO	13 LIB	13 SCO	13 CAP	12 AQU	14 ARI	13 TAU	15 CAN
17 TAU	17 CAN	17 CAN	15 LEO	14 VIR	15 SCO	15 SAG	16 AQU	14 PIS	17 TAU	15 GEM	17 LEO
19 GEM	19 LEO	19 LEO	17 VIR	16 LIB	17 SAG	17 CAP	18 PIS	17 ARI	19 GEM	17 CAN	19 VIR
21 CAN	21 VIR	21 VIR	19 LIB	19 SCO	19 CAP	20 AQU	21 ARI	19 TAU	21 CAN	20 LEO	21 LIB
23 LEO	23 LIB	23 LIB	21 SCO	21 SAG	22 AQU	22 PIS	23 TAU	22 GEM	23 LEO	22 VIR	23 SCO
25 VIR	25 SCO	25 SCO	24 SAG	23 CAP	25 PIS	24 ARI	25 GEM	24 CAN	25 VIR	24 LIB	25 SAG
27 LIB	28 SAG	27 SAG	26 CAP	26 AQU	27 ARI	27 TAU	28 CAN	26 LEO	28 LIB	26 SCO	28 CAP
29 SCO		29 CAP	28 AQU	28 PIS	29 TAU	29 GEM	30 LEO	28 VIR	30 SCO	28 SAG	30 AQU
31 SAG				31 ARI		31 CAN		30 LIB		30 CAP	

JAN	FEB	MAR	APR	MAY	JUN	JUL	AUG	SEP	OCT	NOV	DEC
2 PIS	3 TAU	2 TAU	1 GEM	3 LEO	1 VIR	3 SCO	1 SAG	2 AQU	1 PIS	3 TAU	3 GEM
4 ARI	5 GEM	5 GEM	3 CAN	5 VIR	3 LIB	5 SAG	3 CAP	4 PIS	4 ARI	5 GEM	5 CAN
7 TAU	8 CAN	7 CAN	5 LEO	7 LIB	5 SCO	7 CAP	6 AQU	7 ARI	7 TAU	8 CAN	7 LEO
9 GEM	10 LEO	9 LEO	7 VIR	9 SCO	7 SAG	9 AQU	8 PIS	9 TAU	9 GEM	10 LEO	9 VIR
11 CAN	12 VIR	11 VIR	9 LIB	11 SAG	9 CAP	12 PIS	10 ARI	12 GEM	11 CAN	12 VIR	12 LIB
13 LEO	14 LIB	13 LIB	12 SCO	13 CAP	12 AQU	14 ARI	13 TAU	14 CAN	14 LEO	14 LIB	14 SCO
15 VIR	16 SCO	15 SCO	14 SAG	16 AQU	14 PIS	17 TAU	15 GEM	16 LEO	16 VIR	16 SCO	16 SAG
17 LIB	18 SAG	17 SAG	16 CAP	18 PIS	17 ARI	19 GEM	18 CAN	19 VIR	18 LIB	18 SAG	18 CAP
19 SCO	20 CAP	19 CAP	18 AQU	21 ARI	19 TAU	21 CAN	20 LEO	21 LIB	20 SCO	20 CAP	20 AQU
22 SAG	23 AQU	22 AQU	21 PIS	23 TAU	22 GEM	24 LEO	22 VIR	22 SCO	22 SAG	23 AQU	22 PIS
24 CAP	25 PIS	24 PIS	23 ARI	25 GEM	24 CAN	26 VIR	24 LIB	25 SAG	24 CAP	25 PIS	25 ARI
26 AQU	28 ARI	27 ARI	26 TAU	28 CAN	26 LEO	28 LIB	26 SCO	27 CAP	26 AQU	28 ARI	27 TAU
29 PIS		29 TAU	28 GEM	30 LEO	28 VIR	30 SCO	28 SAG	29 AQU	29 PIS	30 TAU	30 GEM
31 ARI			30 CAN		30 LIB		30 CAP		31 ARI		

2056

JAN	FEB	MAR	APR	MAY	JUN	JUL	AUG	SEP	OCT	NOV	DEC
1 CAN	2 VIR	3 LIB	1 SCO	2 CAP	1 AQU	1 PIS	2 TAU	1 GEM	3 LEO	2 VIR	1 LIB
4 LEO	4 LIB	5 SCO	3 SAG	5 AQU	3 PIS	3 ARI	4 GEM	3 CAN	5 VIR	4 LIB	3 SCO
6 VIR	6 SCO	7 SAG	5 CAP	7 PIS	6 ARI	5 TAU	7 CAN	6 LEO	7 LIB	6 SCO	5 SAG
8 LIB	8 SAG	9 CAP	7 AQU	9 ARI	8 TAU	8 GEM	9 LEO	8 VIR	9 SCO	8 SAG	7 CAP
10 SCO	11 CAP	11 AQU	10 PIS	12 TAU	11 GEM	10 CAN	11 VIR	10 LIB	11 SAG	10 CAP	9 AQU
12 SAG	13 AQU	13 PIS	12 ARI	14 GEM	13 CAN	13 LEO	14 LIB	12 SCO	13 CAP	12 AQU	11 PIS
14 CAP	15 PIS	16 ARI	15 TAU	17 CAN	16 LEO	15 VIR	16 SCO	14 SAG	16 AQU	14 PIS	14 ARI
16 AQU	18 ARI	18 TAU	17 GEM	19 LEO	18 VIR	17 LIB	18 SAG	16 CAP	18 PIS	16 ARI	16 TAU
19 PIS	20 TAU	21 GEM	20 CAN	22 VIR	20 LIB	19 SCO	20 CAP	18 AQU	20 ARI	19 TAU	19 GEM
21 ARI	23 GEM	23 CAN	22 LEO	24 LIB	22 SCO	22 SAG	22 AQU	21 PIS	23 TAU	21 GEM	21 CAN
24 TAU	25 CAN	26 LEO	24 VIR	26 SCO	24 SAG	24 CAP	24 PIS	23 ARI	25 GEM	24 CAN	24 LEO
26 GEM	27 LEO	28 VIR	26 LIB	28 SAG	26 CAP	26 AQU	26 ARI	25 TAU	28 CAN	27 LEO	26 VIR
29 CAN	29 VIR	30 LIB	28 SCO	30 CAP	28 AQU	28 PIS	28 TAU	28 GEM	30 LEO	29 VIR	28 LIB
31 LEO			30 SAG			30 ARI	30 GEM	30 CAN			31 SCO

2057

JAN	FEB	MAR	APR	MAY	JUN	JUL	AUG	SEP	OCT	NOV	DEC
2 SAG	2 AQU	1 AQU	2 ARI	2 TAU	1 GEM	3 LEO	2 VIR	2 SCO	2 SAG	2 AQU	2 PIS
4 CAP	4 PIS	4 PIS	5 TAU	4 GEM	3 CAN	5 VIR	4 LIB	5 SAG	4 CAP	4 PIS	4 ARI
6 AQU	6 ARI	6 ARI	7 GEM	7 CAN	6 LEO	8 LIB	6 SCO	7 CAP	6 AQU	7 ARI	6 TAU
8 PIS	8 TAU	8 TAU	10 CAN	9 LEO	8 VIR	10 SCO	8 SAG	9 AQU	8 PIS	9 TAU	9 GEM
10 ARI	11 GEM	11 GEM	12 LEO	12 VIR	10 LIB	12 SAG	10 CAP	11 PIS	10 ARI	11 GEM	11 CAN
13 TAU	14 CAN	13 CAN	14 VIR	14 LIB	13 SCO	14 CAP	12 AQU	13 ARI	13 TAU	14 CAN	14 LEO
15 GEM	16 LEO	16 LEO	16 LIB	16 SCO	15 SAG	16 AQU	14 PIS	15 TAU	15 GEM	16 LEO	16 VIR
18 CAN	19 VIR	18 VIR	19 SCO	18 SAG	17 CAP	18 PIS	16 ARI	18 GEM	18 CAN	19 VIR	19 LIB
20 LEO	21 LIB	20 LIB	21 SAG	21 CAP	19 AQU	20 ARI	19 TAU	20 CAN	20 LEO	21 LIB	21 SCO
22 VIR	23 SCO	22 SCO	23 CAP	23 AQU	21 PIS	23 TAU	21 GEM	23 LEO	23 VIR	24 SCO	23 SAG
25 LIB	25 SAG	24 SAG	25 AQU	25 PIS	23 ARI	25 GEM	24 CAN	25 VIR	25 LIB	26 SAG	25 CAP
27 SCO	27 CAP	27 CAP	27 PIS	27 ARI	25 TAU	28 CAN	26 LEO	28 LIB	28 SCO	28 CAP	27 AQU
29 SAG		29 AQU	29 ARI	29 TAU	28 GEM	30 LEO	29 VIR	30 SCO	29 SAG	30 AQU	29 PIS
31 CAP		31 PIS			30 CAN		31 LIB		31 CAP		31 ARI

2058

JAN	FEB	MAR	APR	MAY	JUN	JUL	AUG	SEP	OCT	NOV	DEC
3 TAU	1 GEM	1 GEM	2 LEO	2 VIR	1 LIB	2 SAG	1 CAP	1 PIS	1 ARI	1 GEM	1 CAN
5 GEM	4 CAN	3 CAN	4 VIR	4 LIB	3 SCO	4 CAP	3 AQU	3 ARI	3 TAU	4 CAN	4 LEO
7 CAN	6 LEO	6 LEO	7 LIB	6 SCO	5 SAG	6 AQU	5 PIS	5 TAU	5 GEM	6 LEO	6 VIR
10 LEO	9 VIR	9 VIR	9 SCO	9 SAG	7 CAP	8 PIS	7 ARI	8 GEM	8 CAN	9 VIR	9 LIB
13 VIR	11 LIB	10 LIB	11 SAG	11 CAP	9 AQU	11 ARI	9 TAU	10 CAN	10 LEO	11 LIB	11 SCO
15 LIB	14 SCO	13 SCO	13 CAP	13 AQU	11 PIS	13 TAU	11 GEM	13 LEO	13 VIR	14 SCO	13 SAG
17 SCO	16 SAG	15 SAG	15 AQU	15 PIS	13 ARI	15 GEM	14 CAN	15 VIR	15 LIB	16 SAG	15 CAP
19 SAG	18 CAP	17 CAP	18 PIS	17 ARI	15 TAU	18 CAN	16 LEO	18 LIB	17 SCO	18 CAP	17 AQU
22 CAP	20 AQU	19 AQU	20 ARI	19 TAU	18 GEM	20 LEO	19 VIR	20 SCO	20 SAG	20 AQU	19 PIS
23 AQU	22 PIS	21 PIS	22 TAU	22 GEM	20 CAN	23 VIR	21 LIB	22 SAG	22 CAP	22 PIS	22 ARI
25 PIS	24 ARI	23 ARI	24 GEM	24 CAN	23 LEO	25 LIB	24 SCO	25 CAP	24 AQU	24 ARI	24 TAU
28 ARI	26 TAU	26 TAU	27 CAN	27 LEO	25 VIR	28 SCO	26 SAG	27 AQU	27 PIS	27 TAU	26 GEM
30 TAU		28 GEM	29 LEO	29 VIR	28 LIB	30 SAG	28 CAP	28 PIS	28 ARI	29 GEM	28 CAN
		30 CAN			30 SCO		30 AQU		30 TAU		31 LEO

2059

JAN	FEB	MAR	APR	MAY	JUN	JUL	AUG	SEP	OCT	NOV	DEC
2 VIR	1 LIB	3 SCO	2 SAG	2 CAP	2 PIS	1 ARI	2 GEM	3 LEO	2 VIR	1 LIB	1 SCO
5 LIB	4 SCO	5 SAG	4 CAP	3 AQU	4 ARI	3 TAU	4 CAN	5 VIR	5 LIB	4 SCO	3 SAG
7 SCO	6 SAG	8 CAP	6 AQU	5 PIS	6 TAU	5 GEM	6 LEO	8 LIB	7 SCO	6 SAG	6 CAP
10 SAG	8 CAP	10 AQU	8 PIS	8 ARI	8 GEM	8 CAN	9 VIR	10 SCO	10 SAG	8 CAP	8 AQU
12 CAP	10 AQU	12 PIS	10 ARI	10 TAU	10 CAN	10 LEO	11 LIB	13 SAG	12 CAP	11 AQU	10 PIS
14 AQU	12 PIS	14 ARI	12 TAU	12 GEM	12 LEO	13 VIR	13 SCO	15 CAP	14 AQU	13 PIS	12 ARI
16 PIS	14 ARI	16 TAU	14 GEM	14 CAN	15 VIR	15 LIB	16 SAG	17 AQU	17 PIS	15 ARI	14 TAU
18 ARI	16 TAU	18 GEM	17 CAN	16 LEO	18 LIB	18 SCO	18 CAP	19 PIS	19 ARI	17 TAU	16 GEM
20 TAU	19 GEM	20 CAN	19 LEO	18 VIR	20 SCO	20 SAG	21 AQU	21 ARI	21 TAU	19 GEM	19 CAN
22 GEM	21 CAN	23 LEO	22 VIR	21 LIB	23 SAG	23 CAP	23 PIS	23 TAU	23 GEM	21 CAN	21 LEO
25 CAN	23 LEO	25 VIR	24 LIB	24 SCO	25 CAP	25 AQU	25 ARI	25 GEM	25 CAN	23 LEO	23 VIR
27 LEO	26 VIR	28 LIB	26 SCO	26 SAG	27 AQU	26 PIS	27 TAU	27 CAN	27 LEO	26 VIR	26 LIB
30 VIR	28 LIB	30 SCO	29 SAG	28 CAP	29 PIS	28 ARI	29 GEM	29 LEO	30 VIR	28 LIB	28 SCO
				31 AQU		30 TAU	31 CAN				31 SAG

JAN	FEB	MAR	APR	MAY	JUN	JUL	AUG	SEP	OCT	NOV	DEC
2 CAP	1 AQU	1 PIS	1 TAU	1 GEM	2 LEO	1 VIR	3 SCO	2 SAG	1 CAP	2 PIS	2 ARI
4 AQU	3 PIS	3 ARI	4 GEM	3 CAN	4 VIR	4 LIB	5 SAG	4 CAP	4 AQU	4 ARI	4 TAU
6 PIS	5 ARI	5 TAU	6 CAN	5 LEO	6 LIB	6 SCO	8 CAP	6 AQU	6 PIS	6 TAU	6 GEM
8 ARI	7 TAU	7 GEM	8 LEO	8 VIR	9 SCO	9 SAG	10 AQU	8 PIS	8 ARI	8 GEM	8 CAN
11 TAU	9 GEM	9 CAN	10 VIR	10 LIB	12 SAG	11 CAP	12 PIS	10 ARI	10 TAU	10 CAN	10 LEO
13 GEM	11 CAN	12 LEO	13 LIB	13 SCO	14 CAP	14 AQU	14 ARI	12 TAU	12 GEM	13 LEO	12 VIR
15 CAN	14 LEO	14 VIR	15 SCO	15 SAG	16 AQU	16 PIS	16 TAU	14 GEM	14 CAN	15 VIR	15 LIB
17 LEO	16 VIR	17 LIB	18 SAG	18 CAP	18 PIS	18 ARI	18 GEM	17 CAN	16 LEO	17 LIB	17 SCO
20 VIR	18 LIB	19 SCO	20 CAP	20 AQU	21 ARI	20 TAU	20 CAN	19 LEO	19 VIR	20 SCO	20 SAG
22 LIB	21 SCO	22 SAG	23 AQU	22 PIS	23 TAU	22 GEM	22 LEO	21 VIR	21 LIB	22 SAG	22 CAP
25 SCO	23 SAG	24 CAP	25 PIS	24 ARI	25 GEM	24 CAN	25 VIR	24 LIB	24 SCO	25 CAP	24 AQU
27 SAG	26 CAP	26 AQU	27 ARI	26 TAU	27 CAN	26 LEO	27 LIB	26 SCO	26 SAG	27 AQU	27 PIS
29 CAP	28 AQU	29 PIS	29 TAU	28 GEM	29 LEO	29 VIR	30 SCO	29 SAG	29 CAP	30 PIS	29 ARI
		31 ARI		31 CAN		31 LIB			31 AQU		31 TAU

JAN	FEB	MAR	APR	MAY	JUN	JUL	AUG	SEP	OCT	NOV	DEC
2 GEM	1 CAN	2 LEO	3 VIR	3 SCO	1 SAG	1 CAP	2 PIS	1 ARI	2 GEM	1 CAN	2 VIR
4 CAN	3 LEO	4 VIR	3 LIB	5 SAG	4 CAP	4 AQU	5 ARI	3 TAU	4 CAN	3 LEO	5 LIB
6 LEO	5 VIR	7 LIB	5 SCO	8 CAP	6 AQU	6 PIS	7 TAU	5 GEM	7 LEO	5 VIR	7 SCO
9 VIR	7 LIB	9 SCO	8 SAG	10 AQU	9 PIS	8 ARI	9 GEM	7 CAN	9 VIR	7 LIB	10 SAG
11 LIB	10 SCO	12 SAG	10 CAP	13 PIS	11 ARI	11 TAU	11 CAN	9 LEO	11 LIB	10 SCO	12 CAP
13 SCO	12 SAG	14 CAP	13 AQU	15 ARI	13 TAU	13 GEM	13 LEO	12 VIR	13 SCO	12 SAG	15 AQU
16 SAG	15 CAP	17 AQU	15 PIS	17 TAU	15 GEM	15 CAN	15 VIR	14 LIB	16 SAG	15 CAP	17 PIS
18 CAP	17 AQU	19 PIS	17 ARI	19 GEM	17 CAN	17 LEO	17 LIB	16 SCO	18 CAP	17 AQU	19 ARI
21 AQU	19 PIS	21 ARI	19 TAU	21 CAN	19 LEO	19 VIR	20 SCO	19 SAG	21 AQU	20 PIS	22 TAU
23 PIS	22 ARI	23 TAU	21 GEM	23 LEO	21 VIR	21 LIB	22 SAG	21 CAP	23 PIS	22 ARI	24 GEM
25 ARI	24 TAU	25 GEM	23 CAN	25 VIR	24 LIB	23 SCO	25 CAP	24 AQU	26 ARI	24 TAU	26 CAN
27 TAU	26 GEM	27 CAN	26 LEO	27 LIB	26 SCO	26 SAG	27 AQU	26 PIS	28 TAU	26 GEM	28 LEO
30 GEM	28 CAN	29 LEO	28 VIR	30 SCO	29 SAG	29 CAP	30 PIS	28 ARI	30 GEM	28 CAN	30 VIR
			30 LIB			31 AQU		30 TAU		30 LEO	

JAN	FEB	MAR	APR	MAY	JUN	JUL	AUG	SEP	OCT	NOV	DEC
1 LIB	2 SAG	1 SAG	3 AQU	3 PIS	1 ARI	1 TAU	1 CAN	2 VIR	1 LIB	2 SAG	2 CAP
3 SCO	5 CAP	4 CAP	5 PIS	5 ARI	4 TAU	3 GEM	3 LEO	4 LIB	4 SCO	5 CAP	4 AQU
6 SAG	7 AQU	6 AQU	8 ARI	7 TAU	6 GEM	5 CAN	5 VIR	6 SAG	6 SAG	7 AQU	7 PIS
8 CAP	10 PIS	9 PIS	10 TAU	9 GEM	8 CAN	7 LEO	7 LIB	8 CAP	8 CAP	10 PIS	9 ARI
11 AQU	12 ARI	11 ARI	12 GEM	11 CAN	10 LEO	9 VIR	10 SCO	11 AQU	11 AQU	12 ARI	12 TAU
13 PIS	14 TAU	13 TAU	14 CAN	13 LEO	12 VIR	11 LIB	12 SAG	13 PIS	13 PIS	14 TAU	14 GEM
16 ARI	16 GEM	16 GEM	16 LEO	15 VIR	14 LIB	13 SCO	15 CAP	16 ARI	16 ARI	17 GEM	16 CAN
18 TAU	18 CAN	18 CAN	18 VIR	18 LIB	16 SCO	16 SAG	17 AQU	18 TAU	18 TAU	19 CAN	18 LEO
20 GEM	20 LEO	20 LEO	20 LIB	20 SCO	19 SAG	18 CAP	20 PIS	21 GEM	20 GEM	21 LEO	20 VIR
22 CAN	23 VIR	22 VIR	23 SCO	22 SAG	21 CAP	21 AQU	22 ARI	23 CAN	22 CAN	23 VIR	22 LIB
24 LEO	25 LIB	24 LIB	25 SAG	25 CAP	24 AQU	23 PIS	24 TAU	25 LEO	24 LEO	25 LIB	24 SCO
26 VIR	27 SCO	26 SCO	28 CAP	27 AQU	26 PIS	26 ARI	27 GEM	27 VIR	27 VIR	27 SCO	27 SAG
28 LIB		29 SAG	30 AQU	30 PIS	29 ARI	28 TAU	29 CAN	29 VIR	29 LIB	30 SAG	29 CAP
31 SCO		31 CAP				30 GEM	31 LEO		31 SCO		

JAN	FEB	MAR	APR	MAY	JUN	JUL	AUG	SEP	OCT	NOV	DEC
1 AQU	2 ARI	1 ARI	2 GEM	2 CAN	2 VIR	2 LIB	2 SAG	1 CAP	1 AQU	2 ARI	2 TAU
3 PIS	4 TAU	4 TAU	4 CAN	4 LEO	4 LIB	4 SCO	5 CAP	3 AQU	3 PIS	4 TAU	4 GEM
6 ARI	7 GEM	6 GEM	7 LEO	6 VIR	7 SCO	6 SAG	7 AQU	6 PIS	6 ARI	7 GEM	6 CAN
8 TAU	9 CAN	8 CAN	9 VIR	8 LIB	9 SAG	8 CAP	10 PIS	8 ARI	8 TAU	9 CAN	8 LEO
10 GEM	11 LEO	10 LEO	11 LIB	10 SCO	11 CAP	11 AQU	12 ARI	11 TAU	11 GEM	11 LEO	11 VIR
12 CAN	13 VIR	12 VIR	13 SCO	12 SAG	14 AQU	13 PIS	15 TAU	13 GEM	13 CAN	13 VIR	13 LIB
14 LEO	15 LIB	14 LIB	15 SAG	15 CAP	16 PIS	16 ARI	17 GEM	16 CAN	15 LEO	15 LIB	15 SCO
16 VIR	17 SCO	16 SCO	17 CAP	17 AQU	19 ARI	18 TAU	19 CAN	18 LEO	17 VIR	18 SCO	17 SAG
18 LIB	19 SAG	18 SAG	20 AQU	20 PIS	21 TAU	21 GEM	21 LEO	21 VIR	19 LIB	20 SAG	19 CAP
21 SCO	22 CAP	21 CAP	22 PIS	22 ARI	23 GEM	23 CAN	23 VIR	23 LIB	21 SCO	22 CAP	22 AQU
23 SAG	24 AQU	24 AQU	25 ARI	25 TAU	25 CAN	25 LEO	25 LIB	25 SCO	23 SAG	24 AQU	24 PIS
25 CAP	27 PIS	26 PIS	27 TAU	27 GEM	27 LEO	27 VIR	27 SCO	27 SAG	26 CAP	27 PIS	27 ARI
28 AQU		29 ARI	30 GEM	29 CAN	29 VIR	29 LIB	30 SAG	28 CAP	28 AQU	29 ARI	29 TAU
31 PIS		31 TAU		31 LEO		31 SCO			30 PIS		

2064

JAN	FEB	MAR	APR	MAY	JUN	JUL	AUG	SEP	OCT	NOV	DEC
1 GEM	1 LEO	2 VIR	2 SCO	2 SAG	2 AQU	2 PIS	1 ARI	2 GEM	2 CAN	1 LEO	2 LIB
3 CAN	4 VIR	4 LIB	4 SAG	4 CAP	5 PIS	5 ARI	4 TAU	5 CAN	4 LEO	3 VIR	4 SCO
5 LEO	5 LIB	6 SCO	6 CAP	6 AQU	7 ARI	7 TAU	6 GEM	7 LEO	7 VIR	5 LIB	6 SAG
7 VIR	7 SCO	8 SAG	9 AQU	9 PIS	10 TAU	10 GEM	8 CAN	9 VIR	9 LIB	7 SCO	8 CAP
9 LIB	10 SAG	10 CAP	11 PIS	11 ARI	12 GEM	12 CAN	11 LEO	11 LIB	11 SCO	9 SAG	11 AQU
11 SCO	12 CAP	12 AQU	14 ARI	14 TAU	15 CAN	14 LEO	13 VIR	13 SCO	13 SAG	11 CAP	13 PIS
13 SAG	14 AQU	15 PIS	16 TAU	16 GEM	17 LEO	16 VIR	15 LIB	15 SAG	15 CAP	13 AQU	15 ARI
16 CAP	17 PIS	18 ARI	19 GEM	19 CAN	19 VIR	18 LIB	17 SCO	17 CAP	17 AQU	16 PIS	18 TAU
18 AQU	19 ARI	20 TAU	21 CAN	21 LEO	21 LIB	20 SCO	19 SAG	20 AQU	19 PIS	18 ARI	20 GEM
20 PIS	22 TAU	23 GEM	23 LEO	23 VIR	23 SCO	23 SAG	21 CAP	22 PIS	22 ARI	21 TAU	23 CAN
23 ARI	24 GEM	25 CAN	26 VIR	25 LIB	25 SAG	25 CAP	23 AQU	25 ARI	24 TAU	23 GEM	25 LEO
25 TAU	27 CAN	27 LEO	28 LIB	27 SCO	28 CAP	27 AQU	26 PIS	27 TAU	27 GEM	26 CAN	27 VIR
28 GEM	29 LEO	29 VIR	30 SCO	29 SAG	30 AQU	30 PIS	28 ARI	30 GEM	29 CAN	28 LEO	30 LIB
30 CAN		31 LIB		31 CAP			31 TAU			30 VIR	

2065

JAN	FEB	MAR	APR	MAY	JUN	JUL	AUG	SEP	OCT	NOV	DEC
1 SCO	1 CAP	3 AQU	1 PIS	1 ARI	2 GEM	2 CAN	1 LEO	1 LIB	1 SCO	1 CAP	1 AQU
3 SAG	3 AQU	5 PIS	4 ARI	3 TAU	4 CAN	4 LEO	3 VIR	4 SCO	3 SAG	3 AQU	3 PIS
5 CAP	6 PIS	7 ARI	6 TAU	6 GEM	7 LEO	7 VIR	5 LIB	6 SAG	5 CAP	6 PIS	5 ARI
7 AQU	8 ARI	10 TAU	9 GEM	8 CAN	10 VIR	9 LIB	7 SCO	8 CAP	7 AQU	8 ARI	8 TAU
9 PIS	11 TAU	12 GEM	11 CAN	10 LEO	12 LIB	11 SCO	9 SAG	10 AQU	9 PIS	11 TAU	10 GEM
12 ARI	13 GEM	15 CAN	14 LEO	13 VIR	14 SCO	13 SAG	12 CAP	12 PIS	12 ARI	13 GEM	13 CAN
14 TAU	16 CAN	17 LEO	16 VIR	15 LIB	16 SAG	15 CAP	14 AQU	15 ARI	14 TAU	16 CAN	15 LEO
17 GEM	18 LEO	19 VIR	18 LIB	17 SCO	18 CAP	17 AQU	16 PIS	17 TAU	16 GEM	18 LEO	18 VIR
19 CAN	20 VIR	22 LIB	20 SCO	19 SAG	20 AQU	20 PIS	18 ARI	19 GEM	19 CAN	21 VIR	20 LIB
21 LEO	22 LIB	24 SCO	22 SAG	21 CAP	22 PIS	22 ARI	21 TAU	22 CAN	22 LEO	23 LIB	22 SCO
24 VIR	24 SCO	26 SAG	24 CAP	24 AQU	25 ARI	24 TAU	23 GEM	24 LEO	24 VIR	25 SCO	24 SAG
26 LIB	26 SAG	28 CAP	26 AQU	26 PIS	27 TAU	27 GEM	26 CAN	27 VIR	26 LIB	27 SAG	26 CAP
28 SCO	28 CAP	30 AQU	28 PIS	28 ARI	30 GEM	29 CAN	28 LEO	29 LIB	28 SCO	29 CAP	28 AQU
30 SAG				31 TAU			30 VIR		30 SAG		30 PIS

2066

JAN	FEB	MAR	APR	MAY	JUN	JUL	AUG	SEP	OCT	NOV	DEC
2 ARI	3 GEM	2 GEM	1 CAN	1 LEO	2 LIB	2 SCO	2 CAP	3 PIS	2 ARI	1 TAU	3 CAN
4 TAU	5 CAN	5 CAN	4 LEO	3 VIR	4 SCO	4 AQU	4 AQU	5 ARI	4 TAU	3 GEM	5 LEO
7 GEM	8 LEO	7 LEO	6 VIR	6 LIB	6 SAG	6 CAP	6 PIS	7 TAU	7 GEM	5 CAN	8 VIR
9 CAN	10 VIR	10 VIR	8 LIB	8 SCO	8 CAP	8 AQU	8 ARI	9 GEM	9 CAN	8 LEO	10 LIB
12 LEO	13 LIB	12 LIB	10 SCO	10 SAG	10 AQU	10 PIS	11 TAU	12 CAN	12 LEO	11 VIR	13 SCO
14 VIR	15 SCO	14 SCO	12 SAG	12 CAP	12 PIS	12 ARI	13 GEM	14 LEO	14 VIR	13 LIB	15 SAG
16 LIB	17 SAG	16 SAG	14 CAP	14 AQU	15 ARI	14 TAU	15 CAN	17 VIR	17 LIB	15 SCO	17 CAP
18 SCO	19 CAP	18 CAP	17 AQU	16 PIS	17 TAU	17 GEM	18 LEO	19 LIB	19 SCO	17 SAG	19 AQU
21 SAG	21 AQU	20 AQU	19 PIS	18 ARI	19 GEM	19 CAN	20 VIR	21 SCO	21 SAG	19 CAP	21 PIS
23 CAP	23 PIS	23 PIS	21 ARI	21 TAU	22 CAN	22 LEO	23 LIB	23 SAG	23 CAP	21 AQU	23 ARI
25 AQU	25 ARI	25 ARI	23 TAU	23 GEM	24 LEO	24 VIR	25 SCO	26 CAP	25 AQU	23 PIS	25 TAU
27 PIS	28 TAU	27 TAU	26 GEM	26 CAN	27 VIR	27 LIB	27 SAG	28 AQU	27 PIS	26 ARI	28 GEM
29 ARI		30 GEM	28 CAN	28 LEO	29 LIB	29 SCO	29 CAP	30 PIS	29 ARI	28 TAU	30 CAN
31 TAU				31 VIR		31 SAG	31 AQU			30 GEM	

2067

JAN	FEB	MAR	APR	MAY	JUN	JUL	AUG	SEP	OCT	NOV	DEC
2 LEO	3 LIB	2 LIB	1 SCO	2 CAP	1 AQU	2 ARI	1 TAU	2 CAN	1 LEO	3 LIB	3 SCO
4 VIR	5 SCO	4 SCO	3 SAG	4 AQU	3 PIS	4 TAU	3 GEM	4 LEO	4 VIR	5 SCO	5 SAG
7 LIB	7 SAG	7 SAG	5 CAP	7 PIS	5 ARI	7 GEM	5 CAN	7 VIR	7 LIB	7 SAG	7 CAP
9 SCO	10 CAP	9 CAP	7 AQU	9 ARI	7 TAU	9 CAN	8 LEO	9 LIB	9 SCO	10 CAP	9 AQU
11 SAG	12 AQU	11 AQU	9 PIS	11 TAU	9 GEM	12 LEO	10 VIR	12 SCO	11 SAG	12 AQU	11 PIS
13 CAP	14 PIS	13 PIS	11 ARI	13 GEM	12 CAN	14 VIR	13 LIB	14 SAG	13 CAP	14 PIS	13 ARI
15 AQU	16 ARI	15 ARI	14 TAU	16 CAN	14 LEO	17 LIB	15 SCO	16 CAP	16 AQU	16 ARI	15 TAU
17 PIS	18 TAU	17 TAU	16 GEM	18 LEO	17 VIR	19 SCO	18 SAG	18 AQU	18 PIS	18 TAU	18 GEM
19 ARI	20 GEM	19 GEM	18 CAN	21 VIR	19 LIB	21 SAG	20 CAP	20 PIS	20 ARI	20 GEM	20 CAN
21 TAU	23 CAN	22 CAN	21 LEO	23 LIB	22 SCO	23 CAP	22 AQU	22 ARI	22 TAU	23 CAN	22 LEO
24 GEM	25 LEO	24 LEO	23 VIR	25 SCO	24 SAG	25 AQU	24 PIS	24 TAU	24 GEM	25 LEO	25 VIR
26 CAN	28 VIR	27 VIR	26 LIB	28 SAG	26 CAP	27 PIS	26 ARI	27 GEM	26 CAN	28 VIR	28 LIB
29 LEO		29 LIB	28 SCO	30 CAP	28 AQU	29 ARI	28 TAU	29 CAN	29 LEO	30 LIB	30 SCO
31 VIR			30 SAG		30 PIS		30 GEM		31 VIR		

2068

JAN	FEB	MAR	APR	MAY	JUN	JUL	AUG	SEP	OCT	NOV	DEC
1 SAG	2 AQU	2 PIS	1 ARI	2 GEM	1 CAN	1 LEO	2 LIB	1 SCO	3 CAP	1 AQU	1 PIS
3 CAP	4 PIS	4 ARI	3 TAU	5 CAN	3 LEO	3 VIR	4 SCO	3 SAG	5 AQU	3 PIS	3 ARI
5 AQU	6 ARI	6 TAU	5 GEM	7 LEO	6 VIR	6 LIB	7 SAG	6 CAP	7 PIS	6 ARI	5 TAU
7 PIS	8 TAU	8 GEM	7 CAN	9 VIR	8 LIB	8 SCO	9 CAP	8 AQU	9 ARI	8 TAU	7 GEM
10 ARI	10 GEM	11 CAN	10 LEO	12 LIB	11 SCO	10 SAG	11 AQU	11 PIS	11 TAU	10 GEM	9 CAN
12 TAU	13 CAN	13 LEO	12 VIR	14 SCO	13 SAG	13 CAP	13 PIS	12 ARI	13 GEM	12 CAN	11 LEO
14 GEM	15 LEO	16 VIR	15 LIB	17 SAG	15 CAP	15 AQU	15 ARI	15 TAU	15 CAN	14 LEO	14 VIR
16 CAN	18 VIR	18 LIB	19 SCO	19 CAP	17 AQU	17 PIS	17 TAU	16 GEM	18 LEO	16 VIR	16 LIB
19 LEO	20 LIB	21 SCO	19 SAG	21 AQU	20 PIS	19 ARI	19 GEM	18 CAN	20 VIR	19 LIB	19 SCO
21 VIR	23 SCO	23 SAG	22 CAP	23 PIS	22 ARI	21 TAU	22 CAN	20 LEO	23 LIB	21 SCO	21 SAG
24 LIB	25 SAG	26 CAP	24 AQU	25 ARI	24 TAU	23 GEM	24 LEO	23 VIR	25 SCO	24 SAG	24 CAP
26 SCO	27 CAP	28 AQU	26 PIS	28 TAU	26 GEM	26 CAN	26 VIR	25 LIB	28 SAG	26 CAP	26 AQU
29 SAG	29 AQU	30 PIS	28 ARI	30 GEM	28 CAN	28 LEO	28 LIB	28 SCO	30 CAP	29 AQU	28 PIS
31 CAP			30 TAU			30 VIR		30 SAG			30 ARI

2069

JAN	FEB	MAR	APR	MAY	JUN	JUL	AUG	SEP	OCT	NOV	DEC
1 TAU	2 CAN	1 CAN	2 VIR	2 LIB	1 SCO	3 CAP	1 AQU	2 ARI	2 TAU	2 CAN	1 LEO
3 GEM	4 LEO	3 LEO	4 LIB	4 SCO	3 SAG	5 AQU	4 PIS	4 TAU	4 GEM	4 LEO	4 VIR
6 CAN	6 VIR	6 VIR	7 SCO	7 SAG	6 CAP	7 PIS	6 ARI	6 GEM	6 CAN	6 VIR	6 LIB
8 LEO	9 LIB	8 LIB	10 SAG	9 CAP	8 AQU	10 ARI	8 TAU	8 CAN	8 LEO	9 LIB	9 SCO
10 VIR	11 SCO	11 SCO	12 CAP	12 AQU	10 PIS	12 TAU	10 GEM	11 LEO	10 VIR	11 SCO	11 SAG
13 LIB	14 SAG	13 SAG	14 AQU	14 PIS	12 ARI	14 GEM	12 CAN	13 VIR	13 LIB	14 SAG	14 CAP
15 SCO	16 CAP	16 CAP	17 PIS	16 ARI	14 TAU	16 CAN	14 LEO	15 LIB	15 SCO	16 CAP	16 AQU
18 SAG	19 AQU	18 AQU	19 ARI	18 TAU	16 GEM	18 LEO	17 VIR	18 SCO	18 SAG	19 AQU	18 PIS
20 CAP	21 PIS	20 PIS	21 TAU	20 GEM	18 CAN	21 LEO	19 LIB	20 SAG	20 CAP	21 PIS	21 ARI
22 AQU	23 ARI	22 ARI	23 GEM	22 CAN	21 LEO	23 LIB	22 SCO	23 CAP	23 AQU	23 ARI	23 TAU
24 PIS	25 TAU	24 TAU	25 CAN	24 LEO	23 VIR	25 SCO	24 SAG	25 AQU	25 PIS	25 TAU	25 GEM
26 ARI	27 GEM	26 GEM	27 LEO	27 VIR	25 LIB	28 SAG	27 CAP	27 PIS	27 ARI	27 GEM	27 CAN
28 TAU		28 CAN	29 VIR	29 LIB	28 SCO	30 CAP	29 AQU	30 ARI	29 TAU	29 CAN	29 LEO
31 GEM		31 LEO			30 SAG		31 PIS		31 GEM		31 VIR

2070

JAN	FEB	MAR	APR	MAY	JUN	JUL	AUG	SEP	OCT	NOV	DEC
2 LIB	1 SCO	1 SCO	2 CAP	2 AQU	3 ARI	2 TAU	1 GEM	1 LEO	3 LIB	1 SCO	1 SAG
5 SCO	4 SAG	3 SAG	4 AQU	5 PIS	5 TAU	4 GEM	3 CAN	3 VIR	5 SCO	4 SAG	4 CAP
7 SAG	6 CAP	6 CAP	7 PIS	7 ARI	7 GEM	6 CAN	5 LEO	5 LIB	8 SAG	6 CAP	6 AQU
10 CAP	9 AQU	8 AQU	9 ARI	8 TAU	9 CAN	8 LEO	7 VIR	8 SCO	10 CAP	9 AQU	9 PIS
12 AQU	11 PIS	10 PIS	11 TAU	10 GEM	11 LEO	11 VIR	9 LIB	10 SAG	13 AQU	11 PIS	11 ARI
15 PIS	13 ARI	12 ARI	13 GEM	12 CAN	13 VIR	13 LIB	11 SCO	13 CAP	15 PIS	14 ARI	13 TAU
17 ARI	15 TAU	15 TAU	15 CAN	14 LEO	15 LIB	15 SCO	13 SAG	15 AQU	17 ARI	16 TAU	15 GEM
19 TAU	17 GEM	17 GEM	17 LEO	17 VIR	18 SCO	18 SAG	16 CAP	18 PIS	19 TAU	18 GEM	17 CAN
21 GEM	20 CAN	19 CAN	19 VIR	19 LIB	21 SAG	20 CAP	19 AQU	20 ARI	21 GEM	20 CAN	19 LEO
23 CAN	22 LEO	21 LEO	22 LIB	21 SCO	23 CAP	23 AQU	21 PIS	22 TAU	23 CAN	22 LEO	21 VIR
25 LEO	24 VIR	23 VIR	24 SCO	24 SAG	25 AQU	25 PIS	23 ARI	24 GEM	26 LEO	24 VIR	23 LIB
28 VIR	26 LIB	26 LIB	27 SAG	27 CAP	28 PIS	27 ARI	26 TAU	26 CAN	28 VIR	26 LIB	26 SCO
30 LIB		28 SCO	29 CAP	29 AQU	30 ARI	29 TAU	28 GEM	28 LEO	30 LIB	29 SCO	28 SAG
		30 SAG		31 PIS			30 CAN	30 VIR			31 CAP

2071

JAN	FEB	MAR	APR	MAY	JUN	JUL	AUG	SEP	OCT	NOV	DEC
2 AQU	1 PIS	3 ARI	1 TAU	1 GEM	1 LEO	1 VIR	1 SCO	2 CAP	2 AQU	1 PIS	1 ARI
5 PIS	4 ARI	5 TAU	3 GEM	3 CAN	3 VIR	3 LIB	4 SAG	5 AQU	5 PIS	4 ARI	3 TAU
7 ARI	6 TAU	7 GEM	6 CAN	5 LEO	6 LIB	5 SCO	6 CAP	8 PIS	7 ARI	6 TAU	5 GEM
10 TAU	8 GEM	9 CAN	8 LEO	7 VIR	8 SCO	7 SAG	9 AQU	10 ARI	10 TAU	8 GEM	8 CAN
12 GEM	10 CAN	11 LEO	10 VIR	9 LIB	10 SAG	10 CAP	11 PIS	12 TAU	12 GEM	10 CAN	10 LEO
14 CAN	12 LEO	14 VIR	12 LIB	12 SCO	13 CAP	12 AQU	14 ARI	15 GEM	14 CAN	12 LEO	12 VIR
16 LEO	14 VIR	16 LIB	14 SCO	14 SAG	15 AQU	15 PIS	16 TAU	17 CAN	16 LEO	14 VIR	14 LIB
18 VIR	16 LIB	18 SCO	17 SAG	16 CAP	18 PIS	17 ARI	18 GEM	19 LEO	18 VIR	17 LIB	16 SCO
20 LIB	18 SCO	20 SAG	19 CAP	19 AQU	20 ARI	20 TAU	20 CAN	21 VIR	20 LIB	19 SCO	18 SAG
22 SCO	21 SAG	23 CAP	22 AQU	21 PIS	23 TAU	22 GEM	22 LEO	23 LIB	23 SCO	21 SAG	21 CAP
25 SAG	23 CAP	25 AQU	24 PIS	24 ARI	25 GEM	24 CAN	24 VIR	25 SCO	25 SAG	24 CAP	23 AQU
27 CAP	26 AQU	28 PIS	26 ARI	26 TAU	27 CAN	26 LEO	27 LIB	27 SAG	27 CAP	26 AQU	26 PIS
30 AQU	28 PIS	30 ARI	29 TAU	28 GEM	29 LEO	28 VIR	29 SCO	30 CAP	30 AQU	29 PIS	28 ARI
				30 CAN		30 LIB	31 SAG				31 TAU

2072

JAN	FEB	MAR	APR	MAY	JUN	JUL	AUG	SEP	OCT	NOV	DEC
2 GEM	3 LEO	1 LEO	1 LIB	1 SCO	2 CAP	1 AQU	3 ARI	1 TAU	1 GEM	2 LEO	1 VIR
4 CAN	4 VIR	3 VIR	3 SCO	3 SAG	4 AQU	4 PIS	5 TAU	3 GEM	3 CAN	4 VIR	3 LIB
6 LEO	6 LIB	5 LIB	6 SAG	5 CAP	7 PIS	6 ARI	8 GEM	6 CAN	6 LEO	6 LIB	6 SCO
8 VIR	9 SCO	7 SCO	8 CAP	8 AQU	9 ARI	9 TAU	10 CAN	8 LEO	8 VIR	8 SCO	8 SAG
10 LIB	11 SAG	9 SAG	10 AQU	10 PIS	12 TAU	11 GEM	12 LEO	10 VIR	10 LIB	10 SAG	10 CAP
12 SCO	13 CAP	12 CAP	13 PIS	13 ARI	14 GEM	13 CAN	14 VIR	12 LIB	12 SCO	12 CAP	12 AQU
15 SAG	16 AQU	14 AQU	15 ARI	15 TAU	16 CAN	16 LEO	16 LIB	14 SCO	14 SAG	15 AQU	15 PIS
17 CAP	18 PIS	17 PIS	18 TAU	17 GEM	18 LEO	18 VIR	18 SCO	16 SAG	16 CAP	17 PIS	17 ARI
20 AQU	21 ARI	19 ARI	20 GEM	20 CAN	20 VIR	20 LIB	20 SAG	19 CAP	18 AQU	20 ARI	20 TAU
22 PIS	23 TAU	22 TAU	22 CAN	22 LEO	22 LIB	22 SCO	22 CAP	21 AQU	21 PIS	22 TAU	22 GEM
25 ARI	26 GEM	24 GEM	25 LEO	24 VIR	24 SCO	24 SAG	25 AQU	24 PIS	24 ARI	25 GEM	24 CAN
27 TAU	28 CAN	26 CAN	27 VIR	26 LIB	27 SAG	26 CAP	27 PIS	26 ARI	26 TAU	27 CAN	26 LEO
29 GEM		28 LEO	29 LIB	28 SCO	29 CAP	29 AQU	30 ARI	29 TAU	29 GEM	29 LEO	29 VIR
31 CAN		30 VIR		30 SAG		31 PIS			31 CAN		31 LIB

2073

JAN	FEB	MAR	APR	MAY	JUN	JUL	AUG	SEP	OCT	NOV	DEC
2 SCO	2 CAP	2 CAP	3 PIS	3 ARI	1 TAU	1 GEM	2 LEO	1 VIR	2 SCO	1 SAG	2 AQU
4 SAG	5 AQU	4 AQU	5 ARI	5 TAU	4 GEM	4 CAN	4 VIR	3 LIB	4 SAG	3 CAP	4 PIS
6 CAP	7 PIS	7 PIS	8 TAU	8 GEM	6 CAN	6 LEO	6 LIB	5 SCO	6 CAP	5 AQU	7 ARI
9 AQU	9 ARI	9 ARI	10 GEM	10 CAN	8 LEO	8 VIR	8 SCO	7 SAG	8 AQU	7 PIS	9 TAU
11 PIS	12 TAU	12 TAU	13 CAN	12 LEO	11 VIR	10 LIB	11 SAG	9 CAP	11 PIS	10 ARI	12 GEM
14 ARI	14 GEM	14 GEM	15 LEO	14 VIR	13 LIB	12 SCO	13 CAP	11 AQU	13 ARI	12 TAU	14 CAN
16 TAU	17 CAN	16 CAN	17 VIR	17 LIB	15 SCO	14 SAG	15 AQU	14 PIS	16 TAU	15 GEM	17 LEO
18 GEM	19 LEO	19 LEO	19 LIB	19 SCO	17 SAG	16 CAP	17 PIS	16 ARI	18 GEM	17 CAN	19 VIR
21 CAN	21 VIR	21 VIR	21 SCO	21 SAG	19 CAP	19 AQU	20 ARI	19 TAU	21 CAN	20 LEO	21 LIB
23 LEO	23 LIB	23 LIB	23 SAG	23 CAP	21 AQU	21 PIS	22 TAU	21 GEM	23 LEO	22 VIR	23 SCO
25 VIR	25 SCO	25 SCO	25 CAP	25 AQU	24 PIS	24 ARI	25 GEM	24 CAN	26 VIR	24 LIB	25 SAG
27 LIB	27 SAG	27 SAG	28 AQU	27 PIS	26 ARI	26 TAU	27 CAN	26 LEO	28 LIB	26 SCO	27 CAP
29 SCO		29 CAP	30 PIS	30 ARI	29 TAU	29 GEM	30 LEO	28 VIR	30 SCO	28 SAG	30 AQU
31 SAG		31 AQU				31 CAN		30 LIB		30 CAP	

2074

JAN	FEB	MAR	APR	MAY	JUN	JUL	AUG	SEP	OCT	NOV	DEC
1 PIS	2 TAU	1 TAU	3 CAN	3 LEO	1 VIR	1 LIB	1 SAG	2 AQU	1 PIS	2 TAU	2 GEM
3 ARI	5 GEM	4 GEM	5 LEO	5 VIR	3 LIB	3 SCO	3 CAP	4 PIS	3 ARI	5 GEM	4 CAN
6 TAU	7 CAN	6 CAN	7 VIR	7 LIB	5 SCO	5 SAG	5 AQU	6 ARI	6 TAU	7 CAN	7 LEO
8 GEM	9 LEO	9 LEO	10 LIB	9 SCO	7 SAG	7 CAP	7 PIS	9 TAU	8 GEM	10 LEO	9 VIR
11 CAN	12 VIR	11 VIR	12 SCO	11 SAG	9 CAP	9 AQU	10 ARI	11 GEM	11 CAN	12 VIR	12 LIB
13 LEO	14 LIB	13 LIB	14 SAG	13 CAP	11 AQU	11 PIS	12 TAU	14 CAN	13 LEO	14 LIB	14 SCO
15 VIR	16 SCO	15 SCO	16 CAP	15 AQU	13 PIS	13 ARI	15 GEM	16 LEO	16 VIR	16 SCO	16 SAG
17 LIB	18 SAG	17 SAG	18 AQU	17 PIS	16 ARI	16 TAU	17 CAN	18 VIR	18 LIB	18 SAG	18 CAP
20 SCO	20 CAP	19 CAP	20 PIS	20 ARI	19 TAU	18 GEM	20 LEO	20 LIB	20 SCO	20 CAP	20 AQU
22 SAG	22 AQU	22 AQU	23 ARI	22 TAU	21 GEM	21 CAN	22 VIR	23 SCO	22 SAG	22 AQU	22 PIS
24 CAP	25 PIS	24 PIS	25 TAU	25 GEM	24 CAN	23 LEO	24 LIB	25 SAG	24 CAP	25 PIS	24 ARI
26 AQU	27 ARI	26 ARI	28 GEM	27 CAN	26 LEO	26 VIR	26 SCO	27 CAP	26 AQU	27 ARI	27 TAU
28 PIS		29 TAU	30 CAN	30 LEO	28 VIR	28 LIB	28 SAG	29 AQU	28 PIS	29 TAU	29 GEM
31 ARI		31 GEM				30 SCO	30 CAP		31 ARI		

2075

JAN	FEB	MAR	APR	MAY	JUN	JUL	AUG	SEP	OCT	NOV	DEC
1 CAN	2 VIR	1 VIR	2 SCO	1 SAG	2 AQU	1 PIS	2 TAU	1 GEM	1 CAN	2 VIR	2 LIB
3 LEO	4 LIB	3 LIB	4 SAG	3 CAP	4 PIS	3 ARI	5 GEM	3 CAN	3 LEO	4 LIB	4 SCO
6 VIR	6 SCO	6 SCO	6 CAP	5 AQU	6 ARI	6 TAU	7 CAN	6 LEO	6 VIR	7 SCO	6 SAG
8 LIB	9 SAG	8 SAG	8 AQU	8 PIS	9 TAU	8 GEM	10 LEO	8 VIR	8 LIB	9 SAG	8 CAP
10 SCO	11 CAP	10 CAP	10 PIS	10 ARI	11 GEM	11 CAN	12 VIR	10 LIB	10 SCO	11 CAP	10 AQU
12 SAG	13 AQU	12 AQU	13 ARI	12 TAU	14 CAN	13 LEO	14 LIB	13 SCO	12 SAG	13 AQU	12 PIS
14 CAP	15 PIS	14 PIS	15 TAU	15 GEM	16 LEO	16 VIR	17 SCO	15 SAG	15 CAP	15 PIS	15 ARI
16 AQU	17 ARI	16 ARI	17 GEM	17 CAN	19 VIR	18 LIB	19 SAG	17 CAP	17 AQU	17 ARI	17 TAU
18 PIS	19 TAU	19 TAU	20 CAN	20 LEO	21 LIB	20 SCO	21 CAP	19 AQU	19 PIS	19 TAU	19 GEM
21 ARI	22 GEM	21 GEM	22 LEO	22 VIR	23 SCO	23 SAG	23 AQU	22 PIS	21 ARI	22 GEM	22 CAN
23 TAU	24 CAN	24 CAN	25 VIR	25 LIB	25 SAG	25 CAP	25 PIS	24 ARI	23 TAU	24 CAN	24 LEO
25 GEM	27 LEO	26 LEO	27 LIB	27 SCO	27 CAP	27 AQU	27 ARI	26 TAU	26 GEM	27 LEO	27 VIR
28 CAN		29 VIR	29 SCO	29 SAG	29 AQU	29 PIS	29 TAU	28 GEM	28 CAN	29 VIR	29 LIB
30 LEO		31 LIB		31 CAP		31 ARI			31 LEO		31 SCO

JAN	FEB	MAR	APR	MAY	JUN	JUL	AUG	SEP	OCT	NOV	DEC
3 SAG	1 CAP	2 AQU	2 ARI	1 TAU	2 CAN	2 LEO	1 VIR	2 SCO	2 SAG	2 AQU	2 PIS
5 CAP	3 AQU	4 PIS	4 TAU	4 GEM	5 LEO	5 VIR	4 LIB	5 SAG	4 CAP	5 PIS	4 ARI
7 AQU	5 PIS	6 ARI	6 GEM	6 CAN	7 VIR	7 LIB	6 SCO	7 CAP	6 AQU	7 ARI	6 TAU
9 PIS	7 ARI	8 TAU	9 CAN	9 LEO	10 LIB	10 SCO	8 SAG	9 AQU	8 PIS	9 TAU	8 GEM
11 ARI	9 TAU	10 GEM	11 LEO	11 VIR	12 SCO	12 SAG	10 CAP	11 PIS	10 ARI	11 GEM	11 CAN
13 TAU	12 GEM	12 CAN	14 VIR	14 LIB	15 SAG	14 CAP	13 AQU	13 ARI	12 TAU	13 CAN	13 LEO
15 GEM	14 CAN	15 LEO	16 LIB	16 SCO	17 CAP	16 AQU	15 PIS	15 TAU	15 GEM	16 LEO	16 VIR
18 CAN	17 LEO	17 VIR	19 SCO	18 SAG	19 AQU	18 PIS	16 ARI	17 GEM	17 CAN	18 VIR	18 LIB
20 LEO	19 VIR	20 LIB	21 SAG	20 CAP	21 PIS	20 ARI	19 TAU	20 CAN	19 LEO	21 LIB	20 SCO
23 VIR	22 LIB	22 SCO	23 CAP	22 AQU	23 ARI	23 TAU	21 GEM	22 LEO	22 VIR	23 SCO	23 SAG
25 LIB	24 SCO	25 SAG	25 AQU	24 PIS	25 TAU	25 GEM	23 CAN	25 VIR	24 LIB	25 SAG	25 CAP
28 SCO	26 SAG	27 CAP	27 PIS	27 ARI	27 GEM	27 CAN	26 LEO	27 LIB	27 SCO	28 CAP	27 AQU
30 SAG	28 CAP	29 AQU	29 ARI	29 TAU	30 CAN	29 LEO	28 VIR	29 SCO	29 SAG	30 AQU	29 PIS
		31 PIS		31 GEM			31 LIB		31 CAP		31 ARI

JAN	FEB	MAR	APR	MAY	JUN	JUL	AUG	SEP	OCT	NOV	DEC
2 TAU	1 GEM	2 CAN	1 LEO	1 VIR	2 SCO	2 SAG	1 CAP	1 PIS	1 ARI	1 GEM	1 CAN
5 GEM	3 CAN	5 LEO	4 VIR	3 LIB	5 SAG	5 CAP	3 AQU	3 ARI	3 TAU	3 CAN	3 LEO
7 CAN	6 LEO	7 VIR	6 LIB	6 SCO	7 CAP	7 AQU	5 PIS	5 TAU	5 GEM	6 LEO	5 VIR
9 LEO	8 VIR	10 LIB	9 SCO	8 SAG	9 AQU	9 PIS	7 ARI	7 GEM	7 CAN	8 VIR	8 LIB
12 VIR	11 LIB	12 SCO	11 SAG	11 CAP	11 PIS	11 ARI	9 TAU	9 CAN	9 LEO	10 LIB	10 SCO
14 LIB	13 SCO	15 SAG	13 CAP	13 AQU	13 ARI	13 TAU	11 GEM	12 LEO	12 VIR	13 SCO	13 SAG
17 SCO	16 SAG	17 CAP	16 AQU	15 PIS	15 TAU	15 GEM	13 CAN	14 VIR	14 LIB	15 SAG	15 CAP
19 SAG	18 CAP	19 AQU	18 PIS	17 ARI	18 GEM	17 CAN	16 LEO	17 LIB	17 SCO	18 CAP	17 AQU
21 CAP	20 AQU	21 PIS	20 ARI	19 TAU	20 CAN	19 LEO	18 VIR	19 SCO	19 SAG	20 AQU	20 PIS
23 AQU	22 PIS	23 ARI	22 TAU	21 GEM	22 LEO	24 VIR	21 LIB	22 SAG	22 CAP	22 PIS	22 ARI
25 PIS	24 ARI	25 TAU	24 GEM	23 CAN	25 VIR	27 SCO	23 SCO	24 CAP	24 AQU	25 ARI	24 TAU
27 ARI	26 TAU	27 GEM	26 CAN	26 LEO	27 LIB	29 SAG	26 SAG	27 AQU	26 PIS	27 TAU	26 GEM
30 TAU	28 GEM	30 CAN	28 LEO	28 VIR	30 SCO		29 SAG	29 PIS	28 ARI	29 GEM	28 CAN
				31 LIB			30 AQU		30 TAU		30 LEO

JAN	FEB	MAR	APR	MAY	JUN	JUL	AUG	SEP	OCT	NOV	DEC
2 VIR	3 SCO	2 SCO	1 SAG	1 CAP	2 PIS	1 ARI	2 GEM	2 LEO	2 VIR	3 SCO	3 SAG
4 LIB	6 SAG	5 SAG	4 CAP	3 AQU	4 ARI	3 TAU	4 CAN	5 VIR	4 LIB	5 SAG	5 CAP
7 SCO	8 CAP	7 CAP	6 AQU	5 PIS	6 TAU	5 GEM	6 LEO	7 LIB	7 SCO	8 CAP	8 AQU
9 SAG	10 AQU	10 AQU	8 PIS	8 ARI	8 GEM	7 CAN	8 VIR	9 SCO	9 SAG	10 AQU	10 PIS
12 CAP	12 PIS	12 PIS	10 ARI	10 TAU	10 CAN	10 LEO	11 LIB	12 SAG	12 CAP	13 PIS	12 ARI
14 AQU	14 ARI	14 ARI	12 TAU	12 GEM	12 LEO	12 VIR	13 SCO	14 CAP	14 AQU	15 ARI	14 TAU
16 PIS	16 TAU	16 TAU	14 GEM	14 CAN	14 VIR	14 LIB	16 SAG	17 AQU	16 PIS	17 TAU	16 GEM
18 ARI	18 GEM	18 GEM	16 CAN	16 LEO	17 LIB	17 SCO	18 CAP	19 PIS	19 ARI	19 GEM	18 CAN
20 TAU	21 CAN	20 CAN	18 LEO	18 VIR	19 SCO	19 SAG	20 AQU	21 ARI	21 TAU	21 CAN	20 LEO
22 GEM	23 LEO	22 LEO	21 VIR	21 LIB	22 SAG	22 CAP	23 PIS	23 TAU	23 GEM	23 LEO	22 VIR
24 CAN	25 VIR	25 VIR	23 LIB	23 SCO	24 CAP	24 AQU	25 ARI	25 GEM	25 CAN	25 VIR	25 LIB
27 LEO	28 LIB	27 LIB	26 SCO	26 SAG	27 AQU	26 PIS	27 TAU	27 CAN	27 LEO	28 LIB	27 SCO
29 VIR		30 SCO	28 SAG	28 CAP	29 PIS	28 ARI	29 GEM	29 LEO	29 VIR	30 SCO	30 SAG
31 LIB				30 AQU		31 TAU	31 CAN		31 LIB		

JAN	FEB	MAR	APR	MAY	JUN	JUL	AUG	SEP	OCT	NOV	DEC
2 CAP	3 PIS	2 PIS	3 TAU	2 GEM	2 LEO	2 VIR	1 LIB	2 SAG	2 CAP	3 PIS	3 ARI
4 AQU	5 ARI	4 ARI	5 GEM	4 CAN	4 VIR	5 LIB	3 SCO	4 CAP	4 AQU	5 ARI	5 TAU
6 PIS	7 TAU	6 TAU	7 CAN	6 LEO	7 LIB	7 SCO	5 SAG	7 AQU	6 PIS	7 TAU	7 GEM
9 ARI	9 GEM	8 GEM	9 LEO	8 VIR	9 SCO	9 SAG	8 CAP	9 PIS	9 ARI	9 GEM	9 CAN
11 TAU	11 CAN	10 CAN	11 VIR	11 LIB	12 SAG	12 CAP	10 AQU	11 ARI	11 TAU	11 CAN	11 LEO
13 GEM	13 LEO	13 LEO	13 LIB	13 SCO	14 CAP	14 AQU	13 PIS	14 TAU	13 GEM	13 LEO	13 VIR
15 CAN	15 VIR	15 VIR	16 SCO	16 SAG	17 AQU	17 PIS	15 ARI	16 GEM	15 CAN	15 VIR	15 LIB
17 LEO	18 LIB	17 LIB	18 SAG	18 CAP	19 PIS	19 ARI	17 TAU	18 CAN	17 LEO	18 LIB	17 SCO
19 VIR	20 SCO	19 SCO	21 CAP	21 AQU	22 ARI	22 TAU	19 GEM	20 LEO	19 VIR	20 SCO	20 SAG
21 LIB	23 SAG	22 SAG	23 AQU	23 PIS	24 TAU	24 GEM	21 CAN	22 VIR	22 LIB	23 SAG	22 CAP
24 SCO	25 CAP	25 CAP	26 PIS	25 ARI	26 GEM	26 CAN	24 LEO	24 LIB	24 SCO	25 CAP	25 AQU
26 SAG	28 AQU	27 AQU	28 ARI	27 TAU	28 CAN	27 LEO	26 VIR	27 SCO	26 SAG	28 AQU	27 PIS
29 CAP		29 PIS	30 TAU	29 GEM	30 LEO	29 VIR	28 LIB	29 SAG	29 CAP	30 PIS	30 ARI
31 AQU		31 ARI		31 CAN			30 SCO		31 AQU		

2080

JAN	FEB	MAR	APR	MAY	JUN	JUL	AUG	SEP	OCT	NOV	DEC
1 TAU	2 CAN	2 LEO	3 LIB	2 SCO	1 SAG	1 CAP	2 PIS	1 ARI	2 GEM	1 CAN	2 VIR
3 GEM	4 LEO	4 VIR	5 SCO	5 SAG	3 CAP	3 AQU	4 ARI	3 TAU	5 CAN	3 LEO	4 LIB
5 CAN	6 VIR	6 LIB	7 SAG	7 CAP	6 AQU	6 PIS	7 TAU	5 GEM	7 LEO	5 VIR	7 SCO
7 LEO	8 LIB	8 SCO	10 CAP	9 AQU	8 PIS	8 ARI	9 GEM	7 CAN	9 VIR	7 LIB	9 SAG
9 VIR	10 SCO	11 SAG	12 AQU	12 PIS	11 ARI	10 TAU	11 CAN	9 LEO	11 LIB	9 SCO	11 CAP
11 LIB	12 SAG	13 CAP	15 PIS	14 ARI	13 TAU	13 GEM	13 LEO	12 VIR	13 SCO	12 SAG	14 AQU
14 SCO	15 CAP	16 AQU	17 ARI	17 TAU	15 GEM	15 CAN	15 VIR	14 LIB	15 SAG	14 CAP	16 PIS
16 SAG	17 AQU	18 PIS	19 TAU	19 GEM	17 CAN	17 LEO	17 LIB	16 SCO	18 CAP	17 AQU	19 ARI
19 CAP	20 PIS	21 ARI	21 GEM	21 CAN	19 LEO	19 VIR	19 SCO	18 SAG	20 AQU	19 PIS	21 TAU
21 AQU	22 ARI	23 TAU	24 CAN	23 LEO	21 VIR	21 LIB	22 SAG	20 CAP	23 PIS	22 ARI	24 GEM
24 PIS	25 TAU	25 GEM	26 LEO	25 VIR	23 LIB	23 SCO	24 CAP	23 AQU	25 ARI	24 TAU	26 CAN
26 ARI	27 GEM	27 CAN	28 VIR	27 LIB	25 SCO	25 SAG	27 AQU	25 PIS	28 TAU	26 GEM	28 LEO
28 TAU	29 CAN	29 LEO	30 LIB	29 SCO	28 SAG	28 CAP	29 PIS	28 ARI	30 GEM	28 CAN	30 VIR
31 GEM		31 VIR				30 AQU		30 TAU		30 LEO	

2081

JAN	FEB	MAR	APR	MAY	JUN	JUL	AUG	SEP	OCT	NOV	DEC
1 LIB	1 SAG	1 SAG	2 AQU	2 PIS	1 ARI	3 GEM	1 CAN	2 VIR	1 LIB	2 SAG	1 CAP
3 SCO	4 CAP	3 CAP	4 PIS	4 ARI	3 TAU	5 CAN	3 LEO	4 LIB	3 SCO	4 CAP	4 AQU
5 SAG	6 AQU	6 AQU	7 ARI	7 TAU	5 GEM	7 LEO	5 VIR	6 SCO	5 SAG	6 AQU	6 PIS
8 CAP	9 PIS	8 PIS	9 TAU	9 GEM	8 CAN	9 VIR	7 LIB	8 SAG	8 CAP	9 PIS	9 ARI
10 AQU	11 ARI	11 ARI	12 GEM	11 CAN	10 LEO	11 LIB	10 SCO	10 CAP	10 AQU	11 ARI	11 TAU
13 PIS	14 TAU	13 TAU	14 CAN	14 LEO	12 VIR	13 SCO	12 SAG	13 AQU	13 PIS	14 TAU	14 GEM
15 ARI	16 GEM	16 GEM	16 LEO	16 VIR	14 LIB	16 SAG	14 CAP	15 PIS	15 ARI	16 GEM	16 CAN
18 TAU	18 CAN	18 CAN	18 VIR	18 LIB	16 SCO	18 CAP	16 AQU	18 ARI	18 TAU	18 CAN	18 LEO
20 GEM	21 LEO	20 LEO	20 LIB	20 SCO	18 SAG	20 AQU	19 PIS	20 TAU	20 GEM	21 LEO	20 VIR
22 CAN	23 VIR	22 VIR	22 SCO	22 SAG	21 CAP	23 PIS	22 ARI	23 GEM	22 CAN	23 VIR	22 LIB
24 LEO	25 LIB	24 LIB	25 SAG	25 CAP	23 AQU	25 ARI	24 TAU	25 CAN	25 LEO	25 LIB	24 SCO
26 VIR	27 SCO	26 SCO	27 CAP	27 AQU	25 PIS	28 TAU	26 GEM	27 LEO	27 VIR	27 SCO	27 SAG
28 LIB		28 SAG	29 AQU	29 PIS	28 ARI	30 GEM	28 CAN	29 VIR	29 LIB	29 SAG	29 CAP
30 SCO		30 CAP			30 TAU		31 LEO		31 SCO		31 AQU

2082

JAN	FEB	MAR	APR	MAY	JUN	JUL	AUG	SEP	OCT	NOV	DEC
3 PIS	1 ARI	1 ARI	2 GEM	2 CAN	2 VIR	2 LIB	2 SAG	1 CAP	3 PIS	1 ARI	1 TAU
5 ARI	3 TAU	3 TAU	4 CAN	4 LEO	5 LIB	4 SCO	4 CAP	3 AQU	5 ARI	4 TAU	4 GEM
8 TAU	6 GEM	6 GEM	7 LEO	6 VIR	7 SCO	6 SAG	7 AQU	5 PIS	8 TAU	6 GEM	6 CAN
10 GEM	9 CAN	8 CAN	9 VIR	8 LIB	9 SAG	8 CAP	9 PIS	8 ARI	10 GEM	9 CAN	8 LEO
12 CAN	11 LEO	10 LEO	11 LIB	10 SCO	11 CAP	10 AQU	11 ARI	10 TAU	13 CAN	11 LEO	11 VIR
14 LEO	13 VIR	12 VIR	13 SCO	12 SAG	13 AQU	13 PIS	14 TAU	13 GEM	15 LEO	13 VIR	13 LIB
16 VIR	15 LIB	14 LIB	15 SAG	14 CAP	15 PIS	15 ARI	16 GEM	15 CAN	17 VIR	16 LIB	15 SCO
19 LIB	17 SCO	16 SCO	17 CAP	16 AQU	18 ARI	18 TAU	19 CAN	18 LEO	19 LIB	18 SCO	17 SAG
21 SCO	19 SAG	18 SAG	19 AQU	19 PIS	20 TAU	20 GEM	21 LEO	20 VIR	21 SCO	20 SAG	19 CAP
23 SAG	21 CAP	21 CAP	22 PIS	21 ARI	23 GEM	23 CAN	23 VIR	22 LIB	23 SAG	22 CAP	21 AQU
25 CAP	24 AQU	23 AQU	24 ARI	24 TAU	25 CAN	25 LEO	25 LIB	24 SCO	25 CAP	24 AQU	23 PIS
27 AQU	26 PIS	25 PIS	27 TAU	26 GEM	27 LEO	27 VIR	27 SCO	26 SAG	27 AQU	26 PIS	26 ARI
30 PIS		28 ARI	29 GEM	29 CAN	30 VIR	29 LIB	29 SAG	28 CAP	30 PIS	28 ARI	28 TAU
		30 TAU		31 LEO		31 SCO		30 AQU			31 GEM

2083

JAN	FEB	MAR	APR	MAY	JUN	JUL	AUG	SEP	OCT	NOV	DEC
2 CAN	1 LEO	3 VIR	1 LIB	1 SCO	1 CAP	3 PIS	1 ARI	3 GEM	2 CAN	1 LEO	1 VIR
5 LEO	3 VIR	5 LIB	3 SCO	3 SAG	3 AQU	5 ARI	4 TAU	5 CAN	5 LEO	4 VIR	3 LIB
7 VIR	5 LIB	7 SCO	5 SAG	5 CAP	5 PIS	7 TAU	6 GEM	8 LEO	7 VIR	6 LIB	5 SCO
9 LIB	8 SCO	9 SAG	7 CAP	7 AQU	8 ARI	10 GEM	9 CAN	10 VIR	9 LIB	8 SCO	7 SAG
11 SCO	10 SAG	11 CAP	9 AQU	9 PIS	10 TAU	13 CAN	11 LEO	12 LIB	12 SCO	10 SAG	9 CAP
13 SAG	12 CAP	13 AQU	12 PIS	11 ARI	13 GEM	15 LEO	14 VIR	14 SCO	14 SAG	12 CAP	11 AQU
15 CAP	14 AQU	15 PIS	14 ARI	14 TAU	15 CAN	17 VIR	16 LIB	16 SAG	16 CAP	14 AQU	14 PIS
18 AQU	16 PIS	18 ARI	17 TAU	16 GEM	18 LEO	20 LIB	18 SCO	18 CAP	18 AQU	16 PIS	16 ARI
20 PIS	19 ARI	20 TAU	19 GEM	19 CAN	20 VIR	22 SCO	20 SAG	21 AQU	20 PIS	19 ARI	18 TAU
22 ARI	21 TAU	23 GEM	22 CAN	21 LEO	22 LIB	24 SAG	22 CAP	23 PIS	22 ARI	21 TAU	21 GEM
25 TAU	24 GEM	25 CAN	24 LEO	24 VIR	24 SCO	26 CAP	24 AQU	25 ARI	25 TAU	23 GEM	23 CAN
27 GEM	26 CAN	28 LEO	26 VIR	26 LIB	26 SAG	28 AQU	26 PIS	27 TAU	27 GEM	26 CAN	26 LEO
30 CAN	28 LEO	30 VIR	29 LIB	28 SCO	28 CAP	30 PIS	29 ARI	30 GEM	30 CAN	28 LEO	28 VIR
				30 SAG	30 AQU		31 TAU				31 LIB

	JAN	FEB	MAR	APR	MAY	JUN	JUL	AUG	SEP	OCT	NOV	DEC
	2 SCO	2 CAP	1 CAP	1 PIS	1 ARI	2 GEM	1 CAN	3 VIR	1 LIB	1 SCO	1 CAP	1 AQU
	4 SAG	4 AQU	3 AQU	3 ARI	3 TAU	4 CAN	4 LEO	5 LIB	4 SCO	3 SAG	4 AQU	3 PIS
	6 CAP	6 PIS	5 PIS	6 TAU	5 GEM	7 LEO	6 VIR	7 SCO	6 SAG	5 CAP	6 PIS	5 ARI
	8 AQU	9 ARI	7 ARI	8 GEM	8 CAN	9 VIR	9 LIB	10 SAG	8 CAP	7 AQU	8 ARI	7 TAU
	10 PIS	11 TAU	9 TAU	10 CAN	10 LEO	12 LIB	11 SCO	12 CAP	10 AQU	9 PIS	10 TAU	10 GEM
	12 ARI	13 GEM	12 GEM	13 LEO	13 VIR	14 SCO	13 SAG	14 AQU	12 PIS	12 ARI	12 GEM	12 CAN
	14 TAU	16 CAN	14 CAN	15 VIR	15 LIB	16 SAG	15 CAP	16 PIS	14 ARI	14 TAU	15 CAN	15 LEO
	17 GEM	18 LEO	17 LEO	18 LIB	17 SCO	18 CAP	17 AQU	18 ARI	16 TAU	16 GEM	17 LEO	17 VIR
	20 CAN	21 VIR	19 VIR	20 SCO	19 SAG	20 AQU	19 PIS	20 TAU	19 GEM	19 CAN	20 VIR	20 LIB
	22 LEO	23 LIB	21 LIB	22 SAG	21 CAP	22 PIS	21 ARI	22 GEM	21 CAN	21 LEO	22 LIB	22 SCO
	24 VIR	25 SCO	24 SCO	24 CAP	23 AQU	24 ARI	24 TAU	25 CAN	24 LEO	24 VIR	25 SCO	24 SAG
	27 LIB	27 SAG	26 SAG	26 AQU	26 PIS	26 TAU	26 GEM	27 LEO	26 VIR	26 LIB	27 SAG	26 CAP
	29 SCO		28 CAP	28 PIS	28 ARI	29 GEM	29 CAN	30 VIR	29 LIB	28 SCO	29 CAP	28 AQU
	31 SAG		30 AQU		30 TAU		31 LEO			30 SAG		30 PIS

	JAN	FEB	MAR	APR	MAY	JUN	JUL	AUG	SEP	OCT	NOV	DEC
	1 ARI	2 GEM	2 GEM	3 LEO	3 VIR	1 LIB	1 SCO	2 CAP	1 AQU	2 ARI	3 GEM	2 CAN
	4 TAU	5 CAN	4 CAN	5 VIR	5 LIB	4 SCO	4 SAG	4 AQU	3 PIS	4 TAU	5 CAN	5 LEO
	6 GEM	7 LEO	6 LEO	8 LIB	7 SCO	6 SAG	6 CAP	6 PIS	5 ARI	6 GEM	7 LEO	7 VIR
	8 CAN	10 VIR	9 VIR	10 SCO	10 SAG	8 CAP	8 AQU	8 ARI	7 TAU	8 CAN	10 VIR	10 LIB
	11 LEO	12 LIB	11 LIB	12 SAG	12 CAP	10 AQU	10 PIS	10 TAU	9 GEM	11 LEO	12 LIB	12 SCO
	14 VIR	15 SCO	14 SCO	15 CAP	14 AQU	12 PIS	12 ARI	12 GEM	11 CAN	13 VIR	15 SCO	14 SAG
	16 LIB	17 SAG	16 SAG	17 AQU	16 PIS	14 ARI	14 TAU	15 CAN	14 LEO	16 LIB	17 SAG	17 CAP
	18 SCO	19 CAP	18 CAP	19 PIS	18 ARI	17 TAU	16 GEM	17 LEO	16 VIR	18 SCO	19 CAP	19 AQU
	21 SAG	21 AQU	21 AQU	21 ARI	20 TAU	19 GEM	19 CAN	20 VIR	19 LIB	21 SAG	22 AQU	21 PIS
	23 CAP	23 PIS	23 PIS	23 TAU	23 GEM	21 CAN	21 LEO	22 LIB	21 SCO	23 CAP	24 PIS	23 ARI
	25 AQU	25 ARI	25 ARI	25 GEM	25 CAN	24 LEO	24 VIR	25 SCO	23 SAG	25 AQU	26 ARI	25 TAU
	27 PIS	27 TAU	27 TAU	28 CAN	27 LEO	26 VIR	26 LIB	27 SAG	26 CAP	27 PIS	28 TAU	27 GEM
	29 ARI		29 GEM	30 LEO	30 VIR	29 LIB	29 SCO	29 CAP	28 AQU	29 ARI	30 GEM	30 CAN
	31 TAU		31 CAN				31 SAG		30 PIS	31 TAU		

	JAN	FEB	MAR	APR	MAY	JUN	JUL	AUG	SEP	OCT	NOV	DEC
	1 LEO	2 LIB	1 LIB	3 SAG	2 CAP	1 AQU	2 ARI	1 TAU	1 CAN	1 LEO	2 LIB	2 SCO
	3 VIR	5 SCO	4 SCO	5 CAP	5 AQU	3 PIS	4 TAU	3 GEM	4 LEO	4 VIR	5 SCO	4 SAG
	6 LIB	7 SAG	6 SAG	7 AQU	7 PIS	5 ARI	7 GEM	5 CAN	6 VIR	6 LIB	7 SAG	7 CAP
	8 SCO	9 CAP	9 CAP	9 PIS	9 ARI	7 TAU	9 CAN	7 LEO	9 LIB	8 SCO	10 CAP	9 AQU
	11 SAG	12 AQU	11 AQU	11 ARI	11 TAU	9 GEM	11 LEO	10 VIR	11 SCO	11 SAG	12 AQU	11 PIS
	13 CAP	14 PIS	13 PIS	13 TAU	13 GEM	11 CAN	13 VIR	12 LIB	14 SAG	13 CAP	14 PIS	13 ARI
	15 AQU	16 ARI	15 ARI	15 GEM	15 CAN	14 LEO	16 LIB	15 SCO	16 CAP	16 AQU	16 ARI	16 TAU
	17 PIS	18 TAU	17 TAU	18 CAN	17 LEO	16 VIR	18 SCO	17 SAG	18 AQU	18 PIS	18 TAU	18 GEM
	19 ARI	20 GEM	19 GEM	20 LEO	20 VIR	19 LIB	21 SAG	20 CAP	20 PIS	20 ARI	20 GEM	20 CAN
	21 TAU	22 CAN	21 CAN	22 VIR	22 LIB	21 SCO	23 CAP	22 AQU	22 ARI	22 TAU	22 CAN	22 LEO
	23 GEM	24 LEO	24 LEO	25 LIB	25 SCO	24 SAG	25 AQU	24 PIS	24 TAU	24 GEM	24 LEO	24 VIR
	26 CAN	27 VIR	26 VIR	27 SCO	27 SAG	26 CAP	27 PIS	26 ARI	26 GEM	26 CAN	27 VIR	27 LIB
	28 LEO		29 LIB	30 SAG	30 CAP	28 AQU	30 ARI	28 TAU	29 CAN	28 LEO	29 LIB	29 SCO
	31 VIR		31 SCO					30 GEM		31 VIR		

	JAN	FEB	MAR	APR	MAY	JUN	JUL	AUG	SEP	OCT	NOV	DEC
	1 SAG	2 AQU	1 AQU	2 ARI	1 TAU	2 CAN	1 LEO	2 LIB	1 SCO	1 SAG	2 AQU	2 PIS
	3 CAP	4 PIS	3 PIS	4 TAU	3 GEM	4 LEO	3 VIR	5 SCO	3 SAG	3 CAP	4 PIS	4 ARI
	5 AQU	6 ARI	5 ARI	6 GEM	5 CAN	6 VIR	6 LIB	7 SAG	6 CAP	6 AQU	7 ARI	6 TAU
	8 PIS	8 TAU	7 TAU	8 CAN	7 LEO	8 LIB	8 SCO	10 CAP	8 AQU	8 PIS	9 TAU	8 GEM
	10 ARI	10 GEM	9 GEM	10 LEO	10 VIR	11 SCO	11 SAG	12 AQU	11 PIS	10 ARI	11 GEM	10 CAN
	12 TAU	12 CAN	12 CAN	12 VIR	12 LIB	13 SAG	13 CAP	14 PIS	13 ARI	12 TAU	13 CAN	12 LEO
	14 GEM	15 LEO	14 LEO	15 LIB	15 SCO	16 CAP	16 AQU	16 ARI	15 TAU	14 GEM	15 LEO	14 VIR
	16 CAN	17 VIR	16 VIR	17 SCO	17 SAG	18 AQU	18 PIS	18 TAU	17 GEM	16 CAN	17 VIR	17 LIB
	18 LEO	19 LIB	19 LIB	20 SAG	20 CAP	21 PIS	20 ARI	21 GEM	19 CAN	18 LEO	19 LIB	19 SCO
	21 VIR	22 SCO	21 SCO	22 CAP	22 AQU	23 ARI	22 TAU	23 CAN	21 LEO	21 VIR	22 SCO	22 SAG
	23 LIB	24 SAG	24 SAG	25 AQU	24 PIS	25 TAU	24 GEM	25 LEO	23 VIR	23 LIB	25 SAG	24 CAP
	26 SCO	27 CAP	26 CAP	27 PIS	27 ARI	27 GEM	26 CAN	27 VIR	26 LIB	25 SCO	27 CAP	27 AQU
	28 SAG		29 AQU	29 ARI	29 TAU	29 CAN	29 LEO	29 LIB	28 SCO	28 SAG	29 AQU	29 PIS
	30 CAP		31 PIS		31 GEM		31 VIR			31 CAP		31 ARI

2088

JAN	FEB	MAR	APR	MAY	JUN	JUL	AUG	SEP	OCT	NOV	DEC
2 TAU	1 GEM	1 CAN	2 VIR	1 LIB	2 SAG	2 CAP	1 AQU	2 ARI	2 TAU	2 CAN	1 LEO
4 GEM	3 CAN	3 LEO	4 LIB	3 SCO	5 CAP	5 AQU	3 PIS	4 TAU	4 GEM	4 LEO	3 VIR
6 CAN	5 LEO	5 VIR	6 SCO	6 SAG	7 AQU	7 PIS	6 ARI	6 GEM	6 CAN	6 VIR	6 LIB
9 LEO	7 VIR	8 LIB	9 SAG	9 CAP	10 PIS	9 ARI	8 TAU	8 CAN	8 LEO	8 LIB	8 SCO
11 VIR	9 LIB	10 SCO	11 CAP	11 AQU	12 ARI	12 TAU	10 GEM	11 LEO	10 VIR	11 SCO	10 SAG
13 LIB	12 SCO	13 SAG	14 AQU	14 PIS	14 TAU	14 GEM	12 CAN	13 VIR	12 LIB	13 SAG	13 CAP
15 SCO	14 SAG	15 CAP	16 PIS	16 ARI	16 GEM	16 CAN	14 LEO	15 LIB	15 SCO	16 CAP	16 AQU
18 SAG	17 CAP	18 AQU	18 ARI	18 TAU	18 CAN	18 LEO	16 VIR	17 SCO	17 SAG	18 AQU	18 PIS
20 CAP	19 AQU	20 PIS	21 TAU	20 GEM	20 LEO	20 VIR	18 LIB	20 SAG	19 CAP	21 PIS	20 ARI
23 AQU	21 PIS	22 ARI	23 GEM	22 CAN	23 VIR	22 LIB	21 SCO	22 CAP	22 AQU	23 ARI	23 TAU
25 PIS	24 ARI	24 TAU	25 CAN	24 LEO	25 LIB	24 SCO	23 SAG	25 AQU	24 PIS	25 TAU	25 GEM
27 ARI	26 TAU	26 GEM	27 LEO	26 VIR	27 SCO	27 SAG	26 CAP	27 PIS	27 ARI	27 GEM	27 CAN
30 TAU	28 GEM	28 CAN	29 VIR	28 LIB	30 SAG	29 CAP	28 AQU	29 ARI	29 TAU	29 CAN	29 LEO
		30 LEO		31 SCO			31 PIS		31 GEM		31 VIR

2089

JAN	FEB	MAR	APR	MAY	JUN	JUL	AUG	SEP	OCT	NOV	DEC
2 LIB	1 SCO	2 SAG	1 CAP	1 AQU	2 ARI	2 TAU	1 GEM	1 LEO	3 LIB	1 SCO	1 SAG
4 SCO	3 SAG	5 CAP	4 AQU	4 PIS	5 TAU	4 GEM	3 CAN	3 VIR	5 SCO	3 SAG	3 CAP
7 SAG	6 CAP	7 AQU	6 PIS	6 ARI	7 GEM	6 CAN	5 LEO	5 LIB	7 SAG	6 CAP	5 AQU
9 CAP	8 AQU	10 PIS	9 ARI	8 TAU	9 CAN	8 LEO	7 VIR	7 SCO	9 CAP	8 AQU	8 PIS
12 AQU	11 PIS	12 ARI	11 TAU	10 GEM	11 LEO	10 VIR	9 LIB	9 SAG	12 AQU	11 PIS	10 ARI
14 PIS	13 ARI	15 TAU	13 GEM	12 CAN	13 VIR	12 LIB	11 SCO	12 CAP	14 PIS	13 ARI	13 TAU
17 ARI	15 TAU	17 GEM	15 CAN	15 LEO	15 LIB	15 SCO	13 SAG	14 AQU	17 ARI	15 TAU	15 GEM
19 TAU	17 GEM	19 CAN	17 LEO	17 VIR	17 SCO	17 SAG	16 CAP	17 PIS	19 TAU	18 GEM	17 CAN
21 GEM	20 CAN	21 LEO	19 VIR	19 LIB	20 SAG	19 CAP	18 AQU	19 ARI	21 GEM	20 CAN	19 LEO
23 CAN	22 LEO	23 VIR	22 LIB	21 SCO	22 CAP	22 AQU	21 PIS	22 TAU	24 CAN	22 LEO	21 VIR
25 LEO	24 VIR	25 LIB	24 SCO	23 SAG	25 AQU	24 PIS	23 ARI	24 GEM	26 LEO	24 VIR	23 LIB
27 VIR	26 LIB	27 SCO	26 SAG	26 CAP	27 PIS	27 ARI	26 TAU	26 CAN	28 VIR	26 LIB	26 SCO
29 LIB	28 SCO	30 SAG	28 CAP	28 AQU	30 ARI	29 TAU	28 GEM	28 LEO	30 LIB	28 SCO	28 SAG
				31 PIS			30 CAN	30 VIR			30 CAP

2090

JAN	FEB	MAR	APR	MAY	JUN	JUL	AUG	SEP	OCT	NOV	DEC
2 AQU	3 ARI	2 ARI	1 TAU	1 GEM	1 LEO	1 VIR	1 SCO	2 CAP	2 AQU	3 ARI	3 TAU
4 PIS	6 TAU	5 TAU	3 GEM	3 CAN	3 VIR	3 LIB	3 SAG	4 AQU	4 PIS	5 TAU	5 GEM
7 ARI	8 GEM	7 GEM	6 CAN	5 LEO	6 LIB	5 SCO	6 CAP	7 PIS	7 ARI	8 GEM	7 CAN
9 TAU	10 CAN	9 CAN	8 LEO	7 VIR	8 SCO	7 SAG	8 AQU	9 ARI	9 TAU	10 CAN	10 LEO
12 GEM	12 LEO	12 LEO	10 VIR	9 LIB	10 SAG	9 CAP	11 PIS	12 TAU	12 GEM	12 LEO	12 VIR
14 CAN	14 VIR	14 VIR	12 LIB	11 SCO	12 CAP	12 AQU	13 ARI	14 GEM	14 CAN	15 VIR	14 LIB
16 LEO	16 LIB	16 LIB	14 SCO	14 SAG	14 AQU	14 PIS	16 TAU	17 CAN	16 LEO	17 LIB	16 SCO
18 VIR	18 SCO	18 SCO	16 SAG	16 CAP	17 PIS	17 ARI	18 GEM	19 LEO	18 VIR	19 SCO	18 SAG
20 LIB	20 SAG	20 SAG	18 CAP	18 AQU	19 ARI	19 TAU	20 CAN	21 VIR	20 LIB	21 SAG	20 CAP
22 SCO	23 CAP	22 CAP	21 AQU	21 PIS	21 TAU	22 GEM	22 LEO	23 LIB	23 SCO	23 CAP	23 AQU
24 SAG	25 AQU	24 AQU	23 PIS	23 ARI	24 GEM	24 CAN	24 VIR	25 SCO	25 SAG	25 AQU	25 PIS
26 CAP	28 PIS	27 PIS	26 ARI	26 TAU	27 CAN	26 LEO	26 LIB	27 SAG	27 CAP	28 PIS	28 ARI
29 AQU		30 ARI	28 TAU	28 GEM	29 LEO	28 VIR	29 SCO	29 CAP	29 AQU	30 ARI	30 TAU
31 PIS				30 CAN		30 LIB	31 SAG		31 PIS		

2091

JAN	FEB	MAR	APR	MAY	JUN	JUL	AUG	SEP	OCT	NOV	DEC
2 GEM	2 LEO	2 LEO	2 LIB	2 SCO	2 CAP	2 AQU	1 PIS	2 TAU	2 GEM	3 LEO	2 VIR
4 CAN	4 VIR	4 VIR	4 SCO	4 SAG	4 AQU	4 PIS	3 ARI	4 GEM	4 CAN	5 VIR	5 LIB
6 LEO	7 LIB	6 LIB	6 SAG	6 CAP	7 PIS	7 ARI	5 TAU	7 CAN	6 LEO	7 LIB	7 SCO
8 VIR	9 SCO	8 SCO	8 CAP	8 AQU	9 ARI	9 TAU	8 GEM	9 LEO	9 VIR	9 SCO	9 SAG
10 LIB	11 SAG	10 SAG	11 AQU	10 PIS	12 TAU	12 GEM	10 CAN	11 VIR	11 LIB	11 SAG	11 CAP
12 SCO	13 CAP	12 CAP	13 PIS	13 ARI	14 GEM	14 CAN	13 LEO	13 LIB	13 SCO	13 CAP	13 AQU
15 SAG	15 AQU	15 AQU	16 ARI	16 TAU	17 CAN	16 LEO	15 VIR	15 SCO	15 SAG	15 AQU	15 PIS
17 CAP	18 PIS	17 PIS	18 TAU	18 GEM	19 LEO	19 VIR	17 LIB	17 SAG	17 CAP	18 PIS	17 ARI
19 AQU	20 ARI	19 ARI	21 GEM	20 CAN	21 VIR	21 LIB	19 SCO	19 CAP	19 AQU	20 ARI	20 TAU
21 PIS	23 TAU	22 TAU	23 CAN	23 LEO	23 LIB	23 SCO	21 SAG	22 AQU	22 PIS	23 TAU	22 GEM
24 ARI	25 GEM	25 GEM	26 LEO	25 VIR	26 SCO	25 SAG	23 CAP	24 PIS	24 ARI	25 GEM	25 CAN
26 TAU	28 CAN	27 CAN	28 VIR	27 LIB	28 SAG	27 CAP	26 AQU	27 ARI	26 TAU	28 CAN	27 LEO
29 GEM		29 LEO	30 LIB	29 SCO	30 CAP	29 AQU	28 PIS	29 TAU	29 GEM		30 VIR
31 CAN		31 VIR		31 SAG			30 ARI		31 CAN		

JAN	FEB	MAR	APR	MAY	JUN	JUL	AUG	SEP	OCT	NOV	DEC
1 LIB	1 SAG	2 CAP	2 PIS	2 ARI	1 TAU	3 CAN	2 LEO	3 LIB	2 SCO	1 SAG	2 AQU
3 SCO	3 CAP	4 AQU	5 ARI	4 TAU	3 GEM	5 LEO	4 VIR	5 SCO	4 SAG	3 CAP	4 PIS
5 SAG	6 AQU	6 PIS	7 TAU	7 GEM	6 CAN	8 VIR	6 LIB	7 SAG	6 CAP	5 AQU	6 ARI
7 CAP	8 PIS	8 ARI	10 GEM	9 CAN	8 LEO	10 LIB	9 SCO	9 CAP	8 AQU	7 PIS	9 TAU
9 AQU	10 ARI	11 TAU	12 CAN	12 LEO	11 VIR	12 SCO	11 SAG	11 AQU	11 PIS	9 ARI	11 GEM
11 PIS	13 TAU	13 GEM	15 LEO	14 VIR	13 LIB	14 SAG	13 CAP	13 PIS	13 ARI	12 TAU	14 CAN
14 ARI	15 GEM	16 CAN	17 VIR	17 LIB	15 SCO	16 CAP	15 AQU	16 ARI	15 TAU	14 GEM	16 LEO
16 TAU	18 CAN	18 LEO	19 LIB	19 SCO	17 SAG	18 AQU	17 PIS	18 TAU	18 GEM	17 CAN	19 VIR
19 GEM	20 LEO	21 VIR	21 SCO	21 SAG	19 CAP	21 PIS	19 ARI	20 GEM	20 CAN	19 LEO	21 LIB
21 CAN	22 VIR	23 LIB	23 SAG	23 CAP	21 AQU	23 ARI	22 TAU	23 CAN	23 LEO	22 VIR	23 SCO
24 LEO	24 LIB	25 SCO	25 CAP	25 AQU	23 PIS	25 TAU	24 GEM	25 LEO	25 VIR	24 LIB	25 SAG
26 VIR	26 SCO	27 SAG	27 AQU	27 PIS	25 ARI	28 GEM	27 CAN	28 VIR	28 LIB	26 SCO	27 CAP
28 LIB	29 SAG	29 CAP	30 PIS	29 ARI	28 TAU	30 CAN	29 LEO	30 LIB	30 SCO	28 SAG	29 AQU
30 SCO		31 AQU			30 GEM		31 VIR			30 CAP	31 PIS

JAN	FEB	MAR	APR	MAY	JUN	JUL	AUG	SEP	OCT	NOV	DEC
3 ARI	1 TAU	1 TAU	2 CAN	2 LEO	1 VIR	3 SCO	1 SAG	2 AQU	1 PIS	2 TAU	1 GEM
5 TAU	4 GEM	3 GEM	5 LEO	4 VIR	3 LIB	5 SAG	3 CAP	4 PIS	3 ARI	4 GEM	4 CAN
8 GEM	6 CAN	6 CAN	7 VIR	7 LIB	5 SCO	7 CAP	5 AQU	6 ARI	5 TAU	6 CAN	6 LEO
10 CAN	9 LEO	8 LEO	9 LIB	9 SCO	7 SAG	9 AQU	7 PIS	8 TAU	8 GEM	9 LEO	9 VIR
13 LEO	11 VIR	11 VIR	12 SCO	11 SAG	9 CAP	11 PIS	9 ARI	10 GEM	10 CAN	11 VIR	11 LIB
15 VIR	14 LIB	13 LIB	14 SAG	13 CAP	11 AQU	13 ARI	12 TAU	13 CAN	13 LEO	14 LIB	14 SCO
17 LIB	16 SCO	15 SCO	16 CAP	15 AQU	13 PIS	15 TAU	14 GEM	15 LEO	15 VIR	16 SCO	16 SAG
20 SCO	18 SAG	17 SAG	18 AQU	17 PIS	16 ARI	18 GEM	16 CAN	18 VIR	18 LIB	18 SAG	18 CAP
22 SAG	20 CAP	19 CAP	20 PIS	19 ARI	18 TAU	20 CAN	19 LEO	20 LIB	20 SCO	20 CAP	20 AQU
24 CAP	22 AQU	22 AQU	22 ARI	22 TAU	20 GEM	23 LEO	21 VIR	22 SCO	22 SAG	22 AQU	22 PIS
26 AQU	24 PIS	24 PIS	24 TAU	24 GEM	23 CAN	25 VIR	24 LIB	25 SAG	24 CAP	25 PIS	24 ARI
28 PIS	27 ARI	26 ARI	27 GEM	27 CAN	25 LEO	28 LIB	26 SCO	27 CAP	26 AQU	27 ARI	26 TAU
30 ARI		28 TAU	29 CAN	29 LEO	28 VIR	30 SCO	28 SAG	29 AQU	28 PIS	29 TAU	29 GEM
		31 GEM			30 LIB		31 CAP		31 ARI		31 CAN

JAN	FEB	MAR	APR	MAY	JUN	JUL	AUG	SEP	OCT	NOV	DEC
3 LEO	1 VIR	1 VIR	2 SCO	1 SAG	2 AQU	1 PIS	2 TAU	3 CAN	2 LEO	1 VIR	1 LIB
5 VIR	4 LIB	3 LIB	4 SAG	4 CAP	4 PIS	3 ARI	4 GEM	5 LEO	5 VIR	4 LIB	4 SCO
8 LIB	6 SCO	5 SCO	6 CAP	6 AQU	6 ARI	6 TAU	6 CAN	8 VIR	7 LIB	6 SCO	6 SAG
10 SCO	9 SAG	8 SAG	8 AQU	8 PIS	8 TAU	8 GEM	9 LEO	10 LIB	10 SCO	9 SAG	8 CAP
12 SAG	11 CAP	10 CAP	11 PIS	10 ARI	11 GEM	10 CAN	11 VIR	13 SCO	12 SAG	11 CAP	10 AQU
14 CAP	13 AQU	12 AQU	13 ARI	12 TAU	13 CAN	13 LEO	14 LIB	15 SAG	15 CAP	13 AQU	12 PIS
16 AQU	15 PIS	14 PIS	15 TAU	14 GEM	15 LEO	15 VIR	16 SCO	17 CAP	17 AQU	15 PIS	15 ARI
18 PIS	17 ARI	16 ARI	17 GEM	17 CAN	18 VIR	18 LIB	19 SAG	20 AQU	19 PIS	17 ARI	17 TAU
20 ARI	19 TAU	18 TAU	19 CAN	19 LEO	20 LIB	20 SCO	21 CAP	22 PIS	21 ARI	19 TAU	19 GEM
22 TAU	21 GEM	20 GEM	22 LEO	22 VIR	23 SCO	23 SAG	23 AQU	24 ARI	23 TAU	21 GEM	21 CAN
25 GEM	24 CAN	23 CAN	24 VIR	24 LIB	25 SAG	25 CAP	25 PIS	26 TAU	25 GEM	24 CAN	23 LEO
27 CAN	26 LEO	25 LEO	27 LIB	26 SCO	27 CAP	27 AQU	27 ARI	28 GEM	27 CAN	26 LEO	26 VIR
30 LEO		28 VIR	29 SCO	29 SAG	29 AQU	29 PIS	29 TAU	30 CAN	30 LEO	29 VIR	28 LIB
		30 LIB		31 CAP		31 ARI	31 GEM				31 SCO

JAN	FEB	MAR	APR	MAY	JUN	JUL	AUG	SEP	OCT	NOV	DEC
2 SAG	1 CAP	3 AQU	1 PIS	2 TAU	1 GEM	3 LEO	1 VIR	3 SCO	2 SAG	1 CAP	1 AQU
5 CAP	3 AQU	5 PIS	3 ARI	4 GEM	3 CAN	5 VIR	4 LIB	5 SAG	5 CAP	3 AQU	3 PIS
7 AQU	5 PIS	7 ARI	5 TAU	7 CAN	5 LEO	7 LIB	6 SCO	8 CAP	7 AQU	6 PIS	5 ARI
9 PIS	7 ARI	9 TAU	7 GEM	9 LEO	8 VIR	10 SCO	9 SAG	10 AQU	9 PIS	8 ARI	7 TAU
11 ARI	9 TAU	11 GEM	9 CAN	11 VIR	10 LIB	12 SAG	11 CAP	12 PIS	11 ARI	10 TAU	9 GEM
13 TAU	11 GEM	13 CAN	12 LEO	14 LIB	13 SCO	15 CAP	13 AQU	14 ARI	13 TAU	12 GEM	11 CAN
15 GEM	14 CAN	15 LEO	14 VIR	16 SCO	15 SAG	17 AQU	15 PIS	16 TAU	15 GEM	14 CAN	13 LEO
17 CAN	16 LEO	18 VIR	17 LIB	19 SAG	17 CAP	19 PIS	17 ARI	18 GEM	17 CAN	16 LEO	16 VIR
20 LEO	19 VIR	20 LIB	19 SCO	21 CAP	20 AQU	21 ARI	20 TAU	20 CAN	20 LEO	18 VIR	18 LIB
22 VIR	21 LIB	23 SCO	22 SAG	23 AQU	22 PIS	23 TAU	22 GEM	22 LEO	22 VIR	21 LIB	21 SCO
25 LIB	24 SCO	25 SAG	24 CAP	26 PIS	24 ARI	25 GEM	24 CAN	25 VIR	25 LIB	23 SCO	23 SAG
27 SCO	26 SAG	28 CAP	26 AQU	28 ARI	26 TAU	28 CAN	26 LEO	27 LIB	27 SCO	26 SAG	26 CAP
30 SAG	28 CAP	30 AQU	28 PIS	30 TAU	28 GEM	30 LEO	29 VIR	30 SCO	30 SAG	28 CAP	28 AQU
			30 ARI		30 CAN		31 LIB				30 PIS

JAN	FEB	MAR	APR	MAY	JUN	JUL	AUG	SEP	OCT	NOV	DEC
1 ARI	2 GEM	2 CAN	1 LEO	3 LIB	1 SCO	1 SAG	3 AQU	1 PIS	1 ARI	1 GEM	1 CAN
3 TAU	4 CAN	4 LEO	3 VIR	5 SCO	4 SAG	4 CAP	5 PIS	3 ARI	3 TAU	3 CAN	3 LEO
6 GEM	6 LEO	7 VIR	5 LIB	8 SAG	6 CAP	6 AQU	7 ARI	5 TAU	5 GEM	5 LEO	5 VIR
8 CAN	9 VIR	9 LIB	8 SCO	10 CAP	9 AQU	9 PIS	9 TAU	7 GEM	7 CAN	7 VIR	7 LIB
10 LEO	11 LIB	12 SCO	11 SAG	13 AQU	11 PIS	11 ARI	11 GEM	10 CAN	10 LEO	10 LIB	10 SCO
12 VIR	13 SCO	14 SAG	13 CAP	15 PIS	13 ARI	13 TAU	13 CAN	12 LEO	12 VIR	12 SCO	12 SAG
15 LIB	16 SAG	17 CAP	15 AQU	17 ARI	16 TAU	15 GEM	16 LEO	14 VIR	14 LIB	15 SAG	15 CAP
17 SCO	18 CAP	19 AQU	18 PIS	19 TAU	18 GEM	17 CAN	18 VIR	16 LIB	16 SCO	17 CAP	17 AQU
20 SAG	21 AQU	21 PIS	20 ARI	21 GEM	20 CAN	19 LEO	20 LIB	19 SCO	19 SAG	20 AQU	20 PIS
22 CAP	23 PIS	23 ARI	22 TAU	23 CAN	22 LEO	21 VIR	22 SCO	21 SAG	21 CAP	22 PIS	22 ARI
24 AQU	25 ARI	25 TAU	24 GEM	25 LEO	24 VIR	23 LIB	25 SAG	24 CAP	24 AQU	25 ARI	24 TAU
26 PIS	27 TAU	27 GEM	26 CAN	28 VIR	26 LIB	26 SCO	27 CAP	26 AQU	26 PIS	27 TAU	26 GEM
29 ARI	29 GEM	29 CAN	28 LEO	30 LIB	29 SCO	29 SAG	29 AQU	29 PIS	28 ARI	29 GEM	28 CAN
31 TAU			30 VIR			31 CAP			30 TAU		30 LEO

JAN	FEB	MAR	APR	MAY	JUN	JUL	AUG	SEP	OCT	NOV	DEC
1 VIR	2 SCO	2 SCO	3 CAP	3 AQU	1 PIS	1 ARI	2 GEM	2 LEO	2 VIR	2 SCO	2 SAG
3 LIB	5 SAG	4 SAG	5 AQU	5 PIS	4 ARI	3 TAU	4 CAN	4 VIR	4 LIB	5 SAG	5 CAP
6 SCO	7 CAP	7 CAP	8 PIS	7 ARI	6 TAU	5 GEM	6 LEO	6 LIB	6 SCO	7 CAP	7 AQU
8 SAG	10 AQU	9 AQU	10 ARI	10 TAU	8 GEM	7 CAN	8 VIR	9 SCO	8 SAG	10 AQU	10 PIS
11 CAP	12 PIS	11 PIS	12 TAU	12 GEM	10 CAN	9 LEO	10 LIB	11 SAG	11 CAP	12 PIS	12 ARI
13 AQU	14 ARI	14 ARI	14 GEM	14 CAN	12 LEO	11 VIR	12 SCO	14 CAP	13 AQU	15 ARI	14 TAU
16 PIS	17 TAU	16 TAU	16 CAN	16 LEO	14 VIR	14 LIB	15 SAG	16 AQU	16 PIS	17 TAU	16 GEM
18 ARI	19 GEM	18 GEM	18 LEO	18 VIR	16 LIB	16 SCO	17 CAP	19 PIS	18 ARI	19 GEM	18 CAN
20 TAU	21 CAN	20 CAN	21 VIR	20 LIB	19 SCO	18 SAG	20 AQU	21 ARI	20 TAU	21 CAN	20 LEO
22 GEM	23 LEO	22 LEO	23 LIB	22 SCO	21 SAG	21 CAP	22 PIS	23 TAU	23 GEM	23 LEO	22 VIR
24 CAN	25 VIR	24 VIR	25 SCO	25 SAG	24 CAP	24 AQU	25 ARI	25 GEM	25 CAN	25 VIR	25 LIB
27 LEO	27 LIB	27 LIB	28 SAG	27 CAP	26 AQU	26 PIS	27 TAU	27 CAN	27 LEO	27 LIB	27 SCO
29 VIR		29 SCO	30 CAP	30 AQU	29 PIS	28 ARI	29 GEM	30 LEO	29 VIR	30 SCO	29 SAG
31 LIB		31 SAG				31 TAU	31 CAN		31 LIB		

JAN	FEB	MAR	APR	MAY	JUN	JUL	AUG	SEP	OCT	NOV	DEC
1 CAP	2 PIS	1 PIS	2 TAU	2 GEM	2 LEO	2 VIR	2 SCO	1 SAG	1 CAP	2 PIS	2 ARI
3 AQU	5 ARI	4 ARI	5 GEM	4 CAN	5 VIR	5 LIB	5 SAG	3 CAP	3 AQU	5 ARI	5 TAU
6 PIS	7 TAU	6 TAU	7 CAN	6 LEO	7 LIB	6 SCO	7 CAP	6 AQU	6 PIS	7 TAU	7 GEM
8 ARI	9 GEM	8 GEM	9 LEO	8 VIR	9 SCO	9 SAG	10 AQU	8 PIS	8 ARI	9 GEM	9 CAN
11 TAU	11 CAN	11 CAN	11 VIR	10 LIB	11 SAG	11 CAP	12 PIS	11 ARI	11 TAU	11 CAN	11 LEO
13 GEM	13 LEO	13 LEO	13 LIB	13 SCO	14 CAP	14 AQU	15 ARI	13 TAU	13 GEM	14 LEO	13 VIR
15 CAN	15 VIR	15 VIR	15 SCO	15 SAG	16 AQU	16 PIS	17 TAU	15 GEM	15 CAN	16 VIR	15 LIB
17 LEO	17 LIB	17 LIB	18 SAG	17 CAP	19 PIS	18 ARI	20 GEM	18 CAN	17 LEO	18 LIB	17 SCO
19 VIR	20 SCO	19 SCO	20 CAP	20 AQU	21 ARI	21 TAU	21 CAN	20 LEO	19 VIR	20 SCO	20 SAG
21 LIB	22 SAG	21 SAG	23 AQU	22 PIS	24 TAU	24 GEM	23 LEO	22 VIR	22 LIB	22 SAG	22 CAP
23 SCO	24 CAP	24 CAP	25 PIS	25 ARI	26 GEM	26 CAN	25 VIR	24 LIB	24 SCO	24 CAP	24 AQU
26 SAG	27 AQU	26 AQU	27 ARI	27 TAU	28 CAN	28 LEO	28 LIB	26 SCO	26 SAG	27 AQU	27 PIS
28 CAP		29 PIS	30 TAU	29 GEM	30 LEO	29 VIR	30 SCO	28 SAG	28 CAP	29 PIS	29 ARI
31 AQU		31 ARI		31 CAN					31 AQU		

JAN	FEB	MAR	APR	MAY	JUN	JUL	AUG	SEP	OCT	NOV	DEC
1 TAU	2 CAN	1 CAN	2 VIR	1 LIB	2 SAG	1 CAP	2 PIS	1 ARI	1 TAU	2 CAN	1 LEO
3 GEM	4 LEO	3 LEO	4 LIB	3 SCO	4 CAP	4 AQU	5 ARI	3 TAU	3 GEM	4 LEO	4 VIR
5 CAN	6 VIR	5 VIR	6 SCO	5 SAG	6 AQU	6 PIS	7 TAU	6 CAN	6 CAN	6 VIR	6 LIB
7 LEO	8 LIB	7 LIB	8 SAG	7 CAP	8 PIS	8 ARI	10 GEM	8 LEO	8 LEO	8 LIB	8 SCO
9 VIR	10 SCO	9 SCO	10 CAP	10 AQU	11 ARI	11 TAU	12 CAN	10 VIR	10 VIR	10 SCO	10 SAG
11 LIB	12 SAG	11 SAG	12 AQU	12 PIS	13 TAU	13 GEM	14 LEO	13 LIB	12 LIB	12 SAG	12 CAP
13 SCO	14 CAP	14 CAP	15 PIS	15 ARI	16 GEM	16 CAN	16 VIR	15 SCO	14 SCO	15 CAP	14 AQU
16 SAG	17 AQU	16 AQU	17 ARI	17 TAU	18 CAN	18 LEO	18 LIB	17 SAG	16 SAG	17 AQU	17 PIS
18 CAP	19 PIS	19 PIS	20 TAU	20 GEM	20 LEO	20 VIR	20 SCO	19 CAP	18 CAP	19 PIS	19 ARI
21 AQU	22 ARI	21 ARI	22 GEM	22 CAN	22 VIR	22 LIB	22 SAG	21 AQU	20 AQU	22 ARI	21 TAU
23 PIS	24 TAU	24 TAU	25 CAN	24 LEO	24 LIB	24 SCO	25 CAP	23 PIS	23 PIS	24 TAU	24 GEM
26 ARI	27 GEM	26 GEM	27 LEO	26 VIR	27 SCO	27 SAG	27 AQU	26 ARI	25 ARI	27 GEM	26 CAN
28 TAU		28 CAN	29 VIR	28 LIB	29 SAG	29 SAG	29 PIS		28 TAU	29 CAN	29 LEO
30 GEM		31 LEO		30 SCO		31 AQU			30 GEM		31 VIR

2100

JAN	FEB	MAR	APR	MAY	JUN	JUL	AUG	SEP	OCT	NOV	DEC
2 LIB	2 SAG	2 SAG	2 AQU	2 PIS	1 ARI	1 TAU	2 CAN	1 LEO	2 LIB	1 SCO	2 CAP
4 SCO	5 CAP	4 CAP	5 PIS	5 ARI	3 TAU	3 GEM	4 LEO	3 VIR	4 SCO	3 SAG	4 AQU
6 SAG	7 AQU	6 AQU	7 ARI	7 TAU	6 GEM	6 CAN	6 VIR	5 LIB	6 SAG	5 CAP	7 PIS
8 CAP	9 PIS	9 PIS	10 TAU	10 GEM	8 CAN	8 LEO	9 LIB	7 SCO	8 CAP	7 AQU	9 ARI
11 AQU	12 ARI	11 ARI	12 GEM	12 CAN	11 LEO	10 VIR	11 SCO	9 SAG	11 AQU	9 PIS	11 TAU
13 PIS	14 TAU	14 TAU	15 CAN	14 LEO	13 VIR	12 LIB	13 SAG	11 CAP	13 PIS	12 ARI	14 GEM
15 ARI	17 GEM	16 GEM	17 LEO	17 VIR	15 LIB	14 SCO	15 CAP	13 AQU	15 ARI	14 TAU	16 CAN
18 TAU	19 CAN	19 CAN	19 VIR	19 LIB	17 SCO	17 SAG	17 AQU	16 PIS	18 TAU	17 GEM	19 LEO
20 GEM	21 LEO	21 LEO	21 LIB	21 SCO	19 SAG	19 CAP	19 PIS	18 ARI	20 GEM	19 CAN	21 VIR
23 CAN	24 VIR	23 VIR	23 SCO	23 SAG	21 CAP	21 AQU	22 ARI	21 TAU	23 CAN	22 LEO	23 LIB
25 LEO	25 LIB	25 LIB	25 SAG	25 CAP	23 AQU	23 PIS	24 TAU	23 GEM	25 LEO	24 VIR	26 SCO
27 VIR	28 SCO	27 SCO	27 CAP	27 AQU	26 PIS	25 ARI	27 GEM	26 CAN	28 VIR	26 LIB	28 SAG
29 LIB		29 SAG	30 AQU	29 PIS	28 ARI	28 TAU	29 CAN	28 LEO	30 LIB	28 SCO	30 CAP
31 SCO		31 CAP				30 GEM		30 VIR		30 SAG	

2101

JAN	FEB	MAR	APR	MAY	JUN	JUL	AUG	SEP	OCT	NOV	DEC
1 AQU	2 ARI	1 ARI	2 GEM	2 CAN	1 LEO	3 LIB	1 SCO	2 CAP	1 AQU	2 ARI	1 TAU
3 PIS	4 TAU	3 TAU	5 CAN	5 LEO	3 VIR	5 SCO	3 SAG	4 AQU	3 PIS	4 TAU	4 GEM
5 ARI	7 GEM	6 GEM	7 LEO	7 VIR	6 LIB	7 SAG	5 CAP	6 PIS	6 ARI	7 GEM	6 CAN
8 TAU	9 CAN	8 CAN	10 VIR	9 LIB	8 SCO	9 CAP	7 AQU	8 ARI	8 TAU	9 CAN	9 LEO
10 GEM	11 LEO	11 LEO	12 LIB	11 SCO	10 SAG	11 AQU	10 PIS	10 TAU	10 GEM	12 LEO	11 VIR
13 CAN	14 VIR	13 VIR	14 SCO	13 SAG	12 CAP	13 PIS	12 ARI	13 GEM	13 CAN	14 VIR	14 LIB
15 LEO	16 LIB	15 LIB	16 SAG	15 CAP	14 AQU	15 ARI	14 TAU	15 CAN	15 LEO	16 LIB	16 SCO
17 VIR	18 SCO	17 SCO	18 CAP	17 AQU	16 PIS	18 TAU	17 GEM	18 LEO	18 VIR	19 SCO	18 SAG
20 LIB	20 SAG	19 SAG	20 AQU	19 PIS	18 ARI	20 GEM	19 CAN	20 VIR	20 LIB	21 SAG	20 CAP
22 SCO	22 CAP	22 CAP	22 PIS	22 ARI	21 TAU	23 CAN	22 LEO	23 LIB	23 SCO	23 CAP	22 AQU
24 SAG	24 AQU	24 AQU	25 ARI	24 TAU	23 GEM	25 LEO	24 VIR	25 SCO	24 SAG	25 AQU	24 PIS
26 CAP	27 PIS	26 PIS	27 TAU	27 GEM	26 CAN	28 VIR	26 LIB	27 SAG	26 CAP	27 PIS	26 ARI
28 AQU		28 ARI	30 GEM	29 CAN	28 LEO	30 LIB	28 SCO	29 CAP	28 AQU	29 ARI	29 TAU
30 PIS		31 TAU			30 VIR		31 SAG		31 PIS		

What Sign Is Your Ascendant?

THESE UNIQUE ASCENDANT TABLES, specially devised for this book by the astrologer Capel McCutcheon, enable you, simply by laying down two rulers, to ascertain with reasonable accuracy what your Rising sign is.

You will see that there are two tables: one for 40 Degrees North latitude, and one for 30 Degrees North latitude. Both tables will give reasonable accuracy within a 10-degree span. Thus the 40 Degrees North Table can be used for birthplace latitudes from 35 Degrees North to 45 Degrees North. These latitudes roughly cover any birthplace in the top half of the United States, including such cities as New York, San Francisco, Washington, D.C., Chicago, Denver, Philadelphia, St. Louis, Minneapolis, and Seattle. The 30 Degrees North Table can be used for birthplace latitudes from 25 Degrees North to 35 Degrees North, an area roughly covering the bottom half of the United States. This area includes such cities as Los Angeles, Miami, New Orleans, Houston, Dallas, Memphis, Atlanta, and San Diego. (Check an atlas if you are not sure which of these two areas your birthplace is in.)

Of course, you may have been born in London or Rio de Janeiro or Bangkok, in which case your birthplace is not covered by these areas. If you were not born in the United States, the simplest way of discovering your Ascendant is to have a computer calculate it for you. Use the enclosed CD-ROM. In moments, you'll know what sign your Ascendant is—and in what *degree* of this sign it is. You can also surf the web to find sites that will cast your chart for free.

In addition, on page 484 I offer a shortcut method of approximating your Ascendant. If you were born outside the U.S. and cannot use these Ascendant tables—and you have no access to a computer—this shortcut method will provide your approximate Ascendant. But remember, it's just *approximate*.

How to Use the Following Ascendant Tables

To aid in finding your Ascendant, let us find the Ascendant of Oprah Winfrey, whose chart I use in this book as a special example in interpreting a horoscope. (See pages 322 et seq.) Oprah was born January 29, 1954, at 4:30 A.M., in Kosciusko, Mississippi.

1. First decide if your birthplace is in the 30 Degrees North Table or the 40 Degrees North Table. Oprah Winfrey was born in Mississippi, an area represented by the 30 Degrees North Table.

2. Now place a ruler along the line that most closely represents the time of your birth (listed on the left-hand side of the page). You will notice that for each hour of time there are five squares of graph, which means each graph-square represents 12 minutes. Oprah was born at 4:30 A.M.; she would place a ruler across the page in the middle of the third square after 4:00 A.M.

3. The next step is to place a second ruler down the line that most closely represents the day of the month of your birth (listed along the top of the page). You will notice that for each month there are 15 squares of graph, which means each graph-square represents about two days. Oprah was born on January 29; she would place a ruler down the page in the middle of the 15th square (the final square) of January.

4. The last step is to look at the point where the two rulers meet. This point will fall into a specific diagonal band on the graph that is clearly labeled with the name of an astrological sign. That sign is your Ascendant.

For Oprah Winfrey's birth time and birthdate, the two rulers meet in the band marked *Sagittarius*. Therefore, Sagittarius is Oprah's Ascendant.

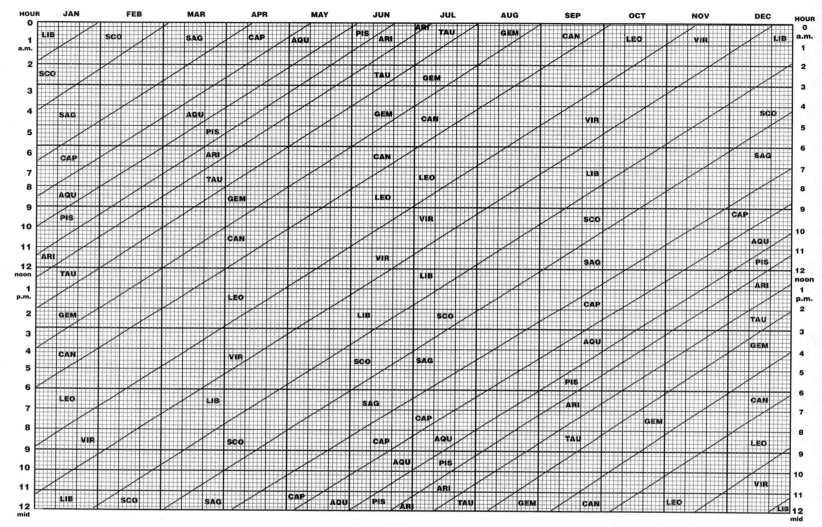

30 DEGREES NORTH

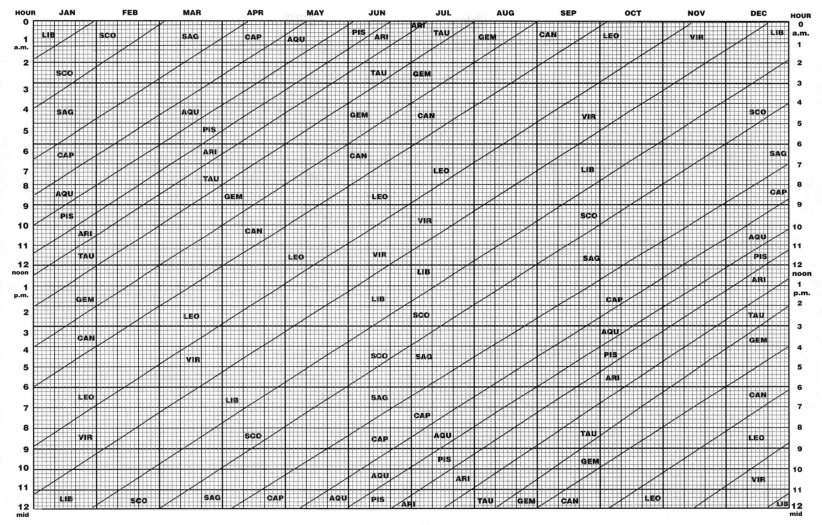

40 DEGREES NORTH

A Shortcut Method of Approximating Your Ascendant

THE FOLLOWING METHOD will give you a simple way of finding your Ascendant. Keep in mind that this shortcut method is a gauge that does not allow for differences in latitude at the place you were born, time changes, etc. Nor does it give you the *degree* of your Rising sign.

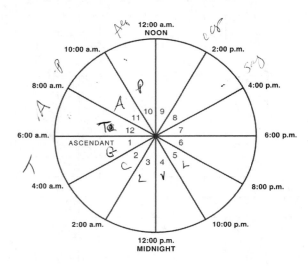

SHORTCUT METHOD

1. What time of day were you born? Locate the segment of the above wheel that contains your birth time.
2. Write the name of your Sun sign in that segment.
3. Going counterclockwise around the wheel, write down in each segment the signs of the zodiac in the order that they follow your Sun sign. (See example below.)

4. The sign that you write down in Segment 1 is your approximate Ascendant.

Example: Person born 7:56 P.M. with Sun in Pisces.*
1. Time of birth, 7:56 P.M., fits into Segment 6.
2. Pisces (Sun sign) is written down in Segment 6.
3. Following the order of the zodiac, the signs of Aries, Taurus, Gemini, Cancer, Leo, Virgo, and Libra are written in Segments 7, 8, 9, 10, 11, 12, and 1 of the wheel.
4. The sign of Libra appears in Segment 1. Libra is this person's Ascendant.

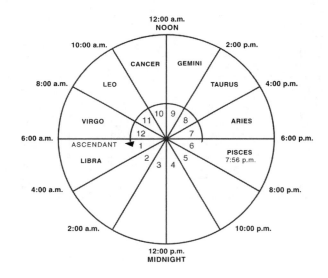

*This person is Elizabeth Taylor, born with the Sun in Pisces and Libra rising.

Where Is Your Mercury?

The following Mercury Tables will tell you what sign Mercury was in on the day of your birth.

First locate the year you were born. Next find the month of your birth (on the left-hand side of the page) and place a ruler across the page under your birth month.

The tables list for your month every date on which Mercury *moved* into a new sign.* Thus, you can quickly ascertain what sign Mercury was in on the day of your birth.

Example: You were born June 1, 1970. Locate the year *1970* and the month *JUN*. You will see that on the 13th of June in 1970 Mercury moved into Gemini. Since you were born on the 1st of June, look at the previous month to find Mercury's position. You will see that Mercury was in Taurus throughout May and did not move into Gemini until the 13th of June. Therefore, on June 1st, your birthday, Mercury was in Taurus.

Example: You were born August 15, 1962. Locate the year *1962* and the month *AUG*. You will see that on the 10th of August Mercury moved into Virgo, and on the 29th of August it moved into Libra. Therefore, on August 15th, your birthday, Mercury was in Virgo.

Note: If you look carefully at the Mercury Tables, you will see that from time to time Mercury enters a new sign and when it moves again reenters a previous sign. For example, in the year 1984 Mercury entered Aries on March 14, entered Taurus on March 31, entered Aries again on April 25, and entered Taurus again in May 15. This backward transit of a planet is called retrograde motion, a term fully described in An Astrologer's Lexicon, page 417. You will notice this phenomenon from time to time in all the Planetary Tables because all the planets, except for the Sun and the Moon, are retrograde at one time or another.

CC - Scorpio
DC - ARIES

JIM - GEMINI
Push - scorpio moved to SAG
on Nov 29th so need exact time

---

*If you were born on a day on which Mercury moved to a new sign, you should use the enclosed CD-ROM to cast your chart. At the *time of day* you were born, Mercury might still have been in the previous sign because it had not yet entered the new sign. Your computer chart will tell you the *exact* sign your Mercury is in as well as the exact degree of this sign.

Mercury Tables

	1900	1901	1902	1903	1904	1905	1906	1907	1908	1909	1910	1911	1912	1913	1914
JAN	8 CAP / 28 AQU	2 CAP / 21 AQU	13 AQU	6 AQU	2 AQU / 13 CAP	CAP	12 CAP	6 CAP / 26 AQU	18 AQU	10 AQU	3 AQU / 30 CAP	CAP	15 CAP	10 CAP / 29 AQU	3 CAP / 22 AQU
FEB	14 PIS	7 PIS	1 PIS / 18 AQU	AQU	15 AQU	9 AQU / 27 PIS	2 AQU / 19 PIS	12 PIS	4 PIS	AQU	15 AQU	12 AQU	6 AQU	16 PIS / 25 PIS	8 PIS
MAR	3 ARI / 29 PIS	PIS	18 PIS	14 PIS	7 PIS / 23 ARI	15 ARI	7 ARI	3 ARI / 13 PIS	ARI	17 PIS	11 PIS / 29 ARI	4 PIS / 20 ARI	11 ARI	4 ARI	PIS
APR	16 ARI	15 ARI	9 ARI / 25 TAU	1 ARI / 16 TAU	7 TAU	1 TAU / 28 ARI	ARI	18 ARI	12 ARI / 29 TAU	5 ARI / 21 TAU	12 TAU / 30 GEM	5 TAU	ARI	7 PIS / 13 ARI	16 ARI
MAY	10 TAU / 26 GEM	3 TAU / 17 GEM	9 GEM / 29 CAN	2 GEM	TAU	15 TAU	14 TAU / 31 GEM	8 TAU / 23 GEM	13 GEM	5 GEM	29 CAN	GEM	TAU	16 TAU / 27 GEM	4 TAU / 19 GEM
JUN	9 CAN / 27 LEO	1 CAN	26 GEM	GEM	14 GEM	8 GEM / 23 CAN	14 CAN / 30 LEO	6 CAN / 27 LEO	6 CAN	CAN	CAN	1 TAU / 11 GEM	12 GEM / 28 CAN	19 CAN	3 CAN / 28 LEO
JUL	LEO	CAN	13 CAN	10 CAN / 25 LEO	1 CAN / 15 LEO	7 LEO / 27 VIR	27 VIR	LEO	26 CAN	13 CAN / 29 LEO	CAN	13 CAN / 29 LEO	12 LEO / 30 VIR	4 LEO / 26 VIR	LEO
AUG	LEO	9 LEO / 25 VIR	2 LEO / 17 VIR	9 VIR / 29 LIB	1 VIR / 28 LIB	VIR	VIR	12 LEO / 31 VIR	6 LEO / 21 VIR	21 VIR / 31 LIB	13 VIR / 31 LIB	LIB	VIR	LEO	11 LEO / 27 VIR
SEP	2 VIR / 18 LIB	11 LIB / 30 SCO	3 LIB / 28 SCO	LIB	7 VIR	VIR	7 VIR / 23 LIB	16 LIB	7 LIB / 28 SCO	7 LIB	28 VIR	LIB	10 VIR / 28 LIB	4 VIR / 20 LIB	12 LIB
OCT	7 SCO / 30 SAG	SCO	15 LIB	LIB	8 LIB / 26 SCO	1 LIB / 19 SCO	11 SCO	4 SCO	SCO	SCO	11 LIB / 31 SCO	31 SCO	6 LIB / 24 SCO	15 SCO	8 SCO / 30 SAG
NOV	18 SCO	SCO	10 SCO / 29 SAG	3 SCO / 22 SAG	14 SAG	7 SAG	1 SAG	SCO	1 LIB / 11 SCO	26 SAG	19 SAG	11 SAG	4 SAG	23 SCO	SCO
DEC	12 SAG	6 SAG / 26 CAP	18 CAP	11 CAP	4 CAP	1 CAP / 9 SAG	6 SCO / 12 SAG	10 SAG / 30 CAP	3 SAG / 22 CAP	15 CAP	8 CAP	2 CAP / 27 SAG	SAG	13 SAG	7 SAG / 27 CAP

	1915	1916	1917	1918	1919	1920	1921	1922	1923	1924	1925	1926	1927	1928	1929
JAN	14 AQU	7 AQU	1 AQU / 17 CAP	CAP	13 CAP	8 CAP / 27 AQU	18 AQU	11 AQU	4 AQU	CAP	14 CAP	11 CAP / 31 AQU	4 CAP / 23 AQU	16 AQU	8 AQU
FEB	2 PIS / 23 AQU	AQU	AQU	14 AQU	10 AQU	3 AQU / 21 PIS	13 PIS	5 PIS	1 PIS / 8 AQU	6 CAP / 13 AQU	13 AQU	7 AQU / 25 PIS	17 PIS	3 PIS / 29 AQU	AQU
MAR	19 PIS	14 PIS	8 PIS / 25 ARI	1 PIS / 17 ARI	9 ARI	2 ARI / 19 PIS	PIS	18 PIS	12 PIS / 30 ARI	5 PIS / 21 ARI	13 ARI	5 ARI	PIS	17 PIS	15 PIS
APR	10 ARI / 26 TAU	2 ARI / 17 TAU	9 TAU	2 TAU	ARI	17 ARI	13 ARI	7 ARI	14 TAU	ARI	5 TAU / 15 ARI	1 TAU	ARI	17 ARI / 27 TAU	3 ARI / 18 TAU
MAY	10 GEM / 29 CAN	2 GEM	TAU	TAU	15 TAU	8 TAU / 23 GEM	1 TAU / 15 GEM / 31 CAN	7 GEM / 31 CAN	1 GEM / 31 CAN	1 GEM	TAU	13 TAU / 29 GEM	6 TAU / 20 GEM	11 GEM / 28 CAN	3 GEM
JUN	CAN	GEM	14 GEM / 24 CAN	14 GEM	2 GEM / 16 CAN	6 CAN	CAN	10 GEM	GEM	12 GEM / 29 CAN	6 GEM / 20 CAN	12 GEM / 29 CAN	4 CAN	CAN	GEM
JUL	CAN	10 CAN / 25 LEO	3 CAN / 17 LEO	9 CAN	1 LEO	LEO	CAN	13 CAN / 31 LEO	8 CAN / 22 LEO	13 CAN / 31 LEO	5 LEO / 26 VIR	LEO	13 CAN	CAN	11 CAN / 27 LEO
AUG	4 LEO / 18 VIR	9 VIR / 28 LIB	2 VIR / 26 LIB	LEO	LEO	2 CAN / 10 LEO / 31 VIR	8 LEO / 23 VIR	15 VIR	7 VIR / 27 LIB	15 VIR	7 VIR / 27 LIB	LEO	11 LEO / 28 VIR	4 LEO / 19 VIR	11 LEO / 30 LIB
SEP	5 LIB / 28 SCO	LIB	LIB	14 VIR	VIR	8 VIR / 25 LIB	16 LIB	LIB	1 LIB / 29 SCO	VIR	VIR	11 VIR / 29 LIB	5 VIR / 21 LIB	13 LIB	LIB
OCT	20 LIB	LIB	9 LIB / 28 SCO	3 LIB / 20 SCO	13 SCO	5 SCO / 30 SAG	SCO	1 SCO / 27 SAG	SCO	4 VIR / 11 LIB	6 LIB / 24 SCO	16 SCO	9 SCO / 31 SAG	3 SCO	24 LIB
NOV	11 SCO	4 SCO / 22 SAG	15 SAG	8 SAG	2 SAG	10 SCO	SCO	8 SCO / 27 SAG	1 SCO / 20 SAG	12 SAG	5 SAG	28 SCO	SCO	11 SCO	5 SCO / 24 SAG
DEC	1 SAG / 20 CAP	12 CAP	5 CAP	1 CAP / 15 SAG	SAG	10 SAG / 31 CAP	24 CAP	16 CAP	9 CAP	2 CAP / 31 SAG	13 SAG	5 SAG	9 SAG / 28 CAP	1 SAG / 20 CAP	13 CAP

	1930	1931	1932	1933	1934	1935	1936	1937	1938	1939	1940	1941	1942	1943	1944
JAN	2 AQU / 22 CAP	CAP	14 CAP	8 CAP / 27 AQU	1 CAP / 20 AQU	12 AQU	5 AQU	1 AQU / 9 CAP	6 SAG / 9 CAP	12 CAP	6 CAP / 25 AQU	16 AQU	9 AQU	3 AQU / 27 CAP	CAP
FEB	15 AQU	11 AQU	4 AQU / 22 PIS	14 PIS	6 PIS	1 PIS / 14 AQU	AQU	13 AQU	8 AQU / 26 PIS	19 PIS	1 AQU / 19 PIS	11 PIS	3 PIS	15 AQU	12 AQU
MAR	9 PIS / 26 ARI	2 PIS / 18 ARI	9 ARI	3 ARI / 25 PIS	PIS	18 PIS	13 PIS / 31 ARI	6 PIS / 22 ARI	14 ARI	7 ARI	4 ARI / 7 PIS	16 PIS	11 PIS / 28 ARI	2 PIS / 19 ARI	2 PIS
APR	10 TAU	3 TAU	ARI	17 ARI	17 ARI	8 ARI / 24 TAU	14 ARI / 30 TAU	6 TAU	1 TAU / 23 ARI	ARI	16 ARI	12 ARI / 28 TAU	5 ARI / 20 TAU	11 TAU	3 TAU
MAY	1 GEM / 17 TAU	TAU	15 TAU	10 TAU / 25 GEM	2 TAU / 16 GEM	8 GEM / 29 CAN	GEM	TAU	16 TAU	TAU	14 TAU / 30 GEM	12 GEM / 29 CAN	4 GEM	26 TAU	TAU
JUN	14 GEM	11 GEM / 26 CAN	2 GEM / 16 CAN	8 CAN / 26 LEO	1 CAN	20 GEM	GEM	13 GEM / 30 CAN	7 GEM / 22 CAN	13 CAN / 30 LEO	13 CAN / 30 LEO	4 CAN	GEM	13 GEM	11 GEM / 26 CAN
JUL	4 CAN / 18 LEO	10 LEO / 28 VIR	2 LEO / 27 VIR	LEO	CAN	13 CAN	8 CAN / 23 LEO	14 LEO / 31 VIR	6 CAN / 26 VIR	LEO	20 CAN	12 CAN / 28 LEO	6 CAN / 20 LEO	6 CAN / 20 LEO	11 LEO / 28 VIR
AUG	3 VIR / 26 LIB	VIR	10 LEO	LEO	9 LEO / 24 VIR	1 LEO / 16 VIR	7 VIR / 27 LIB	VIR	7 VIR	VIR	11 LEO / 29 VIR	12 VIR / 31 LIB	12 VIR / 31 LIB	5 VIR / 26 LIB	VIR
SEP	19 VIR	VIR	9 VIR / 25 LIB	2 VIR / 17 LIB	10 LIB	3 LIB / 30 SCO	28 SCO	LIB	2 LEO / 10 VIR / 30 LIB	6 VIR / 23 LIB	14 LIB	6 LIB / 28 SCO	LIB	25 VIR	VIR
OCT	10 LIB / 29 SCO	4 LIB / 21 SCO	13 SCO	6 SCO / 29 SAG	SCO	12 LIB	LIB	8 LIB / 25 SCO	11 SCO	3 SCO	3 SCO	LIB	6 SCO	11 LIB / 30 SCO	4 LIB / 22 SCO
NOV	17 SAG	9 SAG	2 SAG	15 SCO	SCO	9 SCO / 29 SAG	2 SCO / 20 SAG	13 SAG	6 SAG	1 SAG	SCO	11 SCO	25 SCO	18 SAG	10 SAG
DEC	6 CAP	1 CAP / 20 SAG	20 SAG	11 SAG	6 SAG / 25 CAP	18 CAP	10 CAP	3 CAP	SAG	3 SCO / 13 SAG	9 SAG / 29 CAP	2 SAG / 21 CAP	14 CAP	7 CAP	1 CAP / 23 SAG

Mercury Tables

1945–1959

	1945	1946	1947	1948	1949	1950	1951	1952	1953	1954	1955	1956	1957	1958	1959
JAN	13 CAP	9 CAP, 29 AQU	2 CAP, 21 AQU	14 AQU	6 AQU	1 AQU, 15 CAP	CAP	13 CAP	6 CAP, 25 AQU	18 AQU	10 AQU	4 AQU	CAP	14 CAP	10 CAP, 30 AQU
FEB	5 AQU, 23 PIS	15 PIS	7 PIS	1 PIS, 20 AQU	AQU	14 AQU	9 AQU, 28 PIS	2 AQU, 20 PIS	11 PIS	4 PIS	AQU	2 CAP, 15 AQU	12 AQU	6 AQU, 24 PIS	16 PIS
MAR	11 ARI	4 ARI	PIS	18 PIS	14 PIS	7 PIS, 24 ARI	16 ARI	7 ARI	15 PIS	17 ARI	PIS	17 PIS	11 PIS, 28 ARI	4 PIS, 20 ARI	12 ARI
APR	ARI	1 PIS, 16 ARI	15 ARI	8 ARI, 24 TAU	1 ARI, 16 TAU	8 TAU	1 TAU	ARI	17 ARI	13 ARI, 30 TAU	6 ARI, 21 TAU	12 TAU, 29 GEM	4 TAU	2 TAU, 10 ARI	ARI
MAY	16 TAU	11 TAU, 26 GEM	4 TAU, 18 GEM	8 GEM, 28 GEM	1 GEM	TAU	1 ARI, 14 TAU	14 TAU, 31 GEM	8 TAU, 22 GEM	14 GEM, 30 CAN	6 GEM	GEM	TAU	16 TAU	12 TAU, 28 GEM
JUN	4 GEM, 18 CAN	9 CAN, 27 LEO	2 CAN	28 GEM	GEM	14 GEM	9 GEM, 23 CAN	14 CAN, 30 LEO	6 CAN, 26 LEO	CAN	GEM	GEM	12 GEM, 28 CAN	5 GEM, 19 CAN	11 CAN, 28 LEO
JUL	3 LEO, 26 VIR	LEO	CAN	11 CAN	9 CAN, 25 LEO	2 CAN, 16 LEO	8 LEO, 27 VIR	LEO	28 CAN		13 CAN, 30 LEO	6 CAN, 21 LEO	4 LEO, 29 VIR	26 VIR	LEO
AUG	17 LEO	LEO, 26 VIR	LEO, 17 VIR	10 LEO, 28 LIB	2 LEO, 27 LIB	9 VIR	1 VIR, 30 VIR	LEO, 22 VIR	11 LEO	7 LEO	14 VIR, 26 LIB	5 VIR	VIR	23 LEO	LEO
SEP	10 VIR, 27 LIB	3 VIR, 19 LIB	11 LIB	3 LIB, 27 SCO	LIB	10 VIR	VIR	7 VIR, 23 LIB	15 LIB, 28 SCO	8 LIB	1 LIB	29 VIR	VIR, 28 LIB	10 VIR, 20 LIB	4 VIR
OCT	14 SCO, 30 SCO	7 SCO	1 SCO	16 LIB	LIB	9 LIB, 27 SCO	2 LIB, 19 SCO	11 SCO	4 SCO, 31 SAG	SCO	LIB	11 LIB, 31 SCO	6 LIB, 23 SCO	16 SCO	8 SCO, 30 SAG
NOV	3 SAG	20 SCO	SCO	9 SCO, 29 SAG	3 SCO, 22 SAG	14 SAG	7 SAG	1 SAG	6 SCO, 11 SCO	4 LIB, 11 SCO	8 SCO	18 SAG, 26 SAG	11 SAG	4 SAG	25 SCO
DEC	SAG	12 SAG, 26 CAP	7 SAG	18 CAP	11 CAP	4 CAP	1 CAP, 12 SAG	SAG	10 SAG, 30 CAP	4 SAG, 23 CAP	16 CAP	8 CAP	SAG	28 SAG	13 SAG

1960–1974

	1960	1961	1962	1963	1964	1965	1966	1967	1968	1969	1970	1971	1972	1973	1974
JAN	4 CAP, 23 AQU	14 AQU	7 AQU	1 AQU, 20 CAP	CAP	12 CAP	7 CAP, 26 AQU	19 AQU	12 AQU	4 AQU, 11 AQU	3 AQU, 4 CAP	2 SAG, 13 CAP	11 CAP, 31 AQU	4 CAP, 23 AQU	15 AQU
FEB	9 PIS	1 PIS, 24 AQU	AQU	15 AQU	10 AQU, 29 PIS	3 AQU, 21 PIS	13 PIS	5 PIS	1 PIS	AQU, 11 AQU	13 AQU	7 AQU, 26 PIS	18 PIS	9 PIS	2 PIS
MAR	PIS	18 PIS, 25 ARI	15 PIS	9 PIS	16 ARI	8 ARI	2 ARI, 21 PIS	PIS	17 PIS	12 PIS	5 PIS, 30 ARI	13 ARI, 22 ARI	5 ARI	PIS	2 AQU, 17 PIS
APR	15 ARI	10 ARI, 26 TAU	2 ARI, 17 TAU	9 TAU	1 TAU	ARI	17 ARI	14 ARI	6 ARI, 22 TAU	1 TAU, 30 GEM	ARI, 30 TAU	ARI, 18 ARI	16 ARI	ARI	11 ARI, 27 TAU
MAY	4 TAU, 18 GEM	10 GEM, 28 CAN	3 GEM	2 GEM, 10 TAU	TAU	15 TAU	9 TAU, 24 GEM	1 TAU, 15 GEM, 31 CAN	6 GEM, 29 CAN	GEM	TAU	16 TAU	12 TAU, 29 GEM	5 TAU, 20 GEM	11 GEM, 29 CAN
JUN	2 CAN, 30 LEO	CAN	GEM	14 GEM	9 GEM, 24 CAN	1 GEM, 15 CAN, 31 CAN	7 CAN, 26 LEO	CAN	13 GEM, 15 CAN	GEM	13 GEM, 30 CAN	7 GEM, 21 CAN	11 CAN, 28 LEO	3 CAN, 27 LEO	CAN
JUL	5 CAN	CAN	11 CAN, 26 LEO	3 CAN, 18 LEO	8 LEO, 27 VIR	1 LEO, 31 VIR	LEO	CAN	12 CAN, 24 VIR	7 CAN, 22 LEO	14 LEO, 31 VIR	6 LEO, 26 VIR	LEO	16 CAN	CAN
AUG	10 LEO, 26 VIR	3 LEO, 18 VIR	10 VIR, 29 LIB	3 VIR, 26 LIB	3 LEO, 27 VIR	LEO	LEO	8 LEO, 24 VIR	14 VIR	6 VIR, 27 LIB	VIR	29 LEO	LEO	11 LEO, 28 VIR	5 LEO, 20 VIR
SEP	12 LIB, 27 SCO	4 LIB	LIB	16 VIR, 26 VIR	VIR	8 VIR, 25 LIB	1 VIR, 17 LIB	17 LIB, 29 SCO	1 LIB, 28 SCO	29 SCO	LIB	VIR, 30 LIB	11 VIR, 21 LIB	5 VIR	6 LIB, 27 SCO
OCT	1 SCO	21 LIB	LIB	10 LIB, 28 SCO	2 LIB, 20 SCO	12 SCO	17 LIB, 30 SAG	SCO	7 LIB, 9 LIB	6 VIR	7 LIB	25 SCO	17 SCO, 30 SAG	9 SCO	2 SCO, 26 LIB
NOV	SCO	10 SCO, 30 SAG	4 SCO, 23 SAG	16 SAG	8 SAG, 30 CAP	2 SAG	12 SCO	SCO	8 SCO, 27 SAG	1 SCO, 20 SAG	12 SAG	6 SAG	29 SCO	SCO	11 SCO
DEC	7 SAG, 27 CAP	19 CAP	12 CAP	6 CAP	16 SAG	SAG	11 SAG, 31 CAP	5 SAG, 24 CAP	16 CAP	9 CAP	3 CAP	SAG	12 SAG	8 SAG, 28 CAP	2 SAG, 21 CAP

1975–1989

	1975	1976	1977	1978	1979	1980	1981	1982	1983	1984	1985	1986	1987	1988	1989
JAN	8 AQU	2 AQU, 24 CAP	CAP	13 CAP	8 CAP, 28 AQU	2 CAP, 20 AQU	12 AQU, 31 PIS	5 AQU, 12 CAP	1 AQU	CAP	11 CAP	5 CAP, 24 AQU	17 AQU	10 AQU	2 AQU, 28 CAP
FEB	AQU	15 AQU	10 AQU	4 AQU, 22 PIS	14 PIS	7 PIS	16 AQU	AQU	14 AQU	8 AQU, 27 PIS	18 PIS	11 PIS	3 PIS	AQU	14 AQU
MAR	16 PIS	9 PIS, 26 ARI	2 PIS, 18 ARI	10 ARI	3 ARI, 28 PIS	PIS	17 PIS	13 PIS, 31 ARI	6 PIS, 23 ARI	14 ARI, 31 TAU	6 ARI, 11 PIS	3 ARI	11 AQU	16 PIS	10 PIS, 27 ARI
APR	4 ARI, 19 TAU	10 TAU, 29 GEM	2 TAU, 18 ARI	ARI	17 ARI, 28 PIS	14 ARI	8 ARI, 24 TAU	15 TAU	7 TAU	25 ARI	ARI	17 ARI	12 ARI, 29 TAU	4 ARI	11 TAU, 29 GEM
MAY	4 GEM	19 TAU	TAU	16 TAU	10 TAU, 26 GEM	2 TAU, 16 GEM	8 GEM, 31 CAN	1 GEM	TAU	15 TAU	13 TAU, 30 GEM	7 TAU, 22 GEM	13 TAU, 29 CAN	4 GEM	28 TAU
JUN	GEM	13 GEM, 26 CAN	10 GEM, 17 CAN	3 GEM, 27 LEO	9 CAN	CAN	22 GEM	GEM	14 GEM	7 GEM, 22 CAN	13 CAN, 29 LEO	5 CAN, 26 LEO	CAN	GEM	12 GEM
JUL	12 CAN, 28 LEO	4 CAN, 18 LEO	10 CAN, 28 VIR	2 LEO, 27 VIR	27 VIR	CAN	12 CAN	9 CAN, 24 LEO	1 CAN, 15 LEO	6 CAN, 26 VIR	LEO	23 CAN		12 CAN, 28 LEO	5 CAN, 20 LEO
AUG	12 VIR, 30 LIB	3 VIR, 25 LIB	28 VIR	VIR, 9 VIR	13 LEO	LEO	LEO, 24 VIR	8 VIR, 16 VIR	1 VIR, 27 LIB	VIR, 29 LIB	LEO	11 LEO, 29 VIR	6 LEO, 21 VIR	12 VIR, 30 LIB	4 VIR, 26 LIB
SEP	LIB	21 VIR	VIR	9 VIR, 26 LIB	2 VIR, 18 LIB	9 LIB, 29 SCO	2 LIB, 27 SCO	LIB	5 VIR, 22 LIB	30 LIB	6 VIR	14 LIB, 28 SCO	7 LIB	LIB	26 VIR
OCT	LIB	10 LIB, 28 SCO	4 LIB, 21 SCO	14 SCO	6 SCO, 30 SAG	SCO	13 LIB	LIB	8 LIB, 26 SCO	17 SCO	10 SCO	3 SCO, 31 SAG	31 LIB	LIB, 28 SCO	11 LIB, 30 SCO
NOV	6 SCO, 24 SAG	16 SAG	9 SAG	3 SAG	17 SCO	SCO	9 SCO, 28 SAG	2 SCO, 21 SAG	14 SAG	6 SAG	SCO	SCO	11 SCO	6 SCO, 25 SAG	17 SAG
DEC	13 CAP	6 CAP, 21 SAG	1 CAP	SAG, 24 CAP	12 SAG	5 SAG, 7 SAG	17 CAP	10 CAP, 29 CAP	4 CAP, 22 CAP	1 CAP	4 SCO, 12 SAG	9 SAG, 29 CAP	3 SAG, 22 CAP	14 CAP	7 CAP

Mercury Tables

	1990	1991	1992	1993	1994	1995	1996	1997	1998	1999	2000	2001	2002	2003	2004
JAN	CAP	14 CAP	9 CAP / 29 AQU	2 CAP / 21 AQU	13 AQU	6 AQU	1 AQU / 17 CAP	CAP	12 CAP	6 CAP / 26 AQU	18 AQU	10 AQU	3 AQU	CAP	14 CAP
FEB	11 AQU	5 AQU / 23 PIS	16 PIS	7 PIS	1 PIS / 21 AQU	AQU	14 AQU	9 AQU / 27 PIS	20 PIS	12 PIS	5 PIS	1 PIS / 6 AQU	3 CAP / 13 AQU	12 AQU	6 AQU / 25 PIS
MAR	3 PIS / 19 ARI	11 ARI	3 ARI	PIS	18 PIS	14 PIS	7 PIS / 24 ARI	15 ARI	8 ARI	2 ARI / 18 PIS	PIS	17 PIS	11 PIS / 29 ARI	21 ARI	12 ARI / 31 TAU
APR	4 TAU	ARI	3 PIS / 14 ARI	15 ARI	9 ARI / 25 TAU	2 ARI / 17 TAU	7 TAU	1 TAU	ARI	17 ARI / 29 TAU	12 ARI / 21 TAU	6 ARI / 30 TAU	13 TAU	5 TAU	12 ARI
MAY	TAU	16 TAU / 26 GEM	10 TAU	3 TAU / 18 GEM	9 GEM / 28 CAN	2 GEM	2 GEM	TAU	4 ARI / 12 TAU	14 TAU / 23 GEM	8 TAU	14 GEM / 29 CAN	5 GEM	TAU	16 TAU
JUN	11 GEM / 27 CAN	4 GEM / 19 CAN	9 CAN / 27 LEO	1 CAN	CAN	GEM	13 GEM	8 GEM / 23 CAN	1 GEM / 15 CAN / 30 LEO	6 CAN	26 LEO	CAN	GEM	12 GEM / 29 CAN	5 GEM / 19 CAN
JUL	11 LEO / 29 VIR	4 LEO / 26 VIR	LEO	CAN	2 GEM / 10 CAN	10 CAN / 25 LEO	2 CAN / 16 LEO	8 LEO / 26 VIR	LEO	31 CAN	CAN	12 CAN / 30 LEO	7 CAN / 21 LEO	13 LEO / 30 VIR	4 LEO / 25 VIR
AUG	VIR	19 LEO	LEO	10 LEO / 26 VIR	3 LEO / 17 VIR	9 VIR / 28 LIB	1 VIR / 26 LIB	VIR	LEO	10 LEO / 31 VIR	7 LEO / 22 VIR	14 VIR / 31 LIB	6 VIR / 26 LIB	VIR	24 LEO
SEP	VIR	10 VIR / 27 LIB	3 VIR / 19 LIB	11 LIB / 30 SCO	3 LIB	LIB	12 VIR	VIR	7 VIR / 24 LIB	16 LIB	7 LIB / 28 SCO	LIB	LIB	VIR	10 VIR / 28 LIB
OCT	5 LIB / 22 SCO	15 SCO	7 SCO / 29 SAG	SCO	19 LIB	LIB	8 LIB / 26 SCO	2 LIB / 19 SCO	11 SCO	5 SCO / 30 SAG	SCO	LIB	2 VIR / 11 LIB / 31 SCO	6 LIB / 24 SCO	15 SCO
NOV	10 SAG	4 SAG	21 SCO	SCO	10 SCO / 29 SAG	4 SCO / 22 SAG	14 SAG	7 SAG / 30 CAP	1 SAG	9 SCO	8 SCO	7 LIB / 8 SCO	7 SCO / 26 SAG	19 SAG	12 SAG
DEC	1 CAP / 25 SAG	SAG	12 SAG	6 SAG / 26 CAP	19 CAP	11 CAP	4 CAP	13 SAG	SAG	10 SAG / 31 CAP	3 SAG / 22 CAP	15 CAP	8 CAP	2 CAP / 30 SAG	SAG

	2005	2006	2007	2008	2009	2010	2011	2012	2013	2014	2015	2016	2017	2018	2019
JAN	9 CAP / 30 AQU	3 CAP / 22 AQU	15 AQU	7 AQU	1 AQU / 21 CAP	CAP	13 CAP	8 CAP / 27 AQU	19 AQU	11 AQU / 31 PIS	4 AQU	1 AQU / 8 CAP	4 SAG / 12 CAP	11 CAP / 31 AQU	4 CAP / 24 AQU
FEB	16 PIS	8 PIS / 26 AQU	2 PIS	AQU	14 AQU	10 AQU	3 AQU / 21 PIS	13 PIS	5 PIS	12 AQU	AQU	13 AQU	7 AQU / 25 PIS	17 PIS	10 PIS
MAR	4 ARI	PIS	18 PIS	14 PIS	8 PIS / 25 ARI	1 PIS / 17 ARI	9 ARI	2 ARI / 23 PIS	PIS	17 PIS	12 PIS / 30 ARI	5 PIS / 21 ARI	13 ARI / 31 TAU	6 ARI	PIS
APR	ARI	16 ARI	10 ARI / 27 TAU	2 ARI / 17 TAU	9 TAU / 30 GEM	2 TAU	ARI	16 ARI	13 ARI	7 ARI / 23 TAU	14 TAU / 30 GEM	5 TAU	20 ARI	ARI	17 ARI
MAY	12 TAU / 28 GEM	5 TAU / 19 GEM	11 GEM / 28 CAN	2 GEM	13 TAU	TAU	15 TAU	9 TAU / 24 GEM	1 TAU / 15 GEM / 31 CAN	7 GEM / 29 CAN	TAU	GEM	15 TAU	13 TAU / 29 GEM	6 TAU / 21 GEM
JUN	11 CAN / 27 LEO	3 CAN / 28 LEO	CAN	GEM	13 GEM	10 GEM / 25 CAN	2 GEM / 16 CAN	7 CAN / 25 LEO	CAN	17 GEM	GEM	12 GEM / 29 CAN	6 GEM / 21 CAN	12 CAN / 29 LEO	4 CAN / 26 LEO
JUL	LEO	10 CAN	CAN	10 CAN / 26 LEO	3 CAN / 17 LEO	9 LEO / 27 VIR	2 LEO / 28 VIR	LEO	LEO	CAN	12 CAN / 31 LEO	8 CAN / 23 LEO	13 LEO / 30 VIR	5 LEO / 25 VIR	LEO
AUG	LEO	10 LEO / 27 VIR	4 LEO / 19 VIR	10 VIR / 28 LIB	2 VIR / 25 LIB	VIR	VIR	8 LEO	31 VIR	15 VIR	8 LEO / 23 VIR	7 VIR / 27 LIB	31 LEO	LEO	11 LEO / 29 VIR
SEP	4 VIR / 20 LIB	12 LIB	5 LIB / 27 SCO	LIB	17 VIR / 25 LIB	VIR	9 VIR / 25 LIB	16 LIB	9 LIB / 29 SCO	9 LIB / 27 SCO	2 LIB	LIB	VIR	5 VIR / 29 LIB	14 LIB
OCT	8 SCO / 30 SAG	1 SCO	23 LIB	LIB	9 LIB / 28 SCO	3 LIB / 20 SCO	13 SCO	5 SCO	SCO	10 LIB	LIB	7 LIB / 24 SCO	17 SCO	9 SCO / 30 SAG	3 SCO
NOV	26 SCO	SCO	11 SCO	4 SCO / 23 SAG	15 SAG	8 SAG / 30 CAP	2 SAG	14 SCO	SCO	8 SCO / 27 SAG	2 SCO / 20 SAG	12 SAG	5 SAG	SAG	SCO
DEC	12 SAG	8 SAG / 27 CAP	1 SAG / 20 CAP	12 CAP	5 CAP	18 SAG	SAG	10 SAG / 31 CAP	4 SAG / 24 CAP	16 CAP	9 CAP	2 CAP	SAG	1 SCO / 12 SAG	9 SAG / 28 CAP

	2020	2021	2022	2023	2024	2025	2026	2027	2028	2029	2030	2031	2032	2033	2034
JAN	16 AQU	8 AQU	2 AQU / 25 CAP	CAP	13 CAP	8 CAP / 27 AQU	1 CAP / 20 AQU	13 AQU / 31 PIS	6 AQU	13 CAP	CAP	11 CAP	6 CAP / 25 AQU	16 AQU	9 AQU
FEB	3 PIS	AQU	14 AQU	11 AQU	5 AQU / 23 PIS	14 PIS	6 PIS	18 AQU	AQU	13 AQU	8 AQU / 27 PIS	1 AQU / 19 PIS	11 PIS	3 PIS	AQU
MAR	4 AQU / 16 PIS	15 PIS	9 PIS / 27 ARI	2 PIS / 18 ARI	9 ARI	3 ARI / 29 PIS	PIS	18 PIS	13 PIS / 31 ARI	6 PIS / 23 ARI	15 ARI / 31 TAU	7 ARI	1 ARI / 13 PIS	PIS	16 PIS
APR	10 ARI / 27 TAU	3 ARI / 19 TAU	10 ARI / 29 GEM	3 TAU	ARI	16 ARI	14 ARI	8 ARI / 24 TAU	15 TAU / 30 GEM	7 TAU	28 ARI	ARI	16 ARI	12 ARI / 29 TAU	5 ARI / 20 TAU
MAY	11 GEM / 28 CAN	3 GEM	22 TAU	TAU	15 TAU	10 TAU / 25 GEM	17 GEM	8 TAU / 28 CAN	GEM	TAU	14 TAU	6 TAU / 31 GEM	21 GEM	13 GEM / 29 CAN	5 GEM
JUN	CAN	GEM	13 GEM	11 GEM / 26 CAN	3 GEM / 26 CAN	8 CAN / 26 LEO	1 CAN	26 GEM	GEM	GEM	13 GEM	8 GEM / 22 CAN	14 CAN / 30 LEO	5 CAN / 25 LEO	GEM
JUL	CAN	11 CAN / 27 LEO	5 CAN / 19 LEO	10 LEO / 28 VIR	2 LEO / 25 VIR	LEO	CAN	12 CAN	8 CAN / 23 LEO	1 CAN / 15 LEO / 31 VIR	7 LEO / 26 VIR	LEO	25 CAN	CAN	12 CAN / 29 LEO
AUG	4 LEO / 19 VIR	11 VIR / 30 LIB	4 VIR / 25 LIB	VIR	14 LEO	LEO	9 LEO / 25 VIR	2 LEO / 16 VIR	8 VIR / 27 LIB	26 LIB	VIR	LEO	10 LEO / 29 VIR	6 LEO / 29 VIR	13 VIR / 31 LIB
SEP	5 LIB / 27 SCO	LIB	LIB	23 VIR	VIR	9 VIR / 26 LIB	2 VIR / 18 LIB	10 LIB / 30 SCO	3 LIB / 27 SCO	LIB	8 VIR	VIR	7 VIR / 23 LIB	14 LIB	LIB
OCT	27 LIB	LIB	10 LIB / 29 SCO	4 LIB / 22 SCO	13 SCO	6 SCO / 29 SAG	SCO	SCO	16 LIB	LIB	1 LIB / 18 SCO	11 SCO	3 SCO / 31 SAG	31 SAG	LIB
NOV	10 SCO	5 SCO / 24 SAG	17 SAG	10 SAG	2 SAG	18 SCO	SCO	9 SCO / 29 SAG	2 SCO / 20 SAG	13 SAG	6 SAG / 30 CAP	SAG	3 SCO	2 LIB / 10 SCO	6 SCO / 25 SAG
DEC	1 SAG / 20 CAP	13 CAP	6 CAP	1 CAP / 23 SAG	SAG	11 SAG / 25 CAP	6 SAG	18 CAP	10 CAP / 31 AQU	3 CAP	10 SAG	8 SCO / 10 SAG	9 SAG / 29 CAP	2 SAG / 22 CAP	14 CAP

2035–2049

	2035	2036	2037	2038	2039	2040	2041	2042	2043	2044	2045	2046	2047	2048	2049
JAN	3 AQU / 31 CAP	CAP	13 CAP	9 CAP / 29 AQU	2 CAP / 21 AQU	14 AQU	6 AQU	18 CAP	CAP	12 CAP	6 CAP / 25 AQU	18 AQU	10 AQU / 31 PIS	4 AQU	CAP
FEB	14 AQU	12 AQU	5 AQU / 23 PIS	15 PIS	8 PIS	1 PIS / 23 AQU	AQU	14 AQU	9 AQU / 28 PIS	2 AQU / 20 PIS	12 PIS	4 PIS	9 AQU	7 CAP / 12 AQU	12 AQU
MAR	11 PIS / 28 ARI	3 PIS / 19 ARI	11 ARI	4 ARI	PIS	17 PIS	14 PIS	7 PIS / 24 ARI	16 ARI	7 ARI	1 ARI / 19 PIS	PIS	17 PIS	11 PIS / 29 ARI	4 PIS / 20 ARI
APR	12 TAU / 29 GEM	3 TAU	3 TAU	8 PIS / 6 ARI	15 ARI / 12 ARI	9 ARI / 25 TAU	1 ARI / 16 TAU	8 TAU	1 TAU	ARI	16 ARI	13 ARI / 30 TAU	6 ARI / 22 TAU	12 TAU / 29 GEM	5 TAU
MAY	GEM	TAU	16 TAU	11 TAU / 27 GEM	4 TAU / 18 GEM	9 GEM / 27 CAN	1 GEM	TAU	TAU	14 TAU / 31 GEM	8 TAU / 23 GEM	14 GEM / 30 CAN	14 GEM / 30 CAN	GEM	TAU
JUN	1 TAU / 10 GEM	11 GEM / 27 CAN	4 GEM / 18 CAN	10 CAN / 27 LEO	2 CAN	CAN	CAN	13 GEM	9 GEM / 24 CAN	14 CAN / 30 LEO	6 CAN / 25 LEO	CAN	10 GEM	GEM	12 GEM / 28 CAN
JUL	6 CAN / 20 LEO	11 LEO / 28 VIR	3 LEO / 25 VIR	LEO	CAN	CAN		10 CAN / 25 LEO	2 CAN / 16 LEO	8 LEO / 27 VIR	6 CAN / 25 LEO	LEO	12 CAN / 30 LEO	6 CAN	12 LEO / 29 VIR
AUG	5 VIR / 26 LIB	VIR	21 LEO	LEO	10 LEO / 26 VIR	2 LEO / 17 VIR	9 VIR / 28 LIB	2 VIR / 25 LIB	VIR	LEO	3 CAN / 8 LEO / 31 VIR	7 LEO / 22 VIR	14 VIR	5 VIR / 26 LIB	VIR
SEP	28 VIR	VIR	9 VIR / 27 LIB	3 VIR / 19 LIB	11 LIB	3 LIB / 26 SCO	LIB	14 VIR	VIR	7 VIR / 23 LIB	15 LIB / 28 SCO	8 LIB / 29 SCO	1 LIB	LIB	VIR
OCT	11 LIB / 30 SCO	5 LIB / 22 SCO	14 SCO	7 SCO / 29 SAG	1 SCO	20 LIB	LIB	9 LIB / 27 SCO	2 LIB / 19 SCO	11 SCO / 31 SAG	4 SCO / 29 SAG	SCO	6 LIB	4 VIR / 9 LIB / 31 SCO	6 LIB / 23 SCO
NOV	18 SAG	10 SAG	3 SAG	23 SCO	SCO	9 SCO / 29 SAG	3 SCO / 22 SAG	15 SAG / 30 CAP	8 SAG	SAG	11 SCO	SCO	8 SCO / 27 SAG	18 SAG	11 SAG
DEC	7 CAP	1 CAP / 26 SAG	SAG	12 SAG	7 SAG / 26 CAP	18 CAP / 31 AQU	11 CAP	4 CAP	15 SAG	SAG	10 SAG / 30 CAP	4 SAG / 23 CAP	16 CAP	8 CAP	2 CAP / 31 SAG

2050–2064

	2050	2051	2052	2053	2054	2055	2056	2057	2058	2059	2060	2061	2062	2063	2064
JAN	13 CAP	10 CAP / 30 AQU	4 CAP / 23 AQU	14 AQU	7 AQU	1 AQU / 23 CAP	CAP	12 CAP	7 CAP / 27 AQU	19 AQU	12 AQU / 31 PIS	4 AQU	10 CAP	8 SAG / 10 CAP	11 CAP / 31 AQU
FEB	6 AQU / 24 PIS	17 PIS	9 PIS	1 PIS / 28 AQU	AQU	14 AQU	10 AQU / 29 PIS	3 AQU / 21 PIS	13 PIS	6 PIS	15 AQU	AQU	13 AQU	7 AQU / 26 PIS	18 PIS
MAR	12 ARI / 31 TAU	5 ARI	PIS	17 PIS	15 PIS	9 PIS / 26 ARI	17 ARI	9 ARI	2 ARI	PIS / 25 ARI	17 PIS / 30 ARI	12 PIS / 22 ARI	5 PIS	14 ARI / 31 TAU	5 ARI
APR	15 ARI	ARI	15 ARI	10 ARI / 26 TAU	3 ARI / 18 TAU	10 TAU / 30 GEM	1 TAU	ARI	16 ARI	14 ARI	7 ARI / 22 TAU	14 TAU / 30 GEM	6 TAU	23 ARI	ARI
MAY	16 TAU	12 TAU / 28 GEM	4 TAU / 19 GEM	10 GEM / 28 CAN	3 GEM	17 TAU	TAU	15 TAU	9 TAU / 24 GEM	2 TAU / 16 GEM / 31 CAN	7 GEM / 27 CAN	GEM	TAU	15 TAU	12 TAU / 29 GEM
JUN	5 GEM / 20 CAN	11 CAN / 28 LEO	2 CAN / 26 LEO	CAN	GEM	13 GEM	9 GEM / 24 CAN	2 GEM / 16 CAN	7 CAN / 26 LEO	CAN	19 GEM	GEM	13 GEM / 30 CAN	7 GEM / 21 CAN	12 CAN / 28 LEO
JUL	5 LEO / 25 VIR	LEO	13 CAN	CAN	11 CAN / 26 LEO	4 CAN / 18 LEO	9 LEO / 27 VIR	1 LEO / 26 VIR	LEO	CAN	12 CAN / 31 LEO	8 CAN / 23 LEO	14 LEO / 31 VIR	6 LEO / 26 VIR	LEO
AUG	27 LEO	LEO	10 LEO / 27 VIR	4 LEO / 19 VIR	10 VIR / 29 LIB	3 VIR / 25 LIB	20 VIR	VIR	10 LEO	LEO	8 LEO / 24 VIR	1 LEO / 15 VIR	LEO	VIR	LEO
SEP	10 VIR / 29 LIB	5 VIR / 21 LIB	12 LIB	4 LIB / 26 SCO	LIB	20 VIR	VIR	8 VIR / 25 LIB	1 VIR / 17 LIB	9 LIB / 29 SCO	1 LIB / 26 SCO	LIB	2 VIR	3 LEO / 9 VIR / 30 LIB	5 VIR / 21 LIB
OCT	16 SCO	9 SCO / 30 SAG	1 SCO	24 LIB / 30 SCO	LIB	10 LIB / 28 SCO	3 LIB / 20 SCO	12 SCO / 29 SAG	5 SCO / 20 SAG	SCO	11 LIB	LIB	7 LIB / 25 SCO	17 SCO	9 SCO / 30 SAG
NOV	4 SAG	28 SCO	SCO	10 SCO / 30 SAG	5 SCO / 23 SAG	16 SAG	8 SAG / 30 CAP	1 SAG	16 SCO	SCO	8 SCO / 27 SAG	1 SCO / 20 SAG	12 SAG	6 SAG	SAG
DEC	SAG	12 SAG / 27 CAP	7 SAG	19 CAP	12 CAP	6 CAP / 31 CAP	19 SAG / 24 CAP	SAG / 31 AQU	11 SAG	5 SAG	16 CAP	9 CAP	3 CAP	2 CAP / 6 SAG	2 SCO / 11 SAG

2065–2079

	2065	2066	2067	2068	2069	2070	2071	2072	2073	2074	2075	2076	2077	2078	2079
JAN	4 CAP / 23 AQU	16 AQU	8 AQU	2 AQU / 28 CAP	CAP	13 CAP / 28 AQU	8 CAP / 21 AQU / 22 PIS	CAP	12 CAP / 31 PIS	5 AQU	15 CAP	CAP	11 CAP	5 CAP / 25 AQU	17 AQU
FEB	9 PIS	2 PIS	AQU	14 AQU	10 AQU	4 AQU / 22 PIS	14 PIS	7 PIS	19 AQU	AQU	13 AQU	8 AQU / 27 PIS	1 AQU / 19 PIS	11 PIS	4 PIS
MAR	2 ARI / 8 PIS	7 AQU / 14 PIS	16 PIS	9 PIS / 26 ARI	2 PIS / 18 ARI	10 ARI	3 ARI	PIS	17 PIS	13 PIS / 31 ARI	7 PIS / 23 ARI	14 ARI / 31 TAU	7 ARI	1 ARI / 15 PIS	PIS
APR	16 ARI / 28 TAU	11 ARI / 19 TAU	4 ARI	10 TAU / 28 GEM	3 TAU	ARI	1 PIS / 15 ARI	14 ARI / 24 TAU	8 ARI	7 TAU	30 ARI	ARI	16 ARI	7 TAU / 31 GEM	12 ARI / 29 TAU
MAY	6 TAU / 20 GEM	12 TAU / 28 CAN	4 GEM	25 TAU / 28 GEM	TAU	15 TAU	10 TAU / 26 GEM	2 TAU / 16 GEM	8 GEM / 27 CAN	1 GEM	TAU	13 TAU	13 TAU / 31 GEM	7 TAU / 22 GEM	13 GEM / 29 CAN
JUN	4 CAN / 25 LEO	CAN	GEM	12 GEM / 26 CAN	10 GEM / 17 CAN	3 GEM / 27 CAN	9 CAN / 27 LEO	CAN	28 GEM	GEM	13 GEM / 22 CAN	7 GEM	13 CAN / 29 LEO	5 CAN / 25 LEO	CAN
JUL	20 CAN	CAN	CAN	12 CAN / 28 LEO	4 CAN / 19 LEO	10 LEO / 28 VIR	2 LEO / 25 VIR	LEO	CAN	10 CAN / 24 LEO	9 CAN / 16 LEO	1 CAN / 25 VIR	6 LEO	LEO	CAN
AUG	10 LEO / 28 VIR	5 LEO / 20 VIR	CAN	12 VIR / 30 LIB	3 VIR / 25 LIB	17 LEO	LEO	9 LEO / 24 VIR	1 LEO / 16 VIR	8 VIR / 27 LIB	1 VIR / 26 LIB	VIR	10 LEO / 30 VIR	6 LEO / 22 VIR	LEO
SEP	13 LIB / 27 SCO	6 LIB	LIB	24 VIR	VIR	9 VIR / 26 LIB	3 VIR / 18 LIB	10 LIB / 29 SCO	2 LIB / 26 SCO	LIB	11 VIR / 23 LIB	30 LIB	6 VIR	15 LIB	7 LIB / 28 SCO
OCT	2 SCO	30 LIB / 26 SCO	LIB	10 LIB / 29 SCO	4 LIB / 21 SCO	14 SCO / 29 SAG	7 SCO	SCO	17 LIB / 26 SCO	LIB	8 LIB / 26 SCO	18 SCO / 31 SAG	10 SCO / 30 SAG	3 SCO	SCO
NOV	SCO	10 SCO	6 SCO / 25 SAG	16 SAG / 30 CAP	9 SAG	3 SAG	20 SCO	SCO	9 SCO / 28 SAG	3 SCO / 21 SAG	14 SAG / 29 CAP	6 SAG	SAG	7 SCO	5 LIB / 9 SCO
DEC	8 SAG / 28 CAP	2 SAG / 21 CAP	14 CAP	6 CAP	24 SAG	SAG	12 SAG	5 SAG / 25 CAP	17 CAP / 31 AQU	10 CAP	4 CAP	11 SAG	SAG	9 SAG / 29 CAP	3 SAG / 22 CAP

	2080	2081	2082	2083	2084	2085	2086	2087	2088	2089	2090	2091	2092	2093	2094
JAN	10 AQU	2 AQU	CAP	13 CAP	9 CAP / 29 AQU	2 CAP / 21 AQU	14 AQU	6 AQU	1 AQU / 20 CAP	CAP	12 CAP	6 CAP / 26 AQU	18 AQU	10 AQU / 30 PIS	3 AQU
FEB	2 PIS / 4 AQU	1 CAP / 13 AQU	11 AQU	5 AQU / 24 PIS	16 PIS	7 PIS	1 PIS / 24 AQU	AQU	14 AQU	9 AQU / 28 PIS	2 AQU / 20 PIS	12 PIS	5 PIS	10 AQU	AQU
MAR	16 PIS	10 PIS / 28 ARI	3 PIS / 20 ARI	12 ARI	3 ARI	PIS	17 PIS	14 PIS	7 PIS / 24 ARI	16 ARI	8 ARI / 22 PIS	2 ARI / 22 PIS	12 ARI	16 PIS	11 PIS / 29 ARI
APR	4 ARI / 20 TAU	12 TAU / 29 GEM	4 TAU	1 TAU / 10 ARI	ARI	15 ARI	9 ARI / 25 TAU	2 ARI / 17 TAU	8 TAU / 30 GEM	1 TAU	ARI	16 ARI	12 ARI / 30 TAU	6 ARI / 22 TAU	13 TAU / 29 GEM
MAY	4 GEM	GEM	TAU	16 TAU	11 TAU / 27 GEM	4 TAU / 18 GEM	27 CAN	2 GEM	9 TAU		14 TAU	8 TAU / 24 GEM	14 GEM / 28 CAN	6 GEM / 30 CAN	GEM
JUN	GEM	GEM	11 GEM / 28 CAN	5 GEM / 19 CAN	9 CAN / 26 LEO	2 CAN / 29 LEO	CAN	GEM	13 GEM	8 GEM / 24 CAN	1 GEM / 15 CAN / 30 LEO	7 CAN / 25 LEO	CAN	13 GEM	GEM
JUL	11 CAN / 29 LEO	6 CAN / 20 LEO	12 LEO / 29 VIR	4 LEO / 25 VIR	LEO	6 CAN	CAN	10 CAN / 26 LEO	2 CAN / 16 LEO	8 LEO / 26 VIR	26 VIR	29 VIR	CAN	12 CAN / 30 LEO	7 CAN / 22 LEO
AUG	12 VIR / 30 LIB	5 VIR / 25 LIB	VIR	23 LEO	LEO / 26 VIR		18 VIR	10 VIR / 28 LIB	1 VIR / 24 LIB	10 LIB	VIR	4 LEO	31 VIR	7 LEO / 22 VIR	6 VIR / 26 LIB
SEP	LIB	30 VIR	VIR	10 VIR / 28 LIB	3 VIR	11 LIB / 30 SCO	4 LIB / 26 SCO	LIB	15 VIR	VIR	7 VIR / 24 LIB	16 LIB	7 LIB / 28 SCO	27 SCO	LIB
OCT	LIB	10 LIB / 30 SCO	5 LIB / 23 SCO	15 SCO	7 SCO / 29 SAG	SCO	22 LIB	LIB	8 LIB / 27 SCO	2 LIB / 19 SCO	12 SCO / 29 SAG	5 SCO	SCO	8 LIB	31 SCO
NOV	6 SCO / 25 SAG	18 SAG	10 SAG	4 SAG	24 SCO	SCO	10 SCO / 30 SAG	4 SCO / 22 SAG	14 SAG	7 SAG / 29 CAP	1 SAG	13 SCO	SCO	7 SCO / 26 SAG	19 SAG
DEC	14 CAP	7 CAP	1 CAP / 28 SAG	SAG	11 SAG	6 SAG / 26 CAP	19 CAP	12 CAP	4 CAP	16 SAG	SAG / 31 CAP	10 SAG / 23 CAP	3 SAG	15 CAP	8 CAP

	2095	2096	2097	2098	2099	2100
JAN	1 AQU / 6 CAP	3 SAG / 12 CAP	9 CAP / 30 AQU	3 CAP / 22 AQU	15 AQU	8 AQU
FEB	12 AQU	7 AQU / 25 PIS	16 PIS	9 PIS	2 PIS	AQU
MAR	5 PIS / 21 ARI	12 ARI / 30 TAU	5 ARI	PIS	2 AQU / 16 PIS	15 PIS
APR	5 TAU	17 ARI	ARI	16 ARI	10 ARI / 27 TAU	3 ARI / 19 TAU
MAY	TAU	15 TAU	12 TAU / 28 GEM	5 TAU / 20 GEM	11 GEM / 28 CAN	3 GEM
JUN	12 GEM / 29 CAN	5 GEM / 20 CAN	11 CAN / 27 LEO	3 CAN / 26 LEO	CAN	GEM
JUL	13 LEO / 30 VIR	4 LEO / 24 VIR	LEO	16 CAN	CAN	11 CAN / 27 LEO
AUG	VIR	29 LEO	LEO	10 LEO / 27 VIR	4 LEO / 19 VIR	11 VIR / 29 LIB
SEP	VIR	9 VIR / 28 LIB	4 VIR / 20 LIB	12 LIB	5 LIB / 27 SCO	LIB
OCT	7 LIB / 24 SCO	15 SCO	8 SCO / 29 SCO	1 SCO	27 LIB	LIB
NOV	12 SAG	4 SAG	29 SCO	SCO	10 SCO	5 SCO / 24 SAG
DEC	2 CAP	SAG	11 SAG	8 SAG / 27 CAP	1 SAG / 20 CAP	13 CAP

THE FOLLOWING VENUS TABLES will tell you what sign Venus was in on the day of your birth.

First locate the year you were born. Next, find the month of your birth (on the left-hand side of the page) and place a ruler across the page under your birth month.

The tables list for your month every date on which Venus *moved* into a new sign.* If no date is given and you see only a sign listed, it means Venus was in that sign throughout the entire month.

Example: You were born January 25, 1980. Locate the year *1980* and the month *JAN.* You will see that on the 15th of January in 1980, Venus moved into Pisces; it did not move into the next sign until the 9th of February. Therefore, on January 25th, your birthday, Venus was in Pisces.

Example: You were born July 12, 1964. Locate the year *1964* and the month *JUL.* You will see that Venus was in Gemini throughout the month of July in 1964. Therefore, your Venus is in Gemini.

TC — CANCER
CC — SCORPIO
DC — ARIES

JIM — LEO
Rush SCORPIO

*If you were born on a day on which Venus moved to a new sign, you should use the enclosed CD-ROM to cast your chart. At the *time of day* you were born, Venus might still have been in the previous sign because it had not yet entered the new sign. Your computer chart will tell you the *exact* sign your Venus is in as well as the exact degree of this sign.

1900 – 1914

	1900	1901	1902	1903	1904	1905	1906	1907	1908	1909	1910	1911	1912	1913	1914
JAN	19 PIS	16 CAP	11 PIS	10 AQU	4 SAG / 30 CAP	7 PIS	1 CAP / 25 AQU	SAG	20 PIS	15 CAP	15 PIS / 29 AQU	10 AQU	4 SAG / 29 CAP	7 PIS	1 CAP / 24 AQU
FEB	13 ARI	9 AQU	6 AQU	3 PIS / 27 ARI	23 AQU	2 ARI	18 PIS	6 CAP	13 ARI	8 AQU	AQU	3 PIS / 27 ARI	23 AQU	2 ARI	17 PIS
MAR	10 TAU	5 PIS / 29 ARI	AQU	24 TAU	19 PIS	6 TAU	14 ARI	6 AQU	10 TAU	4 PIS / 29 ARI	AQU	23 TAU	18 PIS	6 TAU	13 ARI
APR	5 GEM	22 TAU	4 PIS	18 GEM	12 ARI	TAU	7 TAU	1 PIS / 27 ARI	5 GEM	22 TAU	5 PIS	17 GEM	12 ARI	TAU	6 TAU
MAY	5 CAN	17 GEM	7 ARI	13 CAN	7 TAU / 31 GEM	9 ARI	1 GEM / 26 CAN	22 TAU	5 CAN	16 GEM	6 ARI	13 CAN	6 TAU / 31 GEM	2 ARI / 31 TAU	1 GEM / 26 CAN
JUN	CAN	10 CAN	3 TAU / 30 GEM	8 LEO	25 CAN	TAU	20 LEO	16 GEM	CAN	9 CAN	3 TAU / 29 GEM	8 LEO	24 CAN	TAU	19 LEO
JUL	CAN	5 LEO / 29 VIR	25 CAN	7 VIR	19 LEO	8 GEM	15 VIR	11 CAN	CAN	4 LEO / 28 VIR	25 CAN	7 VIR	19 LEO	8 GEM	15 VIR
AUG	CAN	23 LIB	19 LEO	17 LIB	13 VIR	6 CAN	10 LIB	4 LEO / 28 VIR	CAN	22 LIB	19 LEO	17 LIB	12 VIR	5 CAN	10 LIB
SEP	8 LEO	17 SCO	13 VIR	5 VIR	6 LIB / 30 SCO	1 LEO	7 SCO	22 LIB	8 LEO	16 SCO	12 VIR	VIR	5 LIB / 30 SCO	1 LEO	7 SCO
OCT	8 VIR	12 SAG	7 LIB / 31 SCO	VIR	25 SAG	21 LIB	9 SAG	16 SCO	8 VIR	12 SAG	6 LIB / 30 SCO	VIR	24 SAG	21 LIB	9 SAG
NOV	3 LIB / 28 SCO	7 CAP	24 SAG	8 LIB	18 CAP	14 SCO	SAG	9 SAG	3 LIB / 28 SCO	7 CAP	23 SAG	8 LIB	18 CAP	14 SCO	SAG
DEC	23 SAG	5 AQU	18 CAP	9 SCO	13 AQU	8 SAG	15 SCO / 25 SAG	3 CAP / 27 AQU	22 SAG	5 AQU	17 CAP	9 SCO	12 AQU	8 SAG	5 SCO / 30 SAG

1915 – 1929

	1915	1916	1917	1918	1919	1920	1921	1922	1923	1924	1925	1926	1927	1928	1929
JAN	SAG	19 PIS	15 CAP	AQU	9 AQU	4 SAG / 29 CAP	6 PIS	24 AQU	2 SAG	19 PIS	14 CAP	AQU	9 AQU	3 SAG / 28 CAP	6 PIS
FEB	6 CAP	13 ARI	8 AQU	AQU	2 PIS / 26 ARI	22 AQU	2 ARI	17 PIS	6 CAP	13 ARI	7 AQU	AQU	2 PIS / 26 ARI	22 AQU	2 ARI
MAR	6 AQU	9 TAU	4 PIS / 28 ARI	AQU	23 TAU	18 PIS	7 TAU	13 ARI	6 AQU	9 TAU	3 PIS / 27 ARI	AQU	22 TAU	17 PIS	8 TAU
APR	1 PIS / 26 ARI	5 GEM	21 TAU	5 PIS	17 GEM	11 ARI	25 ARI	6 TAU / 30 GEM	1 PIS / 26 ARI	5 GEM	21 TAU	5 PIS	16 GEM	11 ARI	19 ARI
MAY	21 TAU	5 CAN	16 GEM	6 ARI	12 CAN	6 TAU / 30 GEM	ARI	25 CAN	21 TAU	5 CAN	15 GEM	6 ARI	12 CAN	5 TAU / 30 GEM	ARI
JUN	15 GEM	CAN	9 CAN	3 TAU / 29 GEM	8 LEO	24 CAN	TAU	19 LEO	15 GEM	CAN	8 CAN	2 TAU / 28 GEM	7 LEO	23 CAN	3 TAU
JUL	10 CAN	CAN	3 LEO / 28 VIR	24 CAN	7 VIR	18 LEO	8 GEM	14 VIR	9 CAN	CAN	3 LEO / 28 VIR	24 CAN	7 VIR	18 LEO	7 GEM
AUG	4 LEO / 28 VIR	CAN	22 LIB	19 LEO	17 LIB	12 VIR	5 CAN	10 LIB	4 LEO / 27 VIR	CAN	21 LIB	17 LEO	17 LIB	11 VIR	5 CAN
SEP	22 LIB	8 LEO	16 SCO	12 VIR	VIR	5 LIB / 30 SCO	1 LEO	7 SCO	20 LIB	8 LEO	15 SCO	11 VIR	VIR	4 LIB / 29 SCO	1 LEO
OCT	16 SCO	7 VIR	11 SAG	6 LIB / 30 SCO	VIR	24 SAG	21 LIB	10 SAG	15 SCO	7 VIR	11 SAG	5 LIB / 29 SCO	VIR	23 SAG	20 LIB
NOV	8 SAG	2 LIB / 27 SCO	7 CAP	23 SAG	7 LIB	17 CAP	13 SCO	SAG	8 SAG	2 LIB / 27 SCO	6 CAP	22 SAG	9 LIB	16 CAP	13 SCO
DEC	2 CAP / 26 AQU	22 SAG	5 AQU	16 CAP	8 SCO	12 AQU	7 SAG / 31 CAP	SCO	2 CAP / 26 AQU	21 SAG	5 AQU	16 CAP	8 SCO	11 AQU	7 SAG / 30 CAP

1930 – 1944

	1930	1931	1932	1933	1934	1935	1936	1937	1938	1939	1940	1941	1942	1943	1944
JAN	23 AQU	3 SAG	18 PIS	14 CAP	AQU	8 AQU	3 SAG / 28 CAP	5 PIS	23 AQU	4 SAG	18 PIS	13 CAP	AQU	8 AQU	2 SAG / 27 CAP
FEB	16 PIS	6 CAP	12 ARI	7 AQU	AQU	1 PIS / 25 ARI	21 AQU	2 ARI	16 PIS	6 CAP	12 ARI	6 AQU	AQU	1 PIS / 25 ARI	21 AQU
MAR	12 ARI	5 AQU / 31 PIS	8 TAU	3 PIS / 27 ARI	AQU	22 TAU	17 PIS	9 TAU	12 ARI	5 AQU / 31 PIS	8 TAU	2 PIS / 26 ARI	AQU	21 TAU	16 PIS
APR	5 TAU / 30 GEM	25 ARI	4 GEM	20 TAU	6 PIS	16 GEM	10 ARI	13 ARI	5 TAU / 29 GEM	25 ARI	4 GEM	20 TAU	6 PIS	15 GEM	10 ARI
MAY	24 CAN	20 TAU	6 CAN	14 GEM	6 ARI	11 CAN	5 TAU / 29 GEM	ARI	24 CAN	20 TAU	6 CAN	14 GEM	5 ARI	11 CAN	4 TAU / 29 GEM
JUN	18 LEO	14 GEM	CAN	8 CAN	2 TAU / 28 GEM	7 LEO	23 CAN	4 TAU	18 LEO	14 GEM	CAN	7 CAN	1 TAU / 27 GEM	7 LEO	22 CAN
JUL	14 VIR	9 CAN	13 GEM / 28 CAN	2 LEO / 27 VIR	24 CAN	7 VIR	17 LEO	7 GEM	14 VIR	8 CAN	5 GEM / 31 CAN	1 LEO / 26 VIR	23 CAN	7 VIR	16 LEO
AUG	10 LIB	4 LEO / 27 VIR	CAN	21 LIB	17 LEO	17 LIB	10 VIR	4 CAN	10 LIB	4 LEO / 27 VIR	CAN	20 LIB	16 LEO	17 LIB	10 VIR
SEP	7 SCO	20 LIB	8 LEO	15 SCO	10 VIR	VIR	3 LIB / 28 SCO	1 LEO	6 SCO	19 LIB	8 LEO	14 SCO	10 VIR	VIR	3 LIB / 28 SCO
OCT	11 SAG	14 SCO	7 VIR	13 SAG	5 LIB / 29 SCO	VIR	23 SAG	19 LIB	10 SAG	13 SCO	6 VIR	13 SAG	4 LIB / 28 SCO	VIR	22 SAG
NOV	22 SCO	7 SAG	1 LIB / 26 SCO	6 CAP	22 SAG	9 LIB	16 CAP	12 SCO	26 SCO	6 SAG / 30 CAP	1 LIB / 26 SCO	6 CAP	21 SAG	9 LIB	16 CAP
DEC	SCO	1 CAP / 25 AQU	21 SAG	5 AQU	15 CAP	8 SCO	11 AQU	6 SAG / 30 CAP	SCO	25 AQU	20 SAG	5 AQU	15 CAP	8 SCO	10 AQU

	1945	**1946**	**1947**	**1948**	**1949**	**1950**	**1951**	**1952**	**1953**	**1954**	**1955**	**1956**	**1957**	**1958**	**1959**
JAN	5 PIS	22 AQU	5 SAG	17 PIS	13 CAP	AQU	7 AQU / 31 PIS	2 SAG / 27 CAP	5 PIS	22 AQU	6 SAG	17 PIS	12 CAP	AQU	7 AQU / 31 PIS
FEB	2 ARI	15 PIS	6 CAP	11 ARI	6 AQU	AQU	24 ARI	20 AQU	2 ARI	15 PIS	5 CAP	11 ARI	5 AQU	AQU	24 ARI
MAR	11 TAU	11 ARI	5 AQU / 30 PIS	8 TAU	2 PIS / 26 ARI	AQU	21 TAU	16 PIS	21 TAU / 31 ARI	11 ARI	5 AQU / 30 PIS	7 TAU	1 PIS / 25 ARI	AQU	20 TAU
APR	7 ARI	4 TAU / 29 GEM	24 ARI	4 GEM	19 TAU	6 PIS	15 GEM	9 ARI	ARI	4 TAU / 28 GEM	24 ARI	4 GEM	18 TAU	6 PIS	14 GEM
MAY	ARI	23 CAN	19 TAU	7 CAN	13 GEM	5 ARI	10 CAN	4 TAU / 28 GEM	ARI	23 CAN	19 TAU	7 CAN	13 GEM	5 ARI / 31 TAU	10 CAN
JUN	4 TAU	18 LEO	13 GEM	29 GEM	7 CAN	1 TAU / 27 GEM	7 LEO	22 CAN	5 TAU	17 LEO	13 GEM	23 GEM	6 CAN	26 GEM	6 LEO
JUL	7 GEM	13 VIR	8 CAN	GEM	1 LEO / 26 VIR	22 CAN	7 VIR	16 LEO	7 GEM	13 VIR	7 CAN	GEM	1 LEO / 25 VIR	22 CAN	8 VIR
AUG	4 CAN / 30 LEO	9 LIB	1 LEO / 26 VIR	2 CAN	20 LIB	16 LEO	VIR	9 VIR	3 CAN / 29 LEO	8 LIB	1 LEO / 25 VIR	4 CAN	19 LIB	15 LEO	VIR
SEP	24 VIR	6 SCO	19 LIB	8 LEO	14 SCO	9 VIR	VIR	3 LIB / 27 SCO	23 VIR	6 SCO	18 LIB	8 LEO	14 SCO	9 VIR	19 LEO / 25 VIR
OCT	18 LIB	16 SAG	13 SCO	6 VIR	10 SAG	4 LIB / 28 SCO	VIR	22 SAG	18 LIB	23 SAG / 27 SCO	12 SCO	5 VIR / 31 LIB	9 SAG	3 LIB / 27 SCO	VIR
NOV	12 SCO	8 SCO	6 SAG / 30 CAP	1 LIB / 25 SCO	5 CAP	20 SAG	9 LIB	15 CAP	11 SCO	SCO	5 SAG / 29 CAP	25 SCO	5 CAP	20 SAG	9 LIB
DEC	6 SAG / 29 CAP	SCO	24 AQU	20 SAG	6 AQU	14 CAP	7 SCO	10 AQU	5 SAG / 29 CAP	SCO	24 AQU	19 SAG	6 AQU	14 CAP	7 SCO

	1960	**1961**	**1962**	**1963**	**1964**	**1965**	**1966**	**1967**	**1968**	**1969**	**1970**	**1971**	**1972**	**1973**	**1974**
JAN	2 SAG / 26 CAP	4 PIS	21 AQU	6 SAG	16 PIS	12 CAP	AQU	6 AQU / 30 PIS	1 SAG / 26 CAP	4 PIS	21 AQU	6 SAG	16 PIS	11 CAP	29 CAP
FEB	20 AQU	1 ARI	14 PIS	5 CAP	10 ARI	5 AQU	6 CAP / 25 AQU	23 ARI	19 AQU	1 ARI	14 PIS	5 CAP	10 ARI	4 AQU / 28 PIS	28 AQU
MAR	15 PIS	ARI	10 ARI	4 AQU / 29 PIS	7 TAU	1 PIS / 25 ARI	AQU	20 TAU	15 PIS	ARI	10 ARI	3 AQU / 29 PIS	6 TAU	24 ARI	AQU
APR	9 ARI	ARI	3 TAU / 28 GEM	23 ARI	3 GEM	18 TAU	6 PIS	14 GEM	8 ARI	ARI	3 TAU / 27 GEM	23 ARI	3 GEM	17 TAU	6 PIS
MAY	3 TAU / 28 GEM	ARI	22 CAN	18 TAU	8 CAN	12 GEM	4 ARI / 31 TAU	10 CAN	3 TAU / 27 GEM	ARI	22 CAN	18 TAU	10 CAN	12 GEM	4 ARI / 31 TAU
JUN	21 CAN	5 TAU	17 LEO	12 GEM	17 GEM	6 CAN / 30 LEO	26 GEM	6 LEO	20 CAN	5 TAU	16 LEO	12 GEM	11 GEM	5 CAN / 30 LEO	25 GEM
JUL	15 LEO	6 GEM	12 VIR	7 CAN / 31 LEO	GEM	25 VIR	21 CAN	8 VIR	15 LEO	6 GEM	12 VIR	6 CAN / 31 LEO	GEM	24 VIR	20 CAN
AUG	9 VIR	3 CAN / 29 LEO	8 LIB	25 VIR	5 CAN	19 LIB	15 LEO	VIR	8 VIR	3 CAN / 28 LEO	8 LIB	24 VIR	5 CAN	18 LIB	14 LEO
SEP	2 LIB / 27 SCO	23 VIR	6 SCO	18 LIB	7 LEO	13 SCO	8 VIR	9 LEO	2 LIB / 26 SCO	22 VIR	6 SCO	17 LIB	7 LEO	13 SCO	8 VIR
OCT	21 SAG	17 LIB	SCO	12 SCO	5 VIR / 31 LIB	9 SAG	2 LIB / 26 SCO	1 VIR	21 SAG	17 LIB	SCO	11 SCO	5 VIR / 30 LIB	9 SAG	2 LIB / 26 SCO
NOV	15 CAP	11 SCO	SCO	5 SAG / 29 CAP	24 SCO	5 CAP	19 SAG	9 LIB	14 CAP	10 SCO	SCO	4 SAG / 28 CAP	24 SCO	5 CAP	19 SAG
DEC	10 AQU	4 SAG / 28 CAP	SCO	23 AQU	19 SAG	6 AQU	13 CAP	7 SCO	9 AQU	4 SAG / 28 CAP	SCO	23 AQU	18 SAG	7 AQU	13 CAP

	1975	**1976**	**1977**	**1978**	**1979**	**1980**	**1981**	**1982**	**1983**	**1984**	**1985**	**1986**	**1987**	**1988**	**1989**
JAN	6 AQU / 30 PIS	1 SAG / 26 CAP	4 PIS	20 AQU	7 SAG	15 PIS	11 CAP	22 CAP	5 AQU / 29 PIS	25 CAP	4 PIS	20 AQU	7 SAG	15 PIS	10 CAP
FEB	23 ARI	19 AQU	2 ARI	13 PIS	5 CAP	9 ARI	4 AQU / 28 PIS	CAP	22 ARI	18 AQU	2 ARI	12 PIS	4 CAP	9 ARI	3 AQU / 27 PIS
MAR	19 TAU	14 PIS	ARI	9 ARI	3 AQU / 28 PIS	6 TAU	24 ARI	2 AQU	19 TAU	14 PIS	ARI	8 ARI	3 AQU / 28 PIS	6 TAU	23 ARI
APR	13 GEM	8 ARI	ARI	2 TAU / 27 GEM	22 ARI	3 GEM	17 TAU	6 PIS	13 GEM	7 ARI	ARI	2 TAU / 26 GEM	22 ARI	3 GEM	16 TAU
MAY	9 CAN	2 TAU / 26 GEM	ARI	21 CAN	17 TAU	12 CAN	11 GEM	4 ARI / 30 TAU	9 CAN	1 TAU / 26 GEM	ARI	21 CAN	17 TAU	17 CAN / 27 GEM	11 GEM
JUN	6 LEO	20 CAN	6 TAU	16 LEO	11 GEM	5 GEM	5 CAN / 29 LEO	25 GEM	6 LEO	19 CAN	6 TAU	15 LEO	11 GEM	GEM	4 CAN / 29 LEO
JUL	9 VIR	14 LEO	6 GEM	11 VIR	6 CAN / 30 LEO	GEM	24 VIR	20 CAN	10 VIR	14 LEO	6 GEM	11 VIR	5 CAN / 30 LEO	GEM	23 VIR
AUG	VIR	8 VIR	2 CAN / 28 LEO	7 LIB	23 VIR	6 CAN	18 LIB	14 LEO	27 LEO	7 VIR	2 CAN / 27 LEO	7 LIB	23 VIR	6 CAN	17 LIB
SEP	2 LEO	1 LIB / 25 SCO	22 VIR	7 SCO	17 LIB	7 LEO	12 SCO	7 VIR	LEO	1 LIB / 25 SCO	21 VIR	7 SCO	16 LIB	7 LEO	12 SCO
OCT	4 VIR	20 SAG	16 LIB	SCO	11 SCO	4 VIR / 30 LIB	8 SAG	1 LIB / 25 SCO	5 VIR	20 SAG	16 LIB	SCO	10 SCO	4 VIR / 29 LIB	8 SAG
NOV	9 LIB	14 CAP	9 SCO	SCO	4 SAG / 28 CAP	23 SCO	5 CAP	18 SAG	9 LIB	13 CAP	9 SCO	SCO	3 SAG / 27 CAP	23 SCO	5 CAP
DEC	6 SCO	9 AQU	3 SAG / 27 CAP	SCO	22 AQU	18 SAG	8 AQU	12 CAP	6 SCO / 31 SAG	8 AQU	3 SAG / 27 CAP	SCO	22 AQU	17 SAG	9 AQU

	1990	1991	1992	1993	1994	1995	1996	1997	1998	1999	2000	2001	2002	2003	2004
JAN	16 CAP	5 AQU / 28 PIS	25 CAP	3 PIS	19 AQU	7 SAG	14 PIS	10 CAP	9 CAP	4 AQU / 28 PIS	24 CAP	3 PIS	18 AQU	7 SAG	14 PIS
FEB	CAP	22 ARI	18 AQU	2 ARI	12 PIS	4 CAP	8 ARI	2 AQU / 26 PIS	CAP	21 ARI	17 AQU	2 ARI	11 PIS	4 CAP	8 ARI
MAR	3 AQU	18 TAU	13 PIS	ARI	8 ARI	2 AQU / 28 PIS	5 TAU	23 ARI	4 AQU	18 TAU	13 PIS	ARI	7 ARI	2 AQU / 27 PIS	5 TAU
APR	6 PIS	12 GEM	7 ARI	ARI	1 TAU / 26 GEM	21 ARI	3 GEM	16 TAU	6 PIS	12 GEM	6 ARI / 30 TAU	ARI	1 TAU / 25 GEM	21 ARI	3 GEM
MAY	3 ARI / 30 TAU	8 CAN	1 TAU / 25 GEM	ARI	20 CAN	16 TAU	GEM	10 GEM	3 ARI / 29 TAU	8 CAN	25 GEM	ARI	20 CAN	16 TAU	GEM
JUN	24 GEM	5 LEO	19 CAN	6 TAU	15 LEO	10 GEM	GEM	3 CAN / 28 LEO	24 GEM	5 LEO	18 CAN	6 TAU	14 LEO	9 GEM	GEM
JUL	19 CAN	11 VIR	13 LEO	5 GEM	11 VIR	5 CAN / 29 LEO	GEM	23 VIR	19 CAN	12 VIR	13 LEO	5 GEM	10 VIR	4 CAN / 28 LEO	GEM
AUG	13 LEO	21 LEO	7 VIR / 31 LIB	1 CAN / 27 LEO	7 LIB	22 VIR	7 CAN	17 LIB	13 LEO	15 LEO	6 VIR / 30 LIB	1 CAN / 26 LEO	7 LIB	22 VIR	7 CAN
SEP	7 VIR	LEO	24 SCO	21 VIR	7 SCO	16 LIB	7 LEO	11 SCO	6 VIR / 30 LIB	LEO	24 SCO	20 VIR	7 SCO	15 LIB	6 LEO
OCT	1 LIB / 25 SCO	6 VIR	19 SAG	15 LIB	SCO	10 SCO	3 VIR / 29 LIB	8 SAG	24 SCO	7 VIR	19 SAG	15 LIB	SCO	9 SCO	3 VIR / 28 LIB
NOV	18 SAG	9 LIB	13 CAP	8 SCO	SCO	3 SAG / 27 CAP	22 SCO	5 CAP	17 SAG	8 LIB	12 CAP	8 SCO	SCO	2 SAG / 26 CAP	22 SCO
DEC	12 CAP / 31 SAG	6 SCO	8 AQU	2 SAG / 26 CAP	SCO	21 AQU	17 SAG	11 AQU	11 CAP	5 SCO / 30 SAG	8 AQU	2 SAG	SCO	21 AQU	16 SAG

	2005	2006	2007	2008	2009	2010	2011	2012	2013	2014	2015	2016	2017	2018	2019
JAN	9 CAP	1 CAP	3 AQU / 27 PIS	24 CAP	3 PIS	18 AQU	7 SAG	14 PIS	8 CAP	CAP	3 AQU / 27 PIS	23 CAP	3 PIS	17 AQU	7 SAG
FEB	2 AQU / 26 PIS	CAP	21 ARI	17 AQU	2 ARI	11 PIS	4 CAP	8 ARI	1 AQU / 25 PIS	CAP	20 ARI	16 AQU	3 ARI	10 PIS	3 CAP
MAR	22 ARI	5 AQU	17 TAU	12 PIS	ARI	7 ARI / 31 TAU	1 AQU / 27 PIS	5 TAU	21 ARI	5 AQU	17 TAU	12 PIS	ARI	6 ARI / 30 TAU	1 AQU / 26 PIS
APR	15 TAU	5 PIS	11 GEM	6 ARI / 30 TAU	11 ARI	25 GEM	20 ARI	3 GEM	15 TAU	5 PIS	11 GEM	5 ARI / 29 TAU	2 ARI	24 GEM	20 ARI
MAY	9 GEM	3 ARI / 29 TAU	8 CAN	24 GEM	ARI	19 CAN	15 TAU	GEM	9 GEM	2 ARI / 28 TAU	7 CAN	24 GEM	ARI	19 CAN	15 TAU
JUN	3 CAN / 28 LEO	23 GEM	5 LEO	18 CAN	6 TAU	14 LEO	9 GEM	GEM	2 CAN / 27 LEO	23 GEM	5 LEO	17 CAN	6 TAU	13 LEO	8 GEM
JUL	22 VIR	18 CAN	14 VIR	12 LEO	5 GEM / 31 CAN	10 VIR	3 CAN / 28 LEO	GEM	22 VIR	18 CAN	18 VIR / 31 LEO	12 LEO	4 GEM / 31 CAN	9 VIR	2 CAN / 27 LEO
AUG	16 LIB	12 LEO	8 LEO	5 VIR / 30 LIB	26 LEO	6 LIB	21 VIR	7 CAN	16 LIB	12 LEO	LEO	5 VIR / 29 LIB	25 LEO	6 LIB	21 VIR
SEP	11 SCO	6 VIR / 30 LIB	LEO	23 SCO	20 VIR	8 SCO	14 LIB	6 LEO	11 SCO	5 VIR / 29 LIB	LEO	23 SCO	19 VIR	9 SCO	14 LIB
OCT	7 SAG	24 SCO	8 VIR	18 SAG	14 LIB	SCO	9 SCO	3 VIR / 28 LIB	7 SAG	23 SCO	8 VIR	18 SAG	14 LIB	31 LIB	8 SCO
NOV	5 CAP	17 SAG	8 LIB	12 CAP	7 SCO	7 LIB / 29 SCO	2 SAG / 26 CAP	21 SCO	5 CAP	16 SAG	8 LIB	11 CAP	7 SCO	LIB	1 SAG / 25 CAP
DEC	15 AQU	11 CAP	5 SCO / 30 SAG	7 AQU	1 SAG / 25 CAP	SCO	20 AQU	15 SAG	CAP	10 CAP	4 SCO / 30 SAG	7 AQU	1 SAG / 25 CAP	2 SCO	20 AQU

	2020	2021	2022	2023	2024	2025	2026	2027	2028	2029	2030	2031	2032	2033	2034
JAN	13 PIS	8 CAP	CAP	2 AQU / 26 PIS	23 CAP	2 PIS	17 AQU	7 SAG	13 PIS	7 CAP / 31 AQU	CAP	2 AQU / 26 PIS	22 CAP	2 PIS	16 AQU
FEB	7 ARI	1 AQU / 25 PIS	CAP	20 ARI	15 AQU	4 ARI	10 PIS	3 CAP	7 ARI	24 PIS	CAP	19 ARI	15 AQU	5 ARI	9 PIS
MAR	4 TAU	21 ARI	6 AQU	16 TAU	11 PIS	27 PIS	6 ARI / 30 TAU	1 AQU / 26 PIS	4 TAU	20 ARI	6 AQU	16 TAU	11 PIS	21 ARI	5 ARI / 29 TAU
APR	3 GEM	14 TAU	5 PIS	10 GEM	4 ARI / 29 TAU	30 ARI	23 GEM	19 ARI	3 GEM	14 TAU	5 PIS	10 GEM	4 ARI / 28 TAU	ARI	23 GEM
MAY	GEM	8 GEM	2 ARI / 28 TAU	7 CAN	23 GEM	ARI	18 CAN	14 TAU	GEM	8 GEM	2 ARI / 27 TAU	7 CAN	23 GEM	1 ARI	18 CAN
JUN	GEM	2 CAN / 26 LEO	22 GEM	5 LEO	17 CAN	5 TAU	13 LEO	8 GEM	GEM	1 CAN / 26 LEO	22 GEM	5 LEO	16 CAN	5 TAU	12 LEO
JUL	GEM	21 VIR	17 CAN	LEO	11 LEO	4 GEM / 30 CAN	9 VIR	2 CAN / 27 LEO	GEM	21 VIR	17 CAN	LEO	10 LEO	4 GEM / 30 CAN	9 VIR
AUG	7 CAN	15 LIB	11 LEO	LEO	4 VIR / 29 LIB	25 LEO	6 LIB	20 VIR	7 CAN	15 LIB	11 LEO	LEO	4 VIR / 28 LIB	24 LEO	6 LIB
SEP	6 LEO	10 SCO	4 VIR / 29 LIB	LEO	22 SCO	19 VIR	10 SCO	13 LIB	5 LEO	10 SCO	4 VIR / 28 LIB	LEO	22 SCO	18 VIR	11 SCO
OCT	2 VIR / 27 LIB	7 SAG	23 SCO	8 VIR	17 SAG	13 LIB	25 LIB	7 SCO	2 VIR / 27 LIB	6 SAG	22 SCO	9 VIR	17 SAG	13 LIB	18 LIB
NOV	21 SCO	5 CAP	16 SAG	8 LIB	11 CAP	6 SCO	LIB	1 SAG / 25 CAP	20 SCO	5 CAP	15 SAG	7 LIB	11 CAP	6 SCO	LIB
DEC	15 SAG	CAP	9 CAP	4 SCO / 29 SAG	7 AQU	24 CAP	4 SCO	19 AQU	14 SAG	CAP	9 CAP	4 SCO / 29 SAG	6 AQU	23 CAP	5 SCO

	2035	2036	2037	2038	2039	2040	2041	2042	2043	2044	2045	2046	2047	2048	2049
JAN	7 SAG	12 PIS	7 CAP / 31 AQU	CAP	1 AQU / 25 PIS	22 CAP	2 PIS	16 AQU	6 SAG	12 PIS	6 CAP / 30 AQU	CAP	1 AQU / 25 PIS	21 CAP	2 PIS
FEB	3 CAP / 28 AQU	6 ARI	24 PIS	CAP	19 ARI	15 AQU	6 ARI	9 PIS	2 CAP / 28 AQU	6 ARI	23 PIS	CAP	18 ARI	14 AQU	8 ARI
MAR	25 PIS	4 TAU	20 ARI	6 AQU	15 TAU	10 PIS	14 ARI	5 ARI / 29 TAU	25 PIS	4 TAU	19 ARI	6 AQU	15 TAU	10 PIS	8 ARI
APR	19 ARI	3 GEM	13 TAU	4 PIS	10 GEM	3 ARI / 28 TAU	ARI	22 GEM	18 ARI	4 GEM	12 TAU	4 PIS	9 GEM	3 ARI / 27 TAU	ARI
MAY	14 TAU	GEM	7 GEM	1 ARI / 27 TAU	6 CAN	22 GEM	2 ARI	17 CAN	13 TAU	GEM	7 GEM	1 ARI / 31 TAU	6 CAN	21 GEM	3 ARI
JUN	7 GEM	GEM	1 CAN / 25 LEO	21 GEM	5 LEO	15 CAN	5 TAU	12 LEO	7 GEM	10 TAU / 25 GEM	25 LEO	21 GEM	5 LEO	15 CAN	5 TAU
JUL	2 CAN / 26 LEO	GEM	20 VIR	16 CAN	LEO	10 LEO	3 GEM / 30 CAN	8 VIR	1 CAN / 26 LEO	GEM	20 VIR	16 CAN	LEO	9 LEO	3 GEM / 29 CAN
AUG	20 VIR	7 CAN	15 LIB	10 LEO	LEO	3 VIR / 28 LIB	24 LEO	6 LIB	19 VIR	7 CAN	14 LIB	9 LEO	LEO	3 VIR / 27 LIB	23 LEO
SEP	13 LIB	5 LEO	9 SCO	3 VIR / 28 LIB	LEO	21 SCO	18 VIR	13 SCO	12 LIB	5 LEO	9 SCO	3 VIR / 27 LIB	LEO	21 SCO	17 VIR
OCT	7 SCO / 31 SAG	1 VIR	6 SAG	22 SCO	9 VIR	16 SAG	12 LIB	12 LIB	6 SCO / 31 SAG	1 VIR / 26 LIB	6 SAG	21 SCO	9 VIR	16 SAG	12 LIB
NOV	24 CAP	20 SCO	5 CAP	14 SAG	7 LIB	10 CAP	5 SCO / 29 SAG	LIB	24 CAP	19 SCO	5 CAP	14 SAG	7 LIB	10 CAP	5 SCO / 29 SAG
DEC	19 AQU	14 SAG	CAP	8 CAP	3 SCO / 28 SAG	6 AQU	23 CAP	6 SCO	18 AQU	13 SAG	CAP	8 CAP	3 SCO / 28 SAG	6 AQU	22 CAP

	2050	2051	2052	2053	2054	2055	2056	2057	2058	2059	2060	2061	2062	2063	2064
JAN	15 AQU	6 SAG	11 PIS	6 CAP / 30 AQU	CAP	24 PIS	21 CAP	2 PIS	15 AQU	6 SAG	11 PIS	5 CAP / 29 AQU	8 SAG / 24 CAP	24 PIS	20 CAP
FEB	8 PIS	2 CAP / 27 AQU	6 ARI	23 PIS	CAP	18 ARI	14 AQU	11 ARI / 28 PIS	8 PIS	1 CAP / 27 AQU	5 ARI	22 PIS	CAP	17 ARI	13 AQU
MAR	4 ARI / 28 TAU	24 PIS	3 TAU	19 ARI	6 AQU	14 TAU	9 PIS	PIS	4 ARI / 28 TAU	24 PIS	3 TAU	18 ARI	6 AQU	14 TAU	9 PIS
APR	22 GEM	18 ARI	4 GEM	12 TAU	4 PIS / 30 ARI	9 GEM	2 ARI / 27 TAU	PIS	21 GEM	17 ARI	5 GEM	11 TAU	4 PIS / 30 ARI	8 GEM	2 ARI / 26 TAU
MAY	17 CAN	13 TAU	GEM	6 GEM / 31 CAN	26 TAU	6 CAN	21 GEM	4 ARI	16 CAN	12 TAU	27 TAU	6 GEM / 30 CAN	26 TAU	5 CAN	20 GEM
JUN	11 LEO	6 GEM	2 TAU / 29 GEM	24 LEO	20 GEM	5 LEO	14 CAN	5 TAU	11 LEO	6 GEM / 30 CAN	TAU	24 LEO	20 GEM	5 LEO	14 CAN
JUL	8 VIR	1 CAN / 25 LEO	GEM	19 VIR	15 CAN	LEO	9 LEO	2 GEM / 29 CAN	8 VIR	25 LEO	1 GEM	19 VIR	15 CAN	LEO	8 LEO
AUG	6 LIB	18 VIR	7 CAN	14 LIB	9 LEO	LEO	2 VIR / 27 LIB	23 LEO	6 LIB	18 VIR	7 CAN	13 LIB	8 LEO	LEO	2 VIR / 26 LIB
SEP	16 SCO	12 LIB	4 LEO / 30 VIR	9 SCO	2 VIR / 26 LIB	LEO	20 SCO	17 VIR	LIB	11 LIB	4 LEO / 30 VIR	8 SCO	2 VIR / 26 LIB	LEO	20 SCO
OCT	4 LIB	6 SCO / 30 SAG	25 LIB	6 SAG	20 SCO	9 VIR	15 SAG	11 LIB	LIB	5 SCO / 30 SAG	25 LIB	6 SAG	20 SCO	9 VIR	15 SAG
NOV	LIB	23 CAP	19 SCO	6 CAP	13 SAG	7 LIB	9 CAP	4 SCO / 28 SAG	LIB	23 CAP	18 SCO	6 CAP	13 SAG	6 LIB	9 CAP
DEC	6 SCO	18 AQU	13 SAG	CAP	7 CAP / 31 AQU	2 SCO / 27 SAG	5 AQU	22 CAP	7 SCO	17 AQU	12 SAG	CAP	7 CAP / 31 AQU	2 SCO / 27 SAG	5 AQU

	2065	2066	2067	2068	2069	2070	2071	2072	2073	2074	2075	2076	2077	2078	2079
JAN	2 PIS	14 AQU	6 SAG	10 PIS	5 CAP / 29 AQU	28 CAP	23 PIS	20 CAP	2 PIS	14 AQU	6 SAG	10 PIS	4 CAP / 28 AQU	30 CAP	23 PIS
FEB	PIS	7 PIS	1 CAP / 26 AQU	5 ARI	22 PIS	CAP	17 ARI	13 AQU	PIS	6 PIS	1 CAP / 26 AQU	4 ARI	21 PIS	CAP	16 ARI
MAR	PIS	3 ARI / 27 TAU	23 PIS	3 TAU	18 ARI	6 AQU	13 TAU	8 PIS	PIS	3 ARI / 27 TAU	23 PIS	3 TAU	17 ARI	6 AQU	13 TAU
APR	PIS	21 GEM	17 ARI	5 GEM	11 TAU	3 PIS / 30 ARI	8 GEM	1 ARI / 25 TAU	PIS	20 GEM	16 ARI	7 GEM	10 TAU	3 PIS / 29 ARI	8 GEM
MAY	4 ARI	16 CAN	12 TAU	21 TAU	5 GEM / 30 CAN	25 TAU	5 CAN	20 GEM	5 ARI	15 CAN	11 TAU	15 TAU	5 GEM / 29 CAN	25 TAU	5 CAN
JUN	5 TAU	11 LEO	5 GEM / 30 CAN	TAU	23 LEO	19 GEM	6 LEO	13 CAN	4 TAU	10 LEO	5 GEM / 29 CAN	TAU	23 LEO	19 GEM	6 LEO
JUL	2 GEM / 28 CAN	7 VIR	24 LEO	2 GEM	18 VIR	14 CAN	LEO	8 LEO	2 GEM / 28 CAN	7 VIR	24 LEO	3 GEM	18 VIR	14 CAN	LEO
AUG	22 LEO	6 LIB	17 VIR	6 CAN	13 LIB	8 LEO	14 CAN / 27 LEO	1 VIR / 26 LIB	22 LEO	6 LIB	17 VIR	6 CAN	12 LIB	7 LEO	6 CAN / 31 LEO
SEP	16 VIR	LIB	11 LIB	3 LEO / 29 VIR	8 SCO	1 VIR / 25 LIB	LEO	19 SCO	16 VIR	LIB	10 LIB	3 LEO / 29 VIR	8 SCO	1 VIR / 25 LIB	LEO
OCT	11 LIB	LIB	5 SCO / 29 SAG	24 LIB	5 SAG	19 SCO	9 VIR	14 SAG	10 LIB	LIB	4 SCO / 28 SAG	24 LIB	5 SAG	19 SCO	9 VIR
NOV	4 SCO / 27 SAG	LIB	22 CAP	18 SCO	7 CAP	12 SAG	6 LIB	9 CAP	3 SCO / 27 SAG	LIB	22 CAP	17 SCO	8 CAP	12 SAG	6 LIB
DEC	21 CAP	7 SCO	17 AQU	12 SAG	31 SAG	6 CAP / 30 AQU	2 SCO / 26 SAG	5 AQU	21 CAP	7 SCO	16 AQU	11 SAG	24 SAG	6 CAP / 30 AQU	1 SCO / 26 SAG

	2080	2081	2082	2083	2084	2085	2086	2087	2088	2089	2090	2091	2092	2093	2094
JAN	19 CAP	2 PIS	13 AQU	5 SAG 31 CAP	9 PIS	4 CAP 28 AQU	SAG	22 PIS	19 CAP	2 PIS	13 AQU	5 SAG 31 CAP	9 PIS	3 CAP 27 AQU	SAG
FEB	12 AQU	PIS	6 PIS	25 AQU	4 ARI	21 PIS	1 CAP	16 ARI	12 AQU	PIS	5 PIS	25 AQU	4 ARI	20 PIS	2 CAP
MAR	8 PIS	PIS	2 ARI 26 TAU	22 PIS	3 TAU	17 ARI	6 AQU	12 TAU	7 PIS 31 ARI	PIS	1 ARI 26 TAU	22 PIS	2 TAU	16 ARI	6 AQU
APR	1 ARI 25 TAU	PIS	20 GEM	16 ARI	8 GEM	10 TAU	3 PIS 29 ARI	7 GEM	24 TAU	PIS	19 GEM	15 ARI	11 GEM	9 TAU	2 PIS 28 ARI
MAY	19 GEM	5 ARI	15 CAN	10 TAU	9 TAU	4 GEM 29 CAN	24 TAU	5 CAN	19 GEM	5 ARI	14 CAN	10 TAU	3 TAU	3 GEM 28 CAN	24 TAU
JUN	13 CAN	4 TAU	10 LEO	4 GEM 29 CAN	TAU	22 LEO	18 GEM	7 LEO	12 CAN	4 TAU	9 LEO	3 GEM 28 CAN	TAU	22 LEO	18 GEM
JUL	7 LEO	1 GEM 27 CAN	7 VIR	23 LEO	4 GEM	17 VIR	13 CAN	30 CAN	7 LEO 31 VIR	1 GEM 27 CAN	6 VIR	22 LEO	4 GEM	17 VIR	13 CAN
AUG	1 VIR 25 LIB	21 LEO	6 LIB	16 VIR	6 CAN	12 LIB	7 LEO 31 VIR	CAN	25 LIB	21 LEO	6 LIB	16 VIR	6 CAN	11 LIB	6 LEO 31 VIR
SEP	19 SCO	15 VIR	LIB	9 LIB	3 LEO 29 VIR	7 SCO	24 LIB	2 LEO	18 SCO	15 VIR	LIB	9 LIB	2 LEO 28 VIR	7 SCO	24 LIB
OCT	14 SAG	9 LIB	LIB	4 SCO 28 SAG	23 LIB	5 SAG	18 SCO	8 VIR	13 SAG	9 LIB	LIB	3 SCO 27 SAG	23 LIB	5 SAG	18 SCO
NOV	8 CAP	2 SCO 26 SAG	LIB	21 CAP	17 SCO	9 CAP	11 SAG	5 LIB	8 CAP	2 SCO 26 SAG	LIB	21 CAP	16 SCO	11 CAP	11 SAG
DEC	4 AQU	20 CAP	7 SCO	16 AQU	11 SAG	18 SAG	5 CAP 29 AQU	1 SCO 25 SAG	4 AQU	20 CAP	8 SCO	15 AQU	10 SAG	11 SAG	5 CAP 29 AQU

	2095	2096	2097	2098	2099	2100
JAN	22 PIS	18 CAP	2 PIS	12 AQU	5 SAG 31 CAP	9 PIS
FEB	15 ARI	11 AQU	PIS	5 PIS	25 AQU	3 ARI
MAR	12 TAU	6 PIS 31 ARI	PIS	1 ARI 25 TAU	21 PIS	3 TAU
APR	7 GEM	24 TAU	PIS	19 GEM	15 ARI	18 GEM 23 TAU
MAY	4 CAN	18 GEM	5 ARI	14 CAN	9 TAU	TAU
JUN	7 LEO	12 CAN	3 TAU 30 GEM	9 LEO	3 GEM 27 CAN	TAU
JUL	24 CAN	6 LEO 31 VIR	26 CAN	6 VIR	22 LEO	6 GEM
AUG	CAN	24 LIB	20 LEO	6 LIB	15 VIR	6 CAN
SEP	4 LEO	18 SCO	14 VIR	LIB	8 LIB	3 LEO 29 VIR
OCT	8 VIR	13 SAG	8 LIB	LIB	3 SCO 27 SAG	23 LIB
NOV	5 LIB 30 SCO	7 CAP	1 SCO 25 SAG	LIB	20 CAP	17 SCO
DEC	25 SAG	4 AQU	19 CAP	8 SCO	15 AQU	11 SAG

σ

Where Is Your Mars?

PISCES

The following Mars Tables will tell you what sign Mars was in on the day of your birth.

First locate the year you were born. Next, find the month of your birth (on the left-hand side of the page) and place a ruler across the page under your birth month.

The tables list for your month the date on which Mars *moved* into a new sign.* If no date is given and you see only a sign listed, it means Mars was in that sign throughout the entire month.

Example: You were born May 10, 1975. Locate the year *1975* and the month *MAY*. You will see that on the 25th of May in 1975, Mars moved into Cancer. Since you were born on the 10th of May, look at the previous month to find Mars's position. You will see that Mars moved into Pisces on the 11th of April and did not move into Aries until the 21th of May. Therefore, on May 10th, your birthday, Mars was in Pisces.

Example: You were born July 4, 1960. Locate the year *1960* and the month *JUL*. You will see that Mars was in Taurus throughout the month of July in 1960. Therefore, your Mars is in Taurus.

TC - PISCES

CC - CAP
JIM - CAP

DC - SCORPIO

RUS - CAP

MOM - CAP
DAO - LEO

*If you were born on a day on which Mars moved to a new sign, you should use the enclosed CD-ROM to cast your chart. At the *time of day* you were born, Mars might still have been in the previous sign because it had not entered the new sign. Your computer chart will tell you the *exact* sign your Mars is in as well as the exact degree of this sign.

Mars Tables

1900–1914

	1900	1901	1902	1903	1904	1905	1906	1907	1908	1909	1910	1911	1912	1913	1914
JAN	21 AQU	VIR	1 AQU	LIB	19 PIS	13 SCO	PIS	SCO	10 ARI	9 SAG	22 TAU	31 CAP	30 GEM	10 CAP	CAN
FEB	28 PIS	VIR	8 PIS	LIB	26 ARI	SCO	4 ARI	5 SAG	22 TAU	23 CAP	TAU	CAP	GEM	19 AQU	CAN
MAR	PIS	1 LEO	18 ARI	ARI		SCO	17 TAU	SAG	TAU	CAP	14 AQU	13 AQU	GEM	30 PIS	CAN
APR	7 ARI	LEO	27 TAU	19 VIR	6 TAU	SCO	28 GEM	1 CAP	6 GEM	9 AQU	GEM	23 PIS	5 CAN	PIS	CAN
MAY	17 TAU	11 VIR	TAU	30 LIB	17 GEM	SCO	GEM	CAP	22 CAN	25 PIS	1 CAN	PIS	28 TAU	LEO	1 LEO
JUN	27 GEM	13 LIB	7 GEM	LIB	30 CAN	SCO	11 CAN	CAP	7 LEO	21 ARI	18 LEO	2 ARI	TAU	16 TAU	25 VIR
JUL	GEM	13 LIB	20 CAN	LIB	CAN	SCO	27 LEO	CAP	LEO	21 ARI	15 TAU	16 VIR	29 GEM	GEM	LIB
AUG	9 CAN	31 SCO	CAN	6 SCO	14 LEO	21 SAG	LEO	CAP	24 VIR	ARI	5 VIR	TAU	GEM	14 LIB
SEP	26 LEO	SCO	4 LEO	22 SAG	LEO	SAG	12 VIR	CAP	LEO	26 PIS	21 LIB	5 GEM	2 LIB	15 CAN	29 SCO
OCT	LEO	14 SAG	23 VIR	SAG	1 VIR	7 CAP	29 LIB	13 AQU	10 LIB	PIS	LIB	GEM	17 SCO	CAN	SCO
NOV	23 VIR	23 CAP	VIR	3 CAP	20 LIB	17 AQU	17 AQU	28 PIS	25 SCO	20 ARI	6 SCO	29 TAU	30 SAG	CAN	11 SAG
DEC	VIR	CAP	19 LIB	12 AQU	LIB	27 PIS	17 SCO	PIS	SCO	ARI	20 SAG	TAU	SAG	CAN	21 CAP

1915–1929

	1915	1916	1917	1918	1919	1920	1921	1922	1923	1924	1925	1926	1927	1928	1929
JAN	30 AQU	LEO	9 AQU	11 LIB	27 PIS	31 SCO	5 PIS	SCO	21 ARI	19 SAG	SAG	SAG	18 CAP	GEM
FEB	AQU	LEO	16 PIS	25 VIR	PIS	SCO	13 ARI	18 SAG	SAG	3 TAU	8 CAP	21 GEM	28 AQU	GEM
MAR	9 PIS	LEO	26 ARI	VIR	6 ARI	SCO	25 TAU	SAG	6 CAP	23 GEM	22 AQU	GEM	AQU	10 CAN
APR	16 ARI	ARI	ARI	VIR	15 TAU	23 LIB	LIB	SAG	15 GEM	24 AQU	AQU	GEM	16 CAN	7 PIS	12 LEO
MAY	25 TAU	28 VIR	4 TAU	VIR	26 GEM	LIB	5 GEM	SAG	30 GEM	AQU	9 CAN	3 PIS	CAN	16 ARI	LEO
JUN	TAU	VIR	14 GEM	23 LIB	GEM	LIB	18 CAN	SAG	CAN	24 PIS	26 LEO	14 ARI	6 LEO	26 TAU	4 VIR
JUL	6 GEM	23 LIB	27 CAN	1 LEO	8 CAN	10 SCO	CAN	SAG	15 LEO	PIS	LEO	ARI	25 VIR	TAU	21 LIB
AUG	19 CAN	LIB	CAN	16 SCO	23 LEO	SCO	3 LEO	SAG	31 VIR	24 AQU	12 VIR	1 TAU	VIR	8 GEM	LIB
SEP	CAN	8 SCO	12 LEO	SCO	LEO	4 SAG	19 VIR	13 CAP	VIR	AQU	28 LIB	TAU	10 LIB	GEM	LIB
OCT	7 LEO	21 SAG	LEO	1 SAG	9 VIR	18 CAP	VIR	30 AQU	17 LIB	19 PIS	LIB	TAU	25 SCO	2 CAN	6 SCO
NOV	LEO	SAG	2 VIR	11 CAP	30 LIB	27 AQU	6 LIB	AQU	LIB	PIS	13 SCO	TAU	SCO	CAN	18 SAG
DEC	LEO	1 CAP	VIR	20 AQU	LIB	26 SCO	11 PIS	3 SCO	19 ARI	27 SAG	SAG	8 SAG	20 GEM	29 CAP

1930–1944

	1930	1931	1932	1933	1934	1935	1936	1937	1938	1939	1940	1941	1942	1943	1944
JAN	CAP	LEO	17 AQU	VIR	AQU	LIB	14 PIS	5 SCO	30 ARI	29 SAG	3 ARI	4 SAG	11 TAU	26 CAP	GEM
FEB	6 AQU	16 CAN	24 PIS	VIR	3 PIS	LIB	21 ARI	SCO	ARI	SAG	16 TAU	17 CAP	CAP	7 GEM	28 CAN
MAR	17 PIS	29 LEO	PIS	VIR	14 ARI	LIB	ARI	12 SAG	12 TAU	21 CAP	CAP	CAP	7 GEM	8 AQU	CAN
APR	24 ARI	LEO	3 ARI	VIR	22 TAU	LIB	1 TAU	SAG	23 GEM	CAP	1 GEM	2 AQU	26 CAN	17 PIS	CAN
MAY	ARI	10 VIR	12 TAU	VIR	TAU	LIB	13 GEM	14 SCO	GEM	24 AQU	17 CAN	AQU	PIS	27 ARI	22 LEO
JUN	2 TAU	VIR	22 GEM	VIR	2 GEM	LIB	25 CAN	SCO	6 CAN	AQU	CAN	CAN	PIS	13 LEO	LEO
JUL	14 GEM	VIR	GEM	6 LIB	15 CAN	29 SCO	CAN	CAN	22 LEO	21 CAP	3 LEO	2 ARI	1 VIR	TAU	11 VIR
AUG	28 CAN	1 LIB	4 CAN	26 SCO	30 LEO	SCO	10 LEO	8 SAG	LEO	CAP	19 VIR	ARI	1 VIR	23 GEM	28 LIB
SEP	CAN	17 SCO	20 LEO	SCO	LEO	16 SAG	26 VIR	30 CAP	7 VIR	23 AQU	VIR	ARI	17 LIB	GEM	LIB
OCT	20 LEO	30 SAG	LEO	9 SAG	17 VIR	28 CAP	VIR	CAP	25 LIB	AQU	5 LIB	ARI	LIB	GEM	13 SCO
NOV	LEO	SAG	13 VIR	19 CAP	VIR	CAP	14 LIB	11 AQU	LIB	19 PIS	20 SCO	ARI	1 SCO	GEM	25 SAG
DEC	LEO	9 CAP	VIR	27 AQU	11 LIB	6 AQU	LIB	21 PIS	11 SCO	PIS	SCO	ARI	15 SAG	GEM	SAG

1945–1959

	1945	1946	1947	1948	1949	1950	1951	1952	1953	1954	1955	1956	1957	1958	1959
JAN	5 CAP	CAN	25 AQU	VIR	4 AQU	LIB	22 PIS	19 SCO	PIS	SCO	14 ARI	13 SAG	28 TAU	SAG	TAU
FEB	14 AQU	CAN	AQU	12 LEO	11 PIS	LIB	PIS	SCO	7 ARI	9 SAG	26 TAU	28 CAP	TAU	3 CAP	10 GEM
MAR	24 PIS	4 PIS	LEO	21 ARI	28 VIR	1 ARI	SCO	20 TAU	SAG	TAU	CAP	17 GEM	17 AQU	GEM
APR	PIS	22 LEO	11 ARI	LEO	29 TAU	VIR	10 TAU	SCO	TAU	12 CAP	10 GEM	14 AQU	GEM	26 PIS	10 CAN
MAY	2 ARI	LEO	20 TAU	18 VIR	TAU	VIR	21 GEM	SCO	1 GEM	(CAP)	25 CAN	AQU	4 CAN	PIS	31 LEO
JUN	11 TAU	20 VIR	30 GEM	17 VIR	9 GEM	11 LIB	GEM	SCO	13 CAN	CAP	CAN	(3 PIS)	21 LEO	7 ARI	LEO
JUL	23 GEM	VIR	GEM	17 LIB	23 CAN	LIB	3 CAN	SCO	29 LEO	3 SAG	11 LEO	PIS	LEO	21 TAU	20 VIR
AUG	GEM	9 LIB	13 CAN	LIB	CAN	10 SCO	18 LEO	27 SAG	LEO	24 CAP	27 VIR	PIS	8 VIR	TAU	VIR
SEP	7 CAN	24 SCO	30 LEO	3 SCO	6 LEO	25 SAG	LEO	SAG	14 VIR	CAP	PIS	23 LIB	21 GEM	5 LIB
OCT	CAN	SCO	LEO	17 SAG	26 VIR	SAG	4 VIR	11 CAP	VIR	21 AQU	13 LIB	PIS	LIB	28 TAU	21 SCO
NOV	11 LEO	6 SAG	LEO	26 CAP	VIR	6 CAP	24 LIB	21 AQU	1 LIB	AQU	28 SCO	PIS	8 SCO	TAU	SCO
DEC	26 CAN	17 CAP	1 VIR	CAP	26 LIB	15 AQU	LIB	30 PIS	20 SCO	4 PIS	SCO	6 ARI	22 SAG	TAU	3 SAG

1960–1974

	1960	1961	1962	1963	1964	1965	1966	1967	1968	1969	1970	1971	1972	1973	1974
JAN	14 CAP	CAN	CAP	LEO	13 AQU	VIR	30 PIS	LIB	9 PIS	SCO	24 ARI	22 SAG	ARI	SAG	TAU
FEB	22 AQU	4 GEM / 7 CAN	1 AQU	LEO	20 PIS	VIR	12 SCO	16 ARI	25 SAG	SAG	CAP	10 CAP	12 CAP	27 GEM
MAR	AQU	CAN	12 PIS	19 ARI	29 ARI	VIR	9 ARI	31 LIB	27 TAU	SAG	12 CAP	26 GEM	GEM	26 AQU	GEM
APR	2 PIS	CAN	CAN	19 ARI	ARI	VIR	17 TAU	LIB	TAU	SAG	18 GEM	CAP	GEM	AQU	20 CAN
MAY	11 ARI	5 LEO	28 TAU	LEO	7 TAU	VIR	28 GEM	LIB	8 GEM	SAG	GEM	3 AQU	12 CAN	7 PIS	CAN
JUN	20 TAU	28 VIR	TAU	3 VIR	17 GEM	28 LIB	GEM	LIB	21 CAN	SAG	2 CAN	AQU	28 LEO	20 ARI	8 LEO
JUL	TAU	VIR	8 GEM	26 LIB	30 CAN	LIB	10 CAN	19 SCO	CAN	SAG	18 LEO	AQU	LEO	ARI	27 VIR
AUG	1 GEM	16 LIB	22 CAN	CAN	CAN	20 SCO	SCO	LEO	5 LEO	SAG	LEO	AQU	14 VIR	12 TAU	VIR
SEP	20 CAN	LIB	LIB	CAN	12 SCO	15 LEO	SCO	9 SAG	21 VIR	21 CAP	2 VIR	AQU	30 LIB	TAU	12 LIB
OCT	CAN	1 SCO	11 LEO	25 SAG	LEO	4 SAG	12 VIR	22 CAP	VIR	CAP	20 LIB	AQU	LIB	29 ARI	28 SCO
NOV	CAN	13 SAG	LEO	LEO	5 VIR	14 CAP	VIR	CAP	9 LIB	4 AQU	LIB	6 PIS	15 SCO	ARI	SCO
DEC	CAN	24 CAP	LEO	5 CAP	VIR	23 AQU	3 LIB	1 AQU	29 SCO	15 PIS	6 SCO	26 ARI	30 SAG	24 TAU	10 SAG

1975–1989

	1975	1976	1977	1978	1979	1980	1981	1982	1983	1984	1985	1986	1987	1988	1989
JAN	21 CAP	GEM	CAP	25 CAN	20 AQU	VIR	AQU	LIB	17 PIS	10 SCO	PIS	SCO	8 ARI	8 SAG	19 TAU
FEB	CAP	GEM	9 AQU	CAN	27 PIS	VIR	6 PIS	LIB	24 ARI	ARI	SCO	2 SAG	20 TAU	22 CAP	TAU
MAR	3 AQU	18 CAN	19 PIS	CAN	PIS	11 LEO	16 ARI	LIB	ARI	5 TAU	SCO	15 TAU	27 CAP	TAU	11 GEM
APR	11 PIS	CAN	27 ARI	10 LEO	6 ARI	LEO	25 TAU	LIB	5 TAU	26 GEM	GEM	CAP	5 GEM	6 AQU	28 CAN
MAY	21 ARI	16 LEO	ARI	LEO	15 TAU	3 VIR	TAU	LIB	16 GEM	GEM	SCO	CAP	20 CAN	22 PIS	CAN
JUN	30 TAU	LEO	5 TAU	13 VIR	25 GEM	VIR	5 GEM	LIB	29 CAN	CAN	SCO	CAP	CAN	PIS	16 LEO
JUL	TAU	6 VIR	17 GEM	VIR	GEM	10 LIB	18 CAN	LIB	CAN	SCO	24 LEO	CAP	6 LEO	13 ARI	LEO
AUG	14 GEM	24 LIB	31 CAN	4 LIB	8 CAN	29 SCO	CAN	3 SCO	13 LEO	17 SAG	LEO	CAP	22 VIR	ARI	3 VIR
SEP	GEM	LIB	CAN	19 SCO	24 LEO	SCO	1 LEO	19 SAG	29 VIR	VIR	SAG	CAP	VIR	ARI	19 LIB
OCT	17 CAN	8 SCO	26 LEO	SCO	LEO	12 SAG	20 VIR	31 CAP	VIR	5 CAP	27 LIB	8 AQU	8 LIB	23 PIS	SCO
NOV	25 GEM	20 SAG	LEO	1 SAG	19 VIR	21 CAP	VIR	CAP	18 LIB	15 AQU	LIB	25 PIS	23 SCO	1 ARI	4 SCO
DEC	GEM	31 CAP	LEO	12 CAP	VIR	30 AQU	15 LIB	10 AQU	LIB	25 PIS	14 SCO	PIS	SCO	ARI	17 SAG

	1990	1991	1992	1993	1994	1995	1996	1997	1998	1999	2000	2001	2002	2003	2004
JAN	29 CAP	20 GEM	9 CAP	CAN	27 AQU	22 LEO	8 AQU	3 LIB	25 PIS	26 SCO	3 PIS	SCO	18 ARI	16 SAG	ARI
FEB	CAP	GEM	17 AQU	CAN	AQU	LEO	15 PIS	VIR	PIS	SCO	PIS	11 ARI	14 SAG	SAG	3 TAU
MAR	11 AQU	GEM	27 PIS	CAN	7 PIS	LEO	24 ARI	8 VIR	4 ARI	SCO	22 TAU	SAG	1 TAU	4 CAP	21 GEM
APR	20 PIS	2 CAN	PIS	27 LEO	14 ARI	LEO	ARI	VIR	12 TAU	SCO	TAU	SAG	13 GEM	21 AQU	GEM
MAY	31 ARI	26 LEO	5 ARI	LEO	23 TAU	25 VIR	TAU	23 GEM	GEM	5 LIB	GEM	3 GEM	28 CAN	CAN	7 CAN
JUN	ARI	LEO	14 TAU	23 VIR	TAU	VIR	12 GEM	19 LIB	GEM	LIB	16 CAN	CAN	CAN	16 PIS	23 LEO
JUL	12 TAU	15 VIR	26 GEM	VIR	3 GEM	21 LIB	LIB	25 CAN	LIB	6 SCO	4 SCO	31 LEO	LEO	13 LEO	PIS	LEO
AUG	31 GEM	VIR	12 CAN	26 SCO	CAN	16 LIB	7 SCO	9 LEO	28 SAG	LEO	2 SAG	16 VIR	8 CAP	VIR	26 LIB
SEP	GEM	1 LIB	12 CAN	SCO	CAN	7 SCO	20 SAG	9 LEO	28 SAG	7 VIR	SAG	16 VIR	8 CAP	VIR	26 LIB
OCT	GEM	16 SCO	CAN	SCO	4 LEO	SCO	20 SAG	30 VIR	SAG	7 VIR	16 CAP	VIR	27 AQU	15 LIB	LIB	PIS	LIB
NOV	GEM	28 SAG	CAN	9 SAG	LEO	LEO	30 CAP	VIR	9 CAP	27 LIB	26 AQU	AQU	3 LIB	PIS	11 SCO
DEC	14 TAU	SAG	CAN	19 CAP	12 VIR	CAP	CAP	VIR	18 AQU	LIB	AQU	23 SCO	8 PIS	1 SCO	16 ARI	25 SAG

	2005	2006	2007	2008	2009	2010	2011	2012	2013	2014	2015	2016	2017	2018	2019
JAN	SAG	TAU	16 CAP	GEM	CAP	LEO	LEO	VIR	AQU	LIB	12 PIS	3 SCO	28 ARI	26 SAG	ARI
FEB	6 CAP	17 GEM	25 AQU	GEM	4 AQU	LEO	22 PIS	VIR	1 PIS	LIB	19 ARI	SCO	ARI	SAG	14 TAU
MAR	20 AQU	GEM	AQU	4 CAN	14 PIS	LEO	1 ARI	VIR	12 ARI	LIB	31 TAU	5 SAG	9 TAU	17 CAP	31 GEM
APR	30 PIS	13 CAN	6 PIS	CAN	22 ARI	LEO	1 ARI	VIR	20 TAU	LIB	TAU	SAG	21 GEM	CAP	GEM
MAY	PIS	CAN	15 ARI	9 LEO	31 TAU	LEO	11 TAU	VIR	31 GEM	LIB	11 GEM	27 SCO	GEM	15 AQU	15 CAN
JUN	11 ARI	3 LEO	24 TAU	LEO	TAU	7 VIR	20 GEM	GEM	GEM	LIB	24 CAN	SCO	4 CAN	AQU	CAN
JUL	28 TAU	VIR	TAU	1 VIR	11 GEM	29 LIB	GEM	3 LIB	13 CAN	25 SCO	CAN	SCO	20 LEO	AQU	1 LEO
AUG	TAU	VIR	7 GEM	19 LIB	25 CAN	LIB	CAN	23 SCO	27 LEO	SCO	LEO	2 SAG	27 CAP	5 VIR	18 VIR
SEP	TAU	7 LIB	28 CAN	LIB	CAN	14 SCO	18 LEO	LEO	SCO	LEO	24 VIR	27 CAP	VIR	10 AQU	VIR
OCT	TAU	23 SCO	CAN	3 SCO	16 LEO	28 SAG	LEO	6 SAG	15 VIR	26 CAP	VIR	CAP	22 LIB	AQU	3 LIB
NOV	TAU	SCO	CAN	16 SAG	LEO	SAG	10 VIR	16 CAP	7 LIB	LIB	12 LIB	9 AQU	LIB	15 PIS	19 SCO
DEC	TAU	5 SAG	31 GEM	GEM	27 CAP	LEO	7 CAP	VIR	25 AQU	7 LIB	4 AQU	LIB	19 PIS	9 SCO	31 ARI	SCO

	2020	2021	2022	2023	2024	2025	2026	2027	2028	2029	2030	2031	2032	2033	2034
JAN	3 SAG	6 TAU	24 CAP	GEM	4 CAP	6 CAN	23 AQU	VIR	3 AQU	LIB	20 PIS	15 SCO	PIS	SCO	12 ARI
FEB	16 CAP	TAU	CAP	GEM	13 AQU	CAN	AQU	21 LEO	10 PIS	LIB	27 ARI	SCO	6 ARI	6 SAG	23 TAU
MAR	30 AQU	3 GEM	6 AQU	25 CAN	22 PIS	CAN	2 PIS	LEO	19 ARI	LIB	LIB	ARI	17 TAU	SAG	TAU
APR	23 CAN	14 PIS	CAN	30 ARI	17 LEO	9 ARI	LEO	27 TAU	7 VIR	8 TAU	SCO	28 GEM	6 CAP	23 CAN
MAY	12 PIS	CAN	24 ARI	20 LEO	ARI	17 LEO	18 TAU	14 VIR	TAU	7 GEM	4 LIB	GEM	19 GEM	SCO	GEM	CAN
JUN	27 ARI	11 LEO	ARI	LEO	8 TAU	17 VIR	28 GEM	VIR	15 LIB	20 CAN	4 LIB	GEM	SCO	11 CAN	CAN
JUL	ARI	29 VIR	5 TAU	10 VIR	20 GEM	VIR	LIB	LIB	1 CAN	SCO	27 LEO	LEO	6 CAP	8 LEO
AUG	ARI	14 LIB	20 GEM	27 LIB	GEM	6 LIB	11 CAN	1 SCO	CAN	7 SCO	15 LEO	25 SAG	LEO	6 CAP	24 VIR
SEP	ARI	14 LIB	GEM	LIB	4 CAN	22 SCO	SCO	27 LEO	4 LEO	23 SAG	LEO	12 VIR	CAP	VIR
OCT	ARI	30 SCO	GEM	11 SCO	CAN	SCO	LEO	15 SAG	23 VIR	SAG	2 VIR	10 CAP	29 LIB	17 AQU	10 LIB
NOV	ARI	SCO	GEM	24 SAG	3 LEO	4 SAG	25 VIR	25 CAP	VIR	3 CAP	21 LIB	20 AQU	LIB	AQU	26 SCO
DEC	ARI	13 SAG	GEM	LEO	15 CAP	VIR	21 LIB	13 AQU	29 PIS	17 SCO	1 PIS	SCO

	2035	2036	2037	2038	2039	2040	2041	2042	2043	2044	2045	2046	2047	2048	2049
JAN	11 SAG	26 TAU	SAG	TAU	11 CAP	CAN	30 AQU	LEO	10 AQU	19 LIB	27 PIS	LIB	7 PIS	SCO	22 ARI
FEB	25 CAP	TAU	1 CAP	4 GEM	20 AQU	CAN	AQU	LEO	18 PIS	12 VIR	PIS	4 SCO	14 ARI	21 SAG	ARI
MAR	CAP	14 GEM	14 AQU	GEM	31 PIS	CAN	10 PIS	LEO	28 ARI	VIR	7 ARI	SCO	26 TAU	SAG	4 TAU
APR	12 AQU	GEM	24 PIS	6 CAN	PIS	CAN	17 ARI	LEO	ARI	VIR	15 TAU	11 LIB	TAU	SAG	16 GEM
MAY	30 PIS	1 CAN	29 LEO	LEO	9 ARI	2 LEO	26 TAU	30 VIR	16 TAU	24 LIB	26 GEM	LIB	19 GEM	SAG	30 CAN
JUN	PIS	18 LEO	4 ARI	LEO	18 TAU	25 VIR	TAU	VIR	16 GEM	24 LIB	GEM	LIB	19 CAN	SAG	CAN
JUL	PIS	LEO	17 TAU	17 VIR	31 GEM	VIR	6 GEM	24 LIB	29 CAN	LIB	8 CAN	15 SCO	CAN	SAG	15 LEO
AUG	PIS	5 VIR	TAU	TAU	14 LIB	19 CAN	LIB	CAN	17 SCO	22 LEO	LEO	4 LEO	SAG	31 VIR
SEP	PIS	21 LIB	11 GEM	3 LIB	18 CAN	29 SCO	CAN	9 SCO	13 LEO	SCO	LEO	7 SAG	20 VIR	17 CAP	VIR
OCT	PIS	LIB	GEM	18 SCO	CAN	SCO	8 LEO	23 SAG	LEO	1 SAG	9 VIR	20 CAP	VIR	CAP	17 LIB
NOV	PIS	6 SCO	12 TAU	SCO	CAN	11 SAG	LEO	SAG	3 VIR	11 CAP	30 LIB	29 AQU	7 LIB	1 AQU	LIB
DEC	1 ARI	20 SAG	TAU	1 SAG	CAN	22 CAP	LEO	3 CAP	VIR	20 AQU	LIB	AQU	27 SCO	12 PIS	3 SCO

	2050	2051	2052	2053	2054	2055	2056	2057	2058	2059	2060	2061	2062	2063	2064
JAN	20 AQU	ARI	10 CAP	TAU	19 CAP	GEM	CAP	LEO	18 AQU	VIR	AQU	LIB	15 PIS	7 SCO	PIS
FEB	SAG	7 TAU	CAP	23 GEM	28 AQU	GEM	8 AQU	4 CAN	25 PIS	VIR	5 PIS	LIB	22 ARI	SCO	1 ARI
MAR	9 CAP	25 GEM	24 AQU	GEM	AQU	14 CAN	17 PIS	CAN	PIS	25 LEO	14 ARI	LIB	ARI	23 SAG	12 TAU
APR	29 AQU	GEM	GEM	17 CAN	9 PIS	CAN	25 ARI	3 LEO	4 ARI	24 VIR	22 TAU	LIB	3 TAU	25 SCO	23 GEM
MAY	AQU	10 CAN	5 PIS	CAN	18 ARI	14 LEO	ARI	LEO	13 TAU	GEM	TAU	LIB	14 GEM	SCO	GEM
JUN	AQU	26 LEO	17 ARI	6 LEO	28 TAU	LEO	3 TAU	10 VIR	23 GEM	8 LIB	2 GEM	15 CAN	26 CAN	SCO	6 CAN
JUL	AQU	LEO	ARI	24 VIR	TAU	5 VIR	14 GEM	VIR	GEM	LIB	15 CAN	30 SCO	CAN	SCO	22 LEO
AUG	AQU	13 VIR	6 TAU	VIR	11 GEM	22 LIB	28 CAN	1 LIB	5 CAN	27 SCO	30 LEO	SCO	11 LEO	14 SAG	LEO
SEP	AQU	29 LIB	TAU	10 LIB	GEM	LIB	CAN	17 SCO	21 LEO	SCO	LEO	18 VIR	27 VIR	VIR	7 VIR
OCT	31 PIS	LIB	TAU	25 SCO	8 CAN	7 SCO	21 LEO	30 SAG	LEO	10 SAG	18 VIR	29 CAP	VIR	3 CAP	24 LIB
NOV	PIS	14 SCO	18 ARI	SCO	19 SAG	LEO	LEO	SAG	15 VIR	20 CAP	11 LIB	CAP	15 LIB	14 AQU	LIB
DEC	23 ARI	29 SAG	10 TAU	8 SAG	7 GEM	30 CAP	LEO	10 CAP	VIR	29 AQU	11 LIB	7 AQU	LIB	23 PIS	11 SCO

	2065	2066	2067	2068	2069	2070	2071	2072	2073	2074	2075	2076	2077	2078	2079
JAN	30 SAG	5 ARI	5 SAG	16 TAU	27 CAP	GEM	7 CAP	CAN	25 AQU	VIR	6 AQU	LIB	23 PIS	21 SCO	1 PIS
FEB	SAG	17 TAU	19 CAP	TAU	GEM	GEM	15 AQU	CAN	AQU	2 LEO	13 PIS	LIB	PIS	SCO	9 ARI
MAR	23 CAP	TAU	CAP	CAP	8 GEM	9 AQU	30 CAN	26 PIS	CAN	5 PIS	LEO	23 ARI	18 VIR	2 ARI	SCO	21 TAU
APR	CAP	2 GEM	4 AQU	26 CAN	18 PIS	CAN	PIS	23 LEO	12 ARI	LEO	ARI	VIR	10 TAU	SCO	TAU
MAY	CAP	18 CAN	19 PIS	CAN	28 ARI	23 LEO	4 ARI	LEO	21 TAU	21 VIR	1 TAU	VIR	11 GEM	21 LIB	GEM	2 GEM
JUN	CAP	CAN	PIS	13 LEO	ARI	LEO	13 TAU	20 VIR	TAU	VIR	11 GEM	14 LIB	GEM	25 SCO	14 CAN
JUL	CAP	4 LEO	8 ARI	31 VIR	9 TAU	12 VIR	25 GEM	VIR	1 GEM	18 CAN	24 CAN	LIB	3 CAN	SCO	30 LEO
AUG	CAP	20 VIR	ARI	VIR	26 GEM	LIB	GEM	9 LIB	14 CAN	LIB	CAN	11 SCO	18 LEO	30 SAG	LEO
SEP	CAP	VIR	ARI	16 LIB	GEM	LIB	9 CAN	24 SCO	CAN	4 SCO	8 LEO	26 SAG	LEO	SAG	15 VIR
OCT	3 AQU	6 LIB	ARI	LIB	GEM	14 SCO	LEO	SCO	1 LEO	18 SAG	28 VIR	VIR	4 VIR	14 CAP	VIR
NOV	22 PIS	21 SCO	ARI	1 SCO	GEM	26 SAG	22 LEO	6 SAG	LEO	28 CAP	VIR	6 CAP	24 LIB	23 AQU	2 LIB
DEC	PIS	SCO	ARI	15 SAG	GEM	SAG	11 CAN	17 CAP	4 VIR	CAP	28 LIB	15 AQU	LIB	AQU	21 SCO

	2080	2081	2082	2083	2084	2085	2086	2087	2088	2089	2090	2091	2092	2093	2094
JAN	SCO	16 ARI	14 SAG	31 TAU	SAG	TAU	14 CAP	12 GEM	CAP	LEO	13 AQU	VIR	31 PIS	LIB	10 PIS
FEB	11 SAG	27 TAU	SAG	TAU	5 CAP	13 GEM	23 AQU	24 CAN	3 AQU	LEO	20 PIS	PIS	PIS	22 SCO	17 ARI
MAR	SAG	TAU	1 CAP	19 GEM	18 AQU	GEM	AQU	CAN	12 PIS	LEO	30 ARI	VIR	9 ARI	12 LIB	29 TAU
APR	22 CAP	11 GEM	18 AQU	GEM	28 PIS	10 CAN	3 PIS	20 ARI	29 TAU	LEO	ARI	VIR	18 TAU	LIB	TAU
MAY	CAP	25 CAN	AQU	5 CAN	PIS	31 LEO	13 ARI	7 LEO	29 TAU	LEO	8 TAU	VIR	28 GEM	LIB	9 GEM
JUN	5 SAG	CAN	10 PIS	22 LEO	8 ARI	LEO	22 TAU	29 VIR	TAU	3 VIR	30 GEM	LIB	GEM	22 SCO	CAN
JUL	SAG	10 LEO	PIS	LEO	24 TAU	20 VIR	TAU	VIR	9 GEM	27 LIB	31 CAN	LIB	11 CAN	21 SCO	CAN
AUG	SAG	26 VIR	PIS	8 VIR	TAU	VIR	4 GEM	17 LIB	22 CAN	LIB	CAN	21 SCO	25 LEO	SCO	6 LEO
SEP	SAG	VIR	PIS	24 LIB	TAU	5 LIB	24 CAN	LIB	CAN	12 LEO	16 LEO	SCO	LEO	10 SAG	22 VIR
OCT	24 AQU	13 LIB	PIS	LIB	TAU	21 SCO	CAN	2 SCO	12 LEO	25 SAG	LEO	5 SAG	12 VIR	23 CAP	VIR
NOV	AQU	28 SCO	PIS	9 SCO	TAU	SCO	CAN	14 SAG	LEO	SAG	7 VIR	15 CAP	VIR	CAP	10 LIB
DEC	6 PIS	SCO	12 ARI	24 SAG	TAU	3 SAG	CAN	25 CAP	LEO	5 CAP	VIR	24 AQU	4 LIB	2 AQU	31 SCO

	2095	2096	2097	2098	2099	2100
JAN	SCO	26 ARI	23 SAG	ARI	SAG	1 TAU
FEB	SCO	ARI	SAG	11 TAU	13 CAP	TAU
MAR	1 SAG	7 TAU	14 CAP	28 GEM	28 AQU	1 GEM
APR	SAG	18 GEM	CAP	GEM	AQU	21 CAN
MAY	SAG	GEM	9 AQU	13 CAN	11 PIS	CAN
JUN	11 SCO	2 CAN	AQU	29 LEO	25 ARI	9 LEO
JUL	25 SAG	17 LEO	AQU	LEO	ARI	28 VIR
AUG	SAG	LEO	AQU	15 VIR	25 TAU	VIR
SEP	24 CAP	2 VIR	AQU	VIR	TAU	13 LIB
OCT	CAP	20 LIB	AQU	1 LIB	2 ARI	29 SCO
NOV	7 AQU	LIB	11 PIS	16 SCO	ARI	SCO
DEC	17 PIS	6 SCO	28 ARI	31 SAG	ARI	11 SAG

♃

Where Is Your Jupiter? — ~~Cancer~~ LEO

THE FOLLOWING JUPITER TABLES will tell you what sign Jupiter was in on the day of your birth. Because Jupiter travels through the zodiac at a much slower rate than Mercury, Venus, or Mars, these Jupiter Tables are much shorter than the tables for previous planets.

DC - ARIES
CC - CANCER
JIM - GEMINI
Rush - CAP

To use these tables, simply locate the year of your birth.* You will see at a glance exactly what signs Jupiter was in during that year. If there is only one sign listed for a specific year, it means Jupiter was in that sign throughout the entire year.

*The computer chart you get using the enclosed CD-ROM will not only tell you the sign your Jupiter is in, but the exact degree of this sign.

1900	**SAG**	
1901	JAN 1 —JAN 18 SAG JAN 19—DEC 31 CAP	
1902	JAN 1 —FEB 5 CAP FEB 6 —DEC 31 AQU	
1903	JAN 1 —FEB 19 AQU FEB 20—DEC 31 PIS	
1904	JAN 1 —FEB 28 PIS FEB 29—AUG 7 ARI AUG 8 —AUG 30 TAU AUG 31—DEC 31 ARI	
1905	JAN 1 —MAR 6 ARI MAR 7 —JUL 19 TAU JUL 20—DEC 3 GEM DEC 4 —DEC 31 TAU	
1906	JAN 1 —MAR 8 TAU MAR 9 —JUL 29 GEM JUL 30—DEC 31 CAN	
1907	JAN 1 —AUG 17 CAN AUG 18—DEC 31 LEO	
1908	JAN 1 —SEP 11 LEO SEP 12—DEC 31 VIR	
1909	JAN 1 —OCT 10 VIR OCT 11—DEC 31 LIB	
1910	JAN 1 —NOV 10 LIB NOV 11—DEC 31 SCO	
1911	JAN 1 —DEC 9 SCO DEC 10—DEC 31 SAG	
1912	**SAG**	
1913	JAN 1 —JAN 1 SAG JAN 2 —DEC 31 CAP	
1914	JAN 1 —JAN 20 CAP JAN 21—DEC 31 AQU	
1915	JAN 1 —FEB 2 AQU FEB 3 —DEC 31 PIS	
1916	JAN 1 —FEB 11 PIS FEB 12—JUN 24 ARI JUN 25—OCT 25 TAU OCT 26—DEC 31 ARI	
1917	JAN 1 —FEB 11 ARI FEB 12—JUN 28 TAU JUN 29—DEC 31 GEM	
1918	JAN 1 —JUL 12 GEM JUL 13—DEC 31 CAN	
1919	JAN 1 —AUG 1 CAN AUG 2 —DEC 31 LEO	
1920	JAN 1 —AUG 26 LEO AUG 27—DEC 31 VIR	
1921	JAN 1 —SEP 24 VIR SEP 25—DEC 31 LIB	
1922	JAN 1 —OCT 25 LIB OCT 26—DEC 31 SCO	

1923	JAN 1 —NOV 23 SCO NOV 24—DEC 31 SAG	
1924	JAN 1 —DEC 17 SAG DEC 18—DEC 31 CAP	
1925	**CAP**	
1926	JAN 1 —JAN 4 CAP JAN 5 —DEC 31 AQU	
1927	JAN 1 —JAN 17 AQU JAN 18—JUN 5 PIS JUN 6 —SEP 9 ARI SEP 10—DEC 31 ARI	
1928	JAN 1 —JAN 21 ARI JAN 22—JUN 2 ARI JUN 3 —DEC 31 TAU	
1929	JAN 1 —JUN 11 TAU JUN 12—DEC 31 GEM	
1930	JAN 1 —JUN 25 GEM JUN 26—DEC 31 CAN	
1931	JAN 1 —JUL 16 CAN JUL 17—DEC 31 LEO	
1932	JAN 1 —AUG 10 LEO AUG 11—DEC 31 VIR	
1933	JAN 1 —SEP 9 VIR SEP 10—DEC 31 LIB	
1934	JAN 1 —OCT 9 LIB OCT 10—DEC 31 SCO	
1935	JAN 1 —NOV 7 SCO NOV 8 —DEC 31 SAG	
1936	JAN 1 —DEC 1 SAG DEC 2 —DEC 31 CAP	
1937	JAN 1 —DEC 18 CAP DEC 19—DEC 31 AQU	
1938	JAN 1 —MAY 13 AQU MAY 14—JUL 28 PIS JUL 29—DEC 28 AQU DEC 29—DEC 31 PIS	
1939	JAN 1 —MAY 10 PIS MAY 11—OCT 28 ARI OCT 29—DEC 19 PIS DEC 20—DEC 31 ARI	
1940	JAN 1 —MAY 15 ARI MAY 16—DEC 31 TAU	
1941	JAN 1 —MAY 25 TAU MAY 26—DEC 31 GEM	
1942	JAN 1 —JUN 9 GEM JUN 10—DEC 31 CAN	
1943	JAN 1 —JUN 29 CAN JUN 30—DEC 31 LEO	
1944	JAN 1 —JUL 24 LEO JUL 25—DEC 31 VIR	
1945	JAN 1 —AUG 24 VIR AUG 25—DEC 31 LIB	

1946	JAN 1 —SEP 24 LIB SEP 25—DEC 31 SCO	
1947	JAN 1 —OCT 22 SCO OCT 23—DEC 31 SAG	
1948	JAN 1 —NOV 14 SAG NOV 15—DEC 31 CAP	
1949	JAN 1 —APR 11 CAP APR 12—JUN 26 AQU JUN 27—NOV 29 CAP NOV 30—DEC 31 AQU	
1950	JAN 1 —APR 14 AQU APR 15—SEP 13 PIS SEP 14—NOV 30 AQU DEC 1 —DEC 31 PIS	
1951	JAN 1 —APR 20 PIS APR 21—DEC 31 ARI	
1952	JAN 1 —APR 27 ARI APR 28—DEC 31 TAU	
1953	JAN 1 —MAY 8 TAU MAY 9 —DEC 31 GEM	
1954	JAN 1 —MAY 22 GEM MAY 23—DEC 31 CAN	
1955	JAN 1 —JUN 11 CAN JUN 12—NOV 15 LEO NOV 16—DEC 31 VIR	
1956	JAN 1 —JAN 16 VIR JAN 17—JUL 6 LEO JUL 7 —DEC 11 VIR DEC 12—DEC 31 LIB	
1957	JAN 1 —FEB 18 LIB FEB 19—AUG 5 VIR AUG 6 —DEC 31 LIB	
1958	JAN 1 —JAN 12 LIB JAN 13—MAR 19 SCO MAR 20—SEP 6 LIB SEP 7 —DEC 31 SCO	
1959	JAN 1 —FEB 9 SCO FEB 10—APR 23 SAG APR 24—OCT 4 SCO OCT 5 —DEC 31 SAG	
1960	JAN 1 —FEB 28 SAG MAR 1 —JUN 8 CAP JUN 9 —OCT 24 SAG OCT 25—DEC 31 CAP	
1961	JAN 1 —MAR 14 CAP MAR 15—AUG 11 AQU AUG 12—NOV 2 CAP NOV 3 —DEC 31 AQU	
1962	JAN 1 —MAR 24 AQU MAR 25—DEC 31 PIS	
1963	JAN 1 —APR 2 PIS APR 3 —DEC 31 ARI	
1964	JAN 1 —APR 11 ARI APR 12—DEC 31 TAU	

1965	JAN 1 —APR 21 TAU
	APR 22—SEP 19 GEM
	SEP 20—NOV 15 CAN
	NOV 16—DEC 31 GEM

CANCER 1966

1966	JAN 1 —MAY 4 GEM
	MAY 5 —SEP 26 CAN
	SEP 27—DEC 31 LEO

1967	JAN 1 —JAN 14 LEO
	JAN 15—MAY 22 CAN
	MAY 23—OCT 18 LEO
	OCT 19—DEC 31 VIR

1968	JAN 1 —FEB 25 VIR
	FEB 26—JUN 14 LEO
	JUN 15—NOV 14 VIR
	NOV 15—DEC 31 LIB

1969	JAN 1 —MAR 29 LIB
	MAR 30—JUL 14 VIR
	JUL 15—DEC 15 LIB
	DEC 16—DEC 31 SCO

1970	JAN 1 —APR 29 SCO
	APR 30—AUG 14 LIB
	AUG 15—DEC 31 SCO

1971	JAN 1 —JAN 13 SCO
	JAN 14—JUN 3 SAG
	JUN 4 —SEP 10 SCO
	SEP 11—DEC 31 SAG

1972	JAN 1 —FEB 5 SAG
	FEB 6 —JUL 23 CAP
	JUL 24—SEP 24 SAG
	SEP 25—DEC 31 CAP

1973	JAN 1 —FEB 22 CAP
	FEB 23—DEC 31 AQU

1974	JAN 1 —MAR 7 AQU
	MAR 8 —DEC 31 PIS

1975	JAN 1 —MAR 17 PIS
	MAR 18—DEC 31 ARI

1976	JAN 1 —MAR 25 ARI
	MAR 26—AUG 22 TAU
	AUG 23—OCT 15 GEM
	OCT 16—DEC 31 TAU

1977	JAN 1 —APR 2 TAU
	APR 3 —AUG 19 GEM
	AUG 20—DEC 29 CAN
	DEC 30—DEC 31 GEM

1978	JAN 1 —APR 10 GEM
	APR 11—SEP 4 CAN
	SEP 5 —DEC 31 LEO

1979	JAN 1 —FEB 27 LEO
	FEB 28—APR 19 CAN
	APR 20—SEP 28 LEO
	SEP 29—DEC 31 VIR

1980	JAN 1 —OCT 26 VIR
	OCT 27—DEC 31 LIB

1981	JAN 1 —NOV 25 LIB
	NOV 26—DEC 31 SCO

1982	JAN 1 —DEC 24 SCO
	DEC 25—DEC 31 SAG

1983	SAG

1984	JAN 1 —JAN 18 SAG
	JAN 19—DEC 31 CAP

1985	JAN 1 —FEB 5 CAP
	FEB 6 —DEC 31 AQU

1986	JAN 1 —FEB 19 AQU
	FEB 20—DEC 31 PIS

1987	JAN 1 —MAR 1 PIS
	MAR 2 —DEC 31 ARI

1988	JAN 1 —MAR 7 ARI
	MAR 8 —JUL 20 TAU
	JUL 21—NOV 29 GEM
	NOV 30—DEC 31 TAU

1989	JAN 1 —MAR 9 TAU
	MAR 10—JUL 29 GEM
	JUL 30—DEC 31 CAN

1990	JAN 1 —AUG 17 CAN
	AUG 18—DEC 31 LEO

1991	JAN 1 —SEP 11 LEO
	SEP 12—DEC 31 VIR

1992	JAN 1 —OCT 9 VIR
	OCT 10—DEC 31 LIB

1993	JAN 1 —NOV 9 LIB
	NOV 10—DEC 31 SCO

1994	JAN 1 —DEC 8 SCO
	DEC 9 —DEC 31 SAG

1995	SAG

1996	JAN 1 —JAN 2 SAG
	JAN 3 —DEC 31 CAP

1997	JAN 1 —JAN 20 CAP
	JAN 21—DEC 31 AQU

1998	JAN 1 —FEB 3 AQU
	FEB 4 —DEC 31 PIS

1999	JAN 1 —FEB 11 PIS
	FEB 12—JUN 27 ARI
	JUN 28—OCT 22 TAU
	OCT 23—DEC 31 ARI

2000	JAN 1 —FEB 13 ARI
	FEB 14—JUN 29 TAU
	JUN 30—DEC 31 GEM

2001	JAN 1 —JUL 11 GEM
	JUL 12—DEC 31 CAN

2002	JAN 1 —JUL 31 CAN
	AUG 1 —DEC 31 LEO

2003	JAN 1 —AUG 26 LEO
	AUG 27—DEC 31 VIR

2004	JAN 1 —SEP 23 VIR
	SEP 24—DEC 31 LIB

2005	JAN 1 —OCT 24 LIB
	OCT 25—DEC 31 SCO

2006	JAN 1 —NOV 22 SCO
	NOV 23—DEC 31 SAG

2007	JAN 1 —DEC 17 SAG
	DEC 18—DEC 31 CAP

2008	CAP

2009	JAN 1 —JAN 4 CAP
	JAN 5 —DEC 31 AQU

2010	JAN 1 —JAN 16 AQU
	JAN 17—JUN 5 PIS
	JUN 6 —SEP 7 ARI
	SEP 8 —DEC 31 PIS

2011	JAN 1 —JAN 21 PIS
	JAN 22—JUN 3 ARI
	JUN 4 —DEC 31 TAU

2012	JAN 1 —JUN 10 TAU
	JUN 11—DEC 31 GEM

2013	JAN 1 —JUN 24 GEM
	JUN 25—DEC 31 CAN

2014	JAN 1 —JUL 15 CAN
	JUL 16—DEC 31 LEO

2015	JAN 1 —AUG 10 LEO
	AUG 11—DEC 31 VIR

2016	JAN 1 —SEP 8 VIR
	SEP 9 —DEC 31 LIB

2017	JAN 1 —OCT 9 LIB
	OCT 10—DEC 31 SCO

2018	JAN 1 —NOV 7 SCO
	NOV 8 —DEC 31 SAG

2019	JAN 1 —DEC 1 SAG
	DEC 2 —DEC 31 CAP

2020	JAN 1 —DEC 18 CAP
	DEC 19—DEC 31 AQU

2021	JAN 1 —MAY 12 AQU
	MAY 13—JUL 27 PIS
	JUL 28—DEC 27 AQU
	DEC 28—DEC 31 PIS

2022	JAN 1 —MAY 9 PIS
	MAY 10—OCT 27 ARI
	OCT 28—DEC 19 PIS
	DEC 20—DEC 31 ARI

2023	JAN 1 —MAY 15 ARI
	MAY 16—DEC 31 TAU

2024	JAN 1 —MAY 24 TAU
	MAY 25—DEC 31 GEM

2025	JAN 1 —JUN 8 GEM
	JUN 9 —DEC 31 CAN

2026	JAN 1 —JUN 29 CAN
	JUN 30—DEC 31 LEO

2027	JAN 1 –JUL 24 LEO JUL 25–DEC 31 VIR	**2047**	JAN 1 –APR 12 ARI APR 13–DEC 31 TAU	**2065**	JAN 1 –DEC 24 SCO DEC 25–DEC 31 SAG
2028	JAN 1 –AUG 23 VIR AUG 24–DEC 31 LIB	**2048**	JAN 1 –APR 21 TAU APR 22–SEP 22 GEM SEP 23–NOV 11 CAN NOV 12–DEC 31 GEM	**2066**	**SAG**
2029	JAN 1 –SEP 23 LIB SEP 24–DEC 31 SCO			**2067**	JAN 1 –JAN 18 SAG JAN 19–DEC 31 CAP
2030	JAN 1 –OCT 21 SCO OCT 22–DEC 31 SAG	**2049**	JAN 1 –MAY 4 GEM MAY 5 –SEP 26 CAN SEP 27–DEC 31 LEO	**2068**	JAN 1 –FEB 6 CAP FEB 7 –DEC 31 AQU
2031	JAN 1 –NOV 14 SAG NOV 15–DEC 31 CAP	**2050**	JAN 1 –JAN 13 LEO JAN 14–MAY 21 CAN MAY 22–OCT 17 LEO OCT 18–DEC 31 VIR	**2069**	JAN 1 –FEB 19 AQU FEB 20–DEC 31 PIS
2032	JAN 1 –APR 10 CAP APR 11–JUN 25 AQU JUN 26–NOV 28 CAP NOV 29–DEC 31 AQU			**2070**	JAN 1 –MAR 1 PIS MAR 2 –DEC 31 ARI
2033	JAN 1 –APR 13 AQU APR 14–SEP 11 PIS SEP 12–NOV 30 AQU DEC 1 –DEC 31 PIS	**2051**	JAN 1 –FEB 25 VIR FEB 26–JUN 14 LEO JUN 15–NOV 14 VIR NOV 15–DEC 31 LIB	**2071**	JAN 1 –MAR 7 ARI MAR 8 –JUL 21 TAU JUL 22–NOV 29 GEM NOV 30–DEC 31 TAU
2034	JAN 1 –APR 20 PIS APR 21–DEC 31 ARI	**2052**	JAN 1 –MAR 29 LIB MAR 30–JUL 12 VIR JUL 13–DEC 14 LIB DEC 15–DEC 31 SCO	**2072**	JAN 1 –MAR 9 TAU MAR 10–JUL 28 GEM JUL 29–DEC 31 CAN
2035	JAN 1 –APR 28 ARI APR 29–DEC 31 TAU			**2073**	JAN 1 –AUG 16 CAN AUG 17–DEC 31 LEO
2036	JAN 1 –MAY 8 TAU MAY 9 –DEC 31 GEM	**2053**	JAN 1 –APR 28 SCO APR 29–AUG 13 LIB AUG 14–DEC 31 SCO	**2074**	JAN 1 –SEP 10 LEO SEP 11–DEC 31 VIR
2037	JAN 1 –MAY 22 GEM MAY 23–DEC 31 CAN	**2054**	JAN 1 –JAN 12 SCO JAN 13–JUN 3 SAG JUN 4 –SEP 9 SCO SEP 10–DEC 31 SAG	**2075**	JAN 1 –OCT 9 VIR OCT 10–DEC 31 LIB
2038	JAN 1 –JUN 11 CAN JUN 12–NOV 15 LEO NOV 16–DEC 31 VIR			**2076**	JAN 1 –NOV 8 LIB NOV 9 –DEC 31 SCO
2039	JAN 1 –JAN 15 VIR JAN 16–JUL 6 LEO JUL 7 –DEC 11 VIR DEC 12–DEC 31 LIB	**2055**	JAN 1 –FEB 5 SAG FEB 6 –JUL 21 CAP JUL 22–SEP 26 SAG SEP 27–DEC 31 CAP	**2077**	JAN 1 –DEC 7 SCO DEC 8 –DEC 31 SAG
2040	JAN 1 –FEB 19 LIB FEB 20–AUG 4 VIR AUG 5 –DEC 31 LIB	**2056**	JAN 1 –FEB 23 CAP FEB 24–DEC 31 AQU	**2078**	SAG
2041	JAN 1 –JAN 10 LIB JAN 11–MAR 19 SCO MAR 20–SEP 4 LIB SEP 5 –DEC 31 SCO	**2057**	JAN 1 –MAR 7 AQU MAR 8 –DEC 31 PIS	**2079**	JAN 1 –JAN 1 SAG JAN 2 –DEC 31 CAP
2042	JAN 1 –FEB 7 SCO FEB 8 –APR 23 SAG APR 24–OCT 3 SCO OCT 4 –DEC 31 SAG	**2058**	JAN 1 –MAR 18 PIS MAR 19–DEC 31 ARI	**2080**	JAN 1 –JAN 20 CAP JAN 21–DEC 31 AQU
2043	JAN 1 –FEB 28 SAG MAR 1 –JUN 8 CAP JUN 9 –OCT 25 SAG OCT 26–DEC 31 CAP	**2059**	JAN 1 –MAR 26 ARI MAR 27–AUG 26 TAU AUG 27–OCT 10 GEM OCT 11–DEC 31 TAU	**2081**	JAN 1 –FEB 2 AQU FEB 3 –DEC 31 PIS
2044	JAN 1 –MAR 13 CAP MAR 14–AUG 8 AQU AUG 9 –NOV 3 CAP NOV 4 –DEC 31 AQU	**2060**	JAN 1 –APR 2 TAU APR 3 –AUG 19 GEM AUG 20–DEC 27 CAN DEC 28–DEC 31 GEM	**2082**	JAN 1 –FEB 11 PIS FEB 12–JUN 26 ARI JUN 27–OCT 21 TAU OCT 21–DEC 31 ARI
2045	JAN 1 –MAR 25 AQU MAR 26–DEC 31 PIS	**2061**	JAN 1 –APR 11 GEM APR 12–SEP 3 CAN SEP 4 –DEC 31 LEO	**2083**	JAN 1 –FEB 13 ARI FEB 14–JUN 29 TAU JUN 30–DEC 31 GEM
2046	JAN 1 –APR 3 PIS APR 4 –DEC 31 ARI	**2062**	JAN 1 –FEB 25 LEO FEB 26–APR 19 CAN APR 20–SEP 27 LEO SEP 28–DEC 31 VIR	**2084**	JAN 1 –JUL 11 GEM JUL 12–DEC 31 CAN
		2063	JAN 1 –OCT 26 VIR OCT 27–DEC 31 LIB	**2085**	JAN 1 –JUL 30 CAN JUL 31–DEC 31 LEO
		2064	JAN 1 –NOV 25 LIB NOV 26–DEC 31 SCO	**2086**	JAN 1 –AUG 25 LEO AUG 26–DEC 31 VIR
				2087	JAN 1 –SEP 23 VIR SEP 24–DEC 31 LIB

2088	JAN 1 —OCT 23 LIB OCT 24—DEC 31 SCO	2093	JAN 1 —JAN 16 AQU JAN 17—JUN 5 PIS JUN 6 —SEP 5 ARI SEP 6 —DEC 31 ARI	2098	JAN 1 —AUG 9 LEO AUG 10—DEC 31 VIR
2089	JAN 1 —NOV 21 SCO NOV 22—DEC 31 SAG	2094	JAN 1 —JAN 21 ARI JAN 22—JUN 3 ARI JUN 4 —DEC 31 TAU	2099	JAN 1 —SEP 8 VIR SEP 9 —DEC 31 LIB
2090	JAN 1 —DEC 16 SAG DEC 17—DEC 31 CAP			2100	JAN 1 —OCT 9 LIB OCT 10—DEC 31 SCO
2091	CAP	2095	JAN 1 —JUN 11 TAU JUN 12—DEC 31 GEM	2101	SCO
2092	JAN 1 —JAN 4 CAP JAN 5 —DEC 31 AQU	2096	JAN 1 —JUN 24 GEM JUN 25—DEC 31 CAN		
		2097	JAN 1 —JUL 14 CAN JUL 15—DEC 31 LEO		

1954- Scorpio

♄

Where Is Your Saturn?

SCORPIO

THE FOLLOWING SATURN TABLES will tell you what sign Saturn was in on the day of your birth. To use these tables, simply locate the year of your birth.* You will see at a glance exactly what signs Saturn was in during that year.

If there is only one sign listed for a specific year, it means Saturn was in that sign throughout the entire year. In some cases, Saturn remains in one sign for two years. For example, Saturn was in Sagittarius throughout 1986 and 1987.

Rush - VIRGO
Jim - Scorpio
Ce - Scorpio
DC - LIBRA

*The computer chart you get using the enclosed CD-ROM will not only tell you the sign your Saturn is in, but the exact degree of this sign.

1900	JAN 1 –JAN 20 SAG		1922		LIB		1947		LEO

1900   JAN 1 –JAN 20 SAG

        JAN 21–JUL 17 CAP
        JUL 18–OCT 16 SAG
        OCT 17–DEC 31 CAP

1901–1902   CAP

1903   JAN 1 –JAN 18 CAP
        JAN 19–DEC 31 AQU

1904   AQU

1905   JAN 1 –APR 12 AQU
        APR 13–AUG 15 PIS
        AUG 16–DEC 31 AQU

1906   JAN 1 –JAN 7 AQU
        JAN 8 –DEC 31 PIS

1907   PIS

1908   JAN 1 –MAR 18 PIS
        MAR 19–DEC 31 ARI

1909   ARI

1910   JAN 1 –MAY 16 ARI
        MAY 17–DEC 13 TAU
        DEC 14–DEC 31 ARI

1911   JAN 1 –JAN 19 ARI
        JAN 20–DEC 31 TAU

1912   JAN 1 –JUL 6 TAU
        JUL 7 –NOV 29 GEM
        NOV 30–DEC 31 TAU

1913   JAN 1 –MAR 25 TAU
        MAR 26–DEC 31 GEM

1914   JAN 1 –AUG 23 GEM
        AUG 24–DEC 6 CAN
        DEC 7 –DEC 31 GEM

1915   JAN 1 –MAY 10 GEM
        MAY 11–DEC 31 CAN

1916   JAN 1 –OCT 16 CAN
        OCT 17–DEC 6 LEO
        DEC 7 –DEC 31 CAN

1917   JAN 1 –JUN 23 CAN
        JUN 24–DEC 31 LEO

1918   LEO

1919   JAN 1 –AUG 11 LEO
        AUG 12–DEC 31 VIR

1920   VIR

1921   JAN 1 –OCT 6 VIR
        OCT 7 –DEC 31 LIB

1922   LIB

1923   JAN 1 –DEC 18 LIB
        DEC 19–DEC 31 SCO

1924   JAN 1 –APR 5 SCO
        APR 6 –SEP 12 LIB
        SEP 13–DEC 31 SCO

1925   SCO

1926   JAN 1 –DEC 1 SCO
        DEC 2 –DEC 31 SAG

1927–1928   SAG

1929   JAN 1 –MAR 14 SAG
        MAR 15–MAY 3 CAP
        MAY 4 –NOV 28 SAG
        NOV 29–DEC 31 CAP

1930–1931   CAP

1932   JAN 1 –FEB 22 CAP
        FEB 23–AUG 12 AQU
        AUG 13–NOV 18 CAP
        NOV 19–DEC 31 AQU

1933–1934   AQU

1935   JAN 1 –FEB 13 AQU
        FEB 14–DEC 31 PIS

1936   PIS

1937   JAN 1 –APR 24 PIS
        APR 25–OCT 16 ARI
        OCT 17–DEC 31 ARI

1938   JAN 1 –JAN 13 ARI
        JAN 14–DEC 31 ARI

1939   JAN 1 –JUL 5 ARI
        JUL 6 –SEP 21 TAU
        SEP 22–DEC 31 ARI

1940   JAN 1 –MAR 19 ARI
        MAR 20–DEC 31 TAU

1941   TAU

1942   JAN 1 –MAY 7 TAU
        MAY 8 –DEC 31 GEM

1943   GEM

1944   JAN 1 –JUN 19 GEM
        JUN 20–DEC 31 CAN

1945   CAN

1946   JAN 1 –AUG 1 CAN
        AUG 2 –DEC 31 LEO

1947   LEO

1948   JAN 1 –SEP 17 LEO
        SEP 18–DEC 31 VIR   Rush – Virgo

1949   JAN 1 –APR 1 VIR
        APR 2 –MAY 28 LEO
        MAY 29–DEC 31 VIR

1950   JAN 1 –NOV 19 VIR
        NOV 20–DEC 31 LIB

1951   JAN 1 –MAR 6 LIB
        MAR 7 –AUG 12 VIR
        AUG 13–DEC 31 LIB

1952   LIB

1953   JAN 1 –OCT 21 LIB
        OCT 22–DEC 31 SCO

1954–1955   SCO

1956   JAN 1 –JAN 11 SCO
        JAN 12–MAY 12 SAG
        MAY 13–OCT 9 SCO
        OCT 10–DEC 31 SAG

1957–1958   SAG

1959   JAN 1 –JAN 4 SAG
        JAN 5 –DEC 31 CAP

1960–1961   CAP

1962   JAN 1 –JAN 2 CAP
        JAN 3 –DEC 31 AQU

1963   AQU

1964   JAN 1 –MAR 22 AQU
        MAR 23–SEP 15 PIS
        SEP 16–DEC 15 AQU
        DEC 16–DEC 31 PIS

1965–1966   PIS

1967   JAN 1 –MAR 2 PIS
        MAR 3 –DEC 31 ARI

1968   ARI

1969   JAN 1 –APR 28 ARI
        APR 29–DEC 31 TAU

1970   TAU

1971   JAN 1 –JUN 17 TAU
        JUN 18–DEC 31 GEM

1972   JAN 1 –JAN 8 GEM
        JAN 9 –FEB 20 TAU
        FEB 21–DEC 31 GEM

1973	JAN 1 –JUL 31 GEM	1995	**PIS**	2018–2019	**CAP**
	AUG 1 –DEC 31 CAN	1996	JAN 1 –APR 6 PIS	2020	JAN 1 –MAR 20 CAP
1974	JAN 1 –JAN 6 CAN		APR 7 –DEC 31 ARI		MAR 21–JUN 30 AQU
	JAN 7 –APR 17 GEM				JUL 1 –DEC 16 CAP
	APR 18–DEC 31 CAN	1997	**ARI**		DEC 17–DEC 31 AQU
1975	JAN 1 –SEP 15 CAN	1998	JAN 1 –JUN 8 ARI	2021–2022	**AQU**
	SEP 16–DEC 31 LEO		JUN 9 –OCT 24 TAU		
1976	JAN 1 –JAN 13 LEO		OCT 25–DEC 31 ARI	2023	JAN 1 –MAR 6 AQU
	JAN 14–JUN 4 CAN				MAR 7 –DEC 31 PIS
	JUN 5 –DEC 31 LEO	1999	JAN 1 –FEB 27 ARI		
			FEB 28–DEC 31 TAU	2024	**PIS**
1977	JAN 1 –NOV 15 LEO				
	NOV 16–DEC 31 VIR	2000	JAN 1 –AUG 8 TAU	2025	JAN 1 –MAY 23 PIS
			AUG 9 –OCT 14 GEM		MAY 24–AUG 31 ARI
1978	JAN 1 –JAN 3 VIR		OCT 15–DEC 31 TAU		SEP 1 –DEC 31 ARI
	JAN 4 –JUL 25 LEO				
	JUL 26–DEC 31 VIR	2001	JAN 1 –APR 19 TAU	2026	JAN 1 –FEB 12 ARI
			APR 20–DEC 31 GEM		FEB 13–DEC 31 ARI
1979	**VIR**	2002	**GEM**	2027	**ARI**
1980	JAN 1 –SEP 20 VIR	2003	JAN 1 –JUN 2 GEM	2028	JAN 1 –APR 11 ARI
	SEP 21–DEC 31 LIB		JUN 3 –DEC 31 CAN		APR 12–DEC 31 TAU
1981	**LIB**	2004	**CAN**	2029	**TAU**
1982	JAN 1 –NOV 28 LIB	2005	JAN 1 –JUL 15 CAN	2030	JAN 1 –MAY 30 TAU
	NOV 29–DEC 31 SCO		JUL 16–DEC 31 LEO		MAY 31–DEC 31 GEM
1983	JAN 1 –MAY 5 SCO	2006	**LEO**	2031	**GEM**
	MAY 6 –AUG 23 LIB				
	AUG 24–DEC 31 SCO	2007	JAN 1 –SEP 1 LEO	2032	JAN 1 –JUL 12 GEM
			SEP 2 –DEC 31 VIR		JUL 13–DEC 31 CAN
1984	**SCO**				
		2008	**VIR**	2033	**CAN**
1985	JAN 1 –NOV 15 SCO				
	NOV 16–DEC 31 SAG	2009	JAN 1 –OCT 28 VIR	2034	JAN 1 –AUG 25 CAN
			OCT 29–DEC 31 LIB		AUG 26–DEC 31 LEO
1986–1987	**SAG**				
		2010	JAN 1 –APR 6 LIB	2035	JAN 1 –FEB 14 LEO
1988	JAN 1 –FEB 12 SAG		APR 7 –JUL 20 VIR		FEB 15–MAY 10 CAN
	FEB 13–JUN 9 CAP		JUL 21–DEC 31 LIB		MAY 11–DEC 31 LEO
	JUN 10–NOV 11 SAG				
	NOV 12–DEC 31 CAP	2011	**LIB**	2036	JAN 1 –OCT 15 LEO
					OCT 16–DEC 31 VIR
1989–1990	**CAP**	2012	JAN 1 –OCT 4 LIB		
			OCT 5 –DEC 31 SCO	2037	JAN 1 –FEB 10 VIR
1991	JAN 1 –FEB 5 CAP				FEB 11–JUL 5 LEO
	FEB 6 –DEC 31 AQU	2013	**SCO**		JUL 6 –DEC 31 VIR
1992	**AQU**	2014	JAN 1 –DEC 22 SCO	2038	**VIR**
			DEC 23–DEC 31 SAG		
1993	JAN 1 –MAY 19 AQU			2039	JAN 1 –SEP 4 VIR
	MAY 20–JUN 29 PIS	2015	JAN 1 –JUN 13 SAG		SEP 5 –DEC 31 LIB
	JUN 30–DEC 31 AQU		JUN 14–SEP 16 SCO		
			SEP 17–DEC 31 SAG	2040	**LIB**
1994	JAN 1 –JAN 27 AQU				
	JAN 28–DEC 31 PIS	2016	**SAG**	2041	JAN 1 –NOV 10 LIB
					NOV 11–DEC 31 SCO
		2017	JAN 1 –DEC 18 SAG		
			DEC 19–DEC 31 CAP		

2042	JAN 1 –JUN 20 SCO JUN 21–JUL 13 LIB JUL 14–DEC 31 SCO	**2063**	**CAN**	**2088**	**TAU**
2043	**SCO**	**2064**	JAN 1 –JUN 27 CAN JUN 28–DEC 31 LEO	**2089**	JAN 1 –MAY 14 TAU MAY 15–DEC 31 GEM
2044	JAN 1 –FEB 20 SCO FEB 21–MAR 24 SAG MAR 25–OCT 30 SCO OCT 31–DEC 31 SAG	**2065**	**LEO**	**2090**	**GEM**
		2066	JAN 1 –AUG 15 LEO AUG 16–DEC 31 VIR	**2091**	JAN 1 –JUN 26 GEM JUN 27–DEC 31 CAN
2045–2046	**SAG**	**2067**	**VIR**	**2092**	**CAN**
2047	JAN 1 –JAN 23 SAG JAN 24–JUL 9 CAP JUL 10–OCT 21 SAG OCT 22–DEC 31 CAP	**2068**	JAN 1 –OCT 9 VIR OCT 10–DEC 31 LIB	**2093**	JAN 1 –AUG 7 CAN AUG 8 –DEC 31 LEO
		2069	**LIB**	**2094**	**LEO**
2048–2049	**CAP**	**2070**	JAN 1 –DEC 24 LIB DEC 25–DEC 31 SCO	**2095**	JAN 1 –SEP 25 LEO SEP 26–DEC 31 VIR
2050	JAN 1 –JAN 20 CAP JAN 21–DEC 31 AQU	**2071**	JAN 1 –MAR 26 SCO MAR 27–SEP 17 LIB SEP 18–DEC 31 SCO	**2096**	JAN 1 –MAR 13 VIR MAR 14–JUN 11 LEO JUN 12–DEC 31 VIR
2051	**AQU**	**2072**	**SCO**	**2097**	JAN 1 –NOV 27 VIR NOV 28–DEC 31 LIB
2052	JAN 1 –APR 15 AQU APR 16–AUG 7 PIS AUG 8 –DEC 31 AQU	**2073**	JAN 1 –DEC 4 SCO DEC 5 –DEC 31 SAG	**2098**	JAN 1 –FEB 20 LIB FEB 21–AUG 17 VIR AUG 18–DEC 31 LIB
2053	JAN 1 –JAN 9 AQU JAN 10–DEC 31 PIS	**2074–2075**	**SAG**	**2099**	**LIB**
2054	**PIS**	**2076**	JAN 1 –DEC 2 SAG DEC 3 –DEC 31 CAP	**2100**	JAN 1 –OCT 25 LIB OCT 26–DEC 31 SCO
2055	JAN 1 –MAR 21 PIS MAR 22–DEC 31 ARI	**2077–2078**	**CAP**	**2101**	**SCO**
2056	**ARI**	**2079**	JAN 1 –FEB 27 CAP FEB 28–AUG 1 AQU AUG 2 –NOV 26 CAP NOV 27–DEC 31 AQU		
2057	JAN 1 –MAY 19 ARI MAY 20–NOV 28 TAU NOV 29–DEC 31 ARI	**2080–2081**	**AQU**		
2058	JAN 1 –JAN 30 ARI JAN 31–DEC 31 TAU	**2082**	JAN 1 –FEB 17 AQU FEB 18–DEC 31 PIS		
2059	JAN 1 –JUL 11 TAU JUL 12–NOV 20 GEM NOV 21–DEC 31 TAU	**2083**	**PIS**		
2060	JAN 1 –MAR 30 TAU MAR 31–DEC 31 GEM	**2084**	JAN 1 –APR 30 PIS MAY 1 –OCT 1 ARI OCT 2 –DEC 31 PIS		
2061	JAN 1 –AUG 31 GEM SEP 1 –NOV 23 CAN NOV 24–DEC 31 GEM	**2085**	JAN 1 –JAN 22 PIS JAN 23–DEC 31 ARI		
2062	JAN 1 –MAY 15 GEM MAY 16–DEC 31 CAN	**2086**	JAN 1 –JUL 26 ARI JUL 27–AUG 24 TAU AUG 25–DEC 31 ARI		
		2087	JAN 1 –MAR 27 ARI MAR 28–DEC 31 TAU		

1954 Was in CANCER

Where Is Your Uranus? — *LEO*

THE FOLLOWING URANUS TABLE will tell you what sign Uranus was in on the day of your birth.* To use this table simply locate the year of your birth. You will see at a glance exactly what signs Uranus was in during that year. Because Uranus moves so slowly through the zodiac, the planet may spend a number of years in one sign. For example, Uranus was in Capricorn all during the years 1905 through 1911.

*The computer chart you get using the enclosed CD-ROM will not only tell you the sign your Uranus is in, but the exact degree of this sign.

1900–1903 **SAG**	**1968** JAN 1 –SEP 27 VIR
	        SEP 28–DEC 31 LIB
		2033 JAN 1 –MAY 21 GEM
		        MAY 22–DEC 31 CAN

1900–1903   **SAG**

1904   JAN 1 –DEC 19 SAG
        DEC 20–DEC 31 CAP

1905–1911   **CAP**

1912   JAN 1 –JAN 29 CAP
        JAN 30–SEP 3 AQU
        SEP 4 –NOV 11 CAP
        NOV 12–DEC 31 AQU

1913–1918   **AQU**

1919   JAN 1 –MAR 30 AQU
        MAR 31–AUG 15 PIS
        AUG 16–DEC 31 AQU

1920   JAN 1 –JAN 21 AQU
        JAN 22–DEC 31 PIS

1921–1926   **PIS**

1927   JAN 1 –MAR 30 PIS
        MAR 31–NOV 3 ARI
        NOV 4 –DEC 31 PIS

1928   JAN 1 –JAN 12 PIS
        JAN 13–DEC 31 ARI

1929–1933   **ARI**

1934   JAN 1 –JUN 5 ARI
        JUN 6 –OCT 8 TAU
        OCT 9 –DEC 31 ARI

1935   JAN 1 –MAR 26 ARI
        MAR 27–DEC 31 TAU

1936–1940   **TAU**

1941   JAN 1 –AUG 6 TAU
        AUG 7 –OCT 3 GEM
        OCT 4 –DEC 31 TAU

1942   JAN 1 –MAY 13 TAU
        MAY 14–DEC 31 GEM

1943–1947   **GEM**

1948   JAN 1 –AUG 29 GEM
        AUG 30–NOV 11 CAN
        NOV 12–DEC 31 GEM

1949   JAN 1 –JUN 8 GEM
        JUN 9 –DEC 31 CAN

1950–1954   **CAN**

1955   JAN 1 –AUG 23 CAN
        AUG 24–DEC 31 LEO

1956   JAN 1 –JAN 26 LEO
        JAN 27–JUN 8 CAN
        JUN 9 –DEC 31 LEO

1957–1960   **LEO**

1961   JAN 1 –OCT 31 LEO
        NOV 1 –DEC 31 VIR

1962   JAN 1 –JAN 9 VIR
        JAN 10–AUG 8 LEO
        AUG 9 –DEC 31 VIR

1963–1967   **VIR**

1968   JAN 1 –SEP 27 VIR
        SEP 28–DEC 31 LIB

1969   JAN 1 –MAY 19 LIB
        MAY 20–JUN 23 VIR
        JUN 24–DEC 31 LIB

1970–1973   **LIB**

1974   JAN 1 –NOV 20 LIB
        NOV 21–DEC 31 SCO

1975   JAN 1 –APR 30 SCO
        MAY 1 –SEP 7 LIB
        SEP 8 –DEC 31 SCO

1976–1980   **SCO**

1981   JAN 1 –FEB 16 SCO
        FEB 17–MAR 19 SAG
        MAR 20–NOV 15 SCO
        NOV 16–DEC 31 SAG

1982–1987   **SAG**

1988   JAN 1 –FEB 13 SAG
        FEB 14–MAY 25 CAP
        MAY 26–DEC 1 SAG
        DEC 2 –DEC 31 CAP

1989–1994   **CAP**

1995   JAN 1 –MAR 31 CAP
        APR 1 –JUN 7 AQU
        JUN 8 –DEC 31 CAP

1996   JAN 1 –JAN 11 CAP
        JAN 12–DEC 31 AQU

1997–2002   **AQU**

2003   JAN 1 –MAR 9 AQU
        MAR 10–SEP 13 PIS
        SEP 14–DEC 29 AQU
        DEC 30–DEC 31 PIS

2004–2009   **PIS**

2010   JAN 1 –MAY 26 PIS
        MAY 27–AUG 12 ARI
        AUG 13–DEC 31 ARI

2011   JAN 1 –MAR 10 ARI
        MAR 11–DEC 31 ARI

2012–2017   **ARI**

2018   JAN 1 –MAY 14 ARI
        MAY 15–NOV 5 TAU
        NOV 6 –DEC 31 ARI

2019   JAN 1 –MAR 5 ARI
        MAR 6 –DEC 31 TAU

2020–2024   **TAU**

2025   JAN 1 –JUL 6 TAU
        JUL 7 –NOV 6 GEM
        NOV 7 –DEC 31 TAU

2026   JAN 1 –APR 24 TAU
        APR 25–DEC 31 GEM

2027–2031   **GEM**

2032   JAN 1 –AUG 2 GEM
        AUG 3 –DEC 11 CAN
        DEC 12–DEC 31 GEM

2033   JAN 1 –MAY 21 GEM
        MAY 22–DEC 31 CAN

2034–2038   **CAN**

2039   JAN 1 –AUG 5 CAN
        AUG 6 –DEC 31 LEO

2040   JAN 1 –FEB 24 LEO
        FEB 25–MAY 14 CAN
        MAY 15–DEC 31 LEO

2041–2044   **LEO**

2045   JAN 1 –OCT 5 LEO
        OCT 6 –DEC 31 VIR

2046   JAN 1 –FEB 7 VIR
        FEB 8 –JUL 21 LEO
        JUL 22–DEC 31 VIR

2047–2050   **VIR**

2051   JAN 1 –DEC 7 VIR
        DEC 8 –DEC 31 LIB

2052   JAN 1 –JAN 30 LIB
        JAN 31–SEP 10 VIR
        SEP 11–DEC 31 LIB

2053–2057   **LIB**

2058   JAN 1 –NOV 2 LIB
        NOV 3 –DEC 31 SCO

2059   JAN 1 –MAY 31 SCO
        JUN 1 –AUG 10 LIB
        AUG 11–DEC 31 SCO

2060–2064   **SCO**

2065   JAN 1 –JAN 9 SCO
        JAN 10–APR 30 SAG
        MAY 1 –OCT 27 SCO
        OCT 28–DEC 31 SAG

2066–2071   **SAG**

2072   JAN 1 –JAN 21 SAG
        JAN 22–JUN 24 CAP
        JUN 25–NOV 10 SAG
        NOV 11–DEC 31 CAP

2073–2078   **CAP**

2079   JAN 1 –MAR 1 CAP
        MAR 2 –JUL 12 AQU
        JUL 13–DEC 22 CAP
        DEC 23–DEC 31 AQU

2080–2086   **AQU**

2087   JAN 1 –FEB 17 AQU
        FEB 18–DEC 31 PIS

2088–2093   **PIS**

2094   JAN 1 –APR 27 PIS
        APR 28–SEP 15 ARI
        SEP 16–DEC 31 ARI

2095   JAN 1 –FEB 17 ARI
        FEB 18–DEC 31 ARI

2096–2101   **ARI**

♆ –

Where Is Your Neptune? Te-Libra

THE FOLLOWING NEPTUNE TABLE will tell you what sign Neptune was in on the day of your birth.* You will notice that Neptune often spends many years in one sign. This is because the planet moves so slowly through the zodiac. Neptune also has long periods of retrograde motion.

1900	**GEM**	
1901	JAN 1 –JUL 18 GEM	
	JUL 19–DEC 24 CAN	
	DEC 25–DEC 31 GEM	
1902	JAN 1 –MAY 20 GEM	
	MAY 21–DEC 31 CAN	
1903–1913	**CAN**	
1914	JAN 1 –SEP 22 CAN	
	SEP 23–DEC 13 LEO	
	DEC 14–DEC 31 CAN	
1915	JAN 1 –JUL 18 CAN	
	JUL 19–DEC 31 LEO	
1916	JAN 1 –MAR 18 LEO	
	MAR 19–MAY 1 CAN	
	MAY 2 –DEC 31 LEO	
1917–1927	**LEO**	
1928	JAN 1 –SEP 20 LEO	
	SEP 21–DEC 31 VIR	
1929	JAN 1 –FEB 18 VIR	
	FEB 19–JUL 23 LEO	
	JUL 24–DEC 31 VIR	
1930–1941	**VIR**	
1942	JAN 1 –OCT 2 VIR	
	OCT 3 –DEC 31 LIB	
1943	JAN 1 –APR 16 LIB	
	APR 17–AUG 1 VIR	
	AUG 2 –DEC 31 LIB	
1944–1954	**LIB**	
1955	JAN 1 –DEC 23 LIB	
	DEC 24–DEC 31 SCO	
1956	JAN 1 –MAR 10 SCO	
	MAR 11–OCT 18 LIB	
	OCT 19–DEC 31 SCO	

1957	JAN 1 –JUN 14 SCO	
	JUN 15–AUG 5 LIB	
	AUG 6 –DEC 31 SCO	
1958–1969	**SCO**	
1970	JAN 1 –JAN 3 SCO	
	JAN 4 –MAY 1 SAG	
	MAY 2 –NOV 5 SCO	
	NOV 6 –DEC 31 SAG	
1971–1983	**SAG**	
1984	JAN 1 –JAN 17 SAG	
	JAN 18–JUN 21 CAP	
	JUN 22–NOV 20 SAG	
	NOV 21–DEC 31 CAP	
1985–1997	**CAP**	
1998	JAN 1 –JAN 27 CAP	
	JAN 28–AUG 21 AQU	
	AUG 22–NOV 26 CAP	
	NOV 27–DEC 31 AQU	
1999–2010	**AQU**	
2011	JAN 1 –APR 3 AQU	
	APR 4 –AUG 3 PIS	
	AUG 4 –DEC 31 AQU	
2012	JAN 1 –FEB 2 AQU	
	FEB 3 –DEC 31 PIS	
2013–2024	**PIS**	
2025	JAN 1 –MAR 29 PIS	
	MAR 30–OCT 21 ARI	
	OCT 22–DEC 31 ARI	
2026	JAN 1 –JAN 25 ARI	
	JAN 26–DEC 31 ARI	
2027–2037	**ARI**	

2038	JAN 1 –MAY 20 ARI	
	MAY 21–OCT 20 TAU	
	OCT 21–DEC 31 ARI	
2039	JAN 1 –MAR 22 ARI	
	MAR 23–DEC 31 TAU	
2040–2050	**TAU**	
2051	JAN 1 –JUL 15 TAU	
	JUL 16–OCT 21 GEM	
	OCT 22–DEC 31 TAU	
2052	JAN 1 –MAY 11 TAU	
	MAY 12–DEC 31 GEM	
2053–2064	**GEM**	
2065	JAN 1 –JUL 2 GEM	
	JUL 3 –DEC 31 CAN	
2066	JAN 1 –JAN 13 CAN	
	JAN 14–APR 30 GEM	
	MAY 1 –DEC 31 CAN	
2067–2077	**CAN**	
2078	JAN 1 –AUG 31 CAN	
	SEP 1 –DEC 31 LEO	
2079	JAN 1 –JAN 5 LEO	
	JAN 6 –JUL 2 CAN	
	JUL 3 –DEC 31 LEO	
2080–2091	**LEO**	
2092	JAN 1 –SEP 3 LEO	
	SEP 4 –DEC 31 VIR	
2093	JAN 1 –MAR 10 VIR	
	MAR 11–JUL 4 LEO	
2093	JUL 5 –DEC 31 VIR	
2094–2101	**VIR**	

*The computer chart you get using the enclosed CD-ROM will not only tell you the sign your Neptune is in, but the exact degree of this sign.

♇

Where Is Your Pluto?

THE FOLLOWING PLUTO TABLE will tell you what sign Pluto was in on the day of your birth.* You will notice that Pluto spends a great many years in each sign.

1900–1911		**GEM**	
1912	JAN 1 –SEP 9	GEM	
	SEP 10–OCT 19	CAN	
	OCT 20–DEC 31	GEM	
1913	JAN 1 –JUL 8	GEM	
	JUL 9 –DEC 26	CAN	
	DEC 27–DEC 31	GEM	
1914	JAN 1 –MAY 25	GEM	
	MAY 26–DEC 31	CAN	
1915–1936		**CAN**	
1937	JAN 1 –OCT 6	CAN	
	OCT 7 –NOV 24	LEO	
	NOV 25–DEC 31	CAN	
1938	JAN 1 –AUG 2	CAN	
	AUG 3 –DEC 31	LEO	
1939	JAN 1 –FEB 6	LEO	
	FEB 7 –JUN 12	CAN	
	JUN 13–DEC 31	LEO	
1940–1955		**LEO**	
1956	JAN 1 –OCT 19	LEO	
	OCT 20–DEC 31	VIR	
1957	JAN 1 –JAN 13	VIR	
	JAN 14–AUG 17	LEO	
	AUG 18–DEC 31	VIR	
1958	JAN 1 –APR 10	VIR	
	APR 11–JUN 9	LEO	
	JUN 10–DEC 31	VIR	
1959–1970		**VIR**	

1971	JAN 1 –OCT 4	VIR	
	OCT 5 –DEC 31	LIB	
1972	JAN 1 –APR 16	LIB	
	APR 17–JUL 29	VIR	
	JUL 30–DEC 31	LIB	
1973–1982		**LIB**	
1983	JAN 1 –NOV 4	LIB	
	NOV 5 –DEC 31	SCO	
1984	JAN 1 –MAY 17	SCO	
	MAY 18–AUG 27	LIB	
	AUG 28–DEC 31	SCO	
1985–1994		**SCO**	
1995	JAN 1 –JAN 16	SCO	
	JAN 17–APR 19	SAG	
	APR 20–NOV 9	SCO	
	NOV 10–DEC 31	SAG	
1996–2007		**SAG**	
2008	JAN 1 –JAN 24	SAG	
	JAN 25–JUN 12	CAP	
	JUN 13–NOV 25	SAG	
	NOV 26–DEC 31	CAP	
2009–2022		**CAP**	
2023	JAN 1 –MAR 22	CAP	
	MAR 23–JUN 9	AQU	
	JUN 10–DEC 31	CAP	
2024	JAN 1 –JAN 19	CAP	
	JAN 20–AUG 31	AQU	
	SEP 1 –NOV 18	CAP	
	NOV 19–DEC 31	AQU	

2025–2042		**AQU**	
2043	JAN 1 –MAR 7	AQU	
	MAR 8 –AUG 30	PIS	
	AUG 31–DEC 31	AQU	
2044	JAN 1 –JAN 18	AQU	
	JAN 19–DEC 31	PIS	
2045–2065		**PIS**	
2066	JAN 1 –JUN 17	PIS	
	JUN 18–JUL 9	ARI	
	JUL 10–DEC 31	PIS	
2067	JAN 1 –APR 7	PIS	
	APR 8 –SEP 26	ARI	
	SEP 27–DEC 31	PIS	
2068	JAN 1 –FEB 22	PIS	
	FEB 23–DEC 31	ARI	
2069–2094		**ARI**	
2095	JAN 1 –JUN 8	ARI	
	JUN 9 –SEP 19	TAU	
	SEP 20–DEC 31	ARI	
2096	JAN 1 –APR 22	ARI	
	APR 23–NOV 13	TAU	
	NOV 14–DEC 31	ARI	
2097	JAN 1 –MAR 9	ARI	
	MAR 10–DEC 31	TAU	
2098–2101		**TAU**	

*The computer chart you get using the enclosed CD-ROM will not only tell you the sign your Pluto is in, but the exact degree of this sign.

BIBLIOGRAPHY

Abadie, M. J., and Bader, Claudia. *Love Planets.* New York: Fireside, 1990.

Adams, Evangeline. *Astrology: Your Place Among the Stars.* New York: Dodd, Mead & Co., 1930.

———. *The Bowl of Heaven.* New York: Dodd, Mead & Co., 1930.

Alexander, Skye. *Planets in Signs.* Atglen, PA: Whitford Press, 1988.

Arnott, Nancy. *The Hidden Meaning of Birthdays.* Kansas City: Ariel Books, 1996.

Astarte. *Astrology Made Easy.* North Hollywood, CA: Wilshire Book Company, 1969.

Avery, Jeanne. *The Rising Sign.* Garden City, NY: Doubleday and Company, 1982.

Bailey, Alice. *Esoteric Astrology: A Treatise on the Seven Rays.* New York: Lucis Publishing Company, 1951.

Banzhaf, Hajo, and Haebler, Anna. *Key Words for Astrology.* York Beach, ME: Samuel Weiser, 1996.

Benjamine, Elbert. *Beginner's Horoscope: Maker and Reader.* Los Angeles: Church of Light, 1972.

Bennett, Judith. *Sex Signs.* New York: St. Martin's Press, 1980.

Brau, Jean-Louis, Weaver, Helen, and Edmands, Allan. *Larousse Encyclopedia of Astrology.* New York: McGraw-Hill Book Company, 1980.

Brenner, Charles. *An Elementary Textbook of Psychoanalysis.* New York: International Universities Press, 1955.

Bulfinch, Thomas. *Bulfinch's Mythology.* New York: Grosset and Dunlap. First edition 1913.

Burt, Kathleen. *Archetypes of the Zodiac.* St. Paul, MN: Llewellyn Publications, 1996.

Camilleri, Stephanie. *The House Book.* St. Paul, MN: Llewellyn Publications, 1999.

Cavendish, Richard, ed. *Encyclopedia of the Unexplained.* New York: McGraw-Hill Book Company, 1974.

Columbia Encyclopedia. New York: Columbia University Press.

Cooper, Michael, and Weaver, Andrew. *An Astrological Index to the World's Famous People.* Garden City, NY: Doubleday and Company, 1975.

Cornell, H. L. *Encyclopedia of Medical Astrology.* New York: Samuel Weiser, 1972.

Crawford, Saffi, and Sullivan, Geraldine. *The Power of Birthdays, Stars, & Numbers.* New York: Ballantine Books, 1998.

Crowmarsh, Preston. *First Steps to Astrology.* New York: Samuel Weiser, 1971.

Crummere, Maria Elise. *Sun-Sign Revelations.* New York: Viking Press, 1974.

Cumont, Franz. *Astrology and Religion Among the Greeks and Romans.* New York: Dover, 1960.

Cunningham, Donna. *An Astrological Guide To Self-Awareness.* Reno, NV: CRCS Publications, 1978.

Davison, Ronald C. *Astrology.* New York: Arco Publishing Company, 1963.

De Vore, Nicholas. *Encyclopedia of Astrology.* New York: Philosophical Library, 1947.

Evers, Joan, ed. *Planets: The Astrological Tools.* St. Paul, MN: Llewellyn Publications, 1989.

Flammarion, Camille. *The Flammarion Book of Astronomy.* New York: Simon and Schuster, 1964.

Frazer, Sir James George. Edited by Theodor H. Gaster. *The New Golden Bough.* New York: Criterion Books, 1959.

Gauquelin, Michel. *The Cosmic Clocks: From Astrology to a Modern Science.* Chicago: Henry Regnery Company, 1967.

Gettings, Fred. *The Hand and the Horoscope.* London: Triune Books, 1973.

Gleadow, Rupert. *The Origin of the Zodiac.* New York: Atheneum, 1969.

Golder, Carole. *The Seductive Art of Astrology.* New York: Henry Holt and Company, 1988.

———. *Moon Signs for Lovers.* New York: Henry Holt and Company, 1992.

Goldschneider, Gary, and Elffers, Joost. *The Secret Language of Birthdays.* New York: Penguin Studio Books, 1994.

———. *The Secret Language of Relationships.* New York: Penguin Studio Books, 1997.

Goodavage, Joseph F. *Write Your Own Horoscope.* New York: New American Library, 1968.

Goodman, Linda. *Linda Goodman's Sun Signs.* New York: Taplinger Publishing Company, 1968.

———. *Linda Goodman's Relationship Signs.* New York: Bantam Books, 1998.

Grant, Michael, and Hazel, John. *Gods and Mortals in Classical Mythology.* Springfield, MA: G. & C. Merriam Company, 1973.

Graves, Robert. *The Greek Myths.* Baltimore: Penguin Books, 1955.

Gray, Eden. *Mastering the Tarot.* New York: Crown Publishers, 1971.

Grebner, Bernice Prill. *Decanates: A Full View.* Tempe, AZ: American Federation of Astrologers, 1980.

Green, Landis Knight. *The Astrologer's Manual.* New York: Arco Publishing Company, 1975.

Greene, Liz. *Star Signs for Lovers.* New York: Stein and Day Publishers, 1980.

———. *The Astrology of Fate.* York Beach, ME: Samuel Weiser, 1984.

Hall, Manly Palmer. *Astrological Keywords.* Los Angeles, CA: Philosophical Research Society, 1958.

———. *The Story of Astrology.* New York: Philosophical Library, 1959.

Harris, Janet. *Astrology for Everyday Living.* North Hollywood, CA: Wilshire Book Company, 1974.

Harvey, Charles & Suzi. *Sun Sign, Moon Sign.* London, England: Thorsons, 1994.

The Holy Bible. King James Version.

Howard, Neale E. *The Telescope Handbook and Star Atlas.* New York: Thomas Y. Crowell Company, 1975.

Ions, Veronica. *Egyptian Mythology.* Middlesex, England: Hamlyn Publishing Group, 1968.

Jayne, Charles. *A New Dimension in Astrology.* Monroe, NY: Astrological Bureau, 1975.

Jones, Marc Edmund. *The Guide to Horoscope Interpretation.* Stanwood, WA: Sabian Publishing Society, 1967.

———. *How to Learn Astrology.* Boulder, CO: Shambhala Publications, 1977.

Jung, C. G. Edited by Violet S. de Laszlo. *Psyche and Symbol.* Garden City, NY: Doubleday and Company, 1958.

Jung, C. G. *Synchronicity: An Acausal Connecting Principle.* New York: Pantheon Books, 1955.

Kaye, Doris. *Your Astrological Guide to Nutrition.* New York: Award Books, 1970.

Keehn, Amy. *Love and War Between the Signs.* Rocklin, CA: Prima Publishing, 1997.

Kramer, Gerard Peter, and Middlehurst, Barbara M. *Telescopes.* Chicago: University of Chicago Press, 1960.

Lamb, Terry. *Born to Be Together.* Carlsbad, CA: Hay House, 1998.

Leach, Judith. *How to Interpret Your Horoscope.* New York: Harper and Row, 1978.

Lee, Dal. *Dictionary of Astrology.* New York: Warner Books, 1968.

Lee, Fleming. *Your Hidden Horoscope.* North Hollywood, CA: Brandon Books, 1971.

Leek, Sybil. *My Life in Astrology.* Englewood, NJ: Prentice-Hall, 1972.

———. *Moon Signs: Lunar Astrology.* New York: Berkley Publishing Corporation, 1977.

Lehner, Ernst and Johanna. *Lore and Lure of Outer Space: Astrology and the Planetary World.* New York: Tudor Publishing Company, 1964.

Leo, Alan. Edited by Vivan E. Robson. *The Complete Dictionary of Astrology.* New York: Astrologer's Library, 1978.

Levine, Joyce. *Breakthrough Astrology.* York Beach, ME: Weiser Books, 2006.

Lewi, Grant. *Heaven Knows What.* St. Paul, MN: Llewellyn Publications, 1978. (1st ed. 1935).

———. *Astrology for the Millions.* St. Paul, MN: Llewellyn Publications, 1979. (1st ed. 1940).

Lewis, James, R. *The Astrology Encyclopedia.* Detroit: Visible Ink Press, 1994.

Lexander, Ren, and Rose, Geraldine. *Seduction By the Stars.* New York: Bantam Books, 1995.

Lindsay, Jack. *Origins of Astrology.* New York: Barnes and Noble, 1971.

Lofthus, Myrna. *A Spiritual Approach to Astrology.* Sebastopol, CA: CRCS Publications, 1983.

Lundsted, Betty. *Astrological Insights into Personality.* San Diego, CA: ACS Publications, 1980.

Lutin, Michael. *SunShine, The Astrology of Being Happy.* New York: Fireside, 2007.

MacNaughton, Robin. *Robin MacNaughton's Sun Sign Personality Guide.* New York: Bantam Books, 1978.

———. *Robin MacNaughton's Moon Sign Personality Guide.* New York: Bantam Books, 1979.

———. *How to Transform Your Life Through Astrology.* New York: Bantam Books, 1983.

———. *Power Astrology.* New York: Pocket Books, 1990.

———. *Goddess Power.* New York: Pocket Books, 1996.

———. *Why Does He Say One Thing and Do Another?* New York: Pocket Books, 1997.

———. *Smart Signs, Foolish Choices.* New York: Citadel Press, 2004

McIntosh, Christopher. *The Astrologers and Their Creed: An Historical Outline.* New York: Frederick A. Praeger, 1969.

———. *Astrology, the Stars and Human Life: A Modern Guide.* New York: Harper and Row, 1970.

Menzel, D. H. *Astronomy.* New York: Random House, 1970.

Meyer, Michael R. *A Handbook for the Humanistic Astrologer.* Garden City, NY: Doubleday and Company, 1974.

Miles, David. *Sex and Astrology.* New York: Paperback Library, 1970.

Moore, Marcia, and Douglas, Mark. *Astrology, the Divine Science.* York Harbor, ME: Arcane Publications, 1971.

Munkasey, Michael. *The Astrological Thesaurus.* St. Paul, MN: Llewellyn Publications, 1993.

Murchie, Guy. *The Music of the Spheres*. Boston: Houghton Mifflin Company, 1961.

Neely, Henry M. *A Primer for Star-Gazers*. New York: Harper and Row, 1970.

Nicholson, Iain. *The Road to the Stars*. New York: William Morrow and Company, 1978.

Norvell, Anthony. *Astrology: Romance, You and the Stars*. North Hollywood, CA: Wilshire Book Company, 1970.

_____ . *Astrology: Your Wheel of Fortune*. New York: Barnes and Noble, 1974.

Oken, Alan. *Alan Oken's Complete Astrology*. New York: Bantam Books, 1980.

Omarr, Sydney. *My World of Astrology*. North Hollywood, CA: Wilshire Book Company, 1965.

———. *Soul-Centered Astrology*. New York: Bantam Books, 1990.

———. *Sydney Omarr's Astrological Guide to Sex and Love*. New York: New American Library, 1970.

———. *Sydney Omarr's Astrological Revelations About You*. New York: New American Library, 1973.

Orr, Marjorie. *Lovers' Guide*. London, England: Aquarian Press, 1994.

Ottewell, Guy. *Astronomical Calendar*. Greenville, SC: Furman University in cooperation with the Astronomical League.

Palmer, Lynne. *Prosperity Signs*. New York: Dell Publishing Company, 1981.

———. *Signs for Success*. New York: Dell Publishing Company, 1982.

Parker, Derek and Julia. *The Compleat Astrologer*. New York: McGraw-Hill Book Company, 1971.

———. *The Compleat Astrologer's Love Signs*. New York: Grosset and Dunlap, 1974.

———. *Parkers' Astrology*. New York: DK Publishing, 1991.

Polansky, Joseph. *Sun Sign Success*. New York: Warner Books, 1977.

Prabhavananda, Swami. *The Spiritual Heritage of India*. London: George Allen & Unwin, 1962.

Prete, Robert J., and Gallo, Angela Louise. *Celebrity Horoscopes*. North Hollywood, CA: Rising Sign Publishing Company, 1975.

Ptolemy, Claudius. Edited and translated by F. E. Robbins. *Tetrabiblos*. London: William Heinemann, 1964.

Quigley, Joan. *Astrology for Adults*. New York: Holt, Rinehart and Winston, 1969.

Robson, Vivian E. *The Fixed Stars and Constellations in Astrology*. New York: Samuel Weiser, 1969.

———. *A Beginner's Guide to Practical Astrology*. New York: Samuel Weiser, 1976. (1st ed. 1930).

Rudaux, Lucien, and de Vaucouleurs, G. *Larousse Encyclopedia of Astronomy*. New York: Prometheus Press, 1967.

Rudhyar, Dane. *The Practice of Astrology*. Baltimore: Penguin Books, 1968.

———. *The Astrology of Personality*. Garden City, NY: Doubleday and Company, 1970. (1st ed. 1936).

———. *The Astrological Houses*. Sebastopol, CA: CRCS Publications, 1972.

———. *Astrology and the Modern Psyche*. Vancouver, WA: CRCS Publications, 1976.

Ryder, Beatrice. *Astrology: Your Personal Sun Sign Guide*. New York: Fleet Publishing Company, 1969.

Sagan, Carl. *Cosmos*. New York: Random House. 1980.

Sakoian, Frances, and Acker, Louis. *The Astrologer's Handbook*. New York: Harper and Row, 1973.

Schulman, Martin. *Karmic Astrology*. York Beach, ME: Samuel Weiser, 1978.

Scott, Oral, E. *The Stars in Myth and Fact*. Caldwell, ID: Caxton Printers, 1942.

Sepharial. *New Dictionary of Astrology*. New York: Arco Publishing Company, 1964.

Smith, Debbi Kempton. *Secrets from a Stargazer's Notebook*. New York: Bantam Books, 1982.

Stearn, Jess. *A Time for Astrology.* New York: Coward, McCann and Geoghegan. 1971.

Stellas, Constance. *Advanced Astrology for Life.* Avon, MA: Provenance Press, 2005.

Sun, Ruth Q. *The Asian Animal Zodiac.* Rutland, VT, and Tokyo: Charles E. Tuttle Company, 1974.

Velikovsky, Immanuel. *Worlds in Collision.* New York: Macmillan Company, 1950.

Vorel, Irys. *Be Your Own Astrologer.* Hackensack, NJ: Wehman Brothers, 1967.

West, John Anthony, and Toonder, Jan Gerhard. *The Case for Astrology.* New York: Coward, McCann and Geoghegan, 1970.

White, Suzanne. *Suzanne White's Book of Chinese Chance.* New York: M. Evans Company, 1976.

———. *The New Astrology.* New York: St. Martin's Press, 1986.

Wulff, Wilhelm Theodor H. *Zodiac and Swastika: How Astrology Guided Hitler's Germany.* New York: Coward, McCann and Geoghegan, 1973.

Zain, C. C. *Astrological Signatures.* Los Angeles: Church of Light, 1972. (1st ed. 1925).

Zolar. *It's All in the Stars.* New York: Fleet Publishing Company, 1962.

———. *The History of Astrology.* New York: Arco Publishing Company, 1972.

RECOMMENDED READING LIST FOR CHART CASTING AND INTERPRETATION

Astrology Made Easy by Astarte. Wilshire Book Company.
Contains chart analyses of twelve well-known figures in history. Also has instructions for chart casting.

Larousse Encyclopedia of Astrology by Jean-Louis Brau, Helen Weaver, and Allan Edmands. McGraw-Hall Book Company.
Excellent reference book.

Astrology by Ronald C. Davison. Arco Publishing Company.
A short, concise, basic textbook.

How to Learn Astrology by Marc Edmund Jones. Shambhala Publications. Distributed by Random House.
First published in 1921, still an excellent introduction to charts for beginning students.

Heaven Knows What by Grant Lewi. Llewellyn Publications.
A classic work on chart interpretation.

Key Words for Astrology by Hajo Banzhof & Anna Haebler. Samuel Weiser, Inc.
An indispensable compendium that gives descriptions and interpretations for every Sign, Planet, House, and Aspect.

The Compleat Astrologer by Derek and Julia Parker. McGraw-Hill Book Company (hardcover); Bantam Books (paperback).
A modern look at chart interpretation. Good planetary tables.

A Beginner's Guide to Practical Astrology by Vivian E. Robson. Samuel Weiser, Publishers.
A classic textbook on the mathematics of constructing a horoscope. First published in 1930.

Be Your Own Astrologer by Irys Vorel. Wehman Brothers.
Concise rundown of signs, planets, horoscope analysis.

Secrets from a Stargazer's Notebook: Making Astrology Work for You by Debbi Kempton Smith. Bantam Books.
A breezy, modern look at planets, signs, houses. The author makes chart interpretation intriguing and fun.

Power Astrology: Make the Most of Your Sun Sign by Robin MacNaughton. Pocket Books.
This is not a book about charts, but an insightful discussion on the deeper psychological issues of each sun sign. I highly recommend this book; it is thought-provoking and immensely interesting.

RECOMMENDED
EPHEMERIDES

American Ephemeris for the 20th Century, The by Neil Michelsen. The years 1900 through 2000 inclusive. The years 2001 through 2050 inclusive. Also available in ten-year editions (1971–1980, 1981–1990, etc.). Also available in one-year editions starting with the year 1977.

Complete Planetary Ephemeris, The. From the Hieratic Publishing Company. The years 1950 through 2000 inclusive. The years 2001 through 2050 inclusive.

Concise Planetary Ephemeris, The. The years 1900 through 1950 inclusive. The years 1950 through 2000 inclusive. The years 2001 through 2050.

Raphael Ephemerides. Published in one-year editions for any year from 1832 through the present year.

Rosicrucian Simplified Scientific Ephemeris. Published for every year from 1857 through 2009. Available in a single-year edition for any of these years. Also published in ten-year editions (1980–1989, 1990–1999, etc.).

SOURCES FOR ASTROLOGICAL BOOKS, EPHEMERIDES, COMPUTER CHARTS AND SOFTWARE

THE FOLLOWING COMPANIES carry a whole range of astrology-related material. Whether you're looking for books or ephemerides, ordering charts or interpretive chart-analyses, or obtaining astrology software for your computer, any of these sources can provide what you need.

American Federation of Astrologers, Inc.
6535 S. Rural Rd
Tempe, AZ 85283-3746
www.astrologers.com

Astro Communications Services
P. O. Box 1646
El Cajon, CA 92022-1646
1-800-514-5070
www.astrocom.com

Astrolabe
P. O. Box 1750
Brewster, MA 02631
1-800-843-6682
www.alabe.com

The Church of Light
2119 Gold Ave SE
Albuquerque, NM 87106-4072
1-800-500-0453
www.light.org

Llewellyn Publications & Astrological Services
2143 Wooddale Drive
Woodbury, MN 55125-2989
1-877-639-9753
www.llewellyn.com

Matrix Software
126 S. Michigan Ave
Big Rapids, MI 49307
1-800-PLANETS
www.astrologysoftware.com

The Rosicrucian Fellowship
222 Mission Ave
Oceanside, CA 92058-2329
www.rosicrucian.com

Samuel Weiser Publications
65 Parker St, Suite 7
Newburyport, MA 01950
1-800-423-7087
www.weiserbooks.com

Wilshire Book Company
9731 Variel Ave
Chatsworth, CA 91311-4315
1-818-700-1522
www.mpowers.com

INDEX

canates of, 156; dominant keyword, 53; duality and, 5, 53; earth sign, 5, 53, 410; erogenous zone, 186; famous people with Moon in, 215; famous people with Sun in, 57; feminine sign, 5, 410; Gemini and, 89, 130; glyph, 53, 321; health, 185–86; Jupiter in, 262–63; legend, 393; Leo and, 101, 130–31; Libra and, 113, 131; and love, 127–32; Mars in, 256; Mercury in, 156, 244–45; Moon in, 156, 214–15; Neptune in, 278, 282; Pisces and, 132, 143; Pluto in, 284, 289; and polarities, 6, 23, 53; quadriplicity, 53; ruled by Saturn, 53, 223, 408, 418; Sagittarius and, 125, 131; Saturn in, 53, 156, 269; Scorpio and, 119, 131; symbol of, 53, 132, 393; Taurus and, 83, 130; traits, 54–56; triplicity, 5, 53, 410; Uranus in, 275; Venus in, 156, 250; Virgo and, 107, 131

Caput Draconis, 415

Caracol observatory, 372

Card reading, 362

Cardinal signs, 6, 408–9, 413; formula, 334. *See also* Aries; Cancer; Capricorn; Libra

Carnac, 372

Caruso, Enrico (Pisces), 66

Casa Grande, 372

Cassini, 265

Cassiopeia (constellation), 147, 377

Castor, 386, 392

Caucasus, Mount, 389

Cauda Draconis, 415

Celestial Branches, 374

Celestial equator, 409

Celestial Stem, 374

Celestial Taskmaster (Saturn), 264

Centaur, 153

Centaurus (constellation), 153

Cepheus (constellation), 158

Cetus (constellation), 147

Chaldeans, 374, 387. *See also* Babylonian astrology

Charioteer. *See* Auriga

Chichen Itza, 372

China, 287

Chinese astrology, 374–75, 413

Chiron (centaur), 238, 392

Chiron (planet), 238

Chopin, Frederic (Pisces), 66

Christianity and astrology, 379, 402

Church of Light, 400

Cicero, 376

City-states, 375, 401

Civil rights, 281, 287

Civil War, 280, 286

Cleopatra, 378

Clytemnestra, 386

Colchis, 384

Compatibility, 364–67

Computer sevices, 223, 349–50, 523

Confucius (Virgo), 374

Conjunctions, 351, 364, 366, 409

Consciousness, 193, 278, 289

Constellations, 383, 399–400, 403–4, 409

Copernicus, Nicolaus (Pisces), 411

Corona Australis (constellation), 156

Corona Borealis (constellation), 153

Corvus (constellation), 153

Coward, Noel (Sagittarius), 50

Crab. *See* Cancer

Crater (constellation), 152

Crete, 385

Cupid, 395

Curie, Marie (Scorpio), 45

Cuspis, 159–66

Cusps, 159–60, 409; Aquarius, 166; Aries, 161; Cancer, 159, 162; Capricorn, 159–60, 165; Gemini, 162; of Houses, 159n, 345; Leo, 159, 163; Libra, 164; Pisces, 166; Sagittarius, 159–60, 165; Scorpio, 164; Taurus, 161; Virgo, 163

Cygnus (constellation), 158

Darwin, Charles (Aquarius), 61, 280

Day-for-a-year method, 362

Decan, 373

Decanate, 373

Decanates, 145–46, 373, 409; Aquarius, 157; Aries, 147; Cancer, 150; Capricorn, 156; Gemini, 149; Leo, 151; Libra, 164; Pisces, 158; Sagittarius, 155; Scorpio, 154; Taurus, 148; Virgo, 152. *See also* subrulers

Dee, John, 379

Degrees, 222, 223, 349–50

Dekanoi, 145, 373

Delphic oracle, 195, 384

Delphinus (constellation), 157

Descendant, 343–44, 345, 409

Deucalion, 394

Diana (goddess), 391

Diet. *See also* Health; *specific signs*

Direct motion, 409

Dispositor, 342, 409

Doyle, Arthur Conan (Gemini), 20

Draco (constellation), 156

Dragon's Head. *See* Nodes

Dragon's Tail. *See* Nodes

Druids, 371–72

Duality, 5, 409–10; Aquarius, 5, 58; Aries, 5, 8; Cancer, 5, 23; Capricorn, 5, 53; Gemini, 5, 18; Leo, 5, 28; Libra, 5, 38; Pisces, 5, 64; Sagittarius, 5, 48; Scorpio, 5, 43; Taurus, 5, 13; Virgo, 5, 33

Ea (god), 393

Earth, 399–400, 403–4, 410

Earth signs, 5, 407, 410, 421; elements formula and, 331–32; love and, 103; Moon and, 197, 199, 201, 203, 205, 207, 209, 211, 213, 215, 217, 219. *See also* Capricorn; Taurus; Virgo

Ecliptic, 383, 399, 404, 410

Edison, Thomas Alva (Aquarius), 61, 214

Ego, theory of, 193